Lecture Notes in Business Information Processing 370

Series Editors

More information about this series at http://www.springer.com/series/7911

Sami Hyrynsalmi · Mari Suoranta ·
Anh Nguyen-Duc · Pasi Tyrväinen ·
Pekka Abrahamsson (Eds.)

Software Business

10th International Conference, ICSOB 2019
Jyväskylä, Finland, November 18–20, 2019
Proceedings

Springer

Editors
Sami Hyrynsalmi
Tampere University of Technology
Pori, Finland

Anh Nguyen-Duc
University of South-Eastern Norway
Bø i Telemark, Norway

Pekka Abrahamsson
University of Jyväskylä
Jyväskylä, Finland

Mari Suoranta
University of Jyväskylä
Jyväskylä, Finland

Pasi Tyrväinen
University of Jyväskylä
Jyväskylä, Finland

ISSN 1865-1348 ISSN 1865-1356 (electronic)
Lecture Notes in Business Information Processing
ISBN 978-3-030-33741-4 ISBN 978-3-030-33742-1 (eBook)
https://doi.org/10.1007/978-3-030-33742-1

This Springer imprint is published by the registered company Springer Nature Switzerland AG
The registered company address is: Gewerbestrasse 11, 6330 Cham, Switzerland

Preface

Welcome to the proceedings of the 10th International Conference on Software Business (ICSOB 2019). This year, ICSOB celebrated its tenth anniversary and returned to Jyväskylä, Finland where the conference series was started in 2010. Jyväskylä is a vibrant university city located in the heart of the beautiful Finnish lake district. The host organization, University of Jyväskylä, is a highly esteemed multidisciplinary university with six faculties, and its Faculty of Information Technology is known for research on computational sciences, software and telecommunications technology, information systems, cognitive science, and educational technology. Additionally, the research of cyber security, computational thinking, and decision-making crosscut all areas mentioned.

For the tenth anniversary of the conference we selected the conference theme "The First Decade and Beyond" and welcomed submissions summarizing the development during the past decade, addressing the future of software-intensive business, as well as studies on new and emerging ideas. Software is pervasively crosscutting all industries and it is nowadays hard to name a business field which has not been revolutionized by software products and services. While software business has a number of similarities with other knowledge-intensive fields, it still has unique features, which has made it a challenging domain for research.

For ICSOB 2019, we received 52 submissions from all over the world. The papers went through a thorough competitive review process by at least three expert reviewers for each paper. The Program Committee deliberated over all the reviews and accepted 18 full and 10 short paper. The accepted papers follow various methodologies and represent the diversity in our research community.

The proceedings open with a keynote presentation paper by Professor Jan Bosch (Chalmers University of Technology, Sweden) on "From Efficiency to Effectiveness: Delivering Business Value Through Software," which provides an overview of trends changing the software-intensive business in the industry as well as presents the requirements for successful digital transformation. Both the second keynote by Dr. Xiaofeng Wang (Free University of Bozen-Bolzano, Italy): "The Rise of Software Startup Research: an In-sider's View" and the third keynote by Professor Slinger Jansen (Utrecht University, the Netherlands): "There's no Business like Software Business: Trends in Software Intensive Business Research" discuss the development and trends in software-intensive business research which excellently pave the way for the versatile and multidisciplinary contents of the ICSOB proceedings. We have organized the papers according to the following themes: Software Ecosystems, Management of Software Products, Continual Improvement and Product Development, Impacts of Digitalization, Software Business Education, Software Startups, and Digital Business.

ICSOB 2019 brought together researchers and practitioners to share their findings and experiences from the field of software-intensive business in academic paper sessions but also in more practice-oriented tutorials and workshops. Tutorials sparked discussions on e.g. the current situation in artificial intelligence, ethics research and practice, as well as guidelines and principles. Workshops continued to delve into emerging fields, artificial intelligence technologies, and their implications on both small and large organizations. Additionally, we learned about software business practices in the Asian context.

As Program Committee chairs, we would like to thank the members of the Program Committee and the additional reviewers for their efforts in evaluating the submissions and ensuring the high quality of the conference. The efforts of the Steering and Organizing Committees and all the chairs were of enormous value in building a successful conference. We extend our heartfelt thanks to all the scholars who submitted papers to the conference, all the authors who presented papers, and to the audience, who participated in very inspirational discussions during the conference.

September 2019

Sami Hyrynsalmi
Mari Suoranta
Anh Nguyen-Duc
Pasi Tyrväinen
Pekka Abrahamsson

Organization

General Chairs

Pekka Abrahamsson	University of Jyväskylä, Finland
Pasi Tyrväinen	University of Jyväskylä, Finland

Program Committee Chairs

Sami Hyrynsalmi	Tampere University, Finland
Mari Suoranta	University of Jyväskylä, Finland

Workshop Chair

Dhrubes Biswas	University of California Berkeley, USA

Short Paper and Poster Chair

Anh Ngyuen Duc	University of South-Eastern Norway, Norway

Social Media Chair

Sonja M. Hyrynsalmi	University of Turku, Finland

Program Committee

Leena Aarikka-Stenroos	Tampere University, Finland
Sergey Avdoshin	National Research University Higher School of Economics, Russia
Richard Berntsson Svensson	University of Gothenhurg, Sweden
Sjaak Brinkkemper	Utrecht University, The Netherlands
David Callele	University of Saskatchewan, Canada
João M. Fernandes	University of Minho, Portugal
Awdren Fontão	Sidia Instituto de Ciência e Tecnologia, Brazil
Samuel A. Fricker	University of Applied Sciences and Arts Northwestern Switzerland (FHNW), Switzerland
Paul Grünbacher	Johannes Kepler University Linz, Austria
Ville Harkke	University of Turku, Finland
Georg Herzwurm	University of Stuttgart, Germany
Helena Holmström Olsson	Malmö University, Sweden
Jukka Huhtamäki	Tampere University, Finland
Slinger Jansen	Utrecht University, The Netherlands

Kai-Kristian Kemell	University of Jyväskylä, Finland
Petri Kettunen	University of Helsinki, Finland
Kai K. Kimppa	University of Turku, Finland
Antti Knutas	Lappeenranta-Lahti University of Technology, Finland
Casper Lassenius	Aalto University, Finland
Ulrike Lechner	Universität der Bundeswehr München, Germany
Valentina Lenarduzzi	Tampere University, Finland
Hongxiu Li	Tampere University, Finland
Andrey Maglyas	Maglyas Consulting, Russia
Tommi Mahlamäki	Tampere University, Finland
Konstantinos Manikas	University of Copenhagen, Denmark
Tiziana Margaria	University of Limerick and Lero, Ireland
John McGregor	Clemson University, USA
Tommi Mikkonen	University of Helsinki, Finland
Jürgen Münch	Reutlingen University, Germany
Matti Muhos	University of Oulu, Finland
Matti Mäntymäki	University of Turku, Finland
Päivi Patja	University of Jyväskylä, Finland
Efi Papatheocharous	SICS, Sweden
Samuli Pekkola	Tampere University, Finland
Henri Pirkkalainen	Tampere University, Finland
Petri Rantanen	Tampere University, Finland
Björn Regnell	Lund University, Sweden
Dirk Riehle	Friedrich-Alexander University of Erlangen-Nürnberg, Germany
Matti Rossi	Aalto University, Finland
Rodrigo Pereira dos Santos	Universidade Federal do Estado do Rio de Janeiro, Brazil
Pertti Seppänen	University of Oulu, Finland
Marko Seppänen	Tampere University, Finland
Kari Smolander	Lappeenranta-Lahti University of Technology, Finland
Jari Soini	Tampere University, Finland
Arho Suominen	VTT Technical Research Centre of Finland, Finland
Kari Systä	Tampere University, Finland
Davide Taibi	Tampere University, Finland
Michael Unterkalmsteiner	Blekinge Institute of Technology, Sweden
Marcus Wagner	Augsburg University, Germany
Xiaofeng Wang	Free University of Bozen-Bolzano, Italy
Karl Werder	University of Cologne, Germany
Krzysztof Wnuk	Blekinge Institute of Technology, Sweden

Additional Reviewers

Sohaib Shahid Bajwa
Luciana Chueri
Orges Cico
Siamak Farshidi
Shan Feng
Francisco Ferreira
Sandro Freire
Harri Keto
Dron Khanna
Gururaj Maddodi
Jorge Melegati
Felipe Cordeiro de Paula
Minna M. Rantanen
Sami Rustholkarhu
Paul van Vulpen

Contents

Emerging Research Topics

Tutorial

Keynote Addresses

From Efficiency to Effectiveness: Delivering Business Value Through Software

Jan Bosch(✉)

Department of Computer Science and Engineering,
Chalmers University of Technology, 41296 Gothenburg, Sweden
jan@janbosch.com

Abstract. Connected products and DevOps allow for a fundamentally different way of working in R&D. Rather than focusing on efficiency of teams, often expressed in terms of flow and number of features per sprint, we are now able to focus on the effectiveness of R&D as expressed in the amount of value created per unit of R&D. We have developed several solutions, such as HYPEX, HoliDev and hierarchical value models, but companies still experience challenges. In this paper, we provide an overview of the trends driving the transition to focusing on effectiveness, discuss the challenges that companies experience as well as the requirements for a successful transformation.

Keywords: Efficiency · Effectiveness · Data-driven development · AI-driven development

1 Introduction

The digital transformation, which we define as software + data + artificial intelligence (AI), is broadly affecting society and industry. Digitalization is disrupting companies at an ever increasing rate as these companies are unable to realize the required pace of change concerning business models, products and services, ways of working and organizational set-up.

As we show in Fig. 1, our research identifies three main areas where digitalization causes fundamental shifts. First, **from ownership to as-a-service**: Especially product companies are traditionally used to a situation where their customers buy an instance of one of their products, own it for several years and then return to buy an updated version of the product. The customers owned the product in the mean time and the company could earn money by providing spare parts and maintenance services. Many companies are now experiencing a transformation from ownership to being asked to provide their products as a service

Supported by Software Center.

S. Hyrynsalmi et al. (Eds.): ICSOB 2019, LNBIP 370, pp. 3–10, 2019.
https://doi.org/10.1007/978-3-030-33742-1_1

to their customers. This causes an interesting shift in business model as rather than getting paid upfront at the time of the sale of the product, the company now monetizes its product portfolio through subscription and other continuous business models. This has many implications, including financial ones in that the company has to finance the product on behalf of the customer.

Second, **from physical to digital offering**: As a consequence of the aforementioned, the nature of the offering transforms from a physical to a digital one. Rather than selling something that consists of atoms, the offer now typical is a digital one that may, for instance, be based on a pay-for-use model. In our research, some of the cases that we studied concerned the company installing its products at selected customers without any upfront fee. The customer instead paid only for the use of the product. The use of digital technologies including connectivity facilitate this transition as products at the customer can be enabled and disabled remotely as well as usage can be remotely recorded for invoicing purposes.

Finally, **from single- to multi-dimensional business ecosystems**: A third area of transformation is move from single- to multi-dimensional business ecosystems. As connected products generate vast amounts of data, this creates business opportunities for companies as other stakeholders may be interested in buying aggregated (and properly anonimized) data sets and streams, meaning that the company now serves multiple customer groups. This may lead to a positive feedback cycle where the monetization of the second customer group allows the company to subsidize the first customer group and in that way increase its market share. That, in turns, increases the value of its data, allowing it to charge and subsidize more. This is how many companies have achieved dominance in their respective industries.

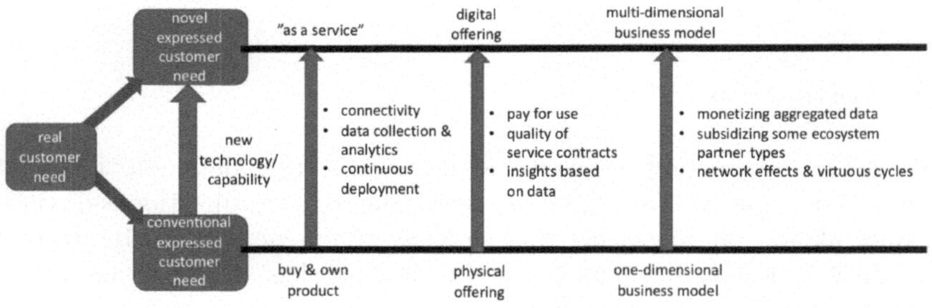

Fig. 1. Three implications of moving to a digital business

The digital transformation, however, has an important impact not only on factors external to the company, but also on the ways of working in R&D. Traditionally, the focus in R&D has been on *efficiency*: building as many features and as much functionality as possible in the given time slot, e.g. per agile sprint, and with the resources available. This is visible throughout the R&D community with, for instance, concepts such as flow being used to measure throughput of R&D teams.

However, with the emergence of connectivity, most software intensive systems products are continuously connected which allows for novel ways of working. Among others, this allows companies to measure the value that their R&D efforts are providing to customers, rather than relying on the qualitative opinions of product managers or feedback from customers. This means that it becomes possible to collect data about the use of features under iterative development as well as to run A/B experiments to evaluate alternatives and optimizations. Generally referred to as DevOps or continuous deployment, this allows for a level of iterative development that was entirely impossible even a decade ago.

Connectivity and DevOps allows for a fundamental shift in R&D approach from a focus on *efficiency* to a focus on *effectiveness*. We define effectiveness as the amount of customer value created per unit of R&D resource. As research by us [3] and others show that half or more of all the features built are hardly, if ever, used, it is clear that the focus on efficiency is fraught with difficulty. Building as many features as possible that nobody uses is, obviously, a monumental waste of R&D resources.

In this short paper, we explore the transition from a focus on efficiency to a focus on effectiveness and we do so in the following way. In the next section, we discuss the background behind this transition and the various technologies enabling or exploiting this. The subsequent section is concerned with the challenges that the companies that we work with experience to realize this transition. Section 4 is concerned with the transition from efficiency to effectiveness and is followed by the conclusion.

2 Background

The basis for the transition from efficiency to effectiveness is driven by the increasing connectivity of products, systems and solutions. This has resulted in the adoption of outcome-driven development where the R&D organizations uses hypotheses and experiments to validate the impact that features and new functionality have on the system and its users. This is predominantly realized in online software-as-a-service (SaaS) systems [6] through A/B experimentation and multi-armed bandit algorithms [9], but as we discuss in [2] also the embedded and internet of things (IoT) industries are adopting these practices now. As the leading companies in the A/B testing space are now running thousands of A/B experiments in parallel, we see the need for automated solutions for continuous experimentation [8]. In Fig. 2, we show the typical process that is used in outcome-driven development where features and functionality are realized iteratively and the additional value delivery from each iteration is constantly measured.

The rapidly increasing availability of data has also resulted in a second technology reaching mainstream deployment: artificial intelligence and specifically machine- and deep-learning (ML/DL). Machine- and deep-learning algorithms benefit immensely from large datasets for training and validation. Combined with the improvements in computational infrastructure, specifically in the area

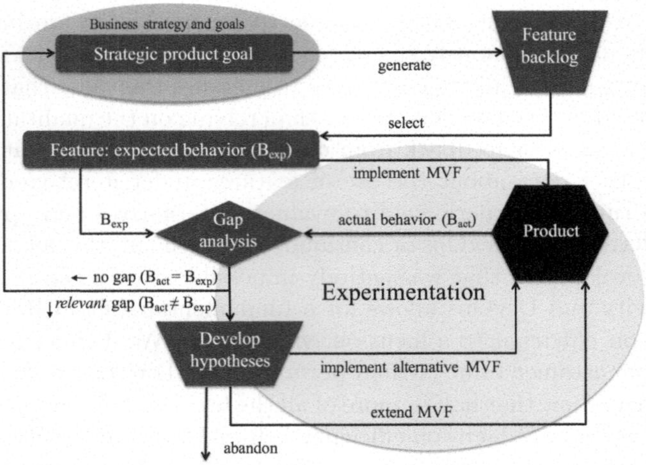

Fig. 2. The HYPEX model

of graphical processing units (GPUs), ML/DL is able to solve problems in a host of domains that earlier were unsolvable or solidly in the purview of humans only. Although industry-strength, production-quality deployment is still a challenge, as we report in [1,7], the use of ML/DL models offers a significant improvement in effectiveness over traditional, programmed approaches.

In earlier research [4,5] we defined the HoliDev model to present how the different approaches to software development are coming together. As shown in Fig. 3, we recognize three approaches to development, i.e. requirements-, outcome- and AI-driven. Each of these development approaches has different purposes and application areas but the results still need to end up in one system and component are subject to continuous monitoring and continuous deployment. One of the key contemporary challenges in software engineering is to seamlessly integrate these different forms of development in a holistic development model and in systems where all functionality is well integrated despite their different pedigrees.

3 Challenges

As has become clear in the previous sections, there is a significant benefit to focusing on effectiveness over efficiency. Still, despite companies having collected data from their products in the field, the vast majority of companies has not adopted the practices that we have discussed so far. This is due to some inhibitors other than the unwillingness or inability of companies to adopt new practices. We have identified several challenges that companies experience and that are holding them back from adopting data-driven and AI-driven practices and consequently fail to transition away from an efficiency focus. Below we discuss some of these challenges in more detail.

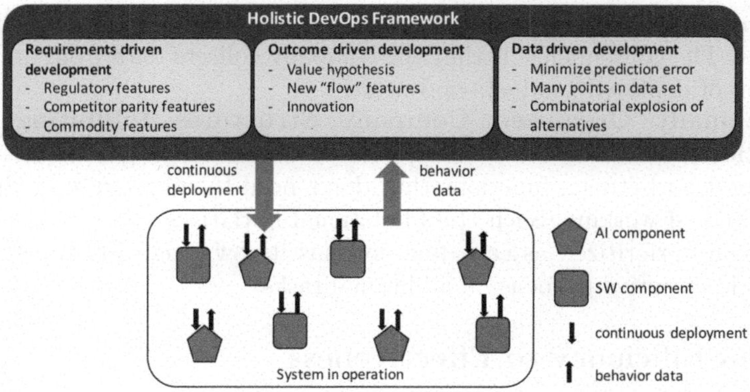

Fig. 3. The HoliDev model

- **Wrong Data**: The first observation that we have made at several companies is that, although the company collects vast amounts of data, this data can not be used for determining whether value is being created for the customer. In most of the cases, the data is concerned with quality related issues, such as defects, error logs and similar topics. Even in the cases where relevant data, such as performance data, is available, it often is collected in such a way that it is difficult to use for the purposes outlined in this paper.
- **Opinions versus Data**: Even in cases where the company has relevant data to use as a basis for decision making, we have experienced several cases where key decision makers prioritized their opinions over the data. Instead, the data was reinterpreted in a way that was in line with the beliefs of the key people in the team or organization. As is the case in many human enterprises, when data meets (deeply held) beliefs, the latter often wins.
- **Illusion of Alignment**: Many teams and organizations maintain an illusion of alignment where, to maintain a sense of community and belonging, teams find ways to abstract the focus of their work to a level that includes everyone and, in that way, are able to gloss over the differences of opinion that are pervasive. When starting to work with quantitative data as a basis, it is virtually impossible to maintain this alignment illusion and consequently many shy away from taking on that challenge.
- **Vocal Customers**: Especially senior leaders are concerned with maintaining good customer relations. This can be exploited by very vocal customers who, by creating a lot of noise, manage to convince key decision makers to take decisions in their favour, even if the data clearly shows that this is not a good use of resources from the perspective of the entire customer base.
- **Unreasonably Strict Interpretation of Legal Constraints**: In companies that have appointed data officers of various kinds with the intent of avoiding legal concerns over the use of data, there often is a tendency by these data officers to decline virtually any use of data from products in the field and their users. Alternatively, these officers ask for such draconian opt-in

measures that the vast majority of users decides to not bother with the whole process. The consequence is that the company collects data from only a tiny fraction of deployed products and users.

- **Functionally Organized Company Structures Inhibiting Cross-Functional Initiatives**: Working with data and focusing on value requires collaboration between functions that don't need to collaborate in the traditional way of working. Such cross-functional initiatives often have a difficult time being prioritized as each function has its own high priority tasks and has little incentive to focus on additional tasks.

4 From Efficiency to Effectiveness

Although most organizations today focus on efficiency as the key metric for R&D, this article argues that the focus should shift to effectiveness. We define effectiveness as the amount of value created per unit of R&D resource. A unit of R&D resource can be defined as a person hour or a person day or a sprint of an agile team. As an example to illustrate this, let us focus on the latter. Assume that a company has a budget for R&D that is 5% of the revenue of the company. The agile teams in the company typically consist of 8 persons and the sprint length is 3 weeks. That means that each agile sprints consumes 24 person weeks of effort or half a person year. If the average cost of an engineer is 100K€ per year, then the cost of an agile team sprint is 50K€. However, the business value that the team has to deliver is 20 times 50K€ = 1M€ as the R&D budget of the company is 5% or 1/20th of the revenue.

The key challenge for most organizations is to develop ways of working and agreed upon models to illustrate that this value is indeed created. This typically requires the creation of a hierarchical value model (HVM). A HVM links the top level business KPIs to middle level system KPIs and, finally, to feature level factors that can be measured. The HVM defines quantitative relationships between higher level and lower level KPIs and factors. These relationships can be tested with "vertical experiments" that are purely intended to quantitatively establish the role of lower level factors in improving or deteriorating higher level KPIs. In Fig. 4 we present this concept graphically. The "horizontal experiments" shown in the figure are the normal A/B and MAB testing that occurs in data-driven development.

Although the transition to effectiveness may seem as a technical and process issue, it actually influences the entire organization. From a business perspective, this allows the company to develop new business models that are much closer aligned with the ways in which its customers make money. For instance, service level agreements where the company gets paid for its performance rather than for delivering a physical product can provide a good approach to connect the fate of the customer with that of the company.

From an organizational perspective, there are several implications of which two are the most relevant here. First, the organization is typically forced to adopt some form of cross-functional, multi-disciplinary teams as the amount of coordination between, for instance, sales, product management, R&D and customer

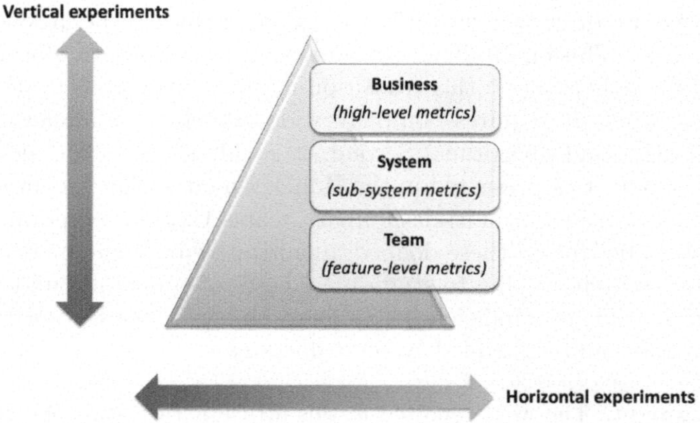

Fig. 4. Illustrating a hierarchical value model

support is increased. In this case, it is typically more efficient to organize a cross-functional team around the development of new functionality as intra-team coordination is orders of magnitude cheaper than inter-team or even inter-function coordination. Second, it allows for a much higher degree of empowerment of teams and individuals as the data allows leaders and managers to define desired outcomes in terms of quantitative data, rather than telling teams how to do their work. This frees up teams to carve their own path to success as the team will get continuous feedback on the impact of its actions.

The key challenge for organizations transitioning from efficiency to effectiveness, though, is that it requires the organization to clearly and quantitatively define what the factors and KPIs are that the company wants to deliver on as well as define the relative priority of these factors and KPIs. Although this may seem like an obvious consequence, our research shows that many companies struggle with reaching precise, aligned definitions of customer value in place across the organization.

5 Conclusion

The focus on R&D efficiency has served a purpose but in a context that was very different from the business reality today. Connected products and DevOps allow for a focus on effectiveness that allows companies to quantitatively measure the amount of value delivered by each R&D initiative. This is achieved by collecting data from products deployed in the field as well as from the users using these products. This data can then be used for outcome-driven development, using A/B and MAB testing approaches, as well as AI-driven development through the use of ML/DL models that are trained using the collected data.

Although the focus on effectiveness may seem a no-brainer, many companies experience challenges to achieve the desired outcome due to a variety of challenges that we discussed earlier in the paper, including the lack of access to relevant data, the illusion of alignment and overly zealous data officers.

Successfully delivering on this transition requires companies to undergo several changes. First, it requires company wide agreement on relevant factors, relative priorities and guardrails. Second, it requires the introduction of new ways of development as presented in the HoliDev model. Third, companies need to adopt cross-functional, multi-disciplinary teams that are empowered to find the best way to deliver on these defined, quantitative outcome metrics.

In future research, we aim to study more cases of companies undergoing the transition from a focus on efficiency to a focus on effectiveness, especially in the software-intensive and embedded systems domains.

Acknowledgment. The work reported in this article is the result of collaborations with many researchers in the context of Software Center, a collaboration between, at the time of writing, thirteen companies and five universities.

References

1. Arpteg, A., Brinne, B., Crnkovic-Friis, L., Bosch, J.: Software engineering challenges of deep learning. In: 2018 44th Euromicro Conference on Software Engineering and Advanced Applications (SEAA), pp. 50–59. IEEE August (2018)
2. Bosch, J., Olsson, H.H.: Toward evidence-based organizations: lessons from embedded systems, online games, and the Internet of Things. IEEE Softw. **34**(5), 60–66 (2017)
3. Bosch, J.: Speed, Data, and Ecosystems: Excelling in a Software-Driven World. CRC Press, Boca Raton (2017)
4. Bosch, J., Olsson, H.H., Crnkovic, I.: It takes three to tango: Requirement, outcome/data, and AI driven development. In: SiBW (2018)
5. Bosch, J.: Towards a digital business operating system. In: Proceedings of RCIS 2019, to appear (2019)
6. Fabijan, A., et al.: Experimentation growth: evolving trustworthy A/B testing capabilities in online software companies. J. Softw.: Evol. Process **30**(12), e2113 (2018)
7. Lwakatare, L.E., Raj, A., Bosch, J., Olsson, H.H., Crnkovic, I.: A taxonomy of software engineering challenges for machine learning systems: an empirical investigation. In: Kruchten, P., Fraser, S., Coallier, F. (eds.) XP 2019. LNBIP, vol. 355, pp. 227–243. Springer, Cham (2019). https://doi.org/10.1007/978-3-030-19034-7_14
8. Mattos I.D., Bosch, J., Olsson, H.H.: Challenges and strategies for undertaking continuous experimentation to embedded systems: industry and research perspectives. In: XP 2018: Agile Processes in Software Engineering and Extreme Programming, pp. 277–292 (2018)
9. Mattos, D.I., Bosch, J., Olsson, H.H.: Multi-armed bandits in the wild: pitfalls and strategies in online experiments. Inf. Softw. Technol. **113**, 68–81 (2019)

The Rise of Software Startup Research: An Insider's View

Xiaofeng Wang(✉)

Free University of Bozen-Bolzano, Bolzano 39100, Italy
xiaofeng.wang@unibz.it

Abstract. Software startup research is an emerging field of study that corresponds to the significance of software startups in the modern economy. The evolution of the software startup research field is inspected in this paper through an examination of the scientific publications and contributing disciplines. The crucial role played by the Computer Science discipline in the development of software startup research is highlighted, as well as the interdisciplinary collaboration happening in the field. An insider's view is also offered on the contribution that a purposeful research network made to grow software startup research.

Keywords: Software startup · Evolution of research field · Scientific discipline · Purposeful research network

1 Software "Eats" the World, Startups Change the World

Around the same time that Marc Andreessen, a cofounder of the renowned venture capital firm Andreessen Horowitz, wrote the later-on famous essay "Why Software is Eating the World" [2] in 2011, the potential of software startups to change the world started to be manifested in a glaring manner with the unprecedented success of new ventures, such as Airbnb, Uber, Netflix, etc. Nowadays, the idea that every company should become a software company is considered almost a cliché, but software startups continue to amaze the world with an astonishing variety of innovative services and products, paving the way for the introduction of disruptive innovations.

Even though sharing common characteristics with other types of startups, such as resource scarcity and a lack of operational history, software startups have their unique attributes [10]. They are often caught up in the wave of technological change frequently happening in software industry, such as new computing and network technologies, and an increasing variety of computing devices. They also need to use cutting-edge tools and techniques to develop innovative software products and services, such as Cloud Computing, Internet of Things (IoTs), Artificial Intelligence, Blockchain, etc. In addition, software products or services are less patentable and protectable compared to hardware or products in other domains,

S. Hyrynsalmi et al. (Eds.): ICSOB 2019, LNBIP 370, pp. 11–18, 2019.
https://doi.org/10.1007/978-3-030-33742-1_2

which leads to continuously innovating and being responsive to change as the primary strategies for software startups to keep their competitive advantages.

Building software startups are challenging endeavours, and it is almost common knowledge that the failure rate is strikingly high. Back in 2011, the Startup Genome Report[1] claimed that "within 3 years, 92% of startups failed". The claim was based on an analysis of 3,200 high-growth web/mobile startups. Fast forward to 2019, there is no reason to believe that the chance of success has increased. The high failure rate indicates the uncertainty and difficulties that software startups need to tackle when turning innovative ideas to concrete products/services and viable businesses. It also leads to unemployment and a huge waste of resources, effort, energy and emotions of startup founders and people and organizations surrounding them.

Despite of the challenges (or better, because of them), software startups keep attracting motivated and committed individuals to join the force. Meanwhile, they represent fascinating phenomena to study. An increasing number of researchers have embarked on the quest for the secret ingredients that could make software startups "unicorns" (startups valued at or over $1 billion), or even "decacorns" (startups valued at or over $10 billion)[2]. Software startups as a research field emerged and evolved against this backdrop.

But before diving into the evolutionary path of the research field, we need to understand better the defining term of the field - software startup.

2 What Is a Software Startup, Exactly?

According to the answers to a Quora.com question[3], the earliest use of the term *startup* was seen in Forbes magazine in 1976, and later in Business Week in 1977. In both cases, the term was used in the context of "the electronic data processing field" and "the fast-growth, high-technology fields". Therefore, it could be argued that the origin of the *software startup* term is as early as *startup* itself.

The modern definitions of *startup* are influenced heavily by the work of the leading figures in the startup community. *Startups* are defined as human institutions designed to create new products/services under the conditions of extreme uncertainty [8], and constantly seek repeatable, profitable and scalable business models and aim at rapid growth [4].

Specific to software startups, given the ubiquitous presence of software in every aspect of modern business, the defining line between software startups and non software startups is extremely blur if not non-existing. However, software does play different roles in different startups, ranging from facilitating and mediating the value creation and delivery processes to being more deeply involved and

[1] http://innovationfootprints.com/wp-content/uploads/2015/07/startup-genome-report-extra-on-premature-scaling.pdf.

[2] https://fortune.com/2015/01/22/the-age-of-unicorns/.

[3] https://www.quora.com/What-is-the-origin-of-the-term-startup-and-when-did-this-word-start-to-appear.

being the core of the value creation of a startup [9]. Applying such a broad spectrum, not only startups that produce software products or services as their core offerings are software startups (e.g., Stripe, Snapchat), so are media-streaming service providers like Spotify, or new e-commerce ventures such as Zalando.

Correspondingly, the innovativeness of a software startup can be derived from different parts of its business model, not necessarily from software itself [7]. It also means that software startups could produce disruptive technical innovations, but it is not necessarily a defining characteristic of a software startup.

3 Evolution of Software Startup Research

In order to examine the evolution of software startup research, a research method, designed by Coccia [6] to analyse the evolution of a research field and which scientific disciplines drive it, was followed.

According to Coccia [6], *discipline* is a concept that derives from Latin *disciplina*, derivation of *discĕre*, which means "to learn". In science, a discipline is a system of norms, theories and principles, organized, systematized and based on specific methods of inquiry that investigate phenomena in nature and society.

A research field, in turn, is a sub-set of a discipline that investigates specific topics and/or phenomena to solve theoretical and practical problems, which generates discoveries and/or scientific advances of applied and/or basic sciences. Software startup research is considered a research field here.

The data used to analyze the evolution of software startup research was collected from Scopus, a source-neutral abstract and citation database commonly used by scholars and research institutions. The "document search" feature at Scopus.com in "Article title, Abstract and Keywords" was used. The search keywords are "software startup*" and "software start-up*". The research method assumes that the disciplines associated with the research field are the subject areas indicated by Scopus, which are decided based on the affiliations of the contributing authors of the publications.

The document search was conducted in the beginning of September, 2019, and resulted in 156 documents. After scrutinising the abstracts, 23 documents were excluded as not relevant. The final dataset contains 133 Scopus-indexed publications that can be considered relevant software startup studies.

Figure 1 shows these published papers over the years.

Among the 133 publications, the first appearance of "software startup" related scientific publications is in IEEE Software, published in 1994, entitled "Anatomy of a Software Start-up". The paper discusses starting and building a software business, what an entrepreneur is, and what sets him or her apart from normal people [3]. After this 1994 article, the "software startup" term would not have been seen until 2000, in another IEEE Software article written by Sutton [10], "Role of Process in a Software Start-up", in which the need of formal development process and methodology for software startups is examined. This is the article widely cited later on as one piece of seminal work in the software startup research field.

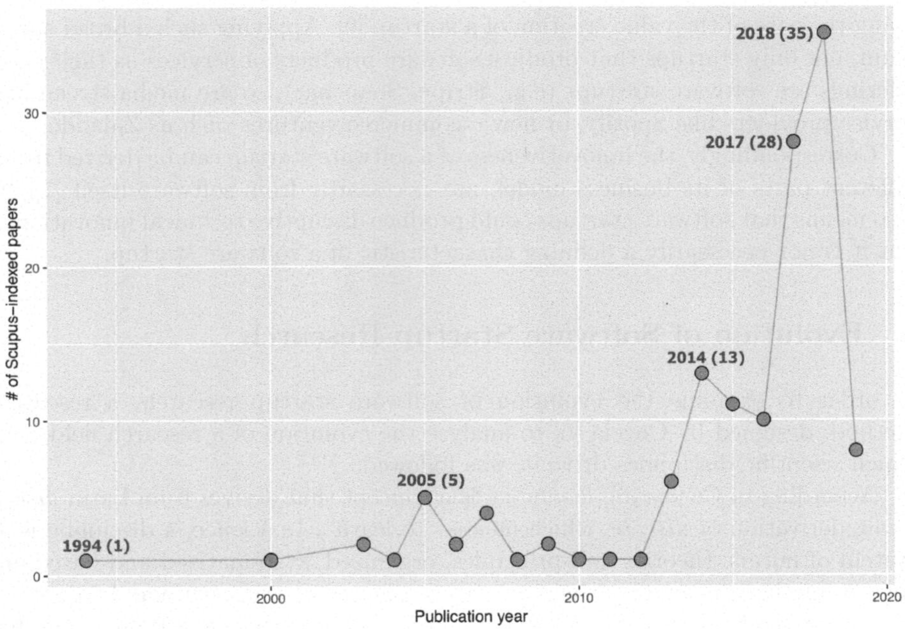

Fig. 1. The published software startup papers over the years

Software startup topics started appearing in scientific literature more regularly since 2003, although the annual number remained low until 2014.

The year of 2014 saw the first significant peak of number of publications in the software startup research field, with 13 publications on the related topics. Despite of the small dip in the following two years, the number of publications has jumped to 28 in 2017, and reached a new peak in 2018 with 35 publications.

It is yet to be seen if this rising trend would be kept in 2019. Due to the incomplete data regarding the 2019 publications and the latency of the indexing by Scopus, it is difficult to predict the trend with the collected data.

Table 1 shows the detailed breakdown of the publications by contributing scientific disciplines. Figure 2 illustrates the contribution from these disciplines using the stacked area chart.

In total, there are 12 disciplines which have contributed to the 133 publications. The most significant contributing disciplines are, in the descending order, Computer Science (D1, 114 publications), Business, Management and Accounting (D2, 48), Mathematics (D3, 38), Engineering (D4, 35), and Decision Science (D5, 30). In comparison, the rest seven disciplines (D6 to D12) contributed marginally to the field of software startup research.

The earliest contribution came from the Computer Science discipline exclusively (the two IEEE Software papers). Meanwhile, Business, Management and Accounting is also among the early contributing disciplines. This reflects the dual business-engineering nature of software startups as a research phenomenon.

Table 1. The breakdown of software startup publications by contributing discipline and year

Disc.	Publication Year																			Total
#	1994	2000	2003	2004	2005	2006	2007	2008	2009	2010	2011	2012	2013	2014	2015	2016	2017	2018	2019	No.
D1	1	1			1	1	2	1		1	1	1	6	9	11	10	26	34	8	114
D2			2	1	2		2		1				3	5	2	3	17	9	1	48
D3							1						3	3	8	5	8	10		38
D4			1		2	1							3	5	2	3	7	10	1	35
D5				1	1		2		1				3	3	2	3	5	8	1	30
D6			1		1			1					1				1	5		10
D7					1									1			1	1		4
D8									1											1
D9																	1			1
D10																		1		1
D11																		1		1
D12																		1		1

Disciplines in the order of descending contribution:

D1: Computer Science
D2. Business, Management and Accounting
D3. Mathematics
D4. Engineering
D5. Decision Sciences
D6. Social Sciences
D7. Economics, Econometrics and Finance
D8. Multidisciplinary
D9. Arts and Humanities
D10. Chemical Engineering
D11. Environmental Science
D12. Biochemistry, Genetics and Molecular Biology

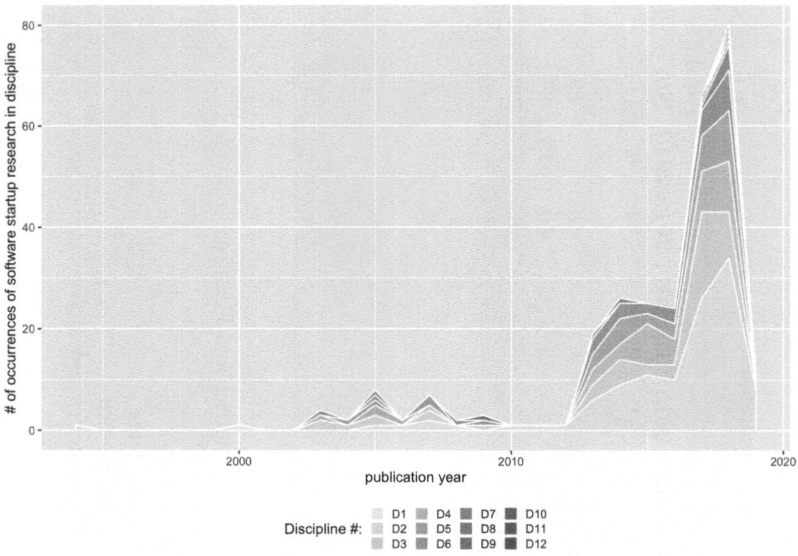

Fig. 2. The published software startup papers, grouped by discipline

Based on the collected data, several patterns could be observed regarding the evolution of software startup research, which are in line with what Coccia [6] found in the evolution of other research fields.

Firstly, the evolution of software startup research is driven by few scientific disciplines that generate more than 80% of the publications in the field (concentration of the scientific production). Based on Table 1, a weighted contribution diagram was generated as Fig. 3. It can be seen that the majority (greater than 80%) of the contributions come from the first 3 to 5 disciplines (D1 to D5).

Secondly, it is evident that Computer Science is the most critical contributing discipline for software startup research. It contributes not only the largest number of publications, but also the seminal ones in the early days of the development of the research field. This pattern can potentially change the view on the relevancy of software startup research to the Computer Science discipline.

Last but not least, the software startup research field is increasingly interdisciplinary during its evolution. For example, there were 35 publications on software startup related topics in 2018, which were authored by the researchers from ten different disciplines. The occurrences of software startup topics in these disciplines amount to 80, which indicates strong interdisciplinary collaboration among these researchers. This is a reassuring tendency since product and business development are highly intertwined and parallel in the lifespan of a software startup, therefore interdisciplinary perspectives and research approaches are appropriate to study startup related phenomena.

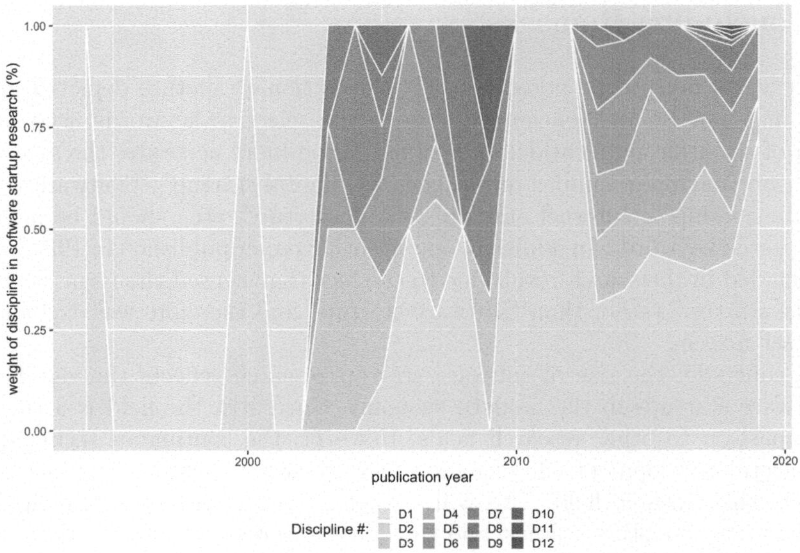

Fig. 3. The weighted contribution of the disciplines to software startup research

4 The Role of a Purposeful Research Network

In an article published in Nature in 2012 entitled "The Rise of Research Networks" [1], Adams emphasized on the importance of research networks forged through co-authoring publications. Even though co-authorship is a good proxy of research networks, a more purposefully constructed research network using various formats of scientific collaborations could contribute greatly to the development of a research field.

Software Startup Research Network (SSRN)[4], in which I have been actively involved, played a crucial role in the development of the software startup research field. Even though it emerged in a bottom-up manner through a small group of researchers sharing the same research interests on software startups, over the course of more than four years (from early 2015 to current time), the network researchers have purposefully promoted and actively built the research field with regular online meetings and network-level initiatives, e.g., defining the research agenda, organising and participating scientific workshops related to software startup research, co-authoring a theme book, and actively seeking for research funding.

The value of this purposeful research network, now composed of researchers distributed in Europe and America, is manifested by the surge of the number of publications in 2018 (as shown in Fig. 1) which could be largely attributed to the network researchers. It is foreseen that the influence of the network in the software startup research field would become increasingly significant in the coming years.

[4] https://softwarestartups.org.

5 Concluding Remarks

Some caveats need to be noted here. The evolutionary picture depicted in this paper may not be 100% accurate, due to the selective keywords used in the search of scientific publications in Scopus. To be more accurate, the synonyms of *software startup* or similar terms, such as "digital startup", "software/digital entrepreneurship", "Internet startup", "Web startup", etc., should be included in the search keywords. In addition, one scientific paper published in 1994 [5] was not included in the search result due to the fact that it used the term "software package startup" rather than "software startup" and therefore was excluded by the exact match.

To conclude, the rise of software startup research reflects the significance of software startups in the modern economy. Currently, the field is a tiny one in comparison to other research fields. However, the continuous technological and societal development will engender more software startups, and instill new topics to this research field. This will attract more researchers to join the force and conduct interesting studies, and thus grow the research field further.

Acknowledgment. My sincere appreciation to the SSRN researchers. Without them, software startup research wouldn't have evolved this far. Special thanks to my colleagues Dron Khanna and Jorge Melegati for their insightful discussion that led to this paper.

References

1. Adams, J.: The rise of research networks. Nature **490**, 335–336 (2012)
2. Andreessen, M.: Why software is eating the world. Wall Street J. **20**, C2 (2011)
3. Bersoft, E.: Anatomy of a software start-up. IEEE Softw. **11**(1), 92–94 (1994)
4. Blank, S., Dorf, B.: The Startup Owner's Manual: The Step-By-Step Guide for Building a Great Company, 1st edn. K & S Ranch, Pescadero (2012)
5. Carmel, E.: Time-to-completion in software package startups. In: Proceedings of the Hawaii International Conference on System Sciences (1994)
6. Coccia, M.: The laws of the evolution of research fields. In: aLab Working Paper, no. 31, pp. 1–44 (2018)
7. Melegati, J., Wang, X.: Do software startups innovate in the same way? A case survey study. In: CEUR Workshop Proceedings (2018)
8. Ries, E.: The lean startup: How today's entrepreneurs use continuous innovation to create radically successful businesses. Crown Books, USA (2011)
9. Steininger, D.M.: Linking information systems and entrepreneurship: a review and agenda for IT-associated and digital entrepreneurship research. Inf. Syst. J. **29**(2), 363–407 (2019)
10. Sutton Jr., S.M.: Role of process in a software start-up. IEEE Softw. **17**(4), 33–39 (2000)

There's No Business Like Software Business: Trends in Software Intensive Business Research

Slinger Jansen(✉)

Utrecht University, Utrecht, The Netherlands
slinger.jansen@uu.nl

Abstract. Software intensive business research is rapidly evolving. Over the last decade we have witnessed a surge in research output but as the field matures, its future remains unsure. In this paper an overview is provided of the highlights and trends of software intensive business research. We briefly discuss the most cited papers in the domain and provide a hype cycle for software intensive business research. With this paper, we hope that researchers can forge more solid research strategies for themselves in the domain, to achieve longevity, academic depth, and impact.

Keywords: Software business hype cycle · Software intensive business · Software ecosystems

1 Introduction to This Keynote Paper

The role of software-intensive solutions is still, after decades, growing in our society. There is hardly a field or an industrial domain where software-intensive solutions have not revolutionized the business. Furthermore, due to the emergence of the platform economy, the role of software solutions and boundary resources, such as the quality of APIs, is rising. The biggest enabler for the growth of software-intensive solutions, is the fact that we are now living in a connected society, where devices, software, and business process can interact at relatively low cost.

Software Intensive Business (SiB) research is a domain that cross–sects software engineering, information systems, and economics. The scientific field of software-intensive business studies organizational arrangements, methods, and tools for value creation, capture, and delivery based on digital products and services. The International Conference on Software Business (ICSOB) was launched to provide a home for this type of research. To follow the trends in SiB research, work is highlighted from the International Conference on Software Business from 2010 to 2016, as these works have been able to amass a significant number of citations. In these works the following major topics are identified: *Software Product Management*, *Continuous X*, *Software Ecosystems*, and *Software Startups*.

S. Hyrynsalmi et al. (Eds.): ICSOB 2019, LNBIP 370, pp. 19–27, 2019.
https://doi.org/10.1007/978-3-030-33742-1_3

In the following Sections we discuss each of these topics. For each topic we highlight some of the most highly cited papers in the domain and identify, using dimensions.ai, the most welcoming forums for these topics.

2 Software Product Management

The domain of *Software Product Management (SPM)* gained its initial traction in the early 2000s, typically in information systems journals and software process conferences. The topic was continuously advanced upon and in 2006 the International Workshop on Software Product Management (IWSPM) was launched, a series that lasted until 2016. The workshop was a success from an academic point of view, as it launched the research area and in a relatively short time professionalized the field of SPM, even to the extent that an initiative was launched for the International Software Product Management Association, an open non-profit association of experts, companies, and research institutes with the goal to foster software product management excellence across industries. In a sense, this association is the culmination of a research domain, where the association actively supports researchers and professionals.

In 2010, when the ICSOB series was launched, it was a logical consequence that SPM would be a main topic of discussion in the conference and it is probably not a coincidence that the best cited paper from 2010 is the seminal work by van de Weerd, Bekkers, and Brinkkemper [18] on developing an SPM maturity model. SPM as a topic is still active, although there appears to be little growth in the domain. Also, the workshop ended in 2016, but that may be in part due to the fact that independent workshops are becoming less common. The main forums where SPM work is published are the Journal of Systems and Software (JSS), Lecture Notes on Computer Science (LNCS), Lecture Notes on Business Information Processing (LNBIP), and the Information and Software Technology Journal (IST).

3 Software Ecosystems

The domain of *Software Ecosystems* was launched with the first International Workshop on Software Ecosystems (IWSECO) in 2009, although earlier works had been using the term [15]. The workshop was launched as an initiative at the International Conference on Software Reuse, as that appeared to be a suitable place for work in this domain. The IWSECO started traveling from conference to conference and was eventually co-located with ICSOB several times. The domain has seen a resurgence in several workshops and is primarily addressed in the software engineering and repository mining communities. The domain is still rapidly growing and works are being written in several new domains, such as blockchain, cryptocurrency, safety and security, platforms, and mobile software.

For the ICSOB community it was logical to also address the topic of software ecosystems, as software ecosystems take a somewhat broader view on the SiB domain. In 2011 the paper with the most citations in the ICSOB community was the work by Jansen and Kabbedijk [12], which presents one of the first in-depth case studies of an open source software ecosystem. In 2013 Bloemendal and Jansen [9] formulate a definition of the concept of an app store at ICSOB and achieve the most citations in that year.

The most welcoming forums for software ecosystems work are JSS, IST, LNBIP, LNCS, the Empirical Software Engineering journal (EMSE), and IEEE Software. The domain is still growing steadily. In this Section we highlight some of the early findings from the creation of an updated research agenda on software ecosystems. The source of the research challenges consists of the notes of a Dagstuhl meeting in 2018 [1] and a series of surveys that has been released to the SiB community.

Engineering Ecosystems. Ecosystems cannot be created: they must be cultivated and grown to enable keystones to gain power from their ecosystems. We find that enabling technologies, such as plug-in architectures, app store architectures, and API architectures create the infrastructure that enables partners to co-create and innovate within an ecosystem. Our first set of challenges centers around enabling partners to engage into the ecosystem through technical infrastructure. There are many enabling technologies for ecosystems, such as plug-in architectures, application stores, and block chains. To engage developers there is a need for code repositories, IDE integrations of ecosystem resources, sand boxes, license protection mechanisms, and even fully integrated development stacks. To monitor and enable partners, there exists a need for incentive systems [16], partner quality monitoring systems, and API performance monitoring. These systems need to be studied more extensively to establish how they contribute to the ecosystem, developer satisfaction, and overall partner performance.

Secondly, there exists a challenge in identifying the barriers to entry for new partners in an ecosystem. We need to study manners to keep thresholds low and employ network effects for the growth of the partner ecosystem.

Analysis of Ecosystem Data. Analyzing ecosystem data is essentially (big) data analytics and techniques from this domain are presently insufficiently applied. Studying a repository such as Github is often compared to drinking water from a fire hose, especially when a research project is focused on the needle in the (Github) haystack. We identify the following data analytics challenges.

First, there is the challenge that most researchers typically limit themselves to a snapshot of one or several ecosystems. However, to answer some of the deeper questions on ecosystem health and attracting new developers and partners to an ecosystems, concrete recipes need to be evaluated in terms of metrics that can be gathered from repositories over time. A large challenge here, is that in software ecosystems data is generally hard to collect. Data is of different types, is hidden behind organizational barriers, and sometimes simply overwritten and unavailable. Monitoring ecosystems over time has become a challenge that requires extensive and long-lasting efforts. Fortunately, with initiatives such as GHTorrent (http://ghtorrent.org/), we are actively curating the data that is needed for durable ecosystem analysis.

Secondly, the concept of ecosystem health, i.e., the propensity for growth of an ecosystem, has been extensively studied. These frameworks have become increasingly elaborate and comprehensive, whereby making them challenging to apply to a research project. Some even call for a customized set of health metrics for every (type of) ecosystem. More research is required into the main performance indicators of ecosystems, the recipes that aim to influence them, and their measurable influence on these performance indicators.

Modeling of Ecosystem Structure and Behavior. Ecosystems are increasingly used as tools for reasoning about an organization's business model [11], market position, opportunities and threats. However, we have not been able to reason at the highest levels of fidelity. There is a need for the development of modeling languages that provide insight and enable analysis at different levels of scale. There are several modeling languages used in the field, such as social network models, goal models, and supply chain models. These models appear to have significant overlap, as they all aim to model actors, software structures, and relationships, and yet each serves a different purpose.

A second challenge is that the current languages do not scale upwards easily. Ecosystems with up to 5 actors can still be modeled in goal modelling languages and power models, but beyond those numbers these models become too complex. Finally, even with such models it becomes complex to monitor and model ecosystems over time.

Management of Developer Ecosystems and Platforms. Ecosystem join decisions are made both on a strategic level but also on an operational level by senior software engineers. Some have coined these software engineers "Kingmakers", as these decisions may lead to long lasting relationships with the technical platform and the keystone organization that supports it.

Software producing organizations address the groups of software engineers in their software ecosystems as "Developer Ecosystems". Managing developer ecosystems is a challenge for software producing organizations in four different ways. First, the platform that the developer ecosystem focuses on needs to be extensible, flexible, robust, evolvable, and provide facilities for rapid development of new solutions. Secondly, the developer community must be managed, by organizing events, coordinating feedback, helping developers help each other, etc. Thirdly, the software producing organization must be ready to accommodate developers, by readily providing them with easy access to the platform as well as to support, knowledge, and advice. Finally, the organization needs to keep track of other ecosystems, the role of open source in the platform, and invest in supporting platforms and ecosystems.

The position of organizations in software ecosystems as a keystone is largely dependent on how they conduct their developer ecosystem, i.e., the ecosystem of collaborating developers that add value to the platform. The field of software ecosystem governance is maturing, but many organizations are still reinventing tools and methods for becoming stronger in a software ecosystem. There is a need for research into the mechanisms that entice, attract, keep, and lock-in developers. These mechanisms range from tools for knowledge sharing, such as joint repositories and API documentation, to release coordination, where release candidates are released to partners early, to enable them to do compatibility checking of their extensions. Another concept that is insufficiently studied is the role of dominant design and standardization in industries. Finally, ecosystem life cycles have not yet been researched comprehensively, and it is as of yet unclear how ecosystems start, grow, develop, die out, and renew again.

4 Continuous X, Agile, and Technical Debt

One topic that has been harder to assign a title to, is the topic of Continuous X, where X can be replaced with testing, improvement, and development. The theme within this domain is the fact that software products are seen decreasingly as finalized artifacts that improve a business process, but increasingly as living artifacts that can be used to evolve with the business process. During the 2018 Dagstuhl meeting on the topic was decided that our field should let go of the 'Software Business' title and move towards "Software intensive Business", a change that can perhaps be attributed to this topical change.

We notice the following patterns in the Continuous X theme and recognize that these are direct lessons from the agile methodology. First, customers should be involved often and early in the development process, to reduce the significant waste that is part of any development process. Secondly, delivery should be frequent, to enable an organization to fail fast and fail often. In industry there are two trends that are at the basis of this research domain: software businesses are maturing into large inflexible organizations and traditional businesses are increasingly finding that they too, are software intensive businesses.

The best cited work of ICSOB 2012 is the work on innovation experiment systems for software products by Jan Bosch [5]. In it, Bosch lays out the first steps towards becoming a more responsive software development organization. Later Fabijan, Ollson, and Bosch [7] again achieve the most cited paper of ICSOB 2015, by elaborating on the methods for data gathering in continuous X processes.

We find that the outlets for work on these topics is best received by IEEE Software, JSS, IST, LNBIP, and LNCS. Also, there appears to be significant growth in this domain, as the number of published papers is steadily increasing.

A topic that deserves more attention from both an academic and a practitioner perspective, is the problem of scaling up from a small to medium software business to a larger one. Even though many companies grow to a healthy five to twenty employees, the hurdle to become a 10 million euro revenue company seems insurmountable for most. We hypothesize that the practices proposed in the domain of Continuous X, together with topics such as agile and aligned autonomy, could support smaller organizations in growing larger; but more research is needed.

5 Software Startups

The topic that has seen the fastest growth over a short time is software startups. With the surge of new startups and startup incubators, there is an audience for deliberate and planned growth of software startups. Several workshops are being started in this domain, but there are few serial academic events. That said, several relatively good articles are published in journals, such as the work by Bajwa, Wang, and Abrahamsson [3].

The community has brought forth several excellent ICSOB papers, such as the best paper of 2014 by Giardino, Wang, and Abrahamsson [8], which proposes a startup behavioral framework that shows reasons for and ways to avoid startup failure. In 2016 the community also has a most cited paper in the ICSOB with work on pivots in startups [2], work that would later be reworked into the journal article in the Empirical Software Engineering Journal (EMSE). Overall, the startup community publishes in forums such as LNBIP, LNCS, Communications of the ACM, JSS, and IEEE Software. A quick analysis of the domain shows a rapid increase in articles year over year and the growith is steadily increasing as well. This makes the topic of startups a relatively safe bet for future work.

6 Software Intensive Business Hype Cycle

In Fig. 1 we illustrate a hype cycle, as inspired by Gartner [14]. First, we address the four themes that can be identified in the best cited papers of ICSOB, being SPM, Software Ecosystems, Continuous X, and Software Startups. Secondly, we place several topics on the hype cycle, to indicate which topics we foresee as potential topics that will yield success in the future.

We identify that robots are an upcoming topic in the field of information systems and could potentially extend the field towards hardware. Secondly, a theme that is increasingly gathering popularity in software engineering and information systems is the application of AI techniques, for instance to support developers in task assignment in large projects. We expect that AI techniques may be able to for instance support task assignment in SPM or be able to support requirements identification in requirements engineering.

We also see a rise in publications on software business and blockchain [4,6] and expect that this is a relatively solid bet for future research in terms of impact and citations. There are two directions that SiB research could take in combination with blockchain. First, there are the cryptocurrencies, which can support new business models in the SiB domain. With cryptocurrencies, software businesses can invent currencies that are only used on their platform, thereby creating complete platform economies, new investment models, and distributed governance mechanisms. Secondly, the blockchain itself can be used to create new software intensive products. Examples are products that enable gateways between cryptocurrencies, products that use smart contracts, or products that can benefit from the fact that the shared distributed ledger is guaranteed to be correct.

One topic that is not addressed in this paper, is the topic of business modeling [13]. This topic is not experiencing the prolific growth of the others and appears not to be gaining much more traction after the seminal work on the business model canvas of Osterwalder and peers [17]. With the word "business"

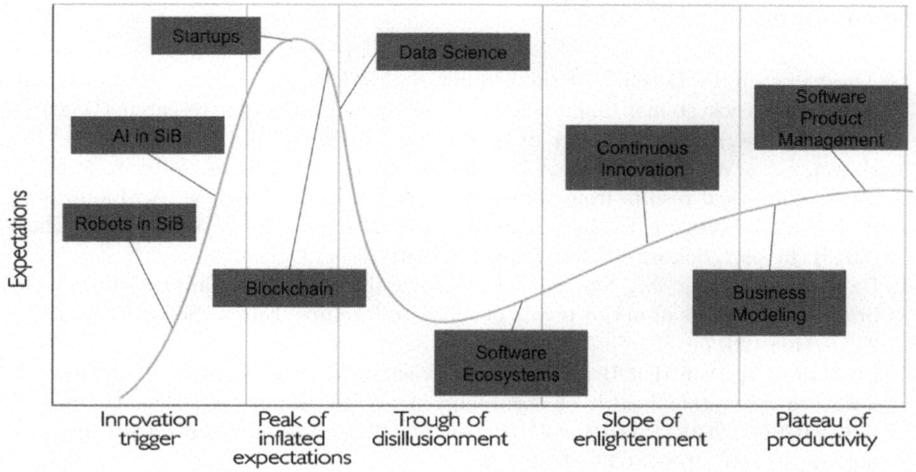

Fig. 1. Software intensive business hype cycle

in the name of the conference, one could have expected more from this domain. However, it is unlikely that the topic of business modeling will experience another surge such as around 2010.

7 Discussion and Conclusions

The future of the domain looks bright. Pockets of researchers will continue their lines on software ecosystems, continuous X, software product management, and software startups. We recognize new trends and research tooling in the domains of data science, artificial intelligence, and blockchain to further facilitate excellent research.

Simultaneously the field suffers from a lack of impact or perhaps a way to signify this impact to the outside world. Few initiatives are undertaken for grant proposal writing in, for instance, a European context. Also, support from companies should be extensive, but only few research groups are supported by industry with data or other resources.

If there is one thing this paper does, it is recognize that there are several sources in which we publish our work. Primarily, SiB work is published in LNCS, LNBIP, IEEE Software, the journal of Information Management, IEEE Computer, JSS, and IST. By recognizing these outlets as our primary outlets, it is perhaps also beneficial to invest heavily in these journals through guest editorships.

Acknowledgement. Please note that parts of the Section on software ecosystems have been discussed by Michael Cusumano, Karl Popp, and myself in an IEEE Software Special Issue on Software Ecosystems [10]. Also, I thank Krzysztof Wnuk for his excellent comments on this paper.

References

1. Abrahamsson, P., Bosch, J., Brinkkemper, S., Mädche, A.: Software business, platforms, and ecosystems: fundamentals of software production research (Dagstuhl seminar 18182). Dagstuhl Rep. **8**(4), 164–198 (2018)
2. Bajwa, S.S., Wang, X., Duc, A.N., Abrahamsson, P.: How do software startups pivot? Empirical results from a multiple case study. In: Maglyas, A., Lamprecht, A.-L. (eds.) Software Business. LNBIP, vol. 240, pp. 169–176. Springer, Cham (2016). https://doi.org/10.1007/978-3-319-40515-5_14
3. Bajwa, S.S., Wang, X., Nguyen Duc, A., Abrahamsson, P.: "failures" to be celebrated: an analysis of major pivots of software startups. Empir. Softw. Eng. **22**(5), 2373–2408 (2017)
4. Berkhout, M., van den Brink, F., van Zwienen, M., van Vulpen, P., Jansen, S.: Software ecosystem health of cryptocurrencies. In: Wnuk, K., Brinkkemper, S. (eds.) ICSOB 2018. LNBIP, vol. 336, pp. 27–42. Springer, Cham (2018). https://doi.org/10.1007/978-3-030-04840-2_3
5. Bosch, J.: Building products as innovation experiment systems. In: Cusumano, M.A., Iyer, B., Venkatraman, N. (eds.) ICSOB 2012. LNBIP, vol. 114, pp. 27–39. Springer, Heidelberg (2012). https://doi.org/10.1007/978-3-642-30746-1_3
6. Boshuis, S., Braam, T.B., Marchena, A.P., Jansen, S.: The effect of generic strategies on software ecosystem health: the case of cryptocurrency ecosystems. In: Proceedings of the 1st International Workshop on Software Health, pp. 10–17. ACM (2018)
7. Fabijan, A., Olsson, H.H., Bosch, J.: Customer feedback and data collection techniques in software R&D: a literature review. In: Fernandes, J., Machado, R., Wnuk, K. (eds.) ICSOB 2015. LNBIP, vol. 210, pp. 139–153. Springer, Cham (2015). https://doi.org/10.1007/978-3-319-19593-3_12
8. Giardino, C., Wang, X., Abrahamsson, P.: Why early-stage software startups fail: a behavioral framework. In: Lassenius, C., Smolander, K. (eds.) ICSOB 2014. LNBIP, vol. 182, pp. 27–41. Springer, Cham (2014). https://doi.org/10.1007/978-3-319-08738-2_3
9. Jansen, S., Bloemendal, E.: Defining app stores: the role of curated marketplaces in software ecosystems. In: Herzwurm, G., Margaria, T. (eds.) ICSOB 2013. LNBIP, vol. 150, pp. 195–206. Springer, Heidelberg (2013). https://doi.org/10.1007/978-3-642-39336-5_19
10. Jansen, S., Cusumano, M., Popp, K.M.: Managing software platforms and ecosystems. IEEE Softw. **36**(3), 17–21 (2019)
11. Jansen, S., Cusumano, M.A., Brinkkemper, S.: Software Ecosystems: Analyzing and Managing Business Networks in the Software Industry. Edward Elgar Publishing, Cheltenham (2013)
12. Kabbedijk, J., Jansen, S.: Steering insight: an exploration of the ruby software ecosystem. In: Regnell, B., van de Weerd, I., De Troyer, O. (eds.) ICSOB 2011. LNBIP, vol. 80, pp. 44–55. Springer, Heidelberg (2011). https://doi.org/10.1007/978-3-642-21544-5_5
13. Khurum, M., Gorschek, T., Wilson, M.: The software value map - an exhaustivecollection of value aspects for the development of software intensiveproducts. J. Softw. Evol. Process. **25**(7), 711–741 (2013)
14. Linden, A., Fenn, J.: Understanding gartner's hype cycles. Strategic Analysis Report No R-20-1971. Gartner, Inc. (2003)

15. Messerschmitt, D.G., Szyperski, C.: Software Ecosystem: Understanding An Indispensable Technology and Industry. The MIT Press, Cambridge (2005)
16. Nakasai, K., Hata, H., Matsumoto, K.: Are donation badges appealing?: a case study of developer responses to eclipse bug reports. IEEE Softw. **36**(3), 22–27 (2019)
17. Osterwalder, A., Pigneur, Y.: Business Model Generation: A Handbook for Visionaries, Game Changers, and Challengers. Wiley, Hoboken (2010)
18. van de Weerd, I., Bekkers, W., Brinkkemper, S.: Developing a maturity matrix for software product management. In: Tyrväinen, P., Jansen, S., Cusumano, M.A. (eds.) ICSOB 2010. LNBIP, vol. 51, pp. 76–89. Springer, Heidelberg (2010). https://doi.org/10.1007/978-3-642-13633-7_7

Software Ecosystems

A SECO Meta-model
A Common Vocabulary of the SECO Research Domain

J. Wouters[1], J. R. Ritmeester[1], A. W. Carlsen[1], Slinger Jansen[1], and Krzysztof Wnuk[2(✉)]

[1] Department of Information and Computing Sciences, Utrecht Universty, 3584 CC Utrecht, The Netherlands
j.wouters1@uu.nl

[2] Department of Software Engineering, Blekinge Institute of Technology, Karlsrkona, Sweden
krw@bth.se

Abstract. Software development companies are venturing towards collaborative approach and software ecosystems (SECO) participation. Over the years, many papers have been written and different modelling languages were proposed to capture the interactions between the SECO participants. What is missing, however, is a comprehensive meta-model describing possible entities and relationships that constitute a SECO. The goal of this paper is to create a common language for academic researchers for software ecosystems by creating such a meta-model. We constructed the meta-model by extracting and grouping entities and relationships from research papers. The meta-model consists of 5 themes: actors and roles, products and platforms, boundaries, ecosystem health and strategy. We advocate that our meta-model allows for easy sharing and comparing of case studies and the generalization of results across studies. We present the results from initial expert evaluation of the meta-model.

Keywords: Software ecosystems · Meta-model · Grounded theory · Literature review · Research synthesis

1 Introduction

Software development companies are venturing towards collaborative approach and software ecosystems participation [15]. The SECO literature is quite rich and offers case studies, experiences and models. A recent systematic literature review on the subject by Manikas [17], summarized 90 papers. They noted the following: *"(a) there is little consensus on what constitutes a software ecosystem and (b) few analytical models of software ecosystems exist"*. A SECO meta-model could be a useful tool for creating consensus and for creating consistent analytical models. Similarly, one of the main challenges in the SECO research agenda was the characterization and modelling of the emerging SECOs [16]. Since 2009, various SECO models [4,24,25] were created, but the domain lacks a meta-model which captures the SECO landscape as a whole.

S. Hyrynsalmi et al. (Eds.): ICSOB 2019, LNBIP 370, pp. 31–45, 2019.
https://doi.org/10.1007/978-3-030-33742-1_4

Accurate context descriptions support generalization and research synthesis across various cases and studies. Briand et al. [5] argue that context-driven research is needed in general since it makes clear working assumptions, and helps to achieve practicality and scalability. Dybået al. [8] propose to use a set of questions (what, who, where, when, why) to characterize the contexts of empirical research results. Petersen and Wohlin [20] provided a context checklist for industrial software engineering research. Ghaisas et al. [9] provide a proposal for reasoning on how to generalize findings across cases. To the best of our knowledge, no study has yet made an attempt to create a unified context description schema for SECO research. Throughout academic literature different terminology is used, which makes it difficult to link different scientific contributions within the domain together.

The goal for this research is *to develop a common language for the Software Ecosystem domain*. This is done by combining models and theories developed earlier by other research partners, utilizing the design science methodology suggested by Wieringa [27]. The main research question is formulated as follows:

What main elements a meta-model for SECO domain should contain?

The rest of this paper is structured as follows. In section two, we present the results from the literature study on SECOs and meta-modelling. In section three, the method used to develop the meta-model is described. In section four, the developed meta-model is presented. In the last section, research opportunities are identified and conclusions are drawn.

2 Related Work in Classification and Meta-models

Bosch developed a software ecosystem taxonomy, where SECOs would be placed on a three-by-three grid based on the category (end-user programming, application and operating system) and platform (desktop, web or mobile) [3]. This taxonomy, however, is not able to show all the aspects of the SECO, it merely positions them based on the output of the SECO. Jansen et al. also developed a classification model, where ecosystems would be classified based on four factors: Base technology, coordinators, extension markets and accessibility [15]. Both these models merely classify a SECO based on some aspects of it.

As the focus of this research is the creation of a SECO meta-model, defined as: *A meta-model provides a unifying framework in which to ensure and check consistency, while at the same time providing the means to distinguish between valid and invalid models, that is, conformance* [19].

The aim is to create a unifying framework by combining entities from existing models. A meta-model can aid in the creation of consistent and unambiguous models, making it easier to reason about SECOs [4].

3 Research Method

We used a design cycle methodology to develop the SECO meta-model [27]. The treatment under design is the SECO meta-model, designed in the four steps outlines in the following text. The following requirements are taken into account for the meta-model:

1. Requirement 1: The meta-model should be applicable to every SECO.
2. Requirement 2: The entities included into the meta-model have to be derived from scientific sources.
3. Requirement 3: The meta-model should be easy to use and understand.
4. Requirement 4: The meta-model should provide an extensive list of universally used terms to make it easier for researchers to discuss SECOs.

3.1 Step 1: Systematic Literature Review

We utilized the recent SLR of Mankikas [17] that contains 90 academic papers relevant for software ecosystems. We also applied the snowballing methodology [28] to identify other relevant papers. The selection criteria include:

1. The paper has to have SECOs as its main object of study.
2. The paper has to present some form of modelling technique, classification technique or characterization about SECOs.
3. The model or theory presented has to be somehow verified using academic techniques, e.g. proof of concept or case study.

Each paper was reviewed by one researcher of our research team. When in doubt, a second researcher was consulted until a consensus was found. All considered papers and inclusion decisions are available from the researchers upon request.

3.2 Step 2: Meta-model Relevant Entity Selection

To extract entities from the selected papers, we utilized open coding procedure in the grounded theory method [6]. The text that described or contained SECO entities was identified and coded. We used the following guidelines for coding:

1. The coding will be done by each researcher individually.
2. All codes need to be related to software ecosystems.
3. For every identified entity, the entire sentence in which this entity is found will be recorded.
4. For every code, a definition will be written, describing what it is and why it was recorded.

The coding process happened in weekly iterations, concluded with a synchronization meeting. In a final meeting, the separate coding files were combined and categorized. To eliminate unnecessary or incorrect codes, we applied the following selection criteria:

1. The entity should be unique (so no synonym), unambiguous and clear, and should not be included in another definition or definitions.
2. The entity should be applicable to all Software Ecosystems.
3. The entity is defined and described in academic literature.
4. The entity is without a doubt important to describe SECOs.

3.3 Step 3: Model Development

The identified entities were clustered according to the similarities and overlaps between them. We also modelled the relationships between the entities. We used the Class Diagram Language as specified by the Object Management Group [18] to depict the SECO meta-model. We described the following relationships:

- Aggregation: entity A consists of entity B. For example; a SECO contains actors.
- Generalization: entity B is a logical generalization of entity a. For example; A bridge is an example of a role.
- Navigated association: entity A is somehow related to entity B. For example; An ecosystem type is based on an extension market.

3.4 Step 4: Expert Review

We reviewed the developed meta-model with an expert in the field of software ecosystems and software business, using a semi-structured interview, in which we discussed the following:

- The completeness of the entities (Req 4).
- The categorization of the entities and the determined themes (Reqs 1, 4).
- The relationships identified and their significance (Req 4).
- The applicability of the meta-model to different kinds of SECOs (Req 1).
- The understandability of the meta-model (Req 3).

The expert review suggestions helped to further improve the meta-model.

4 Results and Analysis

4.1 Step 1: Paper Selection

We reviewed 181 papers (90 papers from the SLR by Manikas et al. [17] and 91 additional papers from the snowballing on the SLR). Based on the exclusion criteria, we included 36 papers and after the full read we left 33 papers[1].

4.2 Step 2: Entity Selection and Theme Construction

Open coding resulted in the identification of 218 entities, each checked on the four criteria defined in Sect. 3.2. After applying the criteria, 114 entities remained. Table 1 shows the number of entities which passed or failed the different criteria[2]. The, entities could have been excluded based on multiple selection criteria.

[1] The final list of selected papers is available online at https://drive.google.com/open?id=1ZzUHA7H22jPm7IfcHSv1AxSRd2hTQ5ye.

[2] The full list of codes and sources for building entities is available at online at https://drive.google.com/open?id=1ZzUHA7H22jPm7IfcHSv1AxSRd2hTQ5ye.

We have clustered the entities into five themes, described below. The full list of entities in available in Table 2.

Table 1. Included and excluded entities per criterion.

Criterium	Passed	Failed
Initial coded	218	–
Criterium 1: Unambigious, unique, clear and no synonym	142	76
Criterium 2: Applicable to (almost) all SECOs	201	17
Criterium 3: Defined and described in academic literature	197	21
Criterium 4: Without a doubt important to describe SECOs	169	49
Incorporated into final meta-model	114	105

Theme 1: Actors and roles. We identified 46 actor entities, outlined in Table 2. Each actor can have one or more roles in a SECO. This theme consists of all the actors and the roles they can take in a SECO. The term actor is not identified in the SLR [17], but can be seen as an overlapping term for all legal entities in a SECO who are taking part in the SECO in some form. The actors were split into two categories: Individuals and organizations. Individuals can be for example customers who are buying something from the SECO [15,25]. Also, hobbyists can be seen as individuals providing extensions to a SECO [7]. Another important individual actor is researcher, as identified by Alves et al. [1]. Organizations can also be part of a SECO. For example, independent software vendors can produce extensions for a base product (discussed below), enabling the keystone (discussed below) to focus on the core products [10]. Also, developer communities are active at SECOs, in certain ecosystems, all users are potential developers and form their own community (for example, in the Android ecosystem) [12].

The role of an actor can be derived from the relationship it has with other actors. A lot of these roles are derived from the work of Jansen et al. [14], e.g. niche player, keystone and dominator, disciple and hedger. The creation of the hub as an overlapping role has been discussed by Dos Santos et al. [23]. Several papers discussed roles which were linked to the roles a keystone fulfils in the ecosystem. For example, a keystone can be seen as an orchestrator, as discussed by Jansen et al. [14], van den Berk et al. [25]. Viljanen et al. also point out that "orchestration is mainly a keystone players' task" [26], which justifies the placement of the orchestrator entity under keystone. Also, a keystone most of the time is a platform leader, as a platform leader is "controlling large parts of an ecosystem", thereby making a platform leader a keystone [15]. As a keystone can fulfill one or multiple of these 'sub-roles', these sub-roles will be modelled as an aggregation. Actor categorization and description helps to map the ecosystem players and their influence on SECO.

Theme 2: Products and platforms. We identified 27 entities in this theme. Each SECO can have one or multiple products and platforms. A product is

Table 2. All entities categorized into five themes.

Theme 1: Actors and roles	**Theme 2: Products and platforms**	**Theme 3: Strategy**
Actor (17, 19)	API (2, 9, 12, 16, 34)	Acquisition strategy (16)
Advertiser (34)	Architecture (2, 3, 7, 8)	Affiliate model (30)
Banks and investors (23, 31)	Base technology (16)	Business strategy (3)
Bridge (14, 16)	Community driven (16)	Cost of development (3)
Broker (14)	Documentation (1, 2, 28)	Ecosystem openness (2, 15, 31, 36)
Buyer (34)	Executable components (2)	Ecosystem strategy (16)
Community leader (1, 28)	Extension market (16)	Entry barrier (14, 16, 30, 31)
Competitor (4, 16, 31)	Hardware product (4)	Licensing (2, 4, 8, 36)
Complementor (34)	Intellectual property (15)	Membership model (30)
Consultancy firms (31)	Open-source component (12)	Orchestration techniques (2, 4, 14,16, 31, 34)
Customer (4, 10, 15, 16, 17)	Operating system (2)	Partnership model (30)
Decision maker (23)	Ownership model (Self-developed)	Platform strategy (16, 31, 34)
Developer communities (32)	Platform (2, 4, 6, 7, 8, 14, 16, 17, 19, 31, 34)	Product lifecycle strategy (16)
Disciple (8, 14)	Platform planning (31)	Risk management (34)
Domain expert (31)	Privately owned (16)	Revenue model (24)
Dominator (8, 6, 14, 16, 31)	Product (Self-developed)	Strategic planning (4)
Governments (1, 23, 31)	Product quality (1)	Technology asset management (34)
Hardware vendor (32)	Programming language (7)	Technology scouting (34)
Hedger (8, 14)	Requirement (11, 27, 34)	Time to market (3)
Hobbyist (9)	SDK (12)	Tipping strategy (34)
Hub (8, 16, 31)	Software artifact (2, 7, 11, 23, 27)	Transaction costs (13)
Ind software vendor (13, 15)	Software concept (16)	
Individual (Self-developed)	Software library (31)	
Influencer (8, 14)	Software product (4, 16, 17, 19, 29, 31)	
Keystone (8, 14, 15, 29, 30, 31, 34)	Software source code component (2)	
Legal entity (6, 12, 32)	Software standard (16)	
Legal firms (31)	Use case (19)	
Manufacturer (9)		
Niche player (8, 14, 16, 29, 31, 32, 34)		
Open source organization (15)		
Orchestrator (14, 30)		
Organization (Self-developed)		
Platform leader (16)		
Platform provider (32)		
Product manager (15)		
Quality assesor (19)		
Regulatory bodies (7, 31)		
Relationship (Self-developed)		
Researcher (1)	**Theme 4: Ecosystem health**	**Theme 5: Boundaries**
Research group (19)	Growth (2)	Abstraction level (17, 19)
Role (8, 14, 23, 30, 34)	Health factors (6, 32)	Ecosystem type (6, 12, 13, 19)
Seller (34)	Maturity (1, 28)	Environment (4)
Supply chain partner (15)	Niche creation (6, 8, 14, 16)	Inputs (4)
Technology provider (15)	Popularity (11)	Legal framework (5)
Third-party developer (9, 15)	Productivity (6, 8, 14, 16)	Market (14, 17, 19)
Value-added reseller (15, 17, 30)	Robustness (6, 8, 14, 16)	Output (4)

defined in this research as either a software standard, hardware product or software artefact that is part of the SECO. A software product is mentioned many times as a part of a SECO by Jansen et al. [15] and Boucheras et al. [4]. A software concept is also discussed by Jansen et al. [15], even naming it a way to discuss software ecosystem types. Other software artefacts were also discussed in different SECO papers. A full list is included in the entity overview in Table 2.

The platform in an ecosystem is a central entity on which different actors can provide their products. Most of the time the platform itself is some form of product, which can be extended by apps or extensions produced by different actors [14,15]. The link between products and platforms can be defined by the entity "base technology", called by Jansen et al. [15] as "the technology underpinning the SECO". In this research, it is argued that the base technology itself is always some form of product, linking the two concepts together. Some key elements about a platform are also identified from the literature, such as a platform planning [2] and an ownership model [15].

Theme 3: Strategy. We identified 21 entities in this theme. The third theme identified is Strategy. Every actor within the ecosystem has certain strategies regarding their products, position in the ecosystem and revenue generations. A lot of these strategies are described by different papers. For example, Dos Santos et al. discussed seven papers which describe strategy in some form [23], Jansen et al. discussed making strategy (platform strategy, acquisition strategy, product lifecycle strategy) explicit [15] and Popp described revenue models for the hybrid software industry [21]. All of these strategies are part of the strategy of an actor within the SECO, and therefore indirectly influence the SECO.

A special kind of strategy is the Ecosystem strategy, which directly influences the ecosystem. Jansen et al. identified developing SECO strategy as one of the main research challenges in the SECO domain [16]. Several papers discussed parts of SECO strategy. For example, the different orchestration techniques discussed by Jansen et al. [14] are part of the SECO strategy, as are the entry barriers set by the keystone(s) of a SECO. Van den Berk et al. discussed a model to measure the SECO strategy in their paper [25], which can be used to formalize the SECO strategy, as well as its underlying entities.

Theme 4: Ecosystem health. We identified 7 entities in this theme. Different papers discuss the health of a certain ecosystem. The health of a SECO is a main theme as it is the main way to measure the current status of an ecosystem. It, therefore, is the main operationalization of the success of an ecosystem thus far. The main factors of measuring health in an ecosystem are identified by Iansiti and Levien [11] to be Niche creation, robustness and productivity. These three factors are further operationalized by Jansen [13]. This research also found some entities which are directly influenced by ecosystem health, such as the growth, maturity and popularity of the SECO.

Theme 5: Boundaries. We identified 7 entities in this theme. The boundaries of a SECO are defined in this research are the defining properties which describe what is part of the SECO, and what is not. The paper of Jansen et al. [14] described some initial boundaries, such as the market the SECO operates in and the ecosystem type the ecosystem at hand has, which is determined based on four factors: base technology, keystone, extension market and accessibility. It also discusses abstraction levels (SECOs level, SECO level or Software Supply

Network level) of SECOs which can be used to further define a SECO. A SECO is further defined by the output it generates and the input it uses to do so [4].

4.3 The SECO Meta-model

The SECO meta-model has gone through four iterations before it reached its current final state. The final version of the meta-model consists of 114 entities and 120 defined relations between them. Figure 1 shows the relationships between a SECO and the main themes. The most important design decisions and relationships are described in the paragraphs that follow.

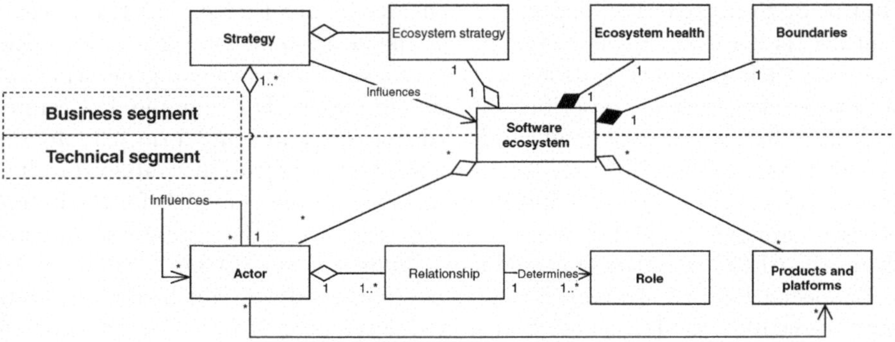

Fig. 1. Part of the model showing the relationships between SECO and main themes

Two segments: Business (strategic) and technical (operational): In the final iteration of the model, it became apparent that two 'segments' of the model can be identified. The first segment is a technical segment. Here, the model describes the actors, products, and platforms the SECO consists of. The other segment, the business segment, describes the SECO on a higher level: it describes the SECOs boundaries, strategy, and health. This will be useful when analyzing the business segment of the SECO in academic situations. Together, these two segments will give a complete overview of the SECO being modelled. If the main aim is to research a SECO in the most complete way, both segments have to be used. Both segments should be used to describe SECO research in the most complete way. Of course, this is not recommended as it glances over the business decisions made about the SECO.

Split between actors and their roles: As identified above, each SECO consists of a number of actors, which can have one or multiple roles. This split has also been made explicit in the meta-model. The 'relationship' entity connects the actor and the roles, as a relationship between actors determines the role a certain actor can have. Special roles are that of the 'niche player' and the 'keystone'. A keystone fulfils certain sub-roles in the SECO, for example; that of platform owner, decision maker, and orchestrator, as discussed above. A keystone does not have to fulfil all of these sub-roles, but when it has at least one of these sub-roles, the actor can be considered as a keystone. See Fig. 2 for a schematic overview of this split.

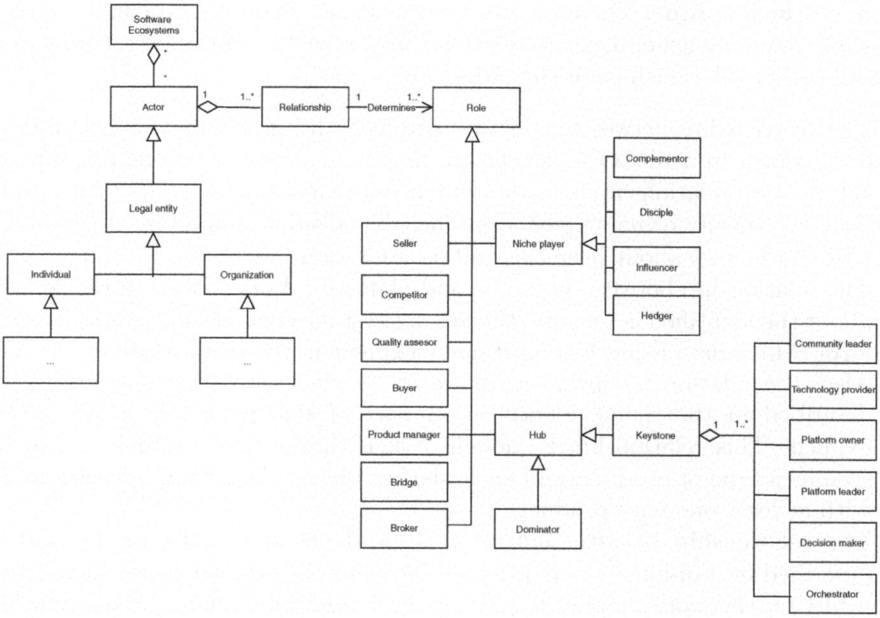

Fig. 2. The part of the model showing the relationships between actors and roles

Strategy and ecosystem strategy: In the business segment, we define a relationship is defined between Strategy and ecosystem strategy. As discussed, different strategies followed by different actors might influence the SECO. Therefore, this relationship is defined as "Strategy influences SECO". To make the link between strategy and the actors having these strategies more explicit, an aggregation relationship from strategy to actor has been defined. The ecosystem strategy, which can be seen as a special kind of strategy, is directly related to the SECO, as each SECO has a SECO strategy determined by the keystone players. Therefore, an aggregation relationship is defined between SECO and SECO strategy. This relationship is also shown in Fig. 1

Links between business and technical segment: The model developed has three links between the business and technical segment. Firstly, the output of a SECO (which is part of the 'boundaries' theme) is linked to the products and platforms theme, as the output generated by SECO can always be described as a product or a platform. Secondly, the ecosystem type (in the 'boundaries' theme), is also linked to two different products and platforms entities and one role entity. This relationship is defined based on the paper of Jansen and Cusumano [15].

This further indicates that both segments are connected to each other, and both have to be modelled to fully represent a SECO. Finally, the relationship between strategy and actor is already described above, but is also a relationship between the two segments of the meta-model.

Other relationships: There are more relationships defined in the meta-model, most of which are generalization relationships derived from the literature. Some notable other relationships in the model are:

- The relationship between actor and product and platforms: Every product or platform in a SECO is developed and/or maintained by one or multiple actors. This relationship is made explicit in the meta-model. The relationship does not specify ownership of a product: This is determined by the strategy a SECO follows about licensing and its affiliation model.
- The relationship between keystone and platform: As described in the section about the identified actors and themes, a keystone controls a platform in some form. This relationship has been made explicit in the meta-model.
- Also, the relationship between platform, product and base technology (as described in the theme identification part of this paper) has been made explicit. This relationship is modelled such that a base technology can be seen as a type of product, and each platform has an aggregation relationship with at least one base product.
- The relationship between output and products and platform: Output is described by Jansen et al. [4] as one of the general characteristics which define a SECO, therefore making it part of the boundaries theme. A relationship can be defined between output and products and platform as the output in the SECO are products and/or platforms and their supporting documents. Therefore, the output entity is modelled to have a generalization relationship with products and platforms.
- Finally, relationships are been made between ecosystem health and three factors which are influenced by the health of an ecosystem: Growth, Maturity and Popularity. As of now, no research has been done on these relationships. Therefore, the direction of this relationship is not made explicit: further research in this subject is needed.

The full meta-model is included in Appendix A.

4.4 Expert Review

The selected expert wrote several papers about Software Ecosystems and is considered an expert in the field of the SECO domain. Because of travel constraints, the interviews were held using Skype. The expert has 15 years of research experiences and 20 years of industrial experience. The results of this expert review are discussed below.

The expert concluded that the technical section was very complete and its entities were all known to him, validating that the entities derived can be seen as common vocabulary in the domain of SECO research. The expert argued that most of the concepts were clearly defined in the literature, and were therefore well-placed in the model.

On the business segment, the experts argued that the strategy entity should be better related to the actor, as the actor follows a certain strategy, and the ecosystem is merely impacted by that strategy but does not contain it (except for the ecosystem strategy). The layout of the meta-model in this stage of the research suggested that all strategies were part of the SECO. In response, we created a new relationship between strategy and actor in the meta-model. The expert also argued that the "boundaries" entity was somewhat unclear. This resulted in the formulation of a definition for the boundaries term, which is described above. The experts also argued that the terms 'transparency level' and 'ecosystem openness' were meaning somewhat the same which resulted in a re-evaluation of the two terms and the dropping of the transparency level entity.

A final remark was to restructure the business segment of the meta-model in three parts: one part about starting the SECO, one part about monetizing on a SECO and one part about the boundaries of a SECO (already included). After consideration, the researchers decided not to include this in the meta-model, as this split was not found in the literature considered and therefore including this split was in contradiction with the third entity-selection criterium.

5 Discussion and Conclusion

5.1 Limitations

There are some limitations to the study at hand. First of all, the researchers are unable to claim completeness: because of time constraints not all papers in the SECO domain could be identified and analyzed. Therefore, the decision was made to use an existing SLR study, and adapt it to the requirements of this research. This could be a threat to the generalizability of this study.

A second limitation is that the model has yet to been evaluated by several case studies. Because of time constraints, only an expert review has been executed, but the meta-model will be further strengthened when there are plenty of case-studies modelled using the technique. Case studies could provide the research field with additional data about the operationalizability of the SECO meta-model developed in this paper. Performing case studies to validate the meta-model is subject to further research.

Another limitation is that we could have missed some papers even after running a snowballing search on the 90 academic from the SLR. Still, snowballing appears to be the most suitable method for following up on previous literature reviews and its nature gives high probability of complete results [28].

Moreover, we are aware that the current meta-model is more of a vocabulary rather than a meta-model and therefore we are planning to apply more sophisticated conceptual modeling and modeling approaches to further develop the main concepts and relationships within the meta-model.

Finally, we are working on creating guidelines for reporting SECO research (similar to [22]) based on the meta-model structure. These guidelines are a necessary element for popularizing the meta-model and unified SECO description that will increase the utility of the meta-model.

5.2 Conclusion

In this paper, we present a SECO meta-model that should help researchers to describe and structure the SECOs they are investigating. The meta-model should also improve communication about SECOs research, making it easier to share case studies or to compare SECOs and research about SECOs. Therefore, the research goal of developing a common language for the SECO domain has been fulfilled.

The meta-model which has been created can be used for different aspects within the SECO domain. Researchers are now able to link their work to the meta-model. By linking their work with a certain entity within the model, it becomes clear to every researcher how their work links within the SECO research domain. The model can, therefore, be used as a basis to link future research about SECOs with the knowledge already available in the field.

In addition, researchers can now make generalizations of certain types of SECOs, as modelling different cases of a SECO type now becomes possible with the meta-model. Shared elements in these models can then be identified, which makes it easier to formalize a SECO type or theory. These types can then be researched more in depth, deriving more general theories about SECOs. This helps to formalize the domain, as most research is now done on a case-by-case basis, which makes it hard to generalize from the results.

5.3 Future Work

We plan to further develop the concepts included into the SECO meta-model. We also plan to create a knowledge repository where, some example actors and software products can be included, to ensure fast modelling possibilities for a SECO. The meta-model created in this paper can be used as a base in developing an extensive reporting technique which enables to report on the structure and policies of a SECO. Additionally, an algorithm can be developed which might be able to support the modelling of a SECO. The algorithm can populate some simple derivable entities from a SECO, like the actors in a SECO based on an app store or the products in an extension market.

Appendix A: The Full Meta-model

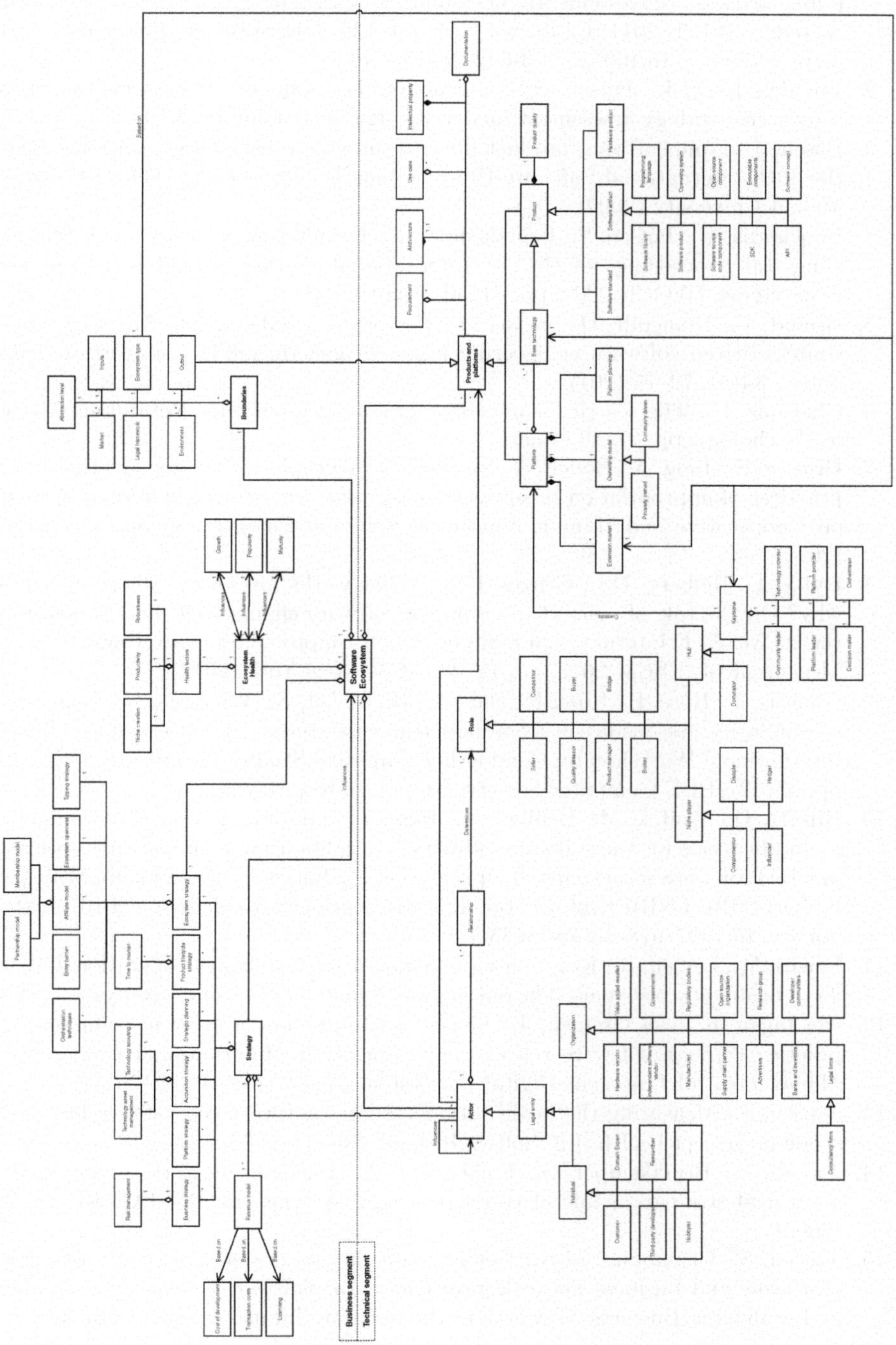
Software Ecosystem
Ecosystem Health
Boundaries
Products and platforms
Strategy
Role
Actor
Relationship
Business segment
Technical segment
Growth
Popularity
Maturity
Robustness
Productivity
Niche creation
Health factors
Abstraction level
Inputs
Ecosystem type
Output
Market
Legal framework
Environment
Requirement
Architecture
Use case
Intellectual property
Documentation
Product quality
Product
Base technology
Platform
Platform planning
Ownership model
Community driven
Privately owned
Extension market
Hardware product
Software artifact
Software standard
Programming language
Operating system
Open-source component
Executable components
Software concept
Software library
Software product
Software source code component
SDK
API
Keystone
Technology provider
Platform provider
Orchestrator
Community leader
Platform leader
Decision maker
Hub
Dominator
Competitor
Buyer
Bridge
Seller
Quality assessor
Product manager
Broker
Niche player
Disciple
Hedger
Complementor
Influencer
Organization
Individual
Legal entity
Value added reseller
Government
Regulatory bodies
Open-source organization
Research group
Developer communities
Hardware vendor
Independent software vendor
Manufacturer
Supply chain partner
Advertiser
Banks and investors
Legal firms
Consultancy firms
Domain Expert
Researcher
Customer
Third-party developer
Hobbyist
Revenue model
Cost of development
Transaction costs
Licensing
Risk management
Business strategy
Platform strategy
Acquisition strategy
Strategic planning
Product lifecycle strategy
Ecosystem strategy
Technology scouting
Technology asset management
Time to market
Orchestration techniques
Entry barrier
Affiliate model
Ecosystem openness
Tipping strategy
Partnership model
Membership model
Based on
Influences
Supports
Determines
Controls

References

1. Alves, A.M., Pessoa, M., Salviano, C.F.: Towards a systemic maturity model for public software ecosystems. In: O'Connor, R.V., Rout, T., McCaffery, F., Dorling, A. (eds.) SPICE 2011. CCIS, vol. 155, pp. 145–156. Springer, Heidelberg (2011). https://doi.org/10.1007/978-3-642-21233-8_13
2. van den Berk, I., Jansen, S., Luinenburg, L.: Software ecosystems: a software ecosystem strategy assessment model, pp. 127–134, January 2010
3. Bosch, J.: From software product lines to software ecosystems. In: Proceedings of the 13th International Software Product Line Conference, pp. 111–119. Carnegie Mellon University (2009)
4. Boucharas, V., Jansen, S., Brinkkemper, S.: Formalizing software ecosystem modeling. In: Proceedings of the 1st International Workshop on Open Component Ecosystems, IWOCE 2009, pp. 41–50, August 2009
5. Briand, L., Bianculli, D., Nejati, S., Pastore, F., Sabetzadeh, M.: The case for context-driven software engineering research: generalizability is overrated. IEEE Softw. **34**(5), 72–75 (2017)
6. Charmaz, K.: The search for meanings-grounded theory. In: Rethinking Methods in Psychology, pp. 27–49 (1996)
7. Draxler, S., Jung, A., Boden, A., Stevens, G.: Workplace warriors: identifying team practices of appropriation in software ecosystems. In: 4th International Workshop on Cooperative and Human Aspects of Software Engineering, pp. 57–60. ACM (2011)
8. Dybå, T., Sjøberg, D.I., Cruzes, D.S.: What works for whom, where, when, and why? On the role of context in empirical software engineering. In: Proceedings of the ACM-IEEE International Symposium on Empirical Software Engineering and Measurement, ESEM 2012, pp. 19–28. ACM, New York (2012)
9. Ghaisas, S., Rose, P., Rose, P., Daneva, M., Sikkel, N., Wieringa, R.: Generalizing by similarity: lessons learnt from industrial case studies. In: Proceedings of the 1st International Workshop on Conducting Empirical Studies in Industry, CESI 2013, pp. 37–42. IEEE Computer Society, United States, May 2013
10. Hilkert, D., Wolf, C.M., Benlian, A., Hess, T.: The "As-a-Service"-paradigm and its implications for the software industry – insights from a comparative case study in CRM software ecosystems. In: Tyrväinen, P., Jansen, S., Cusumano, M.A. (eds.) ICSOB 2010. LNBIP, vol. 51, pp. 125–137. Springer, Heidelberg (2010). https://doi.org/10.1007/978-3-642-13633-7_11
11. Iansiti, M., Levien, R.: Keystones and dominators: framing the operational dynamics of business ecosystems. The operational dynamics of business ecosystems (2002)
12. van Ingen, K., van Ommen, J., Jansen, S.: Improving activity in communities of practice through software release management. In: International Conference on Management of Emergent Digital EcoSystems, pp. 94–98. ACM (2011)
13. Jansen, S.: Measuring the health of open source software ecosystems: beyond the scope of project health. Inf. Softw. Technol. **56**(11), 1508–1519 (2014)
14. Jansen, S., Brinkkemper, S., Finkelstein, A.: Business network management as a survival strategy: a tale of two software ecosystems. In: IWSECO@ICSR 2009 (2009)
15. Jansen, S., Cusumano, M.A.: Defining software ecosystems: a survey of software platforms and business network governance. In: Software Ecosystems: Analyzing and Managing Business Networks in the Software Industry, vol. 13 (2013)

16. Jansen, S., Finkelstein, A., Brinkkemper, S.: A sense of community: a research agenda for software ecosystems. In: ICSE-Companion 2009, pp. 187–190. IEEE (2009)
17. Manikas, K., Hansen, K.M.: Software ecosystems-a systematic literature review. J. Syst. Softw. **86**(5), 1294–1306 (2013)
18. Object Management Group (OMG): Unified Modeling Language (UML) Specification, Version 2.5.1. OMG Document Number formal/17-12-05 (2017). https://www.omg.org/spec/UML/2.5.1/
19. Paige, R.F., Brooke, P.J., Ostroff, J.S.: Metamodel-based model conformance and multiview consistency checking. ACM Trans. Softw. Eng. Methodol. (TOSEM) **16**(3), 11 (2007)
20. Petersen, K., Wohlin, C.: Context in industrial software engineering research. In: 3rd International Symposium on Empirical Software Engineering and Measurement, ESEM 2009, pp. 401–404. IEEE Computer Society, Washington, DC (2009)
21. Popp, K.M.: Hybrid revenue models of software companies and their relationship to hybrid business models. In: IWSECO@ ICSOB Confernece, pp. 77–88 (2011)
22. Runeson, P., Höst, M.: Guidelines for conducting and reporting case study research in software engineering. Empirical Softw. Engg. **14**(2), 131–164 (2009)
23. dos Santos, R.P., Werner, C.M.L.: A proposal for software ecosystems engineering. In: IWSECO@ ICSOB, pp. 40–51 (2011)
24. Van Angeren, J., Kabbedijk, J., Jansen, S., Popp, K.M.: A survey of associate models used within large software ecosystems. Computing **746**, 27–39 (2011)
25. Van Den Berk, I., Jansen, S., Luinenburg, L.: Software ecosystems: a software ecosystem strategy assessment model. In: Proceedings of the Fourth European Conference on Software Architecture: Companion Volume, pp. 127–134. ACM (2010)
26. Viljainen, M., Kauppinen, M.: Software ecosystems: a set of management practices for platform integrators in the telecom industry. In: Regnell, B., van de Weerd, I., De Troyer, O. (eds.) ICSOB 2011. LNBIP, vol. 80, pp. 32–43. Springer, Heidelberg (2011). https://doi.org/10.1007/978-3-642-21544-5_4
27. Wieringa, R.J.: Design Science Methodology for Information Systems and Software Engineering. Springer, Heidelberg (2014). https://doi.org/10.1007/978-3-662-43839-8
28. Wohlin, C.: Guidelines for snowballing in systematic literature studies and a replication in software engineering. In: 18th International Conference on Evaluation and Assessment in Software Engineering, EASE 2014, pp. 38:1–38:10. ACM, New York (2014)

Towards an Understanding of iIoT Ecosystem Evolution - MindSphere Case Study

Dimitri Petrik(✉) and Georg Herzwurm

Graduate School of Excellence Advanced Manufacturing Engineering (GSaME), University of Stuttgart, Nobelstr. 12, 70569 Stuttgart, Germany
{dimitri.petrik, georg.herzwurm}@gsame.uni-stuttgart.de

Abstract. Currently emerging Industrial Internet of Things (iIoT) platforms form open and flexible networks with the aim of facilitating the integration of various stakeholders in the generation of platform-based added value. The ecosystem emergence process is still underresearched and remains a challenge for the platform providers. In this short paper, we analyze the ecosystem development by Siemens for the platform MindSphere to understand its evolution, based on the sequence of entered partnerships, and their interplay with the established platform boundary resources (BR). Based on this case study, our research identifies insights about how Siemens developed its ecosystem during three distinctive phases. Our analysis demonstrates a roadmap, helping to understand how Siemens managed to integrate distinctive company types as partners in the MindSphere ecosystem. The findings add to the theory on platform emergence by embedding it into a complex Business-to-Business (B2B) context of iIoT.

Keywords: Boundary resources · iIoT ecosystem · Ecosystem emergence

1 Introduction

Digital platforms in iIoT are recognized to enable customized value adding services, integrating external resources from complementing third-party companies through open and flexible interfaces [1, 2]. Even large platform-providing companies such as PTC, Siemens or GE do not have sufficient expertise in each of the industrial processes to cope with the functional heterogeneity in iIoT, so they design open interfaces to integrate third-parties with appropriate external expertise. Therefore, platform-enabled services are usually not created by an isolated company, but consist of hardware and software contributions from external partners, and the integration of the customer, resulting in complex end-to-end (E2E) solutions developed by multiple stakeholders [3–5]. BR build a suitable concept to explain governance actions of platform providers to integrate external resources in ecosystems, and develop new insights on platform emergence [6]. Moreover, the platform-providing keystone is in the position to design and control the determinants, influencing the organization logics, which are required to attract external partners, who are not hierarchically controlled by the platform provider [7]. BR offer technological and social mechanisms to build the required organizational

S. Hyrynsalmi et al. (Eds.): ICSOB 2019, LNBIP 370, pp. 46–54, 2019.
https://doi.org/10.1007/978-3-030-33742-1_5

logic, and control the knowledge flows to attract the complementors to create value adding platform-based E2E solutions [4, 5, 7–9]. Despite the popularity of the platform topic in the IS [7], the ecosystem development in the B2B domain of iIoT remains an underresearched topic. Only few studies explored emergence phenomena and partner coping strategies for enterprise software platforms [3, 10]. Although BR are considered as a suitable concept to research theory on digital platforms [7], prior research did not use this concept in context of iIoT ecosystems. Bridging the BR perspective with the development of iIoT ecosystems, the research goal is *to understand how are iIoT ecosystems established in the beginning and evolve over time based on business relationships between the iIoT platform provider and its partners*. To achieve this goal, we conduct an explorative and inductive case study analysis of the MindSphere ecosystem, established by Siemens. We identify patterns how Siemens proceeded to develop its ecosystem, and which partnerships in which order it fostered based on the variety of attracted company types, and their connection with established BR.

This paper is a continuation of another research and relies on its results and the same dataset, used to identify 14 distinctive types of BR used in iIoT ecosystems, provided and evolved by Siemens [5]. Previously identified BR (see Table 2) are used to track BR-related actions of Siemens, and to investigate connections between the provision of BR and establishment of partnerships. Our study extends the previously used dataset [5] by additional data sources, additionally considering the information about business relations (with complements and end customers) in the MindSphere ecosystem.

2 Methodology

We have chosen MindSphere for three reasons. Siemens supports the provision of BR, openly communicating the integration of third-parties and strives for a high degree of technological integration at the connected device level. Being developed since November 2015, MindSphere has reached a certain mature status and offers a sufficient information base for researchers [5, 11].

The methodology of the ecosystem study is based upon the longitudinal case study, conducted by Skog et al. [12]. The ecosystem evolution is studied as a process based on tracking of event streams related to BR (dates of initial provision and following changes or evolving actions) and business relationships (date of partnership establishment). In order to track the BR-related actions, we used the previously identified 14 BR [5] used by Siemens, which helps to understand whether the described action is BR-related or not. The analysis of the business relationships included identification of the company type, the partnership type, the purpose of the partnership and the possible connection to a certain BR. These additional characteristics of the two streams allowed us to discover certain patterns how Siemens proceeded to develop its ecosystem and which partnerships in which order it fostered to conduct analytical generalizations about the development of iIoT ecosystems. Our approach corresponds with the qualitative method of document analysis, developed by Bowen. Study of electronic documents allows the extraction of context-based data regarding the BR-related actions and establishment of partnerships. Furthermore, the documents are suitable to track changes based on their timestamps, thus enabling the researcher to get qualitative knowledge on the ecosystem development based on the available materials in the specific context of iIoT [13, 14]. We relied on the publicly available external articles to verify and enrich the findings [14] from the official press releases. The covered time interval is between early 2016 (public release of MindSphere), and the current time (the 15.08.2019). The developer portal was studied for change logs on relevant BR (such as APIs, SDKs etc.). This approach was effective to track the BR-related actions, but it did not contain a sufficient number of established business relationships between Siemens, and its partners. Therefore, we initiated a follow-up data collection on google.com to track additional partnerships on the websites of the partners. The data analysis included the chronological sorting of the sighted documents as a timeline of events with the help of Aeon Timeline software. Furthermore, we labeled the partner companies according their company type based on the contribution to the iIoT ecosystem and the date of the partnership (either actual date or, if not mentioned in the article, the timestamp of the press release). If an article described something special about a certain partnership (e.g. addition to the platform core technology), then it was labeled as strategic. The list of screened data sources and the number of analyzed articles per data source are depicted in Fig. 1:

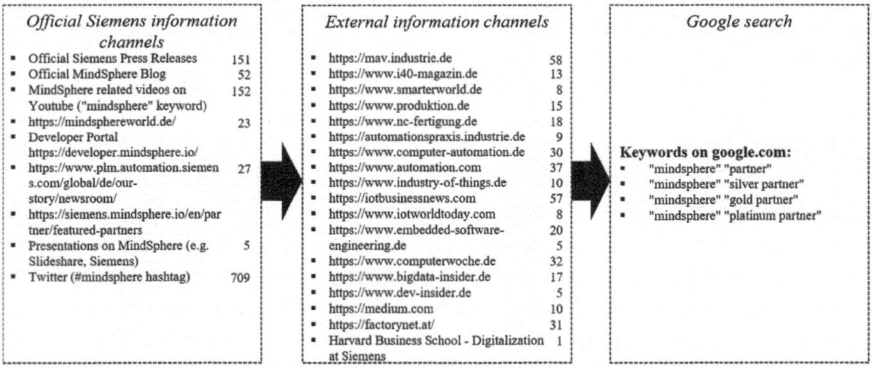

Fig. 1. Data collection overview for boundary resources and ecosystem joins.

3 Results

To observe the development of BR in the MindSphere ecosystem we have divided the timeline between the public release of MindSphere and the 15.08.2019 into three phases, each one is bound to a major release version of the platform. The first phase lasted between the public release of MindSphere and the release of MindSphere 2.0 on the 07.08.2017. The second phase lasted until the release of MindSphere 3.0 on the 01.01.2018. That is when the third phase started and it is currently going on, thus including current Q3 2019. We summarized any new introduction (e.g. support of new cloud infrastructure, or organization of a new type of event), or update (e.g. API patch or documentation update) for each of the 14 previously identified resources [5] in the following matrix of BR-related actions (Table 1). According to the matrix, there were only few BR-related actions (9 in the first and 10 in the second phase of MindSphere), while during the third phase, the ecosystem development process gained momentum, as indicated by the following 155 partner-engaging actions, related to BR.

Table 1. Tracking of events related with installation or maintenance of BR.

Phases		*1.*						*2.*		*3.*						
Timeline		*Q1 2016*	*Q2 2016*	*Q3 2016*	*Q4 2016*	*Q1 2017*	*Q2 2017*	*Q3 2017*	*Q4 2017*	*Q1 2018*	*Q2 2018*	*Q3 2018*	*Q4 2018*	*Q1 2019*	*Q2 2019*	*Q3 2019*
Technical BR	APIs	0	0	0	0	0	0	0	0	0	6	9	7	13	12	3
	Connectivity Libraries	0	0	0	0	0	0	0	0	0	2	1	2	3	0	2
	Support of Open Protocols	0	0	0	0	0	0	0	0	1	0	0	1	1	0	0
	Infrastructure Support	0	0	0	0	0	0	0	0	1	2	1	0	0	0	1
	DevOps Metrics	0	0	0	0	0	0	0	0	0	0	1	0	0	0	0
	SDK	0	0	0	0	0	0	0	0	0	1	0	3	1	4	1
	Cloud Foundry	0	0	0	0	0	1	0	0	1	1	0	0	1	0	0
	App Store	0	0	0	0	1	1	0	0	0	0	0	0	0	0	0
	Model-Driven Development	0	0	0	0	0	0	0	0	0	0	1	0	1	2	2
Social BR	Documentation	0	0	0	0	0	2	2	0	0	3	13	4	9	5	5
	Partner Programs	0	0	0	0	0	0	0	1	1	1	1	1	3	1	3
	Onsite Demonstrators	0	0	0	0	0	2	1	1	0	2	0	0	0	1	0
	Events	0	0	0	0	1	1	1	1	0	1	3	2	3	3	2
	Workshops	0	0	0	0	0	0	1	1	0	0	0	0	0	0	0
	Start-Up Support	0	0	0	0	0	0	1	0	0	0	0	0	0	0	0
Sum		**0**	**0**	**0**	**0**	**2**	**7**	**6**	**4**	**4**	**19**	**30**	**20**	**35**	**28**	**19**

The next step required to build a time series of conducted partnerships between third-parties and MindSphere. During the data collection process, we identified 236 business partnerships around MindSphere, and clustered them based on the company type (full list available online at: https://bit.ly/2k9KJAO). The company types combined with the date of partnership helped to recognize which different company types were systematically attracted by Siemens to collaborate during the three phases of development, and if the partnerships were supported by a provision of certain BR (if mentioned).

Shortly after the launch (during the **first phase**), large consulting companies with development capabilities were attracted to promote MindSphere. At the same time Siemens implemented its first industrial IoT-Gateways, which were based upon the hardware boards provided by Intel to provide easy connectivity with MindSphere, and extend the list of own natively compatible hardware products. In order to promote these gateways, and the iIoT platform, Siemens also fostered partnerships with resellers. Nevertheless, at that time there were only few partnerships with software and machine tool companies. However, some BR-related milestones were set during the first phase, such as the integration of Cloud Foundry as a useful technical BR for the deployment simplification, or the beginning of the opening of digitalization hubs as a social BR.

Table 2. Number of partnerships in the different development phases.

Partners by type	*1. Phase*	*2. Phase*	*3. Phase*
Consulting	5	1	11
Software Technology	2	1	2
Infrastructure	2	1	2
Software as a Service	2	2	44
Reseller	2	0	0
Hardware	1	0	0
Machine Tools	1	2	39
Consumption Goods	1	1	0
Components	1	1	15
Driverless Transport Systems	0	1	0
System Integrator	1	0	7
Data Analysis	1	1	13
Automation	0	0	23
Control Cabinets	0	0	3
Wholesale	0	0	3
Tools	0	0	1
Technology Corporations	0	0	6
Telecommunication	0	1	4
Medical Equipment	0	0	1
Design	0	0	1
Bank	0	0	1
Insurance	0	0	1
Academics	0	0	15
End customer	1	2	10
Sum	**20**	**14**	**202**

During the **second phase,** Siemens initiated various social BR, while the numbers of new partnerships remained low. At that time, the developer portal, first MindSphere application centers, and the first hackathon around MindSphere, were started. Moreover, Siemens started to provide trainings, and finally initiated the startup support initiative to promote them and provide the iIoT platform if needed. Lastly, the official partner program, aiming to facilitate partnerships with software developing companies was launched. Partnerships with consulting companies continued and the startup initiative introduced two new partnerships. Regarding the technology of the platform core, an important strategic partnership was initiated with Software AG to include a device management module in MindSphere. Siemens also started a strategic partnership with Amazon to make MindSphere available on the AWS infrastructure.

In the **third phase**, both the number of new partnerships, and the rates of change for various BR have risen significantly. Shortly after the release of MindSphere 3.0, Siemens started the worldwide user organization “MindSphere World” in six countries in a row, starting with Germany. In the beginning, the user organization primarily included machine tool companies and automation providers. By November of 2018, the organization has received new members with different specializations such as software developing companies, system integrators, banks, industrial wholesalers, and universities. At the same time, the user organization also expanded in Italy, Belgium, Korea, Taiwan, and Japan. Meanwhile, various software developing, and data analysis companies joined the partner program. It is worth mentioning, that some software companies maintain a double membership in the user organization and the partner program. Besides that, three new strategic partnerships were conducted. Hewlett-Packard as a partner enabled platform-based monitoring of additive manufacturing systems. Atos and Rittal were given new strategic roles to foster the development of edge data centres (complementary to the current cloud-based platform). A strategic partnership with the car manufacturer Volkswagen was announced. In total, comparison of BR-related activities and the partner numbers shows similar progressions (see Fig. 2).

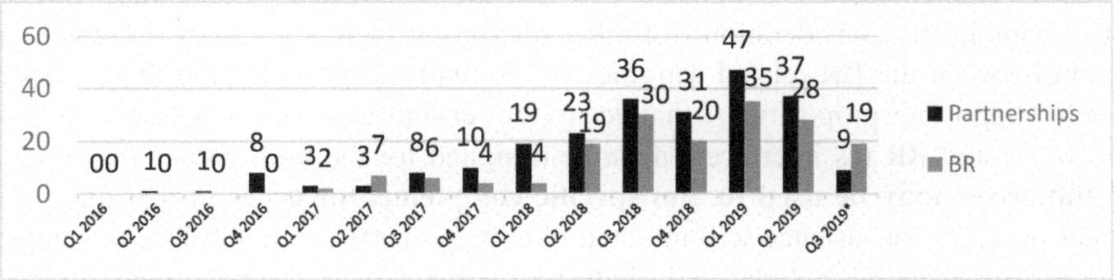

Fig. 2. Values for BR activities and closed partnerships.

The calculated bivariate coefficient indicates a strong correlation based on a value of 0,914800483. The aligning p-value is very low and equals 0,000001784 (see also: https://bit.ly/2k9KJAO). However, the correlation coefficient in this isolated view does not claim to demonstrate a causal relationship between the BR and the ecosystem growth. Interference variables and other dependent variables are not taken into account.

4 Discussion of Key Insights, Limitations and Outlook

Unveiling how Siemens proceeded, we identify **the changing nature of partnerships** as the first contribution. During the first phase, Siemens primarily aimed to cope with infrastructure (SAP, Microsoft) and software technology providers to extend the platform core (Cloud Foundry, IBM). These strategic partnerships expand functional variety and allow a simpler integration of the platform. In comparison, strategic partnerships during the third phase increasingly signaled the maturity of the platform. Exemplary partnerships with Hewlett-Packard and Academics (additive manufacturing), Atos and Rittal (Edge) or Volkswagen (end customer as a global machine operator), demonstrate the platform is mature enough to conquer new industries, and offer new value creation possibilities for partner. The focus of other partnerships changed as well. While the first phase primarily involved consulting companies to support the fist movers in different industries to integrate MindSphere, the focus shifted during the third phase to either complementary hardware (a total of 77 companies providing machines or components), or software and data analytics companies (a total of 57 companies), as these partner types design the value adding E2E solutions. It is also interesting to note the increasing importance of cyber security (partnerships with McAfee and Kaspersky among the 57 software companies) and academic partnerships. These observations provide an inductive blueprint of a roadmap and may help researchers and decision makers to understand how to overcome the chicken-egg-problem (if neither side will find the platform attractive enough to adopt it, without the presence of the other side) in iIoT ecosystems [15]. The heterogeneity of potential industries to enter, and the variety of potential partner types generate this problem for platform providers in iIoT ecosystems.

The next contribution explores **how a platform provider can address specific company types with BR and combine BR to foster the iIoT ecosystem.** The comparison of BR-related actions and partnerships shows a strong correlation between the amount of implemented and updated BR, and the established partnerships with Siemens. Without the consideration of further interfering factors, the data indicates connection between the BR-related activities of the platform provider and the ecosystem growth, supporting propositions, that ecosystem design is a controllable evolutionary process [7] and BR (as interfaces) must be designed for the third-parties [8]. Specific **BR initiatives may be used to aim specific complementor types** in first place. The partner program for instance was initiated to cope primarily with software developers. The user organization included only industrial companies in the beginning, and software developing companies started to join it later. Some partnerships demonstrate **how BR can be combined**. Some of the software companies had a double membership in the partner program and the user organization, and some partners received a membership in the user organization as a reward after their participation in a hackathon. Thus, the general understanding includes possible combinations of BR by the platform provider to promote certain partners, or to bridge the distance between specific partner types. These insights support the theory proposed by Jacobides et al., as the ecosystem emergence requires different types of relationships (i.e. unique and generic), varying in their standardization degree [7]. The growing importance of social BR during the third phase also supports Gawer's idea of unstable and changing platform interfaces during the time [2]. The standardization degree of the initiated partnerships itself seems to increase over time. The quantitative increase of installed or updated BR in 2019 indicates that Siemens increased the standardization rate of its internal processes to release BR updates at a higher rate. The increased frequency reflects positive effects of standardization on coordination costs of the ecosystem [15], and indicates its evolution mechanism [16]. This observation is supported by the parallel increase of partnerships.

Limitations: The investigation was based upon a single case study and the identified mechanisms and business relationships lack the validating consideration of competing iIoT ecosystems. Therefore, there is no comparison of the BR installed by competitors and how their ecosystems have grown as a result of similar measures, thus making the generalization of the results challenging. The second limitation is caused by the interpretative approach, which was used to identify the roadmap patterns conducted by Siemens from publicly available documents. This limitation was partly addressed by mixing the official press releases with external sources. However, future interviews with key informants from Siemens could increase the validity of the interpreted data. Furthermore, the information in the examined domain is relatively confidential. According to the tweet of MindSphere CTO [17] we have identified 78% (236/300) of the existing partnerships at best. Certain partnerships are not advertised publicly, and some companies could deliberately disguise the partnership with Siemens to appear more independent. Thus, future interviews could provide a more complete picture of the ecosystem.

Future work: Further analysis of comparable iIoT ecosystems could help to extend the understanding of domain specific factors on the theory of ecosystem development, and identify real “platform leaders” based on the ecosystem size. The results could be used for a future social network analysis of the MindSphere ecosystem and its visualization, replicating the used research method to study other competing iIoT platforms. This could shed light on the simultaneous relationships of complementors (developer multi homing) in the emerging iIoT ecosystems [16]. The identified BR effects and their changing update frequency may be used to explore the changing developer satisfaction with provided BR [8], during the usage of platform technologies.

References

1. Porter, M.E., Heppelmann, J.E.: How smart connected products are transforming competition. Harv. Bus. Rev. **92**(11), 64–68 (2014)
2. Gawer, A.: Bridging differing perspectives on technological platforms: toward an integrative framework. Res. Policy **43**, 1239–1249 (2014)
3. Schreieck, M., Wiesche, M., Kude, T., Krcmar, H.: Shifting to the cloud – how SAP’s partners cope with the change. In: Proceedings of the 52nd Hawaii International Conference on System Sciences, Hawaii International Conference, pp. 6084–6093 (2019)
4. Hein, A., Weking, J., Schreieck, M., Wiesche, M., Böhm, M., Krcmar, H.: Value co-creation practices in business-to-business platform ecosystems. Electron. Mark. 1–16 (2019). https://link.springer.com/article/10.1007/s12525-019-00337-y
5. Petrik, D., Herzwurm, G.: iIoT Ecosystem development through boundary resources: a siemens MindSphere case study. In: Proceedings of the 2nd ACM SIGSOFT International Workshop on Software Intensive Business: Start-ups, Platforms and Ecosystems (IWSiB 2019), ACM New York (2019)
6. De Reuver, M., Sorensen, C., Basole, R.C.: The digital platform: a research agenda. J. Inf. Technol. **33**(2), 124–135 (2018)
7. Jacobides, M.G., Cennamo, C., Gawer, A.: Towards a theory of ecosystems. Strat. Manag. J. **39**(8), 2255–2276 (2018)
8. Dal Bianco, V., Myllärniemi, V., Komssi, M., Raatikainen, M.: The role of platform boundary resources in software ecosystems: a case study. In: IEEE/IFIP Conference on Software Architecture. IEEE (2014)

9. Yoo, Y., Henfridsson, O., Lyytinen, K.: The new organizing logic of digital innovation: an agenda for information systems research. Inf. Syst. Res. **21**(4), 724–735 (2010)
10. Saadatmand, F., Lindgren, R., Schultze, U.: Configurations of platform organizations: implications for complementor engagement. Res. Policy **48**(8), 103770 (2019)
11. Collis, D., J., Junker, T.: Digitalization at Siemens. Case Study. Harvard Business Review (2017)
12. Skog D.A., Wimelius, H., Sandberg, J.: Digital service platform evolution: how spotify leveraged boundary resources to become a global leader in music streaming. In: Proceedings of the 51st Hawaii International Conference on System Sciences, Hawaii, pp. 4564–4573 (2018)
13. Eisenhardt, K.M.: Building theories from case study research. Acad. Manag. Rev. **14**(4), 532–550 (1989)
14. Bowen, G.A.: Document analysis as a qualitative research method. Qual. Res. J. **9**(2), 27–40 (2009)
15. Tiwana, A.: Platform Ecosystems: Aligning Architecture, Governance, and Strategy. Morgan Kaufmann, Amsterdam (2014)
16. Teixeira, J., Hyrynsalmi, S.: How do software ecosystems co-evolve? A view from openstack and beyond. In: Ojala, A., Holmström Olsson, H., Werder, K. (eds.) ICSOB 2017. LNBIP, vol. 304, pp. 115–130. Springer, Cham (2017). https://doi.org/10.1007/978-3-319-69191-6_8
17. Twitter Homepage. https://twitter.com/AndreasWGeiss/status/1100420422267482112. Accessed 16 Aug 2019

Identifying Architecture Attributes in the Context of Software Ecosystems Based on a Mapping Study

Thaiana Lima[1(✉)], Cláudia Werner[1], and Rodrigo Santos[2]

[1] Computer Science and Systems Engineering Department, COPPE/UFRJ – Federal University of Rio de Janeiro, Rio de Janeiro, Brazil
{thaiana,werner}@cos.ufrj.br

[2] Department of Applied Informatics, UNIRIO – Federal University of the State of Rio de Janeiro, Rio de Janeiro, Brazil
rps@uniriotec.br

Abstract. Currently, software acquirers and suppliers as well as their relations have been investigated as a software ecosystem (SECO). In a SECO, an organization wants to achieve its business objectives supported by technologies based on a common ecosystem platform. Modifications on technologies can make essential systems unsupported or low performance. Thus, IT managers should consider information about technologies and their relationships. Such information may be spread in different documents and/or difficult to analyze due to the lack of support. As such, related attributes assist IT managers and architects in making decisions on the IT architecture modification, i.e., the set of technologies supporting products and services adopted by an organization. This research aims to identify architecture attributes that affect a SECO and its platform and technologies from the literature. With the intention of comparing this research to a well-accepted standard, ISO/IEC 25000 characteristics were analyzed against architecture attributes. Then, we have evaluated such attributes with experts from industry and academia based on a survey research. As a result, 64 attributes were identified and grouped by 11 critical factors. Critical factors are macro attributes that encompass other attributes. Then, a better understanding on how IT managers and architects' choices can affect SECO could help them to take actions to mitigate negative effects.

Keywords: Software ecosystems · Architecture · Survey research · Reuse · Information integration

1 Introduction

Software acquiring organizations generally have an IT management team that plan/establish technologies to be adopted or standardized to support their applications (i.e., software products and services). In this context, an IT architecture is a list of technologies to be used as standard within an organization [14], often classified according to the technology categories used by the organization (e.g., database, programming language etc.). In addition, an IT architecture contributes to meet

S. Hyrynsalmi et al. (Eds.): ICSOB 2019, LNBIP 370, pp. 55–70, 2019.
https://doi.org/10.1007/978-3-030-33742-1_6

organizational business demands through a set of technical decisions [1, 5]. Architecture modifications may involve the adoption of a new technology, removing part of the architecture, or replacing technologies that an organization already uses. Changes in such architecture are not trivial as they affect the development or acquisition of new applications that must be adherent to IT architecture, e.g., new software development projects should use an existing technological standard according to the IT architecture.

In addition, they may reflect on development team's training needs regarding the new technology, aversion to changes and switching licensing costs, or even applications that depend on discontinued technology [16]. Because of rapid technological evolution, organizations frequently need to update/reevaluate their IT architecture. Evaluating the technology in relation to pre-established, manageable, and well-structured criteria provides greater transparency to the process, as IT managers and architects should be able to check/audit the adopted criteria. In [8], one of the most successful actions pointed out by companies is to use a well-defined procedure for IT acquisition. Part of the definition of such procedure is to establish evaluation criteria for technology selection [16]. Revisiting an IT architecture is necessary to maintain the technological platform. Moreover, it is a challenge considering that organizations are relating themselves as a software ecosystem (SECO). SECO involves elements out of the organizational scope, e.g., applications, technologies, internal and external developers, suppliers, and users. As such, there are architecture attributes related to the maintenance of an IT architecture, from organizational or technical nature, not identified or used together in the SECO context [9]. For public companies, this issue has even more restrictions, such as adherence to governmental norms and standards, current legislation, electronic procurement process with less control over technology selection processes, and budget. Private organizations usually have more freedom to choose technologies and applications. However, both types face the lack of indications to guide technologies' modification to maintain IT architecture (and how to collect them) [12].

This research aims to identify architecture attributes that affect a SECO and its platform and technologies from the literature. With the intention of comparing this research to a standard, ISO/IEC 25000 characteristics were also analyzed against architecture attributes. Finally, we have evaluated such attributes with experts from industry and academia based on a survey research. This paper is organized as follows: Sect. 2 presents the background; Sect. 3 brings the mapping study; Sect. 4 presents the survey research; Sect. 5 brings a discussion and Sect. 6 concludes the paper.

2 Background

2.1 Software Ecosystems

SECO is described as a set of actors interacting with technical artifacts such as software products and services based on a common technological platform [4]. As an organization stops developing its independent products, i.e., limited to its internal resources and actors, it creates relationships with companies, suppliers and products that change organizational business [3]. Thus, organizations are more dependent on external partners, suppliers and tools – none of that is controlled by them. Therefore, it is imperative to study not only the platform itself, but also the network of actors and artifacts as a SECO [16].

Actors are people inside and outside the organization who interact in several ways, e.g., developers, users, suppliers, competitors, and external players. Artifacts include software products, components, requirements, documentation, services, among others. According to a recent systematic literature review on the topic [15], health is on the top 25 paper keywords on Business and Management in SECO. A healthy SECO can maintain and increase the number of actors and artifacts, also creating opportunities for its actors. As such, a healthy SECO should be aware of technology management.

2.2 Platform Maintenance

Following SECO platform and its guidelines, it is possible to standardize processes and technologies for the application development. Modifications in platform involve the adoption of a new technology, removal of part of the architecture, or technology replacement. As such, technology change within the platform development must be carefully performed since this action affects the organization's standards. For example, choosing a technology that fails to support a legacy system can be costly, or that generates training costs without sufficient benefits to justify them. There are other organizational constraints that may affect adoption or discontinuation of technologies [16], such as:

- *Organization policies and standards, e.g., encourage open source software or national suppliers, not accepting certain types of proprietary license;*
- *Legislation, e.g., especially in cases of public companies, the country's legislation may affect candidate technologies (taxation and embargoes);*
- *Economic issues, e.g., budget for the period of modification and country's economic situation; and*
- *Organizational culture, e.g., aversion to paradigm shifts, rejection of technologies that reuse external components, and rejection of certain vendors.*

3 Mapping Study

Systematic reviews aim at incorporating evidence and providing a synthesis of the area, while mapping studies are mostly involved in exploring a research area. In addition, there are specific guidelines to expose the result for a systematic study. The type of literature assessment used in mapping studies mainly focuses on structuring a research area and its topics, gathering frequency and definitions. Hence, it offers a general idea of the research area scope. Besides, it also aids the determination of research gaps and tendencies [17]. This study is presented as a Mapping study because it is an exploratory approach for gathering information on the main architectural characteristics of SECO and painting a picture of the literature context.

This work serves as an initial basis to aid IT managers and architects to understand how their choices regarding technology acquisition can affect a SECO platform, as well as provide some actions to diminish harmful effects. With the intention of comparing this research to a well-accepted standard, ISO/IEC 25000 [6] characteristics were also analyzed against the critical factors resulted from the mapping study and validated by the survey, as described in Sect. 4.

The authors of this paper participated in a previous mapping study that primarily investigated how scientific literature studies software architecture in the SECO context, e.g., key characteristics, research needs, and reference architectures. The search string covered title- abstract-keyword with the terms ("software architecture" OR "software architectures") AND ("software ecosystem" OR "software ecosystems"). For each search engine, the search string was adapted according to the syntax rules but keeping terms and logical operators. The search string was run on the Scopus, Springer, IEEE, ACM, and Science Direct search engines. This first mapping study grounded the study presented in this section because, by participating in it, it brought better understanding of the architectural facet of SECO, the most researched topics, and gaps. In addition, its accepted papers and search strings were reused as a starting point for the mapping study to serve as a corpus for the extraction of architecture-related quality attributes for technology selection in SECO. It was not found in the literature a study that concise SECO attributes specific to quality and architecture context. This mapping study complements the literature by offering the list of attributes scattered in literature papers from the main search machines.

3.1 Planning

We defined the following research questions (RQ):

RQ1. What are the architecture-related quality attributes that describe or qualify software ecosystems and their platform regarding the architecture perspective?

RQ2. How do the architecture-related quality attributes relate to each other?

The activities planned for this study were executed in five steps. The set of studies was obtained after executing the mapping study (Step 1). Then, the full reading allowed us to extract the attributes and track the source papers (Step 2), as well as identify relations among attributes described in the selected papers and other possible associations (Step 3). From such relations, it was possible to group the attributes based on similarities, level of abstraction, or interactions reported at the papers (Step 4). Finally, we analyzed the possible effects those attributes could have on a SECO platform (Step 5).

This mapping study followed the same procedure and search string of the previous study. It was conducted by a Master student and supervised by two PhD students and a senior professor. There was not a specific term to be searched for, i.e., papers were scavenged for any term that characterized a SECO as well as its architecture or platform, considering that all the included papers have discussed SECO/architecture. As inclusion criteria, the studies must meet the following requirements: (1) the studies must present a discussion about SECO, its elements and architecture, regardless of which element of the SECO they focused on; and (2) the studies must be written in English and available online.

3.2 Execution

The execution was performed so that we reached as many studies published as possible along with those studies brought from the previous mapping study. In [11], a systematic literature study captured the main keywords related to 'software ecosystem'. The third popular term was "architecture"(s)/"architectural" and they were accompanied by "open", "parallel", "service oriented", and "software" in the papers keyword fields. Since there were no keywords for "technology architecture" or "IT architecture", the search string was generalized for the expression "software architecture" since it represented a very common expression for SECO context according to [11]. The search engines used were ACM, IEEE, ScienceDirect, Springer, and Scopus. In Scopus, some studies were rejected because they already appeared at other search engines. Accepted studies from the previous mapping (34) were also accepted in our mapping. Additionally, 10 new studies were included.

3.3 Results

The final literature base is composed by papers published from 2009. After reading the title, abstract and keywords, few papers were excluded because they fell out of the scope/context of this work by not focusing in any quality related SECO subject or they referenced SECO but did not ground the work on its concepts or research scope. Some papers were not reachable (i.e., full text was not available online, although we requested some of them to the authors) and thus removed from the literature base. From the 44 accepted studies, 16 (36.36%) did not present architecture-related quality attributes concerning SECO or its architecture or platform. Many papers mention the same attribute, e.g., 11 papers cite "integration", even appearing in different SECO contexts. Quality attributes were mentioned as attributes, for example, "openness".

The extraction was manually executed while reading the full text of selected papers and considered attributes seen as technology evaluation criteria. The criteria for identifying an attribute was being explicitly mentioned in the papers as SECO quality attributes, or key factors, properties or challenges. In addition, some papers report on SECO requirements regarding the platform architecture. Other attributes are nouns and adjectives used to describe a specific SECO; in this case, studies or more generic models in the context of architecture or platform. Only 6.2% (4 attributes) has more than five citations. Perhaps the great number of attributes with only one citation (42.2%) since specific SECO contexts are explored in the studies. Although the set is general, it also reaches many contexts. Table 1 shows the classification of attributes according to the papers and how attributes can comprise others as critical factors. The last three critical factors are health measures according to [7]. Critical factors are aggregations based on relationships indicated in the selected papers. Their definition and the references to the papers that mention them are presented in detail in [10]. The mapping does not bring new attributes but adds to the literature in identifying them and gathering its uses.

3.4 Analysis

The extraction resulted in 64 architecture-related quality attributes. The more generic attributes (bold font in the row above quality attributes in Table 1) are critical factors. They help technology assessment as they represent categories of criteria for comparing candidate technologies. Attributes associated with critical factors (subsequent rows in Table 1) can be perceived as different perspectives to assess a factor. Associations were directly extracted from the papers or assigned by the researcher according to critical factors and attributes' definition in the papers. An association happens in cases when an attribute definition includes another one, then the attribute becomes a critical factor related to the attribute contained in the definition, even if both are not explicitly linked as key factors, challenges, or another similar relationship. It might not be necessary to use the whole list of attributes, since a specific organizational context might differ from others. Thus, an organization should decide what information is available or relevant. Attributes cited once might be too specific, new or less relevant. Since it is a long list, practitioners may want to start assessing technologies after using a subset of attributes, e.g., the most popular ones.

Table 1. Results organized as critical factors and attributes

Critical factor: Attributes
CF1 - Configurability: Commonality | Variability
CF2 - Cost: Buildability | Licensing | Openness
CF3 - Extension: Buildability | Extensions' delivery | Extensibility | Extensions' deployment | Modifiability | Standardization across the platform
CF4 - Openness: Accessibility | Availability | Flexibility | Licensing | Performance Reliability | Safety | Security | Synchronization | User experience
CF5 - Quality: Certification | Efficient use of resources | Hard real time requirements | Quality of extensions | Testability
CF6 - Reuse: Composability | Components decoupling | Cost | Dependability | Extensibility | Integration | Modularization | Open interface (for components) | Transparency | Understandability
CF7 - Scalability: Complexity | Extensibility | Interoperability | Performance
CF8 - Stability: Framework stability | Interface stability | Rate of change | Parallel development
CF9 - Support Documentation Shared information
CF10 - User experience: Accessibility | Consistent user interface | Documentation | Simplicity
CF11 - Version compatibility: Backwards compatibility | Maintainability | Portability
CF12 - Niche creation: Innovation | Work facilities
CF13 - Robustness: Availability | Offline capability | Resilience | Stability
CF14 - Productivity: Extensions' delivery | Deployability

The study can also minimize decision bias (commonly based only on manager experience) and better justify technology selection rather than an ad hoc process. For each attribute, an interpretative scale might be associated, e.g., cost: range from feasible to not feasible. IT management team then should choose a value within the range and at the end its members will have a comprehensive comparison of technology candidates. When looking at the literature on software product evaluation based on quality attributes, there are proposed quality models [1, 3, 4]. Assessing quality from standards that compose the ISO/IEC 25000 series, also known as SQuaRE (System and Software Quality Requirements and Evaluation), can help IT management teams in acquisition rounds [6]. However, those guidelines reflect traditional paradigms that leave SECO out of scope. ISO/IEC 25000 defines 8 characteristics and 31 sub-characteristics to assess product quality. They use a similar structure to the one presented in this research, i.e., critical factors/quality attributes would match characteristics/sub-characteristics from ISO/IEC 25000 SQuaRE. Nevertheless, there is a high resemblance in their use and definition. Critical factors and ISO/IEC 25000's characteristics present many similarities (Table 2). Columns show ISO/IEC 25000's characteristics and rows represent SECO's critical factors. If applicable, each cell contains a critical factor or attribute that is related to an ISO/IEC 25000's characteristic, also considering its sub-characteristics. For example, the critical factor "extension" (third row) has an attribute "modifiability" that is similar to "portability" ("adaptability" sub-characteristic).

Table 2. SECO's critical factors versus ISO/IEC 25000's characteristics and sub-characteristics

Critical Factor	**ISO/IEC 25000 Characteristics**							
	Compatibility	**Maintainability**	**Functional Suitability**	**Performance Efficiency**	**Portability**	**Reliability**	**Security**	**Usability**
Configurability	-		-	-		-	-	-
Cost	-	-	-	-		-	-	-
Extension	-	-	-	-		-	-	-
Openness	-	-	-		-			
Quality					-	-	-	-
Reuse	-		-	-	-	-	-	-
Scalability					-	-	-	-
Stability	-	-	-	-	-	-	-	-
Support				-	-	-	-	-
User experience	-	-	-	-	-	-	-	
Version Compatibility	–		-	-		-	-	-
Niche creation	-	-	-	-	-	-	-	–
Robustness	-	-	-	-	-		-	
Productivity	-	-	-	-	-	-	-	

ISO/IEC 25000 models lack characteristics to address SECO concerns related to the external player activities (development of extensions or applications). Those matters are illustrated by quality attributes that had no correspondence, e.g., "extensions' deliver", "extensibility" and "quality of extensions". All ISO/IEC 25000's characteristics are considered by at least one critical factor. On the other hand, "stability" and "niche creation" (SECO's critical factors) are not similar to any ISO/IEC 25000's characteristic (according to the sub-characteristics' definition). "Stability" encompasses "framework stability", "interface stability", "rate of change", and "parallel development".

3.5 Threats to Validity

We can point out some threats to validity as follows: the literature base used for the mapping study could have overlooked some studies with architecture-related quality attributes; attributes might have been incorrectly identified; and attributes might not have been identified from the accepted studies; and the attributes extraction was performed manually and had not followed a formal method. The attributes' extraction was performed manually and did not consider differences among SECO contexts, e.g., mobile sector, health sector or agriculture section. This set of attributes is an initial list and must be broken into subsets according to the suitability for each platform (IT management team's members should select a subset to work with). Surveys participants did not have access to the glossary while the study was conducted. In addition, the survey could benefit from analysis focusing in particular SECO platforms or specific SECOs contexts, e.g., Mobile and Cloud.

4 Survey Research

The survey research used an electronic questionnaire written in English to be filled in 20–30 min. It was sent to the invitees' e-mails who are experts in SECO, technology selection and IT management/architecture. The complete questionnaire is divided as: (1) Research Summary; (2) Term of Consent; (3) Characterization Form; (4) Critical Factors' Relevance; and (5) Critical Factors' Attributes Relevance. Considering the objective of capturing participants' experience, a five-point scale similar to previous surveys run by SECO researchers was used [1, 10]. This objective was to investigate if critical factors (Sect. 3) are relevant for technologies selection in a SECO platform. As a result, experts' opinions on the critical factors and their attributes were collected. From the experts' opinions, critical factors and their attributes were evaluated. In addition, we analyzed if the attributes represent relevant perspectives on the related critical factors. In Table 3, the goal of this survey research is described following the GQM (Goal – Question – Metric) model [2]. Applying GQM approach helps to clarify the study strategy and purpose by specifying a group of targets and how to interpret it. GQM uses Goals representing the Conceptual Level that measures Processes, Products, and Resources. Question means the Operational Level specifying how it is going to be measured. Metric represents the Quantitative Level identifying the data to be collected. The GQM Model structures the questions and goals considering a particular context and point of view. 144 participants were invited from 22 countries. Invitations were

Table 3. GQM for the survey goals

Analyze	List of critical factors and their attributes
With the purpose of	Characterize
With respect to	Relevance
The point of view of	Researchers on SECO, architecture and correlated research areas
In the context of	IT management activities/decision-making

sent by e-mail and participants were chosen from websites of events related to the topics, including: ICSOB[1]; WDES[2]; IWSECO[3]; and WEA[4].

4.1 Execution

From those 144 researchers invited to participate in the survey research, 28 invitees responded the questionnaire (19.4%). A rate of response of 20% is adequate when the sample size exceeds [13], thus this survey response rate is acceptable considering the samples size. Participants had no obligation to answer all the relevance questions from parts (4) Critical Factors' Relevance and (5) Critical Factors' Attributes Relevance.

4.2 Results

Characterization. Participant's experience on the related topics was relatively high, as shown in Fig. 1. Participants' characterization information shows that 86% are Postdoctoral/PhD and 14% of Master and PhD students. It shows their experience as researchers on the related topics and likely strengthens their contribution to this survey. Moreover, participants can be considered experts in the related topics with experience on research (61%) and industry (7%) and both (32%).

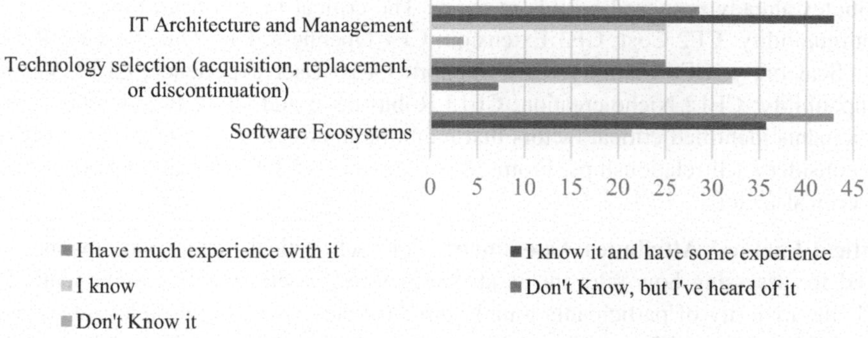

Fig. 1. Participant's responses regarding experience

[1] ICSOB – International Conference on Software Business. Available at: https://icsob2017.wordpress.com/.

[2] WDES – Workshop on Distributed Software Development, Software Ecosystems and Systems-of-Systems. Available at: http://sesos-wdes-2017.icmc.usp.br/.

[3] IWSECO – International Workshop on Software Ecosystems. Available at: https://iwseco.org/.

[4] WEA – Workshop on Software Ecosystem Architectures. Available at: http://wea.github.io/.

Critical Factors. All critical factors were assessed as 'Some relevance' and 'Highly relevant'. As shown in Fig. 2, 'No Relevance', 'Little Relevance' and 'Limited Relevance' answers all together did not reach 50%. It means that experts find those critical factors relevant and therefore applicable for technology selection in a SECO platform. Few features were suggested, some of them already presented as attributes of critical factors.

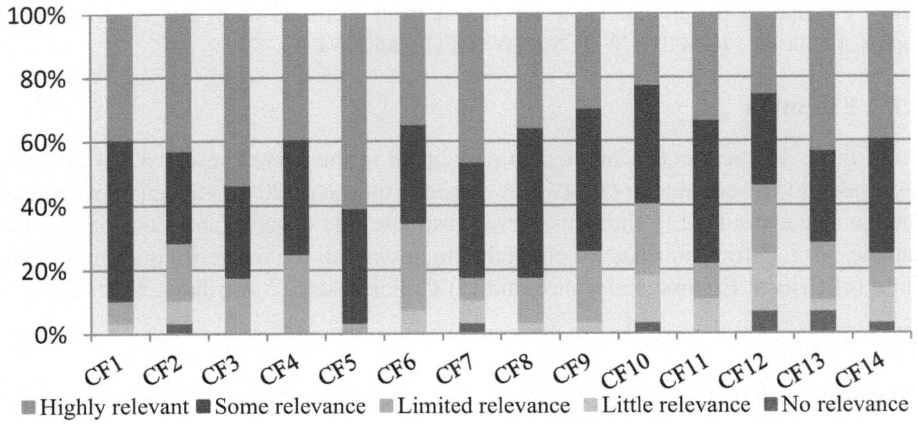

Fig. 2. Critical factors relevance assessment

Participants had not seen the attribute list before the question regarding suggestions of critical factors, so it is positive that they might recommend some features that are attributes already proposed by this research. The critical factors from Fig. 2 are: CF1 Configurability; CF2 Cost; CF3 Extension; CF4 Openness; CF5 Quality; CF6 Reuse; CF7 Scalability; CF8 Stability; CF9 Support; CF10 User experience; CF11 Version compatibility; CF12 Niche creation; CF13 Robustness; and CF14 Productivity. Some participants identified critical factors that might be interrelated, although this study did not consider such relationships. From 28 participants, 15 left general comments about the critical factors.

Critical Factors' Attributes Assessment. For each critical factor, participants were asked for assessing how relevant its attributes were, based on a five-point scale. For CF1, the majority of participants found both attributes to be 'highly relevant' or with 'some relevance'. CF2 attributes are balanced when comparing the sum of 'highly relevant' and 'some relevance'. Those terms are not strange to researchers and are related. For example, a close platform (low openness) might be private software and its licensing may have some cost. CF3 has only one of its six attributes that has been voted as 'no relevance', in fact 'little relevance' is 3.7% in average among its attributes. Those are low rates in comparison to other critical factors reaching over 60% of the top level of relevance in the scale.

CF4 refers to *openness* and was the third most cited quality attribute in the mapping study presented in Sect. 4. The best-evaluated attributes are *flexibility* and *security*, but *availability* is the only one that had no vote for 'no relevance'. CF5 was the top relevant critical factor with 60.7% of 'highly relevant' votes. *Testability* had no vote for the lower two levels of relevance, and it was the attribute with more 'highly relevant' votes. On the other hand, *certification* was not as well evaluated. *Testability* refers to the capability to be tested by anyone and *certification* implies a third party attesting for the quality.

Reuse (CF6) is a critical factor that is hard to find properly in several organizations. The most 'highly relevant' attributes are *extensibility*, *integration*, and *modularization*. Those are the most technical attributes. Attributes such as *transparency*, *understandability*, and *cost* are usual among practitioners, but they were not assessed by the experts with upper level of relevance.

A usual concern when scaling up a platform is that its performance would not keep up with more users or greater data flow. In CF7, *performance* was not considered the most 'highly relevant'. Participants said they did not miss any attribute, not even for *cost*, since it was listed in this research. CF8's most relevant attributes refer to the *stability* of the platform components (frameworks and interface). *Parallel development* may interfere with matters of time, but it was not considered very relevant since it is not a dominant practice in organizations. *Rate of change* might depend on the *framework and interface stability*, since their rate of change can influence the platform's demands for changes.

CF9's attributes assessment is similar. *Documentation* is essential for supporting developers in understanding the functionalities and differences between releases. The *shared information* is not necessary from external parties, e.g., forums and FAQs, but also among the developers and architects working in the platform that also refer to non-technical problems, such as lack of communication. *User experience* (CF10) is essential for a SECO that deals with end users, as they can stop using the platform if user experience fails. User experience is not restricted to the interface they interact with, but also to how easy and simple it is to find and use the platform's functionalities.

Version compatibility (CF11) considers the compatibility of functionalities among the platform versions. In the perspective of developers using the platform for their own development project independently from an organization, it is very harmful to keep changing the stable platform version based on all releases. All attributes are equally 'highly relevant'.

Backwards compatibility and *maintainability* influence the problem a developer has to face during the development process. In a bigger change (e.g., replacing the platform), the project might suffer with specific native functionalities and it should be necessary two separate projects, e.g., developing for different app's versions (Android/iOS).

Niche creation (CF12) is a health indicator for SECO. The more and diverse opportunities the SECO provides, the better its niche creation is. Innovation is the most relevant attribute and directly relates to niche creation. When a SECO produces and promotes innovation, new opportunities and niches are created.

Robustness (CF13) is defined as the capability of a SECO to resist disturbances. Availability is assessed as the most 'highly relevant' attribute. It makes sense since comparing SECO availability before and after a disturbance may be an indication of how much a SECO is robust. For that, other attributes influence a SECO regarding the platform and technologies, e.g., how resilient and stable are the technologies that support the platform. The offline capability was not considered very relevant, perhaps because it is a specific requirement.

Productivity (CF14) reflects how many projects the SECO produces. The relevance of each attribute does not differ much. All attributes refer to the existence of external parties developing on that platform.

Deployability affects how fast a developer is able to deploy and then publish his/her projects, affecting the individual productivity that composes the overall productivity. *Extension's delivery* may stop the projects' developments if the platform extension is not updated (or a new one is not delivered).

Learnability can prevent new projects to begin. If understanding is too difficult, the rate of developers giving up their projects may increase; thus, the overall productivity falls. The majority of participants voted for at least 'some relevance' for all attributes, and then no attribute was removed at first. Collected suggestions were confronted to the assessments to decide whether or not they should be adopted. Putting together votes for the two highest relevance points in the scale ('some relevance' and 'highly relevant'). Only four participants left comments; they mainly expressed concerns about lack of definitions and variations on relevance according to different SECO contexts.

4.3 Threats to Validity

Although most of the terms are common at the literature and participants are experts in the related topics as their characterization profile, some participants might have slightly different conceptions of the same term used for critical factors and attributes. Participants were free to not assess critical factors and attributes, as some questions missed zero, one or two answers. The question with the most absent values had two missing answers compared with the total of 28 participants, then they are not threatening to the study significance. The survey was executed as an electronic questionnaire in order to reach the international community. Interviews might help to collect more data outside the questionnaire (informal), although the survey had questions for comments. Finally, it could not be assured that the sample size was optimal and that they had a high representativeness of the population. Likert scale might not assure that participants used the same criteria for each relevance level.

5 Discussion

The survey shows positive relevance on the use of SECO's critical factors and attributes. Table 4 presents the percentages of the two highest grades in the response scale ('some relevance' and 'highly relevant') for each critical factor. No critical factor was dismissed since no participant asked for removal of any in the questionnaire. Thus, no critical factor was excluded from the list. 57% of the participants said they did not miss any critical factor. Some of them suggested few properties as critical factors: Institutional policies; Vendor trustworthiness; Continuity; Market speed; Flexibility, portability, trustworthiness, sustainability, interoperability; Security, integrity, portability; Innovation; Flexibility and communication; Buildability and learning curve (i.e., how easy it is to learn it); Architecture; Usability; and Supplier reputation.

Table 4. Critical Factors' evaluations in percentage related to number of respondents for each question. (SR = Some Relevance and HR = Highly Relevant)

–	SR	HR	–	SR	HR
CF1	50.0	39.3	**CF8**	46.4	35.7
CF2	28.6	42.9	**CF9**	44.4	29.6
CF3	28.6	53.6	**CF10**	37.0	22.2
CF4	35.7	39.3	**CF11**	44.4	33.3
CF5	35.7	60.7	**CF12**	28.6	25.0
CF6	30.8	34.6	**CF13**	28.6	42.9
CF7	35.7	46.4	**CF14**	35.7	39.3

The set of criteria used in this research (list of critical factors) relate to SECO platform and its architecture/ technologies. Thus, some properties such as *vendor trustworthiness*, *continuity*, *market speed*, *sustainability*, *communication*, and *supplier reputation* were not considered as critical factors.

From all 64 attributes (some of them are repeated from different critical factors), only five had less than 50% when putting together 'some relevance' and 'highly relevant'. In order to decide if they should be removed, we looked into participants' suggestions and comments to find out if anyone expressed an intention of dropping attributes out of the list. As a result, "synchronization" was eliminated from CF4 - Openness and "parallel development" was moved to CF14 - Productivity. Moreover, 68% of participants said they did not think any attribute was misplaced.

After analyzing participants' suggestions as well as consulting their respective proposed relevance levels, the set of critical factors and their attributes was updated after removing, including, copying or moving some attributes, as explained in this section. In addition, some critical factors that appeared as attributes were removed. The final list is presented in Table 5.

Table 5. Final set of critical factor and attributes

Critical factor: Attributes
CF1 - Configurability: Commonality | Variability
CF2 - Cost: Buildability | Licensing
CF3 - Extension: Buildability | Extensions' delivery | Components decoupling | Composability | Extensibility | Extensions' deployment | Interoperability | Modifiability | Standardization across the platform
CF4 - Openness: Accessibility | Availability | Components decoupling | Extensibility | Flexibility | Licensing | Interoperability | Performance | Reliability | Safety | Security

(*continued*)

Table 5. (*continued*)

Critical factor: Attributes
CF5 - Quality: Certification | Efficient use of system resources | Consistent user interface | Hard real time requirements | Quality of extensions | Testability
CF6 - Reuse: Composability | Components decoupling | Dependability | Extensibility | Integration | Modularization | Open interface (for components) |Transparency | Understandability | Interoperability
CF7 - Scalability: Complexity | Extensibility | Interoperability | Performance
CF8 - Stability: Framework stability | Interface stability | Rate of change
CF9 - Support: Documentation | Shared information
CF10 - User experience: Accessibility | Consistent user interface | Documentation | Simplicity
CF11 - Version compatibility: Backwards compatibility | Maintainability | Portability
CF12 - Niche creation: Innovation | Work facilities
CF13 - Robustness: Availability | Offline capability | Resilience
CF14 - Productivity: Extensions' delivery | Deployability | Learnability | Parallel development

6 Final Considerations

SECO's platform is broadly supporting the use and development of software artifacts. In this context, the adopted technologies that support a SECO platform affect what actors enter and keep playing within a SECO. In this paper, we reported on the identification of architecture attributes that affect SECO from the literature. In order to compare results with ISO/IEC 25000 characteristics. Next, we evaluated results with experts from industry and academia based on a survey research. Then, 64 attributes were identified and grouped by 11 critical factors.

In this context, it is necessary to compare the candidate technologies and integrate information with SECO data. The information used to compare needs to cover not only technical properties, but also socio-technical elements, i.e., communities (users, developers and organization), feasibility, quality, cost, and support. This is because the SECO perspective brings information external to the organization/platform and its relationships. Managing platform technologies has many benefits to an organization, e.g., technology standardization, saving money, avoiding unnecessary acquisitions, and supporting a controlled number of technologies. Fast market changes of technologies, deployment of new versions or discontinuation of support require frequent modification and assessment of the SECO platform's reference technologies. In addition, there are effects on finances, users, politics, training, and other perspectives that need to be considered when an organization is changing platform technologies.

As a contribution the research and practice community, we identified and validated a set of architecture attributes to aid IT managers and architects to understand how those choices can affect the SECO platform and technologies and take actions to mitigate the negative effect. Practitioners can use this list as guide for a criterion when comparing technologies in a SECO, since it is necessary to evaluate the technology itself and its relationships to other software artifacts. As future work, we are developing a tool to help IT manager and architects to perform semi-automatic analyses of critical factors and architecture attributes based on the SECO.

Acknowledgements. This study was financed in part by the Coordenação de Aperfeiçoamento de Pessoal de Nível Superior - Brasil (CAPES) - Finance Code 001.

References

1. Albert, B.E., et al.: Software ecosystems governance to enable IT architecture based on software asset management. In: Proceedings of the 2013 7th IEEE International Conference on Digital Ecosystems and Technologies (DEST) Complex Environment Engineering (CEE), Menlo Park, pp. 55–60 (2014)
2. Basili, V.R., et al.: The goal question metric approach. Encycl. Softw. Eng. **1**, 528–532 (1994)
3. Jansen, S., et al.: Managing software platforms and ecosystems. IEEE Softw. **36**(3), 17–21 (2019)
4. Bosch, J.: Speed, data, and ecosystems: the future of software engineering. IEEE Softw. **33**(1), 82–88 (2016)
5. Santos, R.P., Werner, C., Finkelstein, A.: Ecosystems effects on software-consuming organizations: an experience report on two observational studies. In: 2018 12th European Conference on Software Architecture: Companion Proceedings (ECSA), Madrid, pp. 23: 1–23:7 (2018)
6. ISO/IEC 25000: ISO/IEC 25000: Systems and software engineering – Systems and software Quality Requirements and Evaluation (SQuaRE) – Guide to SQuaRE. ISO (2014)
7. Jansen, S.: Measuring the health of open source software ecosystems: beyond the scope of project health. Inf. Softw. Technol. **56**(11), 1508–1519 (2014)
8. Lagerström, R., et al.: Visualizing and measuring software portfolio architectures: a flexibility analysis. J. Mod. Proj. Manag. **3**(2), 14–121 (2014)
9. Lima, T., et al.: A survey on socio-technical resources for software ecosystems. In: Proceedings of the ACM 7th International Conference on Management of Computational and Collective Intelligence in Digital Ecosystems (MEDES), Caraguatatuba, pp. 72–79 (2015)
10. Lima, T.: SECO-AM: an approach for maintenance of IT architecture in software ecosystems. Computer Science and Systems Engineering Department COPPE/UFRJ – Federal University of Rio de Janeiro. Master Dissertation (2018). http://reuse.cos.ufrj.br/files/publicacoes/mestrado/Mes_Thaiana.pdf
11. Manikas, K.: Revisiting software ecosystems research: a longitudinal literature study. J. Syst. Softw. **117**, 84–103 (2016)
12. Manikas, K., Hansen, K.M.: Software ecosystems a systematic literature review. J. Syst. Softw. **86**(5), 1294–1306 (2013)
13. Nulty, D.: The adequacy of response rates to online and paper surveys: what can be done? Assess. Eval. High. Educ. **33**(3), 301–314 (2008)
14. Ross, J.: Creating a strategic IT architecture competency: learning in stages. MIS Q. Executive **2**(1), 31–43 (2003)

15. Barbosa, O., Santos, R.P., Alves, C., Werner, C., Jansen, S.: A systematic mapping study on software ecosystems from a three-dimensional perspective. In: Jansen, S., Brinkkemper, S., Cusumano, M.A. (eds.) (Org.). Software Ecosystems: Analyzing and Managing Business Networks in the Software Industry, Cheltenham/UK & Northampton/USA: Edward Elgar Publishing, pp. 59–81 (2013)
16. Shafia, M.A., Rabadi, N.J., Babakhan, A.R.: The strategies and the factors that influence technology acquisition channels, case study: Iranian die–making industries. Int. J. Manuf. Technol. Manag. **29**(1–2), 48–65 (2015)
17. Petersen, K., Vakkalanka, S., Kuzniarz, L.: Guidelines for conducting systematic mapping studies in software engineering: an update. Inf. Softw. Technol. **64**(1), 1–8 (2015). https://doi.org/10.1016/j.infsof.2015.03.007

Activities and Challenges in the Planning Phase of a Software Ecosystem

Kati Saarni(✉) and Marjo Kauppinen

Department of Computer Science, Aalto University, Espoo, Finland
katimarika.saarni@gmail.com, marjo.kauppinen@aalto.fi

Abstract. Increasing competition forces companies to find new business opportunities by building business ecosystems together. The business ecosystem, where a set of companies develop and provide digital services together for a specific customer segment, can be referred to as a software ecosystem. The planning of ecosystems has been researched in some case studies, but more comprehensive knowledge on how to start building software ecosystems is still needed. The goal of this case study was to investigate activities and challenges in the planning phase of a Finnish software ecosystem. The case study was conducted by interviewing representatives of all six actors of the ecosystem and analyzing the material of the 12 planning workshops. The definition of a vision and objectives, the selection of actors, and the definition of a governance model were the main activities of the planning phase. It was also essential that the actors of the software ecosystem started the conceptualization of digital services and the definition of the business model together. One of the main challenges was that a clear strategy was not defined at the beginning of the planning phase. Furthermore, trust-building between the actors, different decision-making capabilities and a lack of the substance knowledge slowed down the planning phase. The actors also felt that much stronger leadership was needed.

Keywords: Software ecosystem · Digital service · Challenge · Activity · Planning

1 Introduction

Growing competition in markets drives companies to find new business opportunities by building business ecosystems together. The business ecosystem concept was proposed by Moore [17, 18] in the 1990s. The business ecosystem, where digital services are developed and provided, can be considered as a software ecosystem (SECO), where a set of actors interact with a shared market, develop software and services together and operate through the exchange of information, resources and artifacts [10]. The creation of the ecosystem starts from a planning phase, where a basic paradigm of the ecosystem and how value will be created and shared need to be determined [18].

Some earlier studies have reported activities [5, 9, 18, 21] and challenges [e.g. 18, 19, 24, 25] in the planning phase of software ecosystems. However, more comprehensive knowledge of these phenomena is still needed. Manikas and Hansen [14] point out the importance of using existing and real software ecosystems as the subject

S. Hyrynsalmi et al. (Eds.): ICSOB 2019, LNBIP 370, pp. 71–85, 2019.
https://doi.org/10.1007/978-3-030-33742-1_7

of studies. Focusing on specific types of software ecosystems and studying the different aspects of this type can provide results, which can then be applied to different types of software ecosystems. Eventually, this will enable repeatability and theory confirmation [15]. Furthermore, a need to study the life cycles of ecosystems has been recognized. An investigation of processes that steer the creation and dynamics of business ecosystems can bring new understanding about roles of different actors in those life cycles [22].

The goal of this study was to investigate activities and challenges in the planning phase of a software ecosystem, and it was performed by using a descriptive case study method [26]. The study focused on the planning phase of a Finnish software ecosystem, which took place from February to June 2018. This paper describes the main activities and challenges of the planning phase of Case SECO. The main contribution of this study is that companies that are aiming to build a software ecosystem can use the descriptions of the activities as a checklist. In addition, the descriptions of the challenges can help actors to minimize the effects of these challenges when they start building their software ecosystem.

The rest of the paper is organized as follows. Section 2 summarizes the main concepts related to software ecosystems and the activities and challenges of the planning phase of ecosystems identified from the existing literature. The research questions and research methods of the study are described in Sect. 3. The results and answers to the research questions are presented in Sect. 4 and discussed in Sect. 5. Finally, the paper concludes and pinpoints direction for future research.

2 Related Work

2.1 Overview of Ecosystems and Software Ecosystems

In the 1990s, Moore [17, 18] proposed the concept of the business ecosystem, concentrating on how the economic community worked and the interactions between companies, their business environments and business opportunities. Iansiti and Levien [9] have expanded Moore's concept by defining different role types for participating organizations and their strategies. A software ecosystem is a subset of a business ecosystem and the literature contains many definitions of the SECO [e.g. 1, 7, 10, 11]. The main common characteristic for all these definitions of the SECO is the use of software, which differentiates SECOs from other ecosystem types. In this paper, the definition by Jansen et al. [10] of a SECO is used: *"a set of actors functioning as a unit and interacting with a shared market for software and services, together with the relationships among them. These relationships are frequently underpinned by a common technological platform or market and operate through the exchange of information, resources and artifacts."*

Moore [17] defines four *phases* for the ecosystem: birth, expansion, authorities and renewal. Thereafter, Rong and Shi [21] have enriched Moore's definition and defined five phases: emerging, diversifying, converging, consolidating and renewing. Participants in the software ecosystem can be called *actors* and can have different *roles*. For example, Iansiti and Levien [9] define four different roles for the participating organizations:

keystones, dominators, hub landlords and niche players. An actor may have one or more roles in the software ecosystem [12], and the role may also change during the ecosystem's life cycle [16]. Moore [18] highlights the importance of the leaders of an ecosystem, which is further reformulated as "platform leaders" [6]. The leaders need to create and promote mutualism and try to convert individual organizations' competitive relationships into mutualistic ones [18]. Cusumano and Gawer [6] point out that the leaders need to consider the meaning of a scope, a product technology, relationships and an internal organization aspect.

2.2 Activities in the Planning Phase of Ecosystems

Some earlier studies have pointed out activities in the planning phase [e.g. 5, 9, 18, 21]. Definition of a vision and objectives [9, 18, 21] and definition of roles [5, 9] seem to be important activities in the planning phase.

Moore [18] points out the importance of visioning the ecosystem by defining a value proposition and providing it more effectively than the status quo. Rong and Shi [21] emphasize vision-sharing, and Iansiti and Levien [9] recommend defining the vision first, which is then utilized for defining the value creation and sharing methods before the structure and a strategy of an ecosystem can be formulated. The key to a successful ecosystem is to provide real value to the end customers, which will be realized by the combination of actors and contributions involved [18].

Iansiti and Levien [9] also highlight the need to determine roles. Dedehayir et al. [5] identify several key roles in the planning phase, which are classified into four groups: leadership roles, direct value creation roles, value creation support roles and entrepreneurial ecosystem roles. The ecosystem leader role is suggested to be crucial in the planning phase [5]. The leader should be able to conceptualize value chaining and develop strategies by mixing and matching capabilities, processes and organizations to determine the ecosystem with selected key actors [18]. The leader should take care of the governance-related actions, which include the role definition of actors and coordinating interactions between actors [5]. In addition, the leader should forge partnerships by finding relevant partners, enabling collaboration between them and providing opportunities for niche creation [5]. The leader also ensures that the scope of the digital services meets the market needs, and that the ecosystem's offering will accrue all the actors' own value [5].

2.3 Challenges in the Planning Phase of Ecosystems

Some earlier studies have reported challenges, which usually occurs also in the planning phase of ecosystems [e.g. 1, 4, 8, 13, 18–20, 23–25]. Pichlis et al. [20] report that a lack of a clear vision is one of the main challenges of collaborative plan solutions in the software ecosystem. Valenca et al. [24] have also reported that strategies and roadmaps are not fully shared between the partners. To ensure value distribution for the actors, there needs to be a strategy in place [19]. Moore [18] reports competitive challenges around how to protect the idea from others who might be defining a similar offering. Some actors may also have doubts about the market potential [20].

Trust among partners needs to be in place in strategic alliances [4]. It can be challenging to define what each actor brings to the ecosystem, their individual and combined business value, and the value for the customer [20]. There is a need to understand the co-evolution of each actor's offering in the software ecosystem [24]. Moore [18] highlights challenges related to co-operation, such as how to work with the other actors and customers to define a value proposal for a recognized innovation.

The actors may have different structures in their own organizations [13], their decision-making principles may vary [13] and their cultures and ways of communication may be different [13, 19]. The actors may have different substance knowledge which can cause or increase the challenges of conflict [19]. It is also possible that actors are unequally investing resources in and unevenly committed to the construction of the software ecosystem [20]. At the beginning of the ecosystem planning, conflicts of the interests of multiple partners may occur [24, 25]. Having a high number of partners is vital for innovation, but it raises coordination costs and increases complexity [19]. In addition, during the early stages of a software ecosystem, small and medium-sized actors may struggle with the thoughts that are actors in the software ecosystem competitors or collaborators [24]. The roles and relationships between actors in young ecosystems have been recognized as being volatile and flexible [24].

There needs to be leadership in place driving the planning and taking responsibility for the progress [20]. Having more than one leader complicates the ecosystem governance [19]. Effective coordination mechanisms need to be deployed [19]. The clear responsibilities of each role need to be defined and the level of knowledge-sharing decided [24]. Shared responsibility may lead to problems of mutual understanding [24]. Communication channels must be improved to ensure that the purpose, direction and responsibilities are understood [24]. The interaction of different actors and the different levels of knowledge of the actors will present a difficulty, and governance-related issues take time [13].

From the perspective of digital service conceptualization, it is challenging if there is no common value proposition [20] and if a business strategy is defined at a level of abstraction that requires significant interpretation [1]. In addition, earlier studies report challenges around controlling the most valuable product features [24], managing limitations set by the customer and technology maturity [8] and the lack of continuous validation with the customer [8]. Lenkenhoff et al. [13] describe the challenge of the degree of incompatibility of information systems. Schultis et al. [23] have reported challenges where the actors have different requirements based on their business objectives, and if all the actors are involved in the architectural decision-making, it takes time to reach a common agreement on the architecture.

Pichlis et al. [20] report that it is challenging if no common business model is defined. In addition, adapting new business models may be challenging if the offering of the ecosystem requires fundamentally new business models [8].

3 Research Questions and Methods

This study focused on the planning phase of the software ecosystem and the goal was to investigate:

- RQ1: What are the main activities in the planning phase of a software ecosystem?
- RQ2: What are the main challenges in the planning phase of a software ecosystem?

This qualitative research was performed by using a case study research method [26]. A descriptive approach for the case study was used to describe a single-case in depth and to gain deep understanding of the activities and challenges in the planning phase of a software ecosystem. The data was collected from multiple sources by interviewing representatives of all six actors of the software ecosystem and analyzing the material of the 12 planning workshops. We applied the coding and code comparison guidelines of the grounded theory for analyzing the data [3]. The grounded theory method for analysis was selected because it offers systematic and flexible guidelines for analyzing qualitative data [3]. In this case study, we applied the open coding of the grounded theory. Our plan is to conduct case studies in other software ecosystems and apply the axial and selection coding of the grounded theory for the cross-case data analysis.

3.1 Case Description and Research Process

In this case study, the activities and challenges in the planning phase of one Finnish software ecosystem (called Case SECO in this paper) were investigated. The aim of Case SECO was to provide digital services for new entrepreneurs. New entrepreneurs were identified to be a customer segment which did not have enough services at the beginning of a journey to becoming an entrepreneur. The first set of digital services was launched in July 2019. A Fig. 1 shows a timeline of the phases of Case SECO and the main research activities.

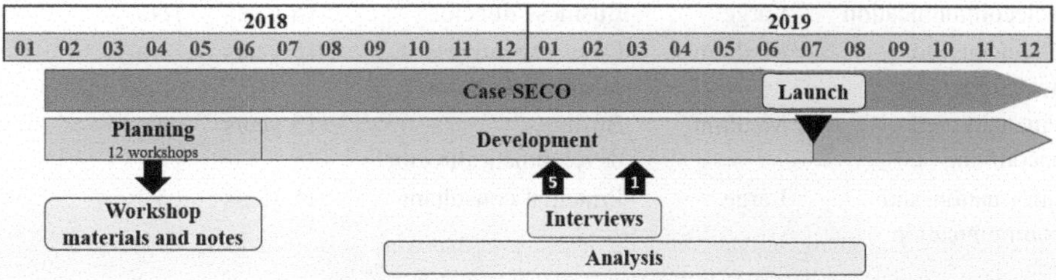

Fig. 1. Timeline of the phases of Case SECO and the main research activities.

The planning of the software ecosystem took place from February to June 2018 and was performed by arranging 12 workshops in which one to three people from each actor participated. The length of the workshops varied from 1 to 4.5 h. In the beginning, there were five actors, and the sixth actor joined to the planning phase in the eighth workshop. The actors represented five different business sectors and two actors were categorized as small and medium-sized companies and four were large companies. All the actors had a keystone role in the planning phase in terms of governing Case SECO. In addition, one actor took the facilitator's role in the planning phase. Each workshop had a predefined agenda, but other topics were also covered during the workshops. The planning was done in an iterative manner.

The answers to RQ1 are based on the workshop materials and notes from the planning phase. First, the first author of this paper read through the workshop materials and notes and added descriptive codes. Then, similar descriptive codes were combined in sub-categories, which were the main tasks of the planning phase. These main tasks were further compared, and the overlapping sub-categories were combined. Finally, the high-level categories were defined. These high-level categories were the activities of the planning phase. The second author of the paper reviewed the results of the analysis. The authors discussed the analysis and the tasks of the planning activities were clarified.

The answers to RQ2 were gained through the results of the semi-structured theme interviews performed in January and March 2019. The interviews were designed by following the guidelines from Boyce and Neale [2]. The themes of the interviews covered main topics related to ecosystem creation. The six actors who were active participants of the planning phase were interviewed. All the interviewees had over 15 years of work experience and had extensive knowledge of their company's business and its development, but only one of them had previous experience of planning ecosystems together with other actors. Table 1 presents a summary of the interviewed actors.

Table 1. Summary of the interviewees.

Business sector	Company size	Role in the company	Work experience	Ecosystem experience
Insurance	Large	Business development director	>15 years	No
Pension insurance	Large	Business development director	>15 years	No
Telecommunication	Large	Business director	>15 years	No
Financial and accounting	Medium	Chief executive officer and owner	>15 years	No
Financial and accounting	Medium	Business development director	>15 years	No
Information and communication	Large	Principal consultant	>15 years	Yes

The interviews were conducted in Finnish, because Finnish was the mother tongue of all the interviewees and we wanted to collect as rich data as possible. The length of each interview varied from 25 min to 55 min. Before each interview, the research objective and structure of the interview was presented to the interviewee. The interviews were recorded and transcribed by a professional external organization. The analysis was done by following the grounded theory method [3]. First the first author read though each transcript separately and added descriptive codes. Then, similar descriptive codes were combined in sub-categories, which were the main challenges. The challenges were further analyzed and categorized against the main activities of the planning phase (RQ1). The second author of the paper reviewed the results of the analysis. The authors discussed the analysis and the categorization and descriptions of the challenges were clarified.

4 Results

4.1 RQ1: Main Activities in the Planning Phase of a Software Ecosystem

Preliminary preparations of the planning phase of Case SECO. Before the actual planning phase, some of the actors refined an idea, which was originally born in discussions during co-operation between the companies in autumn 2017. The companies had recognized that there is a need in the market for comprehensive digital services for new entrepreneurs. They saw that existing digital services do not cover enough of the functions new entrepreneurs require. Based on their own businesses, the companies also saw the potential of this customer segment. Therefore, they were interested in reaching new entrepreneurs in the early phase of their journey to being an entrepreneur and create a targeted offering just for them. The preliminary discussions addressed that creating this kind of digital service offering requires a sufficient set of companies developing it together. *A software ecosystem was recognized as a suitable model for this kind of cooperation.*

The actors started to gather appropriate companies for discussing an interest in joining this software ecosystem creation. Based on the preliminary discussion, potential companies were selected. The potential actors were aware of the idea of the digital services which were going to be planned and that the aim was to build up the software ecosystem together. All participating actors signed a non-disclosure agreement (NDA) to ensure that all further discussions could be undertaken confidentially. One actor took the role of facilitating the planning phase because it had previous experience of ecosystem creation and knowledge of digital services development.

The main activities in the planning phase of Case SECO are summarized in Table 2. One of the first important tasks of the planning phase was to determine the **vision** and main **objectives** for Case SECO, which were defined as *"Case SECO will provide extensive digital services for new entrepreneurs or persons who are aiming to be an entrepreneur. The digital services will be provided through one software platform. The digital services are easy to find, the context is represented in plain language and digital services are offered cost-effectively for end users."*

One significant aim at the beginning of the planning phase was to **introduce** the actors and strengthen the common **motivation** and **capabilities** of the actors to continue the ecosystem planning together. The participating companies agreed that it is better at first to have quite a small **number of actors** to plan the ecosystem, to avoid spreading the idea and to help the planning phase proceed effectively. The actors, however, needed to have an adequate **offering** for the planned digital services. Therefore, the actors analyzed the offering of each actor against the defined vision and objectives of Case SECO and recognized that one more actor may be needed to enable a sufficient set of digital services. The actors decided together to contact one potential new actor, which was then joined into the software ecosystem. This new actor strengthened the service offering of Case SECO.

The actors agreed that all of them had a keystone player's **role** and were in an equal position with each other in **decision-making** during the planning phase. An advisory board was set up consisting of all the actors of this planning phase. The advisory board in the planning phase was the highest decision-making governance body, to enable the

Table 2. Main activities in the planning phase of Case SECO.

Activity	Task
Definition of a vision and objectives	• Definition of a shared vision • Definition of main objectives
Selection of actors	• Introduction of actors • Clarification of motivation and capabilities of actors • Definition of number of actors • Determination of offering of actors
Definition of a governance model	• Definition of roles and responsibilities of actors • Definition of decision-making rules and practices • Creation of a rule book • Creation of needed contracts
Conceptualization of digital services	• Definition of a value proposal • Definition of target groups and customer paths • Benchmarking of existing similar digital services • Creation of a Proof-of-Concept • Determination of the scope of a Minimum Viable Product (MVP) • Definition and prioritization of functionalities • Determination of costs and a schedule
Definition of a business model	• Determination of a business model • Determination of operation roles and practices

planning of the ecosystem and steer the planning of the digital services. The **roles** and **responsibilities**, limitations, cost-sharing principles, rules for co-operation and business model were described in the **rule book**, which is the main guiding document for the governance of Case SECO. The actors agreed that **contracts** for a Proof-of-Concept and a development phase would be created later.

The actors highlighted during the workshops that the conceptualization of the digital services should be based on a determined **value proposal** and well-recognized and defined **target groups and customer paths**. In addition, it required understanding of customer behavior, the current pain points customers are struggling with, and a thoroughly done **benchmarking** of the existing digital services for new entrepreneurs. The value proposal for end users was crystallized around the following terms: *removal of uncertainties, carefree, believable* and the digital services consisted of the following main customer paths: *(1) recommendation of the appropriate company format (2) setting up a company and (3) supporting the growth of the company by offering tools, services and insurances for operating the company.* The actors needed to recognize their interests in the customer paths of planned digital services. A **Proof-of-Concept** was created during the planning phase. The Proof-of-Concept enabled a concrete look-and-feel of the planned digital services e.g. page layouts, main functionalities and interactions.

Based on the defined customer paths and the Proof-of-Concept, there was discussion about the scope of a **Minimum Viable Product (MVP)** and its schedule for the launch. The aim of the MVP was to cover the most valuable customer paths and functionalities for end users and launch it as soon as possible. The **functionalities** were **defined and prioritized** to be included in the MVP, to be implemented in the next versions or recognized as out of the scope of the digital services. After the MVP scope was clarified, a development **schedule** with the main activities and an overall view of the **costs** of the MVP were preliminarily determined.

The actors also defined a **business model** during the planning phase. It was defined that a new company would be set up, which would operate the digital services, and the advisory board would be responsible for steering the digital services development. The actors also discovered that there might be regulatory restrictions on who could own the digital services of the ecosystem and these regulatory restrictions needed to be examined before establishing the new company. In addition, options for how to operate the digital services were discussed. These **operational practices** included customer service activities around the digital services and the technical maintenance of the digital services. Three options were represented; *(1) one single party is responsible for providing the customer service and maintenance of the digital services, (2) one party is responsible for the customer service and another side maintains the digital services, and (3) actors are investing in a new party, who will manage both the customer service and the maintenance of the digital services.* The actors agreed to examine options 1 and 2 further.

The actors defined four **roles for operation**: (1) *a digital service partner*, which has a keystone role in Case SECO's decision-making and is a member of the advisory board, (2) *a digital service operator*: a new company will be set up to operate the digital services, (3) *a customer service provider* will provide the customer service together with each actor's own customer services, (4) *a digital service technical provider* will be responsible for developing and maintaining the digital services.

At the end of the planning phase, the rule book and the Proof-of-Concept were reviewed and accepted. The aim was that the rule book would be updated during Case SECO's life cycle and the Proof-of-Concept act as a starting point for the development of the digital services.

4.2 RQ2: Main Challenges in the Planning Phase of a Software Ecosystem

Table 3 summarizes the main challenges in the planning phase of Case SECO. The challenges are categorized by the main activities of the planning phase (RQ1).

Definition of a vision and objectives. The actors saw that there is a risk of a failure in building a successful software ecosystem if a clear strategy for achieving the defined vision and objectives was not defined at the beginning of the planning phase. Actors did not share their business logics openly together. The motivation for each actor to join to Case SECO was based on their own vision and market understanding.

Selection of actors. Some actors did not know each other at the beginning of the planning. In the beginning, actors were somewhat vigilant and did not openly share all their thoughts and concerns. It required time and meetings to build trust by getting to know each other on a personnel level, getting acquainted with the companies of the software ecosystem, understanding the actors' backgrounds and the way in which they

Table 3. The main challenges in the planning phase of Case SECO.

Activity	Challenge
Definition of a vision and objectives	• A clear strategy was missing • The business logics of the actors were not openly shared
Selection of actors	• Trust-building between actors was time-consuming • Actors had different decision-making capabilities • Actors had different speeds for proceeding in the planning phase • Actors did not have enough substance knowledge • Actors were creating a software ecosystem for the first time
Definition of a governance model	• Stronger leadership was desired • Definitions of the roles of actors were missing at the beginning of the planning phase • Expectations and concrete activities with resource estimations of each role were not determined
Conceptualization of digital services	• It was difficult to understand the needed definition level of digital services • It was difficult to define the scope of the MVP and prioritize functionalities • Lack of substance knowledge made it difficult to define common functionalities
Definition of a business model	• Actors needed to make compromises when defining the business model of the software ecosystem • External regulation had impacts on the selection of a business model

communicate. Some participants changed during the planning phase, and this also affected the trust-building. The trust-building was time-consuming, but the actors felt that it was necessary to achieve enough trust between them.

The decision-making capabilities of the actors varied. Depending on the actor's role in their own company's organization and the size of the company, certain decisions needed to be taken away to their own organization's decision-making process before it could be done in Case SECO. This slowed the planning phase and decreased the dynamics. The actors saw that participating actors need to have enough decision-making authority in their own organization. It takes a lot of time if all, even small, decisions have to be made first in the actors' own organizations.

The actors had different velocities for making decisions and proceeding with tasks during the planning phase. Consequently, it was sometimes difficult to proceed with the topics of the workshops if not all the actors had time to prepare topics beforehand.

The actors did not exactly know what kind of substance knowledge they needed to have during the planning phase. In some cases, they needed to find more knowledge inside their own organization. They felt that there should have been more professionals from business operations, who are responsible for customer segments and the business itself. In addition, the actors considered how much innovation, service design and marketing knowledge was needed.

Most of the actors were participating in a software ecosystem for the first time. They were not familiar with the software ecosystem concept beforehand and did not know what the planning of a software ecosystem and digital services required. The planning phase was a learning process for the actors at the same time as the actual planning was being done. It took time for the actors to become familiar with the software ecosystem concept and how this software ecosystem should be established in.

Definition of a governance model. The leader's role was highlighted in the planning phase. The facilitator enabled the execution of the planning phase, but the actors felt that much stronger leadership was needed. The actors desired that the leader would have defined clear steps and milestones, systemizing the way of working, making work estimations and scheduling the work, and taking care that the needed decisions were made on time and the quality of the digital services was in place. The actors saw that roles in the planning phase, expectations and concrete activities for each role should have been defined in the early phases. This would have given more concreteness on how much and what kind of individual resources from each actor's side were needed and the estimated resource allocation.

Conceptualization of digital services. The actors saw challenging to know how deep and detailed the conceptualization of the digital services needed to be in order to have a sufficient determination of costs and a development schedule. The definition of the MVP scope needed some compromises from the actors. This was seen challenging, but the actors understood that the prioritization is done based on customer paths that had been defined together. The actors knew their own offering well and how their offering could be provided in the digital services in this software ecosystem, and they were capable of defining functionalities based on their own offering. But it was seen challenging to define the common functionalities (e.g. registering, interactions, security and layout) of the digital services. The actors hesitated, considering that they did not have enough substance knowledge to define common functionalities.

Definition of a business model. The business model definition required some compromises and flexibility from the actors. It was understood that the business model must be defined from the perspective of Case SECO and this differed from the business models the actors were used to use in their own organizations. In addition, it was challenging to examine and understand the regulation restrictions which affected the business model definition.

5 Discussion

5.1 Activities and Challenges in the Planning Phase of the Software Ecosystem

In this study, the following **five activities** in the planning phase of the software ecosystem were identified: (1) the definition of a vision and objectives, (2) the selection of actors, (3) the definition of a governance model, (4) the conceptualization of digital services, and (5) the definition of a business model.

The results of the case study indicate that the definition of the vision and objectives was one of the main activities that the actors in a software ecosystem must do at the beginning of the planning phase. The importance of the definition of a vision has also been highlighted in some studies of business ecosystems. For example, Moore [18] emphasizes ecosystem visioning and that it is important to define a value proposition and provide it more effectively than the status quo. Iansiti and Levien [9] also point out that the vision needs to be first in place, and then it can be utilized to define the value creation and sharing methods.

The results of the case study also point out the importance of the selection of actors. It was essential for each actor to clarify their motivation and capabilities for joining the software ecosystem. In addition, the actors needed to have an adequate offering for the planned digital services. Moore [18] also emphasizes that the key to a successful ecosystem is to provide real value to the end customers, which will be realized by the combination of actors and contributions involved.

The results of the case study also indicate that the definition of a governance model was important. The governance model steered the work during the planning phase of the software ecosystem. It was especially important to define the roles and responsibilities of the actors. Iansiti and Levien [9] also highlight a need to determine roles, and the ecosystem leader role is suggested to be crucial in the planning phase [5].

This study shows that the vision and objectives provided information for the actors to start conceptualizing the digital services and defining the business model. It was also essential that the actors of the software ecosystem started conceptualizing the digital services and defining the business model together during the planning phase.

This paper describes a considerable number of **challenges** that actors may encounter during the planning activities of a software ecosystem. One of the main challenges was that a clear strategy was missing at the beginning of the planning phase. The actors saw a risk of a failure in building a successful software ecosystem, because a clear strategy for achieving the vision and objectives of the software ecosystem was not defined at the beginning of the planning phase. Pichlis et al. [20] have also reported that strategies and roadmaps were not fully shared between the partners in a software ecosystem. According to Mukhopadhyay and Bouwman [19], there needs to be a strategy in place to ensure value distribution for the actors.

The results of this study also point out that trust-building between the actors, the different decision-making capabilities and a lack of substance knowledge were challenges that slowed down the planning phase. The actors emphasized the importance of trust-building because it enabled them to share thoughts and ideas openly. Das and Teng [4] also emphasize the importance of creating trust in strategic alliances. We consider strategic alliances as similar to ecosystems. Previous studies have also recognized that actors' decision-making principles vary [13], and the actors may have different substance knowledge [19].

The conflicting interests of multiple partners reported by Valkokari et al. [25] did not arise as a challenge in this study. One reason for not having conflicting interests might be that the existing services of the actors did not overlap.

In this case study, the actors felt that much stronger leadership was needed. According to Pichlis et al. [20], there is a need for leadership in a software ecosystem. The actors desired that the roles, expectations and concrete activities of each actor would have been defined at the beginning of the planning phase. Valenca et al. [24] also report that clear responsibilities for each role in the software ecosystem need to be defined.

The results of this study also point out the challenges related to the conceptualization of digital services. For example, the actors found it challenging to understand the needed definition level of the digital services in order to be able to define preliminary costs and a schedule. In addition, the actors felt that they did not have enough substance knowledge to define the common functionalities of the digital services. The definition of the MVP scope needed some compromises from the actors. This was seen challenging, but the actors understood that prioritization is done based on the customer paths that have been defined together. Valenca et al. [24] also indicate the challenge of prioritizing features in a software ecosystem.

In this study, the actors felt that the definition of the business model required some compromises and flexibility from them and merging it with the actors' own business models was seen challenging. This same challenge has been reported in a multi-case study [8].

5.2 Threats to Validity

Here, we discuss four potential threats to the validity of the results. First, the interviews were conducted six months after the planning phase had ended. This might lead to deviations in the answers. This threat was mitigated by before each interview, the researcher encouraging the interviewees to try to answer as they felt during the planning phase. In addition, the objectives of the study and interviewee's rights and responsibilities were presented to them. The interviewees knew that the interviews were done anonymously, and the material would be kept confidential. Therefore, it could be assumed that the interviewees gave honest answers.

Secondly, one of the limitations of this study is that only one representative from each actor was interviewed. The triangulation of data sources was used to reduce this validity threat. The detailed material from the workshops was another source of data.

The third validity issue concerns investigator triangulation, which we were able to use in a restricted way. The first author of the paper was responsible the design, execution, analysis and reporting of the study, and the second author reviewed the results of the study. The first author started to work in Case SECO after the planning phase, which enabled her to consider the planning phase neutrally. In addition, participation in Case SECO after the planning phase enabled her to understand the context and actors in detail.

The fourth limitation is that the findings of this study are derived from a single-case study, where the case software ecosystem was quite small. It could be assumed that similar findings are achievable by conducting the same research, investigating the planning phase of another software ecosystem or repeating the same research for this case software ecosystem.

6 Conclusions

The results of this study suggest that the definition of a vision and objectives, the selection of actors, and the definition of a governance model are the main activities of the planning phase that place the foundation for the software ecosystem and the co-development of digital services. The results of the study also indicate that the planning phase of the software ecosystem can be demanding, because actors can face many challenges, such as a lack of a clear strategy, trust-building between actors, different decision-making capabilities, the lack of substance knowledge, and weak leadership.

Our future research goal is to gain more detailed knowledge of how actors can conceptualize and develop digital services together in a software ecosystem. We also plan to conduct case studies and gather data from other software ecosystems in order to validate the findings of this study.

References

1. Bosch, J., Bosch-Sijtsema, P.: From integration to composition: on the impact of software product lines, global development and ecosystems. J. Syst. Software **83**(1), 67–76 (2010)
2. Boyce, C., Neale, P.: Conducting in-depth interviews: a guide for designing and conducting in-depth interviews for evaluation input. In: Pathfinder International Tool Series, Monitoring and Evaluation, vol. 2, 16 p. (2006). http://www.pathfind.org/site/DocServer/m_e_tool_series_indepth_interviews.pdf?docID=6301
3. Charmaz, K.: Constructing Grounded Theory: A Practical Guide Through Qualitative Analysis, p. 208. Sage Publications, London (2006)
4. Das, T.K., Teng, B.-S.: Between trust and control: developing confidence in partner cooperation in alliances. Acad. Manage. Rev. **23**(3), 491–512 (1998)
5. Dedehayir, O., Mäkinen, S., Ortt, R.J.: Roles during innovation ecosystem genesis: a literature review. Technol. Forecast. Soc. Change **136**, 18–29 (2018)
6. Cusumano, M.A., Gawer, A.: The elements of platform leadership. MIT Sloan Manage. Rev. **43**(3), 50–58 (2002)
7. Hanssen, G.K.A.: Longitudinal case study of an emerging software ecosystem: implications for practice and theory. J. Syst. Software **85**(7), 1455–1466 (2012)
8. Holmström Olsson, H., Bosch, J.: Strategic ecosystem management: a multi-case study in the B2B domain. In: Proceedings of the 16th International Conference on Product-Focused Software Process Improvement (PROFES), vol. 9459, pp. 3–15 (2015)
9. Iansiti, M., Levien, R.: The Keystone Advantage: What the New Dynamics of Business Ecosystems Mean for Strategy, Innovation, and Sustainability, p. 304. Harvard Business School Press, Boston (2004)
10. Jansen, S., Brinkkemper, S., Finkelstein, A.:. Business network management as a survival strategy: a tale of two software ecosystems. In: 1st International Workshop on Software Ecosystems, IWSECO, vol. 505, pp. 34–48 (2009)
11. Jansen, S., Cusumano, M.A.: Defining software ecosystems: a survey of software platforms and business network governance. In: 4th International Workshop on Software Ecosystems, IWSECO, vol. 879, pp. 40–58 (2012)
12. Knodel, J. and Manikas, K.: Towards a typification of software ecosystems. In: 6th International Conference on Software Business (ICSOB), vol. 210, pp. 60–65 (2015)

13. Lenkenhoff, K., Wilkens, U., Zheng, M., Süße, T., Kuhlenkötter, B., Ming, X.: Key challenges of digital business ecosystem development and how to cope with them. In: 10th Conference on Industrial Product-Service Systems, Procedia CIRP, vol. 73, pp. 167–172 (2018)
14. Manikas, K., Hansen, K.M.: Software ecosystems – a systematic literature re-view. J. Syst. Software **86**(5), 1294–1306 (2013)
15. Manikas, K.: Revisiting software ecosystems research: a longitudinal literature study. J. Syst. Software **117**, 84–103 (2016)
16. Markham, S.K., Ward, S.J., Aiman-Smith, L., Kingon, A.I.: The valley of death as context for role theory in product innovation. J. Product Innov. Manage. **27**(3), 402–417 (2010)
17. Moore, J.F.: Predators and prey: a new ecology of competition. Harvard Bus. Rev. **71**(3), 75–86 (1993)
18. Moore, J.F.: The Death of Competition: Leadership and Strategy in the Age of Business Ecosystems, p. 297. HarperBusiness, New York (1996)
19. Mukhopadhyay, S., Bouwman, H.: Multi-actor collaboration in platform-based ecosystem: opportunities and challenges. J. Inf. Technol. Case Appl. Res. **20**(2), 47–54 (2018)
20. Pichlis, D., Raatikainen, M., Sevón, P., Hofemann, S., Myllärniemi, V., Komssi, M.: The challenges of joint solution planning: three software ecosystem cases. In: Jedlitschka, A., Kuvaja, P., Kuhrmann, M., Männistö, T., Münch, J., Raatikainen, M. (eds.) PROFES 2014. LNCS, vol. 8892, pp. 310–313. Springer, Cham (2014). https://doi.org/10.1007/978-3-319-13835-0_29
21. Rong, K., Shi, Y.: Business Ecosystems – Constructs, Configurations and the Nurturing Process, 263 p. Palgrave Macmillan (2014)
22. Scaringella, L., Radziwon, A.: Innovation, entrepreneurial, knowledge, and business ecosystems: old wine in new bottles? Technol. Forecast. Soc. Change **136**, 59–87 (2017)
23. Schultis, K-B., Elsner, C. and Lohmann, D.: Architecture challenges for internal software ecosystems: a large-scale industry case study. In: Proceedings of the 22nd ACM SIGSOFT International Symposium on Foundations of Software Engineering, pp. 542–552 (2014)
24. Valenca, G., Alves, C., Heimann, V., Jansen, S., Brinkkemper, S.: Competition and collaboration in requirements engineering: A case study of an emerging software ecosystem. In: Proceedings of the IEEE 22nd International Requirements Engineering Conference (RE), pp. 384–393 (2014)
25. Valkokari, K., Seppänen, M., Mäntylä, M., Jylhä-Ollila, S.: Orchestrating innovation ecosystems: a qualitative analysis of ecosystem positioning strategies. Technol. Innovat. Manage. Rev. **7**(3), 12–24 (2017)
26. Yin, R.K.: Case Study Research: Design and Methods, Third Edition. Sage Publications, Applied Social Research Methods, vol. 5, 179 p. (2003)

API Management Challenges in Ecosystems

Sebastien Andreo[1(✉)] and Jan Bosch[2]

[1] Siemens AG Corporate Technology, Erlangen, Germany
sebastien.andreo@siemens.com
[2] Department of Computer Science and Engineering,
Chalmers University of Technology, Göteborg, Sweden
jan.bosch@chalmers.se

Abstract. The API has become a cornerstone of software ecosystems, providing ways to drive innovation inside and outside the organization. Because of this criticality, we should manage APIs. The purpose of this study is to identify and classify the challenges that organizations evolving into internal ecosystems are facing as they have to deal with APIs. We performed a qualitative research study on three Siemens internal ecosystems with different sizes, technologies, and age. The results reveal that even if we are talking about the API economy, organizations are struggling with different aspects of API management related to Business, Architecture, Process, and Organization. The challenges identified in this paper provide a basis for future research.

Keywords: API · API management · Case study

1 Introduction

Not a day goes by that a company, or a governmental organization argues for or presents a plan to accelerate its digitalization and digital transformation. A cornerstone of those transformations is to make the digital services available to customers, and this is mostly realized using application programming interfaces (APIs). The development of APIs is not new and has been widely used since its inception in 1972 [1], but nowadays the monetization of API usage and the requirement to deliver software continuously to customers puts additional pressure on the development and the maintenance of APIs. As APIs are critical [2], any organization has to find measures to mitigate the risks of failure.

An API presents two sides. The first is a technical side and as a first definition we can use: an API is a technical answer to a business problem. The second is a business side because an API is a business enabler. In the simplest terms, we can define APIs as a set of requirements that govern how applications can interact and exchange data and how we want to deliver value to the customers. Because of the critical aspect of the APIs a form of management is required to mitigate the risks of failure. In this paper we consider the term API management

S. Hyrynsalmi et al. (Eds.): ICSOB 2019, LNBIP 370, pp. 86–93, 2019.
https://doi.org/10.1007/978-3-030-33742-1_8

as described by Jan Stafford in [3] where he compares, the API management to application life-cycle management: observing and controlling an API from creation to retirement.

In this paper, we highlight the challenges regarding API management in internal software ecosystems (ISECOs). To define an internal ecosystem, we used the definition proposed by [4]: an internal ecosystem is characterized by self-contained profit centers with their own business objectives, organizationally independent with their own product management, and have to a wide extent autonomous processes and software-engineering life cycles. To this end, we investigate the following research question to support our study: What are the major challenges for API management in internal ecosystems?

The challenges in this paper are based on the analysis of three internal ecosystems inside Siemens. The ecosystems present different aspects regarding the way they are integrating the different partners, the technologies involved, and also the size of the project itself.

The contribution of this paper is to provide evidence that even if the API economy has become a key driver of digital businesses, organizations evolving in internal ecosystems still face business and technical challenges to take advantages of this transformation.

The paper is organized as follows. The next section defines the research methodology we used to collect the challenges and presents the internal cases studied, while Sect. 3 describes the challenges we identified about API management. We used the BAPO model [5] to cluster the challenges in order to reflect the impact of API management often considered as a technical challenge in all other product development concerns. Section 4 summarizes and orders the challenges. Then in Sect. 5, we discuss threats to validity as well as implications for practitioners and researchers. In Sect. 6, we provide an overview of related work. Finally, we conclude the paper in Sect. 7.

2 Research Methodology

This section describes the research settings of the three ISECOs we investigated and outlines our research method.

2.1 Case Study Systems

The cases in this paper are based on the study of large ISECOs at Siemens. All case study systems, ISECO-A ISECO-B, and ISECO-C present a similar ecosystem structure, comprising a keystone which is a member of the software ecosystem that owns, operates and evolves a platform and multiple clients that build applications upon it. The ISECOs have established products in industrial and healthcare domains. However the ISECOs present distinctions in term of age, development size, technology and deployment, and finally in term of marketing: the keystone name is the market identifier, or the apps on top of the keystone are the identifiers. We summarized the characteristics in Table 1.

Table 1. ISECOs key data

Ecosystems	ISECO-A	ISECO-B	ISECO-C
# years of development	16	12	5
# deployment	Client server	Desktop	Web
# of keystone devs	200	300	50–100
# of internal partners	6–8	6–8	5–10
# of external partners	2–5	5–10	5–10
# of apps	40–50	10–20	5–10

2.2 Research Method

A participant observer approach and well-established case-study methods have been applied [6,7]. The case data were collected directly from people working in different organizations. Principally two modes of collaboration were in place:

- Assessment: our role was to provide an external opinion and recommendations about the API management practices in place within the organization. To this end, we performed semi-structured interviews with relevant stakeholders: software architects responsible for the definition and evolution of the APIs and developers or key developers responsible for the implementation and the maintenance of the APIs. The interviews followed a guideline to guarantee that we collect the same areas of information from each interviewee, but also we leave space for a conversational approach to facilitate the interaction and to allow the interviewee to bring new topics to the discussion. If a new topic presented a high relevance for our assessment, we re-interviewed the previous stakeholders especially on that topic.
- Joint development: In this case, we worked closely with the organizations to develop tools and strategies to improve the API management in their existing software development landscape.

3 Challenges

In this section, we present our findings resulting from the study. We have chosen to cluster them according to the Business, Architecture, Process, and Organization (BAPO) perspectives [5] to reflect the impact of API management often considered as a technical challenge in all other product development concerns.

3.1 Business Challenges

As described in BAPO, the 'B' stands for Business, how do we generate revenue and profits.

Finding the Optimal Innovation Speed for All Partners. In our internal ecosystem cases, the platform is the principal provider of new technologies, and consequently, one of the innovation enablers. Its role is to provide an optimum speed to provide innovations to the partners without becoming a development bottleneck. To innovate means add, evolve, and change existing functionalities to create new customer added value. Unfortunately, each change has a cost: development cost for the provider and potentially a migration cost for the consumer. In the three cases we studied, we observed different strategies by the customers regarding the integration of the new platform's functionalities. From one side the innovators, who move as fast as possible behind the platform's intermediate releases. At the other end, the laggards who would postpone the migration as long as they can because they do not want it, do not have the resource to pay the migration or have other priorities. This heterogeneity comes from a divergence in the business model and the business goal as well as the staffing of the partners even if the domains are identical. From a business unit point of view, the platform can not favor one or the other partner type and has to compromise to satisfy both of them. The consequences are a slowing down the innovator partners and taking the risk they do not feel comfortable with "new" innovation speed and increasing the cost of development of the platform.

Finding B: Organizations suffer difficulties to provide an optimal innovation speed between all the ecosystem's partners by taking into account the heterogeneity of their business goals.

3.2 Architecture Challenges

As described in BAPO, the 'A' stands for Architecture and relates to technologies and structure to build the system.

Managing API Dependencies. Knowing which partner is using which API of the platform and how the partners are using these APIs is beneficial for the platform provider. It gives insight about the usage, the popularity and the criticality. Thereby, this data can help to get better decisions about the platform evolution direction.

In all cases, we encountered a similar pattern: a keystone provides a platform, and multiple clients build applications upon it. To separate the responsibilities and to encapsulate certain functionalities, architects have structured different layers of APIs and created public, internal, and in some cases, partner-specific APIs. If the platform is a kind of centralized application (like facebook.com) and the keystone provider controls it, it makes it easy to track the API dependencies between the platform and applications. However, if the platform is a shipping application, delivered as a set of binaries or if the development processes and release cycles are somewhat independent, the detection of undesired dependencies to the API surface becomes difficult or even impossible.

Finding A: In an internal ecosystem, maintaining an overview of the partners API usage gives the organization advantages to optimize its speed and customer added value.

3.3 Process Challenges

As described in BAPO, the 'P' stands for Process and relates to activities and way of working.

Handling of Deprecation Process. As we indicate in the introduction, the API has a birth, a life, and a death: a life-cycle. If birth and life are unproblematic, the death implemented by a deprecation creates more struggles for organizations. We have noticed that finding the "good" date for a deprecation tends to be impossible and even more the date to altogether remove the API. Again the structure of the software ecosystem reveals several conflicting forces. From one side, we want to follow the ecosystem strategy to be able to create new business models and embrace the change and gain in speed. On the other side, we want to keep the current API stable, even if in our case not removing the API will cause additional costs for the maintenance of the software as well as potentially increase the complexity of the code and architecture. Which information and tools are missing to enable the customer to accept the deprecation? In [8] a beginning of an answer is provided: specifying the severity of change and the deadline or version of the deprecation. This, offers more transparency for the ISECO partners but, from the customer point of view, the effort of migration will still stay the same.

Finding P: A deprecation process is mandatory for the financial and technical health of the platform. When implementing it, it is difficult because of contradictory forces in internal ecosystems.

3.4 Organisation Challenges

Finally, the 'O' of BAPO, which stands for Organization, relates to teams and responsibilities.

Lack of Education of the Developers. In the three projects at Siemens, we observed that these involve several technologies. This heterogeneity and multiplicity of technologies drastically increase the challenges for all the developers to understand those technologies and to master the subtleties. Another aspect of this lack of education is not related to the technology itself, but the awareness that manipulating APIs requires additional activities. At Siemens, we conducted worldwide dozens of internal training focused on API evolution, and the significant finding was that the ability to design and code an API is not depending on the seniority. Regarding the quality in term of usability and evolvability, the seniority has advantages, but we observed that a trivial aspect like controlling the visibility of the API was often forgotten. Even if the developer is experienced, the trap is laid, API design and evolution need another mindset and another process.

Finding O: API design and evolution need a different mindset, awareness and continuous education of development teams to achieve better API quality

4 Relating Findings to the Cases

In this section, we will present the relevance of the finding for each case. We performed interviews with team architects and system architects for each project (3 to 4 per case) to characterize the importance of the identified challenges. After the presentation of a finding, the interviewees had to rank the relevance of the finding for their own case between 1 not relevant and 10, highly relevant. The average for each finding, and each case is presented in Table 2.

Table 2. Findings relevance for each case

	ISECO-A	ISECO-B	ISECO-C	Average	Std. deviation
B	7.5	8.7	7.0	7.7	0.9
A	7.0	8.7	8.3	8.0	0.9
P	9.0	8.7	6.0	7.9	1.7
O	9.5	7.3	8.3	8.4	1.1

As depicted in Table 2, for the three ISECOs, the relevance of the challenges are almost equivalent with a value around 8.0 of 10.0. The major difference observed is related to Sect. 3.3, when ISECO-A and ISECO-B indicate high relevance, ISECO-C tends to a medium relevance. ISECO-A and ISECO-B are comparable in term of development size and also in term of API Surface. Both have a wide API surface and different technology stacks to express APIs. Unlike ISECO-C, which has a narrow API surface and a single technology as API. The other explanation can be the age of the projects. ISECO-A and ISECO-B are older than ISECO-C.

5 Discussion

In the following section, we discuss construct, internal, and external validity threats.

Threats to Construct Validity is related to the relation between theory and observation. As we performed interviews, we relied on a potentially subjective statement of the participants. To reduce the effect, we listed only findings that have been mentioned several times. We also performed a two paths validation: collecting the challenges in each organization, reformulating the challenge independently from the organization and requiring an evaluation of the relevance on the reformulated findings.

Threats to Internal Validity is related to a co-factors that may affect our results. In our case, interviewees might have given answers that do not fully reflect reality or have been exaggerated due to the current project stress situation regarding API Management. We worked for the three ecosystems for an extended period: two to three years, with different roles, assessor and co-worker, which gave us an overall measure and reduced the risk of an isolated measure. Furthermore, we anonymized and reformulated the challenges and proceeded to individual validation by the software architects and system architects.

Threats to External Validity is related to the generalization of our results. In our case, the main thread is the representativeness of our cases. We investigated three Siemens ISECOs. The results can be specific to them. However, the collection of data was performed independently on several organizations.

6 Related Work

The problem of API management is not a new topic, but it has become more prominent in recent years. Study has already been performed [9] to evaluate the reaction of API evolution and to a deprecation. The need for continuous API Management is generally described in [10]. The authors propose several guidelines to balance the desire for agility and speed with the need for robust and scalable operations. Specifically to software ecosystems, Hammouda et al. [11] point out the necessity of a regular re-assessment of API architectural and design decisions to be able to balance the tradeoff between offering a current and modern API with offering a stable and backward compatible API.

Several tools and frameworks have also been developed to help the organizations to check/design their APIs. Lindman et al. [12] proposed a framework to help managers, designers, and developers to discuss API management. On a source code point of view, Brito et al. [13] proposed an APIdiff tool to detect syntactic breaking changes.

7 Conclusion

In this paper, we have given an empirical overview of the challenges, organizations implementing internal ecosystems are facing to realize effective API strategies. The empirical study was performed on three Siemens internal ecosystems.

Even if in a first sense, an API can easily be viewed as something technical, we realized that many interconnections exist with other concerns of software development. We found 4 challenges, and we clustered around the BAPO model. The main focus of the paper does not provide solutions, but rather highlights areas of improvements and open topics for further research.

The API economy is there, but to enable all organizations to benefit in a sustainable way from this possibility to innovate, further research and development is needed to increase the impact of APIs.

References

1. Parnas, D.L.: On the criteria to be used in decomposing systems into modules. Commun. ACM **15**(12), 1053–1058 (1972). https://doi.org/10.1145/361598.361623
2. Bloch, J.: How to design a good API and why it matters. In: Companion to the 21st ACM SIGPLAN Conference on Object-Oriented Programming Systems, Languages, and Applications - OOPSLA 06 (2006)
3. Why use new lifecycle tools in API management platforms? https://searchmicroservices.techtarget.com/feature/Why-use-new-lifecycle-tools-in-API-management-platforms
4. Schultis, K.-B., Elsner, C., Lohmann, D.: Architecture challenges for internal software ecosystems: a large-scale industry case study. In: Proceedings of the 22Nd ACM SIGSOFT International Symposium on Foundations of Software Engineering, FSE 2014, pp. 542–552. ACM, New York (2014). http://doi.acm.org/10.1145/2635868.2635876
5. van der Linden, F.J., Schmid, K., Rommes, E.: Software Product Lines in Action: The Best Industrial Practice in Product Line Engineering. Springer, Heidelberg (2007). https://doi.org/10.1007/978-3-540-71437-8
6. Eisenhardt, K.M.: Building theories from case study research. Acad. Manag. Rev. **14**(4), 532 (1989)
7. Walsham, G.: Interpretive case studies in is research: nature and method. Eur. J. Inf. Syst. **4**(2), 74–81 (1995). https://doi.org/10.1057/ejis.1995.9
8. Sawant, A.A., Aniche, M., van Deursen, A., Bacchelli, A.: Understanding developers' needs on deprecation as a language feature. In: Proceedings of the 40th International Conference on Software Engineering, ICSE 2018, pp. 561–571. ACM, New York (2018). http://doi.acm.org/10.1145/3180155.3180170
9. Hora, A., Robbes, R., Valente, M.T., Anquetil, N., Etien, A., Ducasse, S.: How do developers react to API evolution? A large-scale empirical study. Softw. Qual. J. **26**(1), 161–191 (2018). https://doi.org/10.1007/s11219-016-9344-4
10. Medjaoui, M., Wilde, E., Mitra, R., Amundsen, M.: Continuous API Management: Making the Right Decisions in An Evolving Landscape. OReilly, Sebastopol (2018)
11. Hammouda, I., Knauss, E., Costantini, L.: Continuous API design for software ecosystems. In: 2015 IEEE/ACM 2nd International Workshop on Rapid Continuous Software Engineering, pp. 30–33, May 2015
12. Lindman, J., Horkoff, J., Hammouda, I., Knauss, E.: Emerging perspectives of API strategy. IEEE Softw., 1 (2018)
13. Brito, A., Xavier, L., Hora, A., Valente, M.T.: APIDiff: detecting API breaking changes. In: 2018 IEEE 25th International Conference on Software Analysis, Evolution and Reengineering (SANER), pp. 507–511, March 2018

Management of Software Products

The Product Roadmap Maturity Model DEEP: Validation of a Method for Assessing the Product Roadmap Capabilities of Organizations

Jürgen Münch[1(✉)], Stefan Trieflinger[1(✉)], and Dominic Lang[2(✉)]

[1] Reutlingen University, Alteburgstraße 150, 72768 Reutlingen, Germany
{juergen.muench, stefan.trieflinger}@reutlingen-university.de

[2] Department of IT Coordination, Robert Bosch GmbH, 71636 Ludwigsburg, Germany
dominic.lang2@bosch.com

Abstract. **Context:** Organizations are increasingly challenged by high market dynamics, rapidly evolving technologies and shifting user expectations. In consequence, many organizations are struggling with their ability to provide reliable product roadmaps by applying traditional roadmapping approaches. Currently, many companies are seeking opportunities to improve their product roadmapping practices and strive for new roadmapping approaches. A typical first step towards advancing the roadmapping capabilities of an organization is to assess the current situation. Therefore, the so-called maturity model DEEP for assessing the product roadmapping capabilities of companies operating in dynamic and uncertain environments has been developed and published by the authors. **Objective:** The aim of this article is to conduct an initial validation of the DEEP model in order to understand its applicability better and to see if important concepts are missing. In addition, the aim of this article is to evolve the model based on the findings from the initial validation. **Method:** The model has been given to practitioners such as product managers with the request to perform a self-assessment of the current product roadmapping practices in their company. Afterwards, interviews with each participant have been conducted in order to gain insights. **Results:** The initial validation revealed that some of the stages of the model need to be rearranged and minor usability issues were found. The overall structure of the model was well received. The study resulted in the development of the version 1.1 of the DEEP product roadmap maturity model which is also presented in this article.

Keywords: Product roadmapping · Maturity model · Agile development · VUCA · Product management

S. Hyrynsalmi et al. (Eds.): ICSOB 2019, LNBIP 370, pp. 97–113, 2019.
https://doi.org/10.1007/978-3-030-33742-1_9

1 Introduction

For each company it is essential to provide a strategic direction in which the product offering will be developed over time in order to achieve the corporate vision. In general, the purpose of a roadmap is to provide essential understanding, proximity, direction and some degree of certainty regarding the planning of a course [1]. In companies, roadmaps are strategic tools, which can take various forms such as product roadmaps, technology roadmaps, industry roadmaps or science roadmaps [2]. From the product management's point of view, a good roadmap is a strategic communication tool, a statement of intend and direction. It should focus on the value it aims to deliver to its customers and the organization itself in order to rally support and coordinate effort among stakeholders [3]. Currently, the product roadmaps of many companies cover long time horizons and specific products, features or services together with precise release dates [4]. This approach works well in market environments that are predictable, stable and reliable. However, through increasing market dynamics, rapidly evolving technologies and shifting user expectations coupled with the adoption of lean and agile practices, it becomes almost impossible to predict which products, features or services will satisfy the needs of the customers and the organization in the future [3, 5]. As a result, companies are facing the challenge of deciding between breaking promises by constantly adjusting the roadmap or staying on course according to a plan made months ago that seems increasingly outdated. By recognizing the mismatch between traditional roadmaps and dynamic and uncertain market environments, most companies have realized that new approaches and procedures regarding the development and handling of product roadmaps are required. They need to identify and prioritize opportunities to improve their roadmapping processes and capabilities [3, 6]. A typical first step towards advancing the roadmapping abilities of an organization is to assess the current situation. Therefore, the so-called maturity model DEEP version 1.0 for assessing the product roadmapping capabilities of companies operating in dynamic and uncertain environments has been developed by the authors. The model is called DEEP as it comprises the principles "deliver value", "embrace learning", "evolve with change", and "prioritize ruthlessly". The model is especially suited for companies that operate in a dynamic and uncertain market environment. Practitioners can use the model in order to assess their current situation and identify potentials for a sustainable improvement of their product roadmapping practices. The model is designed in a way that a high assessment score should indicate a higher probability of product success in dynamic and uncertain environments than a low score. Product risks, for instance, are systematically and considered at an early stage and planning and implementation waste is avoided on higher maturity levels. However, having a high score does not guarantee product success and vice versa. This maturity model predominantly aims at raising the odds of product success. The DEEP V1.0 model has been previously published [7]. In this article, we extend this published article [7] with the description of the initial validation of the model. In addition, this article presents the new version DEEP V1.1 of the model and justifies the evolution of the model. This article is organized as follows: Sect. 2 sketches related work. Section 3 presents the initial model DEEP V1.0. Section 4 presents the study approach including the research questions, the validation process and the execution of the study. The results of the study as well as limitations of the findings are discussed in Sect. 5. This includes a description of how the model has been changed based on the findings. Afterwards, a summary and an outlook on future research is given. The new version 1.1 of the DEEP model can be found in the Appendix.

2 Related Work

In the scientific literature some maturity and assessment models can be found with respect to product roadmapping. Lombardo et al. [3] provide a so-called Roadmap Health Assessment Checklist. By scoring 15 questions the user assesses the status of his current product roadmapping practices. The calculated score indicates how the user can evolve his roadmapping practices either through a course correction or through a full relaunch. The questions are clustered around five dimensions that represent recommended product roadmapping practices (i.e., strategic context, focus on value, embrace learning, rally the organization around priorities, get customers excited) and two dimensions that represent bad product roadmapping practices (i.e., avoid overpromising, avoid overdesigning and over planning). The health check can be seen as a quick assessment that covers main issues. In contrast to the model presented in this paper, the model by Lombardo et al. does not explicitly show different stages for each dimension and does not consider specific organizational aspects (e.g., who is responsible for the roadmap or who can place items on the roadmap). Due to the different stages for each dimension of the model presented in this article, we expect to be able to provide more specific recommendations for improvement, i.e., on how to move from one stage to a higher one. Van de Weerd et al. [8] present a maturity matrix that helps users to assess their current product management practices. In contrast to the model presented in this article the approach of van de Weerd et al. is developed for traditional product management. A similar model is the so-called Roadmapping Value Scorecard published by Albright [9]. Although published in 2003, it already covers some key aspects of agile product management such as continuous reviewing and updating of the roadmap or linking the roadmap to value creation. A main difference of Albright's approach, compared to the approach presented in this article, is, that the scorecard aims at tracking a roadmapping team's progress as they first create a roadmap. Petrick [10] has developed a roadmapping maturity model with six stages. A major difference to the model presented in this article is, that it is described on a meta level (e.g., "[Roadmapping] balances market-pull and technology-push investments in new product development.") and that it lacks a clear guide on how to execute an assessment. In order to identify the current state of the art in the field of product roadmapping in dynamic and uncertain environments, Münch et al. consolidated the existent body of knowledge related to product roadmapping with a systematic literature review [4]. The authors identified 23 scientific papers that have a close relation to product roadmapping. The literature review showed that there is very little knowledge available in the scientific literature about how to address the challenges of product development in a dynamic and uncertain market environment.

3 The DEEP Product Roadmap Maturity Model V1.0

In the following, we present the initial version DEEP V1.0 of the model based on Münch et al. [7]. The maturity model was developed with the goal to be easy to use as a tool for self-assessing the product roadmapping capabilities of organizations in dynamic market environments with high uncertainties. In order to develop the model, the authors identified important aspects (so-called dimensions) of product roadmapping in which companies differ. The development of the model followed the principles of design science research as this approach combines practical and scientific research. In detail, 15 interviews were conducted with experts from 13 different German companies which operate in the digital sector and face a dynamic and uncertain market environment. The authors were able to obtain a deeper understanding of the usage of product roadmapping in practice as well as the challenges and success factors associated with product roadmapping. The analysis of the expert interviews showed, that the status quo of product roadmapping practices is very heterogeneous with respect to the dimensions. Therefore, it was decided to use five stages for each dimension that represent some kind of increase of maturation. Based on this information the stages for each dimension were defined.

D1: Items to be Found on the Roadmap. A suitable roadmap for product development in dynamic environments contains items of varying granularity (from products to themes to the vision). A product roadmap should not only describe what will be built but also why it should be built. This requires that roadmap items are connected to outcome-oriented goals, i.e., customer- or business-oriented goals. The product roadmap items should contribute to delivering value to customers and the business. The roadmap also needs to be aligned with the product vision (Table 1).

Table 1. Dimension "Items to be found on the product roadmap" in DEEP V1.0

Dimension	Stage of maturity				
Items to be found on the product roadmap	1 point Products	3 points Features	8 points Customer-oriented goals	15 points Topics (e.g., connected mobility or smart home) and customer/business-oriented goals	20 points Product vision, themes (i.e., high-level customer and system needs), customer/business-oriented goals and short-term features

D2: Adequacy of Item Detailing Based on Timeline. Items should be more detailed the closer they are in time. For example, the roadmap should not contain a detailed long-term planning. The reason is that features often need to be discovered and validated first before they are planned in detail. Defining detailed features in the long-term planning usually leads to unnecessary upfront efforts and might lead to promises that engineering cannot deliver on (Table 2).

Table 2. Dimension "Adequacy of item detailing based on the timeline" in DEEP V1.0

Dimension	Stage of maturity				
Adequacy of item detailing based on the timeline	1 point Next steps are planned ad-hoc and there is no mid- to long-term planning. Only short-term planning exists	3 points All tasks are planned and worked out in detail for short-, mid- and long-term	10 points The detailing of the items is not done systematically and does not reflect the necessity for detailing	12 points There is a clear correlation between time and level of detail. The timelier items are more detailed	20 points The detailing depends on the timeframe. Short-term items are detailed, prioritized, estimated and validated. Mid-term items are under validation or being discovered. The long-term timeframe contains themes only

D3: Reliability. Reliability can be seen as the trustworthiness of a roadmap and its ability to give orientation for an organization and its teams. This mainly depends on the roadmap's stability and how adjustments are done. A roadmap should be stable in a way that changes are only done systematically and justifiably. There should be reasons for changes of the roadmap and there should be a regular cadence for revisiting and refreshing the roadmap. Ad-hoc and not sufficiently justified changes should be avoided. This helps to get a better understanding of what should be delivered in the next cycle and to avoid that uncertain features are perceived as a promise to deliver (Table 3).

Table 3. Dimension "Reliability" in DEEP V1.0

Dimension	Stage of maturity				
Reliability	1 point The product roadmap is subject to permanent ad-hoc adjustments	3 points The product roadmap is subject to frequent ad-hoc adjustments	10 points Adjustments of the product roadmap are done in regular review cycles	10 points The product roadmap is subject to systematic change management and adjustments are done mainly reactively	16 points The product roadmap is subject to systematic change management and adjustments are done mainly proactively

D4: Confidence. Confidence describes the trust in a roadmap item regarding its ability to fulfill the respective goal/s at appropriate cost. It also illustrates the tentative nature of roadmap items in the mid-term planning. The short-term planning should consider only roadmap items with a high confidence in their contribution to the respective goals. The mid-term planning should indicate the degree of confidence of potential roadmap items with respect to contributing to goals (Table 4).

Table 4. Dimension "Confidence" in DEEP V1.0

Dimension	Stage of maturity				
Confidence	1 point The effects/impacts of product roadmap items are not considered	4 points The effects/impacts of product roadmap items are considered but only estimated	7 points The effects/impacts of product roadmap items are considered and determined based on the past (e.g., statistics)	10 points The effects/impacts of product roadmap items are considered and partly validated	14 points The effects/impacts of product roadmap items are considered and systematically validated

D5: Discovery. This dimension describes the ability of a company to identify and validate the right items on the roadmap before implementation. The seamless integration of discovery activities in the product development process helps to avoid building features that nobody wants or needs. Using product discovery techniques (such as customer interviews, split testing, prototyping, or Wizard of Oz) before deciding about features to implement can be seen as an indicator for high maturity in product roadmapping in dynamic technological and market environments (Table 5).

Table 5. Dimension "Discovery" in DEEP V1.0

Dimension	Stage of maturity				
Discovery	1 point No discovery activities. Typically, a manager is defining the roadmap items	2 points No discovery activities. Product roadmap items are identified based on expert knowledge	4 points No discovery activities. Product roadmap items are identified based on customer requests	8 points Professional discovery activities but no or only lose integration with delivery activities	10 points Close integration of discovery and delivery activities

D6: Responsible for Placing Items on the Roadmap. Responsibility refers to the question "Who is responsible for the definition of the roadmap and the conduction of the product roadmapping process?" A clear responsibility is necessary for pursuing the product strategy and coordinating stakeholder needs at the same time. Product management or cross-functional product teams should be established in a way that they can take over the responsibility of placing items on the roadmap (Table 6).

Table 6. Dimension "Placing features on the product roadmap" in DEEP V1.0

Dimension	Stage of maturity				
Placing features on the product roadmap	1 point Tools are used to decide if items are placed on the roadmap (e.g., decision matrix)	2 points Higher-level management	2 points Middle management	3 points Specific roles (e.g., portfolio manager)	6 points Product management or cross-functional product teams in liaison with key stakeholders

D7: Prioritization of Product Roadmap Items. This dimension describes how roadmap items are prioritized and which factors are taken into consideration. The prioritization should aim at finding the most efficient and effective way to deliver value to the customer and the business. Having a clear prioritization process helps to integrate all stakeholder needs early and to align these around the priorities. With an insufficient prioritization the most important items might not be done first and chances of reaching them later might be compromised (Table 7).

Table 7. Dimension "Prioritization of product roadmap items" in DEEP V1.0

Dimension	Stage of maturity				
Prioritization of product roadmap items	1 point First in first out	2 points Opinions determine priority	3 points Prioritization is based on the capability to deliver (e.g., low hanging fruits)	3 points Prioritization is based on short-term benefit (e.g., shareholder value)	6 points Prioritization is done with an established process and focuses on delivering value to customers and the business

D8: Extent of Alignment. This dimension specifies the depth and width of the alignment of the roadmap, i.e., how many stakeholders are covered by the roadmap and how good the alignment is. The product roadmap will not fulfill its purpose without alignment and buy-in of the key stakeholders. All stakeholders need to have individualized but consistent representations of a common product roadmap that reflects their information needs. A process for achieving alignment and buy-in needs to be in place (e.g., through regular cross-functional meetings and workshops) (Table 8).

Table 8. Dimension "Extent of alignment" in DEEP V1.0

Dimension	Stage of maturity				
Extent of alignment	1 point No alignment. No one or only one stakeholder such as high-level management has a product roadmap that is not communicated to others	1 point Several loosely connected pro-duct roadmaps for internal stakeholders exist	2 points Several loosely connected product roadmaps for internal and external stakeholders (such as customers or investors) exist	3 points One central product roadmap exists for different internal and external stakeholders	3 points One central product roadmap exists that allows to derive different representations for different stakeholders. A process for achieving alignment and buy-in is in place

D9: Ownership of the Product Roadmap. Ownership refers to the question "Who owns the roadmap and is accountable, i.e., signs and approves the roadmap?" The owner of the roadmap should not be separated from those who create the roadmap. Having no ownership might lead to conflicts and inconsistencies (Table 9).

Table 9. Dimension "Ownership of the product roadmap" in DEEP V1.0

Dimension	Stage of maturity				
Ownership of the product roadmap	1 point No owner defined	1 point Managers	2 points Ownership is shared between multiple roles	3 points Strategy or portfolio planning	3 points Product management or product teams

Based on the assessment of each dimension a total score is calculated that reflects the overall maturity of the roadmapping practices (see [7] for details). The total score is mapped to five maturity levels. If an organization is on level 1 or 2, the authors of the DEEP model recommend conducting a complete reset of the roadmapping process. If an organization is on level 3 or higher, we recommend improving the roadmapping practices in small steps (see Table 10).

Table 10. Levels of the maturity model

Maturity level	Score	High-level recommendation
1	9–18	Complete reset of roadmapping practices
2	19–30	
3	31–57	Incremental improvement of roadmapping practices
4	58–83	
5	84–100	

As mentioned before, the DEEP maturity model was developed for assessing the roadmapping capabilities of companies operating in dynamic and uncertain market environments. Leaders as well as teams (e.g., product teams) can benefit from the model. This DEEP model can be used by, but is not limited to, the following roles:

- Leaders and teams - to assess and reflect the current roadmapping activities.
- Leaders and teams - to see how product roadmapping practices could be improved.
- Leaders - to support and guide product teams in improving their roadmapping capabilities.
- Leaders and teams - to decide about next steps for improvement.
- Teams - to evaluate the progress in improving roadmapping practices.
- Leaders - to harmonize and integrate roadmapping practices in an organization.
- Coaches and consultants - to accompany the organizational transformation towards agile product management or a product-led organization.

The term "leaders" refers to roles such as management, head of product, head of design, head of engineering, or project manager. Teams might include specific roles such as product owner, scrum master, business analyst, developer, UX designer, sales or marketing.

4 Research Approach

This section gives an overview of the validation study approach. The aim of the study is to conduct an initial validation of the DEEP model in order to understand its applicability better and to see if important concepts are missing. The aim of this study is not to justify the design of the model itself. This has been the focus of a previous study [7]. The section starts with presenting the research questions and continues with the description of the validation process. Afterwards the details of the study's execution are presented, especially the data collection with practitioners who voluntarily participated in the validation process.

This study addresses following research questions:

RQ1: Can practitioners easily and efficiently use the model provided in the form of a questionnaire for self-assessing the product roadmap maturity of their organization or organizational unit?

RQ1.1: Do practitioners understand the questions, dimensions and stages of the self-assessment model?

RQ1.2: Can practitioners easily map the dimensions and stages to their organizational context to conduct the self-assessment?

RQ2: Do practitioners miss important information (such as dimensions or stages) in the product roadmap maturity model?

Data Collection and Analysis

In order to validate and evolve the model, we provided the developed DEEP V1.0 product roadmap maturity model (in the form of a self-assessment questionnaire) to practitioners without any explanations and instructions. This was done with the aim to ensure that the participants apply the DEEP model unbiased and to get feedback regarding interpretability and usability of the model. In the next step we conducted interviews with each practitioner in order to identify improvement potentials (e.g., ambiguities) of the DEEP model. All interviews were conducted by phone and by the same researcher. The average length of the interviews was 47 min with the range being between 31 and 81 min. All interviews were conducted in German language. In order to focus and structure the interviews and to ensure thematic comparability, we developed an interview guide which consisted of the following questions: (1) What do you think, are the strengths and weaknesses of the model? (2) Which phrases did you find difficult to understand during the application? (3) Does the calculated score reflect the status of your current product roadmapping process?

We recruited 14 experts, who operate in a dynamic and uncertain market environment with high uncertainties. The selection of those participants was based on their experience in product roadmapping and role in the organization (team lead, etc.). The search for suitable participants and the subsequent establishment of contact took place via a social business platform. Table 11 gives an overview of the participants in this study. The column "experience" refers to the amount of years in which the person was involved in product roadmapping activities. Each interview was recorded. We analyzed the audio files by extracting main responses, key statements and quotes and revised the model based on the participants statements.

Table 11. Participating interviewees (size classification: small <50, large >250)

Interviewee	Position	Experience	Company Size by no. of employees
Interviewee 1	Product Manager	15 years	Large
Interviewee 2	Product Manager	7 years	Small
Interviewee 3	Head of Product Management	11 years	Large
Interviewee 4	Head of Product Management	6 years	Large
Interviewee 5	Head of Product Management	8 years	Medium
Interviewee 6	Product Manager	14 years	Medium
Interviewee 7	Product Manager	4 years	Large

(*continued*)

Table 11. (*continued*)

Interviewee	Position	Experience	Company Size by no. of employees
Interviewee 8	Product Manager	18 years	Large
Interviewee 9	Product Manager	9,5 years	Small
Interviewee 10	Head of Product Management	9 years	Large
Interviewee 11	Head of Product Management	12 years	Medium
Interviewee 12	Software Engineer	5 years	Medium
Interviewee 13	Board member (CEO)	16 years	Small
Interviewee 14	Product Manager	9 years	Medium

Based on the findings from the interviews we made changes to the DEEP model. Additionally, we discussed these changes with a practitioner of the Robert Bosch GmbH with many years of experience in the field of product roadmapping in order to obtain a subject-specific opinion.

5 Validation Results

This section outlines the feedback that was gathered during the interviews. First, we present general feedback. Afterwards we structure the feedback according to those model dimensions that generated feedback we considered valuable for modifications in the model (or respectively the self-assessment questionnaire). In addition, we describe how we changed the model based on the feedback.

Overall, the current version of our model was described as comprehensible and applicable. For example, one participant stated: *"It is obvious that the model is designed to increase the customer value when developing products. From my perspective the model provides useful insights to improve the current product roadmapping practice." (product manager)* Another participant mentioned: *"I think the model supports the identification of weaknesses regarding the current product roadmapping process and gives good insights in order to improve it." (head of product management)* Another participant reported: *"What I find particularly pleasant about this model is the possibility to review the current roadmapping practice as well as to learn which other possibilities exist in order to create and handle a product roadmap. I think that the model helps to identify relevant factors to improve the product roadmapping practice." (head of product management)* The validation showed that all participants understood that they had to select the stage that represents their current practices best for each dimension. In addition, the participants had no ambiguities regarding our developed scoring system. In detail, each participant understood that each dimension is assigned to a certain score, so that the total score is calculated by summing up the points of each selected stage (which determines the maturity level). Nevertheless, in order to further increase the usability, we slightly improved the design of our model. In detail, we added a question for each dimension so that the different stages serve as the answers to these questions. This provides a clearer instruction to the user that has to answer the question by selecting one stage for each dimension. Besides the general feedback, the interviews provided comments and recommendations for the improvement of specific dimensions. These comments and recommendations as well as the changes we made to the model will be discussed in the following.

Dimension: Items to be Found on the Product Roadmap

During the interviews five participants mentioned difficulties to match the roadmap items they use in their current practice with a corresponding stage in the model. The reason is that their companies are using several roadmap items such as features, goals, topics or themes together in the roadmap. Since our model (in the version 1.0) asked only for one type of item per stage (e.g., only products in the first stage), it was difficult for the participants to identify the stage that matches best to their current roadmapping practices. Consequently, they did not know, which stages to choose. However, after the participants considered the second dimension "adequacy of item detailing based on the timeline", the answer got clearer. Therefore, we changed the sequence of the first two dimensions. In addition, we modified the phrasing of the different stages in order to emphasize those items that can mainly be found in a roadmap of a certain stage (Table 12).

Table 12. Revised dimension "Roadmap items" in the new version DEEP V1.1

Dimension	Stage of maturity				
Roadmap items - Which items are on your product roadmap?	1 point Mainly products	3 points Mainly products, features	10 points Mainly business goals, products, features	12 points Mainly customer and business goals, products, features and for the long-term timeframe topics (e.g., smart home)	20 points Mainly product vision, customer and business goals, products, features and for the long-term timeframe themes (i.e., high-level customer needs)

Dimension: Discovery

Regarding this dimension the expert interviews showed that the comprehensibility and evaluation of the different stages provided several challenges. First, the participants did not fully see the difference between the second and the third stage. For example, one participant asked: *"Does the stage 'No discovery activities. Product roadmap items are identified based on customer requests' only refer to the identification of requirements based on customer requests or does it also include expert knowledge?" (head of product management)* In order to make it clear that each stage is considered separately from each other, we introduced the word "mainly" in the second stage (i.e., "Product roadmaps items are *mainly* defined based on expert knowledge."). This ensures that only those organizations select the second stage that mainly use the knowledge of experts in order to define their product roadmap items. Similarly, in the third stage we introduced the word “mainly” (i.e., “Product roadmap items are *mainly* defined based on customer requests”). We chose the word “mainly”, because it provides more flexibility. As a result, our model covers situations where the organization concerned identifies not only its roadmap items through customer requests but also uses the knowledge of experts.

Another challenge for the participants posed the term “professional” regarding the wording of the fourth stage “Professional discovery activities but no or only lose integration with delivery activities”. It was not completely clear to the participants which requirements had to be fulfilled in order to characterize their discovery activities as “professional discovery activities”. To counter the confusion regarding the word “professional” within the third stage we replaced “professional discovery activities but no or only lose integration with delivery activities” with “Several discovery activities are conducted (e.g., user research) but they are not or only loosely integrated with delivery activities”. This ensures that each user obtains a better understanding of what is required for the fourth stage (Table 13).

Table 13. Revised dimension “Discovery” in the new version DEEP V1.1

Dimension	Stage of maturity				
Discovery – How do you conduct product discovery?	1 point No discovery activities. Typically, a manager is defining the roadmap items	2 points Product roadmap items are mainly defined based on expert knowledge	4 points Product roadmap items are mainly defined based on customer requests	8 points Several discovery activities are conducted (e.g., user research) but they are not or only loosely integrated with delivery activities	10 points Close integration of discovery and delivery activities

Dimension: Responsible for Placing Features on the Product Roadmap

Within this dimension several participants saw potential to improve the description of the stage with the highest maturity level. As an example, one participant mentioned: “*In the current model, the highest level of responsibility for placing items on the pro-duct roadmap is called: ‘Product management or cross-functional product team in liaison with key stakeholders’. In my opinion the product management working in a cross-functional way with other teams and the management is the highest form of maturity.” (head of product management)* Another participant mentioned: “*I think, in an agile company usually different collaborating teams are responsible for placing items on the product roadmap.” (product manager)* Besides that, two participants stated that according to their experience middle management plays a smaller role compared to the high-level management. In this context one participant said: *“My experience is that decisions regarding the product roadmap are discussed less by the middle management and more often by the high-level management.” (product manager)*

According to this feedback we summarized the two separate stages "high-level management" and "middle management" into one stage. The practitioners saw the product management in cross-functional collaboration with other teams as the highest maturity level. In order to integrate this insight into the model, we phrased the fifth stages in the version 1.1 as follows: "Product management with cross-functional product teams in liaison with key stakeholders" (i.e., we changed "or" to "with"). In addition, the expert interviews revealed that most practitioners considered an organization as more mature if the product management is responsible for placing items on a product roadmap instead of the management. For this reason, we defined the fourth stage in a way that product management is responsible for placing items on the roadmap (Table 14).

Table 14. Revised dimension "Responsibility" in the new version DEEP V1.1

Dimension	Stage of maturity				
Responsibility – Who is responsible for placing items on the roadmap?	1 point Tools are used to decide if items are placed on the roadmap (e.g., decision matrix)	2 points Management	2 points Specific roles (e.g., portfolio manager)	3 points Product Management	6 points Product Management with cross-functional product teams in liaison with key stakeholders

Overall, the validation revealed that some of the stages of the model need to be rearranged as well as minor usability issues. Anyhow, the overall structure of the model was well received. The results from applying the assessment model (i.e., the maturity levels) were widely in agreement with the own perceptions of the study participants. The new version of the model can be found in the Appendix of this article.

Considering the validity of the results, it should be mentioned that the study scope was limited to a set of German companies that are developing software-intensive products in dynamic and technical market environments with high uncertainties. The results cannot be directly transferred to other contexts, although an analytical generalization may be possible for similar contexts. Moreover, the reported results are based on the personal perceptions of each participant. Interviewees may have given answers which do not fully reflect the reality of their companies. This threat to validity is mitigated by the fact that the interviewees had no apparent incentive to polish the truth. Since contact with the participants was brief, misunderstandings on the researcher's side cannot be excluded. In order to mitigate this threat to validity, email clarifications were requested from the interviewees when in doubt.

6 Summary and Further Research

In summary, the article presents an initial validation of the DEEP V1.0 product roadmap maturity model and shows how the model evolved based on the findings from the validation. Overall, the model was well received by practitioners. The validation led to the rearrangement of some stages of the model. In addition, changes with the aim to improve the usability of the model were done. The practitioners participating in the validation did not identify major incompleteness or inaccuracies of the model. In future research we plan to conduct further validation of the model (e.g., with more practitioners and in specific industry sectors). Moreover, we plan to develop an industry benchmark with the model that reflects the current state of product roadmapping in practice. We also intend to empirically develop an instrument that guides companies through the improvement process. In order to do that we plan to carry out an analysis of how to transition from one stage to the next and to analyze transition costs and organizational implications in our future research. This should lead to more detailed recommendations of the model based on the assessment score. It might also include a cost-benefit analysis of some sort with respect to improving the maturity. Most practitioners that participated in the study clearly see the current assessment model DEEP as a good starting point for companies to advance their product roadmapping capabilities. The avenues for future research can be based on a variety of empirical data and can therefore be considered as highly promising.

Acknowledgements. We wish to thank the participants in the study for their time and contributions. All feedback collected from the interviews gave us great insights and motivates us to continue our research and to refine the model.

Appendix 1: DEEP V1.1

PRODUCT ROADMAP MATURITY ASSESSMENT

DEEP Version 1.1

Dimension	Question	Option 1	Option 2	Option 3	Option 4	Option 5
ROADMAP DETAILING	How adequate is your roadmap detailed with respect to the timeline?	1: Next steps are planned ad-hoc and there is only short-term planning	3: All tasks are planned and worked out in detail for short-, mid- and long-term	8: There is some correlation between time and level of detail but the detailing of the items is not done systematically	15: There is a clear correlation between time and level of detail. Timelier tasks are more detailed.	20: Short-term items are detailed, prioritized, estimated and validated. Mid-term items are under validation or being discovered. The long-term timeframe contains themes.
ROADMAP ITEMS	Which items are on your product roadmap?	1: Mainly products	3: Mainly products, features	10: Mainly business goals, products, features	12: Mainly customer and business goals, products, features and for the long-term timeframe topics (e. g., smart home)	20: Mainly product vision, customer and business goals, products, features and for the long-term timeframe themes (i.e., high-level customer needs)
RELIABILITY	How often do you adjust your product roadmap?	1: Permanent ad-hoc adjustments	3: Frequent ad-hoc adjustments	10: Mainly in regular review cycles (e.g., every 3 months)	10: Adjustments are mainly done reactively on demand.	16: Adjustments are mainly done proactively,
CONFIDENCE	How confident are you that the roadmap items have the expected impacts on goals?	1: The impacts are not considered.	4: The impacts are mainly estimated by experts.	7: The impacts are mainly determined based on data from the past (e.g., statistics)1	10: The impacts are partly validated.	14: The impacts are systematically validated.
DISCOVERY	How do you conduct product discovery?	1: No discovery activities. Typically a manager is defining the roadmap items.	2: Product roadmap items are mainly defined based on expert knowledge.	4: Product roadmap items are mainly defined based on customer requests.	8: Several discovery activities are conducted (e.g., user research) but they are not or only loosely integrated with delivery activities.	10: Close integration of discovery and delivery activities
PRIORITIZATION	How do you prioritize items?	1: First in, first out	2: Opinions determine priority.	3: Prioritization is based on the capability to deliver (e.g., low hanging fruits).	3: Prioritization is based on short-term benefit (e.g., shareholder value).	8: Prioritization is done with an established process and focuses on delivering value to customers and the business.
EXTENT OF ALIGNMENT	How do your align stakeholders?	1: No one or only one stakeholder such as high-level management has a product roadmap that is not communicated to others.	1: Several loosely connected product roadmaps for internal stakeholders exist.	2: Several loosely connected product roadmaps for internal and external stakeholders exist.	3: One central product roadmap exists for different internal and external stakeholders.	6: One central product roadmap exists that allows to derive different representations for different stakeholders. A process for achieving alignment is in place.
RESPONSIBILITY	Who is responsible for placing items on the roadmap?	1: Tools are used to decide if items are placed on the roadmap (e. g., decision matrix).	2: Management	2: Specific roles (e.g., portfolio manager)	3: Product management	3: Product management with cross-functional product teams in liaison with key stakeholders
OWNERSHIP	Who owns the product roadmap and is accountable?	1: No owner defined	2: Managers	3: Ownership is shared between multiple roles	4: Strategy or portfolio planning	3: Product management with cross-functional product teams

MATURITY
Please sum up the number of points for the fields you selected.

Total points:	Maturity level:	1	2	3	4	5
	Score:	9 – 18 pts	10 – 30 pts	31 – 57 pts	58 – 83 pts	84 – 100 pts
	Recommendation:	Complete reset of roadmapping practices		Incremental improvement of roadmapping practices		

CREATED BY: Jürgen Münch, Stefan Trieflinger, Dominic Lang

References

1. Kostoff, R.N., Schaller, R.: Science and technology roadmaps. IEEE Trans. Eng. Manag. **48**(2), 132–143 (2001)
2. Kameoka, A., Kuwahara, T., Li, M.: Integrated strategy development: an integrated roadmapping approach. In: Portland International Conference on Management of Engineering and Technology Management for Reshaping the World, PICMET 2003, Portland, OR, USA, pp. 370–379 (2003)
3. Lombardo, C.T., McCarthy, B., Ryan, E., Conners, M.: Product Roadmaps Relaunched - How to Set Direction While Embracing Uncertainty. O'Reilly Media Inc., Sebastopol (2017)
4. Münch, J., Trieflinger, S., Lang, D.: Product roadmap – from vision to reality: a systematic literature review. In: ICE/IEEE ITMC: International Conference on Engineering, Technology and Innovation, Valbonne, France (2019)
5. Brynjolfsson, E., McAfee, A.: How the Digital Revolution is Accelerating Innovation, Driving Productivity, and Irreversibly Transforming Employment and the Economy. Digital Frontier Press Lexington, Massachusetts (2018)
6. Münch, J., Trieflinger, S., Lang, D.: Why feature based roadmaps fail in rapidly changing markets: a qualitative survey. In: International Workshop on Software-Intensive Business: Start-ups, Ecosystems and Platforms, Espoo, Finland, pp. 202–218 (2018)
7. Münch, J., Trieflinger, S., Lang, D.: DEEP: the product roadmap maturity model – a method for assessing the product roadmapping capabilities of organizations. In: International Workshop on Software-Intensive Business: Start-ups, Ecosystems and Platforms, Tallinn, Estonia (2019)
8. Weerd, I.v., Bekkers, W., Brinkkemper, S.: Developing a maturity matrix for software product management. In: Tyrväinen, P., Jansen, S., Cusumano, M.A. (eds.) Software Business, ISCOB 2010, pp. 76–89 (2010)
9. Albright, R.E.: A unifying architecture for roadmaps frames a value scorecard. In: Proceedings. Managing Technologically Driven Organizations: The Human Side of Innovation and Change IEMC 2003, pp. 383–386 (2003)
10. Petrick, I.: Developing and Implementing Roadmaps – A Reference Guide. White Paper - Pennsylvania State University (2008)

Towards a SaaS Pricing Cookbook: A Multi-vocal Literature Review

Andrey Saltan[1,2(✉)] and Kari Smolander[2]

[1] HSE University, Moscow, Russian Federation
asaltan@hse.ru
[2] LUT University, Lappeenranta, Finland
kari.smolander@lut.fi

Abstract. Informed SaaS pricing decision-making requires the involvement of different business units and integrated pricing approaches. Achieving both appears to be challenging for a lot of SaaS providers, and despite its declared importance, pricing is one of the most under-managed business processes. Small and medium-sized companies do not have the resources for or the understanding of how to make informed decisions on pricing strategy and tactics. Pricing is a topic of interest in several research domains including economics, management science, digital and service marketing, and, increasingly, in software engineering. Still, the lack of integration between studies creates inconsistency in research. A comprehensive SaaS pricing body of knowledge is missing, as is a coherent action-oriented "Cookbook". This multi-vocal literature review both brings together results from these research domains and matches practitioner expertise with academic research outcomes to promote the advancement of SaaS pricing theory and practice.

Keywords: SaaS · Software-as-a-Service · Pricing · Multi-vocal literature review

1 Introduction

Pricing is recognized as one of the crucially important elements of business strategy and tactics in the majority of product and service companies [39]. Software companies, including SaaS providers, are not an exception. For them, pricing is crucial and requires sophisticated decision-making [13,38]. There is a keen interest in and need for better pricing methods and solutions in the software industry, which is experiencing a transition towards the service paradigm. Therefore, a growing number of practitioners and researchers are seeking pricing methods and solutions. However, the body of knowledge in pricing is vast and full of isolated pricing-related approaches and recommendations that can induce radically different pricing tactics and strategies.

By its nature, pricing lay on the intersection of different responsibilities, including Development, Sales, Marketing, Finance, Support, and informed

S. Hyrynsalmi et al. (Eds.): ICSOB 2019, LNBIP 370, pp. 114–129, 2019.
https://doi.org/10.1007/978-3-030-33742-1_10

decisions that require coherent effort coordination and collaboration between them [12]. The Software Product Management Body of Knowledge [27] specifies pricing as one of the core areas of responsibility of product managers. However, pricing requires sophisticated analyses based on internal and external information and product management requires extensive analytical support. Facing these challenges, large tech companies, including SaaS providers, employ highly qualified economists in cooperation with qualified product and project managers who are capable of coping with these pricing challenges [5]. However, SMEs do not have the resources and understanding to make informed decisions on pricing strategy and tactics. Inconsistent knowledge of SaaS pricing and the complications of proper implementation of all pricing-related processes and practices leads to a scattered and under-managed pricing process in many software and SaaS developing companies [12,52].

Incoherent pricing in the industry is mirrored in academic literature. There is no single "home" for studies on software and SaaS pricing in the academic community. Pricing is a growing field of research within several different research domains, including economics, management science, digital and service marketing, as well as software engineering and computer science. Still, the current theory does not offer coherent and verified solutions to assist product managers in selecting among the millions of options while designing and implementing pricing. Rare attempts to provide such guidance do not bring utilitarian value for practitioners [51].

The eventual goal of SaaS pricing research should be a body of knowledge that defines the scope and content of knowledge on SaaS pricing and a "Cookbook" that offers appropriate SaaS pricing designs to product managers based on parameters and objectives of a given situation. There should be no illusions that one SaaS pricing framework could be applicable to all types of products in all types of SaaS providers. Moreover, product managers and their teams remain responsible for deciding which SaaS pricing processes and practices should be applied to the specific product, taking into account product characteristics and overall business model and strategy. However, a "Cookbook" that consists of compartmentalized pricing frameworks, step-by-step solutions, and easy-to-use decision-support mechanisms could support product managers and in the long run improve pricing in SaaS industries.

As pricing is both a critical business function and a subject of academic research, we have searched for articles for this literature study from both pricing practitioners and leading scholars. Combining these two sources of literature in the systematic multi-vocal literature review allows us to explore existing pricing frameworks and systematize a diverse range of recommendations and guidance grounded either in research or practical experience. We explored available academic literature on SaaS pricing across various scientific databases and digital libraries ("white" literature, 76 items), as well as materials produced by practitioners and industry experts outside the traditional academic community ("grey" literature, 151 items). As a result, this research attempts to contribute to developing a concise and practical SaaS pricing "Cookbook" and comprehensive Body of Knowledge by comparing and analyzing thirteen existing SaaS pricing frameworks.

2 Background

2.1 SaaS Definition

The most common definition of SaaS is the one presented in 2011 by the United States National Institute of Standards and Technology (NIST) [35]. NIST defines the Cloud computing in general as: "*a model for enabling ubiquitous, convenient, on-demand network access to a shared pool of configurable computing resources (e.g., networks, servers, storage, applications, and services) that can be rapidly provisioned and released with minimal management effort or service provider interaction*". Further, SaaS itself is defined as one of three service models cloud computing could be deployed along with Platform-, and Infrastructure-as-a-Service. Specifically, Software as a Service (SaaS) is "*the capability provided to the consumer is to use the provider's applications running on a cloud infrastructure*". The applications are accessible from various devices through a thin client interface or an application. The consumer does not manage or control the underlying cloud infrastructure, with the possible exception of limited user-specific application configuration settings.

Being widely accepted by practitioners in the software industry, quite often we can see that researchers in academia use interchangeable notions depending on their research domain instead of SaaS. Depending on the research context, terms "cloud services" [31], "online services" [40] and "information services" [6] among others are widely used as synonyms to SaaS.

2.2 SaaS Pricing

In most types of businesses, pricing has always been recognized as an essential component of overall business strategy with an impact on profits and revenues [33]. Software companies became an example of those whose commercial success is very dependent on an adequate pricing strategy due to the nature of the market, cost structures, and network effects [53]. Decisions on designing and implementing a pricing strategy have always been challenging for software companies [9].

The transition towards the SaaS business model enabled new opportunities for software companies in software development, delivery, and operations. These opportunities have implications on pricing by creating and magnifying the number of pricing design, experiment, and control mechanisms are available for SaaS companies. These mechanisms include, for example, recurring subscription fees, new mechanisms to ensure efficient price discrimination, and real-time usage tracking: [15,18,28]. However, these new opportunities can also cause obstacles for companies when old pricing principles and practices become obsolete and companies' understandings of how the new ones should be designed are unclear [38].

There is no unified approach to determining the pricing strategy, its implementation, or tactics. We still lack a comprehensive discussion and analysis of this issue. When considering quite extensive literature overviews in background sections of several research papers (i.e., [22,29,38]), we were able to identify only one paper that explicitly performed a literature review on the pricing of all three pillars of cloud computing including SaaS, PaaS, and IaaS [54]. All these reviews and overviews lack a systematic approach and cover only a narrow body of literature.

2.3 SaaS Pricing Body of Knowledge and "Cookbook"

A comprehensively defined and structured set of knowledge is now commonly referred to as a Body of Knowledge. Such Bodies of Knowledge exist in a range of disciplines and associated professional areas and provide complete guides to various areas of knowledge, concepts, terms, competences, and activities within a particular domain [10]. However, few of these Bodies of Knowledge define knowledge with the stress on general factors and most often do not provide easy-to-use solutions in a step-by-step or exemplifying style. For these purposes, Body of Knowledge could be supplemented with more action-oriented "Cookbooks" helpful in making decisions and organizing processes and practices more systematically and efficiently.

So far, SaaS pricing lacks successful attempts to provide a widely accepted Body of Knowledge that defines the scope and content of knowledge regarding SaaS pricing, clarifying its place, and setting the boundary concerning other processes and activities inside SaaS developing companies. As a result, even the same terms of pricing strategy, tactics, and structure can have different meanings to researchers and practitioners, and the amount of such confusing terms is large [51]. Roughly the same situation is found with action-oriented approaches and cookbook-style recipes for consistent analyses and decision-making regarding SaaS pricing.

By now, the very best attempts to develop SaaS pricing Body of Knowledge or "Cookbooks" can be considered books titled "The Anatomy of SaaS Pricing" by Campbell [12] and "Mastering SaaS Pricing" by Poyar [43]. In a narrative style, both books cover a wide range of pricing-related issues crucial for SaaS companies and undoubtedly delivers great value for practitioners. However, these books lack thorough discussions of concepts, terminology, and knowledge areas within SaaS pricing, nor do they provide coherent and comprehensive ready-to-use solutions and step-by-step guidelines.

3 Research Approach

3.1 Research Scope and Research Questions

The theory and practice of SaaS pricing have advanced over the last fifteen years since first SaaS solutions have been introduced. However, SaaS pricing has not arisen from scratch. Existing SaaS pricing practices are largely grounded in earlier pricing practices in software, internet, and service-oriented industries. Exploring and alignment existing pricing frameworks and approaches proposed by both academic researchers and experienced practitioners seem to be the first step towards a better understanding of how SaaS solutions are and should be priced. Thus, the research question can be defined as follows:

RQ: What pricing frameworks have been proposed and how they can support pricing-related decision-making?

To address **RQ** and to promote further studies on SaaS pricing, we conducted a multi-vocal literature review across various research areas and sources of literature ("white" or "grey"). To answer these questions, we classified the existing literature across various dimensions. Cross-domain and cross-sourced analysis of the research trends, contribution, and challenges allowed us to compare and match them. Both similarities and differences can indicate the potential for further studies, as well as highlight promising research avenues in SaaS pricing. The multi-vocal literature review was conducted following the research protocol outlined from the guidelines [21].

3.2 Search Strategy and Study Selection

The literature review consisted of two stages of searching for literature. In the first stage, we collected "white" literature using multiple scientific databases and digital libraries. We defined the list of the primary search terms that could form the basis of search queries for major scientific databases and libraries as well as set search limitations regarding time, publication type, and research area.

In the search query we dealt with the difference in terminology regarding the notion of SaaS by creating a list of possible synonyms, which were linked during the search procedure using the operator **OR**: "SaaS", "software as a service", "software service", "cloud service", "information service", "digital service" and "internet service". The second part of the search query consisted of words "price" and "pricing" linked with the operator **OR**. Both parts of the search query were linked with the operator **AND**. The search procedure was applied to three fields (title, abstract, and keywords) that contain the most accessible information about the paper.

Once the search terms were settled, we defined a list of sources of relevant scientific literature. We selected the following scientific databases and libraries that cover the most significant journals and conference proceedings: ScienceDirect, SpringerLink, Scopus, JSTOR, IEEE Xplore, and ACM Digital Library. The search procedure was conducted in June 2019. To ensure the exhaustiveness of the collected body of literature, we complemented automated search with backward and forward chaining manual search using the Google Scholar search engine.

"White" literature search produced 99 studies without duplicates. All papers were stored for further revision of Inclusion/Exclusion criteria. The Inclusion Criteria (IC) was applied for screening titles, keywords, and abstracts. The IC helped to identify papers that meet research scope and implicitly investigate any aspects of SaaS pricing. The Exclusion Criteria (EC) allowed us to exclude papers from those that have already been included based on the full-text analysis. We excluded papers where SaaS and its pricing were the context of the study rather than the topic and papers that did not provide any documented evidence to support research findings. As a result, the "white" literature for further analysis consisted of 76 items that meet the following requirements:

- **[IC]** Full texts of the paper are available;
- **[IC]** Published in peer-reviewed journals or conference proceedings;
- **[IC]** The study is not a duplicate of another study;
- **[IC/EC]** The study covers any aspect of SaaS pricing;
- **[EC]** Research goals and approach are clearly defined;
- **[EC]** The research provides evidence for the results obtained and pieces of evidence for the results are rigorously reported;

In the second stage, we collected "grey" literature following a similar protocol. Using the Google search engine instead of scientific databases, we ran the same search query and explored the first one hundred items provided. We manually explored each web-resource identified within the search procedure. The collected body "grey" literature consists of 151 items with content that satisfies the following requirements:

- Is publicly available (i.e., not behind a pay-wall/registration);
- Discusses certain SaaS pricing aspect;
- Is a standalone material written under a real name or published under the name of the organization;
- The material content is original.

3.3 Data Extraction

The multistage formal content analysis process was implemented to extract a taxonomy of pricing frameworks with further analyzing and reporting.

For both sources of literature, we extracted the following information: *Title*, *Author(s)*, *Date (Year)*, *Publication Type*, *SaaS Type*, *Market Type*, *Considered SaaS Pricing Aspects*, *Identified SaaS Pricing Factors*, *Key Findings*. Additionally, for the "white" literature items we extracted such fields as *Publication Venue*, *Research Approach*, *Research Aim*, *Research Questions*. The corresponding list of additional fields for "grey" literature includes *Company/Project*, *Analytical Approach*, and *Web Address*. Tables with the information on the collected body of "white" and "grey" literature items including extracted fields are available online[1].

After the data extraction was completed, we made excerpts of publications describing pricing frameworks, schemes, or approaches. These publications were further reviewed to extract information regarding the framework and answer the defined research question **RQ**.

[1] https://1drv.ms/x/s!AplKvkJggBgQuABgBypTTEs0STz4.

3.4 Comparison and Analysis

The most widely accepted definition of the term "framework" states that a framework is "*the system of concepts, assumptions, expectations, beliefs, and theories that supports and informs research*" [34,48]. Besides, a framework is a visual or written product explains, either graphically or in narrative form, main issues behind certain phenomena, key factors, concepts, or variable, and the presumed relationships among them. Within our study, we tried to keep our comparison analysis as full as possible and will include in the scope all pieces of research that intend to provide any systematization or decision-making support for any SaaS pricing aspects. However, the total number of publications that we were able to classify as providing SaaS pricing frameworks was not high.

Quite a lot of publications written by practitioners list possible pricing strategies, mechanisms, options with hints on their applicability in different contexts (i.e., [1,58]) or provide an extensive range of guidelines in narrative form and not being adequately systemized (i.e., [12,50]). While all these resources provide a wide range of recommendations that altogether cover all SaaS pricing aspects and consider all factors that could influence pricing decision, however, we did not treat them as frameworks and did not include them in our comparison. Similarly, many papers in academic literature provide frameworks where pricing is the context or an integral part, still not the objective (i.e., licensing frameworks [49,57]) or propose models designed to highlight specific SaaS pricing issues (i.e., [32,37,56]). We were not able to include them in our comparison. In total we identified and selected thirteen SaaS pricing frameworks, seven of which (F1–F7) were proposed in "white" literature and the rest (F8–F13)—in "grey".

Pricing frameworks are difficult to compare due to their comprehensiveness, variability in basic assumptions, and even confusing terminology. We compared frameworks within a defining list of five characteristics. The following characteristics were considered: Perspective, Scientific Origins, Framework Structure, Pricing Aspects Covered, and Pricing Factors Considered.

The *Perspective* of the framework specifies whether the framework employs a prescriptive or descriptive perspective. Prescriptive or action-oriented frameworks provide guidelines on how pricing should be done. In contrast, descriptive or analysis-oriented frameworks do not assign specific actions to be taken. Instead, they conceptualize certain pricing aspects and systematically classify various pricing-related options. The *Framework Structure* describes the structure and the logic of the framework. The *Scientific Origins* means the background on which the framework is based and approaches used to design. Some of the frameworks originated from purely philosophical principles or mathematical/statistical rules, while others are grounded into extensive literature overview, previous frameworks, or even based on personal experience.

Pricing Aspects Covered and *Pricing Factors Considered* respectively specify SaaS pricing areas addressed in these frameworks and factors influencing pricing-related decision-making processes. Both characteristics were grounded in the typologies provided in [51]. *Pricing Aspects Covered* were classified across three groups: Pricing strategy, Pricing tactics, and Pricing operations. *Pricing Factors*

Considered were classified across four categories named Market, Consumers, Company, and Product.

The comparison of identified pricing frameworks is presented in Tables 1 and 2. Frameworks classifications based on *Pricing Aspects Covered* and *Pricing Factors considered* are presented in Tables 3 and 4 respectively.

Table 1. Academic SaaS pricing frameworks comparison

#	Name	Ref.	Perspective	Framework structure	Scientific and practical origins
F1	Customer-centric value-based pricing framework	[7,8]	Analysis-oriented	Customer-centric two-staged framework: 1: Pre-purchase phase (Communication & Transparency) 2: Post-purchase phase (Dynamism & Service)	Literature overview (esp. [14,26,28,36]) Series of in-depth interview
F2	Customer-value based pricing framework	[22,23]	Action-oriented	Depicts the interconnection between three pillars: 1: Customer characteristics 2: Company objectives 3: Pricing objectives and strategy	Literature overview (esp. [19])
F3	Pricing process framework	[59]	Analysis-oriented	Three-stage pricing process structure: 1: Data collection 2: Strategy analysis 3: Strategy establishment	Literature overview (esp. [11,16])
F4	Competitive forces based framework	[38]	Analysis-oriented	Four-layer model: 1: Competitive forces 2: Factors impacting 3: Revenue models 4: Competitive advantage	Literature overview (esp. [41,42])
F5	Software products pricing typology	[30]	Analysis-oriented	Typology based on six pricing parameters: 1: Formation of price, 2: Structure of payment flow, 3: Assessment base, 4: Price discrimination, 5: Price bundling, 6: Dynamic pricing strategies	Literature overview (esp. [9]) Series of in-depth interviews
F6	Cloud solution pricing framework	[28]	Analysis-oriented	Typology based on seven pricing parameters: 1: Pricing scope 2: Structure of payment flow 3: Assessment base 4: Price discrimination 5: Price bundling 6: Dynamic pricing strategies	Literature overview (esp. [25,30]) Market survey
F7	Pricing strategy guideline framework	[2,55]	Action-oriented	Five layers of pricing within Corporate and Sales & Marketing Strategies: 1: Value Creation + Business Case, 2: Pricing Structure, 3: Price and Value Communication, 4: Price Policy + Sales Mechanism 5: Price Level	Literature overview (esp. [4,24,26,41,42])

Table 2. Practice SaaS pricing frameworks comparison

#	Name	Ref.	Perspective	Framework structure	Scientific and practical origins
F8	Pricing canvas framework	[20]	Action-oriented	Six-segment pricing canvas: 1: Customer Segments, 2: Value Proposition, 3: Cost Structure, 4: Competitors and Market, 5: Pricing Strategy, 6: Price Model	Not specified
F9	Pricing strategies decision framework	[17]	Action-oriented	Six-step framework: 1: What is the Customer's Value of the Product? 2: Is the Customer Aware of this Value? 3: Can the Customer Base be Segmented? 4: Is the Customer's Demand Variable or Uncertain? 5: Establish a Price Floor 6: What are the value metrics that are most important to the customer?	Case-studies (own experience) Pacific Crest SaaS Company Survey, Totango Reports on SaaS Metrics
F10	PWC pricing management framework	[47]	Analysis-oriented	Four pricing management segments: 1: Pricing strategy, 2: Price formulation, 3: Transaction management, 4: Performance management	Case-studies (own experience)
F11	Mastering pricing framework	[43]	Action-oriented	Pricing pillars: 1: Pricing at the Seed Stage 2: Pricing at the Expansion Stage 3: Pricing at the Growth Stage	Large-scale survey and market research
F12	ACCION pricing framework	[3]	Action-oriented	Four-step framework: 1: Define your upper bound 2: Define your lower bound 3: Identify any reasons to charge less than max value 4: Structure your pricing model as a compromise between upper bound and lower bound	Not specified
F13	Product Focus pricing framework	[44, 46]	Action-oriented	Pricing pillars: 1: Pricing constraints 2: Pricing cycle 3: Pricing Evolution	Case-studies (own experience)

Table 3. SaaS pricing aspects coverage

Category	Aspect	Framework												
		F1	F2	F3	F4	F5	F6	F7	F8	F9	F10	F11	F12	F13
Pricing strategy	Structure and models	×	×	×	×	×	×	×	×	×	×	×	×	×
	Evaluation and evolution	×									×	×		×
Pricing tactics	Customer analytics and segmentation	×	×	×					×	×	×	×	×	×
	Transparency and communication	×						×	×	×		×	×	×
	Offering design and promotion							×	×	×	×	×	×	×
Pricing operations	Ownership and decision-making									×				×
	Monitoring and control										×	×		×

4 Research Findings

Several publications authored by practitioners aim to deliver the desired SaaS pricing «Cookbook» or even more comprehensive body of knowledge (i.e., [12,43, 45]). Being systematically combined in a single book the myriad of blogposts by L. Murphy[2] and C. Mele[3] could serve the same purpose. These publications could provide valuable support for SaaS companies in designing and implementing their pricing. However, their crucial limitation is the lack of systematic approach and frameworks that structure the content, insights, and ideas provided. In this study, we were able to identify SaaS pricing frameworks that addressed various pricing aspects and employed different pricing methods. All thirteen frameworks for SaaS pricing vary significantly in their theoretical content, their purpose, and the way they conceptualize pricing. This variety reflects the diversity of research questions and purposes addressed by these different frameworks. One framework cannot serve all purposes of research and be applicable for all kinds of cases.

Seven out of thirteen frameworks (F1–F7) were introduced in academic literature, and six by practitioners (F8–F13). We classified six as *Analysis-oriented* (developed mostly by researchers) and seven—as *Action-oriented*. In comparison to practical frameworks, academic ones include better documentation of their logic, goals, and principles as well as traces of their groundings in previous studies. However, these academic frameworks do not do much to describe their actual implementations in practice, and they are not referred to extensively in grey literature [51]. On the other hand, frameworks provided by practitioners are not so well-documented. With some of them, we had to extract information from only very brief presentations. It is possible that many of these frameworks provided by practitioners are made for consulting business. They do not provide reliable evidence of their implementations in practice. Often their relevancy comes from the reputation of the companies (i.e., PWC [47] or Product Focus [45]) or the expert (i.e., K. Poyar [43]) behind them.

2 https://sixteenventures.com.

3 https://softwarepricing.com.

Table 4. SaaS pricing factors consideration

Group	Factor	Framework												
		F1	F2	F3	F4	F5	F6	F7	F8	F9	F10	F11	F12	F13
Market	Market size and maturity	×	×	×					×	×	×	×	×	×
	Market structure and competition	×	×	×	×			×	×	×	×	×	×	×
	Types of customers	×	×	×		×	×		×	×	×	×		×
	Barriers and constraints							×						
Consumers	Perceived value	×	×					×	×	×	×	×	×	×
	Willingness-to-pay		×	×				×	×	×		×		
	Adoption readiness				×									
	Switching costs							×		×		×		×
	Network effect							×		×		×		
Company	Business goals and opportunities		×		×	×	×	×	×	×		×		×
	Company size and maturity										×	×		×
	Resources availability		×		×							×		
	Cost structure	×	×	×	×			×	×	×	×	×	×	×
Product	Product category					×	×		×	×	×	×		
	Lifecycle stage										×	×		×
	Competitive advantage	×			×			×	×	×	×	×	×	×
	Experience required							×		×				
	Scalability potential											×		

Frameworks vary significantly regarding SaaS pricing aspects covered (Table 3). While all frameworks address pricing *Structure and Models* and many of them additionally incorporate issues related to *Customer Analytics and Segmentation*, few of them deal with pricing *Evaluation and Evolution* or other SaaS pricing tactics and operations. In general, practical frameworks address more pricing aspects and they are more informal and less structured than academic frameworks. Their decision-support is often just a structured set of recommendations or a list of items to consider (i.e., *Monitoring and Control* or *Offering design and Promotions* in [43, 45]).

Correspondingly, less systematic practical frameworks (i.e., F11, F13) consider more pricing-affecting factors (Table 4) than academic ones. Still, the support for decision-making often remains unclear. Moreover, it is challenging for SaaS companies to proceed with these factors in decision-making without collecting data to assess these factors (i.e., measuring network effects strength that this particular SaaS solution creates, or consumers' willingness-to-pay). Additionally, the pricing frameworks do not incorporate engineering aspects of SaaS factors related to the market, consumers, and company itself. While some frameworks consider *Scalability potential* and *Lifecycle stage*, none connects pricing decisions with *Quality attributes* and *Functional requirements and features sets*.

5 Discussion and Conclusion

Pricing is often a difficult and uncertain process. SaaS providers vary widely in how they organize, execute, and evaluate pricing decisions. The implementation of proper SaaS pricing is one of the most complex activities that any company can attempt. It impacts many processes inside the company, affects different business units, and requires sophisticated analysis. Many organizations, while understanding the complexity of pricing and its strategic role in product and company success, find themselves not capable of performing proper pricing. More importantly, the academic community has failed to equip the industry with trustworthy pricing approaches, frameworks, and guidelines.

To the best of our knowledge, this research is the first attempt to bridge academic research and practice employing a multi-vocal literature review to obtain a better understanding of SaaS pricing in general and what frameworks now exist to guide SaaS companies designing and implementing pricing strategies, policies, and practices. We provided a comparison of thirteen frameworks found in academic and practitioner literature. Some of these have been developed for specific aspects, whereas others have a broader purpose. This comparison goes beyond identifying the benefits and limitations of provided frameworks. As stated below, although the amount of literature on SaaS pricing is growing, the comprehensive body of knowledge on SaaS pricing is missing. Following the approaches of existing mature bodies of knowledge in other disciplines, an SaaS pricing body of knowledge should promote a consistent view of SaaS pricing and clarify its place with respect to other business functions by defining key terms and concepts, knowledge areas, and SaaS pricing-related tasks and techniques. Grounded in this body of knowledge, a cookbook-style guideline and a compendium of recommendations could be introduced. They will equip product managers with verified step-by-step pricing frameworks and easy-to-use approaches, addressing different pricing aspects from different perspectives, supplemented with structured decision-making systems.

Bringing together theoretical analysis and practical experience is an essential step toward developing a SaaS pricing "Cookbook". However, much more research is needed to achieve the goal of having the "Cookbook" mentioned above. Academic research on SaaS pricing seems to somewhat lag behind in terms of practical expertise, observations, and opinions. While existing academic literature on SaaS consists of relatively small and fragmented studies that belong to different research domains, practitioners are active in publishing and sharing

SaaS pricing advice, observations, and even frameworks. Moreover, many non-academic studies performed without scientific rigor provide more value for the industry. Pricing contains many opportunities for research. Many of the studies in this review identify relevant research topics. Furthermore, none of the significant areas of pricing are "closed". There are great opportunities to extend the current state-of-the-art in pricing. We intend to provide some guidelines in follow-up publications concerning this study.

Understanding how prices are set, communicated, and updated is a fundamental pre-condition for prescribing pricing approaches. The vast majority of «grey» literature publications do not provide comprehensive pricing frameworks nor report extensive reviews; instead, they offer bits of advice, guidelines, and suggestions usually outside of the personal experience or non-systematic observations. The value of each recommendation can be modest; some of them can even look trivial or unconvincing. Furthermore, these sources do not equip SaaS companies with usable decision-making instruments instead of diverse ranges of recommendations. However, they can bring about an understanding of real-world pricing practices, reveal the pricing challenges that companies and product managers face, and, if adequately synthesized, be useful in designing SaaS pricing ready-to-use solutions and step-by-step guidelines.

Academic papers, especially those in the fields of economics and management science, quite often aim at demonstrating the market consequences of implementing certain SaaS pricing mechanisms at a model level. In explicit form, these models can hardly be applied by real-world companies; still, insights grounded in the analysis of these models could be of value. In order to attain this value, these academic literature outcomes should be classified and matched with recommendations derived from «grey» literature. Doing so will not only allow the verification of practical recommendations (often of an intuitive nature) but will also allow the design of powerful decision-support instruments.

While within this paper, we provide a fundamental comparison of SaaS pricing frameworks, many issues can only be explored through practical use and further investigation. This includes, but is not limited to: frameworks' effectiveness, easy-to-use, and adaptability. As far as we are aware, there have been no attempts to assess pricing frameworks from these perspectives or to validate the total effects of using different SaaS pricing frameworks.

Acknowledgment. The paper was prepared within the framework of the HSE University Basic Research Program and funded by the Russian Academic Excellence Project '5–100'. The research was also supported by Liikesivistysrahasto (The Foundation for Economic Education, Finland) under research grant number: 14-7518.

References

1. Aaron, J.: 12 Different "SaaSy" Pricing Strategies (2016). https://bit.ly/2HKud4o
2. Abdat, N., Spruit, M., Bos, M.: Software as a service and the pricing strategy for vendors. In: Digital Product Management, Technology and Practice: Interdisciplinary Perspectives. IGI Global (2011)

3. Accion: Pricing your SaaS product (2015). https://bit.ly/2YzYEm5
4. Amit, R., Zott, C.: Value creation in e-business. Strat. Manag. J. **22**(6–7), 493–520 (2001)
5. Athey, S., Luca, M.: Economists (and economics) in tech companies. J. Econ. Perspect. **33**(1), 209–230 (2019)
6. Balasubramanian, S., Bhattacharya, S., Viswanathan, K.: Pricing information goods: a strategic analysis of the selling and pay-per-use mechanisms. Mark. Sci. **34**(2), 218–234 (2015)
7. Baur, A.W., Bühler, J., Bick, M.: How pricing of business intelligence and analytics SaaS applications can catch up with their technology. J. Syst. Inf. Technol. **17**(3), 229–246 (2015)
8. Baur, A.W., Genova, A.C., Bühler, J., Bick, M.: Customer is king? A framework to shift from cost- to value-based pricing in software as a service: the case of business intelligence software. In: Conference on e-Business, e-Services and e-Society (I3E) Proceedings, pp. 1–13 (2014)
9. Bontis, N., Chung, H.: The evolution of software pricing: from box licenses to application service provider models. Internet Res. **10**(3), 246–255 (2000)
10. Bourque, P., Fairley, R.E.: SWEBOK Guide V3.0 Guide to Software Engineering Body of Knowledge (2014). www.swebok.org
11. Braeutigam, R.R.: An analysis of fully distributed cost pricing in regulated industries. Bell J. Econ. **11**, 182–196 (1980)
12. Campbell, P.: The Anatomy of SaaS Pricing Strategy. Price Intelligently (2016)
13. Campbell, P.: The Price is Right: Essential Tips for Nailing Your Pricing Strategy (2016). https://bit.ly/2LZ2CyG
14. Court, D., Elzinga, D., Mulder, S., Vetvik, O.J.: The consumer decision journey. McKinsey Q. **3**(3), 96–107 (2009)
15. Cusumano, M.: The changing labyrinth of software pricing. Commun. ACM **50**(7), 19–22 (2007)
16. Daripa, A., Kapur, S.: Pricing on the internet. Oxf. Rev. Econ. Policy **17**(2), 202–216 (2001)
17. Deeter, B., Jung, R.: Software as a Service Pricing Strategies (2013)
18. Dutt, A., Jain, H., Kumar, S.: Providing Software as a Service: a design decision(s) model. Inf. Syst. e-Bus. Manag. **16**(2), 327–356 (2018)
19. Forbis, J.L., Mehta, N.T., et al.: Value-based strategies for industrial products. Bus. Horiz. **24**(3), 32–42 (1981)
20. Garlet, F., Wirth, C.: Pricing Strategy (2018)
21. Garousi, V., Felderer, M., Mäntylä, M.V.: Guidelines for including grey literature and conducting multivocal literature reviews in software engineering. Inf. Softw. Technol. **106**, 101–121 (2018)
22. Harmon, R., Demirkan, H., Hefley, B., Auseklis, N.: Pricing strategies for information technology services: a value-based approach. In: Hawaii International Conference on System Sciences (HICSS) Proceedings, pp. 1–10 (2009)
23. Harmon, R., Raffo, D., Faulk, S.: Value-based pricing for new software products: strategy insights for developers. In: Portland International Conference on Management of Engineering and Technology (PICMET) Proceedings, pp. 1–24 (2004)
24. Hogan, B.J., Nagle, T.: What is strategic pricing? SPG Insights by Strategic Pricing Group, pp. 1–7 (2005)
25. Iveroth, E., Westelius, A., Petri, C.J., Olve, N.G., Cöster, M., Nilsson, F.: How to differentiate by price: proposal for a five-dimensional model. Eur. Manag. J. **31**(2), 109–123 (2013)

26. Kittlaus, H.B., Clough, P.: Software Product Management and Pricing: Key Success Factors for Software Organizations. Springer, Heidelberg (2008). https://doi.org/10.1007/978-3-540-76987-3
27. Kittlaus, H.B., Fricker, S.A.: Software Product Management: The ISPMA-Compliant Study Guide and Handbook. Springer, Heidelberg (2017). https://doi.org/10.1007/978-3-642-55140-6
28. Laatikainen, G., Ojala, A., Mazhelis, O.: Cloud services pricing models. In: International Conference on Software Business (ICSOB) Proceedings, pp. 117–129 (2013)
29. Lee, I.: Pricing schemes and profit-maximizing pricing for cloud services. J. Revenue Pricing Manag. **18**, 112–122 (2019)
30. Lehmann, S., Buxmann, P.: Pricing strategies of software vendors. Bus. Inf. Syst. Eng. **1**(6), 452–462 (2009)
31. Lei, S., Chen, F., Li, M.: Pricing cloud service considering heterogeneous customers. In: International Asia Conference on Industrial Engineering and Management Innovation (IEMI) Proceedings, pp. 1063–1073 (2016)
32. Ma, D., Seidmann, A.: Analyzing software as a service with per-transaction charges. Inf. Syst. Res. **26**(2), 360–378 (2015)
33. Marn, M.V., Rosiello, R.L.: Managing price, gaining profit. Harv. Bus. Rev. **70**(5), 84–94 (1992)
34. Maxwell, J.A.: Qualitative Research Design: An Interactive Approach. Applied Social Research Methods, vol. 41, 3rd edn. Sage Publications, London (2012)
35. Mell, P.M., Grance, T.: The NIST Definition of cloud computing. Technical report, National Institute of Standards and Technology Special Publication 800–145 (2011)
36. Mohr, J.J., Sengupta, S., Slater, S.F.: Marketing of High-Technology Products and Innovations. Pearson Prentice Hall, Upper Saddle River (2010)
37. Nan, G., Li, X., Zhang, Z., Li, M.: Optimal pricing for new product entry under free strategy. Inf. Technol. Manag. **19**(1), 1–19 (2018)
38. Ojala, A.: Adjusting software revenue and pricing strategies in the era of cloud computing. J. Syst. Softw. **122**, 40–51 (2016)
39. Özer, Ö., Phillips, R.: Introduction. In: Özer, Ö., Phillips, R. (eds.) The Oxford Handbook of Pricing Management, pp. 1–9 (2012)
40. Pang, M.S., Etzion, H.: Research Note: analyzing pricing strategies for online services with network effects. Inf. Syst. Res. **23**(4), 1364–1377 (2012)
41. Porter, M.E.: Competitive advantage: Creating and sustaining competitive advantage (1985)
42. Porter, M.E.: The five competitive forces that shape strategy. Harv. Bus. Rev. **86**(1), 25–40 (2008)
43. Poyar, K.: Mastering SaaS Pricing: How to Price Your Product from the Seed Stage through IPO (2017). https://bit.ly/2YGtwxc
44. Product Focus: How to price: strategies for setting prices effectively. Prod. Manag. J. **5**, 4–9 (2014)
45. Product Focus: Pricing. Setting the optimum price. Tips, tactics and theory (2014). https://bit.ly/31pRVZJ
46. Product Focus: The psychology of pricing: making prices tick. Prod. Manag. J. **5**, 10–14 (2014)
47. PWC: The future of software pricing excellence: SaaS pricing (2013). https://pwc.to/2DrYGzz
48. Robson, C., McCartan, K.: Real World Research. Wiley, Hoboken (2016)
49. Rohitratana, J., Altmann, J.: Impact of pricing schemes on a market for Software-as-a-Service and perpetual software. Future Gener. Comput. Syst. **28**(8), 1328–1339 (2012)

50. Saha, M.: The Overlooked Opportunity: Successfully Designing Pricing for Upsells and Expansion. https://bit.ly/2gdABmb
51. Saltan, A.: Do we know how to price SaaS: a multi-vocal literature review. In: ACM SIGSOFT International Workshop on Software-Intensive Business: Start-ups, Platforms and Ecosystems (IWSiB) Proceedings, pp. 7–12 (2019)
52. Saltan, A., Jansen, S., Smolander, K.: Decision-making in software product management: identifying research directions from practice. In: Software-intensive Business Workshop on Start-ups, Platforms and Ecosystems (SiBW) Proceedings, pp. 164–176 (2018)
53. Shapiro, C., Varian, H.R.: Information Rules: A Strategic Guide to the Network Economy. Harvard Business School Press, Boston (1999)
54. Soni, A., Hasan, M.: Pricing schemes in cloud computing: a review. Int. J. Adv. Comput. Res. **7**(29), 60–70 (2017)
55. Spruit, M., Abdat, N.: The pricing strategy guideline framework for SaaS vendors. Int. J. Strat. Inf. Technol. Appl. **3**(1), 38–53 (2012)
56. Sundararajan, A., Xin, M.: Nonlinear Pricing of Software with Local Demand Inelasticity (2018)
57. Wu, S., Wortmann, H., Tan, C.W.: A pricing framework for software-as-a-service. In: International Conference on the Innovative Computing Technology (INTECH) Proceedings, pp. 152–157 (2014)
58. Zavadskaya, V.: SaaS Pricing Models: How the Right Pricing Will Help You Earn a Fortune (2017). https://bit.ly/2pGpuHr
59. Zheng, Y.: Practical application of FDC in software service pricing. In: IEEE International Conference on e-Business Engineering (ICEBE) Proceedings, pp. 1–6 (2006)

Managing Commercial Conflicts of Interest in Open Source Foundations

Florian Weikert, Dirk Riehle, and Ann Barcomb(✉)

Friedrich-Alexander-Universität Erlangen-Nürnberg,
Martensstr. 3, 91058 Erlangen, Germany
florian@weikert.it, dirk@riehle.org, ann@barcomb.org
https://oss.cs.fau.de, https://dirkriehle.com/

Abstract. When companies opt to open source their software, they may choose to offer the project to an open source foundation. Donating the software to an open source foundation offers a number of advantages, such as access to the foundation's existing tools and project management. However, in donating the software, the company relinquishes control of the software and grants other foundation members—including competitors—the same rights to the software. Using a multiple-case study research approach, this paper examines how foundations manage conflicts of interest in the open sourcing donation scenario. We find that foundations primarily use a set of well-defined mechanisms to prevent such conflicts from arising, and that the use of these mechanisms can depend on the foundation type.

Keywords: Open source foundations · Sponsored open source · Commercial open source · Open source software

1 Introduction

Open source software (OSS) is ubiquitous in today's world. OSS is widely used within companies, not only for tooling and infrastructure, but also as a critical component of the supply chain [1,17,38]. Companies are not only using OSS, but are also contributing to OSS projects [2,3] and *open sourcing,* or releasing as OSS, millions of lines of source code [31]. Although many *single vendor open source* companies opt to retain intellectual property rights to their software, some companies donate their software to non-profit foundations [12,25,33,34, 36]. Becoming a *donor* can help companies create open standards, lower their development costs, increase sales of complementary products or services, and take advantage of faster innovation [35,39], but it comes at a price.

By transferring their intellectual property rights to a non-profit foundation, these companies give up the control over their software [43] and have only the same privileges as other members of the foundation. Foundation members may even compete with each other, potentially introducing conflicts and tensions because of differing interests [15,20].

S. Hyrynsalmi et al. (Eds.): ICSOB 2019, LNBIP 370, pp. 130–144, 2019.
https://doi.org/10.1007/978-3-030-33742-1_11

In the context of donated projects, our research question is:

- **RQ**: How do foundations handle the conflicting interests of their members, when one member is a donor?

We investigate these questions through an exploratory multiple-case case study of four OSS projects which were created by companies, and subsequently donated to non-profit foundations.

The contributions of this paper are:

- A theory of conflict prevention in open source foundations.
- A discussion of the different types of foundations and the impact of foundation type on the use of conflict prevention mechanisms.

The rest of this paper is structured as follows: related work is reviewed in Sect. 2. Section 3 outlines the research process and Sect. 4 describes the results of our research. Limitations and suggestions for future work are discussed in Sect. 5. Finally, Sect. 6 concludes this paper.

2 Related Work

We identified three areas of research that were relevant to our topic: open source foundations, the evolution of company-created projects into open source, and conflicts in open source projects.

2.1 Open Source Foundations

Open source foundations are not all the same. For example, comparisons of the Apache Software Foundation (ASF) and the Eclipse Foundation have shown significant differences. Riehle [37] describes differences in legal status, mission, philosophy and governance structures. Furthermore, the power within the Eclipse Foundation is concentrated on the executive director, while the ASF gives most of its power to the board of directors [32]. Our work differs from previous work on conflict in open source foundations by explicitly considering the type of foundation involved.

The benefits of foundations are that they can handle donations [53]; provide communities with tools to handle corporate interests [23,27,28]; and manage and protect projects, intellectual property rights and communities [35]. Foundations enable shared development of software, thus reducing costs, helping to create a common standard, and increasing both reputation and visibility of members [35].

2.2 Project Evolution: From Company-Founded to Community-Managed

West and O'Mahony classify projects based on whether they are currently managed by a community (*autonomous*) or by a sponsoring company (*sponsored*) [52]. As projects may evolve from sponsored to autonomous, they also introduce the categories *synthetic* (sponsor-created, i.e. started as a sponsored project) and *organic* (community-created, i.e. started as an autonomous project) to describe the original state of the project [30]. In this work, we consider the origin of the project as a possible source of conflict within foundations, and specifically examine projects which are synthetic and autonomous according to this framework.

If a project receives its initial resources and code from a company, it can also be described as a *spinout* [51]. Spinouts build on an established code base and are usually supported by their creators. However, this also means that new contributors face a steep learning curve because they must understand the existing code before they can contribute. As a result, the original sponsor may remain the largest contributor after spinning out the project. For example, even several years after it was donated, the majority of the source code in OpenStack was created by its donor, Rackspace [19].

2.3 Conflicts in Open Source Projects

One source of conflicts arises from the different interests of corporate and individual participants. For example, corporate sponsors have tried to steer the development via financial rewards or wanted to close parts of the code, thus violating the philosophy of open source software [13,42]. Other companies exploit OSS by taking more than they contribute [2]. As a result, tensions can be seen as a consequence of corporate behavior: that is, whether companies respect and give back to the community [7].

Another source of conflicts is within companies. Individuals who participate in OSS as employees of a company do not always promote the technical or business interests of their employers [3,29,40,47].

Finally, there can be conflicts between companies which are members of the same foundation. Sometimes, companies can collaborate on OSS and compete in the same market, without obvious conflicts [45]. This 'community of competitors' coordinates OSS development for mutual benefit by focusing on non-differentiating components [15]. However, inter-company rivalry can manifest in several ways. When companies make contributions without a complementary donation of intellectual property such as patents, it hinders innovation and limits the commercial benefit of OSS [50]. When multiple companies are contributing to a project, a company has to invest more resources to influence the project [16,41]. Companies can also be concerned about losing key developers to competitors [40]. Our emphasis is on the conflicts that can arise between foundation members, specifically in the case where one member is the project donor.

Van Wendel de Joode [46] argues that conflict management is mandatory for the success of software projects and identifies four mechanisms for managing conflict: third party intervention through mediators or arbitrators, code modularity to increase independence, parallel development lines to allow multiple solutions and the option to fork the project. Other techniques which have been proposed to resolve conflict are the promotion of shared beliefs and values, and discussions on persistent and public channels such as mailing lists [10,24].

3 Research Process

Our research is an exploratory investigation of conflict in open source foundations, and we wanted to consider different foundations in order to develop a broader understanding of how conflict between donors and other foundation members is handled. We chose an exploratory multiple-case case study research approach combined with grounded-theory-based analysis [6,54].

3.1 Case Study Design

A multiple-case case study allows researchers to employ replication logic to generalize case findings [54]. Our study consists of non-profit foundations as the primary unit of analysis. Our embedded, or sub-units of analysis, were made up of the different legal entities involved: the foundation itself, as well as individual companies.

As shown in Tables 1 and 2, we selected four cases based on their unique characteristics (age of the foundation, acceptance of corporate members, public versus member benefit, and whether they existed prior to the donation), thus using theoretical sampling [6] of polar types. Because of our grounded theory approach, we did not start with a preexisting theory [11]. Following Yin [54], we used a case study protocol and a case study database.

Table 1. Overview of cases

Case	Project	Donor	Creation date	Donation date
ACS	Apache CloudStack	Citrix Systems, Inc.	2008	2012[a]
CF	Cloud Foundry	Pivotal Software, Inc.	2011	2014
EC	Eclipse	IBM Corporation	2001	2004
OSt	OpenStack	Rackspace US, Inc.[b]	2010	2012

[a] CloudStack entered the Apache Incubator in 2012 and graduated to a top-level project in 2013.
[b] Parts of the project were donated by NASA.

Table 2. Overview of foundations

Case	Foundation	Creation date	Benefit[c]	Corporate members
ACS	Apache Software Foundation	1999	Public	No
CF	Cloud Foundry Foundation	2014	Member	Yes
EC	Eclipse Foundation	2004	Member	Yes
OSt	OpenStack Foundation	2012	Member	Yes

[c] Foundations for public benefit were established as "charitable organizations" based on Section 501(c)(3) of the United States Internal Revenue Code, while foundations for member benefit were incorporated as 501(c)(6) organizations ("trade associations").

3.2 Data Sources

We utilized a broad array of data sources, including documents (e.g. foundation bylaws and rules, protocols of board meetings, mailing list discussions, blog posts and press releases), podcasts and conference videos. We also conducted interviews with selected foundation representatives. More specifically, we contacted potential interview partners who had been active in the project for several years and who were (former) employees of the respective donor. With the exception of Cloud Foundry, we had one semi-structured interview per foundation. The interviews lasted between 45 and 90 min and were conducted via Skype, recorded and then transcribed. We refined our questions after each interview [6]. The case study protocol, interview protocols, and the case study database are published in an appendix [48].

As displayed in Table 3, our research incorporated more than 280 data sources, which we used for triangulating the insights and the resulting theory.

Table 3. Data sources by case and step of analysis

	Preliminary	Grounded theory			
Case	Documents	Interviews	Documents	Podcasts	Videos
ACS	24	1	20	4	3
CF	69	-	17	1	-
EC	15	1	10	-	3
OSt	81	1	26	5	4

3.3 Data Analysis

As is typical for grounded theory research, data collection and analysis happened simultaneously [5]. The whole process was iterative because we re-visited previously collected data and findings after new insights had emerged.

First, we started with a preliminary analysis step by creating a chronology of the most important events in the histories of the foundations and by identifying governance structures as well as the most important entities within the foundation. Moreover, we created an overview of participating companies and tracked the affiliations of contributors and board members.

Next, we used a software for qualitative data analysis (MAXQDA) to analyze the documents, all interview transcripts and the partial transcripts of the videos and podcasts while following the grounded theory approach of Corbin and Strauss [6].

We labeled text fragments with codes that emerged from the data (open coding). For example, when interview partners cited structures and rules that were borrowed from existing foundations, we assigned the code *learning from existing foundations*. Codes and text fragments were constantly compared to each other. Furthermore, we revised the codings after each interview in order to incorporate new insights.

The next step entailed combining codes into categories based on shared concepts (axial coding). For instance, the category *limited foundation power* included the codes *no authority over volunteers* and *prioritizing project health over vendor dominance*.

Finally, we started selective coding in order to reduce our model to a core category. Although *conflict resolution* appeared to be a suitable candidate, we discovered that the category *conflict prevention* was central to our findings. We focused on this category by further developing its subcategories such as *governance*, *strategies*, *culture*, *screening processes* as well as *values* and *common motivation*. Moreover, we identified the causal relation of *bad behavior* and the influencing factor *foundation type*.

We wrote analytic memos throughout analysis [5] and compared the emerging theory to existing literature. This paper uses a theory-building logic [54] where individual case reports are omitted in favor of a comprehensive theory.

4 Results

Our research question concerned the mechanisms foundations use to handle conflicting interests between members, when one member is a donor. Our analysis identified the main category of *conflict prevention*, as described in Sect. 4.2. We also observed that the concrete strategies were influenced by the type of the foundation as described in Sect. 4.3.

4.1 Sources of Conflict

Since the foundations attracted a diverse audience of individuals and sometimes companies, the existence of different interests and goals was hardly surprising. However, this led to conflicts when members tried to enforce their own interests at the expense of other foundation members (*bad behavior*). For example, some wanted to take over specific projects or committees. This was especially likely when corporate members were competing with each other, thus having conflicting interests. Competition was especially fierce when these members targeted the same users, the market potential was huge or the technology was disruptive. The interview partners were also aware that this could ultimately threaten the success of the foundation.

However, foundations and their members not only expected but even encouraged competing companies to join. For example, the donors welcomed some of their competitors if those would help them fight a single dominant competitor (see Table 4).

Table 4. Dominant competitors as common motivation

Case	Quote
ACS	"CloudStack is Citrix's effort to take on VMware and enlist the rest of the vendor community in doing so."
EC	"Having others joining was exactly what should have happened, right? I mean you had in a way 'One enemy' and that one enemy was Microsoft. Everybody else - whether they were a competitor or not for you - was not really it. It was not really an issue. You wanted to get unified against Microsoft."
OSt	"Rackspace knew that in order to compete with Amazon they needed to have software that was like Amazon's. And the only way to get software like Amazon's was to band together every competitor of Amazon and develop that software."

4.2 Conflict Prevention

Figure 1 depicts our theory of conflict prevention in open source foundations. The five major subcategories from the code system were (1) *screening processes*, (2) *governance rules*, (3) *prevention strategies*, (4) *common interests* and (5) *culture and values*. We now describe these major categories and their relationships.

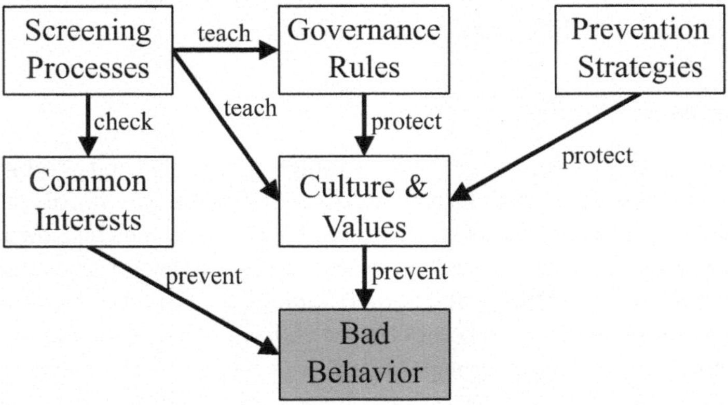

Fig. 1. Mechanisms for conflict prevention and their relations.

Screening Processes. Potential new members and projects had to pass specific screening processes before being accepted in a foundation (see Table 5). These processes had two goals.

First, they tried to identify *common interests* and to assess the motivation of potential members. Moreover, the technical, cultural and strategic fit of new projects was determined. If a new project was proposed for donation, the foundation also wanted to make sure that the donor was interested in its long-term support while tolerating other participants.

Second, foundations—in particular the ASF—used an incubation process to teach both their *governance rules* and *culture and values* to new projects.

Additionally, these processes were described as *two way vetting processes* (ACS) since they did not only allowed the foundation to assess new members, but also allowed the potential members to see whether the foundation suited their needs.

Table 5. Different types of screening processes

Subject	Example
Committers	Committed enough for the task and matched the human attitudes required to work well with others (ACS)
Companies	They need to acknowledge that they have in mind the fact that the success of the foundation is the success of their own business (OSt)
Projects	The community has learned and demonstrated that it understands the principles and processes laid by the Apache Software Foundation and that it can now operate more autonomously. (ACS)

Governance Structures and Rules. As shown in Table 6, foundations had established formal governance structures and rules that were codified in their bylaws. Corporate members required such clearly-defined structures.

For example, *transparent affiliations* meant that individual contributors had to disclose their affiliations when joining the foundation. Moreover, any changes in status had to be communicated immediately. *Distributed decision-making* through clearly defined voting processes enabled a large base of members to voice their opinions. If the foundation was organized as a *meritocracy*, privileges such as the right to vote or write-access to source code repositories had to be earned through contributions. Consequently, even employees of smaller companies could reach high ranks in the foundation because of their individual contributions. Although some foundations accepted corporate members, they made sure that the amount of control through sponsorship was limited (*decoupling funding from control*). The foundations in this paper also established a *separation of powers* by transferring the technical authority to specific committees. As a result, the board of directors could only make legal and management decisions. In order to address the resource inequality of participating companies and individuals, some foundations offered different *tiers of membership*, depending on the size and financial possibilities of their members. As a result, these tiers could send their own representatives to the board. However, some foundations had established *representation limits* which limited the number of employees a single company could have on the board. Finally, the foundations and their committees saw themselves as *independent entities*. They made sure that their success did not depend on just a few companies by recruiting independent staff and by monitoring the behavior of corporate members.

Table 6. Examples of governance structures and rules

Rule	Example
Transparent Affiliations	I will promptly update any change in my Affiliate status as defined in the Bylaws. (OSt)
Distributed Decision-Making	The decisions are made by the vote, as required in our by-laws. (ACS)
Meritocracy	It is [a] meritocracy and he did a good job that is why he is in the position he is. (ACS)
Decoupling Funding From Control	You cannot just, you know, shower the foundation in money and then you get all of the power. It is not going to happen. (EC)
Separation of Powers	There is also very strong separation between the technical decisions and the other things like the management in general, the general management of the foundation. (OSt)
Tiered Membership	Tiered structure is exactly to give representation to big companies and to smaller companies and to individuals who are part of a larger free software and open source community who want to care about this project. (OSt)
Representation Limits	No more than two directors shall be Affiliated (the 'Director Diversity Requirement'). (OSt)
Independent Entities	The Executive Director may not be an employee, officer, director or consultant of any Member of the Eclipse Foundation. (EC)

Explicit Strategies. In addition to creating governance structures, the foundations also employed a set of explicit prevention strategies to protect their *culture and values* (Table 7).

Because of transparent processes, foundations could *monitor the behavior* of their members and act accordingly. They also tried to *allow community participation* by including the larger community in as many decision-making processes as possible. For example, proposed governance changes were made subject to community review. This required the foundations to *enforce public communication* by announcing and discussing decisions on public mailing lists. Finally, they could use *project-specific strategies* if a project was dominated by a single corporate member. This could mean sending in independent contributors, terminating the project or creating a competing project.

Common Interests. Even if members were competing with each other, they shared some common interests. For example, their contributors were described as *engineers by heart* (EC) who valued merit and the technical value of solutions more than corporate agendas and employment relations.

Common interests were also observed on the business side. Companies participated for pragmatic business reasons as they had commercial dependencies on the foundations' projects. Some of them saw foundations as a possibility to create a common platform against a dominant competitor (see Table 4).

Consequently, these companies were interested in growing their former projects by attracting new allies who had the same enemy. However, this could only work if they behaved in a collaborative way. Moreover, *bad behavior* was limited by the costs it would incur: *the money you spend and the outcome you get out of this is the big equalizer in this game.* (EC)

Culture and Values. Interview partners cited the existence of a good culture and shared values as essential for project success. While they helped to prevent *bad behavior*, the absence of such values could even destroy a project.

Openness describes not only open access to the source code, but also to decision processes, committees and documents. Interview partners pointed out that too much openness slowed down decision processes and could scare away potential commercial members. *Transparency* was as important as openness. Consequently, foundations tried to restrict the use of non-public communication like private mailing lists. If a foundation allowed corporate members, *equality* of opportunity was important to attract smaller companies and individual members: *The main role of the foundation is to make sure there is a level playing field where everybody feels safe* (OSt). The foundations also valued *merit* by acknowledging the amount of work contributors spent on the projects. *Neutrality* was named *the single most important thing of all* (EC). Consequently, foundations should not prefer single members. Instead, a truly vendor-neutral foundation would create a safe place where even competitors could collaborate. Similar to equality, a lack of neutrality would scare away contributors. Having competing members inside a foundation was seen as a sign of its *independence*. Moreover, foundations did not want to depend on specific members. Finally, they valued *diversity* of their members to benefit from different experiences and backgrounds.

4.3 Different Types of Foundations

We noticed that the ASF differed from the other foundations in several characteristics. For example, it tried to minimize corporate influence by allowing only individual members and by discouraging the display of member affiliations (*non-affiliation*). Our interview partners explicitly described the ASF as a *user-led* foundation, while the others were *vendor-led*. As a result, the ASF could not employ rules such as *transparent affiliations* and *representation limits*.

Instead, it emphasized culture and values more than the other foundations did. For example, its cultural principles—the Apache Way—and meritocracy were explicitly mentioned in its bylaws. This could be explained with the origin of the ASF: unlike vendor-led foundations, it was founded by a group of individuals

Table 7. Examples of prevention strategies

Strategy	Example
Monitor Behavior	The mission of the foundation is to make sure that all the companies and all the groups that are involved into development of the project actually behave. (OSt)
Allow Community Participation	Bylaws and legal documents for community review. (OSt)
Enforce Public Communication	The Apache mantra is, if it doesn't happen on the list it didn't happen kind of thing. (ACS)
Project-Specific Strategies	So at this very moment we sent in a few committers to also have the other implementation in that project. (EC)

(Apache Group), a "'grass roots' community of user-developers" [51, p. 1]. While companies are motivated by formal rules and structures [20,23,49], communities reflect the cultural beliefs and values [9] of traditional open source.

5 Limitations and Future Work

5.1 Limitations of the Study

Guba [21] proposed that the quality of qualitative work should be evaluated by its *credibility*, *transferability*, *dependability*, and *confirmability*, in place of measures which are appropriate for quantitative studies. For instance, a qualitative case study cannot claim statistical generalizability to a population, but this does not mean that it cannot offer theoretical generalizability, for instance through careful selection of polar cases [4,6,54].

Credibility can be established through triangulation. Case studies are a form of research which naturally incorporate data triangulation. We examined four cases, with three of them being backed by our interviews. However, we compensated for this fact by analyzing more than 200 other documents. While we cannot claim to have reached theoretical saturation, several researchers have noted that four cases might be reasonable due to pragmatic reasons [8].

Transferability concerns claims of theoretical generalizability [4], as described above. Our four cases were selected to vary by age of the foundation, acceptance of corporate members, public versus member benefit, and whether the foundation existed before the software donation. The differences between the ASF and the other foundations studied suggests that the dimension of membership was especially relevant.

Confirmability describes the extent to which researcher bias is mitigated. Any grounded theory analysis might be subject to coding errors or misinterpretations, and could have been influenced by previous knowledge of the researchers [11]. However, one way of reducing bias is through venting, which entails sharing the results with professional colleagues to ensure that the findings are consistent with their experiences [18]. Moreover, our consideration of extant literature enhanced the objectivity of our study [8].

Dependability is increased through maintaining a record of the research process. We maintained both a case study protocol and a case study database to improve reliability [54]. Furthermore, we applied constant comparison and memoing during grounded theory analysis to increase theoretical sensitivity [22].

5.2 Future Work

In our research, we identified two particularly interesting topics which could benefit from further study.

Role of Trust. Since individual members were volunteers, the foundations did not have formal authority over them, thus having to trust them and their motivations. Trust was also cited by one foundation member as important for conflict resolution. However, existing literature makes opposing claims. For example, Gallivan [14] regards control as far more important while other researchers stress the importance of trust in open source projects [26,44].

Effectiveness of Non-Affiliation. It is not clear whether non-affiliation solves the problems of commercial interests instead of merely hiding them, as the underlying economic motivations still existed. Additionally—unlike foundations—companies do have formal authority over their contributors. However, there have been multiple reported cases where employees prioritized community needs over those of their employers [29,47], so this question needs to be studied with a nuanced understanding of affiliation.

6 Conclusions

In this paper, we examined four non-profit open source foundations that managed projects originally created by companies. More specifically, we investigated how these foundations handled potential conflicts of interests of their corporate members.

By conducting a multiple-case study combined with grounded theory analysis, we established a theory of conflict prevention. We identified a combination of screening processes, governance rules, prevention strategies, culture, values and common interests to discourage bad behavior of foundation members. This is of practical value to new foundations, as well as to companies which are considering donating to a foundation. For researchers, our work contributes to the understanding of cooperation between competitors in open source foundations by explaining how conflict is prevented.

Finally, we highlighted potential future work when we discussed the role of trust and non-affiliation. The limitations of our process and a theory-testing approach might also warrant future research on this topic.

Acknowledgments. We would like to thank our interview partners for sharing their time and expertise with us: Mark Hinkle, Stefano Maffulli and the anonymous member of the Eclipse Foundation.

References

1. Ayala, C.P., Cruzes, D.S., Hauge, O., Conradi, R.: Five facts on the adoption of open source software. Softw. IEEE **28**(2), 95–99 (2011)
2. Bonaccorsi, A., Rossi, C.: Contributing to the common pool resources in open source software. a comparison between individuals and firms. Technical reports, Working Paper, Sant'Anna School of Advanced Studies Institute for Informatics and Telematics (August 2003)
3. Butler, S., et al.: On company contributions to community open source software projects. IEEE Transactions on Software Engineering (2019)
4. Cavaye, A.L.: Case study research: a multi-faceted research approach for IS. Inf. Syst. J. **6**(3), 227–242 (1996)
5. Charmaz, K.: Grounded theory as an emergent method. In: Leavy, P., Nagy Hasse-Biber, S. (eds.) Handbook of Emergent Methods, chap. 7, pp. 81–110. Gilford Press, New York (2008)
6. Corbin, J.M., Strauss, A.L.: Grounded theory research: procedures, canons, and evaluative criteria. Qual. Sociol. **13**(1), 3–21 (1990)
7. Dahlander, L., Magnusson, M.G.: Relationships between open source software companies and communities: observations from Nordic firms. Res. Policy **34**(4), 481–493 (2005)
8. Eisenhardt, K.M.: Building theories from case study research. Acad. Manag. Rev. **14**(4), 532–550 (1989)
9. Elliott, M.S., Scacchi, W.: Communicating and mitigating conflict in Open Source software development projects. Projects & Profits (2002)
10. Elliott, M.S., Scacchi, W.: Free software development: cooperation and conflict in a virtual organizational culture. In: Koch, S. (ed.) Free/Open Source Software Development, pp. 152–173. Idea Group Publishing (2004)
11. Fernández, W.D.: The grounded theory method and case study data in IS research: issues and design. In: Information Systems Foundations: Constructing and Criticising Workshop at The Australian National University, pp. 43–59 (July 2004)
12. Fitzgerald, B.: The transformation of open source software. MIS Q. **30**(3), 587–598 (2006)
13. Freeman, S., Siltala, J.: Freedom and profit: how suits and hackers are working it out on the desktop (2004), working paper presented in 4/EASST Joint Meeting, Paris 26/08/04
14. Gallivan, M.J.: Striking a balance between trust and control in a virtual organization: a content analysis of open source software case studies. Inf. Syst. J. **11**(4), 277–304 (2001)
15. Germonprez, M., Allen, J.P., Warner, B., Hill, J., McClements, G.: Open source communities of competitors. Interactions **20**(6), 54–59 (2013)
16. Germonprez, M., Kendall, J.E., Kendall, K.E., Mathiassen, L., Young, B., Warner, B.: A theory of responsive design: a field study of corporate engagement with open source communities. Inf. Syst. Res. **28**(1), 64–83 (2016)
17. Germonprez, M., Link, G.J., Lumbard, K., Goggins, S.: Eight observations and 24 research questions about open source projects: Illuminating new realities. In: Proceedings of the ACM on Human-Computer Interaction 2(CSCW), 57 (2018)

18. Goetz, J., LeCompte, D.: Ethnography and Qualitative Design in Educational Research. Academic Press, Cambridge (1984)
19. González-Barahona, J.M., Izquierdo-Cortazar, D., Maffulli, S., Robles, G.: Understanding how companies interact with free software communities. IEEE Softw. **30**(5), 38–45 (2013)
20. González-Barahona, J.M., Robles, G.: Trends in Free, Libre, Open Source Software Communities: From Volunteers to Companies/Aktuelle Trends in Free-, Libre-, und Open-Source-Software-. Information Technology (2013)
21. Guba, E.G.: Criteria for assessing the trustworthiness of naturalistic inquiries. Educ. Technol. Res. Dev. **29**(2), 75–91 (1981)
22. Hallberg, L.: Some thoughts about the literature review in grounded theory studies. Int. J. Qual. Stud. Health Well-being **5**, PMC2915820 (2010)
23. Hunter, P., Walli, S.: The rise and evolution of the open source software foundation. Int. Free Open Source Softw. Law Rev. **5**(1), 31–42 (2013)
24. Jensen, C., Scacchi, W.: Collaboration, leadership, control, and conflict negotiation and the Netbeans.org open source software development community. In: Proceedings of the 38th Annual Hawaii International Conference on System Sciences (2005)
25. Krishnamurthy, S.: An analysis of open source business models. In: Feller, J., Fitzgerald, B., Hissam, S.A., Lakhani, K.R. (eds.) Making Sense of the Bazaar: Perspectives on Open Source and Free Software, vol. 54, pp. 267–278. The MIT Press, Cambridge (2003)
26. Lattemann, C., Stieglitz, S.: Framework for governance in open source communities. In: Proceedings of the 38th Annual Hawaii International Conference on System Sciences (2005)
27. O'Mahony, S.: Guarding the commons: how community managed software projects protect their work. Res. Policy **32**(7), 1179–1198 (2003)
28. O'Mahony, S.: Nonprofit foundations and their role in community-firm software collaboration. In: Feller, J., Fitzgerald, B., Hissam, S.A., Lakhani, K.R. (eds.) Perspectives on Free and Open Source Software, pp. 393–413. The MIT Press, Cambridge (2005)
29. O'Mahony, S., Bechky, B.A.: Boundary organizations: enabling collaboration among unexpected allies. Adm. Sci. Q. **53**(3), 422–459 (2008)
30. O'Mahony, S., West, J.: What makes a project open source? migrating from organic to synthetic communities. Academy of Management conference, Technology and Innovation Management division, Honolulu, August 2005, p. 39 (2005)
31. Pearce, J.: 9.9 million lines of code and still moving fast - Facebook open source in 2014 (2014). https://code.facebook.com/posts/292625127566143/9-9-million-lines-of-code-and-still-moving-fast-facebook-open-source-in-2014/
32. Prattico, L.: Governance of Open Source Software Foundations: Who Holds the Power? Technology Innovation Management Review (2012)
33. Riehle, D.: The economic motivation of open source software: stakeholder perspectives. Computer **40**(4), 25–32 (2007)
34. Riehle, D.: The commercial open source business model. In: Proceedings of the Fifteenth Americas Conference on Information Systems. vol. AMCIS 2009, pp. 1–10 (2009)
35. Riehle, D.: The economic case for open source foundations. Computer **43**(1), 86–90 (2010)
36. Riehle, D.: The single-vendor commercial open course business model. Inf. Syst. E-Bus. Manag. **10**(1), 5–17 (2012)

37. Riehle, D., Berschneider, S.: A model of open source developer foundations. In: The 8th International Conference on Open Source Systems (OSS 2012), pp. 7–28. Springer (2012)
38. Riehle, D., Harutyunyan, N.: License Clearance in Software Product Governance, chap. 5, pp. 83–96. NII Shonan, Tokyo, Japan (2017)
39. Rossi, C., Bonaccorsi, A.: Why profit-oriented companies enter the OS field?: intrinsic vs. extrinsic incentives. In: ACM SIGSOFT Software Engineering Notes. vol. 30, pp. 1–5. ACM (2005)
40. Schaarschmidt, M., Stol, K.J.: Company soldiers and gone-natives: role conflict and career ambition among firm-employed open source developers. In: Thirty ninth International Conference on Information Systems. Association for Information Systems (AIS) (2018)
41. Schaarschmidt, M., Walsh, G., von Kortzfleisch, H.F.: How do firms influence open source software communities? a framework and empirical analysis of different governance modes. Inf. Organ. **25**(2), 99–114 (2015)
42. Siltala, J., Freeman, S., Miettinen, R.: Exploring the tensions between volunteers and firms in hybrid projects (2007), center for Activity Theory and Developmental Work Research. (Working Paper 36)
43. Skerrett, I.: Best practices in multi-vendor open source communities. Open Source Business Resource (2011)
44. Stewart, K.J., Gosain, S.: The impact of ideology on effectiveness in open source software development teams. MIS Q. **30**(2), 291–314 (2006)
45. Teixeira, J.: Understanding coopetition in the open-source arena: the cases of WebKit and OpenStack. In: Proceedings of The International Symposium on Open Collaboration, p. 39. ACM (2014)
46. Van Wendel de Joode, R.: Managing conflicts in open source communities. Electron. Markets **14**, 104–113 (2004)
47. Wagstrom, P., Herbsleb, J., Kraut, R., Mockus, A.: The impact of commercial organizations on volunteer participation in an online community. In: 2010 Academy of Management Meeting. Montreal, Canada (2010)
48. Weikert, F.: How Open Source Foundations Handle Conflicting Interests in Company-Started Projects. Master's thesis, Friedrich-Alexander-Universität Erlangen-Nürnberg (2014)
49. Weiss, M.: Control and diversity in company-led open source projects. Open Source Business Resource (2011)
50. Wen, W., Ceccagnoli, M., Forman, C.: Opening up intellectual property strategy: implications for open source software entry by start-up firms. Manag. Sci. **62**(9), 2668–2691 (2015)
51. West, J., O'Mahony, S.: Contrasting community building in sponsored and community founded open source projects. In: Proceedings of the 38th Annual Hawaii International Conference on System Sciences (2005)
52. West, J., O'Mahony, S.: The role of participation architecture in growing sponsored open source communities. Ind. & Innov. **15**(2), 145–168 (2008)
53. Xie, Z.: Open Source Software Foundations. Open Source Business Resource (2008)
54. Yin, R.K.: Case Study Research: Design and Methods, 5th edn. SAGE Publications, Thousand Oaks (2013)

Dynamic Data Management for Machine Learning in Embedded Systems: A Case Study

Hamza Ouhaichi[1(✉)], Helena Holmström Olsson[1(✉)], and Jan Bosch[2(✉)]

[1] Malmö University, Malmö 205 06, Sweden
{hamza.ouahichi,helena.holmstrom.olsson}@mau.se
[2] Chalmers University of Technology, Gothenburg 412 96, Sweden
jan.bosch@chalmers.se

Abstract. Dynamic data and continuously evolving sets of records are essential for a wide variety of today's data management applications. Such applications range from large, social, content-driven Internet applications, to highly focused data processing verticals like data intensive science, telecommunications and intelligence applications. However, the dynamic and multimodal nature of data makes it challenging to transform it into machine-readable and machine-interpretable forms. In this paper, we report on an action research study that we conducted in collaboration with a multinational company in the embedded systems domain. In our study, and in the context of a real-world industrial application of dynamic data management, we provide insights to data science community and research to guide discussions and future research into dynamic data management in embedded systems. Our study identifies the key challenges in the phases of data collection, data storage and data cleaning that can significantly impact the overall performance of the system.

Keywords: Dynamic data · Embedded systems · Machine learning · Data management · Business outcomes

1 Introduction

In data management, dynamic data or transactional data is information that is periodically updated, meaning it changes asynchronously over time as new information becomes available [1]. Continuously evolving sets of records are essential for a wide variety of today's data management applications [2]. However, the dynamic nature of data makes it challenging to transform it into machine-readable forms [3]. Sensor data produced by a specific device can be used concurrently in multiple applications by different teams which make goals definition challenging from an organizational perspective [4]. Already, there exists several studies that identify the challenges faced by industry when developing AI-enabled systems [4–14]. While many of these studies focus on the technological aspects of AI-enabled systems, we focus also on the industrial and business aspects of these systems. Nevertheless, all the improvements have not been viewed from a certain industrial and business perspectives. Thus, there is a need for a detailed understanding of the characteristics of these systems as well as

S. Hyrynsalmi et al. (Eds.): ICSOB 2019, LNBIP 370, pp. 145–154, 2019.
https://doi.org/10.1007/978-3-030-33742-1_12

generic tools and techniques that can support practitioners and businesses in managing and ensuring high-quality data. In this paper, we discuss a real-world industrial application of dynamic data management -Data Factory (DF): a data pipeline that process dynamic data and make it ready to training and various types of analytics- in a company with high experience in developing embedded systems, highlighting the key challenges in the phases of data collection, storage and cleaning that can significantly impact the overall performance of ML system. We analyze how the company is shifting from opinions to data-driven development [4]. We conduct this research within the company through a direct collaboration with the development team and we were involved in the development process. The contribution of this paper is the identification of the main challenges encountered during the development of the Data Factory system in the case company. These challenges are of high priority because they influence the business outcomes significantly.

The rest of this paper is organized into six sections. In Sect. 2, we describe the background and we review related work. In Sect. 3, we present the research methodology adopted for conducting this research and we describe the case company. In Sect. 4, we present the findings of our study and we identify the challenges encountered at each stage of the dynamic data management process. In Sect. 5, we discuss the threats to validity of our study. Finally, in Sect. 6, we conclude the paper and we outline future research opportunities.

2 Background (Related Work)

Building on the Big Data era, AI and specifically ML and DL is increasingly widely adopted in industry. As these technologies rely on large amounts of data, the data management, both on the device and accumulated in the cloud, is challenging and some researchers have described general data management challenges in ML and DL [15], [7–9]. The DIVS (Dynamic Intelligent Virtual Sensors) concept was introduced in previous work [5] to extend and generalize the notion of a virtual sensor to a dynamic setting with heterogenous sensors.

2.1 Data and Business Decision-Making

Data science involves principles, processes, and techniques for understanding phenomena via the (automated) analysis of data, and its goal is improving decision making, as this generally is of paramount interest to business. The use of Business Intelligence (BI) applications aids a knowledge enterprise by using analytical methods to provide valuable decision-making knowledge to minimize operating costs and to forecast market trends. Using detailed survey data on the business practices and information technology investments of 179 large publicly traded firms in [17], they found that firms adopting data driven decision making have output and productivity that is 5–6% higher than what would be expected given their other investments and information technology usage. Furthermore, the relationship between data driven decision making and performance also appears in other performance measures such as asset utilization, return on equity and market value.

2.2 Dynamic Data Management

In this study, the concerned data is generated by a device with multiple sensors (different dimensions and different data attributes) producing continuously updated sets of records. This data is then stored in the same database table which creates inconsistency in the data structure. In addition, the structure of the data from individual sensors is frequently changed and can be used in multiple applications developed by different teams. Designing and building robust processes and tools that make it easier to analyze, validate, and transform data that is used for data analytics or for large-scale machine learning poses several data management challenges. To prepare data for analytics or for training machine- and deep-learning systems, three stages are typically recognized [14], i.e. collection, cleaning and labeling of the data. In the sections below, we discuss each stage in more detail.

2.2.1 Data Collection

The data collection stage follows the initial definition of the overall system or application goals. Research shows that there are several limitations associated with the available techniques for gathering data from large-scale, non-stationary data streams [11, 12] as well as difficulties associated with establishing ground truth due to errors and faulty data [12]. Lack of metadata, data granularity, lack of "depth" (number of data points) in data samples, the lack of techniques for sharing, tracking and data storage were identified as the main challenges of data collection in [7]. Existing data collection and storage mechanisms for software-intensive systems are originally not set-up for ML systems [8].

2.2.2 Data Cleaning

In the data science community, unclean or noisy data is often referred to as dirty data [7]. There is significant risk associated with using noisy data, because it can affect the results dramatically [1]. Data cleaning is the process of transforming a dirty data so that it can be used for analytics and ML/DL model training. Cleaning is often challenging for a variety of reasons. First, many users of the data are no experts in the application domain. Hence, it is difficult for these users to identify data issues as the semantics are not understood. Second, in many cases data originates from different sources, causing the data to be formatted differently [13]. Mechanisms for critical analysis of training data, proper logging and data cleaning are lacking and require significant domain understanding as well as manual labor [8].

2.2.3 Data Labelling

Manual labelling is very expensive as it is extremely effort and time consuming. Especially in the case of heterogeneous data sources, the result often exhibits different label qualities and labelling costs. As studied in [15], the use of outsourcing for the labelling process to external companies may result in trust issues and must be verified with known labels [15]. Wrongly labelled samples may increase the imbalance or mask actual disproportions [1]. Scarcity of labelled data, imbalanced training sets cause a lack of well-established ground truth [12]. ML/DL models cannot operate on alphanumeric label values as it requires all input variables in the numeric form [7].

This often requires the mapping of alphanumeric data to numeric values, or categories, such as one-hot encoding [7]. When there are thousands or millions of categories, the complexity of the data management problem increases significantly.

3 Research Method

This paper reports on an action research study with the main goal of identifying dynamic data management challenges in building a Data Factory system in an industrial case-company context. For this purpose, we conducted an action design research study in collaboration with a multinational engineering and technology company in the embedded systems domain. Action Design Research (ADR) is a research method for generating prescriptive design knowledge through building and evaluating ensemble IT artifacts in an organizational setting [18]. The method conceptualizes the research process as containing the inseparable and inherently interwoven activities of building the IT artifact, intervening in the organization, and evaluating it concurrently.

3.1 Case Company

The case company is a multinational engineering and technology company in the embedded systems domain and a large supplier to the automotive industry. It has established a software development center with a focus on applications for embedded systems, connected devices and mobile solutions. The company is building a Recognition System based on data generated from different sensors using statistical and machine learning algorithms. In doing this, the company recognizes the importance of developing a data management and processing system, i.e. a 'Data Factory', that takes care of data collection, data cleaning and data labeling. By having such a tool in place, the reliability and the accuracy of the recognition system can be increased.

3.2 Research Process

We conducted this study following the four stages guidelines of the Action Design Research [18]: (1) Problem formulation, (2) Building, intervention and evaluation, (3) Reflecting and learning, (4) Formalization of the learning. This research is an ongoing project, and in this paper, we report on the first three months of our study (June – August 2019) in which a significant part of the development was conducted as this period coincides with the commencement of the project at the company. Below we describe each of the four phases of our study and we detail the activities within each of these.

3.2.1 Problem Formulation

In the first phase of this research, we met with several of the key people at the case company who were actively involved and responsible for the project of developing the recognition system. As one of the key people, the data engineer with responsibility on the data management infrastructure. In our discussions, we were introduced to the recognition system and its application, the associated data resources and the data management processes used in the company. As a result of these initial meetings, we got an understanding of the nature of the data as well as how to format and arrange it to be successfully used for analytics and for ML training model.

3.2.2 Building, Intervention and Evaluation

During this study, we worked closely with the development team at the case company. One of the authors of this paper spent two/three days every week at the case company to observe, engage and intervene with the team and in the development of the system. This required active use of tools and techniques applied at the company and taking part of the development of the data conversion tools. Semi-structured interviews were conducted with each practitioner. In the interviews, we focused on the following themes: (1) previous professional experience, (2) current role and responsibilities in the development of the data management system for the recognition system, and (3) the main challenges encountered in the initiation and execution of this project. Additionally, we participated in daily stand up meetings during the first month of this study. In these meetings, five practitioners participated (see Table 1) and they provided a detailed understanding of the on-going work. Also, it gave us the opportunity to continuously discuss and present the research perspective of the work and to align on goals with the practitioners.

3.2.3 Reflecting and Learning

At this stage of the study, all interviews and meetings were carefully transcribed and examined with the aim to identify repeated and frequent concepts as is common in open coding techniques [16]. In our analysis, all interviews were read several times by the researchers. Also, and as part of our close collaboration, potential misunderstandings could be discussed immediately with the team members to get a second view and explanation of a statement or a quote. In addition to the interview transcripts, notes were taken during all meetings to capture the discussions, and white board illustrations were documented.

Table 1. List of practitioners' roles and number of times they reached out in the standup meetings, and number of times they were interviewed.

ID	Role	Standup meetings	Duration minutes	Individual interviews	Duration minutes
P1	Data engineer	7	20 to 40	4	30 to 60
P2	Algorithm analyst	8	20 to 40	1	20
P3	Mobile developer	8	20 to 40	1	14
P4	Mobile developer	8	20 to 40	1	12
P5	Test engineer	8	20 to 40	1	35
P6	Product owner	8	20 to 40	1	10

3.2.4 Formalization of the Learning

At this phase, we formalized and generalized the learnings from our empirical data and from the experience we had gained by intervening with the team and the company over a time frame of three months. As a result, we identified the challenges in building the Data Factory system, each of the challenges were defined and associated to a description of the organizational and business outcomes. While we are aware that the challenges we identified were derived based on our close collaboration with one case company, we believe that the nature of these may well occur also in other companies with similar systems. Therefore, the challenges we identified can be regarded generic principles and a basis for future solutions of the problems they represent.

4 Findings

Collecting, processing, storing and analyzing data is different and more complex in an embedded systems context as compared to SaaS deployments [20]. By engaging in an action research study, and based on interventions such as interviews, workshops and active participation in the development team at the case company, we identified challenges encountered when developing the Data Factory system. Below, we present our findings and we discuss each challenge in detail.

4.1 Expensive and Error-Prone Collection of Labeled Sensor Data Sequences

The collected data consisted of multisensory data sequences generated by wearable devices. The labels refer to the physical activity performed by a human (the activity to be recognized) which imply that the labels should be assigned by the same person. To generate the data, each activity that is expected to be recognized is performed by a human who manually starts and stops the data collection sequence and labels the sequence using available tools. The data collection and labeling is done initially by employees at the case company. As part of the action design research underlying this study, one of the authors of this papers was involved in this task. The experience we had from this, and confirmed by employees of the company, is that this task is extremely time consuming and expensive because it requires human dedication and it cannot be performed automatically. As the task requires a lot of attention and is routinely long, it is very easy to introduce erroneous data. Practitioners have also expressed that the amount of available data is very low and always limited to the number of employees involved and the need for sophisticated tools for data collection. A solution that the company is considering in the future is a data collection campaign, in which several people will be hired to run the simulations and collect more data in a shorter time, but it will be a very expensive solution. Additionally, this solution doesn't represent any guarantees to data quality.

4.2 Difficulties Maintaining Semantics of Dynamically Evolving, Heterogenous Data

The company should use standards, and structures for organizing data, to facilitate data re-use and interchange. The data generated by our device was coming from different sensors at the same time. Each sensor delivered different information which has different dimensions and diverse structures. All these data were stored in the same table and it was continuously updated throughout the project. As was remarked by practitioners, the most challenging thing, is to fit all the data from all sensors into one data storage. Also, they mentioned that working with different versions of files and different versions of data is more difficult. Development teams at the company had to use the same data source for multiple and various aims. Practitioners confirmed that it was very confusing to decide a final data structure for the whole dataset.

4.3 Unclean and Noisy Data

Data quality is a major concern, and dirty data can lead to incorrect decisions and unreliable analysis. Analysts must consider the effects of dirty data before making any decisions, and as a result, data cleaning has been a key area of database research [1]. In the case study [10] all practitioners agreed that they have faced this unclean data issue in all the cases. We observed that, first, inconsistent data generation practices during development and manual data collection causes noisy and unclean data. Second, the dynamicity and the unstructured nature of data causes data holes and numerous empty fields in the dataset.

4.4 Restrictive Security Constraints

Security constraints can become very restrictive to the extent of preventing or making it very complicated to use external tools and technologies. With the noticeable advancement of SaaS products almost all digitalized companies that are not specialized in data management are dependent to such services, and it is completely unpractical to build a whole data management platform from scratch. The team members stated that the company receives around one many network attacks every day and it is quite reasonable why they have such security constraints. The case company was in a situation where practitioners needed use external tools for data storing and processing "e.g. Azure", at the same time the company presented overly restrictive security constraints which is obstructing the progress of the development process, consequently this results in reducing the business value.

4.5 Difficulty of Heterogeneous and Dynamic Data Interpretation

At the case company, the dynamic and multimodal nature of data makes it challenging to transform them into machine-readable and machine-interpretable forms. Determining how to annotate the data and make them machine- interpretable is an important issue. Ontology construction and semantic annotation was used to resolve this issue. People at the company claimed the work involved reverse engineering to understand the algorithms to apply on the data. In [6], an initial ontology based on the semantic sensor network for dynamic IoT sensor data was firstly built. Then, historical sensor data are used to extract knowledge. They adopted the K-means clustering method to obtain and group the data set. The concept of virtual sensors provides a step towards making sense of the sensor data in an efficient and effective manner to provide users with relevant services. However virtual sensors are often used to denote homogeneous types of data, generally retrieved from a predetermined group of sensors.

4.6 Lack of Well-Defined Goals

Several practitioners at the case company didn't know much about the final goal or the application of the project. Lack of alignment concerning overall goals for data collection, causes conflicting initiatives. Practitioners mentioned that the requirements were not clear, and it was not easy to understand what it is possible to do with the data. Different teams use the data in different ways and need it for various aims, which make an unclear idea of the type of analytics that will be done on this data after the preparation. All the challenges are listed with a brief description in Table 1.

5 Threats to Validity

Our research was conducted in close collaboration with the case company and it is dependent on the context of the company. However, in the findings section we present challenges that were experienced and observed in this study that might be valid also in broader contexts. Specifically, we believe that the findings we present are applicable to software development units inside an organization that aims to apply advanced data analytics and machine learning (ML) to improve their business and decision-making processes (Table 2).

Table 2. Challenges faced by the company during the development of the data factory system.

Challenge	Description
Expensive and error-prone collection of labeled sensor data sequences	Lack of automated techniques for collecting labeled sensor data sequences
Difficulties maintaining semantics of dynamically evolving, heterogenous data	Multisensory data stored under the same table. This data is continuously updated overtime and used concurrently in multiple applications by different teams
Unclean and noisy data	Inconsistent data generation practices and manual data collection causes noisy and unclean data, and data dynamicity causes data holes or empty fields
Restrictive Security constraints	Overly restrictive security constraints reduce business value because it obstructs the data management process

(*continued*)

Table 2. (*continued*)

Challenge	Description
Difficulty of heterogeneous and dynamic data interpretation	The dynamic and multimodal nature of data makes it challenging to transform them into machine-readable and machine-interpretable forms
Lack of well-defined goals	Lack of alignment concerning overall goals for data collection, causes conflicting initiatives

6 Conclusion

Business infrastructures are progressively built with data as key for business operations and decisions [4]. Constantly updated datasets are fundamental for a broad range of nowadays data management applications. However, the dynamic and multimodal nature of data makes it challenging to transform it into machine-readable and machine-interpretable forms. In this paper, we report on an action research study conducted within a multinational company with high experience in developing embedded systems. Our study identifies the main challenges that the company encountered in the phases of data collection, data storage and data cleaning. We provided insights to highlight the challenges involved for companies aiming to implement data-driven development approaches and offer a guide for future research in dynamic data management in embedded systems. Based on the experiences gained in this study, we plan to continue research and collaboration with the case company to better understand how data management impact the organization and the business outcomes. Moreover, we plan to develop solutions that address the identified challenges and further explore the benefits of investing in data management processes and data-driven development.

References

1. Darema, F.: Dynamic data driven applications systems: a new paradigm for application simulations and measurements. In: Bubak, M., van Albada, G.D., Sloot, P.M.A., Dongarra, J. (eds.) ICCS 2004. LNCS, vol. 3038, pp. 662–669. Springer, Heidelberg (2004). https://doi.org/10.1007/978-3-540-24688-6_86
2. Polyzotis, N., Roy, S., Whang, S.E., Zinkevich, M.: Data lifecycle challenges in production machine learning: a survey. SIGMOD Record **47**, 17–28 (2018)
3. Kennedy, O., Ahmad, Y., Koch, C.: DBToaster: agile views for a dynamic data management system. In: CIDR 2011 - 5th Biennial Conference on Innovative Data Systems Research, Conference Proceedings, pp. 284–295 (2011)
4. Tegen, A., Davidsson, P., Mihailescu, R.C., Persson, J.A.: Collaborative sensing with interactive learning using dynamic intelligent virtual sensors. Sensors (Basel, Switzerland) **19**(3), 477 (2019). https://doi.org/10.3390/s19030477
5. Charles, H., Bellarnyz, R., Ericksonz, T., Burnett, M.: Trials and tribulations of developers of intelligent systems: a field study, pp. 162–170 (2016). https://doi.org/10.1109/vlhcc.2016.7739680

6. Polyzotis, N., Roy, S., Whang, S.E., Zinkevich, M.: Data management challenges in production machine learning. pp. 1723–1726 (2017). https://doi.org/10.1145/3035918.3054782
7. Arpteg, A., Raj, A., Brinne, B., Crnkovic-Friis, L., Bosch, J.: Data Management Challenges of Deep Learning, pp. 50–59 (2019). https://doi.org/10.1109/seaa.2019.00018
8. Kumar, A., Boehm, M., Yang, J.: Data Management in Machine Learning: Challenges, Techniques, and Systems, pp. 1717–1722 (2017). https://doi.org/10.1145/3035918.3054775
9. Delaye, E., Sirasao, A., Dudha, C., Das, S.: Deep learning challenges and solutions with Xilinx FPGAs, pp. 908–913 (2017). https://doi.org/10.1109/iccad.2017.8203877
10. Lwakatare, L.E., Raj, A., Bosch, J., Olsson, H., Crnkovic, I.: A Hilltironomy of Software Engineering Challenges for Machine Learning Systems: An Empirical Investigation (2019). https://doi.org/10.1007/978-3-030-19034-7_14
11. Zhou, L., Pan, S., Wang, J., Vasilakos, A.: Machine learning on big data: opportunities and challenges. Neurocomputing **237**, 350–361 (2017). https://doi.org/10.1016/j.neucom.2017.01.026
12. Chu, X., Ilyas, I., Krishnan, S., Wang, J.: Data Cleaning: Overview and Emerging Challenges, pp. 2201–2206 (2016). https://doi.org/10.1145/2882903.2912574
13. Krawczyk, B.: Learning from imbalanced data: open challenges and future directions. Progress Artif. Intell. **5**, 221–232 (2016)
14. Ahuja, S., Angra, S.: Machine learning and its Applications: A Review (2017). https://doi.org/10.1109/icbdaci.2017.8070809
15. Hedgebeth, D.: Data-driven decision making for the enterprise: an overview of business intelligence applications. VINE **37**(4), 414–420 (2007)
16. Maxwell, J.A.: Qualitative Research Design: An interactive approach, 2nd edn. SAGE Publications, Thousands Oaks (2005)
17. Berthold, M.R., Borgelt, C., Höppner, F., Klawonn, F.: Guide to Intelligent Data Analysis. TCS. Springer, London (2010). https://doi.org/10.1007/978-1-84882-260-3
18. Broy, M.: Challenges in automotive software engineering. In: Proceedings of the 28th International Conference on Software Engineering (ICSE 2006), ACM, New York, NY, USA, pp. 33–42 (2006)

Continual Improvement and Product Development

Fostering Continuous Innovation with Engaging IT-Assisted Transparent Information Sharing: A Case Study

Petri Kettunen[1(✉)], Susanna Teppola[2], and Jari Partanen[3]

[1] University of Helsinki, Helsinki, Finland
petri.kettunen@helsinki.fi
[2] VTT Technical Research Centre of Finland Ltd., Espoo, Finland
susanna.teppola@vtt.fi
[3] Bittium Wireless Ltd., Oulu, Finland
jari.partanen@bittium.com

Abstract. Continuous innovation (CI) in large, established companies aiming to both produce incremental innovations as well as to create more radical ones is complex and complicated. It is affected by many simultaneous hard and soft factors and interrelationships. One suggested way how CI performance can potentially be improved is by increasing transparency in the innovation process, through which better employee participation to the process can possibly be achieved. Modern information/knowledge management and sharing IT tools can support that in practice. In this paper, we investigate those questions in an industrial software-intensive B2B company case. The company augmented its former, formal stage-gate based innovation process with new practices in order to accelerate the business innovation decision-making with validated information. We collected empirically rich qualitative and quantitative data and analyzed it to extract a set of statements grounded on the data. Those statements suggest that it is central to engage and connect right people and key information for effective and efficient idea generation, idea development, and business incubation. However, in different phases various stakeholder feedback and expert knowledge are critical for successful innovation progress. Increased transparency supported by integrated and versatile innovation, and knowledge management IT tools can intensify them. In effect, the clock speed of the organization for connecting people, ideas, knowledge (even tacit), and business decisions is accelerated. Overall the CI process should be flexible but at the same time it should frame the central direction. Consequently, it is hard to measure CI performance fully decisively with traditional KPIs.

Keywords: Continuous innovation · Innovation performance · Idea management system

S. Hyrynsalmi et al. (Eds.): ICSOB 2019, LNBIP 370, pp. 157–174, 2019.
https://doi.org/10.1007/978-3-030-33742-1_13

1 Introduction

Companies producing software-intensive solutions are living in a rapidly changing market environment, where they have to continuously look for ways how to efficiently produce new appealing products and services for various customers while sustaining their current products and businesses [1]. This is not straightforward for B2B technology companies developing complex technical solutions, which need to be maintained throughout their typically long life spans.

For achieving business-driven innovations in which technology push and market pull are high, it is suggested that companies should evolve towards high-speed experimentation and continuity in their innovation [2]. Continuity should be developed in a way that supports both the company's operative efficiency and profitability in their current business, and also the flexibility to develop their future business opportunities. The continuous innovation approach has been proposed for binding the operational and strategic planning processes closer to each other, and for providing a way for continuous and efficient contribution to the company's strategic planning activities [3]. Experimentation, on the other hand, is an approach that supports radical rethinking of ideas and early collection of feedback to cope with high uncertainties related to new business ideas.

To achieve continuity and radical innovations, it is suggested to increase the stakeholders' participation in innovation, remove the bottlenecks in the innovation process and adopt an experiment-driven approach [4–6]. Organizational structures and innovation management systems should support those [7]. Knowledge transfer and learning are essential elements of continuous innovation [8].

Transparency has been identified as one contributing factor for continuous innovation [9, 10]. However, it has not been widely studied how it actually affects innovation process performance. There appear to be few empirical studies on how transparency of information is facilitated in order to gain positive process performance effects (e.g., [11]). Moreover, it is important to realize what particular information and knowledge should be managed and shared transparently between different actors [8].

We have been investigating those topics with a case study in one industrial company. This paper is the continuation of our prior work with the case company [12]. The earlier paper described how transparency of information is realized in our case company's continuous innovation practice and examined performance measurements with selected key performance indicators (KPIs). The objective was mostly descriptive, concentrating just on the particular company situation while generality was not of primary importance. This paper advances from that point of view by taking a wider and more in-depth view at the collected research material to conceptualize and frame the findings in order to draw more general conclusions, informed suggestions, and propositions for replicating studies. We also widen our longitudinal research scope by several months, in total ranging now from February 2014 to October 2016, spanning 33 months in the company. During this time, several data collection occasions and frequent observations were made by the researchers together with the case company representatives. In this paper we are thereby interested in the following research questions motivated and informed by our prior work:

- RQ1. *What factors affect continuous innovation (CI) performance?*
- RQ2. *How does transparency impact it?*
- RQ3. *What is the role of IT tools?*

The paper is structured as follows. In Sect. 2, prior research and motivation for this research are outlined. The case research design is explained in Sect. 3. Section 4 presents the empirical results followed by analysis and discussion in Sect. 5. Finally, Sect. 6 concludes the paper, suggesting further research.

2 Background

2.1 Continuous Innovation

Modern software-intensive companies are inclined toward continuous improvement particularly in conjunction with agile and lean software development methods. However, in many current business environments more than that is needed: innovation, even continuously. Companies should be able to innovate overtime consistently and in a sustained manner [13].

In what is called Continuous Innovation, continuous improvement, learning, and innovation are converged [14]. The overall goal of continuous innovation capability is to enable ongoing interaction between operations, incremental improvement and learning (exploitation processes), and radical innovation and change (exploration processes) [15]. The key principle of continuous innovation is that it is integrated into the daily work of the organization [16]. Relevant research questions are then how continuously innovative organizations look like (processes, technology, people, organization and management), and what can be learned from the change process of successful development of continuous innovation capability [15].

In general, industrial innovation involves many challenges related both to the ideation and the implementation [1]. Incremental (sustaining) innovations are improvements exploiting the existing knowledge while radical (discontinuous) innovations require exploration and new knowledge acquisition. Realizing both needs ambidexterity in the capabilities to get flexibility in decision-making and conducive culture.

Established firms may have challenges in responding to and generating discontinued innovations when their idea screening processes filter away discontinuous ideas, and because the idea management is aimed at generating patents only [17]. Advancing from incremental product innovation only to further the business model, discontinuous and open innovation requires balancing of open-mindedness and visibility of innovation, but in a structured way to avoid chaotic ideation [5]. Organizational change management should promote innovativeness by considering knowledge an asset and a resource, and developing future awareness for innovation orientation [18].

2.2 Innovation Performance

Innovation, in particular continuous innovation, should be actively managed and measured with performance measurements linking innovation performance to firm performance [16]. Such comprehensive measurement frameworks require conceptualizing the innovation capability. Innovation capability is suggested to cover the potential (e.g., know-how, organizational communication and culture, individual creativity), the processes (systems and activities), and the results of innovation activities [19].

Continuous innovation measurements should be multidimensional and integrated, focusing on the company-specific business success factors (business innovation capability) [16]. Such potential measurement items could be, for instance, leadership toward continuous innovation, employees' idea generation, employees' expertise, and internal processes supporting and reflecting continuous innovation.

Fostering and sustaining innovation consistently over time requires a comprehensive view of innovation, comprising the innovation capability (inputs, activities, determinants), innovation outputs, impacts on performance (direct, indirect), and learning (feedbacks) [13]. However, there is a lack of empirically validated innovation metrics and measurement models.

2.3 Transparency

In the context of continuous innovation, transparency concerns in particular visibility of relevant information and knowledge of innovation targets, ideas, and the innovation activities. When product ideas, features, and their related information are visible in real time, including links between the different items, generated ideas may trigger new ideas [5]. Moreover, transparent idea feedback channels and traceability facilitate idea maturation. In addition, visibility of innovation metrics provides transparency to the internal workings of the organization's innovation process [13].

Transparent sharing and communication of internal information and knowledge, such as open dialogue of company's vision, strategy and innovation targets and re-exploring of existing ideas and concepts, may improve innovation performance [18, 20]. Potential measures of innovation capability thus include communication channels [19].

2.4 Innovation Management Systems, Information Sharing and Knowledge Management IT Tools

Modern IT tools enable systematic and efficient handling of ideas by making it highly interactive [17]. Such idea management systems give structure to the early phases of the innovation process. Searchable idea banks make it rational for ideas to be refined, exchanged and re-used in different projects. Discontinuous ideas can be stored and (re) used later. Information and knowledge management IT tools can support different views of information based on the needs of the teams, project managers, and product management, visible globally in real time [5].

Collaborative IT platforms promote and stimulate idea generation and employee engagement, and they can even serve as management tools for creativity [20]. Virtual idea campaigns and virtual innovation spaces encourage and enable all employees to participate. Moreover, such platforms give critical experts the opportunity to contribute on right times in the idea development process [5].

Overall, knowledge management IT systems can support organization and innovativeness development by making organizational knowledge actionable [18]. However, notably, IT barriers for information sharing and knowledge utilization could also hinder innovativeness. More research is needed to understand the impact of collaborative tools on idea generation and innovation development, and on the impact of IT on knowledge sharing in the innovation process for firms' innovation capability [20].

3 Research Design

3.1 Case Account

The case company is a B2B provider of embedded systems for the wireless industry, having around 30 years of expertise in advanced radio communication technologies with more than 500 employees in four countries. The company had used the traditional stage-gate model for their ideation well over ten years [21]. In the stage-gate innovation process, the collected ideas focused only on creating intellectual property rights (IPR), which was confidential information and which involved only a limited number of experts. In general, there were challenges with the daily operative work, which did not allow designers and experts to participate much in the innovation.

The used tools and processes were inadequate for continuous idea handling and instead the innovation process was based on heavy control mechanisms and decision making procedures. Without a common, well-known practice to present ideas for business decision makers, and without well-defined criteria to assess the potential business value of the ideas, the quality of the ideas varied a lot and missed the link to company business targets. Consequently, the lead time of idea handling varied as well and many of the ideas remained unresolved. All this decreased employees' motivation to propose ideas. There was a real need to increase the amount of ideas, especially in the areas which were significant for company strategic business targets.

During the research period the company went through a big organizational change in which a significant part of the company was divested to another company. This provided the company a unique and excellent opportunity to renew its innovation processes, and revise their business strategies in a large scale. This also made the company an excellent sample for this research as the single-case study.

To improve the abovementioned situation, the company set a grand innovation strategy to have more radical innovations (products or applications) to scale the business by utilizing the full potential of the entire organization. The improvement focused on radical new business innovations but covered product and process innovations as well [21]. First, the company decided to adopt a more experimental approach in their idea harvesting, focusing, and validation. It was assumed that employees who work daily in operative work have many good ideas, which could support the company's business planning, but in the beginning there was no way to collect them. It was assumed that increasing the transparency of the innovation process and making it more agile with experimentation as well as adding frequent screening practices would lead to a greater number of harvested ideas and an improved idea fit for the company's business targets. As a consequence, it was expected that this would increase the overall innovation performance in the company and lead to achieving of more radical business innovations. The concrete targets of the improvements are shown in Table 1.

Table 1. Case company innovation process improvement targets.

Target	Description
T1	Harvest more ideas within the company
T2	Grow ideas faster into business innovations
T3	Capture ideas with better fit for purpose
T4	Improve the participation of various company stakeholders in the innovation process

In order to measure the impacts of the improvements on continuous innovation performance, the company set up the following KPIs (Table 2).

Table 2. Case company KPIs.

KPI#	Definition
KPI1	Number of harvested ideas (T1 in Table 1): *Continuous number of ideas*
KPI2	Number of people participating in the innovation process (T4): *Number of people who participated in the processing of ideas*
KPI3	Quality of ideas in the idea pool (T3): *Number of ideas in business validation*
KPI4	Throughput from idea to business innovation (T2): *Cycle time of an idea (from idea to potential business case demonstration)*
KPI5	Frequency of business innovations growing from the idea database (T2): *Frequency of potential business idea demonstration*

Several actions were conducted to improve the innovation practices in the company [21]. Figure 1 illustrates the timeline of the observation period during which the improvement actions were conducted.

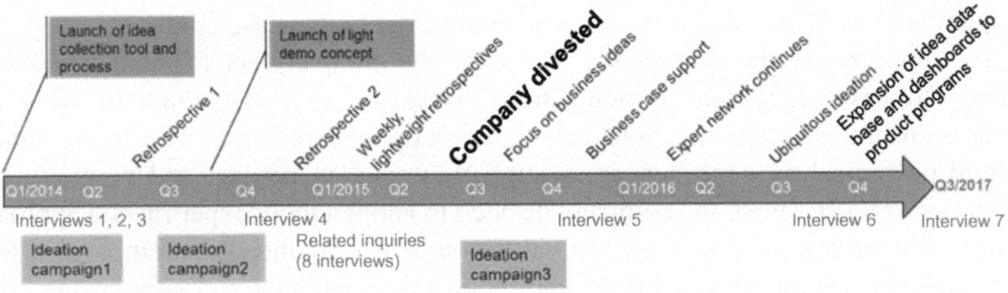

Fig. 1. Timeline of the improvement actions in the case company.

The first step in the journey of improving continuous innovation was the deployment of an innovation management information system tool for collecting all ideas and covering the innovation process from idea harvesting until the business validation. The tool system makes the ideas, their current status, and related information continuously transparent to stakeholders. The tool provides important support for the process implementation. The KPI data collection and follow-up is automated in the tool system. In this paper we call it as the *Ideas Tool* (idea collection, ideation, idea management tool [21]).

Another significant change in the innovation approach was that the continuous innovation process was copied to various places across the organization to support idea creation on a local level. The company began to call this approach as a ubiquitous ideation approach. This meant that ideas could also be submitted directly to a product program where they were handled first, e.g., in epic evaluation before moving to relevant development backlog.

In summary, the new continuous innovation process of the case company included three main phases: idea harvesting, focusing, and validation phase (Fig. 2). This process also illustrates the maturity of individual ideas.

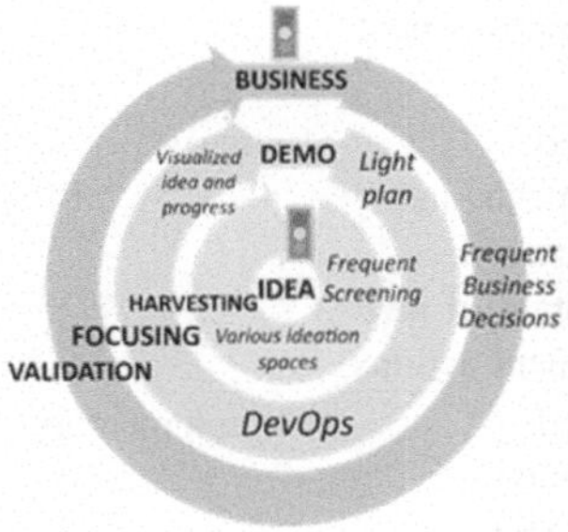

In the idea harvesting phase an idea is a simple, textual description – no more than a couple of sentences. When idea evolves and enters the demo phase, idea is already more focused and able to provide proof of concept solution that can be demonstrated. Entering the demo phase requires business decision (so called "traffic light feedback") although demos are lightweight and not involve more than 2-3 days of work. After the demo is successful and it is agreed that it employs business potential, the idea is ready to enter the final validation phase. Therein, an R&D project is established following company's end-product-process guidelines in order to develop a product or product improvement targeting a real, selected market segment. Entering the validation phase i.e., R&D project, requires business decision as well as naturally project plans, resource and cost estimates.

Fig. 2. Continuous innovation process of the case company.

3.2 Methodology

The main approach for the research is an exploratory single-case study [22, 23]. The research is longitudinal, spanning Q2/2014 to Q4/2017. The case company provided a possibility to investigate the continuous innovation phenomenon deeply and measure it throughout the process. This made it possible to discover different performance influencing factors in practice and to evaluate the performance effects during the long observation period. Intensive long-term collaboration together with the case company representatives and researchers increased the in-depth understanding of how the innovation process evolved in the company, and what impacts and experiences were gained, as well as provided multiple sources for rich data collection and triangulation.

Data Collection. For empirical data gathering, several sources and techniques were used to collect evidence for the case study as presented in Table 3 (c.f., Fig. 1). Frequent meetings with the company representatives (Head of Quality and the Innovation Management (IM) consultant) were conducted to verify the researchers' interpretations and emerging conclusions. The representatives continuously followed the company internal data, including the KPI measurements.

Table 3. Empirical data collection.

ACTS (Fig. 1)	Themes, topics	Subjects	Methods	Data types – contents	Use in analysis
Related inquiries	Continuous planning	Various managerial levels	Semi-structured interviews	Qualitative – operative planning practices across organization	Complementary
Interview 1	CI process: current status and targets	Head of Quality, IM consultant	Semi-structured interview	Current state challenges, targets, plan and scope	Primary
Interview 2	CI process: status and targets	Head of Quality, IM consultant	Semi-structured interview	Targets, goals and current problems	Primary
Interview 3 workshop	CI process improvement status, first use experiences	Lead of Tools Dev, Head of Quality, IM consultant	Current state analysis – workshop	Current state process map, improvement points; experiences of improvements, further improvement needs	Primary
Interview 4	CI: progress status and next goals	IM consultant	Semi-structured interview, numerical data show	Conducted improvements and experiences, identification of new improvement actions	Primary
Interview 5	CD, information and process transparency	Tech team Lead, Tech specialists (2), QM	Brain-storming	Conducted improvement activities and experiences, next steps	Complementary
Interview 6	CI acceleration methods, usage and experiences	Head of Quality, IM consultant	Semi-structured interview	Qualitative data – used methods, experiences; next steps	Primary
Interview 7	Enrichment and validation	Head of Quality, IM consultant	Semi-structured interviews	Conducted activities and experiences; enhanced, verified research conclusions	Primary

The role of the IM consultant was central in the development of the company innovation process as a participative insider expert. Thus, s(he) was a key informant both as a data source and for the validation of the research conclusions.

Data Analysis. The principal method of the empirical data analysis was the constant comparison method [24]. The collected, mostly qualitative data was explored and grouped with respect to our research themes (RQ1–3) to form a set of statements. They were then examined to discover the underlying themes and potential explanations of the underlying phenomenon to build more theoretical propositions. The complementary data in Table 3 related to continuous planning practices in business processes and continuous engineering in R&D processes. It helped framing and comprehending the innovation process in the case company business and R&D operations context.

4 Results

4.1 Measurements

During the longitudinal case study observation period the company Ideas Tool recorded the quantitative KPI measures defined in Table 2. Figure 3 shows the trends of the harvested ideas (KPI1) and the validated business ideas (KPI3). The trend charts are mapped here to the timeline of the company innovation process improvement activities and the research events (c.f., Fig. 1). Table 4 presents numerically how the different KPI values changed over the observation period. Note Table 1 for the target state.

Table 4. Case company KPI evolutions during the observation period.

KPI (Table 2)	Initially	Finally (end of observations, Q4/2016)
KPI1 (# of harvested ideas)	Could not be measured in the beginning because there was no mechanism to do that	By the end of the observation period, the number was 10–20 ideas per month
KPI2 (# of people participating)	Less than 5% of the company employees participated in the innovation process	The number had exceeded 10% of the total number of employees
KPI3 (# of ideas in business validation)	less than 26% of the total number of ideas	That value was 35%
KPI4 (cycle time of an idea)	There was no mechanism to measure it in the beginning	The best measurements were determined to be less than 8 weeks from idea registration to business decision
KPI5 (frequency of potential business idea demonstration)	one month	one week

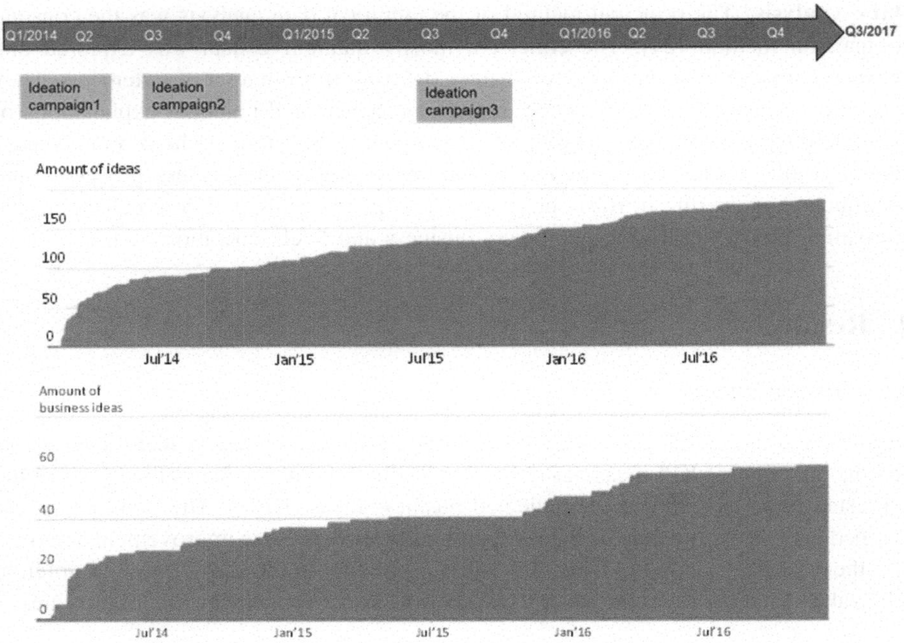

Fig. 3. Cumulative trends of the submitted ideas and the business ideas in validation during the observation period.

4.2 Observations and Findings

In the qualitative data analysis the empirical observations and discoveries were formulated as statements grounded on the data and grouped according to the research questions RQ1–RQ3. Altogether we noted 52 such items. Table 5 presents the ones which we evaluated to be the most essential ones.

Table 5. Key empirical observations.

LABEL	Statements
<S1>	By keeping the threshold to submit ideas low and by not isolating ideation process away from the operative context triggers employees more actively participate in the process
<S2>	Ubiquitous ideation practice makes employees more confident to submit ideas because they trust that sufficient experts of the relevant business and technology domain will review their ideas
<S3>	Innovation work is supported by a systematic but lightweight screening process, enabling fast and regular feedback between management and developers
<S4>	Light demo planning is iterative process and visible in the Ideas Tool, which supports continuous learning and feedback. This means that many ideas start to reach the maturity level for business decisions

(*continued*)

Table 5. *(continued)*

LABEL	Statements
<S5>	The process pushing the fast incremental growth of ideas with frequent screenings and collection of versatile feedback and early feedback ensures that ideas will reach the maturity level needed for business decisions in proper time
<S6>	The use of a frequent and systematic screening process, which was a practice in the old stage-gate model, ensures that idea growth is systematic and validated, but at the same time is flexible enough to handle rapid experimentation as well
<S7>	Synchronization between business planning, budgeting and operative work enables the flow in the innovation process
<S8>	It is important to enable opportunities for creative people, share relevant information (e.g., strategic needs, customer and technology demands, ideas, feedback), organize events and actions so that the innovation process stays continuous and focused, but give flexibility for ideas to grow and connect together
<S9>	The process and the flow how an idea grows to an innovation, or ends up being canceled or put on hold, is all the time visible in the Ideas Tool, making sure that all the steps and the overall progress of the idea is known by all stakeholders
<S10>	Transparent idea feedback is a way for any stakeholder to see what is discussed and decided regarding an idea. This also enables extremely busy specialists to participate in the idea growth
<S11>	The main triggers for more efficient idea focusing is that the Ideas Tool is integrated to existing tool chains in the company ensuring that ideas are connected to dependent items and business cases from the beginning

The statement items were then mapped to the continuous innovation process phases of idea harvesting, focusing, and validation illustrated in Fig. 2. In the following, Tables 6 and 7 present the mappings of the items in Table 5. In the data analysis we compiled a full mapping of all the 52 items of which these tables are thus subsets.

Table 6. Mapping of factors affecting continuous innovation performance (RQ1).

<table>
<tr><th>IDEA HARVESTING</th><th>IDEA FOCUSING</th><th>IDEA VALIDATION</th><th>Business Incubation, Project</th></tr>
<tr><td><S1></td><td></td><td></td><td></td></tr>
<tr><td><S2></td><td></td><td></td><td></td></tr>
<tr><td></td><td><S3></td><td></td><td></td></tr>
<tr><td></td><td colspan="2"><S4></td><td></td></tr>
<tr><td></td><td colspan="3"><S5></td></tr>
<tr><td colspan="3"><S6></td><td></td></tr>
<tr><td colspan="4"><S7></td></tr>
<tr><td colspan="2"><S8></td><td></td><td></td></tr>
</table>

In these tables each row represents individual items shown in Table 5. The column shadings indicate the ideation life-cycle spans that the items concern primarily.

In Table 6 the rows are clustered according to the performance targets defined in Table 1. In addition they are partially ordered following the flow of ideas from idea generation to business decision.

Table 7 categorizes what particular visibility and information sharing impacted the continuous innovation performance (positively). Like in Table 6, the rows are partially ordered following the flow of ideas from idea generation to business decision. Notably, contrasting, we were also interested in finding out whether the lack of certain transparency has restrained innovation performance. Our empirical evidence suggests that the open sharing of idea information was perceived to improve idea development and progress compared to the former, limited-access IPR-focused innovation process. In addition there was some evidence indicating that initially the lack of linking ideas to product program roadmaps made it complicated to achieve a comprehensive overview.

Table 7. Mapping of impact of transparency (RQ2).

<table>
<tr><th>IDEA HARVESTING</th><th>IDEA FOCUSING</th><th>IDEA VALIDATION</th><th>Business Incubation, Project</th></tr>
<tr><td colspan="4"><S9></td></tr>
<tr><td></td><td><S10></td><td></td><td></td></tr>
<tr><td></td><td><S11></td><td></td><td></td></tr>
</table>

Considering the role of IT tools (RQ3), in our case company the Ideas Tool was the main innovation (idea) management and information sharing IT tool (see Sect. 3.1). In Tables 6 and 7 it is explicitly noted in <S9>, <S4> and <S11>.

5 Analysis and Discussion

5.1 Principal Empirical Conclusions

In the following Table 8 we separate out our key empirical observations presented in Sect. 4.2. It suggests a mapping to the associated components of innovation capability leaning on the conceptual framework introduced in Sect. 2.2 (exploitation of the company innovation potential, activities of its innovation process, and the results of the activities) proposed in [19]. The capital X letters indicate what we discern to be the major associations.

Table 8. Innovation capability associations from the key empirical observations and findings.

Statements (see Table 5)	Innovation capability elements					
	People, interactions	Data, information, knowledge	Process	Tools	Products, business	Organization, culture
<S8>	X	x	x		x	
<S1>	X		x			x
<S2>	X		x	x	x	x
<S9>	X	x	x	x		
<S10>	X	x	x			x
<S3>			X			x
<S4>		x	X	x	x	x
<S5>			X		x	
<S6>			X		x	
<S7>			X		x	
<S11>		x		x	X	x

5.2 Related Studies

Table 9 compares the main results, findings and suggestions of the related research reviewed in Sect. 2 against our key results by reflecting the statements presented in Table 5. Only the central points are highlighted here.

Table 9. Comparing selected related research and this case.

Publications	Related focal points	*Our research*
Continuous Innovation Performance (RQ1)		
[17]	• dualistic idea management to encourage and handle both continuous and discontinuous ideas	<S6>
[5]	• ideas coming from different sources across and beyond the organization	<S1>
[19]	• realizing linkages and potential cause–effect relationships of innovation and business performance	<S7>
[16]	• managing and developing continuous innovation utilizing varieties of performance measurements	<S5>
[18]	• self-reliant individuals as innovators	<S1>
[13]	• determinants of innovation (e.g., organization resources, knowledge/information, tool support) influencing the innovation capability	<S8>
Transparency (RQ2)		
[5]	• idea owners able to follow up the status and progress of their ideas, ideas handled in a transparent way	<S9>
[13]	• providing transparency to the organization's innovation related internal workings	<S9>

(*continued*)

Table 9. (*continued*)

Publications	Related focal points	*Our research*
[20]	• transparent idea screening criteria	<S3>
[19]	• Potential measures in different business performance perspectives: flexibility of decision-making with effective information flows, effectiveness of problem-solving with history information	<S4>
[18]	• Individual employees have open possibilities to access and acquire relevant information and competence to generate ideas.	<S8>
Innovation Management and Information/Knowledge Management IT Tools (RQ3)		
[17]	• IT tools enabling systematic and efficient handling of ideas	<S9>
[20]	• IT platform contributions to the innovation process by involving different stakeholders for idea generation and decision-making (cross-functional, cross-department innovation)	<S10>
[5]	• ubiquitous idea management systems accessible anywhere at any time and through different media channels, allowing distributed staff to participate in the ideation	<S2>
[18]	• data utilization with accessible and integrated IT systems	<S11>

By and large our empirical case study results tend to correspond with the related research. However, our contribution is to frame the individual items with respect to the whole innovation process (from ideation to R&D and business) and the organizational continuous innovation capability as portrayed by our research questions (RQ1–3).

Our research contributes to the knowledge gaps and research needs identified in the prior works (Sect. 2). With this industrial in-depth case study we have portrayed how a continuously innovating company looks like and in what ways the company has been developing its innovativeness. We have compiled a set of statements and propositions for explaining mechanisms affecting innovation performance. Furthermore, we have examined how certain performance metrics (KPIs) manifest themselves in practical innovation activities. We have already analyzed them in our previous works [12].

5.3 Implications

Managerial Implications. In general, all the items in Tables 6, 7 and 8 have some managerial impacts and concerns. Consequently, companies should contemplate them from their points of view. However, in our view – informed by the case company insights – particular managerial emphasis should be put on the people-related and organization culture items like suggested in Table 10.

Efficient information systems (IT tools) can be developed and utilized to support to implement the suggestions in Table 10 in practice. That is particularly central in order to achieve the benefits of transparency across the entire organization and in real time. Moreover, the information systems facilitate building and cultivating versatile and

Table 10. Primary managerial implications stemming from the empirical observations and findings.

Statements	Implications
(not shown in Table 5)	Trigger increasing the amount of harvested ideas is by *collecting ideas systematically*, *sharing them among stakeholders* and *learning from them* throughout the life-cycle
<S1>	Encourage employees to participate more actively in the innovation process by keeping *threshold to submit ideas low* and by incorporating the *ideation process into the operative contexts*
<S2>	Raise employee confidence in regard to submitting ideas by using *ubiquitous ideation practice*
(not shown in Table 5)	Create pull toward the overall innovation process by continuous *transparency of harvested ideas*, continuous *communication of innovation targets and strategic business needs*, and through constructive *feedback by managers and experts*
(not shown in Table 5)	Foster and steer people to contribute with relevant business ideas by *transparent and integrated idea-related information*
<S10>	Engage relevant stakeholders and critical specialists to participate in the idea development by *transparent feedback*

integrated organizational memory over time. They furthermore support engaging intra-organizational networking of people and knowledge.

With respect to transparency, it is important to consider both the ideas-related information transparency (e.g., business cases) and the innovation process transparency (e.g., screening). Considering the former type of transparency, not only the visible information in information systems but also tacit knowledge and informal (even face-to-face) communications are relevant. One of our findings was for instance that some ideas submitted to the Ideas Tool were seen to be already in the first stage thought-out and mature suggesting that the ideators may have discussed intensively with their colleagues and interacted with the business owners and domain experts already before submitting their ideas formally.

In the innovation process transparent idea handling may increase awareness and accountability between management and employees. In our case company in the ideation campaigns (c.f., Fig. 3) business owners and technology experts communicated needs and targets in pitches. It was possible to submit ideas face-to-face and to get immediate feedback from the business owners. The frequent screening and idea reviews were perceived to be (interview quote) "the engine of the innovation process". Every new idea was assigned to relevant specialists to foster discussion for the idea to grow further and to find relevant owners.

In all, it is important to realize that continuously high innovation performance requires that the entire value network of idea generation, idea development, R&D, and commercialization works successfully. Inefficiencies or obstacles in any of the above elements may lower the total innovation system performance. The grand challenge for each organization is to realize their full innovation potential and to be able to fully utilize it.

Theoretical Implications. Exploratory case studies are typically conducted as initial investigations to derive new hypotheses and build theories. In the early stages of our research work we have asked exploratory research questions in order to understand the phenomena of and around continuous innovation (RQ1) in practical industrial organization context. In doing so we have tentatively attempted to identify and understand the key concepts, constructs, and their relations. Transparency (RQ2) and IT tool support (RQ3) have been our particular key elements of interests.

The statements in Table 5 can be elaborated and formulated as generalized propositions. The following exemplifies that (see <S1> in Table 5):

- **Proposition 1a**: when *Threshold to submit ideas low and by not isolating ideation process away from the operative context => Employees participate more actively in the process*
- **Proposition 1b**: when *Not isolating ideation process away from the operative context => Employees participate more actively in the process*
- **Proposition 1c**: when *Employees participate more actively in the process* => Improved innovation performance

These propositions can be tested as hypotheses in future research (confirmatory case studies). Naturally they must be operationalized with testable measures, such as our KPIs in Table 2. Such tests could also explain our observed trends in Fig. 3.

5.4 Limitations and Threats to Validity

This study is based on a single-case setting and was conducted within one company context. The case selection stems from our long-term research collaboration relationships with the company (convenience sampling). We acknowledge that this may have caused some sampling bias. We also refrain from evaluating how representative our case company is within the industry sector. Multiple-case analysis could provide stronger support for theory development [25].

During the data analysis we did not have direct access to the company's confidential information of the individual idea items. Statistical analysis was thus not possible. We were also not able to detail either the types of different ideas (i.e., product, process, organizational, business) or the radicalness of the innovations. The plan was also to measure and analyze concrete examples of radical innovations in the future. However, that was not realized due to the confidentiality of the actual company business needs and the performance information. Overall, the innovation process improvement was aiming to increase the share of business innovations in the long term. Based on the results from first two years (2015–2016, c.f., Fig. 3) the new innovation approach could be seen to be effective as the share of business innovations has been constantly raising. However, it is for further study to confirm such cause–effect relationships (propositions in Sect. 5.3).

We recognize certain threats to validity [23]. Considering the construct validity, one particular threat may be that we did not present any specific definition of 'transparency' (RQ2). Internal validity may be a concern when causal relations are investigated. In this study we have extracted propositions with some suggestions for possible cause–effect relations. However, we do not confirm them decisively here. With respect to the external validity the intention of the presented propositions is to enable analytical generalization for extending to cases in other companies with similar characteristics. Finally, the data collection interviews (see Table 3) were mostly conducted by the same one researcher. They were semi-structured, some of them with partially informal interview protocols and only manual note-taking. Those may be concerns for the reliability.

6 Conclusions

In this empirical study we have investigated how one established industrial high-technology B2B company has fostered continuous innovation with people-engaging, transparent IT tool-supported information sharing. A longitudinal, single case study was performed in the case company which was conducting significant changes in innovation practices at the time.

Grounded on the collected empirical data in the single-case company context we compiled a set of statements and propositions of the continuous innovation process and its performance factors. By and large our results and findings align with the previous related research. However, we emphasize the subtle, agile and lean organizational factors of orienting and encouraging employees for creative but fitting idea generation, and engaging key experts and business stakeholders to idea development at right times in a transparent manner. These work in conjunction to transparent innovation process practices (e.g., screening) and information sharing IT tools. Potential performance measurements (KPIs) for continuous innovation process improvement have been evaluated in this case.

We suggest further research for comparable analysis and business performance measures, in particular with respect to knowledge creation and utilization to harness the full innovation capability and its business performance effects. Our future research plans are to expand the case with additional industrial cases of innovation capability development. Cross-case analysis would make it possible to compare and contrast our statements (Table 5) in more general and test the propositions (Sect. 5.3).

References

1. Ormala, E., Tukiainen, S., Mattila, J.: Industrial Innovation in Transition. Aalto University, Helsinki (2014)
2. Tuulenmäki, A., Välikangas, L.: The art of rapid, hands-on execution innovation. Strat. Lead. **39**, 28–35 (2011)
3. Smeds, R., Boer, H.: Continuous innovation and learning in industrial organizations. Knowl. Process. Manag. **11**(4), 225–227 (2004)
4. Tonnesen, T.: Continuous innovation through company wide employee participation. TQM Mag. **17**(2), 195–207 (2005)
5. Pikkarainen, M., Codenie, W., Boucart, N., Heredia Alvaro, J.A. (eds.): The Art of Software Innovation: Eight Practice Areas to Inspire Your Business. Springer, Heidelberg (2011). https://doi.org/10.1007/978-3-642-21049-5

6. Paju, S.: Managing uncertainty in innovative projects: alternative for causal project plans. In: Huizingh, E., Conn, S., Torkkeli, M., Bitran, I. (eds.) Proceedings of the XXV ISPIM Conference (2014)
7. O'Connor, G.C., DeMartino, R.: Organizing for radical innovation: an exploratory study of the structural aspects of RI management systems in large established firms. J. Prod. Innov. Manag. **23**, 475–497 (2006)
8. Boer, H., et al.: Knowledge and continuous innovation: the CIMA methodology. Int. J. Oper. Prod. Manag. **21**(4), 490–503 (2001)
9. Björk, J., Karlsson, M.P., Magnusson, M.: Turning ideas into innovation – introducing demand-driven collaborative ideation. Int. J. Innov. Reg. Dev. **5**, 429–442 (2014)
10. Denning, S.: Reinventing management: the practices that enable continuous innovation. Strat. Lead. **39**(3), 16–24 (2011)
11. Berner, M., Augustine, J., Maedche, A.: The impact of process visibility on process performance: a multiple case study of operations control centres in ITSM. Bus. Inf. Syst. Eng. **58**(1), 31–42 (2016)
12. Teppola, S., Kettunen, P., Matinlassi, M., Partanen, J.: Transparency of Information to Improve Continuous Innovation Experimentation Performance. In: 17th International CINet Conference. Continuous Innovation Network (CINet) (2016)
13. Edison, H., Bin Ali, N., Torkar, R.: Towards innovation measurement in the software industry. J. Syst. Softw. **86**, 1390–1407 (2013)
14. Gertsen, F.: Editorial: continuous innovation. Int. J. Technol. Manag. **26**(8), 801–804 (2003)
15. Boer, H., Kuhn, J., Gertsen, F.: Continuous innovation. Managing dualities through co-ordination. Continuous Innovation Network, Working Paper Series WP2006-1 (2006)
16. Saunila, M.: Managing continuous innovation through performance measurement. Compet. Rev. **27**(2), 179–190 (2017)
17. Sandström, C., Björk, J.: Idea management systems for a changing innovation landscape. Int. J. Prod. Dev. **11**, 310–324 (2010)
18. Väyrynen, H.: Constructing Innovativeness in the Organization: Knowledge Management and Information Technology Management Perspective. Dissertations 77. Tampere University, Finland (2019)
19. Saunila, M., Ukko, J.: A conceptual framework for the measurement of innovation capability and its effects. Balt. J. Manag. **7**(4), 355–375 (2012)
20. Elerud-Tryde, A., Hooge, S.: Beyond the generation of ideas: virtual idea campaigns to spur creativity and innovation. Creat. Innov. Manag. **23**(3), 290–302 (2014)
21. Partanen, J., Matinlassi, M.: Applying agile and lean elements to accelerate innovation culture in a large organization – key learnings after one year journey. In: Lassenius, C., Dingsøyr, T., Paasivaara, M. (eds.) XP 2015. LNBIP, vol. 212, pp. 262–269. Springer, Cham (2015). https://doi.org/10.1007/978-3-319-18612-2_26
22. Yin, R.K.: Case Study Research: Design and Methods. SAGE Publications, Los Angeles (2003)
23. Runeson, P., Höst, M.: Guidelines for conducting and reporting case study research in software engineering. Empir. Softw. Eng. **14**, 131–164 (2009)
24. Seaman, C.B.: Qualitative methods in empirical studies of software engineering. IEEE Trans. Softw. Eng. **25**(4), 557–572 (1999)
25. Eisenhardt, K.M., Graebner, M.E.: Theory building from cases: opportunities and challenges. Acad. Manag. J. **50**(1), 25–32 (2007)

Change Management Practices for Continuous Delivery - A Systematic Literature Mapping

Telcio Elui Cardoso(✉), Alan R. Santos, Rafael Chanin, and Afonso Sales

School of Technology, PUCRS, Porto Alegre, RS 90619-900, Brazil
telcio.cardoso@edu.pucrs.br
{alan.santos,rafael.chanin,afonso.sales}@pucrs.br

Abstract. The agility proposed by new software development practices such as Continuous Delivery and Continuous Deployment may introduce challenges to the teams who adopt such practices. One of these challenges is the change management process. The goal of this systematic literature mapping is to understand which change management practices are used in environments that adopted CDE or CD, focused on practices that could benefit application support teams, an important stakeholder in the software development life-cycle. Our study indicates the change management practices, in environments where CDE and CD have been adopted, have not been deeply explored and documented, an opportunity for future researches.

Keywords: Continuous Delivery · Continuous Deployment · Agile Software Development · Change Management · Knowledge Management · Software Configuration Management · Application Support

1 Introduction

There is a general pressure in the software industry for ever shorter development cycles, and this is particularly pronounced in highly competitive, market-driven sectors [16].

In this context of agility, software engineering approaches, such as Continuous Delivery (CDE) and Continuous Deployment (CD), have evolved in the recent years to support agile software development practices. Environments where software changes are continuously delivered to users, might be challenging from a Change Management perspective. The goal of this study is to perform a literature systematic mapping [10], in order to understand which practices of change management are used by companies who adopted Continuous Delivery and Continuous Deployment practices on their software development processes.

S. Hyrynsalmi et al. (Eds.): ICSOB 2019, LNBIP 370, pp. 175–182, 2019.
https://doi.org/10.1007/978-3-030-33742-1_14

2 Background

In this section we present the main concepts regarding Continuous Delivery, Continuous Deployment and Change Management, and define a problem statement.

2.1 Continuous Delivery

Continuous Delivery (CDE) is the practice of ensuring that software is always ready to be deployed. It relies on the principle of creating and delivering products to customers, in small releases.

The concept of Continuous Delivery became popular after the launch of the book *Continuous Delivery: Reliable Software Releases Through Build, Test and Deployment Automation* [14], in August of 2010, and, since then, several companies have adopted its principles and practices. The foundation of CDE is the deployment pipeline, which, in essence, is an automated implementation of its application's build, deploy, test, and release process [14].

2.2 Continuous Deployment

According to Pittet [18], Continuous Deployment (CD) goes one step further than CDE. With this practice, every change that passes all stages of the production pipeline is released to customers. There is no human intervention, and only a failed test will prevent a new change to be deployed to production.

2.3 Software Configuration Management

The Change Management process, in Software Engineering, consists in requesting, determining attainability, planning, implementing and evaluating the changes in a given system [15].

Given the inevitability of change, stakeholders should agree on the means by which requirements and scope are to be reviewed and revised (for example, change management procedures, iterative cycle retrospectives) [16].

Software configuration management (SCM) is a supporting-software life cycle process that benefits project management, development and maintenance activities, quality assurance activities, as well as the customers and users of the end product. SCM procedures should provide verification, validation, and audit of each step required to identify, authorize, implement, and release the software product [16].

According to Parnin et al. [19], companies such as Netflix and Facebook perform deployments of their products in ranges from 1,000 times daily to once or twice yearly.

Considering such change management needs, how companies, which practice CDE and CD, such as Netflix and Facebook, keep their main stakeholders up to date regarding the changes introduced to their software, every new deploy? Based on this question, in the following section we state the problem this study aims to answer.

2.4 Problem Statement

A software release may introduce changes or new functionalities to an existing application, which may require specific documentation to help end users to use such features or to better understand the changes introduced. In this context, application support teams are key stakeholders, being the bridge between end users and development teams, by providing guidance on how to better use such applications as well as by being responsible for recording and documenting bugs and feature requests reported by end users [17].

Considering the importance of application support teams in the software development and maintenance life-cycle, it is important to understand how application support teams are communicated and trained in order to be up to date regarding changes introduced on applications, in environments where Agile, Continuous Delivery and Continuous Deployment practices were adopted, and where several new software releases are delivered to end users on a daily basis, that is the case for companies such as Netflix and Facebook, which perform deployments of their products on a range of 1,000 times daily [19].

In order to better understand the problem stated, we have performed a literature systematic mapping according to Petersen et al. [10]. In the following section, we provide further details about the research method adopted for this study.

3 Research Method

In order to understand the impacts of CDE and CD on application support teams, we applied a literature systematic mapping [10,13] to the Software Engineering area. In order to drive our research, the following research questions were defined:

RQ1: *How the adoption of Agile Software Development, Continuous Delivery or Continuous Deployment practices impact Application Support Teams?*
RQ2: *Which Change Management practices are used by software development teams that adopted Agile Software Development, Continuous Delivery or Continuous Deployment?*

The search terms were defined based on the main terms related to the subject of this research and structured in terms of population, intervention, comparison, and outcome [12]. Based on these terms, the final search string used in this study is presented in Table 1.

Table 1. Search string

Type	String
Population	(software engineering OR software development) AND
Intervention	(continuous deployment OR continuous delivery OR agile methods OR agile development OR agile software development) AND
Outcome	Change management

Relevant keywords that may describe Application Support teams, such as *"Application Support"*, *"Service Desk"* and *"Help Desk"*, were initially part of the search string. However, they have restricted the results to a very few number of studies. Therefore, in order to ensure we would not miss relevant studies, these keywords were removed from the search string and non-relevant studies were discarded in the subsequent steps of the systematic mapping.

The following inclusion and exclusion criteria were applied as described in Table 2.

Table 2. Exclusion/inclusion criteria

Type	Description
Exclusion	Event keynotes, summaries, extended abstracts
Exclusion	Papers with less than 4 pages
Exclusion	Year lower than 2010
Exclusion	Language different than English
Exclusion	Bibliometrics and Courses

3.1 The Process

Following a systematic mapping process, the research questions were used to search for relevant information on the IEEE, ACM and Scopus online databases. Our initial search results returned 605 articles, which were filtered according to the steps described in Fig. 1 resulting on nine full papers read.

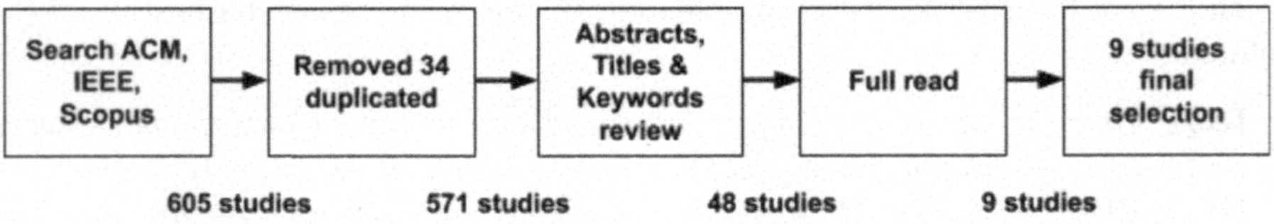

Fig. 1. Search steps

The systematic mapping process allowed us to select relevant studies related to the researched area, which will have the results presented in the following sections.

4 Results

Our systematic mapping process resulted in nine studies, which could provide insights to answer the questions **RQ1** and **RQ2**, formulated in the beginning of this research (Sect. 3). Table 3 shows the nine studies selected as part of the systematic mapping process.

In the following section we provide details about the nine studies evaluated.

Table 3. Selected studies

ID	Title	Author	Year
1	Challenges in agile software development: A systematic literature review	Fitriani, W. R., Rahayu, P	2016
2	Knowledge Management in Agile Software Development	Indumini, U., Vasanthapriyan, S	2018
3	Analyzing the modes of communication in agile practices	Bhalerao, S., Ingle, M	2010
4	The Challenges of Staying Together While Moving Fast: An Exploratory Study	Rubin, J., Rinard, M	2016
5	A Framework for Managing Mission Needs, Compliance, and Trust in the DevOps Environment	Farroha, B., Farroha, D	2014
6	Systematic literature review on the impacts of agile release engineering practices	Karvonen, T., Behutiye, W., Oivo, M., Kuvaja, P	2017
7	Agile development as a change management approach in software projects: Applied case study	Alawairdhi, M	2016
8	Obstacles in moving to agile software development methods; At a Glance	Gandomani, T., Zulzalil, H., Ghani, A., Sultan, M., Nafchi, M	2013
9	Perceived productivity threats in large agile development projects	Hannay, J., Benestad, H	2010

5 Discussion

In order to answer RQ1 we will describe some of the agile influcences on CD as part of this section. According to Alawairdhi [11], in agile environments, it is vital to make sure that quick knowledge sharing is ensured between various stakeholders, which was something extremely difficult in face of strict and quick deadlines. Furthermore, according to the author, communication between end-users, project managers and team members had a profound impact in the project progress.

According to Indumini et al. [1] knowledge transfer in Agile Software Development (ASD) is a recent research and knowledge types which are used in ASD are not identified correctly in the organizations. The author highlighted the main benefits of Knowledge Management in Agile Software Development, such as the increase of effectiveness, competitive advantages, cost reduction and productivity increase.

In the study conducted by Bhalerao et al. [3] the author concludes that email provides the most convenient and cost effective mode of communication in Agile Software Development (ASD) projects and as well in global and distributed software teams.

According to the study conducted by Rubin et al. [5], the pressure to deliver new products and functionalities to the market imposes several challenges related to documentation and communication to the development teams. Furthermore, according to the challenges, based on the survey results of this study, the author mentions the vast majority of participants mentioned issues related to the collaborative nature of the work: availability and discoverability of documented knowledge, communication within and between teams, coordination and integration with work produced by others.

Farroha et al. [6] emphasizes the importance of having development and operations teams working closer in order to support the business competitiveness and velocity, presenting a DevOps (Development and Operations) framework. According to the authors, the implementation of a DevOps framework brings several benefits, being one of them the collaboration and communication between Development and Operations teams, which at the end, implies in more reliable releases to the end-users.

According to Karvonen et al. [7], in Agile Release Engineering (ARE), changes do not break the user experience, therefore, the user can fluently adopt the changes and continue using the product/service normally, otherwise, proper notifications and training should be given to the user. Such statement suggests that just some product changes may require formal user notification and training. However, in some cases, even minor changes, may have impact on knowledge management practices, such as end-user documentation, which is also used by application support teams and has to reflect exactly what is available to the end users.

Gandomani et al. [4], evaluated the challenges of adopting agile software development and emphasized the importance of documentation and the challenges of documentation and knowledge management in ASD. According to the author, in ASD documentation is limited and knowledge is mostly tacit and reside in the head of the development team members. This challenge could be decreased by defining appropriate knowledge management strategy and distribution of knowledge in different level of organization. In the study conducted by Hannay et al. [8], a large agile project has been used to evaluate productivity aspects. The author explores some productivity threads faced by a large agile project, emphasizing the importance of communication in such environments.

According to Fitriani et al. [2], the key barriers to adopt agile are usually associated with culture, including company culture, change management, resistance to change, and management support. Moreover, according to the author, documentation, customer, training and communication are some of the agile software development challenges. Table 4 summarizes the insights provided by the articles analyzed.

In this sense, based on the analysis of the selected studies in order to answer RQ2 we have build a list of Change Management practices available at Table 4.

Table 4. Change management practices

ID	Insight	Author
1	Distributed environments may represent a challenge for face-to-face communication	Bhalerao et al. [3], Gandomani et al. [4]
2	Email as a common and cost effective communication channel	Bhalerao et al. [3]
3	Artifacts such as user-stories and use cases could be used to communicate changes to Application Support Teams	Bhalerao et al. [3]
4	Development and Application Support teams working closer through DevOps practices	Farroha et al. [6]
5	Changes that don't break the user experience may not require notifications and training	Karvonen et al. [7]

6 Conclusions

Challenges of agile software development, such as communication, change management and knowledge management were commonly cited in the articles analyzed. However, even providing relevant insights, none of the studies answered the main questions we had, which suggests this is an area which still requires further research. Most of the studies analyzed by this research, focused on software development teams and end-users as being the key stakeholders in the software development life-cycle. However, other stakeholders are part of this process. Therefore, the impact of CDE and CD practices adoption on other stakeholders could be further explored by future research.

Change Management challenges, more specifically documentation and knowledge sharing, in ASD, CDE and CD environments, could be further explored by additional researches, once, based on this study, the practices adopted by the market remain unclear.

References

1. Indumini, U., Vasanthapriyan, S.: Knowledge management in agile software development- a literature review. In: 2018 National Information Technology Conference (NITC), pp. 1–7 (2018)
2. Fitriani, W. R., Rahayu, P., Sensuse, D.I.: Challenges in agile software development: a systematic literature review. In: 2016 International Conference on Advanced Computer Science and Information Systems (ICACSIS), pp. 155–164 (2016)
3. Bhalerao, S., Ingle, M.: Analyzing the modes of communication in agile practices. In: 2010 3rd International Conference on Computer Science and Information Technology, pp. 391–395 (2010)
4. Gandomani, T., Zulzalil, H., Ghani, A., Sultan, M., Nafchi, M.: Obstacles in moving to agile software development methods: at a Glance. J. Comput. Sci. **9**(5), 620–625 (2013)

5. Rubin, J., Rinard, M.: The challenges of staying together while moving fast: an exploratory study. In: 2016 IEEE/ACM 38th International Conference on Software Engineering (ICSE), pp. 982–993 (2016)
6. Farroha, B., Farroha, D.: A framework for managing mission needs, compliance, and trust in the DevOps environment. In: 2014 IEEE Military Communications Conference, pp. 288–293 (2014)
7. Karvonen, T., Behutiye, W., Oivo, M., Kuvaja, P.: Systematic literature review on the impacts of agile release engineering practices. In: 2017 Information and Software Technology, pp. 87–100 (2017)
8. Hannay, J., Benestad, H.: Perceived productivity threats in large agile development projects. In: Proceedings of the 2010 ACM-IEEE International Symposium on Empirical Software Engineering and Measurement, pp. 1–10 (2010)
9. Hasnain, E.: An overview of published agile studies: a systematic literature review. In: Proceedings of the 2010 National Software Engineering Conference, pp. 3:1–3:6 (2010)
10. Petersen, K., Feldt, R., Mujtaba, S., Mattsson, M.: Systematic mapping studies in software engineering. In: Proceedings of the 12th International Conference on Evaluation and Assessment in Software Engineering, pp. 68–77 (2008)
11. Alawairdhi, M.: Agile development as a change management approach in software projects: applied case study. In: Proceedings of 2016 International Conference on Information Management, pp. 1–5 (2016)
12. Kitchenham, B.: Procedures for undertaking systematic reviews. Technical Report TR/SE-0401. Department of Computer Science, Keele University and National ICT, Australia Ltd., Joint Technical Report (2004)
13. Bailey, J., Budgen, D., Turner, M., Kitchenham, B., Brereton, P., Linkman, S.: Evidence relating to object-oriented software design: a survey. In: Proceedings of the 1st International Symposium on Empirical Software Engineering and Measurement (ESEM 2007), pp. 482–484 (2007)
14. Humble, J., Farley, D.: Continuous Delivery. Pearson Education, London (2010)
15. Crnkovic, I., Asklund, U., Dahlqvist, A.: Implementing and Integrating Product Data Management and Software Configuration Management. Artech House Computing Library), Artech Print on Demand (2003)
16. Bourque, P., Fairley, R.: SWEBOK v3.0: Guide to the Software Engineering Body of Knowledge. IEEE Computer Society Products and Services (2018)
17. Steinberg, R.: Service Operation ITIL, Version 3. Stationery Office (2011)
18. Atlassian. https://www.atlassian.com/continuous-delivery/principles/continuous-integration-vs-delivery-vs-deployment. Accessed June 2019
19. Parnin, C., et al.: The top 10 adages in continuous deployment. IEEE Software **34**, 86–95 (2017)

Leveraging Business Transformation with Machine Learning Experiments

David Issa Mattos[1(✉)], Jan Bosch[1], and Helena Holmström Olsson[2]

[1] Department of Computer Science and Engineering, Chalmers University of Technology, Hörselgången 11, 412 96 Göteborg, Sweden
{davidis, jan.bosch}@chalmers.se

[2] Department of Computer Science and Media Technology, Malmö University, Nordenskiöldsgatan, 211 19 Malmö, Sweden
helena.holmstrom.olsson@mau.se

Abstract. The deployment of production-quality ML solutions, even for simple applications, requires significant software engineering effort. Often, companies do not fully understand the consequences and the business impact of ML-based systems, prior to the development of these systems. To minimize investment risks while evaluating the potential business impact of an ML system, companies can utilize continuous experimentation techniques. Based on action research, we report on the experience of developing and deploying a business-oriented ML-based dynamic pricing system in collaboration with a home shopping e-commerce company using a continuous experimentation (CE) approach. We identified a set of generic challenges in ML development that we present together with tactics and opportunities.

Keywords: Machine learning · Continuous experimentation · Retail industry · Dynamic pricing · Business transformation

1 Introduction

The deployment of production-quality ML solutions, even for simple applications. is a complex task that requires significant software engineering effort [1]. Many companies fail to fully understand the consequences and the business impact of ML-based systems, prior to the development of these systems. However, in order to minimize investment risks while evaluating the potential business impact of an ML system, both software and non-software companies can utilize continuous experimentation (CE) techniques [2]. CE allows companies to systematically develop and evaluate solutions, based on early prototypes and field data. The combination of ML development with CE can guide companies towards investing in solutions that have a real business impact.

Based on action research, we report on the experience of developing and deploying a business-oriented ML-based dynamic pricing system in collaboration with a home shopping e-commerce company using a continuous experimentation (CE) approach.

S. Hyrynsalmi et al. (Eds.): ICSOB 2019, LNBIP 370, pp. 183–191, 2019.
https://doi.org/10.1007/978-3-030-33742-1_15

In this research, we identified a set of generic challenges in ML development that we present together with tactics and opportunities. These challenges, tactics and opportunities can aid other companies in directing their efforts and overcoming known challenges during the planning the development of ML systems on business units.

2 Background and Related Work

Continuous Experimentation. The basic idea behind CE is to constantly formulate hypotheses for which experiments can be built, measured and evaluated so companies can make better development and business decisions. Each experiment generates learnings that can be used for further experiments and help to both identify and better prioritize new hypotheses [3]. CE is used to evaluate from prototypes, new products and features to smaller product changes [3, 4]. One of the methods to operationalize CE is the HYPEX (Hypothesis Experiment Data-Driven Development) model [4]. The HYPEX model is a development process model for companies aiming to shorten the feedback loop to customers. Instead of spending engineering efforts on large pieces of functionality that were not validated by customers, the HYPEX model reinforces the need for an iterative and incremental approach in what is called Minimal Viable Feature (MVF). MVF is the smallest possible part to implement a feature that can be measured, deployed and that adds value to the customers. Although there are other models for CE, this work utilizes the HYPEX model in the CE approach.

Dynamic Pricing in the Retail Industry. Dynamic pricing, also known as demand pricing, is a pricing strategy in which the company sets flexible prices for the products based on market demands. This strategy allows companies to increase or maintain a profit margin while reducing losses generated by having an excess stock level or the loss of having an under-stock level. Time-based dynamic pricing has been extensively used in industry with examples in airline companies, Uber and Amazon. Dynamic pricing consists of two main continuous activities, the first is the price-based demand forecasting that investigates the price demand elasticity of the products. The second activity consists of optimizing the price based on a utility function given a set of constraints. ML is extensively used in the first activity, as often other factors beyond price influence in the product demand [5, 6].

3 Research Method

The goal of this research is to understand the business impact of deploying an ML system in the retail industry and how CE can support this process. We conducted a collaborative action research (AR) [7] study with a home shopping and e-commerce company on the deployment of an ML-based system, from June 2018 to June 2019. The case company is a home shopping and e-commerce company based in one of the Nordic countries. The company is one of the leading e-commerce companies in the Nordics but also operates other European and Asian markets.

1 - Understanding the Problem and the Context
The company sees an increased need to combining both internal and external data sources to increase the confidence in their prediction systems not only to capture new product and consumer trends but also to avoid both under and overestimations of product demand. We started this research understanding and discussing ways of providing better stock estimates and profit for the end-of-season sale utilizing data analytics and ML. In this first step, we conducted a workshop with a duration of 4 h and involving nine stakeholders. In this workshop, we discussed the problems, the context and we prioritized several ideas in terms of feasibility and return on investment.

2 - Creating Hypotheses and Planning Interventions
We decided to move towards a dynamic pricing strategy already adopted by several industries, as it provided a faster return on investment, involved a smaller number of stakeholders while generating new expertise in applying ML and data analytics to the decision process. In this step, we conducted a second workshop with a duration of 3 h and involving 6 stakeholders. In this second workshop, we scoped and refined the dynamic pricing application limiting it to a group of products in the Christmas markdown period and planned a timeline for the implementation of the system.

3 - Applying the Intervention
During the development of the dynamic pricing MVP, we conducted bi-weekly meetings to refine the solution scope and to understand how it could be integrated and used in the business units. These meetings were conducted with business planners and IT specialists of the case company. Additionally, the case company shared relevant historical data to test and train the pricing system prior to deployment.

4 - Evaluating the Interventions
We evaluated the system utilizing both qualitative data from the business planners and the control and purchase manager, and quantitative data comparing how the system performed in historical data and in live data. The quantitative analysis was done as an experiment in the CE approach and is presented in the online appendix.

5 - Reflecting on the Results
In this report, we present our reflections of this experience together with identified challenges, tactics and open problems. Reflections on the CE process and discussion on the dynamic pricing solution are presented in the online appendix.

Data Collection and Analysis. We identified the challenges and tactics based on thematic coding on recurring themes seen in meeting notes, discussions with multiple stakeholders, as well as reflections in the software development process. For some of these challenges, we provided tactics and lessons learned from both our experience as well as from other academic research works, while the other challenges are still open challenges and present opportunities for both research and engineering.

Validity Considerations. Our research was conducted in close collaboration with the case company and it is dependent on the context of the company. In Sect. 4, we tried to abstract the observed challenges to a broader context in triangulation with existing research. However, some discussion points might be applicable only non-software development units and to the retail industry. In conjunction with the online appendix, we describe the context, the problem, the results and decision points throughout this research process aiming at making it recoverable to interested outsiders [8].

4 Challenges Tactics and Opportunities

In this section, we discuss the identified challenges, tactics and opportunities identified from the collected data. The challenges were grouped in four themes: data, integration, assessment and model development challenges. Figure 1 summarizes the identified challenges and correspondent tactics.

1 - Model Development Challenges

The Trade-off Balance Between Model Accuracy and Explainability
Recent success stories in ML often present complex deep-learning and ensemble (aggregation of multiple models into a single one) models capable of making precise predictions and classifications based on several input sources and in highly unstructured data formats. However, we observed that in phases 2 and 3 of the AR, that the delivery speed and the explainability of the solution were more relevant than the accuracy of the model in the initial stages of the project. This creates a challenge to balance on how to balance the accuracy with explainability and development speed of the model.

Tactic: An initial and early prototype with a minimum viable model allowed the case company to understand what kind of data can be relevant and how they want to approach the integration with their existing systems and practices. We borrowed the term minimum viable model from CE literature to represent the simplest model capable of delivering value in the early prototype. Explainability helps to generate insights in the data for further refinement of the model and the process, as well as increasing trust in the solution and the application of an ML process in a traditional business area. If the solution is validated in terms of the delivered value, with the minimum viable model, the new insights into the data and the process can drive the refinement of the system

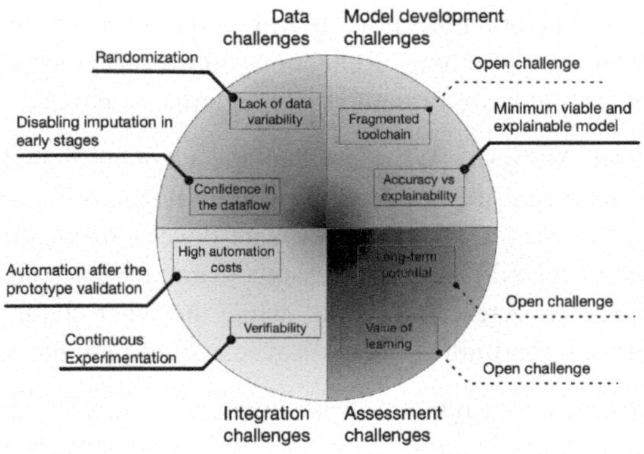

Fig. 1. Summary of the identified challenges and the correspondent tactics. The groups of challenges are represented by the different colors in the circle while the specific challenges are represented by boxes. A summary of the tactics is represented by the black lines. Open challenges are represented by the dotted line.

towards a more complex and accurate prediction model that has less explainability, e.g. deep-learning models. During this project, we utilized a minimum viable and explainable model based on the time series model ARMA-X (autoregressive moving average with exogenous variables).

Fragmented Toolchain Hinder ML Prototyping Activities
The business unit of the company utilizes an integrated business intelligence solution for their internal analysis, pricing strategies among others. However, the tool currently does not support the dynamic and custom analysis required by machine learning. This led to a very fragmented pipeline, from accessing market data, processing it and outputting the final result to the e-commerce platform. This fragmented toolchain slowed down the process as several steps required manually importing, converting and preparing data to be transferred between different software and increases cost in terms of training and licensing. A combination of these factors among others hinders the possibilities of business analysts to conduct ML experiments and test early prototype ideas.

Open Challenge: Recently, companies started pushing machine learning features into their business intelligence software. However, these tools often provide limited functionality and flexibility to be integrated seamlessly with the company process. An integrated toolchain of ML technologies with business tools would allow business analysts to quickly generate prototypes ML ideas to be experimented with. It is worth reinforcing that these solutions would not be integrated into a large-scale production system, but they could be used to make the first evaluation and gap analysis of ML ideas.

2 - Data Challenges

Lack of Data Variability
Training even the simplest models in ML requires some variability in the data for the whole prediction range (both dependent and independent variables) [9]. However, often issues with variability appear during the prototype development phase but can also occur during deployment. In this project, the historical data did not have enough variability for the full range of prices, therefore the prediction for some of these extreme ranges (30–50% discount) was not as good in terms of accuracy as for the rest of the range (0–30%). In this project for a few items in the beginning, we inserted randomized discounts in the 30–50% range, to introduce some variability in the data. Lack of data variability decreases the accuracy of the model, increases the development time and can delay the deployment of the MVP.

Tactic: Based on this experience, companies would benefit to analyze first if they have enough variability and run a simple randomization trial to generate variability on the data. This randomization procedure could be enough to give new insights into the data and better evaluate the gap and the potential benefits of the ML application. If combined with an experimental design, it can infer causal effects, giving a first evaluation of the hypothesis.

Lack of Confidence in the Dataflow Due to Missing and Duplicated Data
One of the challenges faced in this project during phase 2 and 3 was how to handle missing and duplicated data. Although this is a well-known challenge in research [9, 10], from the perspective of training ML models, companies need to investigate why and how data errors appear in the system. The occurrence of missing or duplicated data might be expected behavior, however, it can indicate problems in the dataflow and quality of the data. In phase 2 of the AR, one occurrence of missing data was due to the default settings of the business intelligence tool. In the case where a product hasn't sold any items on a particular day, the tool would exclude the item from the automated report. Although this is the preferred behavior for the company business analysts, it would introduce missing data and additional complexity for the MVP and the ML model.

Tactic: Understanding when missing and duplicated data appears in the system and knowing how to handle it helps to identify problems in the dataflow. Therefore, we suggest in the MVP stage to turn-off all automatically imputation methods for handling missing and duplicated data from the algorithms in the first iterations of the MVP, until the dataflow is validated, and these cases are well-understood.

3 - Integration Challenges

High Cost in the Integration and Automation of the Solution
One of the challenges often seen in machine learning applications is the complexity in integrating, deploying and scaling a solution [10, 11]. Integrating the different parts of the pipeline can require significant development effort and creates cost barriers when testing ideas and developing prototypes that depend on integration with larger external systems such as business intelligence tools. For non-development organizations, this software integration cost is often prohibitive in particular with prototyping solutions, since they might require external collaborators and can take a significant amount of time.

Tactic: Deploying manual solutions in the prototype stage (both input and output data are handled manually), helps to validate the dataflow, the process and the value delivered by an ML system with small cost compared to engineering effort of automating and integrating a non-validated application with in-house and third-party systems. As a tactic, we suggest that the tight integration and the automation of the dataflow should occur only after the solution is validated with an MVP.

Verifiability for Trustable Business Integration
The development of ML solutions that can impact the decision-making process needs to consider the verifiability of the solution. Verifiability refers to the fact that the whole ML solution and specifically the ML model can be verified in terms of the correctness of the dataflow, absence of data leakage [9], the accuracy of the prediction or classification accuracy and backtracking the decision to identify possible unintended feedback loops and data drifts. With respect to the ML models, some training algorithms and models are less dependent on initialization factors, random seeds and hyperparameters, and produce more consistent and verifiable models [12]. In the context of this project, verifiability was often discussed during phases 1–3 of the AR.

Tactic: For the business perspective, it is important to be able to trace back the decisions and verify the solution and models, especially if they do not deliver the expected value. One of the first aspects to be questioned in case of an unexpected output is the prediction model and the dataflow. If the root cause for the unexpected behavior cannot be identified, the analysts have less trust in the ML solution and are less likely to accept its output. Although verifiability depends on many different aspects, we suggest the usage of a CE process along with a simplified ML pipeline during the prototype. Combined with the other discussed tactics, the system is developed incrementally with continuous feedback from the business allowing faster alignment and increased trust in the solution.

4 - Assessment Challenges

Accounting for the Value of Learning
At the end of this project (phases 4 and 5 of the AR), the company evaluated the impact of the project and the experiment very positively. The developed system allowed the company to optimize their profit and validate the idea of utilizing a dynamic pricing solution in markdown sales. However, the case company decided not to use the solution. The ML dynamic pricing solution sparked a discussion into the analysis of how pricing determination was being made, which type of discounts should be applied to which products, the frequency on how price updates should be made and especially how customers behaved towards pricing. The challenge consists of how to evaluate the impact of a project even if the prototype is not shipped.

Open Challenge: The decision of not continuing investing in an ML system, or even if a prototype did not deliver the expected value, does not represent failure as the company can generate learnings and further iterate on other ideas [3]. Since these learnings can lead to deeper and more impactful business transformations beyond the developed prototype, it is still an open challenge how to quantify and assess the value of these learnings in the context of CE and ML.

Assessing the Long-Term Potential Value of the Prototype
CE can be used to assess the value of a prototype or changes in product in the short-term. However, it is hard to understand the benefits and negative impacts of an ML prototype for the long-term.

Open Challenge: The understanding and separation of short-term from long-term effects it is still an open research challenge. ML prototypes results of short-term metrics should be combined and triangulated with long-term observations from research from other fields. For the retail industry, factors such as psychological anchoring prices, perception in comparison with competition, brand image and effects on future markdowns can be impacted by such systems in the long-term [13]. For example, Levy et al. [13] discuss different effects of pricing strategies, indicating that customers already expect that products sold at fashion retailers will be priced lower than the suggested manufacturer retail price, a different market perception than 30 years ago. In the long-term, a dynamic pricing solution should account for this change, and the solution should be re-evaluated.

5 Conclusion

In this paper, we report on an action research study focusing on the experience of developing and deploying a business-oriented ML-based dynamic pricing system in collaboration with a home shopping and e-commerce company following a CE approach. We identified generic challenges, provided appropriated tactics and discussed opportunities for both engineering and research. In particular, we observed that the effort in building complex and precise models and in integrating and automating the ML system with the rest of the project can be wasted efforts if the delivered value of the ML system is not confirmed. Experiments with ML prototypes can lead companies to observe benefits more impactful than the accuracy of the model and potentially transform their business.

Acknowledgments. This work was partially supported by the Wallenberg Artificial Intelligence, Autonomous Systems and Software Program (WASP) funded by the Knut and Alice Wallenberg Foundation and by the Software Center.

Online Appendix

The online appendix, available at https://github.com/davidissamattos/icsob-2019, presents additional information regarding the CE process, the analysis of the experiment and the developed ML dynamic pricing system

References

1. Breck, E., Cai, S., Nielsen, E., Salib, M., Sculley, D.: The ML test score: a rubric for ML production readiness and technical debt reduction. In: Proceedings - 2017 IEEE International Conference Big Data, Big Data 2017, vol. 2018, pp. 1123–1132 (2018)
2. Lindgren, E., Münch, J.: Raising the odds of success: the current state of experimentation in product development. Inf. Softw. Technol. **77**, 80–91 (2016)
3. Fagerholm, F., et al.: The RIGHT model for continuous experimentation. J. Syst. Softw. **123**, 292–305 (2017)
4. Olsson, H.H., Bosch, J.: From opinions to data-driven software R&D: a multi-case study on how to close the 'Open Loop' problem. In: 2014 40th EUROMICRO Conference on Software Engineering and Advanced Applications, pp. 9–16 (2014)
5. Huang, H., Huang, H., Liu, Q.: Intelligent retail forecasting system for new clothing products considering stock-out. Fibres Text. East. Eur. **25**(121), 10–16 (2017)
6. Ferreira, K.J., Lee, B.H.A., Simchi-Levi, D.: Analytics for an online retailer: demand forecasting and price optimization. Manuf. Serv. Oper. Manag. **18**(1), 69–88 (2016)
7. Dos Santos, P.S.M., Travassos, G.H.: Action research can swing the balance in experimental software engineering. Adv. Comput. **83**, 205–276 (2011)
8. Checkland, P., Holwell, S.: Action research: its nature and validity. Syst. Pract. Action Res. **11**(1), 9–21 (1998)

9. Raj, A., Bosch, J., Olsson, H.H., Arpteg, A., Brinne, B.: Data management challenges for deep learning. In: 45th Euromicro Conference on Software Engineering and Advanced Applications (SEAA), pp. 1–8 (2019)
10. Lwakatare, L.E., Raj, A., Bosch, J., Olsson, H.H., Crnkovic, I.: Agile Processes in Software Engineering and Extreme Programming, vol. 149. Springer, Berlin (2013). https://doi.org/10.1007/978-3-642-38314-4
11. Sculley, D., et al.: Machine Learning : The High-Interest Credit Card of Technical Debt, pp. 1–9 (2014)
12. Pineau, J.: Building reproducible, reusable, and robust machine learning software. In: 41st ACM/IEEE International Conference on Software Engineering (ICSE 2019) (2019)
13. Levy, M., Grewal, D., Kopalle, P., Hess, J.: Emerging trends in retail pricing practice: implications for research. J. Retail. **80**(3), 13–21 (2004)

Intertwined Development of Business Model and Product Functions for Mobile Applications: A Twin Peak Feature Modeling Approach

Sebastian Gottschalk(✉), Florian Rittmeier, and Gregor Engels

Software Innovation Lab, Paderborn University, Paderborn, Germany
{sebastian.gottschalk,florianr,engels}@uni-paderborn.de

Abstract. Mobile app stores like Apple's AppStore or Google's PlayStore are highly competitive markets for third-party developers wanting to develop successful applications. During the development process, many developers focus on the multitude of product functions but neglect the business model as an equally important part. As a result, developers often fail to meet customer needs, leading to unnecessary development costs and poor market penetration. This, in turn, raises the question of how we intertwine the business model and product functions during the development process to ensure a better alignment between the two.

In this paper, we show this intertwined development by adapting the concept of Twin Peaks to the business model and product functions. Based on feature modeling as an abstraction layer, we introduce the concept of a Business Model Decision Line (BMDL) to structure the business model decisions and their relation to product functions structured in a Software Product Line (SPL). The basis of our feature models is the analysis of top listed applications in the app stores of Apple and Google. To create and modify both models, we provide an incremental feature structuring and iterative feature selection process. This combination of abstraction layer and development process supports third-party developers to build successful applications both from a business and a product perspective.

Keywords: Intertwined development · Twin peaks · Feature model · Business model · Product functions

1 Introduction

Mobile app stores are highly competitive markets for third-party developers. The analytics company AppAnnie [2] reports for 2018 that 194 billion apps are

This work was partially supported by the German Research Foundation (DFG) within the Collaborative Research Center "On-The-Fly Computing" (CRC 901, Project Number: 160364472SFB901).

S. Hyrynsalmi et al. (Eds.): ICSOB 2019, LNBIP 370, pp. 192–207, 2019.
https://doi.org/10.1007/978-3-030-33742-1_16

just downloaded from Apple's AppStore and Google's PlayStore which lead to revenues of $101 billion for paid apps and in-app purchases. Over 70% of this revenue is paid out to the third-party developers. With additional revenue from transactions outside the store and advertisements, the monetarization potential becomes even larger. In contrast to that, there are over 2 million apps in these stores and the average end-user uses less than 40 of them within a month. Moreover, Gartner [6] has predicted that in 2018 less than 0.01% apps would becoming financially successful, while 90% of the applications are downloaded less than 500 times (study not validated until September 2019). In order to develop a successful app, developers must consider both the business model and product functions [3]. For this intertwined development, a common abstraction layer is required, which is researched less due to the different application areas of business and product modeling.

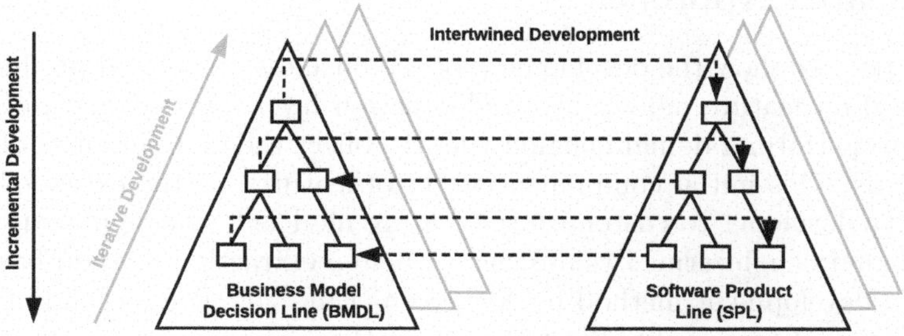

Fig. 1. Twin Peaks of BMDL-based business model and SPL-based product functions

In this paper, we show this intertwined development by adapting the concept of Tweak Peaks, which originally "intertwines software requirements and architectures to achieve incremental development and speedy delivery" [21]. Instead of the software requirements and the architectures, we intertwine the development of the business model and product functions, as seen in Fig. 1, by defining a structure and a development process. To abstract the business model and product functions due to the separation of concerns, we are using feature models as a structure. The corresponding development process is twofold: At the beginning, we create an initial structure using Incremental Development. After that, we update the structure with an Iterative Development based on customer needs.

The feature modeling of product functions can be done with the existing concept of a Software Product Line (SPL) which is a "set of software-intensive systems sharing a common, managed set of features that satisfy the specific needs of a particular market segment or mission and that are developed from a common set of core assets in a prescribed way" [4]. We adopt the concept of SPL to the structuring of the business model by creating a Business Model Decision Line (BMDL), where each feature represents a business model decision. The structure of the BMDL is based on the nine building blocks (Customer Segments, Value Proposition, Channels, Customer Relationships, Key Activities, Key Resources,

Key Partners, Revenue Streams, Cost Structure) of the widely-adopted Business Model Canvas [22] and is refined with a domain engineering of literature and top listed mobile applications. The domain engineering provides an initial set of features which can be extended by the third-party developer for his applications. We show the validity of our approach by providing concrete instances of our BMDL and SPL together with the development process based on a case study of streaming applications.

In the following, Sect. 2 describes our research approach to derive the BMDL and SPL. Section 3 shows both feature models by focussing on the BMDL as a new concept. The validity of both feature models is shown on concrete examples of streaming applications in Sect. 4. After that, in Sect. 5, we introduce the intertwined development based on Twin Peaks. Section 6 considers the related work. Finally, we give a conclusion in Sect. 7.

2 Research Approach

In the paper, we show the development of the business model and product functions based on feature models as an abstraction layer. For the feature models, we need to perform a domain engineering to collect the main features of mobile applications. This initial comprehensive set of features can be extended by the third-party developer to customize the feature models for his applications.

For domain engineering, we are using a 3-step extraction method based on a taxonomy development method by Nickerson et al. [20]. The method of Nickerson can be used to classify objects based on their common characteristics. We model each business model decision and product function as a characteristic of a mobile application. To use the method, we need to define meta-characteristics and ending conditions together with empirical-to-conceptual and conceptional-to-empirical iteration steps. The meta-characteristics are the most comprehensive characteristics that can be used as the basis for the choices in the taxonomy. Based on this meta-characteristics, we are running combinations of empirical-to-conceptional and conceptual-to-empirical iterations. After each iteration, the taxonomy is checked against objective and subjective ending conditions. While this section just briefly introduces the research approach, the intermediate results can be looked up in our technical report [9].

The creation process of the feature models consists of the initialization of the process, followed by three execution steps and ends with deriving of the feature models and the creation of the dependencies between them.

At the beginning of the process, we need to define the overall meta-characteristics together with the ending conditions. To model the business model decisions we are using the nine building blocks of the Business Model Canvas [22] as the most-comprehensive characteristics. We refine these blocks by the categories of the book Business Model Generation [22] to support the information extraction process. The objective ending conditions are the examination of all selected applications and papers for the corresponding execution step. As subjective conditions, we want to create an appropriate and cross-application usable model that can be easily extended by the third-party developer.

1. **Study Existing Material:** In the first step, we get an overview of different types of apps and their business models. Within the conceptual-to-empirical iteration, we analyze selected literature [5,7,10,15,18,19,23,26] from a literature search by Jazayeri et al. [13]. In the empirical-to-conceptual iteration, we look at the information of 150 apps[1] from the top lists of mobile ecosystems. Based on our updated taxonomy and different app categories, we select a comprehensive subset of the 150 applications to conduct a deeper analysis.
2. **Analyse Existing Applications:** In the second step, we conduct a deeper analysis of the product functions of the selected apps and their business model. In the conceptual-to-empirical iteration, we analyze business model decisions and product functions based on literature (e.g. analyses, news articles), which we obtain using Google Search. Within the empirical-to-conceptual iteration, we execute the apps and analyze their business model.
3. **Abstract Existing Features:** In the third step, we abstract the business model decisions and product functions to create a domain model for our taxonomy. This abstraction is especially relevant for the value propositions, which depend highly on the respective product functions. Moreover, we refine the naming and granularity of the features.

At the end of the process, we derive the feature models of the business model decisions and the product functions. Based on that, we create dependencies between these models. The result of the process is the BMDL and the corresponding SPL for the domain of mobile applications.

3 Business Model and Product Functions

In this section, we present the Business Model Decision Line (BMDL) together with the Software Product Line (SPL). While the construction and feature analysis for SPLs is well-studied in the literature [27], we focus on the BMDL. Based on the concept of Domain Engineering [27], we create a generic feature model for the construction of different business models. The model is based on an extractive product line approach, which is flexible enough to add new business model decisions in a reactive way [14].

For both feature models, we are using basic methods of hierarchical feature modeling (see Fig. 4 for a legend). Features can be mandatory or optional for the model instances. Moreover, there can be Or (at least one sub-feature is selected) and Alternate (exactly one sub-feature is selected) relationships between a parent and a child feature. To refine the model instance, cross-tree constraints for requiring and excluding dependencies can be made.

3.1 Business Model Decision Line

In this section, we present the Business Model Decision Line as the result of our analysis. In the beginning, we present the business model decisions by using

[1] Top 25 in Free, Paid and Grossing for Apple's App Store and Google Play Store.

the Business Model Canvas. After describing the translation from the canvas representation to a feature model, we describe important dependencies inside the feature model.

Canvas Representation. The canvas representation of the business model decisions can be seen in Fig. 2. As a structure, we are using the Business Model Canvas, which consists of nine building blocks. Due to the impact to the customer needs, we are focusing on the Value Propositions, Customer Segments, Customer Relationships, Channels and Revenue Streams in this paper. Nevertheless, the Key Partners, Key Activities, Key Resources and Cost Structures are described in our technical report [9].

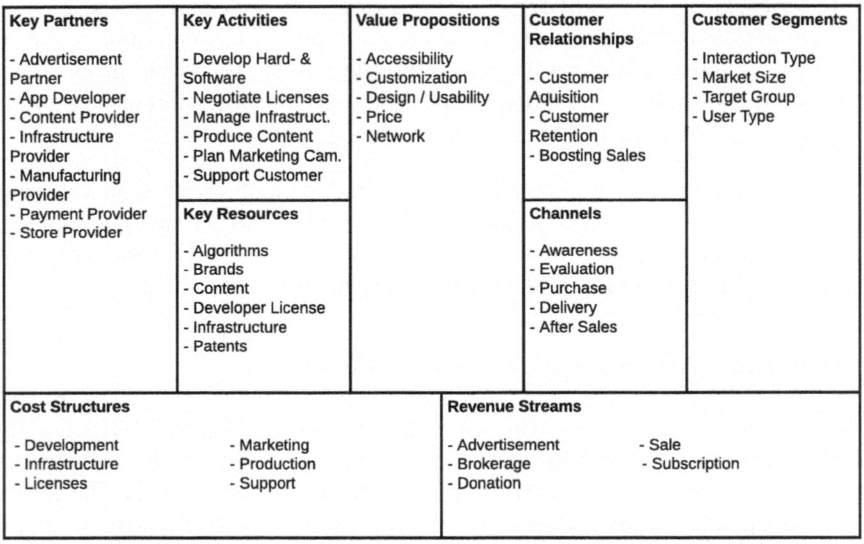

Fig. 2. Business model decisions for the third-party developer

The **Value Propositions** are the promise of the third-party developer to a certain customer segment. Here, the *Accessibility* relates to the access strategy of the app which can be for example anonymous access, the simplified usage of single-sign-on services or the accessibility from different devices. To get a personalized experience the developer can use the concept of *Customization.* Examples of this customization are the usage of personalized recommendations or changeable user interfaces [18]. This user interfaces is also important for the *Design/Usability* decisions. To propose good usability, the developer can reduce the execution steps or use design patterns from existing applications. Part of the value proposition can also be a *Price* promise. Examples here are a low-price strategy [10] or a money-back guarantee. The last point is the *Network* aspect, which plays a role if multiple customers are connected through an application. Here, the quantity and quality of other customers can be proposed.

The **Customer Segments** are a distinct customer group which a developer wants to reach in the mobile app store. The *Interaction Type* describes the interaction of a customer with other customers of the app. A customer can use the app only himself (called Single-User), interacting with the same type of customer (called Single-Sided-Market) or with customers of another type (called Multi-Sided-Market). Moreover, the *Market-Size* of a customer segment can be classified as a Niche- or a Mass-Market. Another point in the customer segment is the *Target Group*. The target group can be described by different characteristics like gender (e.g. Male), interests (e.g. Gamer) or relationship (e.g. Singles). The last point, we found out, is the *User Type* which relates to the decision if the customer is a private or professional one.

The **Customer Relationships** are relationships the developer wants to establish and maintain with each customer. The first step is the establishment of a relationship called *Customer Aquisition*. Examples of this acquisition step are the usage of advertisements or the implementing of a friend invitation system. After this step, the relationship is maintained within the *Customer Retention*. For the retention features like Locked-In [7], gamification or good customer support can be provided. To increase the revenue from existing customers there can be *Sales Boosting* techniques implemented. An example is the usage of Forced-Stops in games when the customer is not willing to spend money.

Inside the **Channels** the different phases of the value creation process are described. The *Awareness* is the first step to attract attention to their own application. Examples for the attraction are distribution via Word-Of-Mouth or a good store placement [10]. After creating this attraction, the customer needs an *Evaluation* of the benefits of the application. Here, the developer can use a Freemium model [19] or improve the rating and reviews in the store. This step is followed by the *Purchase* and *Delivery* of the applications. Depending on the mobile ecosystem, the payment for and the download of the application can be provided within the ecosystem or via an external system. The last step is called *After Sales*, where the customer receives value after the purchase process. Examples here are regular application and content updates.

Within the **Revenue Streams** different types of income can be generated. The most common way of generating income is the placing of *Advertisements* inside the app for example with In-App-Ads [19]. Moreover, the developer can also provide a *Brokerage* service between different customers and receives a transaction fee. In non-commercial applications sometimes also the *Donation* for the service is possible. Another possible option is the one-time *Sale* of the app or the usage of In-App-Payments for additional functions. To generate recurring revenue the developer can also use a *Subscription* model.

Feature Representation. The canvas representation can be translated directly to the feature representation as seen in Fig. 3. After the translation of the model, the mandatory features have to be chosen. From the developer perspective, only the development of the application and the publishing and, if needed, the access to infrastructure, are mandatory. From a business perspective, there should be at least sales and marketing be considered. For sales, there should be at least one Revenue Stream and, if needed, the corresponding Channel to Purchase used. For marketing, there should be strategies for Customer Aquisition and Customer Retention chosen, which can lead to marketing costs. The rest of the mandatory features, especially the Value Propositions, depend highly on the specific application.

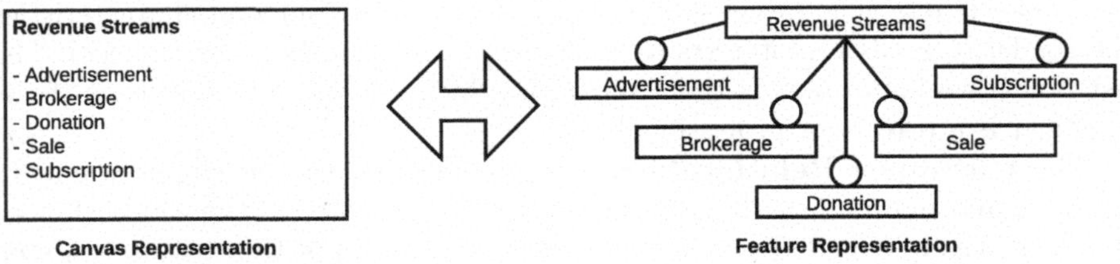

Fig. 3. Canvas representation vs. feature representation

Dependency Management. The structure of the BMDL can be refined by using dependencies. These dependencies can be divided into mandatory and optional dependencies.

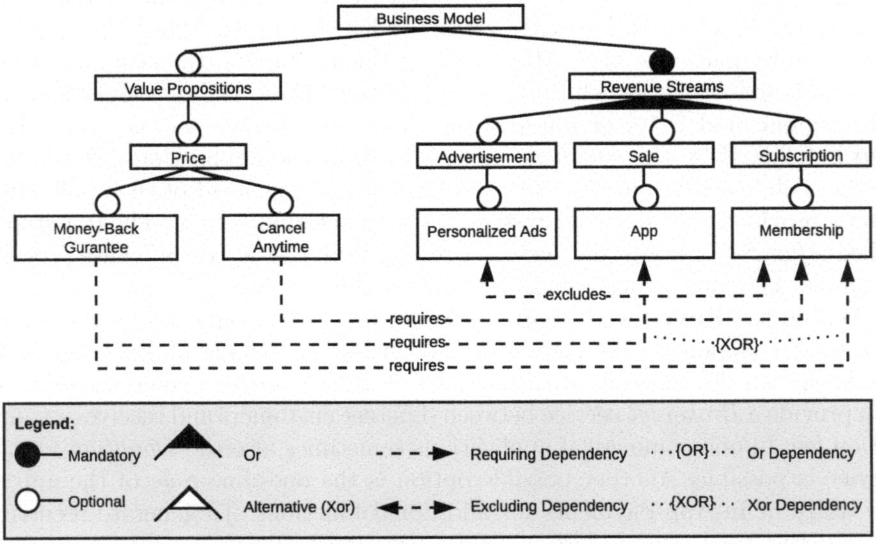

Fig. 4. Feature dependencies of the Business Model Decision Line

The mandatory dependencies are defined mostly on the third hierarchy level of the BMDL. Here the child features of Key Activities, Key Partners and Key

Resources require specific child features in the Cost Structures. Moreover, the child features of Channels, Customer Relationships, Value Propositions, and Revenue Streams require specific Customer Segments. The optional dependencies, which are flexible choices of the developers, are defined mostly on the fourth and lower levels of the hierarchy.

An example of the dependency management can be seen in Fig. 4. Here, the usage of Personalized Ads and a Membership are excluded from each other and the Value Proposition to Cancel Anytime requires a Membership. Moreover, for a Money-Back Guarantee, there has to be used at least one payment model (i.e. Sale, Subscription).

3.2 Software Product Line

The SPL of the product functions can be seen in Fig. 5. It consists of three feature groups of General Functions (Home Screen, Settings), User (Management, Interaction) and Item (List, Consumption, Provision).

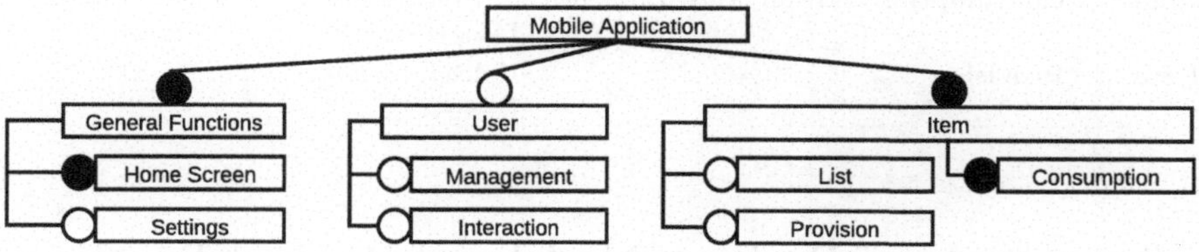

Fig. 5. Product functions of mobile applications

The *General Functions* are the most common features, which are used within an application. In our analyzed application these where a home screen with some starting information and the settings for the application. If a customer can register to the application and used an account, a *User Management* needs to be implemented. In Single-Sided- and Multi-Sided-Markets there is often used some kind of *User Interaction*. Here the different users can edit their profiles, establish friendships with each other or send messages. In nearly every app there are some items (e.g. Movies, Songs, Products, Weather Information) which are displayed and processed. The *Item List* provides different parts to structure these items (e.g. Categories, Search). Within the *Item Comsumption* it is possible to interact with these items (e.g. Play, Comment, Rate). The last feature group is the *Item Provision* where content can be provided (e.g. Create Content, Upload Videos).

4 Describing Existing Mobile Applications with Feature Modeling

To show the validity of our approach, we provide concrete instances of the BMDL and the SPL for the streaming applications of Netflix, YouTube, and Spotify.

For the BMDL, we focus in Table 2 on the Value Propositions (VP), Customer Segments (CS), Channels (Ch) and Revenue Streams (RS) as the most customer-related variability points. The instances of the Key Partners (KP), Key Activities (KA), Key Resources (KS) and Costs Structures (Co), which contain business-related variabilities, are described in our technical report [9]. The corresponding instances of the SPL can be seen in Table 1.

Table 1. Describing the streaming apps based on the SPL

Feature	Subfeature	Netflix	YouTube	Spotify
General	**Home Screen**	Home Screen		
General	**Settings**	Settings		
User	**Management**	Register, Password Lost, Login, Logout		
User	**Interaction**	–	Profiles, Friendships, Messages, Shared Playlists	Profiles, Shared Playlists
Item	**List**	Categories, Highlights, Search/Filter, Recommendations		
Item	**Consumption**	Stream, Rate, Download	Stream, Comment, Like, Download	Stream, Like, Download
Item	**Provision**	–	Upload, Update, Delete	–

5 Twin Peaks of Business Model and Product Functions

To intertwine the development of the business model and the product functions, we are using the concept of Twin Peaks [21]. In this concept, Nuseibeh discusses the general issue of the alignment of requirements and architecture within software development. Instead of considering the areas separately, both areas are developed at the same time. With this incremental development of both equally weighted areas (i.e. Twin Peaks), Nuseibeh improves the flexibility of the development process, which can adapt rapidly on changing requirements.

We adopt his concept by modeling the business model and product functions as Twin Peaks and using feature modeling as an abstraction layer (see Fig. 6). To create an initial feature model structure, we are using Incremental Development, while further changes are adopted using Iterative Development.

The *Incremental Development* provides an initial structure of the business model and product functions and consists of a Starting Step, an arbitrary number of Refinement Steps and an Ending Step.

1. **Starting Step:** In the first step, we are using the feature models of our predefined BMDL and SPL as the initial layer of our mobile application.
2. **Refinement Step(s):** In every refinement step, we select the features in the current layer of the mobile application and define a more detailed layer of features and dependencies within and between the business model and product functions.

Table 2. Describing the streaming apps based on the BMDL

Block	Decision	Netflix	YouTube	Spotify
VP	**Access**	Paid Account	No Account, Free Account, Paid Account	Free Account, Paid Account
VP	**Customization**	Personalized Recommendations		
VP	**Design/Usabillity**	Responsible Design, Easy Usability		
VP	**Price**	Low-Price	Freemium	Equal-Price-Strategy
VP	**Network**	–	Quantity of other Market-Side, Share Content, Connect with other Users	Share Playlists, Connect with other Users
CS	**Interaction Type**	Single-User	Multi-Sided-Market	Single-Sided-Market
CS	**Market Size**	Mass-Market		
CS	**Target Group**	Content-Consumer	Content-Creator, Content-Consumer	Content-Consumer
CS	**User Type**	Private User		
Ch	**Awareness**	Advertisement, Word-of-Mouth, Store Position		
Ch	**Awareness**	–	3rd-Party-Integration	3rd-Party-Integration, Distributable Codes
Ch	**Evaluation**	Rating, Reviews		
Ch	**Evaluation**	Free Month	Free Month	–
Ch	**Purchase**	Homepage	Homepage, App	Homepage, App
Ch	**Delivery**	App-Store		
Ch	**After Sales**	App-Updates, Content-Updates, Push-Notifications		
CR	**Customer Aquisition**	Single-Sign-In, Invite Friends		
CR	**Customer Retention**	Content-Updates, Self-Service	Locked-In, Self-Service	Content-Quantity, Self-Service
CR	**Boosting Sales**	–		
RS	**Advertisement**	–	Advertisement without Account, Advertisement with Free Account	Advertisement with Free Account
RS	**Brokerage**	–	Money for Content Creators	–
RS	**Donation**	–		
RS	**Sale**	–	Sell Movies, Lend Movies	–
RS	**Subscription**	Subscription for Content	Subscription for Premium Content	Subscription for Premium Features

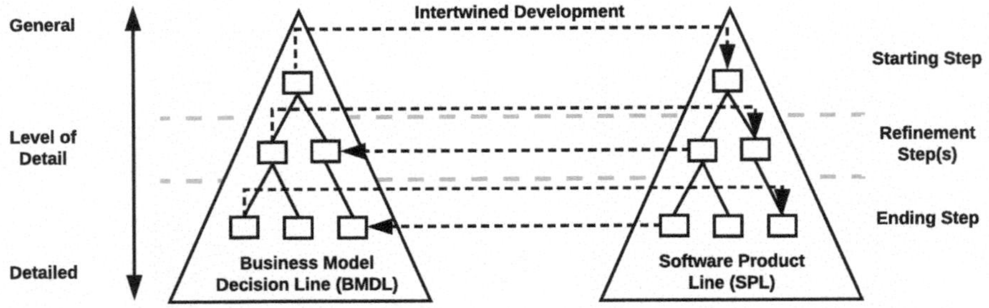

Fig. 6. Incremental development of the Twin Peaks (based on Nuseibeh [21])

3. **Ending Step:** In the last step, we select the features of the current layer of the mobile application and determine the business model and product functions.

An example of the incremental development based on streaming applications is illustrated in Fig. 7. In the *Starting Step*, we are modeling the Value Propositions (e.g. Price) and Revenue Streams (e.g. Advertisement, Subscription) as BMDL and how they are related to the product functions for the user (e.g. Management) and the item (e.g. Consumption, Provision) as SPL. For example, we can decide if we want to use an Advertisement or Subscription as an income model and notice that User Management is required for Subscription. In the *Refinement Step*, we select the Price as Value Proposition and the Subscription model and the required User Management. Moreover, we define new features for the Business Model (e.g. Cancel Anytime) and Product Functions (e.g. Upgrade) together with the creation of dependencies within and between the models (e.g. Cancel Anytime requires Membership, Adv. Features requires Upgrade). In the *Ending Step*, we choose that the user can Cancel Anytime with a corresponding Membership model. For the product functions, the user can Register, Play and Rate the existing items and Upload new items.

The *Iterative Development* provides to ability to rapidly change both models based on changing customer needs. The development can be divided into operations of Feature Selection Change and Feature Evolvement Change.

1. **Feature Selection Change:** A feature selection change is an activation and deactivation of features without changing the structure of the feature model. The change can be made directly in the model and verified with a consistency check. If consistency errors occur, the error needs to be resolved by returning to the specific layer in the incremental development and repeat the incremental development from this layer.
2. **Feature Evolvement Change:** A feature evolvement change is adding or deleting of features in the structure of the model. The change is done by returning to the specific layer in the incremental development, add or delete the specific feature and repeat the incremental development from the layer.

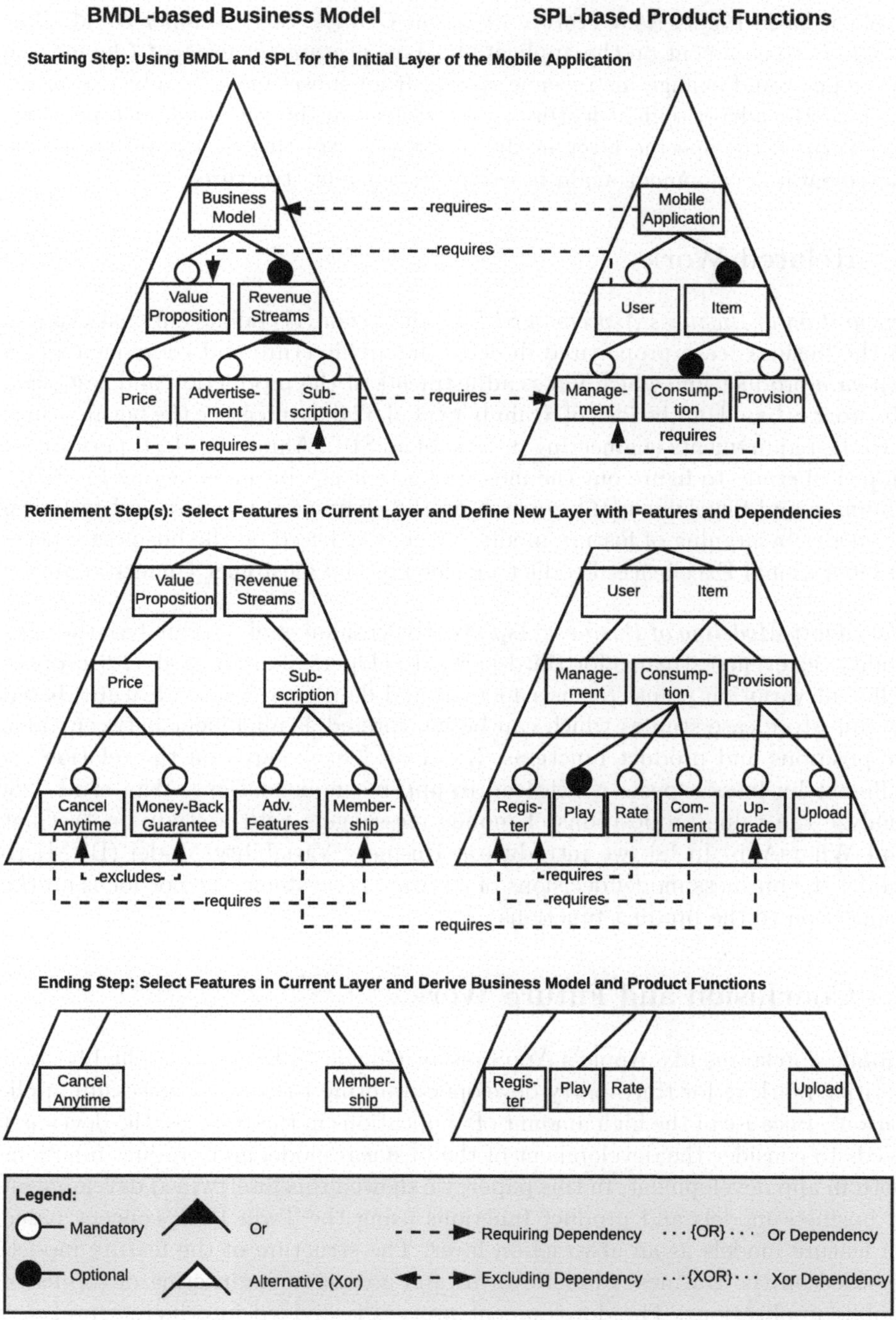

Fig. 7. Incremental development process of a streaming app

An example of the iterative development can be given based on the streaming application in Fig. 7. As a *Feature Selection Change*, the developer could allow the users to comment on the application. As a *Feature Evolvement Change*, the developer could change his revenue stream from subscription to advertisement. Because the advertisement feature is not evolved in the feature model, he needs to return to the specific layer in the model (i.e. Starting Step) and starts the incremental development again based on the current structure.

6 Related Work

Integration of Business Aspects in SPL's. McGregor [17] points out that changes in the business case propagated directly the architecture and components of a software product line which forces adjustments of the production and test plan. His work is based on the idea of Svahnberg et al. [24] to integrate the business unit into the requirements engineering process of an SPL. Ahmed et al. [1] perform an empirical study to figure out the most important key business factors for SPLs. Mannion and Savolainen [16] research on the aligning of business and technical strategies by arguing of feature model granularity based on the business aspects of Operational Excellence, Product Leadership and Customer Understanding.

Variability Modeling of Business Aspects. Hyrynsalmi et al. [11] analyze the variability of revenue streams for third-party developers. Jansen et al. [12] propose different variation points for user-focused and developer-focused features based on app store case studies which can be interpreted as alignment between value propositions and product functions. Xu et al. [28] research on the relations of different business aspects which lead to app recommendations. Wan et al. [25] analyze the value propositions of mobile messengers with a study on WeChat and WhatsApp. In [8], we introduce a Business Variability Model (BVM) to model the business model decisions of software ecosystems but not focus on the connection to the product functions.

7 Conclusion and Future Work

Mobile app stores like Apple's AppStore or Google's PlayStore are highly competitive markets for third-party developers wanting to develop successful applications. Because of the high amount of applications in these stores, the developer needs to consider the development of the business model and product functions both in app development. In this paper, we showed this intertwined development of business models and product functions using the Twin Peak concept based on feature models as an abstraction layer. The structure of the feature models is based on the Business Model Canvas and a domain engineering of top-listed mobile applications. The development process is divided into incremental and iterative development. At the beginning of the process, we used an incremental development for the initial model, while the iterative development is used to update the model based on customer needs. This combination of abstraction layer and development process supports third-party developers to build successful applications both from a business and a product perspective.

While our current approach is made for mobile applications, it can be easily transferred to other domains. To do this the collected information in the domain engineering (i.e. Papers, Applications) needs to be exchanged with information about the new domain. This exchange will change the structure of BMDL and SPL, while the development process remains the same.

Our future work is twofold: First, we want to evaluate the structure and development process of our approach by conducting an empirical study with third-party developers. Second, we want to apply feature model mining to our approach so that the BMDL and SPL can be automatically derived from examples, which simplifies the domain engineering process.

References

1. Ahmed, F., Capretz, L.F.: Managing the business of software product line: an empirical investigation of key business factors. Inf. Softw. Technol. **49**(2), 194–208 (2007). https://doi.org/10.1016/j.infsof.2006.05.004
2. App Annie Inc: The State of Mobile 2019. https://www.appannie.com/en/go/state-of-mobile-2019/
3. Chesbrough, H.: Business model innovation: it's not just about technology anymore. Strat. Leadsh. **35**(6), 12–17 (2007). https://doi.org/10.1108/10878570710833714
4. Clements, P., Northrop, L.: Software Product Lines: Practices and Patterns, 7th edn. Addison-Wesley, Boston (2009)
5. Fontao, A.d.L., dos Santos, R.P., Dias-Neto, A.C.: Mobile software ecosystem (MSECO): a systematic mapping study. In: Annual Computer Software and Applications Conference (COMSAC), pp. 653–658. IEEE (2015). https://doi.org/10.1109/COMPSAC.2015.121
6. Gartner Inc: Predicts 2014: Mobile and Wireless. https://www.gartner.com/en/documents/2620815
7. Gonçalves, V., Walravens, N., Ballon, P.: "How about an App Store?" enablers and constraints in platform strategies for mobile network operators. In: Ninth International Conference on Mobile Business and Ninth Global Mobility Roundtable (ICMB-GMR), pp. 66–73. IEEE (2010). https://doi.org/10.1109/ICMB-GMR.2010.41
8. Gottschalk, S., Rittmeier, F., Engels, G.: Business models of store-oriented software ecosystems: a variability modeling approach. In: Shishkov, B. (ed.) BMSD 2019. LNBIP, vol. 356, pp. 153–169. Springer, Cham (2019). https://doi.org/10.1007/978-3-030-24854-3_10
9. Gottschalk, S., Rittmeier, F., Engels, G.: Intertwined development of business model and product functions for mobile applications: a twin peak feature modeling approach. Technical report (2019). https://cs.uni-paderborn.de/fileadmin/informatik/fg/dbis/IntertwiningBMandPF.pdf
10. Holzer, A., Ondrus, J.: Mobile application market: a developer's perspective. Telemat. Inform. **28**(1), 22–31 (2011). https://doi.org/10.1016/j.tele.2010.05.006

11. Hyrynsalmi, S., Suominen, A., Mäkilä, T., Järvi, A., Knuutila, T.: Revenue models of application developers in android market ecosystem. In: Cusumano, M.A., Iyer, B., Venkatraman, N. (eds.) ICSOB 2012. LNBIP, vol. 114, pp. 209–222. Springer, Heidelberg (2012). https://doi.org/10.1007/978-3-642-30746-1_17
12. Jansen, S., Bloemendal, E.: Defining app stores: the role of curated marketplaces in software ecosystems. In: Herzwurm, G., Margaria, T. (eds.) ICSOB 2013. LNBIP, vol. 150, pp. 195–206. Springer, Heidelberg (2013). https://doi.org/10.1007/978-3-642-39336-5_19
13. Jazayeri, B., Platenius, M.C., Engels, G., Kundisch, D.: Features of IT service markets: a systematic literature review. In: Sheng, Q.Z., Stroulia, E., Tata, S., Bhiri, S. (eds.) ICSOC 2016. LNCS, vol. 9936, pp. 301–316. Springer, Cham (2016). https://doi.org/10.1007/978-3-319-46295-0_19
14. Krueger, C.W.: Easing the transition to software mass customization. In: van der Linden, F. (ed.) PFE 2001. LNCS, vol. 2290, pp. 282–293. Springer, Heidelberg (2002). https://doi.org/10.1007/3-540-47833-7_25
15. Lee, S.M., Kim, N.R., Hong, S.G.: Key success factors for mobile app platform activation. Serv. Bus. **11**(1), 207–227 (2017). https://doi.org/10.1007/s11628-016-0329-y
16. Mannion, M., Savolainen, J.: Aligning product line business and technical strategies. In: 17th International Software Product Line Conference (SPLC), vol. 6287, pp. 406–419. ACM (2013). https://doi.org/10.1145/2491627.2493900
17. McGregor, J.D.: The evolution of product line assets. Technical report CMU/SEI-2003-TR-005 (2003)
18. Menychtas, A., et al.: 4CaaSt marketplace: an advanced business environment for trading cloud services. Futur. Gener. Comput. Syst. **41**, 104–120 (2014). https://doi.org/10.1016/j.future.2014.02.020
19. Müller, R.M., Kijl, B., Martens, J.K.J.: A comparison of inter-organizational business models of mobile app stores: there is more than open vs. closed. J. Theor. Appl. Electron. Commer. Res. **6**(2), 13–14 (2011). https://doi.org/10.4067/S0718-18762011000200007
20. Nickerson, R.C., Varshney, U., Muntermann, J.: A method for taxonomy development and its application in information systems. Eur. J. Inf. Syst. **22**(3), 336–359 (2013). https://doi.org/10.1057/ejis.2012.26
21. Nuseibeh, B.: Weaving together requirements and architectures. Computer **34**(3), 115–119 (2001). https://doi.org/10.1109/2.910904
22. Osterwalder, A., Pigneur, Y.: Business Model Generation: A Handbook for Visionaries, Game Changers, and Challengers. Wiley, Hoboken (2010)
23. Roma, P., Ragaglia, D.: Revenue models, in-app purchase, and the app performance: evidence from Apple's App Store and Google Play. Electron. Commer. Res. Appl. **17**, 173–190 (2016). https://doi.org/10.1016/j.elerap.2016.04.007
24. Svahnberg, M., Bosch, J.: Evolution in software product lines: two cases. J. Softw. Maint. Res. Pract. **11**, 391–422 (1999). https://doi.org/10.1002/(SICI)1096-908X(199911/12)11:6⟨391::AID-SMR199⟩3.0.CO;2-8
25. Sze Wan, W., Dartane, O., Mohd Satar, N.S., Ma'arif, M.Y.: What WeChat can learn from WhatsApp? Customer value proposition development for mobile social networking (MSN) apps: a case study approach. J. Theor. Appl. Inf. Technol. **97**, 1091–1117 (2019)
26. Tuunainen, V.K., Tuunanen, T., Piispanen, J.: Mobile service platforms: comparing Nokia OVI and apple app store with the IISIn model. In: International Conference on Mobile Business (ICMB), pp. 74–83. IEEE (2011). https://doi.org/10.1109/ICMB.2011.42

27. van der Linden, F., Schmid, K., Rommes, E.: Software Product Lines in Action. Springer, Heidelberg (2007). https://doi.org/10.1007/978-3-540-71437-8
28. Xu, C., Peak, D., Prybutok, V.: A customer value, satisfaction, and loyalty perspective of mobile application recommendations. Decis. Support. Syst. **79**, 171–183 (2015). https://doi.org/10.1016/j.dss.2015.08.008

The Role of the Customer in an Agile Project: A Multi-case Study

Erno Vanhala[1(✉)] and Jussi Kasurinen[2]

[1] Tampere University, Tampere, Finland
erno.vanhala@tuni.fi
[2] LUT University, Lappeenranta, Finland
jussi.kasurinen@lut.fi

Abstract. In this multi-case study we report the findings from three software projects conducted with SCRUM agile development framework. Each project took approximately a little less than a year to design, develop and test before the launch to the user groups. All project vendors utilized SCRUM framework customized to suit their processes, and included customer as a participant in the overall process. Due to this fact, this study focuses on the role of the customer in daily life of an agile project. The findings show what is actually required from the customer – especially when the sprint length is only one week and the development process is very time-intensive. Although a one week sprint cycle can lead to improved efficiency it required a full time worker from the customer side and it burdened also the developers. Based on our observations, as the developer teams and customer were located in various places around Europe, smooth communication was a key for success. In all cases the asynchronous communication tools, such as Slack, were highly praised, although also direct communications were used to handle more complex issues. According to our findings, these agile projects did not have significant issues caused by the online communication being the preferred way of communication. All of the cases had difficulties in fitting the agile project to the fixed budget, but good collaboration, partnership and trust alleviated most of these problems.

Keywords: Agile software development · SCRUM · Customer relationship · Multi-case study

1 Introduction

Software engineering fundamentals are not very swift to change. For example, the nowadays commonly used agile methods such as eXtreme Programming (XP) and Scrum, are already more than twenty years old [15]. Even the agile manifesto itself is turning twenty in two years [2], and it more or less codifies software process expertise, which was already known fifty years ago [15]. Agile software engineering methods have been studied from various perspectives; yet, the role and especially the requirements set for the customer in an agile software project

S. Hyrynsalmi et al. (Eds.): ICSOB 2019, LNBIP 370, pp. 208–222, 2019.
https://doi.org/10.1007/978-3-030-33742-1_17

require deeper understanding since there seem to be only few works where this issue is even mentioned [16,22].

The agile manifesto itself states how interaction and customer collaboration are important parts of software development [2]. How the actual software design, development and testing lifecycle is then carried out depends on the case and the study. The reported issues are different whether the research concentrates on customer side, developer side or both (e.g. [16,20]). To get more in-depth understanding of the customer problems and issues with the communication between the customer and the vendor, in this study it was decided to get interview data from both sides to see how the role of the customer is formed. On the software process aspects, it was interesting to understand what the customers actually do or understand, and how they relate themselves to the rest of the development team. Based on earlier work, we had an understanding that the most common ways of customer participation was on the first stages in definition phases, and on the last stages in acceptance testing [12]. But was this still the case with the agile development practices and if not, how had the adoption of the agile methods in large scale affected this dynamic?

In this work we discuss and analyze this role of the customer with the following research questions:

1. How do the customers consider working in an agile project?
2. What are the appropriate communications mechanisms and how effective are they?
3. What do the participants from software organizations expect from the customers in an agile project?

With these research questions in mind we studied three software projects conducted in 2018–2019 and present the results in this article.

The rest of the article contains first related research in Sect. 2, description of research process in Sect. 3, results in Sect. 4 and discussion of findings in Sect. 5. Section 6 concludes the study.

2 Related Research

The agile world has embraced change happening in the software development [13,30]. Yet, especially public organizations have preferred fixed pricing when buying software [7]. This has created an equation, which has been described problematic, but also manageable [1,4]. Agile software development has nevertheless become the new norm [9] in all but the most heavily regulated areas of the industry.

When talking about agile software development one is describing an umbrella term: the agile world consists of many different process models, frameworks and development strategies which may vary to a large degree from each other [2]. In the beginning of this millenia eXtreme programming (XP) was discussed a lot in industry and also in academia, but the shift has then been towards scrum, albeit the continuous development models lean heavily on the principles first introduced with the XP approaches [10].

In general, XP and the Continuous models are strongly related to the actual software-in-development while SCRUM or Dynamic System Development Model (DSDM) are more project management methods. Other methodologies, such as, Feature Driven Development (FDD) or Kanban can be considered between those two [18].

Agile methods have been studied from various point of views; Google scholar return hundreds of results when searching for agile method in title. In their systematic literature review Dybå and Dingsøyr identified 36 articles discussing empirical studies of agile software development [3], but only a handful of those focused on the participation of the customer and collaboration. There are studies discussing agile methods and user centric design [24] and the role of user stories [23]. And it has been discussed how daily communication with the customer and the vendor reduces overruns [17,22]. Martin et al. [20] discuss how important the role of the customer is in XP project. The role of the customer includes not only to provide user stories and acceptance testing, but also communication to external stakeholders and keeping the trust between the vendor and the funder; the customer is the glue keeping the project together. The overall communication, collaboration and coordination is important and it has been even discussed how these elements ensure quality and productivity in an agile project [11,21]. Also Korkala et al. [14] present their findings on how lesser communication with customer reflects on the higher defect rates. They embrace face-to-face communication but also accept online video collaboration when participants are remote.

Sprint length in SCRUM development is usually 2–6 weeks [6,28] and conventionally it has been preferred that the development teams are physically in the same place [13]. However, this has changed with the improved Internet connections and online communication and collaboration tools [26], to the point where it has been reported how distributed teams can be as productive as collocated teams [27].

In a nutshell: agile methods, which are many, have been studied quite a lot, yet the role of the customer has not been in the focus.

3 Research Process

This study is a multi-case study and it follows the frameworks and principles presented by Gable [8] and Eisenhardt [5]. We followed seven steps: defining the strategy, reviewing the literature, developing the case study protocol, conducting a pilot case study, conducting a multiple case study, developing a conceptual model and interpreting the findings.

The research questions, presented in section one, determine the overall strategy. Section two illustrates the related literature. The case study was based on two interview rounds where the first one was conducted with the customer representatives and the second one with the vendor representatives. Data was collected through interview rounds where the first author interviewed the customer and the vendor representatives and the second author validated the interview questions and interview recordings. The case organizations were selected from the pool of professional contacts, which were working with a software project utilizing an agile method. The aim was to interview the project managers and leaders – the persons who worked most for the project – from the customer side and the main architect and/or project manager from the vendor side. Typically one interview lasted for one hour, and included approximately ten semistructured questions, with subquestions, which allowed also open discussions. Key information of the interviewees is presented in Table 1.

Table 1. Information on the interviewed persons

Case A	Case B	Case C
Customer product owner (PO) ***	Customer PO **	Customer PO A ***
Customer secondary PO **	Customer secondary PO, head of content production *	Customer PO B **
Vendor chief architect ***	Vendor chief architect ***	Vendor project manager ***

All the projects had a person dedicated to the project and responsible for budgeting, reporting and taking care of running the project from the customer side, this is called product owner (PO). Secondary PO is the person who helps the most and works as a PO when the real PO is not present (e.g. on holidays). The PO of Case C was changed during the project. Asterisks illustrate how extensive project work experience that person had (* = none, ** = some, *** = extensive). Product owners were not software engineering professional – with the exception of Customer PO A, who had software engineering background and formal training to act as PO.

3.1 Description of the Cases

This study discussed three cases. The customer organization built three systems almost simultaneously. Cases A and B were developed by Vendor 1 and Case C was delivered by Vendor 2. Although some of the customer's people were working on all of the case projects the projects also had their dedicated product owners from the customer side.

With Case A there was a strict deadline when the system needed to be in production and there was no option to miss the date. With Case B it would have been optimal if the system had been up and running with the same date as Case A, but that deadline was not that crucial. With Case C the schedule was more flexible as the first ideas were to finish the Case C before Case A, but it was also acceptable to postpone the release of Case C after the Case A and that was also the final outcome.

3.2 Details of the Cases

Table 2 presents the key figures of the cases. The software in Cases A and B were bought from the Vendor 1 and Case C was delivered by Vendor 2. All the software were browser-based aimed to provide tools to share information and materials to both users in the organization and to the public, and to integrate to a larger framework utilizing for example Drupal and WordPress. There had been some requirements for analysis and specification with consults before the vendors were selected. The GDPR, data security and system validation requirements of all the observed systems were similar, and generally comparable to each other.

Table 2. Key figures of the case projects

	Case A	Case B	Case C
Vendor	V1	V1	V2
Schedule criticalness	Release date cannot be missed, features can be compromised	Both release date and feature richness can be flexible	Feature completeness is more important than the release date
Expected number of authenticated users	Hundreds	Tens of thousands	Hundreds
Software development framework	Scrum	Scrum	Scrum
Sprint length	1 week	1 week	2 weeks
Dailies mandatory for product owner	Yes	Yes	No
Customer testing	Weekly	Weekly	Before the release
Software framework	Drupal	Custom React code + Drupal	WordPress
Vendor team size	ca. 10 persons	ca. 10 persons	ca. 5 persons
Customer team size[a]	ca. 10 persons	ca. 5 persons	ca. 5 persons
Vendor documentation platform	Google Drive	Google Drive	Google Drive
Customer documentation platform	Wiki, O365	Wiki, O365	Wiki, O365
Communication tool	Skype for Business, Zoom, Slack	Skype for Business, Zoom, Slack	Google Meet, Slack
Tool to handle product related daily tasks	Jira	Jira	Jira
Pricing	Time & material	Target price	Fixed price
Budget	Hundreds of thousands of euros	Hundreds of thousands of euros	Tens of thousands euros
Estimated project duration (achieved)	7 months (10)	6 months (8)	7 months (10)

[a]Does not include content production team

4 Results

In this section the results are discussed. Overall, we observed seven main aspects which greatly influenced the customer participation and client roles in the software projects. This includes discussion of general frameworks utilized, what tools and documents were used, how communication was carried out, what happened to the budget and scheduling and how transparent the project work was. These relations are illustrated in the Fig. 1.

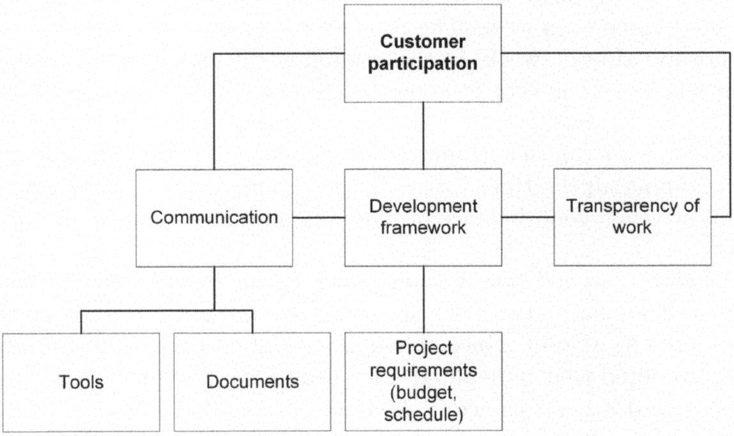

Fig. 1. The most common observed related aspects on the topic "customer participation".

The customer participation was observed to be associated with communication policies, the development framework of the projects and transparency aspects. These aspects were further defined by the applied tools, documents and the general project requirements, especially budgets and schedules, which affected the way the customer participated in the development work. There might also be further underlying aspects, but within our data and our observed projects, these were the most meaningful influences which affected the roles and types of the participation. In the following subsections, we discuss the different aspects separately, and define how they affect the customer participation and working roles.

4.1 Framework

On the general topic of the first research question, the applied process models were investigated to understand how the development work is done in general and how much these approaches demand cooperation and customer participation. The vendor of Cases A and B utilized a scrum framework customized for their organization. The key points of this customization were: estimated 60% workload for a person from the customer organization and the utilization of sprint length of one week instead of the de facto two week length.

Although the vendor required only 60% of time to be scheduled for the project the reality was different. Almost double work was required from the product owner.

"In fact I spent 120% of my time on the project." - product owner of Case A.

"My workload was something between 60 and 100%." - product owner of Case B.

Besides the workload, also the meaningfulness of the one week sprint length was questioned. Although it was also considered good when there were more issues to be decided each week. The product owner was also expected to participate dailies five times a week. In the beginning the customer's role was just to listen, but when everyone got to known each other the customer was also giving feedback.

"The one week sprint length produced a huge load of overhead. It was meetings and planning all the time." - secondary product owner of Case A.

"I think it was a good balance of planning and developing" - product owner of Case B.

The Vendor 1 argued how the one week sprint length had increased their productivity. They had a two week sprint length, but the move to one week had been considered as a good choice. Though it resulted in increased productivity, they had also noted that it required a lot from both developers and customers. It was considered a good choice if the developer could work in a maintenance project for a while after scrum development project had ended. This is an opposite finding when compared to, for example [17], where one month sprint length was used. Still the Vendor 1 considered one week sprints most suitable.

"In one week period we can really be sure what we need to do." - chief architect of Vendor 1.

Vendor 2, which developed the Case C, utilized two weeks sprints and did not require customers participation as much as Vendor 1. Dailies were held only internally and no customer participation was required or even offered. Although there was less participation, there was still much to do for the customer: sprint meetings, testing, design decisions, to name a few.

Testing was very different between the two vendors. With Vendor 1 the customer tested the new features each sprint week and had to do quite a lot of work with testing. This was also noted in the interviews:

"It looks like I am working in Vendor 1. Sometimes it feels like I am doing their jobs" - product owner of Case B.

It was criticised how the testing responsibility was on the customer side – although this is in line with the findings in [11]. For example all the integrations needed to be verified by the customer and in many cases it was reported how one field here and another there was missing. It created a burden. Vendor 1 also noted this.

"The customer's role in testing has been too big. It has to be also noted how pedantic the customer has been. There has been very little bugs in the production." - chief architect of Vendor 1.

With Vendor 2 in Case C the testing workload was smaller and stressed the project group merely in the end of the release cycle, not on a weekly basis. The philosophies of Vendor 1 and Vendor 2 can be considered quite different, yet they both worked.

4.2 Tools and Documents

On more in-depth topic regarding cooperation and work, the communication mechanisms and cooperation-enabling tools were also an area of interest. Fundamentally, all case projects included collaborative work with various documents, such as requirements and customer testing. In all cases the work was done in Google Drive environment. Both customer and vendors were satisfied with these tools. With Case A it was reported that documents were made, but not updated that much during the project. With Cases B and C both customer and vendor reported that all non-temporary documents were kept updated and used during the project.

"All the documents created were really in use, but with meeting memos there were problems when same issues were discussed in various meetings and the results were not consistent" - product owner B of Case C.

"All the documentation was in Google Drive and all the documents were linked in Jira. The developer could always go from Jira ticket to up-to-date information found from Google Drive." - project manager of Vendor 2 (Case C).

Both vendors used Atlassian Jira as the issue and bug tracking project management tool. Although some project members from the customer side had never used it before and described it as "spooky" when first seen, the utilization of story and bug reporting in Jira was a success.

4.3 Communication

Besides tools, the methods and volume of communication between the client and the developer were assessed, since the communications and exchange of information between organizations are considered one of the key values of agile approaches. Both vendors used Slack online discussing tool as the main communication method. The Vendor 1 also used Zoom and Vendor 2 Google Meet. Also Skype for Business was used, especially internally on the customer side. Both vendors also arranged live meetings. Email was disfavoured although still used occasionally. Especially with Vendor 1 there were several face to face designing sessions before the implementation part that led to intensive work as partners from the beginning. Although both Case A and Case B had disagreements between the customer and the vendor no conflicts arose. The product owner of Case B felt it good how the work was intensive between the vendor and the customer:

"They have become like colleagues", product owner of Case B.

Vendor 1 had developers in several cities in two different countries. Some of them never visited the customer physically, yet they still fit in the project group and were considered as good partners as those who were met face to face. Slack and Zoom were found to be sufficient tools to handle day-to-day communication. This is a method of work that was not emphasized in the early XP visions [13], yet it is common and effective nowadays [26].

Although almost all key customer persons had at least some experience in working in software development project, there were still some problems with the communication, especially in Case B, where the key persons had the least of experience.

"The customer always responded, but sometimes we only got a fragment of what we needed and after that piece by piece. In this sense we build the software from hand to mouth." - chief architect of Vendor 2.

The product owner of Case B mentions how it was felt straight from the beginning that resources were not enough.

"We should have had more resources internally in this project" - product owner of Case B.

It was not a problem that the vendor would be the bottleneck, but the customer who could not respond in time or get all the necessary information. Also too optimistic schedules from the Vendor's side contributed to the missing of the deadline. Thus there was a mismatch in communication that resulted in missed deadlines; wrong requirements in correct date and vice versa.

With Case C the communication was not that intensive with the vendor and the customer and there were days when no messages were delivered. Still the Vendor 2 considered it supportive when the project communication was successful and helped when the customer and the vendor did not see eye to eye.

The overall view was that in the beginning of the projects face to face meetings were more common. When people started to know each other and the broad lines were set, and the actual work started, the need for physical meetings decreased but online communication – both textual and with voice – was fortified and it was considered working well.

4.4 Transparency of the Project Work

With one week sprints Vendor 1 was able to communicate the project progression weekly and the customer was using Jira tool from day one, so that the project was all the time under an expressive supervision of the product owners of Case A and Case B. There was also a need for transparency the towards steering groups and the end users, but the lack of time prevented that.

"There simply was not enough time to communicate all the things in the project group not even mentioning the need to communicate with the end users." - product owner of Case A.

With Case C the customer was not that intensively included in the daily work, but rather in testing features when they were announced. Sometimes some features were presented even if they were not required and the customer was not sure if they were the ones they needed. Still the overall feeling within the vendor was that everything went smoothly.

"It was nice to see how the customer liked to work in this project" - project manager of Vendor 2 (Case C).

It seemed that the transparency required intensive collaboration that also required resources from the customer side so that it cannot be described only to have good parts. If resources are not a problem on the customer side, a deep communication can improve the transparency.

4.5 Budget and Schedule

Finally, all projects are subject to some restrictions and objectives, usually defined by time, money, resources or quality to assess the success rate of the project. Although the customer and the vendor were in intense communication all the time, all the cases missed their budget and/or schedule in some way. This was especially bad with the Case B as it meant that the content needed to be updated simultaneously in old systems and in the production environment of the new system where the new guidelines of content production were set. Finally the product was released more than a month late and with beta-status. It was already decided in the beginning of the project that the first release was nothing but final, but the lack of features was still overwhelming.

There was also an enormous pressure to get the Case A done in time as the deadline was strict and could not be missed. There had already been delays for weeks in the previous beta and soft launches, which led to reducing features from the release. These features were then implemented after the release and that was also considered a burden as customer's representatives were eager to move on with other tasks in hand.

With Case C everything else went smoothly but the authentication with the organization wide method was not easy to integrate to WordPress and that lead to missing the final deadline. The project had also a problem with the key developer's sick leave as there was no replacement available.

"We had quite good resources for this project and could keep the deadlines. Although the injured developer had negative effect to meet the final deadline." - project manager of Vendor 2 (Case C).

"I think the only problem with the schedule was the sick leave and a little lightweight know-how, that caused delays" - product owner B of Case C.

The Case C utilized a fixed price model and managed to get all done within the budget although they did not manage to do it in the time they had set internally, thus they used their own resources to get everything done.

"Fixed price and agile project – is it even possible? I think it is" - project manager of Vendor 2 (Case C).

With Case B there were negotiations after it was realized that the estimated work amount would exceed and with Case A fixed pricing was not even tried. This underlines how fixed price and agile project are challenging to combine.

4.6 Conclusion of the Findings

It was found how in these three cases agile software development required resources from the customer more than they anticipated and the product owners were overwhelmed by the workload the project gave them. The one week sprint length in Cases A and B was considered exhausting; yet the vendor had experienced its power.

From the actual tasks testing was considered the most burden. There was much more to test than the traditional waterfall acceptance testing.

Cloud environments as the backend for document sharing and collaborative editing were highly praised. As were also online communication tools that were used.

All the projects missed their budget or schedule in some way and it was noted how the customer had too little dedicated resources – i.e. manpower – that was a bottle neck in various occasions and also produced the lack of necessary communications.

5 Discussion

In the beginning we set three research questions: (1) How do the customers consider working in an agile project? (2) What are the appropriate communications mechanisms and how effective are they? and (3) What do the participants from software organizations expect from the customers in an agile project?

Four key points arose from interview after interview:

- Agile sprints require a lot from the customer; the customer has to provide information on a short notice and live with the schedules and workloads even if they are incompatible with their own organization.
- Communication through modern asynchronous online tools works as well as face to face; direct communications between the client and the developer are not considered overtly intrusive.
- Close collaboration and trust between the partner organizations can alleviate most of the problems; most of the issues are based on the lack or limited amount of communications between the client and the customer organizations.
- Agile project with a fixed budget is still a tricky concept; the amount of revisions and redesigns are difficult to estimate beforehand especially with a new client.

Especially Vendor 1 required a lot from the customer. They had experienced how one week sprint length is efficient and they put a heavy load of testing responsible to the customer. On one hand this burdens the customer, but on the other hand it guarantees that the customer gets what he wants and no unnecessary work is done when the sprint length is kept short. The problem is that the burden might be too much if the customer is not prepared for the workload. Within this study the customer had experience of agile software work, but the workload was still considered too heavy on many times. If the vendor is working with the customer with no prior knowledge of software projects there could be a significant risk that the customer rejects the working method and the project fails. *We recommend that the agile software vendors communicate the responsibilities beforehand and underline how the customer's participation is crucial for the success of the project.*

XP has traditionally emphasized close physical proximity [13], yet these projects embraced online communication tools. Discussions popping up all the time in Slack – questions getting answered, bugs being fixed – illustrated that the tools we have today are sufficient to diminish the need for continuously physically shared spaces. And when textual chatting was not enough Skype and Zoom brought the customer and the developers to the same virtual room to discuss the issues at hand. In the beginning of the project physical meetings were held, but when approaching the release online communication had replaced the physical meetings almost entirely. *We recommend the customers and the vendors make a point of creating digital work space for all participants, and apply modern online communication tools whether they would be as sufficient as this study describes.*

Although none of these projects were complete successes, there was never real blaming from either side. The customer could always trust that the vendor gets all done even if it would mean being late few months or requiring more work. A deep collaboration and partnership helped all cases to overcome problems that could lead to courthouse. *We recommend to begin a software project with partnership in mind so that the problems are tackled together and not by blaming each other.*

Monetary issues were not the main research theme, but they arose from the interviews. With Case A it was decided that fixed pricing was not to be used, with Case B target pricing was used, but budgeting was an issue and with Case C fixed pricing was used and the customer was satisfied, but it resulted the vendor doing some development without payment. This emphasises how agile software development and fixed pricing is still a concept that needs a careful thinking whether it is suitable for the project or should some other pricing model be used. *We recommend to avoid strict fixed pricing with an agile project method, and to consider for example target price or similar more adjustable pricing.*

To summarize the findings in a nutshell: agile project requires more expertise from the customer and flexibility from the budget than traditional plan-driven projects to succeed, and the current online communications and collaboration tools enable agile development teams to locate physically all over the globe.

In qualitative studies, the validity issues concentrate on the generalizability and bias aspects of the researchers reflecting their own expectations on the data [25]. In this work, the research data was analyzed and documented by a team of researchers, and the qualitative data was collected from a group of experts representing different viewpoints in the software development project. In qualitative studies, the key aspects are integrity, authenticity, credibility and criticality [29]. In our work, we selected organizations and people directly involved in these projects to gain first hand information, and conducted the interviews personally, getting observations from several roles to establish several viewpoints into the analyzed projects. In this sense, the integrity, authenticity and credibility of our observations should establish a firm chain-of-evidence between our observations, and the activities which have taken place in these development projects. As for generalizability, the qualitative studies in general cannot be generalized into all-encompassing theories such as in mathematics or physics but in transferability [19], with the study results being treated as areas of interest, or enhancement proposals, when transferred outside the original study ecosystem.

6 Conclusion

In this article, we present our qualitative multi-case study on the customer expectations and the roles in different types of agile processes. The concept was to study the effect the customer has on the software process, and by observing real-life software development projects, understand the benefits and risks of active/non-active customer participation in the development work. Our research work included three real life software projects, several different viewpoints and experts from both customer and vendor organizations to the study. The results were analyzed and agreed upon by a group of researchers, and the strongest leads based on the qualitative chain of evidence were reported as results.

Based on our results, the customer participation has a significant impact on the quality assurance activities and to the overall success of the agile project. Additionally, we observed that the customer participation does not require physical presence as documented in some agile practices such as XP, but for a meaningful participation it is sufficient that the customer participates for example via shared digital workspace. In fact, we did not find strong indicators of added benefits from the on-site presence by the customer representatives at the development team.

Finally, it seems that we have a number of attributes which affect the customer role and have impact on the overall project outcome. As a future research, it would be interesting to test these attributes for example with larger quantitative surveys to further validate our observations, or assess how software projects succeed, when the client behavior, responsibilities and representative requirements are specified to ease the identified problematic process areas.

References

1. Banerjee, U., Narasimhan, E., Kanakalata, N.: Experience of executing fixed price off-shored agile project. In: Proceedings of the 4th India Software Engineering Conference on - ISEC 2011, pp. 69–75. ACM Press, Thiruvananthapurama (2011). https://doi.org/10.1145/1953355.1953364
2. Dingsøyr, T., Nerur, S., Balijepally, V., Moe, N.B.: A decade of agile methodologies: towards explaining agile software development. J. Syst. Software **85**(6), 1213–1221 (2012). https://doi.org/10.1016/j.jss.2012.02.033

3. Dybå, T., Dingsøyr, T.: Empirical studies of agile software development: a systematic review. Inf. Software Technol. **50**(9–10), 833–859 (2008). https://doi.org/10.1016/j.infsof.2008.01.006
4. Eckfeldt, B., Madden, R., Horowitz, J.: Selling agile: target-cost contracts. In: Agile Development Conference (ADC 2005), pp. 160–166. IEEE Comput. Soc, Denver (2005). https://doi.org/10.1109/ADC.2005.39
5. Eisenhardt, K.M.: Building theories from case study research. Academy of management. Acad. Manage. Rev. **14**(4), 532 (1989). http://search.proquest.com/docview/210938650?accountid=27292, copyright - Copyright Academy of Management Oct 1989; Last updated - 2010–06-08
6. Flora, H., Chande, S.: A systematic study on agile software development methodlogies and practices. Int. J. Comput. Sci. Inf. Technol. **5**(3), 3626–3637 (2014)
7. Franklin, T.: Adventures in agile contracting: evolving from time and materials to fixed price, fixed scope contracts. In: Agile 2008 Conference, pp. 269–273. IEEE, Toronto (2008). https://doi.org/10.1109/Agile.2008.88
8. Gable, G.G.: Integrating case study and survey research methods: an example in information systems. Eur. J. Inf. Syst. **3**, 112–126 (1994)
9. Hoda, R., Salleh, N., Grundy, J.: The rise and evolution of agile software development. IEEE Softw. **35**(5), 58–63 (2018). https://doi.org/10.1109/MS.2018.290111318
10. Humble, J., Farley, D.: Continuous Delivery: Reliable Software Releases through Build, Test, and Deployment Automation. Pearson Education (2010)
11. Kautz, K.: Customer and user involvement in agile software development. In: Abrahamsson, P., Marchesi, M., Maurer, F. (eds.) XP 2009. LNBIP, vol. 31, pp. 168–173. Springer, Heidelberg (2009). https://doi.org/10.1007/978-3-642-01853-4_22
12. Kettunen, V., Kasurinen, J., Taipale, O., Smolander, K.: A study on agility and testing processes in software organizations. In: Proceedings of the 19th International Symposium on Software Testing and Analysis - ISSTA 2010, p. 231. ACM Press, Trento (2010). https://doi.org/10.1145/1831708.1831737
13. Kircher, M., Jain, P., Corsaro, A., Levine, D.: Distributed extreme programming. In: Proceedings of the International Conference on eXtreme Programming and Flexible Processes in Software Engineering, pp. 66–71. Sardinia, Italy, May 2001
14. Korkala, M., Abrahamsson, P., Kyllonen, P.: A case study on the impact of customer communication on defects in agile software development. In: AGILE 2006, AGILE 2006. pp. 76–88. IEEE, Minneapolis (2006). https://doi.org/10.1109/AGILE.2006.1
15. Larman, C., Basili, V.R.: Iterative and incremental developments. A brief history. Computer **36**(6), 47–56 (2003). https://doi.org/10.1109/MC.2003.1204375
16. Lohan, G., Lang, M., Conboy, K.: Having a customer focus in agile software development. In: Pokorny, J., et al. (eds.) Inf. Syst. Dev., pp. 441–453. Springer, New York (2011)
17. Mann, C., Maurer, F.: A case study on the impact of scrum on overtime and customer satisfaction. In: Agile Development Conference (ADC 2005), pp. 70–79. IEEE Comput. Soc, Denver (2005). https://doi.org/10.1109/ADC.2005.1
18. Margini, A., Cutrona, G., Fantuzzi, C.: Comparison of different agile methodologies and fit assessment in an industrial context. Int. J. Adv. Res. **5**(7), 673–690 (2017). https://doi.org/10.21474/IJAR01/4768
19. Marshall, M.N.: Sampling for qualitative research. Fam. Pract. **13**(6), 522–526 (1996)

20. Martin, A., Biddle, R., Noble, J.: The XP customer role in practice: three studies. In: Agile Development Conference, pp. 42–54. IEEE, Salt Lake City (2004). https://doi.org/10.1109/ADEVC.2004.23
21. Mishra, D., Mishra, A.: Effective communication, collaboration, and coordination in eXtreme programming: human-centric perspective in a small organization. Hum. Factors Ergon. Manuf. **19**(5), 438–456 (2009). https://doi.org/10.1002/hfm.20164
22. Molokken-Ostvold, K., Furulund, K.M.: The relationship between customer collaboration and software project overruns. In: AGILE 2007 (AGILE 2007), pp. 72–83. IEEE, Washington, DC, August 2007. https://doi.org/10.1109/AGILE.2007.57
23. O'hEocha, C., Conboy, K.: The role of the user story agile practice in innovation. In: Abrahamsson, P., Oza, N. (eds.) LESS 2010. LNBIP, vol. 65, pp. 20–30. Springer, Heidelberg (2010). https://doi.org/10.1007/978-3-642-16416-3_3
24. Raison, C., Schmidt, S.: Keeping User Centred Design (UCD) alive and well in your organisation: taking an agile approach. In: Marcus, A. (ed.) DUXU 2013. LNCS, vol. 8012, pp. 573–582. Springer, Heidelberg (2013). https://doi.org/10.1007/978-3-642-39229-0_61
25. Robson, C.: Real World Research, 2nd edn. Blackwell Publishing, Oxford (2002)
26. Stotts, D., Williams, L., Nagappan, N., Baheti, P., Jen, D., Jackson, A.: Virtual teaming: experiments and experiences with distributed pair programming. In: Maurer, F., Wells, D. (eds.) XP/Agile Universe 2003. LNCS, vol. 2753, pp. 129–141. Springer, Heidelberg (2003). https://doi.org/10.1007/978-3-540-45122-8_15
27. Sutherland, J., Viktorov, A., Blount, J., Puntikov, N.: Distributed scrum: agile project management with outsourced development teams. In: 2007 40th Annual Hawaii International Conference on System Sciences (HICSS'07), pp. 274a–274a. IEEE, Waikoloa (2007). https://doi.org/10.1109/HICSS.2007.180
28. Vlaanderen, K., Jansen, S., Brinkkemper, S., Jaspers, E.: The agile requirements refinery: applying SCRUM principles to software product management. Inf. Softw. Technol. **53**(1), 58–70 (2011). https://doi.org/10.1016/j.infsof.2010.08.004
29. Whittemore, R., Chase, S.K., Mandle, C.L.: Validity in qualitative research. Qual. Health Res. **11**(4), 522–537 (2001). https://doi.org/10.1177/104973201129119299
30. Williams, L.: Agile software development methodologies and practices. In: Advances in Computers, vol. 80, pp. 1–44. Elsevier (2010). https://doi.org/10.1016/S0065-2458(10)80001-4

Impacts of Digitalization

Cloud-Based Solution for Construction Documentation and Quality Management – Examination of the Value-in-Use

Taina Eriksson(✉)

University of Turku, Turku, Finland
taina.eriksson@utu.fi

Abstract. This study examines the customers' experience of value added they gain from the use of a cloud-based solution for documentation and quality management in construction industry. The industry is a laggard in the adoption of digital solutions. Currently it struggles with very low productivity increases, and the need to develop the operations to respond to new needs. Digitalizing documentation and potentially also quality management is one possibility for the industry towards better productivity. The empirical study was conducted through qualitative interviews with industry experts and organizations that have implemented a cloud-based solution for documentation and quality management. The findings of the study show that using a cloud-based solution for construction documentation generates numerous different kind of value in use benefits. In addition to the time savings in employees' daily job, the use of the solution provides gains in documentation quality and contributes even to the company image for both the (potential) employees and external stakeholders. Most importantly, the use of the solution enhances keeping track of the big picture as it adds to the accessibility and transparency of the data. The industry experts envision that digitalized solutions can be used for developing completely new business models in the industry.

Keywords: Construction industry · Customer perceived value · Digitalization · Documentation · Quality management · Solution

1 Introduction

Construction industry is struggling globally with stagnant productivity developments [1]. Projects typically exceed both the duration and costs budgeted, there are safety issues and long-lasting circles of claims and counterclaims [2]. Important factor contributing to the aforementioned issues is the lack of standards; each project is treated as unique regardless of the recurring elements [2, 3]. However standardizing processes and work flows is an important condition for enabling benefits from digitalization.

The use of digital tools is expected to cut costs and thus improve productivity as it reduces information waste and data inaccuracies. Most importantly, digitalizing information flows reduces the costs caused by human error and oversight [4]. Even though there is already some evidence of successful cases where digitalizing work

S. Hyrynsalmi et al. (Eds.): ICSOB 2019, LNBIP 370, pp. 225–236, 2019.
https://doi.org/10.1007/978-3-030-33742-1_18

flows or processes has led to cost savings in construction [5, 6], the benefits are difficult to achieve, because they necessitate thorough digital transformation.

In an established industry like construction, the transformation is all but easy. Similar to any other context, it must be lead from the top. In addition, the transformation also necessitates a culture that supports it [7]. The transformation calls for commitment from the top management [7]. Nonetheless, getting digitalization to the boardroom agenda in the construction industry can be challenging, since the traditional approaches to costs make investments in ICT unattractive to many construction decision-makers [8].

Equally importantly, successful digital transformation is based on and driven by strategy, not technology [7, 9]. It calls for an end-to-end approach (as opposed to improving specific functions only) and a fundamental change in thinking, by emphasizing profitability rather than resource utilization and by being more selective on the work they target [10].

Successful digital transformation enables the organization to generate value in the use of digital tools. The value generated in the use of any digital solution cannot be predefined by the provider but is created as a joint process between the provider and the customer. The value depends on the provider's resources and processes, the customer's resources and processes as well as the joint resource integration process [11]. This means that the features of the solution and the provider's ability to deliver are only part of the realized value in use. Therefore, this study addresses the following research question:

What kind of value construction industry customers derive from the use of a software solution for documentation and quality control?

The main research question is divided into three sub-questions:

1. Which factors contribute as value for the customer?
2. What is the role of the solution provider in delivering the value?
3. What is the role of the customer in generating the value?

Answers to these questions are sought in a qualitative empirical study focusing on the solutions developed by a company called Congrid Oy. In addition to multiple meetings with the solution provider, the study includes interviews with five selected customers of the company.

The paper is structured as follows. After the introduction is a short overview of the state of digitalization of construction documentation. This is followed by theoretical discussion on value of software solutions. Research methods are introduced in Sect. 4 of the paper, followed by discussion on the research findings. The paper ends with conclusions and suggestions for further research.

2 Digitalization of Documentation in Construction

Construction industry is a laggard in technology adoption and digitalization [1]. There are obvious obstacles, some of which were already mentioned in the introduction. In addition, digital transformation necessitates risk taking and tolerance for failure. It is critical that management is willing to take risks and show a tolerance for failed initiatives [12–15].

Generally, the biggest challenges in digital transformation include the lack of vision, impetus and urgency on the firm, but also on the industry level [16]. These factors are highly relevant also in the context of construction industry. Despite the nonexistent productivity growth, the present operating modes have been satisfactory to the industry. In addition to the lack of impetus, the transformation is hindered also by the fact that it would impact current power structures [16].

In the context of construction, it has been found that BIM diffusion is influenced by: individual, environmental, managerial and technical factors [17]. I.e. numerous factors have an influence. Particularly the resources and capabilities for innovation and coordination are noteworthy [16]. In practice this means that adapting a novel solution or a system represents an innovation to the organization. It has to re-examine its processes whether the old ways of doing things enable benefiting from the novel tools. It is highly likely that processes need to be at least adapted. In addition, the interfaces between the firm and its partners need to be re-examined to find out whether the new tools have implications on them.

Documentation is an essential part of any construction project. Documentation is focal part of all parts of the project, since it is the only way to record what has been done. Despite documentation being very well established and widely accepted part of the industry projects, there exist countless different practices for documenting. One could almost say that there are as many different processes as there are individuals making the documents.

In construction industry, it is important that the documented data can be shared with or delivered to the parties that need it (be those the authorities or the customer) [1]. Even though digitalization of documentation is an essential step in enabling the data to flow where it is needed, the established working methods change very slowly. There is, though, a growing number of cases where novel methods and solutions have produced value and possibly also competitive edge. To better understand where the benefits emerge from, the following section takes a look at the concept of value-in-use.

3 Solution Value-in-Use

In academic examination of customer value, the focus has been mainly on quality as an antecedent to customer value [18] even though presumably also other aspects besides the quality have an impact on the value experienced by the customer. For instance, Macdonald et al. [19] have identified that the benefits of solutions may relate to the customer's:

- improved operational performance
- innovativeness
- competitive advantage
- reduced financial risk (because the provider bears some of the risk)
- dependence avoidance (avoiding putting all the eggs in one basket)
- employees' ability to do their job quicker, easier, or with less stress

- employees' having better control over processes/resources
- employees' having to deal with less uncertainties
- employees' personal reputation as being viewed as competent by others or feeling comfortable with the other people related to their job.

These broad categories cover a versatile set of value experiences and based on their diversity, it can be expected that also many other factors beyond quality influence the customer's experience. For instance, value of using a technology can also be derived from expanding the user network. Increasing number of users adds to the incentives of others to start using the solution [20].

The concept value-in-use refers to "*all customer-perceived consequences arising from a solution that facilitate or hinder achievement of the customer's goals*" [19]. Hence, value-in-use as a concept does not necessarily take a stand on the antecedents of the value.

When a customer implements a new solution, they expect to derive benefits. The customer's expectation of the value in use is formed as they hypothesize an outcome based on the solution features [19]. In addition to the features of the solution, the customer actually plays an equally significant role in value formation. The customer must have resources and capabilities to make use of the solution to realize the benefits and extract value. From this it follows that instead of the value being predetermined, it is continually optimized in use [19].

Value in use is actually phenomenological, in that different people at the customer organization may have different perceptions of it [21]. Hence, it is important to examine value in use on both the organizational as well as the individual levels [19]. On the level of an individual manager for instance, better transparency of data improves the managers' overview of the situation. This is expected to reduce the stress level caused by lack of information [22].

4 Research Design

After reviewing earlier literature on value in use and charting the situation of digitalization in the construction industry. The empirical part of this study was conducted with qualitative research methods. Two sets of qualitative research interviews were conducted with altogether ten interviewees.

First, four industry experts were interviewed on the overall picture of digitalization in the industry and in particular in the area of documentation, the generic potential benefits, expected developments. Second, five different customer organizations using the Congrid solution were interviewed to scrutinize the benefits the customers perceive to derive from the use of the solution.

The experts interviewed were from Finland (two experts), Denmark and Norway. All of them represent an organizations that operate for the benefit of the construction industry (associations or public organizations). The Finnish experts were selected based on their position in the Finnish ecosystem around construction industry. The Danish and Norwegian experts were selected based on the recommendations of the Finnish experts. Two of the expert interviews were conducted face to face and two over Skype.

The five customer organizations were selected together with Congrid to include different types of organizations to cover the full range of different customer groups.

Three of the customer interviews were conducted face to face and two over Skype. In four of the interviews there was one interviewee and in the fifth one there were two interviewees. The main user of the solution was interviewed from each company. They were responsible for giving access to all new users and organizing training as well as solving problems and communicating the company needs with the solution provider. In addition to the responsibility as the main user, most of the interviewees also had first-hand experience of using Congrid in the daily operations of the company.

All of the nine interviews were recorded to enable more detailed analyses. In addition the interviewer made detailed notes during the interview to capture which issues were emphasized. Details of the interviews are presented in Table 1.

Table 1. Interview details

Interviewee position	Duration (min)	Face-to-face/Skype
Expert interviews		
Head of digital innovation	53	F2F
CEO	56	F2F
R&D manager	54	Skype
Director of digitalization development	36	Skype
Customer interviews		
Project manager	30	Skype
Quality manager & CTO	50	F2F
War room engineer	56	F2F
Quality manager	51	Skype
Property developer engineer	49	F2F

The data from expert interviews was used to deepen the literature-based understanding of the state of digitalization and in particular the state of digitalization of documentation and the foreseeable developments. Each interview was scrutinized and the notes written during the interview were supplemented.

The data from the customer organizations was analyzed in relation to the different value dimensions the interviewees brought up. The key value adding dimensions of the solution use were extracted from the data [24]. The data was further reduced in the analysis through categorization into different value classes [23]. Insights on the roles of the solution provider and the customer were derived from the customers' stories of their experience of the solution use reflected against the experts' views and earlier literature.

5 Empirical Insight into the Value of Digitalized Documentation in Construction

5.1 Digitalization of Documentation in the Industry – State of the Art

The interviewed experts shared the impression that digitalization is about to hit the construction industry thoroughly very soon. There are countless solutions available for digitalizing for instance documentation in the industry. Nevertheless, the solutions remain isolated and data does not flow between systems. This implies that the accumulated data cannot be utilized optimally or as widely as possible. Therefore, the data does not produce value for its owners. There can be identified various obstacles for progress. Most importantly, firms' willingness and capabilities to buy software and solutions are low. The firms are used to a purchasing process that is different from how software solutions are generally bought. In addition to putting very high emphasis on the cost, they would prefer buying also software of the shelf.

Once the purchasing decision has been made, the firms are prone to fail (or at least stumble) in the implementation process. Due to the inability to handle the implementation process as an organizational transformation process, the benefits from the solution remain meagre. The experts have seen many cases where even a very successful piloting has not lead to success in organization-wide implementation. Lack of understanding of e.g. the importance of managerial support and the fact that some processes may need to change to leverage the acquired solution [16] lead to sub-optimal use.

All in all, the companies in the construction industry invest only a small share of their turnover in development. Typically the managers' time in the firms is spent "fire-fighting" very acute and extremely acute issues, which leaves no time for forward-looking reflection.

On the other hand, the experts could see numerous potential benefits from digitalizing construction documentation. The state of data management in the industry is currently poor and improvements can yield many benefits. Most importantly, better data management would enable reducing waste (in terms of time and materials, and hence waste on money). More efficient utilization of data helps in allocating the right amount of the right materials and human resources in the right place at the right time. It also reduced the need to do things multiple times. When data is recorded so that it can be utilized for multiple purposes workers' time is saved.

In addition to the potential benefits for the industry, there are notable opportunities for the software/solution providers. Solution providers need to take into account the very highly networked structure of the industry, and the fact that the network is constantly changing since each project is done with somewhat different group of companies. Hence, the companies have the need to include new partners easily in the system and exclude the ones that are no longer part of the network. Optimally this is taken into account also in pricing. The solution provider may also enhance the implementation through consultation for instance. This, however presupposes that the customer understands the importance of the implementation process and acknowledges their own role on creating value in the use of the solution.

5.2 The Customers' Perceptions of Value in Use

The Congrid Solution

Congrid is a cloud-based solution for documentation, quality and safety management in the construction industry. It is used on mobile devices on the construction sites where the inspections are made. All observations made on-site are recorded in the system with details and photos. Hence, the data is accessible to anyone who might need it at any stage of the project. The system generates reports based on templates specified by the customer and the recorded data. In addition, when an inspector observes an issue that calls for action, they are able to assign responsibility for corrective actions to a specific foreman for instance. Hence, documenting the observations in the cloud-based system makes the process of fixing the issue more transparent and easier to follow. Moreover, the solution can be somewhat tailored for the customer's needs.

The company behind the solution is a small, but growing firm that was founded in 2013. The company employs approximately fifteen people and the turnover in 2018 was 1,3M€. The company references include a large share of the construction companies in the Finnish market (including all of the biggest ones), multiple design companies and many property developers. The interviewed five customer organizations using the Congrid solution reported that they are not yet utilizing the solution in the extent they envision, but have gotten off to a good start.

Customers' Experience of the Value in Use

The customers were asked systematically about specific value factors that could be expected to be meaningful based on the Congrid value proposition, the features of the solution and the perceived customer needs. In addition, the interviewees were allowed to bring up things that are beyond the categorization. The systematic categories were:

- costs
- time
- quality
- risk management
- safety at work

The aforementioned factors are naturally linked to each other; costs in particular are related to the other factors. However, by asking specifically about all of these factors, it was possible to find out which factors the solution users prioritize.

Above all, the interviewees emphasized that the use of the solution adds considerably to data transparency and accessibility in their company and with their subcontractors. Having real-time knowledge of what is happening on the site is important for effective project management; yet it has not been reality in the industry thus far. Projects have been, and largely continue to be managed with very poor visibility to the current actual situation. The use of a cloud-based solution is one step in the process of building real-time visibility of the site. One of the interviewed companies has put a lot of efforts in this and they tell that having the real-time visibility to all of the sites where they operate is very important for management. It enables better resource allocation and much better planning. Hence, the customers seem to rate the improved transparency and the most notable benefit. Transparency makes it possible to keep track of the big picture both on the site level and on the company level.

Second, all of the customers reported that using the solution for documentation makes it easier for them to keep to the schedule. Once the observations are recorded directly into the system at site, the time from the observation to the repair (if repair is needed) shortens. In addition, the interviewees tell that they are able to produce higher quality documentation with less time. This is particularly relevant to companies that deliver reports to their customers, but plays a role also in the ones that produce reports for internal use and the authorities. The ones that deliver reports to their customers, tell that it is beneficial for their company that the reports are more consistent in terms of content, quality and the visual representation.

Three out of the five interviewed companies also utilize the solution for quality control. These companies report that defects are more consistently reported when the system is used, because the observations are recorded directly into the system as opposed to someone noticing a defect and trying to remember to tell that to someone whom they might not see today, but only next week etc. Nonetheless, it must be noted that only by changing the peoples' behavior so that all of the observations truly are recorded in the system when they are made, the system can yield these benefits. The customers also told that it is good to be able to assign the responsibility for fixing the defect in the system. Yet, at the same time, all of the interviewees emphasized that the system does not replace human to human interaction. So, these two are both needed for an effective end result.

Three of the examined customers also utilize the possibility of recording safety observations in the system. These interviewees told that similar to the quality management, the use of the solution in safety management calls for a systematic approach, where all observations are indeed recorded when they are made. Only then the companies get the benefits of sharing the data within the company and with partners. Having the process in the system, makes following progress from observation towards fixing the issue visible and more reliable, since it is not dependent only on someone remembering to do or say something.

In addition, once the observations are systematically recorded in the system, it becomes possible to examine whether there can be seen some trends that call for action. For instance multiple observations on serious safety issues concerning a particular subcontractor's operations is an issue that needs to be handled. The interviewees emphasized that the safety issues need to be dealt with in person, however the system is a good aid in improving safety.

An additional and very interesting value factor that two of the customers brought up spontaneously was the company image. Using this relatively new solution is seen to be part of the company image. They want profile themselves as an employer that offers modern tools for its employees and thus e.g. attract talent into the company, but also improve the motivation and job satisfaction of current employees. Thus, it is part of employer branding. On the other hand, the interviewees also told that they want to profile the company as an operator that wants to introduce change and progress into the industry. This kind of value factor was not anticipated based on earlier research, but there could be found an analogy from the consumer context, where it has been recognized that the expected value in use may include also promotional goals such as looking good to others [25].

Challenges in Generating Value in Use

Based on the interviews with both the firm representatives and the industry experts, there could be identified two main categories of obstacles that may hinder deriving value from the use of the solution:

1. The internal organizational capabilities
2. The industry culture

The capabilities refer to the customer organizations skill in implementing a software solution. As it is known based on earlier literature [10] the implementation process includes examination of the current processes and their suitability for the situation in which the new solution is in use. Most probably some changes need to be made in the processes to make the best use of the solution. Hence, the big issue is in the customer organizations' ability to manage a digital transformation process.

Second, the industry culture does not drive the successful digitalization of documentation in construction industry. For example, there is no tradition of sharing data between firms. Therefore, there has not been much emphasis on enabling data to flow between systems or even on organizing visibility to the data for anyone who might need it in their work. In addition, from the perspective of digital transformation, it has not been customary in the industry to drive (or even force) change in the organization from the top. Top management rarely forces organization-wide implementation processes, but lets individual managers decide for their teams whether they want to implement novel tools and when they want to do so. Therefore, moving from pilots to organization-wide implementations is often very slow. In addition, the benefits from novel tools remain unevenly distributed in the organization, inconsistent and superficial.

6 Conclusions and Further Research

Digitalizing documentation may not seem very radical or innovative, but in the context of construction industry it is an important and strengthening trend. Companies are not yet very advanced in their digital transformation that aims at developing their systems. THe goal in construction is to have detailed real-time data of the progress of each site. In practice this means for instance data on the progress of and potential quality issues encountered in installing door handles on-site. Currently, the construction companies do not yet have this data and hence the management does not have a full picture of what is going on in the construction sites. This leads to waste of resources in various forms: time, quality and materials.

Even though the Finnish construction industry is quite advanced in global benchmarking, only a hand full of companies engage in true digital transformation. It is only the leading companies where a good digital strategy (or equivalent) meets a culture and leadership that drive the digital transformation [7]. In these companies the top management has a vision of the digitalization goals of the company and the employees trust the leaders and their vision [7].

The Factors Generating Value in Use

Most importantly, the customers find the increased transparency of the data to add value to their operation. Transparency is a critical factor for building the real-time understanding of progress on-site. The second focal value factor related to time: utilizing cloud-based solution for documentation enhances keeping to the schedule and saves time in reporting.

Together these two factors are very important issues considering the global need in the industry for improving productivity development. Reliable data on the progress and quality issues on the construction sites is critical for better productivity. Awareness of the situation is necessary condition for efficient resource allocation and material deliveries.

In addition, the ease of acquiring and implementing the solution seem to be value-adding factors for the customer. Lack of experience in purchasing software-based solutions makes it difficult for the potential customer to engage in a purchasing process that would serve successful acquisition. Implementation is the second critical hurdle before the customer can derive benefits from the use of the solution. Hence, it is very important to make these easy for the potential customer. (Discussed more in the following section on relation to the role of the solution provider).

Also the ease of including partner network in the use is very important. In construction, the partner network is very fluid in the sense that each site has potentially different orchestra of partners. Therefore, including new partners and excluding the obsolete ones needs to be very convenient and cost effective so that the customer can derive benefits from the use.

The Role of the Customer and the Solution Provider

All in all, the value factors that add value to the customer relate largely to the systematic approach and the structure the software solution introduces to the process. Nonetheless, the systematic procedures need to be put in place in the customer organization. To enable the benefits, the customer organization needs to transform the old processes so that novel tools can be utilized optimally. In addition, it is important that the implementation is organization-wide so that consistent benefits can be gained throughout the firm. Achieving an organization-wide implementation appear to be challenging, yet it can be achieved with top management commitment and support. Also management needs to commit to a systematic approach and enforce the implementation.

The customer organization is also responsible for developing its internal culture in relation to data sharing for instance. They may also need to develop the organizational capabilities to fully leverage the potential of the solution. The minimum requirement is to develop an understanding of the need for implementing the solution.

As discussed in the beginning of the paper, both organization, the customer and the provider have an important role in value creation. The role of the provider begins with the solution and its feature, but does not end there. The provider can play an important role in supporting the customer towards the implementation of the solution.

The ease of acquiring, the ease of implementing as well as the ease of including and excluding partners all are highly linked to choices made by the solution provider. Therefore, these are issues that need to be considered in the development work and even more importantly in building the business model around the solution. Offering complementary services to support the customer may be a clever strategy. For example, offering a person to be part of the implementation process (e.g. doing the user training) can make it a lot easier for the customer to commit to the solution.

At its best, the relationship between the solution provider and the customer is dialogical where both parties engage in constructive discussion around the customer's needs, the solution features and the envisioned development paths. All of the examined customer companies testified to this.

Further Research and Limitations

The goal of the study has been to develop deeper understanding of the value factors for a construction industry customer and the roles that the solution provider and the customer play in generating the value. The study naturally has some limitations.

As it is based on review of literature and nine qualitative research interviews, the findings are not generalizable to wider group of companies. However, analytical generalizations to similar contexts may be fruitful. In addition, the study focuses on one very specific industry that is clearly a laggards in digitalization. Hence the findings do not necessarily apply in any other industry context.

Further research is certainly needed. One avenue for further research is deeper examination of the roles of the solution provider and the customer and particularly the potential benefits of collaborative relationship. In addition, the potential contributions of utilizing novel solutions on the company image and on the job satisfaction among the current employees warrant more attention. Moreover, it would be important to find which ones of the value factors can be measured and with which indicators.

References

1. How to build more efficiently; construction. The Econ. **424**, 10 (2017)
2. Singh, D., Tiong, R.L.K.: A fuzzy decision framework for contractor selection. J. Constr. Eng. Manag. **131**, 62–70 (2005). 1(62)
3. Fulford, R., Standing, C.: Construction industry productivity and the potential for collaborative practice. Int. J. Proj. Manag. **32**, 315–326 (2014). https://doi.org/10.1016/j.ijproman.2013.05.007
4. Liu, R., Chua, V.C.: Theoretical digitalization of information flow in the construction supply chain. Int. J. Manag. Res. Bus. Strat. **5**, 10–27 (2016)
5. Agarwal, R., Chandrasekaran, S., Sridhar, M.: The digital future of construction & in global infrastructure initiative (2018)
6. Araszkiewicz, K., Tryfon-Bojarska, A., Szerner, A.: Modern information management throughout a construction project life cycle – selected issues concerning digitization in construction and a case study (2017). https://doi.org/10.4467/2353737xct.17.127.6878
7. Kane, G.C., Palmer, D., Phillips, A.N., Kiron, D., Buckley, N.: Strategy, not technology, drives digital transformation (2015)
8. Al Moldof: A boardroom discussion: strategic planning around information technology in the construction industry. Constr. Acc. Tax. **25**, 40 (2015)
9. Agarwal, R., Chandrasekaran, S., Sridhar, M.: Imagining construction's digital future & insights on capital projects & infrastructure (2016)

10. Blanco, J.L., Janauskas, M., Ribeirinho, M.J: Transforming construction operations to improve productivity (2016)
11. Storbacka, K.: A solution business model: capabilities and management practices for integrated solutions. Ind. Mark. Manag. **40**, 699–711 (2011). https://doi.org/10.1016/j.indmarman.2011.05.003
12. Hornsby, J.S., Kuratko, D.F., Zahra, S.A.: Middle managers' perception of the internal environment for corporate entrepreneurship: assessing a measurement scale. J. Bus. Ventur. **17**, 253–273 (2002). https://doi.org/10.1016/S0883-9026(00)00059-8
13. Kuratko, D.F., Montagno, R.V., Hornsby, J.S.: Developing an intrapreneurial assessment instrument for an effective corporate entrepreneurial environment. Strat. Manag. J. **11**, 49–58 (1990)
14. Burgelman, R.A.: Corporate entrepreneurship and strategic management. Manag. Sci. **29**, 1349–1364 (1983)
15. Stopford, J.M., Baden-Fuller, C.W.F.: Creating corporate entrepreneurship **15**, 521–536 (1994). https://doi.org/10.1002/smj.4250150703
16. Fitzgerald, M., Kruschwitz, N., Bonnet, D., Welch, M.: Embracing digital technology: a new strategic imperative. MIT Sloan Manag. Rev. **55**, 1 (2014)
17. Merschbrock, C., Munkvold, B.E.: Effective digital collaboration in the construction industry – a case study of BIM deployment in a hospital construction project **73**, 1–7 (2015). https://doi.org/10.1016/j.compind.2015.07.003
18. Ulaga, W., Kohli, A.K.: The role of a solutions salesperson. Ind. Mark. Manag. **69**, 161–168 (2018)
19. Macdonald, E.K., Kleinaltenkamp, M., Wilson, H.N.: How business customers judge solutions: Solution quality and value in use **80**, 96–120 (2016). https://doi.org/10.1509/jm.15.0109
20. Viardot, E.: Six principles to make a technology standard **16**, 23–28 (2005). https://doi.org/10.1111/j.0955-6419.2005.00370.x
21. Vargo, S., Lusch, R.: Institutions and axioms: an extension and update of service-dominant logic. J. Acad. Mark. Sci. **44**, 5–23 (2016). https://doi.org/10.1007/s11747-015-0456-3
22. Molio: Digital transformation in construction (2018)
23. Miles, M.B., Huberman, A.M.: Qualitative Data Analysis An Expanded Sourcebook. Sage, Thousand Oaks (1994)
24. Sandelowski, M.: Qualitative analysis: what it is and how to begin **18**, 371–375 (1995). https://doi.org/10.1002/nur.4770180411
25. Chitturi, R., Raghunathan, R., Mahajan, V.: Delight by design: the role of hedonic versus utilitarian benefits **72**, 48–63 (2008). https://doi.org/10.1509/jmkg.72.3.048

Initial Coin Offering (ICO) as a Fundraising Strategy: A Multiple Case Study on Success Factors

Aleksei Panin, Kai-Kristian Kemell(✉), and Veikko Hara

University of Jyväskylä, Jyväskylä, Finland
alexsey.panin@gmail.com,
{kai-kristian.o.kemell, veikko.k.hara}@jyu.fi

Abstract. Cryptocurrencies and Initial Coin Offerings (ICO) are some of the more prominent examples of currently used blockchain technology applications. Especially software startups have leveraged ICOs to gain funding early on in their lifecycles, going on to develop and create new blockchain based applications. Recently, larger companies such as Facebook have also begun to show interest in cryptocurrency, although thus far not for funding purposes in the form of ICOs. In this paper, we investigate factors that positively affect the abilities of companies to meet their fundraising goals via ICOs. We first identify a set of factors from extant literature and then seek to further confirm the effect of these factors while uncovering new ones by means of a multiple case study of eight firms that have carried out an ICO with varying success. Based on the data, we highlight success factors for ICOs in funding use.

Keywords: Initial Coin Offering · Success factor · Cryptocurrency · Blockchain · Fundraising · Crowd sale · Token

1 Introduction

Interest in blockchain technologies has grown rapidly in the recent years both among the academia and out on the field, especially following the spike in the price of Bitcoin in the autumn of 2017, which made the cryptocurrency a prominent topic of discussion in mainstream media for months. Various blockchain applications have been explored by banks, governments and private businesses alike [20]. The properties of blockchain related to security and traceability are of particular interest to the various parties exploring the possibilities of blockchain [20].

Initial Coin Offering is a method of financing projects through the Internet, in which new ventures sell tokens to a crowd of investors [7]. They are usually, as Fenu et al. [6] define them *"public offers of new cryptocurrencies in exchange of existing ones, aimed to finance projects in the blockchain development arena"*. ICOs have been utilized as a form of crowdfunding [18], particularly by software startups. This method of funding can simplify the process of acquiring it compared to various traditional means. On the other hand, various fraudulent funding ICOs have already been witnessed [14]. Only a fraction of projects using ICOs as a source of funding were ultimately productive and

S. Hyrynsalmi et al. (Eds.): ICSOB 2019, LNBIP 370, pp. 237–251, 2019.
https://doi.org/10.1007/978-3-030-33742-1_19

innovative, although this is consistent with the failure rates of software startups and small companies in general. The way in which ICOs have sparked hype can at times seem reminiscent of the Dot Com Bubble of the 1990s, although some of the hype has since died down following the downward trend of Bitcoin after its Autumn 2017 spike.

Nonetheless, ICOs show promise as a novel way of acquiring funding for firms and especially software startups. Software startups regularly struggle with funding as they search for a scalable, or even sustainable, business model early on in their lifecycles. While extant research has shown that the successful acquisition of funding has little bearing on the success of software startups [16], and that it can even influence it negatively [8], external funding is nonetheless a necessity for most software startups should they wish to keep operating. With hundreds of projects raising billions of dollars in total via ICOs in the United States alone, ICOs as a source of funding are becoming increasingly noteworthy [9].

In this paper, we seek to better understand what makes an ICO succeed. Few extant studies on the topic exist [1, 2, 6, 7] and all of these studies are quantitative in nature, conducted by utilizing secondary sources (more specifically, public information available on the Internet). To tackle this gap in the area, we conduct a qualitative study on the topic using primary data gathered directly from firms. We first look at extant literature in order to look at success factors already discovered, following which we conduct eight case studies of companies that have carried out an ICO in search of funding. Data from these cases is collected by means of semi-structured interviews. Specifically, we tackle the following research question:

RQ: What are the most important factors positively affecting the ability of firms to acquire funding by means of an ICO?

2 Background

In this section, we first discuss the general background of ICOs in terms of blockchain and cryptocurrencies. Then, in the second subsection, we discuss ICOs in detail. In the third and final subsection, we examine extant literature on ICO success factors. As academic literature on the topic is still scare, some grey literature sources are cited, although scientific ones are used where available.

2.1 Blockchain, Cryptocurrencies, and ICOs

While blockchain technology is often associated with cryptocurrency, and especially BitCoin [11], the technology itself is not exclusive to cryptocurrency. Blockchain transactions are validated and recorded in a peer-to-peer network, becoming permanent, irreversible, and verifiable. This makes them notably secure and well-suited for all manners of financial transactions [4]. Indeed, as blockchain as a technology matures, it has become possible to tokenize various assets in addition to (digital) currency [17]. Though they both refer to cryptocurrency and are sometimes used interchangeably, a coin (e.g. Bitcoin) refers to a *standalone* cryptocurrency that functions on its own blockchain (platform), while a token refers to a cryptocurrency that requires a separate (coin) blockchain to function [2].

The Ethereum project has been considered a turning point in blockchain, allowing for the creation of a large variety of decentralized applications and digital tokens created using blockchain and consequently making it possible to represent a wide range of assets [3, 4]. In the wake of this development, the possibility of tokenizing entire projects and using ICOs to fund them also dawned on developers [4].

In 2012, Willett [19] wrote about the possibility of using ICOs as a source of funding. Since then, thousands of projects have utilized ICOs to raise funding [9]. ICOs are an attractive way to raise funding primarily due to (1) the lack of regulation surrounding them; (2) cost efficiency resulting from the absence of intermediary costs; (3) a larger pool of potential investors resulting from there being no restrictions on investment or marketing; and (4) rapid liquidity for investors upon successful listing, as tokens can be sold almost immediately, at virtually no detriment to the project [2].

2.2 Carrying Out ICOs in Practice

ICOs are highly varied due to being nearly unregulated. The firm carrying out the ICO is free to choose whether to utilize an existing blockchain platform or develop a new one. Similarly, ICOs vary in duration, and the firm is free to decide what its minimum (soft cap) and maximum investment (hard cap) goals are, who can participate in the ICO, and which cryptocurrencies they accept.

In an attempt to more specifically categorize ICOs, Kaal and Dell'Erba [10] outlined a roadmap depicting the average ICO process. According to their roadmap, ICO projects are typically first announced to the cryptocurrency community on one of the many community forums, such as Reddit. Then, an executive summary of the project is presented to project investors. The next step of the process typically involves drafting a whitepaper describing the project in further detail which can be likened to a business plan. Out of the 253 ICOs studied by Adhami et al. [1], 16% did not have a whitepaper publicly available, underlining the quite varied nature of ICOs. The final step of this preliminary phase is drafting a yellowpaper which discusses the technical specifications of the project, as far as they are clear in such an early stage [10].

An ICO is then launched in steps. Ryshin [15] list three stages an ICO may have once the sale begins: private sale, pre-sale, and crowd sale. The earlier stages are generally for seeking larger investments from fewer investors who expect discounts. Some ICOs only feature a crowd sale, although a pre-ICO is typically first made available to selected investors. After the pre-ICO offers are signed, the public ICO is announced. This marks the start of a public marketing campaign. Once the crowd sale begins, the tokens can be listed for trade on cryptocurrency exchanges [10].

2.3 ICO Success Factors in Existing Literature

Due to the novelty of ICOs as a fundraising strategy, few studies on the topic currently exist. Four extant studies [1, 2, 6, 7] studying the success factors for ICOs were identified as of April 2019. The factors studied in these four papers are summarized in Table 1 below, along with the effect (positive, negative, mixed) of these factors.

If a factor was studied in multiple extant studies, the effect column is based on the average result of the relevant studies. E.g. if one study found a factor to have no effect while one study found that same factor to have a positive effect, the effect is considered nonetheless positive across those two studies. If one study found a positive effect and one study found a negative one, the effect is considered mixed.

Table 1. ICO success factors studied in extant literature

Factor	Effect	Studies and Explanation
White paper	Mixed	No effect [1]. Page length increased chance of success [2]. A bad whitepaper decreases chance of success [7]
Use of Ethereum	Positive	Using Ethereum as a platform positively impact the chance to secure minimum funding goals [2, 6, 7]. On the other hand, it decreased overall funding received, possibly because big projects often develop their own platforms [2]
Code availability on GitHub	Positive	Positive effect [1, 2]. Good ratings on GitHub had a more positive impact [7]. GitHub generates transparency, allowing those interested to both ascertain code quality and track progress
Pre-ICO	Mixed	Adhami et al. [1] argued pre-ICOs to have a positive impact. Amsden and Schweizer [2] found it to have a negative one. Pre-ICOs can signal uncertainty to investors
Jurisdiction	Positive	Specifying jurisdiction in whitepaper had a positive effect [1]. Utilizing tax haven jurisdiction had no effect [2]
Social media use	Positive	Twitter had no impact [1, 7], possibly because nearly every firm had had one [7]. Use of Telegram impacted positively [2]
Accepting FIAT	Negative	Could make developers seem insecure about their ICO success. Considered to make project more liable to interventions by law enforcement and regulators (e.g. freezing bank accounts) [2]
ICO Bonus Schemes	Positive	Unaffected (2017). Slightly positive effect in terms of the token at least becoming tradable [2]
Use of utility tokens	Positive	Tokens that grant contributor(s) an access to the service and tokens which give profit rights positively affect ICO success [1]
Team	Positive	Not comprehensively studied. A CEO with a large network on LinkedIn (500+) seems to have a positive effect [2]. Team size had a positive effect in one study [2] but no effect in another [6]
Return and Volatility	Mixed	Return and volatility of the currency (e.g. Bitcoin) associated with the underlying blockchain seemed to have no effect [1] or a negative or positive effect depending on the situation [2]. Specifically, higher Ethereum price decreased the likelihood of investing in ICOs while higher volatility increased it [2]

3 Research Methodology

This section is split into two subsections. First, we describe the eight case firms. We then discuss our data collection and analysis methodologies in the second subsection.

3.1 Cases

The eight case companies all wished to remain anonymous upon data collection and thus the case companies are presented as companies A to H. Table 2 presents the general characteristics of the eight case companies.

Table 2. General case firm characteristics

Case	Industry	Team size	Founded in	# Advisors
A	Advertising	19	2017	11
B	Finance	29	2017	7
C	Finance	10	2017	6
D	Finance	No info	2015	2
E	Finance	9	2014	No info
F	Cloud storage	16	2016	4
G	Gambling	7	No info	9

Below, in Table 3, we list the characteristics of the ICO of each company. The data we collected are based on the previous studies discussed in the preceding background section. E.g. use of Telegram is included because an extant study [2] linked ICO success with Telegram use. Jurisdiction refers to the jurisdiction of reference for the token sale, which can be different from the physical location of the firm.

Table 3. ICO characteristics by case firm

	A	B	C	D	E	F	G	H
Whitepaper	Yes	Yes	Yes	Yes	Yes	Yes	Yes	Yes
ICO Year	2017–2018	2018	2017	2017	2017	2017	2017	2018
Prototype	No	No	No	No	No	No	No	Yes
Hard Cap	10 k ETH	50 m USD	200 k ETH	13.5 m USD	70 k ETH	29,6 m USD	12 m EUR	25 m EUR
% of hard cap reached by ICO	100%	100%	30%	104%	71%	39%	17%	78%
Platform	Ethereum	Ethereum	Ethereum	Nem	Ethereum	Ethereum	Ethereum	Ethereum
Code on GitHub	No	Yes	No	No	Yes	Yes	Yes	Yes
Telegram	Yes	Yes	Yes	Yes	Yes	Yes	Yes	Yes
Pre-ICO	Yes	Yes	Yes	Yes	No	Yes	No	No
Jurisdiction	Canada	UK	Estonia	Vanuatu	Singapore	Singapore	Austria	Gibraltar

Finally, in Table 4 are the financial details of the ICOs of each case firm. Some of these are details are discussed in relation to our findings later.

Table 4. Financial details of the ICOs of the eight case firms

Case	Accepted cryptocurrencies	Accepted Fiat during ICO	ICO bonuses	Role of token	ROI as of 22 Mar 2019
A	ETH	No	Token discounts, bouncy program	Utility token	0.60x ETH
B	ETH, BTC	USD	Token discounts	Utility token	0.89x ETH
C	ETH	No	Token discounts, bouncy program	Utility token	0.43x ETH
D	ETH, BTC, LTC	No	Token discounts	Utility token	0.43x ETH
E	ETH, BTC	No	Airdrops	Utility token	0.39x ETH
F	ETH	No	Token discounts	Utility token	0.43x ETH
G	ETH	No	Bounty program	Utility token	0.25x ETH
H	ETH	No	No	Utility token	37.84x ETH

3.2 Data Collection and Analysis

Data from the eight cases were collected by means of semi-structured, qualitative interviews. The interviews were conducted by the first author. The interviews of six cases were conducted over video, using Google Hangouts, and recorded. The interviews of two cases were conducted by having the respondents reply in writing due to scheduling issues. Where possible, we interviewed multiple respondents from each company, although in most cases we ultimately only interviewed one respondent. The titles of the respondents were highly varied from founder to marketing manager.

At the start of each interview, the respondents were asked to describe the most essential factors they felt had contributed to the success of their ICO. This was a question that had been sent to each respondent prior to the interviews, in order to let them think about their responses properly. To this end, they were also asked to discuss the question with their team if possible.

This approach to collecting success factors from companies was adapted from a study by Ojala and Tyrväinen [12] where they studied success factors in Japanese software markets. The respondents were asked to name the top five success factors in this fashion, and to rank the factors from one to five in order of importance. The definition of ICO success used here was adapted from Adhami et al. [1], i.e. the criteria for success was reaching the ICO soft cap set by the company.

Following this initial question, we went over each of the success factors studied in extant literature ([1, 2, 6, 8], as summarized in Table 1) in the following fashion: "Do you think that [factor] affected the success of your ICO? How? Why did you choose to use it?". Then, at the end of each interview, the companies whose ICOs had not reached their hard caps were asked why they thought this was the case, and what they would have done differently in retrospect.

For the purpose of data analysis, the interview recordings were transcribed. From the transcripts, factors affect ICO either positive, negatively, or ones that had had no notable effect (neutral) were highlighted. The effect of each factor was also briefly described in the transcripts. These edited transcripts were then sent back to the respondents who corrected any inaccuracies before sending them back.

Ordinal scale measurement method was used to analyze which factors were the most important ones from the point of view of the firms. This is again in line with the work of Ojala and Tyrväinen [12] on success factors in another context.

Finally, to ascertain (some of) the claims made by the respondents in the interview data and to collect additional data on the case companies, we consulted secondary sources such as the websites of the companies, their (ICO) project whitepapers, and from external sources such as Icobench and Icowatchlist.

4 Results

In Table 5, below, we present our analysis of the respondents' five most important success factors. The factors are scored based on the respondents' factor rankings.

Table 5. Scores of each success factor as assigned by case firms

Factor	A	B	C	D	E	F	G	H	Avg.	Total score
Inspiring idea that will sell		2.5	2	5	5	5		5	3.1	18.6
Efficient building of a community of supporters		1	3		1	3	4	4	2	12.0
Effective marketing/SMM	2		3	3	2		3	3	2	12.0
Professional team		2.5	4.5		4			2	1.6	6.4
Clarity of problem and solution	5	3.5				4			1.6	4.8
Partnership/advisors	3				3				0.8	1.6
Perceived vs. actual progress	4					2			0.8	1.6
Transparency/creating trust				4			2		0.8	1.6
PR	1					1			0.3	1.6
Legal compliance								5	0.6	0.6
Market research/potential		0.5		1					0.2	0.4
Correct timing			2						0.3	0.3
Translations		2							0.3	0.3
Real business practice				2					0.3	0.3

(*continued*)

Table 5. (*continued*)

Factor	A	B	C	D	E	F	G	H	Avg.	Total score
Video content/campaign							1		0.1	0.2
Token economics		1.5							0.2	0.2
Passion/trust in success								1	0.1	0.1
Technical preparation			0.5						0.1	0.1
YouTube influencers		1							0.1	0.1
Telegram use		0.5							0.1	0.1

The scores were distributed so that the top of choice of each respondent received five points, the second choice received four points, and so on. Each firm thus allocated 15 points (5 + 4 + 3 + 2 + 1) to their top five choices. In cases where multiple respondents were interviewed in one case company, the score values placed by each respondent were divided by the number of the respondents for that case. I.e. each firm could only assign the total of 15 points no matter how many respondents represented it.

All the recognized success factors are arranged in decreasing order of importance based on their total score (total score = average * frequency, where average = sum/number of cases) in the table. In the subsections of this section, we then discuss further the top five success factors arising from this data. We omitted frequency from Table 5 as an explicit column, as it can be determined from the firm-specific scores.

In the following subsections, we discuss the five most important factors that emerged from this analysis in detail. The following five Subsects. 4.1–4.5 discuss one factor each, elaborating on them based on the interview data. Subsection 4.6 then presents our results in relation to the negative factors uncovered, and in Sect. 4.7 we compare our results to extant literature. Finally, Subsect. 4.8 summarizes our results.

4.1 Inspiring Idea that Will Sell

The most important success factor based on the scores given was the idea itself, with four case companies ranking it as their number one success factor. Specifically, as firm D elaborated, the idea should showcase real use of a blockchain technology as opposed to a speculative new cryptocurrency. They felt that it was important for the idea to show a blockchain technology that has the potential to improve the current state of the (blockchain) field or to create a useful product or an entirely new industry.

The idea or value proposition was considered important not only in relation to being attractive in the eyes of potential investors but also in keeping the team motivated. Company H noted that at the start of their project, the team was working full day with no pay and half of the team was even living together in order to work more effectively. This, they felt, was only possible because they truly believed in their own idea.

4.2 Efficient Building of a Community of Supporters

Many of the respondents felt that building a community begins before a whitepaper is published or even before the company has a website. Community building should start when the idea is formulated, and it never truly ends as long as the firm operating. All case firms agreed that finding supporters who love the project and share the mission or vision, and who are ready to spread the idea in their own networks are important for the project and specifically for its ICO success.

Some firms entered the crowdsale or public phase of their ICO with their soft cap already reached. Firm C discussed what they referred to as "book building" as a form of community building, referring to the idea of approaching investors in private before the ICO and ensuring their participation in the upcoming ICO. This, they added, was important because it helped them build momentum for the very first moments of the actual ICO. Seeing other investors choose to invest into a new ICO can encourage potential investors who may otherwise be on the fence about doing so. This idea of momentum was shared by firm F in relation to community building in general. A small community had to exist for the community to grow at all.

Firms C, G, and H also discussed the importance of community management in building a community. The respondents felt that it was important to interact with the community on the level of individual community members or investors. The firm should answer every question the members may have, actively support active members, and encourage new members to become active by means of various incentives.

4.3 Effective Marketing

Going global, the firms felt, was the key to success in marketing in preparation for an ICO. However, according to firms A and C, it was notably challenging to gain exposure with how much competition there was. Ways of advertising cryptocurrency projects are limited, and companies largely have to invest into crypto-specific advertisement networks to reach the relevant audiences. Another way of advertising discussed by the respondents was engaging industry influencers such as big Youtube channels.

One specific facet of marketing discussed by the companies was memorability to e.g. website visitors. While actively advertising the project was also needed, the companies felt that it was also important to make people talk about the project to their own contacts. E.g., the respondents of firm C felt that the interactive cartoon characters on their website and the overall design of their website had been a big factor in making people talk about their project.

Social media use was a prominent theme discussed by the case firms in relation to marketing. According to firm D, most, if not all, investors first look at the social media profiles of the firm or the project to gauge how active, engaging, and popular they are. Social media should be used actively (e.g., one post a day). The social media content should display progress on the project or have a clear and interesting message. The team members should also eventually show their faces to the community, e.g. by making video content, in order to generate trust. Utilizing platforms aimed at cryptocurrency enthusiasts such as bitcointalk.org was also considered mandatory.

As the effect of Telegram use was studied in the past, we asked the respondents how they felt their use of Telegram had affected their success. In response, all respondents agreed that it had had a positive effect, with firm D noting that Telegram was the preferred messenger application in cryptocurrency communities. However, the firms noted that focusing on just one channel is not enough, as different channel are useful for reaching different audiences.

4.4 Professional Team

An anecdotal wisdom often heard in relation to startup firms is that an idea alone is worth nothing until a capable team manages to execute it. According to firm C, the team has to have the required capabilities and resources to carry out the project. However, this alone is not enough, as the team also has to be attractive to potential investors, assuring them that they do have the needs to carry out the project.

To this end, the LinkedIn profiles and the personal GitHub profiles of the team members are often used by investors to evaluate the team. For example, some of the respondents noted that the CEO's lack of prior experience had reflected poorly on the project in the eyes of potential investors. The firms felt that an experienced CEO was a positive factor to ICO success. Firm B advised that an inexperienced team should focus on having a prototype to show in place of past achievements and experience.

In gauging the credibility of a team, firms A and G added that team size is also important. Investors typically look at team size in gauging whether the team has the resources to carry out the project. While team size can help a team carry out more tasks simultaneously, the firms stressed quality over quantity. This was also true for project advisors. Firms A, B, C, D, F, and G all agreed that the number of quality of advisors was more important than quantity. One advisor famous in the crypto community can be worth more than ten unknown ones in the eyes of investors.

4.5 Clarity of Problem and Solution

No matter how attractive the idea is, it has to be communicated well. In communicating the problem and solution, one should formulate a clear message explaining: (1) why it is important to solve the problem; (2) how the firm intends to solve it, (3) whether they have all the capabilities required to do so; and (4) why their particular solution is the best one to solve it. Clear use cases help sell the service, as people are then able to understand why they (or someone else) would need it.

Firm F summarized this by noting that there are very smart people out there with very good ideas to solve existing problems, but who are bad at branding themselves and communicating their ideas. This, they added, applies to ideas, projects, or even entire companies. Ultimately, this ties to the idea of effective marketing as well.

4.6 Negative Impact Factors

Case firms C, E, F, G, and H did not reach the hard caps of their ICOs. We thus asked these firms why they felt that they had fallen short of their goal in relation to their hard caps, even if their ICOs had been successful in reaching their soft caps. The firms listed the following reasons they felt had in part prevented them from reaching their hard caps:

- Time pressure (finding and satisfying early investors)
- Being late to the market
- Hard cap too high
- Fraudulent activities by attackers (e.g. phishing sites)
- Ethereum price crash
- Legislative changes (ICO ban in China)
- Lack of knowledge about the target (customer) group in the crypto sphere
- Underestimating the needed marketing budget.

While the focus of this study is on success factors, we collected this data to potentially provide better managerial implications in this study. We relate these findings to extant research in the discussion.

4.7 Findings in Relation to Success Factors Studied in Extant Research

In addition to studying which factors the firms considered most important for ICO success, we also asked the respondents how important they thought the factors studied so far in academic literature had been for their ICO success. These factors were ultimately considered to be of little importance, as their absence in Table 5 indicates. Our findings in relation to these factors are compared to extant literature in Table 6 below.

E.g., while code availability on GitHub was perceived generally positive due to its role in enabling investors to see tangible progress on the project, it was not considered to have had a notable impact on ICO success. Moreover, in relation to GitHub specifically, the respondents noted that it could also be negative because the code could be utilized by attackers looking for weaknesses.

Table 6. Comparison of our data in relation to factors studied extant literature

Factor	Effect in extant research	Our results
Whitepaper	Mixed [1, 2, 7]	Not studied
Ethereum platform	Positive [2, 6, 7]	Positive or Neutral
Code on GitHub	Positive [1, 2, 7]	Positive
Pre-ICO	Mixed [1, 2]	Mixed
Jurisdiction	Positive [1] Neutral [2]	Positive or Neutral
Accepting FIAT	Negative [2]	Positive or Neutral. Only one company actually accepted FIAT, leading their answers to be speculative
Bonus schemes	Neutral. Techniques vary [2]	Mixed. Different firms had different opinions of different types of bonuses
Return and volatility	No effect [1]. High value decreases ICO investments while high volatility increases them [2]	Mixed. Firms could only speculate how the return and volatility could have affected their ICOs, aside from considering the early 2018 crypto crash negative

4.8 Results Summary

To summarize our results, we present them as four Primary Empirical Conclusions (PECs). These PECs are also utilized to present a clearer discussion of our results:

PEC1: The most important success factors for ICO success are: (1) inspiring idea that will sell, (2) efficient building of a community of supporters, (3) effective marketing, (4) professional team, and (5) clarity of problem and solution.
PEC2: Factors that can negatively affect ICO success are: (1) time pressure; (2) hared cap too high; (3) fraudulent activities by attackers; (4) Ethereum (or other associated cryptocurrency) price crash; (5) legislative changes; (6) lack of knowledge about the target (customer) group in the crypto sphere; (7) underestimating the needed marketing budget.
PEC3: Our data supports the notion in extant literature that the utilization of Telegram and the use of utility tokens have a positive effect on ICO success.
PEC4: Factors from extant literature other than those in PEC3 that play a role (positive, negative, or neutral) in ICO success, depending on the project: whitepaper, use of Ethereum platform/ERC20 token, code availability on GitHub, pre-ICO, choice of jurisdiction, accepting FIAT, bonus schemes, BTC/ETH price and volatility prior to and during ICO. Team size and number of advisors are included in PEC1 under professional team as one key success factor.

5 Discussion

Our results present some novel findings in the context of ICO success in the academic literature. Extant studies on the topic have been quantitative in nature, relying on secondary data available online. While we looked at the factors studied in these extant studies, we wished to uncover ones not present in them.

PEC1 (see PECs 1–4 in Sect. 4.8 above) summarizes the five most important factors uncovered across the eight cases of this study. Out of these factors, two have been studied in existing studies while others are new in the context of ICOs, although not new in business studies in general. First, teams in relation to ICOs have only been studied in terms of team size, number of advisors, and the LinkedIn network size of the CEO. As the case firms of this study emphasized the importance of team member and CEO experience and public image, we consider our findings to be in line with the idea the networks of a CEO affecting ICO success. Secondly, the positive effect of Telegram use found in existing literature [2] could be likened to effective marketing.

Otherwise, these five success factors have not been studied in the context of ICOs. However, e.g. teams and marketing have been widely studied across disciplines. Our findings thus point to the factors unique to ICOs not bearing a particularly notable impact on ICO success. Companies seeking funds via ICOs seem to be similar to any other mature firm or startup operating in another market. Indeed, we would highlight Business Model Canvas (BMC) [13] in this context. All of these top five factors of PEC1 can be allocated to some of the nine building blocks of the business model canvas. E.g. “inspiring idea that will sell” and “the clarity of the problem and solution” can be likened to the value proposition of the BMC, while investors at different ICO stages are customer segments for such a firm. Following this line of thought, we would urge firms seeking to carry out ICOs to utilize this tool, and to follow established good business practices in general.

In this regard, we would also highlight the importance of the team as perceived by the case firms. The team behind the project was considered important both in terms of capabilities required to carry out the project, as well as in terms of public image so as to be able to convince potential investors to invest. The importance of the team is also an anecdotal wisdom among startup investors. This brings us to suggest that the BMC [13] may in fact be lacking a team component, given the importance placed on the team by the teams themselves as well as investors in various business contexts.

Out of the negative factors discussed in PEC2, only one has been studied thus far. Amsden and Schweizer [2] found that higher Ethereum price decreased the likelihood of participation in ICOs while a higher level of volatility increased it. The "Ethereum price crash" in our data, on the other hand, referred to the particularly notable cryptocurrency crash of early 2018 that (negatively) affected the value of most if not all larger cryptocurrencies at the time, including Ethereum and Bitcoin. Thus this particularly noteworthy event can hardly be linked to the findings of Amsden and Schweizer [2] either, leaving it a rather context-specific occurring.

Among the other factors of PEC2, most are not unique to ICOs. Lack of knowledge about one's target customer group or segment is a common business issue, as are a hard cap too high (i.e. overestimated target goal in fundraising), time pressure, and underestimating the required marketing budget. These have been studied in other business-related literature in various contexts and our findings offer little to these discussions past the notion of them also being relevant in the context of ICOs.

On the other hand, PEC3 fully supports extant literature on ICOs. All firms agreed that the use of utility tokens had a positive effect on their ICO success, in line with the findings of Adhami et al. [1]. Utility tokens make legal compliance easier, and among our case firms supported the use cases of some of the firms well. As for the use of Telegram, all companies agreed that having a Telegram channel for a bi-directional communication with a community positively affected ICO success, which is in line with findings of Amsden and Schweizer [2]. However, the firms also agreed that the social media use of a company preparing for an ICO should not be limited to just a Telegram but include other channels as well.

Finally, the factors listed in PEC4 have been noted to have varying effects across studies. Our findings in terms of these factors (Table 6) are largely in line with extant literature. The one clear exception is the firms' perception on the acceptance of FIAT. However, only one of our eight case companies actually accepted FIAT while the other firms could only speculate what effect it could have on an ICO. We thus do not consider our findings to go against extant literature in this regard.

Finally, we would highlight PEC1 in relation to whitepapers (Table 6). As the purpose of a whitepaper is to ultimately describe the idea of a firm, it is likely that the idea described therein and how well it is described (marketing and clarity of problem and solution in PEC1) are far more important than the mere existence of a whitepaper. We thus consider PEC1 in relation to whitepapers to partially support the findings of Amsden and Schweizer [2] who found the length of a whitepaper to have a positive effect on ICO success. Longer papers are likely to better describe ideas, although a needlessly long one may also indicate a lack of clarity in describing one's idea.

5.1 Limitations of the Study

The generalizability of the findings of case studies in theory building is a long-standing topic of discussion. We turn to Eisenhardt and Graebner [5], in arguing that case studies are useful for novel research areas. In this case, while some studies have been conducted in relation to ICOs, they have relied solely on secondary sources. We thus consider our approach novel in this area and we consider our results to contribute to the budding discussion in the area. Moreover, Eisenhardt and Graebner [5] argue that 4 to 10 cases is usually a good number of cases. Our eight cases fall inside this range.

6 Conclusions

In this study, we have conducted a multiple case study on the success factors affecting the success of an ICO. By conducting semi-structured interviews in eight case companies that successfully carried out ICOs in the past, we have sought to understand what factors the firms themselves considered to have been most important to the success of their ICOs. This approach, we argue, filled a gap left by extant studies which have been quantitative, focusing on secondary sources publicly available online.

To answer our research question, we argue that the five most important success factors affecting ICO success are: (1) inspiring idea that will sell, (2) efficient building of a community of supporters, (3) effective marketing, (4) professional team, and (5) clarity of problem and solution. These findings point towards firms conducting ICOs being similar to any other type of firm. We thus suggest that companies seeking to carry out ICOs should apply existing good business practices. While we uncovered some success factors specific to ICOs (such as the use of Ethereum platform), the case firms did not rate these factors highly in discussing their importance.

Further research on the topic should seek to study these success factors in-depth. This could be done by e.g. comparing different marketing strategies used prior to ICOs, or by comparing the effect of different bonus techniques on overall ICO success. Our findings point towards ICO companies not being unique on a higher level of abstraction, but e.g. firms looking to conduct ICOs for crypto projects may find some marketing strategies far more effective than other types of firms. Further research on the topic could also take on the point of view of advisors. While a team may only have experience with one ICO, advisors have often witnessed multiple ICOs, letting them thus compare their experiences with different ICOs.

References

1. Adhami, S., Giudici, G., Martinazzi, S.: Why do businesses go crypto? An empirical analysis of Initial Coin Offerings. J. Econ. Bus. **100**, 64–75 (2018)

2. Amsden, R., Schweizer, D.: Are blockchain crowdsales the new 'Gold Rush'? Success Determ. Initial. Coin Offer. (2018). https://doi.org/10.2139/ssrn.3163849
3. Buterin, V.: A next-generation smart contract and decentralized application platform [Whitepaper]. Ethereum (2014). https://www.weusecoins.com/assets/pdf/library/Ethereum_white_paper-a_next_generation_smart_contract_and_decentralized_application_platform-vitalik-buterin.pdf
4. Chen, Y.: Blockchain tokens and the potential democratization of entrepreneurship and innovation. Bus. Horiz. **61**(4), 567–575 (2018)
5. Eisenhardt, K.M., Graebner, M.E.: Theory building from cases: opportunities and challenges. Acad. Manag. J. **50**(1), 25–32 (2007)
6. Fenu, G., Marchesi, L., Marchesi, M., Tonelli, R.: The ICO phenomenon and its relationships with ethereum smart contract environment. In: 2018 International Workshop on Blockchain Oriented Software Engineering (IWBOSE), pp. 26–32. IEEE (2018)
7. Fisch, C.: Initial coin offerings (ICOs) to finance new ventures: an exploratory study. J. Bus. Ventur. **34**(1), 1–22 (2019)
8. Hadley, B., Gloor, P.A., Woerner, S.L., Zhou, Y.: Analyzing venture capital influence on startup success: they might not be good for you (2017)
9. Icobench: Top Countries and ICOs. https://icobench.com/stats. Accessed 16 July 2019
10. Kaal, W., Dell'Erba, M.: Initial coin offerings: emerging practices, risk factors, and red flags. In: Möslein, F., Omlor, S. (eds.) Fintech Handbook. Verlag C.H. Beck (2018). U of St. Thomas (Minnesota) Legal Studies Research Paper No. 17–18 (2018). http://dx.doi.org/10.2139/ssrn.3067615
11. Nakamoto, S.: Bitcoin: A Peer-to-Peer Electronic Cash System (2008). https://bitcoin.org/bitcoin.pdf
12. Ojala, A., Tyrväinen, P.: Best practices in the Japanese software market. Glob. Bus. Organ. Excel. **27**(2), 52–64 (2008)
13. Osterwalder, A., Pigneur, Y.: Business Model Generation: A Handbook for Visionaries, Game Changers, and Challengers. Wiley, Hoboken (2010)
14. Roubini, N.: The Big Blockchain Lie (2018). https://www.project-syndicate.org/commentary/blockchain-big-lie-by-nouriel-roubini-2018-10?barrier=accesspaylog. Accessed 10 May 2019
15. Ryshin, L.: Diving Into The ICO: The Crowdsale, Presale & Private Sale (2018). https://news.ibinex.com/2018/09/22/diving-into-the-ico-the-crowdsale-presale-private-sale/. Accessed 15 June 2019
16. Suominen, A., Hyrynsalmi, S., Still, K., Aarikka-stenroos, L.: Software Start-up failure An exploratory study on the impact of investment. In: Proceedings of the 2017 Workshop on Software-Intensive Business, Espoo, Finland, pp. 55–64 (2017)
17. Tapscott, D., Tapscott, A.: Realizing the Potential of Blockchain. World Economic Forum (2017). http://www3.weforum.org/docs/WEF_Realizing_Potential_Blockchain. Accessed 25 June 2018
18. Wall Street Journal: Initial Coin Offerings Surge Past $4 Billion- and Regulators are Worried (2017). https://www.wsj.com/articles/initial-coin-offerings-surge-past-4-billionand-regulators-are-worried-1513235196
19. Willett, J.R.: The Second Bitcoin Whitepaper (2012). https://sites.google.com/site/2ndbtcwpaper/
20. Zhao, J.L., Fan, S., Yan, J.: Overview of business innovations and research opportunities in blockchain and introduction to the special issue. Financial Innovation, vol. 2 (2016)

Enabling Circular Economy with Software: A Multi-level Approach to Benefits, Requirements and Barriers

Juha-Matti Väisänen, Valtteri Ranta(✉), and Leena Aarikka-Stenroos

Tampere University, Korkeakoulunkatu 7, 33720 Tampere, Finland
valtteri.ranta@tuni.fi

Abstract. Digital and software-based solutions have been identified as key enablers of circular economy, a recently emerged phenomenon that promises more sustainable business through better systemic material efficiency. Opportunities reside on multiple implementation levels. For example, optimizing resource use within processes, engaging in business models enabled by software development, sharing information to optimize resource use on a network level, and creating infrastructures that support systemic tracking and optimization of resource usage.

This conceptual paper contributes to both circular economy and information systems research by identifying the most prolific technologies underlying software-based solutions enabling circular economy. Furthermore, this paper discusses requirements and barriers for successful implementation of identified solutions residing on each of the application, network, and infrastructure levels, providing a framework for researchers analyzing digital solutions and software business in the context of circular economy, and for practitioners seeking to leverage the potential of digital technologies for their customers.

Keywords: Circular economy · Software-intensive business · Digitalization · Micro-meso-macro perspective

1 Introduction

Software-based solutions have recently been identified as a crucial step towards improving sustainability of business through circular economy (CE) [1, 12]. In comparison to traditional consumption called the linear economy model, circular economy is a new model for material flows, which strives to improve sustainability through maintaining the value of products and materials at their highest possible level for longer, thus reducing the need for production of new products, the extraction of virgin materials from our finite planet, and reducing the amount of materials being disposed of as waste [5].

In order to maintain the value of products and materials at the highest possible level, information is needed for efficient management of processes that maintain the value, such as remanufacturing products [8]. Similarly, as circular economy often

S. Hyrynsalmi et al. (Eds.): ICSOB 2019, LNBIP 370, pp. 252–259, 2019.
https://doi.org/10.1007/978-3-030-33742-1_20

leverages the idea that waste for one actor is a resource for another [12], information is required to match the resources that are considered of low value with the actors that have higher value uses for the resource. Software solutions provide the means to collect, disseminate, and analyze this information. While developing technologies thus play a role of crucial enablers for circular economy, research on how to successfully capture these opportunities is still scarce. To address this gap, we adopt the multilevel approach [5], and address the implementation of software solutions on a micro-level, i.e. applications that a single company implements to improve the circularity of their operations, meso-level, i.e. systems that networks of companies collaboratively leverage to improve circularity between them, and macro-level, i.e. infrastructural digital technologies that improve systemic resource efficiency.

Our paper aims to answer four distinct research questions. To map out the underlying technologies for software-intensive solutions in circular economy we seek to answer: *what are the technologies that enable circular economy?* Acknowledging that circular economy actions take place on multiple levels (micro, meso, and macro) by different stakeholders [5], we answer: *how the technologies affect different levels of circular economy?* To address the potential pre-requisites for successfully enabling CE through software solutions, we answer: *what are the requirements to implement the solutions on the different levels of CE?* Lastly, to identify existing barriers that can undermine the potential of software-based business in CE, *we answer what are the barriers on each level?* Through answering these questions, we create a comprehensive framework for identifying and analyzing the feasibility of implementing a digital solution to enable circular economy, suitable for use by practitioners and academics.

2 Circular Economy and Software Solutions

Circular economy challenges the old linear economy approach to production and consumption, by implementing ways to reduce landfill and emissions, and instead keeping materials and products in circulation [4]. Traditional linear economy focuses on maximizing the results by maximizing production, whereas circular economy aims to break the relation between economic growth and use of resources by redesigning economic processes and maximizing the values of resource use [5]. The focus of the reduction is both in the inputs and outputs of material flows and the aim is to keep the materials in the cycle.

The level of impact or implementation of circular economy principles can be divided into three categories: Micro-, Meso- and Macro-levels. The Micro-level refers to actions and effects regarding products, applications, companies and consumers, the Meso-level refers to Eco-industrial parks (EIP) formed together by organizations and societies and the Macro-level covers the largest scale including cities, regions, nations and even global actions [5]. Thus, on the Micro-level, software solutions enabling circular economy to focus on singular applications, Meso-level implementations focus on applications used within a network of actors, and Macro-level implementations focus on digital infrastructure. The Meso-level differs from micro-level especially through the inclusion of public authorities and the decision-making process of the political system. Even though immediate circular decisions and effects can be hard to achieve on the Macro-level, the importance of wide discussion and cooperation is valuable to the promotion of circular economy implementation. Fundamental changes towards circular economy require simultaneous actions on each level of impact [9].

Software solutions are key enablers of circular economy and the development of the emerging technologies are driving the change towards circular thinking and innovation [9, 10]. Emerging digital technologies are relevant in every part of the product lifecycle [2], and through improving ways of data gathering and analysis, products are transformed into value-creating systems [16]. New solutions are breaking down the barriers on implementation of circular economy principles and forming new ways of operation in the form of new revenue streams generated by new possibilities and the implementation of new business models [19], but also by helping companies increase their resource efficiency and close the material loops of the material cycles [2]. Some identified benefits of software solutions that help drive circular economy are new business models and product service systems [15], enhanced product life cycle management [21], loop-closing platforms [16] and more efficient supply-chain management [17], which is why circular economy has attracted major global companies in the hopes of large financial, social and environmental benefits [10].

3 Research

To evaluate the factors and development of software solutions in circular economy, we use the multi-level approach by analyzing existing literature with the aim to form an understanding of the current technologies, requirements for their implementation and the barriers for implementation on each level of impact. The research was done by searching information on uses of digital technologies in the context of circular economy. Scopus and Web of Science were used as primary databases by searching information with phrases such as digi* AND CE or digi* AND "circular economy" between April and May in 2019. The research is conducted by approaching the findings through the different levels of the multi-level approach resulting in better understanding of each level and categorization of the technologies, benefits, implementation and barriers based on their uses in literature. Additionally, the findings and the ways they can be used were discussed with experts, to provide further insight and reliability for the results. Questions one and two are addressed in Sect. 3.1, the third question in Sect. 3.2 and the fourth in Sect. 3.3.

3.1 Mapping the Technologies and Their Benefits

The technologies that can be identified to be used in the context of circular economy are: radio-frequency identification (RFID) [6], internet of things (IoT) [11], big data and analytics [1], cloud computing [19], cyber physical systems, [13], additive manufacturing [8], distributed ledger technologies [16] and artificial intelligence and machine learning [15]. Many of the technologies are used together and may require the use of other technologies to be relevant, for example the RFID sensor technology is a key enabler of other digital technologies, which enables data gathering and communication between objects [17].

On the micro-level many technologies and benefits can be identified through the innovative solutions provided by companies. Internet of things, cloud manufacturing, cyber physical systems (CPS), and additive manufacturing can be used to develop the design, production and logistic processes in a company to promote circular economy [8]. On a company level, internet of things and RFID technologies help companies gather information on product usage, CPS can be used to help with waste sorting and production assembly [13] and also to avoid overproduction [7]. Cloud computing helps companies to handle massive data amounts and reduces energy consumption and additionally it can be used to help logistic processes in selective waste collection [13]. The bundling of IoT solutions with big data analytics, allow the large amount of data gathered to be used in strategic analysis and support decision-making [3] The results gained from big data analytics can be further developed with artificial intelligence solutions which support the process and system optimization even further [15]. New business models are also increasingly being taken into consideration and IoT related emerging technologies seem to be the missing link to enable the use of service business models [7].

On meso-level the digital technologies in circular economy are focusing around the ways of cooperation in the networks. In network communication distributed ledger technologies are being developed to allow safe sharing of information and databases between the different operators [16]. By closing the loops with network cooperation, product lifecycle management needs to be effective to keep track of the quality and availability of products [21]. The RFID and IoT technologies are used to create so called "product passports" to enable the possibilities of reusing products and collaborating in production processes [6]. On meso-level the technologies enable the transformation towards a collaborative environment and the use of platform-type operating [16]. In the available research and literature, the use of technologies on macro-level are not addressed and have been researched only limitedly. Many of the technologies could undoubtedly promote circularity on macro level, but clear examples of the technologies being utilized in the macro level were not found in the context of circular economy during the research.

3.2 Identifying Requirements

The change to favor new disruptive innovations not only require large investments in the technologies [2], but also support from institutions, governments and foreign investors [14]. Information management is a key part in implementing data-based CE-solutions, and the realization of the data-information-knowledge-wisdom-cycle helps to understand the requirements and components in the data structure [20]. When handling data as core business problems, companies need to also cover new knowledge areas for example relating to data security [3].

Development of software for circular economy would benefit from an integration and redesign of industrial systems, infrastructure and delivering services [5], to better facilitate data-driven systemic resource efficiency [5]. Systematic development of the public sector is also needed as it plays a key role as part of the potential networks [18]. The economy needs to support investments as they are a key part in implementing new technologies and building the digital infrastructure and the regulation needs to support circular solutions for example, in the form of favorable taxation and standardization [4]. Lastly, the general awareness of circular economy needs to improve among the consumers and companies, to make the transformation intriguing for companies [4].

3.3 Identifying Barriers

There are still some risks in the development of the technologies, for example in printed QR-codes, which result in 15% failed scans in testing [6]. The reliability between machines is a critical problem, so the barrier of technical development is relevant [8]. Many companies use old information systems which might prevent implementing CE solutions [20] The technologies need to also be coordinated across different organizational areas simultaneously [8]. Circular economy being a new trend that brings in new thoughts and innovations, lack of talent may also form a barrier for corporations, if they have not implemented circular solutions before [8]. At the transition phase, digital and circular competences inside the organization need to be combined [1].

On the consumer perspective, the new service focused business models might affect the behavior of consumers through the loss of ownership. If consumers do not acknowledge the effectiveness of the new business models both for the customers and the service providers, the implementation of new business models enabled by software solutions might fail. However, through servitization, often enabled with software solutions, the financial and operational risks transfer from the customer to the service provider. This might encourage the consumers towards switching from owning products to using services, but the companies need to be able to cover the risks [2].

On the meso-level the challenges are realized in networks and cooperation management. Collaboration and ownership, sharing and access of data can be identified as challenges for CE implementation in meso-level [1]. The ownership of information is a problem that needs to be solved, for example in the cases of jointly created information. In shared data bases, which are used in innovation processes, the ownership of the information and thus the innovation might be unclear [16]. At the same time, the integrity of data might cause problems in collaborating databases and networks [8].

On macro level the barriers coordinate with the requirements identified on the same level. Wrong focus on taxation creates a strong barrier to the development of circular economy and thus the need for software solutions supporting it. Through political decisions the attitudes towards implementing circular decisions are formed as the taxation affects the profitability for circular transformation [8]. Through the national decision-making the general awareness also forms a barrier for the circular solutions to be implemented nationally as the society needs to accept the transition towards circularity [4].

4 Discussion and Conclusions

The distinction between the different levels can be seen clearly in Table 1, displaying the results. Reported possibilities and examples of software supporting circular economy reside mostly in the micro level. On the meso-level, the findings are related to the cooperation and networking of organizations, helping to build a collaborating environment to promote circular economy. On the macro-level, the findings are only limited to identifiable requirements and barriers, indicating that circular economy is not yet thoroughly achieved on the macro-level or the solutions are not applied yet on large scale.

Table 1. Identified technologies, benefits, requirements and barriers

	Technologies	Benefits	Requirements	Barriers and challenges
Micro	• Radio Frequency Identification • Internet of Things • Cloud computing • Additive manufacturing • Cyber physical systems • Big Data analytics • Artificial intelligence and machine learning	• Development and optimization of operational processes • Gather information on product usage • Help in waste sorting • Avoid Overproduction • Data management • Resource and energy efficiency • Support decision-making • Enable service business models	• Investments • support from the public sector • Information management • Data Security • Knowledge on materials and product development • Skills in circular economy • New business models • Reverse cycle development	• Coupling of resource use and economic growth • Development of the technologies • Old information systems in use • Indoor organizational coordination • Lack of talent • the loss of ownership. • Financial and operational risks
Meso	• Distributed ledger technologies • Radio Frequency Identification • Internet of Things	• Allow safe sharing of information and databases • Keep track of the quality and availability of products • Enable the transformation towards a collaborative environment • Platform-type operating	• Dedicated network • Allowing information sharing • Platforms for collaboration • Shared vision	• Coupling of resource use and economic growth • Collaboration • Data ownership • Data sharing • Data access • Data integrity
Macro	• No identified results	• No identified results	• Development of the infrastructure • General awareness • Legislation • Good economical phase that supports investments	• Coupling of resource use and economic growth • Taxation • General awareness

Based on the results, digital technologies can be seen to drive the circular transformation from micro-level towards the meso- and macro-levels. The broader implementation of software-based business requires large grounds of digital infrastructure, and from the perspective of circular economy, industrial companies are the key operators in the infrastructural development due to their closeness to material and energy flows. The solutions that are achieved on a micro-level can be further utilized on the upper levels, when the digital infrastructure on public and national operators are developed as well and the micro-level solutions can be generalized.

Meso-level requirements and barriers rely heavily on networking and collaboration, which leads to focusing on data management. The rise of distributed ledger technologies like blockchain are key for enabling safe collaboration and data sharing. Though the data technologies are developing fast the questions related to the ownership of data still remain unsolved. The success of meso-level implementation is only achieved if all the operators dedicate to operating towards a common goal, which might be a challenge to organize and bring out new challenges related to operating methods and general cooperation. The simultaneous competition and co-development might be hard to fit into certain ecosystems, which is why meso-level implementations might not work even though the software technologies could be utilized.

The slow development of the macro level infrastructure might be one of the key reasons why software is not utilized more in the context of circular economy. On the other hand, the development of circularity seems to need the development of the lower levels, before macro-solutions and benefits might be achieved. Even though, the macro-level benefits are yet unrealized, the actions towards circular economy on macro-level are important, as support to the transition on lower levels. The support of the public sector and government can tip the scales on whether new business models and other new forms of operations are profitable and thus motivate organizations to pursue them.

The concluded study contributes to the prior research done on the areas of circular economy, software-intensive solutions and their combined effects. The study develops the understanding on the technologies, benefits, requirements and barriers among each level on the perspective of software solutions supporting circular economy and provides information on the differences between the levels.

The results of the conducted study are conceptual and limit only to the available literature and the findings that have been reported in previous research. The focus of the findings is mainly on the theoretical side, which is supported by few concrete examples on individual operators or cases. Thus, we suggest that further research should be made with a case-based empirical focus on the software solutions and their effects on circular economy on each levels of the multi-level approach. The use and effects of the technologies should be researched in an organizational environment that already focuses on software solutions and have the infrastructure ready for circular development in order to empirically test the findings and provide information for circular economy development. We also suggest that the macro-level solutions need to be researched thoroughly as the current findings on this level are very limited.

Acknowledgments. This research was conducted within the projects CICAT2025, Circular Economy Catalysts: From Innovation to Business Ecosystems funded by the Academy of Finland, Strategic Research Council (decision no 320194, 26.11.2018, updated 10.01.2019) and 6Aika: CircVol funded by the European Regional Development Fund (decision no EURA 2014/6291/09 02 01 01/2018/UML).

References

1. Antikainen, M., Uusitalo, T., Kivikytö-Reponen, P.: Digitalisation as an enabler of circular economy. Procedia CIRP **73**(2018), 45–49 (2018)
2. Bressanelli, G., Adrodegari, F., Perona, M., Saccani, N.: Exploring how usage-focused business models enable circular economy through digital technologies. Sustainability **10**(3), 1–21 (2018)
3. Bressanelli, G., Adrodegari, F., Perona, M., Saccani, N.: The role of digital technologies to overcome Circular Economy challenges in PSS Business Models: an exploratory case study. Procedia CIRP **73**(2018), 216–221 (2018)
4. Ellen MacArthur Foundation: Towards a Circular Economy: Business Rationale for an Accelerated Transition (2015)
5. Ghisellini, P., Cialani, C., Ulgiati, S.: A review on circular economy: the expected transition to a balanced interplay of environmental and economic systems. J. Clean. Prod. **114**, 11–32 (2016)
6. Gligoric, N., et al.: Smarttags: IoT product passport for circular economy based on printed sensors and unique item-level identifiers. Sens. (Switz.) **19**, 3–5 (2019)
7. Hansen, E.G., Alcayaga, A.: Smart-circular systems: a service business model perspective. Plate **2017**(2017), 10–13 (2017)

8. de Sousa Jabbour, A.B.L., Jabbour, C.J.C., Filho, M.G., Roubaud, D.: Industry 4.0 and the circular economy: a proposed research agenda and original roadmap for sustainable operations. Ann. Oper. Res. **270**(1–2), 273–286 (2018)
9. Kirchherr, J., Reike, D., Hekkert, M.: Conceptualizing the circular economy: an analysis of 114 definitions. Resour. Conserv. Recycl. **127**, 221–232 (2017)
10. Lewandowski, M.: Designing the business models for circular economy-towards the conceptual framework. Sustainability. **8**(1), 1–28 (2016)
11. Lieder, M., Rashid, A.: Towards circular economy implementation: a comprehensive review in context of manufacturing industry. J. Clean. Prod. **115**, 36–51 (2016)
12. Merli, R., Preziosi, M., Acampora, A.: How do scholars approach the circular economy? A systematic literature review. J. Clean. Prod. **178**(2018), 703–722 (2018)
13. Nascimento, D.L.M., et al.: Exploring Industry 40 technologies to enable circular economy practices in a manufacturing context. J. Manuf. Technol. Manag. **30**, 607–627 (2018)
14. Nasiri, M., Tura, N., Ojanen, V.: Developing disruptive innovations for sustainability: a review on Impact of Internet of Things (IOT). In: Proceedings of PICMET 2017 - Portland International Conference on Engineering and Technology Management for the Interconnected World, pp. 1–10 (2017)
15. Pagoropoulos, A., Pigosso, D.C.A., McAloone, T.C.: The emergent role of digital technologies in the circular economy Procedia CIRP **64**, 19–24 (2017)
16. Rajala, R., Hakanen, E., Mattila, J., Seppälä, T., Westerlund, M.: How Do Intelligent Goods Shape Closed-Loop Systems? Calif. Manage. Rev. **60**(3), 20–44 (2018)
17. Rajput, S., Singh, S.P.: Connecting circular economy and Industry 4.0. Int. J. Inf. Manage. **49**, 98–113 (2019)
18. Ruohomaa, H., Kantola, J., Salminen, V.: Value network development in Industry 4.0 environment. In: Kantola, J., Barath, T., Nazir, S. (eds.) AHFE 2017. AISC, vol. 594, pp. 28–39. Springer, Cham (2018). https://doi.org/10.1007/978-3-319-60372-8_4
19. Stock, T., Obenaus, M., Kunz, S., Kohl, H.: Industry 4.0 as enabler for a sustainable development: A qualitative assessment of its ecological and social potential. Process Saf. Environ. Prot. **118**, 254–267 (2018)
20. Valkokari, P., Tura, N., Ståhle, M., Hanski, J., Ahola, T.: Advancing Circular Business: from data to wisdom: approaches enabling circular economy (2018)
21. Watanabe, C., Naveed, N., Neittaanmäki, P.: Digitalized bioeconomy: planned obsolescence-driven circular economy enabled by Co-Evolutionary coupling. Technol. Soc. **56**, 8–30 (2019)

Implementing AI Ethics in Practice: An Empirical Evaluation of the RESOLVEDD Strategy

Ville Vakkuri(✉) and Kai-Kristian Kemell

Faculty of Information Technology, University of Jyväskylä, Jyväskylä, Finland
{ville.vakkuri,kai-kristian.kemell}@jyu.fi

Abstract. As Artificial Intelligence (AI) systems exert a growing influence on society, real-life incidents begin to underline the importance of AI Ethics. Though calls for more ethical AI systems have been voiced by scholars and the general public alike, few empirical studies on the topic exist. Similarly, few tools and methods designed for implementing AI ethics into practice currently exist. To provide empirical data into this on-going discussion, we empirically evaluate an existing method from the field of business ethics, the RESOLVEDD strategy, in the context of ethical system development. We evaluated RESOLVEDD by means of a multiple case study of five student projects where its use was given as one of the design requirements for the projects. One of our key findings is that, even though the use of the ethical method was forced upon the participants, its utilization nonetheless facilitated of ethical consideration in the projects. Specifically, it resulted in the developers displaying more responsibility, even though the use of the tool did not stem from intrinsic motivation.

Keywords: Artificial intelligence · Ethics · Design methods · Ethical tool · RESOLVEDD · Developer commitment

1 Introduction

As Artificial Intelligence (AI) and Autonomous Systems (AS) become increasingly ubiquitous, real-life incidents, such as the recent Cambridge Analytica one, begin to highlight the importance of AI ethics. AI systems are unique in that one cannot opt out of using them. Even if one does not own an autonomous vehicle, it would seem that one nonetheless has to drive on the roads with them. Similarly, one cannot avoid being tracked by AI-based surveillance systems even if one does not consent to being surveilled. In this fashion, the very idea of an active user in the context of AI systems becomes blurred as human actors e.g. become mere objects of data collection.

An early version of this paper was presented in the Euromicro Conference on Software Engineering and Advanced Applications (SEAA 2019).

S. Hyrynsalmi et al. (Eds.): ICSOB 2019, LNBIP 370, pp. 260–275, 2019.
https://doi.org/10.1007/978-3-030-33742-1_21

As the enormous impact of AI systems becomes increasingly clear, calls for privacy and fairness in these systems grow more prominent. The city of San Francisco already voted to ban facial recognition from being used to track and profile its citizens[1], underlining that regulations and laws directed at AI systems are likely to grow in number as further progress on AI is made. With laws and regulations (e.g. GDPR) starting to necessitate ethical consideration in AI design, and with the general public demanding more ethical systems, those utilizing or designing these systems should become familiar with AI ethics.

Organizations developing and deploying AI systems will arguably benefit from focusing on fair systems that respect the privacy of their users in the future. With such trends as environmental awareness and user privacy, ethics seem to be becoming a global mega trend. As users become more aware of their privacy and how data is handled by various AI systems, ethical development is likely to become a selling point for such systems.

Studies in the area of AI ethics should seek to bridge this gap between research and practice by turning to the field of behavioral Software Engineering (SE) [18]. If the goal is to make ethics a part of AI system development, the focus should be on the developers. In practice, it is the developers who build the ethical principles into the system, as no AI system is at present capable of evaluating and deciding on its own ethical principles. In doing so, developers build their own values into the systems, which end up reflecting their views [2]. Yet, it is known that developers are not well-informed of ethics in software engineering [19].

This, combined with the current lack of tools and methods in AI ethics, has resulted in a situation where developers do not have the means to implement ethics. The methods that exist have not seen widespread adoption [26] and lack empirical validation or are immature [21]. In developing methods for this area, the focus should be on understanding the developers, focusing on behavioral SE [18].

Currently, ethical issues seem to be often simplified or neglected entirely during development. This can be costly when they then later surface during the operational life of the system, as was e.g. the case when Amazon's recruitment AI[2] was found to be biased towards women, having been trained using past recruitment data which featured predominantly male recruits.

Studies into implementing AI ethics in practice are currently lacking. Moreover, the methods and tools that we presently have are also lacking in empirical validation [21]. To provide empirical data into this area of research, in this paper we test an ethical tool from business ethics, the RESOLVEDD strategy [22], in the context of AI design. We do so by means of a multiple case study of five different prototype projects where the use of RESOLVEDD was one of the requirements for the projects. The goal of this study is to further our understanding

[1] https://www.bbc.com/news/technology-48276660.

[2] https://www.reuters.com/article/us-amazon-com-jobs-automation-insight/amazon-scraps-secret-ai-recruiting-tool-that-showed-bias-against-women-idUSKCN1MK08G.

on how to provide actionable tools for implementing AI ethics. In this paper, we approach this problem through the following two research questions: **Q1** Does the use of an ethical tool enhance ethical consideration in the design process? **Q2** How does the ethical tool RESOLVEDD perform in the AI context?

2 Background

2.1 Ethically Aligned Design

In the field of IT and ICT, ethics has historically been discussed in different contexts. It has been discussed in relation to (1) applying traditional ethical theories in the context of ICT; (2) as a branch of professional ethics for ICT; and (3) as a set of specific ethical issues such as internet privacy and security in ICT [5]. For example, traditional ethical theories such as Kantian ethics and virtue ethics have been applied in the context of ICT. Moreover, specific, practical questions related to professional ethics have been addressed in the ACM Code of Ethics [13]. In this paper, we define ethics from the point of view of ICT as follows: "the analysis of the nature and social impact of computer technology and the corresponding formulation and justification of policies for the ethical use of such technology" [20]. Another central construct used in this paper, Ethically Aligned Design [10], on the other hand refers to the involvement of decision-making in practice and ethical consideration in a the practice and design AI and autonomous systems and technologies.

The continuing progress in the field of AI calls for new and concrete methods to manage the ethical issues arising from these new innovations [2,6]. Indeed, Allen et al. [2] argue that AI and AI-based systems produce new kinds of needs to consider. Specifically, they propose that designers implicitly embed values in the technologies they produce [2]. AI and other complex systems force designers to consider what kind of values are embedded in the technologies and also how the practical implementation of these values could be done and how these systems can be governed [6].

To better incorporate human values into the design process of AI systems, some AI-specific values have been proposed. For example, the importance of transparency in AI systems was emphasized by Bryson and Winfield [4]. Dignum [7] presented two more values in addition to transparency by presenting the ART principles (Accountability, Responsibility, Transparency) to guide ethical development of AI systems [7]. Finally, fairness and freedom from machine bias have also become important as core values expected from AI systems [12].

To direct the discussion on aligning ethics with system design, the IEEE Global Initiative on Ethics of Autonomous and Intelligent Systems was launched. The initiative was branded under a concept titled Ethically Aligned Design (EAD), a construct we briefly discussed at the start of this section. The initiative aims to encourage practitioners to consider and prioritize ethics in the development of AI. So far, the initiative has defined values and ethical principles that prioritize human well-being in a given cultural context. These guidelines have been published online (latest Edition1 2019) [10]. These guidelines revolve around presenting different AI ethics issues and then suggesting ways of tackling each issue through extant literature, but ultimately offer very little in terms of actionable practices or tools, with most of the focus being on discussing the issues.

Arguably, the key audience of EAD are, or should be, the developers. AI development, much like conventional software development, is a cognitive activity [14] where humans play a significant role in deciding how the system behaves. Extant research has established that developers' interests are driven by work related concerns [1]. Concerns are the foundation of developer commitment development in his/her work. Commitment is important as it directs attention and helps in maintaining the chosen course of action [1]. Should EAD practices become used by the developers, it should be meaningful to them, contributing to their work related concerns and thus helping them accomplish their tasks.

Experiencing meaningfulness in the work place plays a significant role in understanding the ethical aspects related to one's work. Bowie [3] states that an overall experience of meaningfulness while working supports the individual's moral development related to that activity. Understanding the ethical aspects of one's work stems from understanding the meanings of one's own actions and responsibility for the well-being of others [3]. In this regard, the challenge in software and interactive systems development and design is that the developers may not fully understand the consequences of their actions and how their decisions eventually affect others once the system is operational. In other words, in order for EAD to be possible, ethics needs to become meaningful for developers. For ethics to become meaningful for developers, it needs to help developers accomplish work tasks, instead of being something extra they have to take into consideration e.g. because the product manager tells them to.

In summary, there are multiple methods that could potentially be used to implement AI ethics. However, we argue that AI calls for new, actionable methods to address the new ethical issues presented by these systems, specifically tailored for the context of AI. In the next section, we further discuss an existing tool for ethical decision-making that we focus on in this study, RESOLVEDD.

2.2 The RESOLVEDD Strategy

The RESOLVEDD strategy was first introduced by Pfeiffer and Forsberg [22]. It is a step-by-step decision-making method, originally intended for teaching practical ethics to bachelor students. The method is aimed at those who do not have prior knowledge of ethics or philosophy to evaluate ethical principles in practice. This aspect of the RESOLVEDD strategy makes it particularly appealing in the field of Software Engineering (SE) where few curricula have traditionally included studies in ethics or philosophy.

The RESOLVEDD strategy is based on professional ethics and approaches ethics from the point of view of personal ethical problems in work contexts. It is not connected to any specific ethics theory and does not enforce any set of values on its would-be users. Instead, RESOLVEDD is intended to support its users in taking into account ethical issues and tackling them through their own set of values or through an ethics theory of their choice [22].

The strategy is presented as a series of nine concrete steps (Fig. 1) portraying the rational ethical decision-making process. By using the method, one is able to justify and explain the decision-making process leading up to whatever actions were ultimately taken. It is intended to help its users understand the ethical issues present in their work and encourages them to address them in the way they deem best, though nonetheless without compromising ethical principles. Though it originates from the field of business ethics, the method can also be utilized for tackling ethical issues outside the field of business [22].

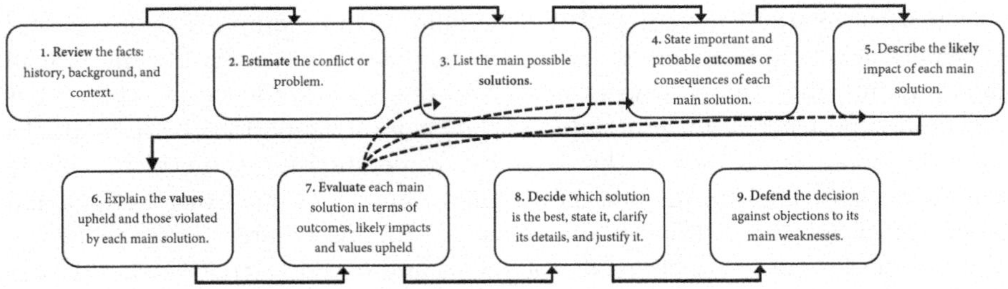

Fig. 1. The nine steps of the RESOLVEDD strategy

In extant research, the RESOLVEDD strategy has been applied in the field of biology where it was used to teach ethics [17]. Based on their study, Johansen [17] note that the method introduces a capability to produce a description of various solutions and viewpoints to a single problem. However, they also criticize the method for being time-consuming, and for giving no feedback to its users on whether they succeeded in implementing ethics. Indeed, as RESOLVEDD does not directly offer any solutions to the ethical issues it may help discover, it is up to its users how to address them, or whether to address them at all.

3 Research Model

In addressing ethics as a part of AI development, various principles have been discussed in academic literature. For the time being, the discussion has centered on four constructs: Transparency [4,7,10], Accountability [7,10], Responsibility [7,10] and Fairness e.g. [12]. A recent EU report [11] also discussed Trustworthiness as a goal AI systems should strive for. Moreover, the field of AI ethics can be divided into three categories: (1) Ethics by Design (integration of ethical reasoning capabilities as a part of system behavior e.g. ethical robots); (2) Ethics in Design (the regulatory and engineering methods); and (3) Ethics for Design: (codes of conduct, standards etc.) [8]. In this paper, we focus on the ethically aligned development process.

Out of the aforementioned four main principles for AI Ethics, we consider accountability, responsibility, and transparency (the so-called ART principles, formulated by Dignum [7]) a starting point in understanding the involvement of ethics in AI projects. We have selected these three constructs as the basis of our research framework (Fig. 2).

Transparency is defined in the ART principles of Dignum [7] as transparency of the AI systems, algorithms and data used, their provenance and their dynamics. i.e. transparency refers to understanding how AI systems work by being able to inspect them. Transparency can be argued to currently be the most important of these principles or values in AI ethics. Turilli and Floridi [25] argue that transparency is the key pro-ethical circumstance that makes it possible to implement AI ethics. It is also one of the key ethical principles in EAD [10].

In the research framework of this study, transparency is considered on two levels: (a) transparency of data and algorithms, as well as (b) transparency of systems development. The former refers to understanding the inner workings of the system in a given situation, while the latter refers to understanding what decisions were made by whom during development. It is a pro-ethical circumstance that makes it possible to assess accountability and responsibility.

Accountability refers to determining who is accountable or liable for the decisions made by the AI. Dignum [7] defines accountability to be the explanation and justification of one's decisions and actions to the relevant stakeholders. Transparency is required for accountability, as we must understand why the system acts in a certain fashion, as well as who made what decisions during development in order to establish accountability. Whereas accountability can be considered to be externally motivated, closely related but separate construct responsibility is internally motivated. In the context of this research framework, accountability is used not only in the context of systems, but also in a more general sense.

Dignum [7] defines responsibility in the ART principles as a chain of responsibility that links the actions of the systems to all the decisions made by the stakeholders. We consider it to be the least accurately defined part of the ART principles, and thus have taken a more comprehensive approach to it in our research framework. According to the EAD, responsibility can be considered to be an attitude or a moral obligation [10].

Responsibility in the context of this study connects the designer to any stakeholders of the system. In order to be responsible, one must make weigh their own actions and to consciously evaluate their choices. A simplified way to approach responsibility is to ask "would I be fine with using my own system?".

To link this AI ethics discussion with SE practice, we have adopted the Commitment Net Model of Abrahamsson [1] to study AI Ethics in the context of Software Process Improvement (SPI). As we approach AI Ethics from the point of view of implementing it into practice in SE, we consider the utilization of extant theories in SPI useful for this purpose.

Developers' interests are driven by work-related concerns [1]. From the point of view of the developers, an important question to pose is: why would the developer act responsibly and take into account ethical issues? In order to understand commitment, we should first seek to understand the concerns of the developers which lead to actions, and together, form commitment. A task that may be perceived as time consuming, boring, or otherwise lacking in motivational elements, will still be executed because it plays a role in the developer's commitment behavior.

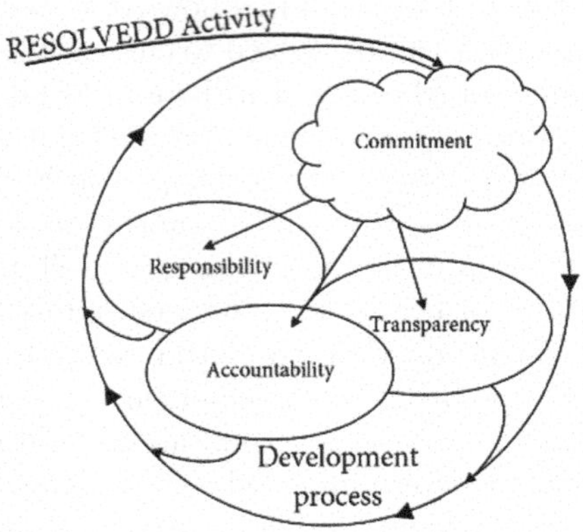

Fig. 2. Research framework for ethically aligned design

Commitment, accountability, responsibility and transparency can therefore be seen as a cycle with links (Fig. 2). These links are explorative as little empirical data is currently available. We can hypothesize that by strengthening commitment towards the RESOLVEDD strategy, ethics will be implemented in the system through its use. Ethics, as defined by EAD, is made apparent through an increase in responsibility in design and the clarity of accountability, in order to help produce more transparency in AI development. Transparent project culture can likewise influence commitment, responsibility and accountability in design. In order to achieve this goal, the RESOLVEDD strategy should (1) support responsibility and responsible culture, (2) help developers to make more meaningful decisions in their own work, and (3) take into consideration ethical principles such as accountability, privacy, autonomy, and fairness.

4 Study Design

The RESOLVEDD strategy was empirically through a multiple case study. More specifically, we studied five student projects in which the RESOLVEDD strategy was utilized. Yin [27] explains that the use of multiple case study makes it possible to have multiple data sources with rich in-depth investigations that would not be possible with a survey. This approach also made it possible to analyze each case separately and to then validate the observations by cross-referencing.

The study was conducted in an Information Systems (IS) course at the University of Jyväskylä. Bachelor level students were introduced to the RESOLVEDD strategy as a part of system design and development methods. In the course, the students were given the task of developing a concept and prototype of a futuristic innovation that could be possible in the near future, but which was not considered currently plausible. The projects were carried out in five groups of 4–5 students. Choosing from a list, the students had to select one technology they would utilize as a part of their solution. For example, a team could choose to utilize Augmented Reality (AR) as a part of their solution in this fashion.

In the project, the use of the ethical method, RESOLVEDD, was given as one of the design requirements. The course spanned 10 weeks and consisted of eight weekly 5–6-h workshop sessions and a project demonstration event held in the final week. During the workshop sessions, the students were introduced to the RESOLVEDD strategy in two lectures: (1) how to use the method, and (2) how to report their ethical considerations. The student were also given step-by-step instructions to the method and the project groups also had periodic RESOLVEDD strategy sessions with the teaching team where they had a chance to pose questions related to the method. At the end of the course, the teams presented their work in a project demonstration event. In the event they presented a demo of their solution and a poster where they had visualized the ethical issues, solutions to these issues and a justification to the actions taken in the design process.

Data for this study were collected by means of semi-structured interviews conducted after the course had concluded. The goal of the interviews was to (1) understand how the RESOLVEDD strategy had been used in practice in each project, and (2) how the ethical decision-making had been carried out in the projects, if at all. The interview questions were formulated based on the research framework. The semi-structured approach was applied to allow the respondents to elaborate on themes beyond the prepared questions. The interviews were conducted as group interviews with one project team at a time, and recorded. The records were later transcribed and the analysis was conducted using the transcripts.

Given the novelty of applying new ethical methods in AI ethics, and the current lack of existing literature related to our research questions, we adapted a qualitative approach, using open-ended interview questions. Moreover, we utilized a grounded theory inspired approach to analyzing them. We followed the recommendations of Heath and Cowley [15] in selecting a method that best suited our cognitive style and research environment. We utilized elements of the grounded theory approach proposed by Strauss and Corbin [24], aside from naming of the coding phases.

In practice, the transcripts were analyzed in the following manner. First, the transcripts were coded quote by quote and each quote was given a code describing its contents. Secondly, based on these codes, more abstract categories were introduced to group the individual quotes from each interview into general, re-occurring themes. Thirdly, this higher-level categorizing was validated by comparing the data from each interview. In this stage, we also sought to discover reoccurring themes across the five interview cases. From these reoccurring themes, core categories were formed and then compared to the research framework in order to determine how the principles of EAD were present in the projects (responsibility, meaningfulness, transparency and accountability), and what kind of commitment the developers exhibited towards implementing them. In discussing our findings, we present our key observations as Primary Empirical Conclusions (PECs).

5 Findings

The findings from the analysis of the empirical data are reported here as topic-related Primary Empirical Conclusions (PEC). In total 5 PECs were formulated in the analysis. This section is structured into four sub-sections according to the research framework discussed in the preceding section. We illustrate some of our findings with relevant quotes from the respondents. However, our arguments are not solely based on the quotes but on our data in general.

5.1 Commitment to Ethically Aligned Design

All five teams had rather critical sentiments towards dealing with ethical issues or using ethical tool as a part of their product design. Using an ethical tool was perceived as something completely novel to them, and they did not seemingly place value on considering the ethical aspects on their project. This was despite of the fact that the employed method is focused on helping its users detect ethical issues. When considering commitment to EAD, it is important to understand what the true concerns of the developers are. In this case, the teams were more concerned about the usefulness and viability of their product than its ethical aspects.

> "We don't want to do anything so absurd that it can't be actualized and that was probably our biggest motivator." -team 2

Aside from the usefulness and viability of their planned product, completing the projects on time and competing with the other teams were higher on teams' lists on concerns than ethics. The teams had difficulties seeing the ethical aspects as an activity that would help them to create better and more sustainable designs.

> "We spent time and effort on those tasks but it always felt very artificial because there was nothing to gain from it." -team 1

> "RESOLVEDD was a nice addition, but not absolutely necessary in this project. In another one it could be better." -team 4

The application of the RESOLVEDD strategy was part of the project requirements. Still, even after projects concluded, none of the teams thought that considering the ethical aspects of their product had been crucial to their success.

"It [RESOLVEDD] was a burden for us. It was just there in the background, and we only remembered it was there when we had already designed something. We were not proactive with it." -team 2

Difficulties to develop concerns that would relate to ethics may also come from the nature of ethics itself. For the teams, ethics was something completely new. The educational system in IS studies directs the attention towards project requirements and other matters, and ethics are seldom discussed in relation to IS. Developing the ethical thinking of the students during the projects did not have the same kind of clear goals as the operational aspects of the project (e.g. were the requirements fulfilled). Similarly, some of the teams were frustrated that there were no "right" answers to the ethical issues that they faced:

"At its best, an ethical tool would be tool that would inspire you to do good design. But RESOLVEDD didn't give us any answers to anything! If you put data into RESOLVEDD, you would not get anything out of it." -team 3

The teams also faced difficulties with RESOLVEDD. The teams were normatively committed to using RESOLVEDD to address the ethical issues faced in design. The normative commitment in this case was only externally enforced and thus not very strong.

"Using RESOLVEDD felt forced since we didn't have that many ethical issues" - team 1

"For us, the goal was not clear. We just needed to have some kind of product that supervisor would be ok with."- team 4

The teams did not consider RESOLVEDD helpful in reaching the project goals. Therefore, it was not considered useful by the teams. On the contrary, the teams considered it to be something that hindered their performance or drew their attention away from what they considered to be more important work. The teams did utilize it and reported their use of the tool, but only because it was required (= normative, external force). Notably, the teams remarked that the method needed to be adapted to better suit their context:

"It [RESOLVEDD] felt like it didn't fit into our design process, so we had to adapt it, almost forcing it to work. So as an instrument it was not working." - team 3

"For us it [RESOLVEDD] didn't work. We got much more out of having good conversations about ethical issues among the team. After those discussions, we just had to select some angle in order to force it into RESOLVEDD to get that requirement done." - team 2

The teams were, however, able to adapt successfully. They held group discussions where they discussed and addressed the ethical issues faced in their design processes. Thus, in practice, the teams used different methods to actually manage their ethical thinking. The RESOLVEDD strategy was then used to report their ethical thinking as a part of the course deliverables. None of the teams developed affective reasons to continue using the method after the projects concluded.

PEC1: While normative commitment to the use of Ethically Aligned Design brings immediate results, it will seize to exist when the external pressure is taken away. The RESOLVEDD strategy needs adaptation in application context. In practice, group discussions were seen effective in addressing the ethical issues.

5.2 Transparency in Design

Even though the teams were not affectively committed to using the ethical tool in their design process, they were required to follow the steps of the RESOLVEDD strategy and to produce documents that increased the transparency of the teams' decision-making processes. The teams adapted RESOLVEDD to fit their needs in order to carry out ethical analysis. The external pressure to use a specific method did not please the teams. Nonetheless, the necessitated use of the RESOLVEDD strategy method did increase transparency and ensured that the ethical discussions of the teams were documented for later use. The teams remained skeptical, however, whether their documentation would be beneficial.

> "Visualization of the RESOLVEDD-method seemed to be a waste of time and effort. Nobody would understand the drawn thing and all those lines in our picture." -team 3

The RESOLVEDD strategy primarily produced transparency in the design process itself rather than transparency in terms of the systems being designed. This may be in part due to the project setting where the focus was mostly on conceptualizing the product rather than the technical details. Furthermore, the developers were novices with little to no experience in AI development in practice. This may explain why the typical AI transparency issues, such as the black box thinking and understandability of the system actions, were omitted from the ethical considerations of the teams.

PEC2: When the RESOLVEDD strategy is followed step-by-step a paper trail is born where each decisions made and the respective justification can be found. This produces transparency in the design process, but it does not promote transparency at the product layer.

5.3 Accountability in Design

The question of accountability divided the teams. It was not clear to the teams who could be held accountable for the design. Teams defended their position (not being accountable) by arguing that the systems are only concepts and prototypes. They outsourced the issue of accountability to the end user, or they were simply unable to explain how it would be managed from the legal or social viewpoints.

> "If this was a real life application, we would have had to think that if somebody steals the product and kills somebody with it, who would sue us? We didn't actively concern ourselves with studying any legal matters, we only considered those we realized by ourselves." -team 3

This all implies that the RESOLVEDD strategy did not support the idea of accountability or help the teams gather the needed knowledge for resolving the accountability issues.

PEC3: The RESOLVEDD strategy does not deliver accountability.

5.4 Responsibility in Design

Expecting the teams to engage in EAD and supporting their engagement in EAD by introducing an ethical tool made it possible to discuss ethical issues related to their current projects with the teams. However, our introduction to the RESOLVEDD strategy could have been better based on the data.

> "We did have a very independent and self-oriented group, but we knew that in the case of problems there would have been somebody there to help us. — Then when RESOLVEDD came along, it was more like a nitpicking stuff. It wasn't very understandable." -team 4

In spite of the negative feelings expressed by the teams, reflecting on the ethical aspects became socially acceptable in the teams and in their development work. The developers shared their views on the responsibility issues among the team members in group discussions. These discussions activated reflections on the developers' own responsibility and raised the level of the developers' sense of responsibility.

> "We thought about the ownership issues and how it would be possible to misuse the [product]. Then we decided that it would be used as a vehicle and would be registered biometrically so no one else could use it." - team 3

> "We considered the loss of jobs and entire professions [resulting from AI]." - team 5

PEC4: Requiring Ethically Aligned Design activated reflections on the developers' own sense of responsibility.

So far, we have established that the RESOLVEDD strategy promotes the use of EAD as described in PECs 2 and 4. However, we also found that the teams were not keen on using the method, nor were they satisfied with the results they obtained by doing so. External pressure for the use of the tool nonetheless created tangible results, promoted EAD, and even supported the developers' sense of responsibility. It remains an open question whether this is a merit to the RESOLVED strategy or whether this kind of improvement would have been achieved with any other ethical method as well.

PEC5: The mere presence of an ethical tool has an effect on ethical consideration creating more responsibility even when it the use of the method is not voluntary.

6 Discussion

On a general level, this study begins to bridge a gap discussed in existing literature. The IEEE guidelines for Ethically Aligned Design discuss a gap between research and practice in the area, underlining that work on the guidelines, as well as implementing AI ethics overall, has not carried over onto the field. In a similar vein, Morley et al. [21] note that the area is lacking in empirical studies actually testing the methods and tools that do exist. In this paper, we have begun to address these gaps by evaluating one ethical tool. Outside evaluating the specific tool, RESOLVEDD, our findings provide some insights into implementing AI ethics using any method or tool.

Indeed, PEC1 gives us some insights into commitment in the context of implementing ethics. By enforcing the use of an ethical tool top-down, it is possible to create normative commitment to implementing ethics (PEC4). This commitment, however, ceases to exist once the external pressure to utilize the tool ceases to exist. While this does support the implementation of ethics by making developers more responsible, if only while utilizing the tool, it does not result in any intrinsic motivation to implement ethics (PEC5). This is interesting, however, as responsibility is typically considered to be intrinsically motivated and an attitude [10].

As for RESOLVEDD in particular [22], the tool supports one out of the two ethical principles that are currently considered to be the most important ones EAD: transparency and accountability. The use of RESOLVEDD produced transparency in the design process (PEC2). In utilizing it, the developers produced documentation on their decision-making, including reasoning behind their ethical choices as well as documenting alternate solution ideas that were ultimately discarded. Though transparency is considered required for accountability to be possible [10], RESOLVEDD did not produce accountability in the projects studied in this paper (PEC3). However, RESOLVEDD is not an ethical tool for AI ethics in particular, and thus does not account for the technical side of the system but only its overall design. It produces transparency of systems development (paper trail regarding decisions) but no transparency of data or algorithms.

Top-down adoption of ethical methods in organisations would seem to produce the wanted results, at least to some extent, and depending on the tool or method on question. Nonetheless, supporting the participatory adoption of such methods, as Morley et al. [21] suggest, would likely result in more ethical consideration from the developers. If they are intrinsically more motivated to implement ethics, they are arguably more likely to do so more meticulously.

On the other hand, adopting methods top-down is not a new proposition, especially in the context of SE. Many organisations made the move from waterfall to Agile development top-down after the management became convinced about the positive effects of Agile development, regardless of what the developers thought. While this induces change resistance, the developers will ultimately have to comply. Moreover, it can be difficult for developers to convince management, or even other developers, about the importance of ethics. Thus, while ethical methods should be designed with developers in mind, the point of entry into organisations for these methods may in fact be e.g. the product manager.

Finally, the research framework formed in this study also has practical implications by making the level of Ethically Aligned Design evaluable. We have shown, initially, that while it is possible to introduce EAD by force, results will not sustain over time. The RESOLVEDD strategy needs to be adjusted in practice. One important adjustment done by our case teams was the introduction of group discussions as the primary means to do EAD in practice. Thus, a possible avenue for tailoring is to identify what are the practices that actually lead to favorable outcomes increasing transparency, responsibility and accountability.

6.1 Limitations of the Study

The primary potential limitation of this study are its sample size and the use of student projects. However, in relation to using students as subjects for data collection, Höst et al. [16] argued that the differences between students and professionals in SE is minor and not statistically significant. In fact, they recommend the use of students in SE studies. Runeson [23] found similar improvement trends between undergraduate, graduate and professional study groups. For a novel topic in the field (such as EAD here), the students provide an excellent platform for an empirical evaluation, method development and experimentation.

Additionally, in relation to our sample size, we acknowledge that five projects is not a large sample. Nonetheless, Eisenhardt [9] note that 4 to 10 cases typically work well in case study research, outside particularly in-depth case studies, which may utilize fewer cases. They also highlight the suitability of case studies for novel research areas [9]. While AI ethics is not a novel area as such, empirical studies in the area are lacking, especially in relation to methods.

7 Conclusions and Future Work

In this study, we have evaluated the RESOLVEDD strategy for ethical decision-making through an exploratory, multiple case study of five student projects. The main results of this study are as follows: (1) While normative commitment to the use of Ethically Aligned Design brings immediate results, it will cease to exist when the external pressure is taken away. (2) An ethical method (RESOLVEDD) that necessitated tracking the decisions that were made produced transparency in the design process. (3) The RESOLVEDD strategy does not deliver accountability. (4) Requiring Ethically Aligned Design from the developers also resulted in responsibility in the developers. (5) The mere presence of an ethical tool has an effect on the ethical consideration exerted by developers, creating more responsibility even when the use of the method is not voluntary.

Thus, forcefully implementing an ethical tool or method can further the implementation of ethics. A top-down approach to introducing a tool or method for implementing ethics can serve as a starting point for ethical development in an organization. However, normative commitment does not seem to result in any intrinsic motivation to implement ethics among developers. i.e. this does not motivate the developers to implement ethics out of their own volition.

Based on these results, the following theoretical implications can be made. The formed research framework where ethical principles are combined with concept of commitment is a functional approach for evaluating the inclusion of ethics in design. Understanding the mechanics related to the developers' commitment(s) has a crucial role in furthering the inclusion of ethics in design.

References

1. Abrahamsson, P.: Commitment nets in software process improvement. Ann. Softw. Eng. **14**(1), 407–438 (2002). https://doi.org/10.1023/A:1020526329708
2. Allen, C., Wallach, W., Smit, I.: Why machine ethics? IEEE Intell. Syst. **21**(4), 12–17 (2006). https://doi.org/10.1109/MIS.2006.83
3. Bowie, N.E.: A kantian theory of meaningful work. J. Bus. Ethics **17**(9), 1083–1092 (1998)
4. Bryson, J., Winfield, A.: Standardizing ethical design for artificial intelligence and autonomous systems. Computer **50**(5), 116–119 (2017). https://doi.org/10.1109/MC.2017.154
5. Bynum, T.: Computer and information ethics. In: Zalta, E.N. (ed.) The Stanford Encyclopedia of Philosophy. Metaphysics Research Lab Stanford University (2018). https://plato.stanford.edu/archives/sum2018/entries/ethics-computer/
6. Charisi, V., et al.: Towards moral autonomous systems (2017). arXiv preprint arxiv.org/abs/1703.04741
7. Dignum, V.: Responsible autonomy (2017). arXiv preprint arXiv:1706.02513, https://arxiv.org/abs/1706.02513
8. Dignum, V.: Ethics in artificial intelligence: introduction to the special issue. Ethics Inf. Technol. **20**(1), 1–3 (2018). https://doi.org/10.1007/s10676-018-9450-z
9. Eisenhardt, K.M.: Building theories from case study research. Acad. Manag. Rev. **14**(4), 532–550 (1989)
10. Ethically aligned design: a vision for prioritizing human well-being with autonomous and intelligent systems, first edition (2019). https://standards.ieee.org/content/ieee-standards/en/industry-connections/ec/autonomous-systems.html
11. Ethics guidelines for trustworthy ai (2019). https://ec.europa.eu/digital-single-market/en/news/ethics-guidelines-trustworthy-ai
12. Flores, A.W., Bechtel, K., Lowenkamp, C.T.: False positives, false negatives, and false analyses: a rejoinder to "machine bias: there's software used across the country to predict future criminals, and it's biased against blacks". Fed. Probation **80**(2), 38 (2016)
13. Gotterbarn, D.W., et al.: ACM code of ethics and professional conduct (2018). https://www.acm.org/code-of-ethics
14. Graziotin, D., Wang, X., Abrahamsson, P.: Are happy developers more productive? In: Heidrich, J., Oivo, M., Jedlitschka, A., Baldassarre, M.T. (eds.) Product-Focused Software Process Improvement, pp. 50–64. Springer, Berlin (2013). https://doi.org/10.1007/978-3-642-39259-7_7
15. Heath, H., Cowley, S.: Developing a grounded theory approach: a comparison of glaser and strauss. Int. J. Nurs. Stud. **41**(2), 141–150 (2004). https://doi.org/10.1016/S0020-7489(03)00113-5

16. Höst, M., Regnell, B., Wohlin, C.: Using students as subjects-a comparative study of students and professionals in lead-time impact assessment. Empirical Softw. Eng. **5**(3), 201–214 (2000). https://doi.org/10.1023/A:1026586415054
17. Johansen, C.: Teaching the ethics of biology. Am. Biol. Teacher **62**(5), 352–358 (2000)
18. Lenberg, P., Feldt, R., Wallgren, L.G.: Behavioral software engineering: a definition and systematic literature review. J. Syst. Softw. **107**, 15–37 (2015). https://doi.org/10.1016/j.jss.2015.04.084
19. McNamara, A., Smith, J., Murphy-Hill, E.: Does ACM's code of ethics change ethical decision making in software development? In: Proceedings of the 2018 26th ACM Joint Meeting on European Software Engineering Conference and Symposium on the Foundations of Software Engineering. pp. 729–733. ESEC/FSE 2018, ACM, New York, NY, USA (2018). DOI: https://doi.org/10.1145/3236024.3264833
20. Moor, J.H.: What is computer ethics? *. Metaphilosophy **16**(4), 266–275 (1985)
21. Morley, J., Floridi, L., Kinsey, L., Elhalal, A.: From what to how. an overview of AI ethics tools, methods and research to translate principles into practices (2019). arXiv preprint arXiv:1905.06876, https://arxiv.org/abs/1905.06876
22. Pfeiffer, R.S., Forsberg, R.P.: Ethics on the Job: Cases and Strategies. Wadsworth Publishing Company, California (1993)
23. Runeson, P.: Using students as experiment subjects - an analysis on graduate and freshmen student data. In: Proceedings of the 7th International Conference on Empirical Assessment in Software Engineering, p. 95 (2003). http://lup.lub.lu.se/record/708340
24. Strauss, A., Corbin, J.: Basics of Qualitative Research: Techniques and Procedures for Developing Grounded Theory, 2nd edn. Sage Publications Inc, Thousand Oaks (1998)
25. Turilli, M., Floridi, L.: The ethics of information transparency. Ethics Inf. Technol. **11**(2), 105–112 (2009). https://doi.org/10.1007/s10676-009-9187-9
26. Vakkuri, V., Kemell, K., Kultanen, J., Siponen, M.T., Abrahamsson, P.: Ethically aligned design of autonomous systems: Industry viewpoint and an empirical study (2019). arXiv preprint arxiv.org/abs/1906.07946
27. Yin, R.K.: Qualitative Research from Start to Finish, 1st edn. Guilford Press, New York (2010)

Towards a Better Society

An Analysis of the Value Basis of the European eGovernment and Data Economy

Minna M. Rantanen(✉) and Jani Koskinen

Turku School of Economics, University of Turku, Turku, Finland
{minna.m.rantanen,jasiko}@utu.fi

Abstract. Motivation behind electronic government (eGovernment) is generally creating of a better society. However, many eGovernment projects have failed due to the complex nature of these ecosystems. In the future eGovernment are starting to form larger data ecosystems due to initiatives such the European Single Market. The current trend of moving from national initiatives to international cooperation will make these projects even more complicated and thus, even more vulnerable to failures. Multiple large groups of stakeholders should be considered in the governance of these ecosystems, but there are little effective ways for that. It has been argued that values play an integral role in the success of eGovernment. Thus, in this paper we present a constructive analysis of values in eGovernment that aims to clarify the complexity around the matter. First, different levels and types of values affecting eGovernment are considered and then existing values guiding the governance of eGovernment are analysed. Based on these preliminary analyses it is noted, that there are some justified values, but more work is needed to create ethical governance model for eGovernment and data ecosystems that they are a part of to avoid failures and perhaps reach the goal of better society.

Keywords: eGovernment · Ecosystem · Single market · Values · Value-sensitive design

1 Introduction

Electronic government (eGovernment) has long been defined as digitalisation of governmental services [2,24]. In the last decade, governments all over the world have moved from offering information online to providing vast variety of online services to their citizens that did not exist before. Services that offer citizens constant possibilities to participate in democratic processes (eDemocracy) have been taken into use in several countries [43,45]. However, development of eGovernment is not stopping there. It still continues as development of new innovations.

Latest phase of eGovernment exceeds the digitalisation of former services of governments. New innovative technologies are used to offer more personalised

S. Hyrynsalmi et al. (Eds.): ICSOB 2019, LNBIP 370, pp. 276–290, 2019.
https://doi.org/10.1007/978-3-030-33742-1_22

and customised services to the public sector, citizens, organisations and non-governmental stakeholders. This development, driven by the ideals of government 3.0, is characterised by openness and transparency of government and development, sharing of data, increased communication and collaboration between stakeholders, reorganisation of government through integration and interoperability and use of new technologies [45]. Development of eGovernment is not no longer the case of national initiatives, but a larger cooperation between different nations. Innovative and more cooperative forms of eGovernment are promoted for example by the European Union in a form of the Single Market - an Union wide data economy ecosystem [1,38] Thus, we can no longer say that eGovernment is just digitalisation of governmental services, because in reality we are talking about developing data ecosystems instead of standalone information systems.

Often mentioned potential benefits of eGovernment include but are not limited to greater efficacy and transparency government, and better inclusion of citizens [2,24]. In general, it is stated, that the purpose of eGovernment is to create value to the public and in the end as a mean to create public good and better societies [31,35]. Despite the noble cause, potential benefits of eGovernment seem hard to achieve, since many of eGovernment initiates fail [27,28]. One of the biggest issues is that adoption rates of the eGovernment services are fairly low [2,43]. This poses a threat to also to the new eGovernment solutions and innovations, but also to development of the Single Market. Thus, it is timely to consider, the problem that stands in the way of good society that is pursued through governmental data ecosystems.

One of the potential reasons for eGovernment project failures could be inability to address the legitimate but diverse interests of many stakeholders involved in the development of these information systems [27]. Understanding and fulfilling the needs of the stakeholders has been acknowledged in several socio-technical design methods such as participatory design [22]. However, in eGovernment stakeholders are often large and heterogeneous group, which makes the participatory development hard or even impossible. This, however, does not make it any less important to acknowledge true needs of stakeholders when designing and governing eGovernment ecosystems.

It has been suggested that values play an integral role in success of eGovernment. Rose et al. [28] suggest that problems of eGovernment might stem from different value traditions that do not meet and that might steer development process to failure. From the perspective of use value conflicts can lead to mis-use or non-use of an information system [17,46]. And since ecosystems are by people they are never value free [18,23,36], careful consideration should be done in selection of the values that drive the development [5].

Value-sensitive design (VSD) takes into account human values in the design project and aims into implementing them in technology. As a methodology VSD is a tripartite, integrative and iterative. VSD consists of conceptual, empirical and technical investigations to study information systems and values with several techniques [11,12]. The conceptual investigation is exploration of the concepts and values with philosophically informed analyses, empirical investigation contains participant evaluation of values selected in conceptual phase and technical investigation is the integration of values in the technical system. The last phase can be seen as an investigation of existing properties of the technical system and focusing on how these properties support or conflict with human values, or as designing a system that supports values identified in the earlier phases [12].

In this paper we aim to clarify the complex relationship of values, and focus on conceptual phase of VSD. In the next section, we clarify different perspectives on values. We explore personal, organisational and ethical values, that all have their place in the development of eGovernment. In the Sect. 3 we review the values of the European Union in context of eGovernment. These values guide the development of eGovernment in the member nations, so their role is significant in many national eGovernment projects, but also as future values of the Single Market. In the Sect. 4 these values are discussed through ethics to justify which values should be selected. Finally, we conclude in the Sect. 5.

2 Three Perspectives on Values

2.1 Personal and Cultural Values

From the perspective of personal values, values can be defined as something that a person or a group find important in their life [13,30]. Each person holds numerous values with different level of importance. These values form value sets that are hierarchical by nature. Values and value systems also vary between persons – something that is important to one person, might be unimportant to another [30]. Values subjective rather permanent beliefs that affect peoples actions, goals and judgements [11,26,30]. Thus, values play an important role also in relation technology and people's willingness to use it.

Since values affect our actions and the goals, values also affect the way that we design, develop, implement, use and govern. Technological systems are made to serve certain goals, that reflect the values of the individuals behind them, thus information systems are never value-free [18,23,36]. Thus, also eGovernment systems have values embedded in them. However, also people that are supposed to use these systems have values that they act upon. Value conflicts have been noted to lead misuse and non-use of information systems [17,46]. Thus, acknowledging the values of citizens and other stakeholders in the development and governance of eGovernment ecosystems could help to increase the adoption rates and ultimately realise potential benefits of eGovernment.

Although people do value different things in their life some consistency can be found in value sets of people of same culture. This is due to the fact that values are belief that evolve but are not inherited. Social norms of cultures affect the values of individuals and thus it is more likely that people from similar cultures have similar value sets [14,26]. Hofstede et al. [15] call cultures programming of the mind, since it teaches individuals the ideas of what should be considered important. However, cultural values do not represent fully the values of individuals, but an rough estimate of shared values of people sharing a culture. Due to globalisation one could also argue that we are affected by cultures instead of a culture through out our lives.

Thus, in search for value basis of eGovernment ecosystems, we should find an another approach to simplify the plurality of personal values. Schwartz [29,30] has developed a theory of basic values (see Fig. 1) that can be found in all cultures and that cover a large portion of personal values.

Fig. 1. Schwartz's basic values and categories (based on [29,30])

The basic values are likely universal, since they are grounded in one or more universal requirements of human existence. These requirements are (1) needs of individuals as biological organisms, (2) requisites of coordinated social interaction, and (3) survival and welfare needs of groups [30]. Thus, Schwartz's theory of basic values offers a framework to make sense of value complexity of large groups of people. It does not however help us resolve the question about the value basis of eGovernment on its own. To answer that question we should study individuals values in this context and compare them to values behind the governance of these ecosystems.

2.2 Organisational Values

Similarly, as the individual's values guide their actions core values of an organisation can be seen as guiding principles that guide actions of people in an organisational context. Collins and Porras [6] define organisational core values as *"The organisation's essential and enduring tenets—a small set of general guiding principles; not to be confused with specific cultural or operating practices; not to be compromised for financial gain or short-term expediency"*. Thus, organisational core values are seen as relatively permanent features of an organisation similarly as personal values to a person. However, it must be noted that organisational values are selected set of values, thus not in similar sense learned and subjective as personal values. Also, organisational values are highly contextual, since they are often effectual in only that organisation. Thus, organisational values are more norms of a certain organisation than personal values, although it is possible that employees share some of the organisational values.

Having organisational values that the employees can adapt to have been prove to lead to many benefits such as distinctiveness to the organisation [7,20] and better functioning organisation and greater job satisfaction [8]. It has been indicated that companies that are explicitly value-led, outperform others and are also perceived as better companies by potential employees that share those values [34]. Thus, clear and meaningful organisational values can make an organisation to flourish.

However, all of the companies do not have explicit core values, or these values can be hollow which can do more harm to company than good. Lencioni [20] states, that *"Most values statements are bland, toothless, or just plain dishonest. And far from being harmless, as some executives assume, they're often highly destructive. Empty values statements create cynical and dispirited employees, alienate customers, and undermine managerial credibility."* He further argues that building authentic organisational values takes a lot of work, but fixing the problems created by poorly understood role and nature of organisational values is even harder [20]. This demonstrates well the complexity of values and their effects in an organisation.

A large portion of the research about organisational values has been done in the private sector. However, there are differences between private and public organisations, despite that it can be argued that also governments have adopted more business-like management styles [28,42]. Difference between public and private sectors have become apparent in the field of eGovernment, where IT implementations have proven to be even more complex than in public sector due to plurality of stakeholders, intricate decision-making and accountability of systems. Complexity of a eGovernment ecosystems make it challenging to the developers and managers to maintain a clear sense of purpose in ecosystems that are characterised by an urge to get (new) technological solutions implemented to solve complex challenges. Problems of eGovernment initiatives could be rooted in value traditions of management in eGovernment development [28]. Thus, paying attentions to values of individuals that are part of these ecosystems could lead to more efficient development with clearer purpose.

The latest trend of eGovernment also opens the governmental ecosystems to the private sector [45]. Thus, "organisation" around eGovernment is neither public or private, but both. Nevertheless, organisational values of the organisations play an integral role in the way that the future economy build around eGovernment will work. Hence, it should also be crucial to consider what kind of organisational values or guiding principles are suitable and justifiable for developing eGovernment. Based on the research done about organisational values, it should be assured that values of eGovernment are clearly written and communicated by the organisation initiating change to people taking part in the development of the system. To do this, the initiator should also be aware of the values and value traditions of different stakeholders in this complex system, so that values can become shared, and divergence and negative consequences can be avoided. However, assuring that this hybrid system of public and private organisations shares values regarding eGovernment is not an easy task.

2.3 Moral and Ethical Values

Since eGovernment and its stakeholders hold a plurality of values that might be in contraction with each other we need a way to assess what values we should accept as the core values of the eGovernment ecosystem governance. One way to do this is assess the values through ethics, which has a long joint history with values. Ethics have been occasionally subsumed to value theories and sometimes values have been viewed only as part of ethics [11]. Within this history many moral philosophers have pondered values, their nature and properties. For example, Plato [25] distinguished instrumental and intrinsic values and Frankena [10] made distinction between moral and non-moral values. Thus, also ethical values should be considered, and ethics could be used as tool to assess the values of eGovernment.

Before proceeding to ethical values, we need to consider concept of morality, since ethics can be considered as philosophical study of morality [9]. Rokeach [26] distinguished moral values as one type of personal values. He argues that moral values refer mainly to modes of behaviour and so not necessarily include values that concern the end-states of existence. Thus, moral values can be seen as instrumental values. Moral values are characterised by an "oughtness" factor that originates within the society and is an objective demand that concerns member of society. However, the "oughtness" is often more like and experience of what is good or bad and thus, hard to explicitly explain.

Thus, like values the moral values or codes can be and usually are different between individual, groups and societies. Because of this people usually live under three different level of moral codes: their own code, codes shared by people they are interacting with and codes of society they are living in. Similarly, as values in general and moral values can be conflicting. People may value overwhelming wealth and understand that creed is not good thing. Problem with moral is that in many cases moral codes are not rational or well argued and thus analysing conflict between values and morals seem to be unfruitful.

Stahl [32] explains that morality can be seen as normativity, that can be divided in four levels. First, there is the level of moral intuition, that forms a basis for explicit morality. This explicit morality is then reflected on ethical theory, that requires reflection and meta-ethics which in return help to clarify ethical theories, which then justify explicit morality that informs moral intuition [32]. Thus, all of the levels of normativity are interviewed and needed in conceptualisation of ethical values.

As shown the values are not similar or static and comparing and their "worth" or "goodness" is not task to be achieved by merely measuring values by surveys or empirical observation. The problem is that different values are not equal in ethical sense. Some values are more important and more valuable than others from ethical perspective. For example, can anyone say that a right to have job is more important than right to live without fear of death or violence? Thus, we have different values that should be seen in the larger context where different values exist and are conflicting other ones and yet, we should be able to distinguish a hierarchy between them.

We argue, that due to ethics relation to moral and morals relation to values ethics is a suitable tool "philosophically informed analyses" in conceptual phase of the VSD. As ethics is brand of philosophy - based on rational and scientific argumentation - that aims to find what is good and bad in normative sense, it seems promising basis to find a way to analyse what values are worth of cherishing and what should be altered or even rejected. One could say that democracy is the way to achieve right values. However, democracy as a mean has two critical problems – the authority of majority and the alienation. Majority has in history suppressed the right and values of minorities. By alienation we refer the complex situation, where individuals possibility to make a difference by political system is actually lost. Other aspect of alienation is the focus of politics that has shifted form real issues towards populism and it effects that complex problems are bypassed or oversimplified. Thus, we need also ethical analysis to deal with values in our societies to seek more good society.

There has been different attempts to seek more clear frameworks for ethicality (proper and justified values) instead of creating an ethical theory. One promising framework is Brey's [5] framework for just society. Framework is analysing the role of technology for good society and its main idea is to evaluate how technology impacts and shapes society. Brey's presents values that are either intrinsic and instrumental for the desirable goal of good society that should be also embedded in technology. Intrinsic values are values that are most fundamental ones and valuable in themselves. Brey argues that intrinsic values for good society are well-being and justice. Instrumental values are necessary values that are important as they provide people possibility to seek other ends than those values itself. Instrumental values in this context are freedom, democracy and sustainability [5].

Like Brey notes, there are probably more instrumental values but at least those three should be taken account [5]. Indeed, if we compare these values to the basic values (see Fig. 1) there are a lot of other values to consider, but In comparison to Schwartz's theory [29,30] these Brey's values reflect similar basis: survival, welfare and social nature of human species. Thus, to analyse what values are more important and what are secondary values, the notions of intrinsic and instrumental could be used to see in selection of values that the eGovernment should be based on.

3 Organisational Values Behind eGovernment

The ecosystem of eGovernment is highly complex and there are many stakeholders that should be considered. Rose et al. [28] focused on managers of eGovernment, but there is still need for studying values of governmental officials, citizens and organisations that are either using or developing government systems. So that one can further analyse the values of a eGovernment we must aim to understand the values that these ecosystems are currently build on.

Many development of eGovernment ecosystems in Europe are aiming to fullfill the needs of the European Single Market [40]. Thus, one can argue that the issues that the European union emphasises as valuable issues in regards of eGovernment form a good starting point for research of organisational values. Thus, to clarify the value complexity around eGovernment, in this paper we analyse documents published by the European Commission about the topic of eGovernment.

Values of these documents could be considered as the values of eGovernment that meant to guide the members of the European Union. However, it must be noted that reviewed documents are not explicitly meant to be present organisational values of eGovernment, although they are meant to guide the development of it. The aim of this review is to clarify the potential core values of eGovernment. These values are further analysed through ethics in the next section.

3.1 The European Union and Values of eGovernment

The European Union has had an action plan for eGovernment since 2006 [37]. The latest action plan was published in 2016. From the perspective of the European commission the eGovernment Action Plans have been political instruments to advance the modernisation of public administrations across the European Union supporting coordination and collaboration [38]. Successful eGovernment in EU is also key element in the success of the digital Single Market that aims to open up digital opportunities for people and enhance Europe's position as a world leader in the digital economy [38,41]. Thus, the success of eGovernments around Europe could enable much more than just more efficient governance.

Previous action plans have had positive impact on the development of eGovernment in Member States. Positive impacts have been coherence of national eGovernment strategies, exchange of best practices, and interoperability of solutions [38]. The action plan is developed in cooperation with stakeholders – EU citizens, company representatives, public administrations and supply side of eGovernment services. [40] and thus, it also should reflect the personal of the individuals and organisational values of the represented companies.

The Action Plan 2016–2020 includes both motivation and the goal of eGovernment development in the EU level. Action Plan 2016–2020 presents the vision and underlying principles of eGovernment action plan as well as policy priorities and actions that the European Commission will conduct between 2016 and 2020 [38]. The vision of the action plan, that guides the development is: *"By 2020, public administrations and public institutions in the European Union should be open, efficient and inclusive, providing borderless, personalised, user-friendly, end-to-end digital public services to all citizens and businesses in the EU. Innovative approaches are used to design and deliver better services in line with the needs and demands of citizens and businesses. Public administrations use the opportunities offered by the new digital environment to facilitate their interactions with stakeholders and with each other."* [38] As it can be noted, the vision compresses a lot of values. Openness, efficiency, inclusiveness and benevolence seem to be the main values that are expressed, although "innovation approaches" also reflect openness to change.

In the Action plan [38] these values are further emphasised. Repeatedly eGovernment is represented as a way to improve quality of services and increasing efficiency. Quality of services is mentioned through the action plan and it is described as a benefit for the stakeholders. Efficiency is almost as repeated theme than quality and it is often paired with effectiveness, that could also be interpreted as expression of benevolence.

However, it is also stated that digital public services will *"reduce administrative burden on businesses and citizens by making their interactions with public administrations faster and efficient, more convenient and transparent, and less costly"* and that eGovernment will result in *"faster, cheaper, more user-oriented digital public services"* [38]. Speed or acceleration, lower costs and practicality for users are as well mentioned throughout the action plan. From the value perspective these kind of statements do highlight moral values such benevolence through transparency and user-orientation, but also achievement and authority through economical values. Also openness translates in some cases to "growth and competitiveness" since opening the public data and services to third parties can contribute to them.

The action plan also includes policy principles that should be followed. The policy principles were also approved by all the stakeholders [38]. These principles resemble organisational values as defined by Collins and Porras [7], since they can be interpreted as essential and enduring tenets of eGovernment that are mean to guide Member States. The policy principles and their explanations are presented in the Table 1.

The policy principles provide actual guidelines for what should be taken into account in eGovernment. Principles highlight values such transparency, easiness, inclusiveness, and accessibility, but also practicality. In some sense, they also provide the "oughtess" and thus, set some moral ground to eGovernment and the Single market.

In the European Commission's eGovernment bench-marking from 2016 [39] similar values recur, because the survey is based on the action plan's [38] policy priorities. However, there are small differences. The four top-level benchmarks in the survey are: user-centricity, transparency of government, cross-border mobility. Special emphasis is given to the support of eGovernment in different life events that vary between even and odd years. The 2016 bench-marking focused on starting up a business (economic), losing and finding a job (employment), studying (education) and family life. From these, family life was included in 2016, whereas others have been measured since 2012. In odd years life events are regular business operations economic) and starting a small claims procedure (justice), moving (general administration) and owning and driving a car (transport). Life events are measured to cover as much as possible eGovernment services and the customer journeys [39]. Thus, bench-marking covers more aspects of eGovernment. It mainly focuses on practical issues and seems to emphasis the eGovernment's support to well-being.

Table 1. Policy principles [38].

Policy principle	Description
Digital by default	Public administrations should deliver services digitally (including machine readable information) as the preferred option (while still keeping other channels open for those who are disconnected by choice or necessity). In addition, public services should be delivered through a single contact point or a one-stop-shop and via different channels
Once only principle	Public administrations should ensure that citizens and businesses supply the same information only once to a public administration. Public administration offices take action if permitted to internally re-use this data, in due respect of data protection rules, so that no additional burden falls on citizens and businesses
Inclusiveness and accessibility	Public administrations should design digital public services that are inclusive by default and cater for different needs such as those of the elderly and people with disabilities
Openness and transparency	Public administrations should share information and data between themselves and enable citizens and businesses to access control and correct their own data; enable users to monitor administrative processes that involve them; engage with and open up to stakeholders (such as businesses, researchers and non-profit organisations) in the design and delivery of services
Cross-border by default	Public administrations should make relevant digital public services available across borders and prevent further fragmentation to arise, thereby facilitating mobility within the Single Market
Interoperability by default	Public services should be designed to work seamlessly across the Single Market and across organisational silos, relying on the free movement of data and digital services in the European Union
Trustworthiness and security	All initiatives should go beyond the mere compliance with the legal framework on personal data protection and privacy, and IT security, by integrating those elements in the design phase. These are important pre-conditions for increasing trust in and take-up of digital services

4 Discussion

Thus, based on these documents, the values of European eGovernment seem to be various. When interpreted through Schwartz's basic values [30] the values of the European eGovernment and the Single market seem to be based on universalism, benevolence, power, achievement, and well-being. It is interesting that values of conservation are often seen only as enablers, such as security and trust as enablers of use, but not valuable as in them self, whereas other values seem to serve as intrinsic values. It is notable, that Brey's [5] intrinsic values for a good society – well-being and justice – are rather implicitly stated in the action plan, but more strongly presented in the bench-marking survey. From Brey's advocates for instrumental values that are necessary for a good society (freedom, democracy and sustainability) only democracy and sustainability are mentioned. In the action plan [38] sustainability, however, does not refer to sustainability of natural ecosystem, but to the sustainability of the digital ecosystem.

All the presented values seems as reasonable, but to justify the values of eGovernment and forthcoming data economy the governance of the framework should be grounded in ethics. It should at least cover the three big normative ethical branches: Consequentialism, deontology, and virtue ethics as proposed by Stahl et al. [33]. The first ethical approach is consequentialism where the evaluation of ethicality of actions is based on the what kind of outcome of an action will provide. Utilitarianism (the classical consequentialist theory) is simplified evaluation of different possibilities of action by outcome utilities of those alternatives. The term utility refers "the good" that is evaluated, and it can be different in different context. Originally are utilities are described as hedonic "goods" such as pleasure or satisfaction like philosophers Bentham [4] and Mill [21] defined it in their ground works on Utilitarianism. However, from this perspective the goodness of is evaluated and action which produces it most is the most ethical act.

Through consequentalism the values of a universalism, benevolence and well-being are the most ethically justified values. Universalism can be justified through "most good for most people" and benevolence through "do no harm". Well-being is a subjective matter, thus a rather hedonic value, but it should undoubtedly be an outcome that should be valued. Power is not a value that is easily justified, since the power in this context reflects more power over citizens than citizens power over their issues (freedom, autonomy). If power would be considered as latter, it could be more easily justified as ethical value from consequentalist perspective because then it could be seen as instrumental value for well-being if we assume that people know their needs and act to fulfil them. Similarly achievement of a government can not be considered as justified value unless it translates to well-being of the citizens.

The second approach is (Kantian) Deontology. It is branch of ethics where ethicality of action is based on action itself not the consequences it produces [16]. This means that the focus is on intention of an action, not on the outcome of an action. There are rules that must be followed to action to be good. From this perspective universalism and benevolence are the values that can be justified, since other values are more outcomes than descriptors of actions. The values that are based on deontology may even be conflicting with consequentialist values. As example: Health information collected from individuals would help to create new treatments and increase overall utility of population. However, the patient right over information is seen as deontological value that protects the autonomy(that is basis for freedom) of human beings and it cannot be thus overridden by mere utility outcome [19,44].

The third approach is virtue ethics, that in Aristotelian tradition is ethical view where focus is not it consequences nor rules but in goodness of character of people [3]. Thus, in the context of eGovernment adopting a virtue ethics as an approach means that we should focus on governing eGovernment ecosystem that supports the fruition of good citizens that are e.g. empathic, just, and equal by character. Again, universalism and benevolence are easily justified as values of eGovernment, whereas power and achievement are not. Well-being certainly supports fruition of good citizens, but it seems far fetched that people that are not well have bad characters. In ecosystems the citizens should give more control over their actions and let their choose to make their decisions and cultivate their own character that is not done by mere force. As example, voting is something that we could force by legislation but more likely we can get more devoted citizen by education and transparency.

It seems that universalism and benevolence are values that are good from all theories and thus, most likely is ethical values that should be incorporated in to government governance. Values that fail to fulfil the demands of some theories should be analysed in more detail to find the problem of those values. Also universalism and benevolence should be analysed further to find a way to incorporate them in practice to eGovernment governance However, we leave this framework development for future research as even it is needed the aim of this paper is to show the complexity of values and give visibility for underlying – even hidden – level of values that are set in eGovernment and policies which guide its development and governance.

5 Conclusions

As demonstrated, the nature and characteristics of values are complex. Values can be viewed from personal, organisational and society level. Values also have an integral role in the success of any information system. In the case of eGovernment values of all different stakeholders should be considered to reach potential benefits. Aiming for value congruence could also lead to other, yet unrealised benefits.

However, due to the complexity of eGovernment and value systems embedded in it, we need to find a way to distinguish intrinsic and instrumental values and be able to justify the ones that are selected. In this ethical justification through multiple approaches could be fruitful. However, since eGovernment systems have already been developed, we cannot discard the values already embedded in them. Thus, in this paper we considered the values of eGovernment in the European union which guide the development of eGovernment initiatives and creation of the Single Market data economy ecosystem. Based on the brief analysis it seems that universalism, benevolence, power, achievement, and well-being are intrinsic values of eGovernment, whereas security and trust are seen as instrumental values.

From these values universalism and benevolence seem to cover the three big normative ethical branches: consequentialism, deontology, and virtue ethics as ethical values. Well-being that is seen as intrinsic value by Brey, does require more analyses as value due to its subjective nature. To analyse well-being further it is necessary to focus more on the citizens and individuals affected by the eGovernment ecosystems. Thus, this paper is merely a preliminary construction of values in eGovernment and much still needs to be done, so that we can find justified values for eGovernment that can be shared by the all stakeholders. The eGovernment should always be justified, not only by instrumental or hedonistic values that aim to serve few.

Future research could follow the phases of VSD. The empirical research of the personal values of individuals in eGovernment and data economy in general, further and deeper ethical analysis of the organisational and personal values found, and finally incorporating the values in the governance guidelines of the eGovernment ecosystems and data ecosystems so that we can reach a better society through this development.

References

1. Digital single market. https://ec.europa.eu/digital-single-market/. Accessed 08 Aug 2019
2. Al-Hujran, O., Al-Debei, M.M., Chatfield, A., Migdadi, M.: The imperative of influencing citizen attitude toward e-government adoption and use. Comput. Hum. Behav. **53**, 189–203 (2015)
3. Aristotle: The Nicomachean ethics. Oxford University Press, Oxford (2009). translated and edited by Ross, W. D., and Brown, L
4. Bentham, J.: An Introduction to the Principles of Morals and Legislation. Batoche, Kitchener (1781)
5. Brey, P.: The strategic role of technology in a good society. Technology in Society (2017). advance online publication
6. Collins, J.C., Porras, J.I.: Built to Last: Successful Habits of Visionary Companies. Harper Business, New York (1994)
7. Collins, J.C., Porras, J.I.: Building your company's vision. Harv. Bus. Rev September-October **1996**, 65–77 (1996)
8. Edwards, J.R., Cable, D.M.: The value of value congruence. J. Appl. Psychol. **94**, 654–677 (2009)
9. Feldman, F.: Introductory Ethics. Prentice-Hall Inc., Upper Saddle River (1978)
10. Frankena, W.K.: Ethics, 2nd edn. N.H J. Prentice Hall, Englewood (1973)
11. Friedman, B., Kahn, P.H., Borning, A., Huldtgren, A.: Value sensitive design and information systems. In: Doorn, N., Schuurbiers, D., van de Poel, I., Gorman, M.E. (eds.) Early engagement and new technologies: Opening up the laboratory. PET, vol. 16, pp. 55–95. Springer, Dordrecht (2013). https://doi.org/10.1007/978-94-007-7844-3_4

12. Friedman, B., Kahn, P.H.J., Borning, A.: Value sensitive design: Theory and methods. Technical Report, 02–12-01, UW CSE Technical Report, The address of the publisher (2001)
13. Helkama, K., Myllyniemi, R., Liebkind, K.: Johdatus Sosiaalipsykologiaan. Edita Prima Oy, Helsinki (2010)
14. Hofstede, G.: Dimensionalizing cultures: the hofstede model in context. ORPC **2**, 8 (2011)
15. Hofstede, G., Hofstede, G.J., Minkov, M.: Cultures and Organizations: Software of the Mind: Intercultural Cooperation and Its Importance for Survival, 3rd edn. London McGraw-Hill, New York (2010)
16. Kant, I.: Grundlegung zur Metaphysic der Sitten [main translation: Liddel B. Kant on the foundation of morality - a modern version of the Grundlegung]. Indiana University Press, Indiana (1785/1970)
17. Kolkowska, E., Karlsson, F., Hedström, K.: Towards analysing the rationale of information security non-compliance: devising a value-based compliance analysis method. J. Strateg. Inf. Syst. **26**, 39–57 (2017)
18. Koskinen, J.S., Heimo, O.I., Kimppa, K.K.: A viewpoint for more ethical approach in healthcare information system development and procurement: the four principles. In: Exploring the Abyss of Inequalities: 4th International Conference on Well-Being in the Information Society, WIS (2012)
19. Koskinen, J., Kimppa, K.K.: An unclear question: who owns patient information? In: Kreps, D., Fletcher, G., Griffiths, M. (eds.) HCC 2016. IAICT, vol. 474, pp. 3–13. Springer, Cham (2016). https://doi.org/10.1007/978-3-319-44805-3_1
20. Lencioni, P.: Make your values mean something. Harv. Bus. Rev. **80**(7), 113–117 (2002)
21. Mill, J.S.: Utilitarianism. Green and Company, Longmans (1895)
22. Mumford, E.: The story of socio-technical design: reflections on its successes, failures and potential. Inf. Syst. J. **16**, 317–342 (2006)
23. Nissenbaum, H.: Computing and accountability. Commun. ACM **37**, 72–80 (1994)
24. Panagiotopoulos, P., Al-Debei, M.M., Fitzgerald, G., Elliman, T.: A business model perspective for icts in public engagement. Gov. Inf. Q. **29**, 192–202 (2012)
25. Plato: Valtio [org. The Republic], 3rd edn. Otava, Keuruu (2012)
26. Rokeach, M.: The Nature of Human Values. Free Press, New York (1973)
27. Rose, J., Flak, L.S., Sæ bØ, O.: Stakeholder theory for the e-government context: framing a value-oriented normative core. Gov. Inf. Q. **35**, 362–374 (2018)
28. Rose, J., Persson, J.S., Heeager, L.T., Irani, Z.: Managing e-government: value positions and relationships. Inf. Syst. J. **25**, 531–571 (2015)
29. Schwartz, S.H.: Universals in the content and structure of values: Theory and empirical tests in 20 countries, vol. 25, 3 edn., pp. 1–65. Academic Press, New York (1992)
30. Schwartz, S.H.: An overview of the schwartz theory of basic values. Gov. Inf. Quart. **2**, 362–374 (2012)
31. Scott, M., DeLone, W., Golden, W.: Measuring egovernment success: a public value approach. Eur. J. Inf. Syst **25**, 187–208 (2015)
32. Stahl, B.C.: Morality, ethics, and reflection: a categorization of normative is research. J. Assoc. Inf. Syst. **13**, 636–656 (2012)
33. Stahl, B.C., Eden, G., Jirotka, M., Coeckelbergh, M.: From computer ethics to responsible research and innovation in ICT: the transition of reference discourses informing ethics-related research in information systems. Inf. Manag. **51**, 810–818 (2014)

34. Sullivan, W., Sullivan, R., Buffton, B.: Aligning individual and organisational values to support change. J. Change Manag. **2**, 247–254 (2001)
35. Talbot, C.: Measuring Public Value - A Competing Values Approach. The Work Foundation, London (2008)
36. Tavani, H.T.: Ethics & Technology: Ethical Issues in an Age of Information and Communication Technology. John Wiley & Sons, Hoboken (2007)
37. The European Commission: The European eGovernment Action Plan 2011–2015 - Harnessing ICT to promote smart, sustainable & innovative Government. Brussels: Communication from the Commission to the European Parliament, the Council, the European Economic and Social Committee and the Committee of the Regions. The European Commission (2010)
38. The European Commission: Communication from the Commission to the European Parliament, the Council, the European Economic and Social Committee and the Committee of the Regions: EU eGovernment Action Plan 2016–2020, Accelerating the digital transformation of government, Brussels. The European Commission (2016)
39. The European Commission: eGovernment Benchmark 2017 - Taking stock of user-centric design and delivery of digital public services in Europe. Final Background Report - volume 2, A study prepared for the European Commission DG Communications Net-works, Content & Technology. The European Commission (2016)
40. The European Commission: Report on the public consultation and other consultation activities of the European Commission for the preparation of the EU eGovernment Action Plan 2016–2020. Public services. The European Commission, Directorate-General for Communications Networks, Content and Technology (2016)
41. The European Commission: eGovernment Benchmark 2017, Taking stock of user-centric design and delivery of digital public services in Europe, Final Insight Report - Volume 1, A study prepared for the European Commission DG Communications Networks, Content & Technology. The European Commission (2018)
42. Van Der Wal, Z., De Graaf, G., Lasthuizen, K.: What's valued most? Similarities and differences between the organizational values of the public and private sector. Public Adm. **86**, 465–482 (2008)
43. Venkatesh, V., Thong, J.Y.L., Chan, F.K.Y., Hu, P.J.H.: Managing citizens' uncertainty in egovernment services: the mediating and moderating roles of transparency and trust. Inf. Syst. Res **27**, 87–111 (2015)
44. Wiesing, U.: Immanuel kant, his philosophy and medicine. Med. Health Care Philos. **11**(2), 221–236 (2008)
45. Yli-Huumo, J., Päivärinta, T., Rinne, J., Smolander, K.: Suomi.fi – towards government 3.0 with a national service platform. In: Parycek, P., et al. (eds.) EGOV 2018. LNCS, vol. 11020, pp. 3–14. Springer, Cham (2018). https://doi.org/10.1007/978-3-319-98690-6_1
46. Zhou, Z., Jin, X.L., Fang, Y., Vogel, D.: Toward a theory of perceived benefits, affective commitment, and continuance intention in social virtual worlds: cultural values (indulgence and individualism) matter. Eur. J. Inf. Syst **24**, 247–261 (2015)

Software Business Education

Educational Innovations and Gamification for Fostering Training and Testing in Software Implementation Projects

Zornitsa Yordanova(✉)

University of National and World Economy, 8mi dekemvri, Sofia, Bulgaria
zornitsayordanova@unwe.bg

Abstract. Much research have proven the advantages of innovation in education and training as well as of gamification in different areas of business and engaging people. These both concepts have been used in software implementation projects but still there is a knowledge gap on how they impact such projects. This explorative study aims at undertaking two experiments so as to reveal how educational innovation may impact the training process as part of a business software implementation project and how gamification may influence the testing phase and process of the same project. The experiments have been performed in an ERP implementation project. Before them, a literature review analyses the nature of educational innovation, gamification and ERP implementation to bridge the gap between these three concepts of this multidisciplinary approach for knowledge transfer between different management areas. The results of the experiments show concrete examples of game design elements and educational innovations for their application within training and testing phase of business software implementation project. The results of the experiments showed unconditionally the relevance of these two approaches in training and testing of business software.

Keywords: Business software training · Business software testing · Educational innovation · Gamification · Project management · ERP implementation

1 Introduction

Software implementation projects often struggle from high level of failure and user rejection. Training of users and user testing are amongst the most crucial phases in software implementation. This experimental study explores how educational innovations may foster user training and how gamification may influence positively the user testing process.

The educational innovation has always been from a great interest of researchers and educational organizations. However, most of the research presenting either case studies or researching the impact of applying innovative methods or technologies in different educational use cases for the purpose of continuous quality improvement [1]. The case of innovating for the purposes of problem solving [2, 3] and fundamental improvement [4] of real educational challenges is missing [5]. In few cases where this is not true, the

S. Hyrynsalmi et al. (Eds.): ICSOB 2019, LNBIP 370, pp. 293–305, 2019.
https://doi.org/10.1007/978-3-030-33742-1_23

research approach does not focus on the identified educational problems and challenges but rather on the pressure for innovating [6]. Utilizing the idea of problem driven innovation [7], the current research aims at extracting some commonly identified problems and challenges in user training as part of a business software implementation because of the understanding that these would be the directions for innovating this process [8].

Gamification on the other hand, has recently gained much interest of both practitioners and academics. Ordinary, gamification is used as a tool for better understanding of a particular material or topic and also to illustrate a specific scenario or a case in which demonstration and empathy are required [9]. It has been used for greater commitment to a cause (representing the topic as a game, not an obligation or responsibility). Other case studies show gamification utilization for increasing results and bringing reality closer through role play (in which situations the user would be in an artificial environment and would not be able to show his potential) [10]. Gamification is used as well to accommodate intergenerational differences in the setting of objectives and tasks (particularly between the different thinking of millenniums - born around and after 2000 and their possible leaders from previous generations). Gamification is applied for many other purposes, its main idea is the use of game elements in a non-business context in order to achieve concrete and better results [11] Thus, the generalized perceptions of gamification give reasons for the researchers to believe that it would be a particularly useful and applicable tool for increasing the learning outcomes and the business results as a whole [12]. Bearing in mind the scale of the concept and the wide spectre and scope of its application, the proper usage and application of gamification is a difficult task especially for achieving particular goals. No matter of the large quantity of research during the latest years analysing and digging the gamification, the topic is still not fully scoped. Even more, the concept is increasingly attracting more interest from different industries for achieving different purposes. On the other hand, the large number of discussions, research and case studies give reasons for reckoning the topic as a hot one. The explanation of gamification of Nicholson [13] showing gamification as the use of gameful and playful layers to help a user find personal connections that motivate engagement with a specific context for long-term change and it motivates the current research for testing it in an experiment with user testers in software implementation.

2 Literature Background

Bearing in mind the complex and multidisciplinary nature of the current research, in this section of the paper, different literature background objectives take place. These are: educational innovation from the prism of its application for training in software development and implementation of ERP systems, gamification as a tool for fostering user testing in business system implementation and ERP implementation as an objective of the both experiments in the research.

2.1 Educational Innovation

Educational innovations are defined by Taylor et al. [14] as any novel teaching technique, strategy, tool, or learning resource that could be used by an instructor to lead to effective (or promising) instructional techniques that benefit student learning and engagement. According to Fullan [15], educational innovation must contain three elements: use of new revised materials (curriculum materials or technologies); use of new teaching approaches (teaching strategies or activities); alteration of beliefs (pedagogical assumptions). Regardless of the exact definition and scope of educational innovations, their management seems to be an unsolved challenge through the years [16, 17]. Havelock [18] pointed out in his book The Change Agent's Guide to Innovation in Education that the innovation management in education should be performed on multi-level layers simultaneously and this complication is the main burden for educational institutions.

The identified problem, which motivates this research is the usually missing link between innovating and real problem solving. Tidd and Bessant [19] have put it as the tendency of organizations to follow and fit research and innovation into contemporary fads, rather than to face real and fundamental challenges and problems. This is relevant for software training per se. Most of the educational and training innovations are focused on using innovative methods for teaching and learning [20], applying technology [21], networking or collaboration for open innovation [22] or modernizing the education in general [23] as a primary reason for exploring and research. The educational innovations start usually not from fundamental problems and challenges, which would scale training at a next level, but rather extend the body of knowledge of educational innovation with experimental case studies. On the other hand, there are much of research on educational innovation that also extend the educational innovation theory by providing research on non-educational topics which are rather related to research on knowledge transfer from other fields. In this research we are trying to achieve exactly extending the understanding of educational innovations in business field such as the process of training in business software implementation project.

Educational innovations divide into different categories: Innovation in teaching; Innovation in the administration of universities; technological innovations in training; Innovations to achieve more active learning/learning; Innovations to stimulate science at a university; innovation training and education, etc. Many research focus on teaching innovation as the importance of innovative pedagogies provides an opportunity to implement innovation amongst both students and environment [24]. Technology also provides a reason and insight for innovations in education and they are second-rated usually in terms of popularity in case studies in educational innovation. An interesting point in technological educational innovation resent analysis is that technology is a crossing bridge between education and business [25]. Supporting this thesis, many research in general innovation studies originally focused on technological innovation, having historical roots in the manufacturing sector which topics have been largely research by Carlborg et al. [26], Djellal et al. [27].

Many researchers observe educational innovation from their perspective to be an open dialogue to future innovative practice in any other industry [28]. Bearing in mind these both stated opinions on enlarging technology usage in education and openness, technologies are more and more utilized for collaboration and changing the classical models of class-attendance. This reveals much more opportunity for interdisciplinary learning activities and for students to approach complex problems [29] and to improve their practical experience and knowledge.

2.2 Gamification

Play as a phenomenon is older than culture, economy, all socio-cultural and socio-economic system as we know them today prior to human society and human civilization [30]. The author makes an analogy with animal games that resemble and etymologically represent the same process, which suggests that games as a phenomenon may have existed even before the birth of mankind. Analysing the game as a concept, Huizinga [30] concludes that it is more than just a physiological phenomenon or a psychological reflex. It goes beyond purely physical or purely biological activity. This is a significant feature – i.e. has some meaning and serves not only on its own, isolated from side factors and purposes, it is a function of human being. The importance of games as a phenomenon is also confirmed by pedagogical research, which determines games as an essential and critical element of the maturation process. After the brief preface, which puts the games at the center of human development since its inception, the concept of gamification is brand new, yet significant and promising for its development.

Among the first to define the concept of gamification as a modern concept is Pelling [31] who saw it back in 2002 as a process that makes the interface of different products, in his case, electronic transactions, more fun, faster and more playful. The gamification process defined by Deterding et al. [32] is the use of game elements in non-game contexts. In depth, this definition is dealt with in another authors' study [33], where they explain that it is a matter of game elements, not a game in general. While games are usually played, play itself is a different and broader category than the game itself. Games, on the other hand, are characterized by rules and competition, or the struggle with concrete and persistent results or goals on the part of those involved. The authors in the literature make a clear distinction between the term "serious games" and "gaming". While serious games describe the use of incomplete games for non-entertainment purposes, the use of games and the use of gaming elements is a way of diversifying existing approaches for better performance. A link between the concept of gaming and serious games, however, is that both concepts use games for purposes other than their normal use for entertainment. In addition, gamification is also defined as a process of using gaming mechanisms and game thinking to solve problems from Deterding itself. In another study, [33] claim that gamification as a term derives from the digital media industry. Lee and Hammer [34] believe that gamification is the use of gaming mechanisms, dynamics, and frameworks to promote desired behavior. Kapp [35] defines gamification as the use of game-based mechanics, aesthetics and playful thoughts to make people loyal, to motivate action, to encourage learning, and to solve problems. The key point of gamification is the inclusion of gaming tasks that players have to perform [36]. McGonigal [37] summarizes in a study that, since the beginning of the 21st century, a lot of research interest has been on games as a phenomenon through which can be conveyed an element of joy and excitement in serious work situations and their solution. Shpakova et al. [38] defines gamification as "the process of doing activities in non-game contexts such as games". Another definition in the literature interprets gamification as an informal term for the use of video game elements in non-gaming systems to improve user experience and user engagement [39]. Huotari and Hamari [40] divide gamification into three parts: (1) implementing elements of the game in non-gaming activities, (2) making psychological changes, and (3) visible changes in user behavior.

As a summary of the analysed definitions, it can be concluded that gamification is a concept for using game elements [32, 41, 42] in a different non-game context [32, 42] for the purpose of increasing consumer engagement [40–42]. Again for the purpose of systemizing and summarizing, Jakubowski [43] concludes that he considers the following two definitions to be the most focused: (1). Gaming is the use of game elements in non-game contexts [32]; (2). Ignoring is the process of gaming and gaming mechanics for consumer engagement and problem solving [41]. The table below summarizes the definitions in the scientific literature (Table 1).

Table 1. Gamification definitions in the literature

Authors	Definition
Pelling (2011)	"A process that makes the interface of different products, more fun, faster and more playful"
Deterding et al. (2011)	"Using game elements in non-game contexts"
Deterding et al. (2011)	"The process of using gaming mechanisms and game thinking to solve problems by yourself"
Deterding et al. (2011)	"Term for using video game elements in non-gaming systems to improve user experience and user engagement"
Lee and Hammer (2011)	"Using gaming mechanisms, dynamics and frameworks to promote desired behavior"
Kapp (2012)	"Use of game-based mechanics, aesthetics and playful thoughts to make people faithful, to motivate action, to promote learning and to solve problems"
Shpakova et al. (2017)	"The inclusion of gaming tasks that players must perform"
Huotari and Hamari (2012)	"Implementing elements of the game in non-games activities, making psychological changes and visible changes in user behavior"
Zicherman and Cunningham (2011)	"A process of using thinking and mechanics to engage users"
Burke (2012)	"Using game mechanics and game design techniques in non-game contexts of design behavior, skills development, or engaging people in innovation"
Werbach and Hunter (2012) [44]	"Using gaming elements and game design techniques in non-gaming contexts"
Huotari and Hamari (2012)	"A process of improving the service with the ability to play games to maintain the overall value creation of the user"
Werbach (2014) [45]	"Process of turning activities into more playful situations"

For the research purposes after the performed literature analysis on the concept of gamification, the author uses the following definition:

> "Gamification is using of game elements, techniques and mechanism in non-game context to achieve specific goals"

The result of the analysis of all the definitions and understanding of gamification in the literature provides a contribution with (1). Unifying all the mentions ingredients of game within the concept, i.e. elements, technics and mechanism; and (2). Clarifying that gamification concept aims at delivering results on particular topics and already set goals. This second deliverable from the literature analysis motivates the experiment of try using gamification to deliver particular results in the testing process in a software implementation project.

2.3 ERP Implementation

Enterprise Resource Planning is an integrated management approach for enterprises, which encompasses enterprise activities into a systemic process moving as an integrated entity. In the current corporate landscape, these systems are usually integrated into an information system due to the large scope and diversity of business applications and capacity to handle huge transaction-base. ERP systems are also defined to be integrated software packages, which include necessary ingredients that would support the smooth flow of work in a pre-defined process using a common database [46]. ERP systems propose various benefits to enterprises such as ease to use, enabling real-time decision making, resource for decision support systems, by integrating multiple organizational functions into a unique system [47]. ERP systems are expensive by cost and require significant resources including time for implementation and this is why their better and faster implementation are from a great researchers and practitioners interest. ERP systems are prone to high risk of failure leading to disruption in business continuity and operational work processes [48] potentially affecting the customer satisfaction. Hence ERP implementations are considered as complex and challenging, and often result as unsuccessful [49, 50].

All these reasons have motivated researchers to focus their studies on the critical failure factors of ERP implementation [51–53] and concluded that more flexible and business orientated methods are needed to fill the gaps in overcoming the barriers. The research aims at experimenting mainly to contribute to decreasing the failure in implementation of these crucial for the business success business software systems.

3 Research Methodology

Designing the research methodology starts from the statement of Campbell and Stanley [54] that by experiment we refer to that portion of research in which variables are manipulated and their effects upon other variables are observed. In this context, the author believes in the experimental approach in innovation research as well as in project research. Reasons for this are the unique nature of the referred concepts: innovation and project which both has a meaning of uniqueness, multi-factories, multi-disciplinary and complex essence, changing in the diverse use cases of their application [55].

Two experiments took place in this research. They were performed during an ERP implementation project by an IT company, developing an ERP product for a large corporate. These two experiments were focused on the fourth project phase of the implementation, i.e. training and testing phase. They are recognized as main challenges in ERP implementation and crucial factors for success of these projects [56]. The covered modules by the system were: ERP testing; Finance – general ledger; Finance – fixed assets; Accountancy – customer payments; Accountancy – vendor payments; Accountancy – bank management; supply chain management – vendor management; supply chain management – purchase order management; supply chain management – return management; Procurement – vendor offers; Procurement – master planning; sales and marketing – customer management; sales and marketing – sales order management; human resource management – employee management; human resource management – payroll management; Inventory – product management (items, BOM, services); Inventory – warehouse management; customer relationship management – lead and prospect management; customer relationship management – offering process; production – master planning; production – production management processes; Reporting – standard ERP reports; Reporting – BI extended reports.

3.1 Educational Innovation in Training Phase

The training phase included a training of 15 key users from different departments on the whole functionality of the system. Usually the challenges in such trainings in business software implementation are related to: lack of concentration by the trainees, not deep knowledge on the whole business cycle processes, covered by the system, weak engagement, user resistance, routine devolution to the old system or process, inability of trainees to accept novelties, etc. These 15 key users were divided into two groups who had parallel training sessions: the first one with ordinary training approach and the second one – with embedded educational innovations for teaching and learning. For the first training, the training design included power point slides and working directly in the implemented ERP product. During the experiment with teaching and learning innovations in the second group, we used video guiding process, collaborative work, digital materials, combinatory approach in presenting the lectures material, gamification techniques, collective thinking, critical thinking and problem solving approaches, embedded experimental conditions, interactive learning approach, music and sport activates. The parallel sessions continued one full week. The assessment at the end of the training was designed as an ordinary test scenario where the trainees should demonstrate individually the knowledge and experience gained with the system. The testing scenario covered all the implemented modules, took an hour, it was computer-based and electronically evaluated the right answers and actions by the trainees. The maximum result was 100%.

3.2 Gamification in Testing Phase

During the testing phase, as per the ERP project plan, the same key users took part. The testing phase started in two weeks after the training took place. For avoiding the risk of selective choice of better performing users for the innovative approaches in the experiments, the groups were inverted this time. Now, the first group of testers was part of the gamification experiment (the same one which had been trained with ordinary approach in the training phase) and the second one was part of a standard testing approach. The used gamification techniques were: virtual goods, cooperation in the field of competition, achievements, levels, opportunities for rewarding, gifts, challenges. The purpose of the testing and its successful performing was assessed by comparing the bugs found by the two groups. Both testing sessions were again parallel and covered the same modules as the testers had been already trained in.

4 Results

The detailed results from the training experiment are presented in Table 2. They show some of the tested metrics, relevant to the difference in the performance of both groups.

Table 2. Summarized results from experimenting with education innovations in ERP implementation project.

Performance metric	Result
Test results for all trainees	72,53%
Test results of the first group (average)	69,14%
Test results of the second group (average)	75,50%
Max test result	91%
Min test result	49%
Standard deviation	0,1272198

The average results of the evaluation after the week of training were 72,53%. Definitely higher performance has been achieved by the second group of trainees who were trained with teaching and learning innovations. In Table 3 are shown all the results as well as the role of the key user. No linkage between users' role and the achieved results has been observed.

Table 3. Detailed results from experimenting with education innovations in ERP implementation project.

Users	Performance	Position
User 1 (1st group)	89,00%	Accountant
User 2 (1st group)	71,00%	Process specialist (lean)
User 3 (1st group)	66,00%	Administration
User 4 (1st group)	62,00%	Supply chain
User 5 (1st group)	49,00%	Logistics
User 6 (1st group)	91,00%	Software department

(continued)

Table 3. (*continued*)

Users	Performance	Position
User 7 (1st group)	56,00%	Marketing
User 8 (2nd group)	61,00%	Supply chain
User 9 (2nd group)	91,00%	Accountant
User 10 (2nd group)	78,00%	Sales
User 11 (2nd group)	77,00%	Logistics
User 12 (2nd group)	75,00%	Process specialist (lean)
User 13 (2nd group)	68,00%	Marketing
User 14 (2nd group)	66,00%	Accountant
User 15 (2nd group)	88,00%	Software department

Apart from the quantitative results of the final tests after the training, some informal interviews with the users proved the reason for the better performance of the second group. The interviews confirmed the increased engagement, interaction and commitment of those students and made them more interested in the next phase of the project.

The second experiment in the testing phase of the ERP implementation showed the following results presented in Table 4. In this second iteration of the experiment, the first group was part of the gamification experiment and the second one received an ordinary approach.

Table 4. Summarized results from experimenting with gamification in ERP implementation project.

Performance metric	Result
Bugs found by all testers	153
Bugs found by the first group	112
Bugs found by the second group	41

The results from the second experiment showed a big different of the results between both groups involved in the testing. 73% of the found bugs within the testing phase were discovered by the group in which the action research experimented with some gamification elements and techniques. After the unconditional results, the software implementation company shared that usually during testing in similar projects for the same ERP project and same customer profile, no more than 50 bugs have been discovered by the key users.

5 Conclusion

The research provides a general information on how educational innovation (teaching and learning innovations in particular) and gamification impact training and testing phases as part of an ERP implementation project. The results support some already achieved results in other studies with different focus but again emphasizing on educational innovation and gamification application [57]. The research showed results from two experiments which explicitly demonstrated the relevance of usage of both techniques in software implementation. The obtained results in this action research convinced both the customer (company employed the key users who had been trained and used as testers in the project of implementation) and the ERP implementer itself, that educational innovation and gamification would impact positively the effectiveness in business software implementation projects. They are even much relevant when it comes to project members with no IT background [58].

Acknowledgments. The paper is supported by the BG NSF Grant No M 15/4-2017 (DM 15/1), KP-06 OPR01/3-2018, and NID NI 14/2018.

References

1. Roffe, I.M.: Conceptual problems of continuous quality improvement and innovation in higher education. Qual. Assur. Educ. **6**(2), 74–82 (1998). https://doi.org/10.1108/09684889810205723
2. von Hipple, E.: "Sticky information" and the locus of problem solving: implications for innovation. Manag. Sci. **40**(4), 429–439 (1994)
3. Terwiesch, C., Xu, Y.: Innovation contests, open innovation, and multiagent problem solving. Manag. Sci. **54**(9), 1529–1543 (2008). https://doi.org/10.1287/mnsc.1080.0884
4. Boer, H., Gertsen, F.: From continuous improvement to continuous innovation: a (retro)(per) spective. Int. J. Technol. Manag. **26**(8), 805–827 (2003)
5. Hopkins, D.: School Improvement for Real. Routledge Falmer (2001)
6. Clack, L., Ellison, R.: Innovative approaches to management education. J. Manag. Policies Pract. **6**(1), 6–9 (2018). https://doi.org/10.15640/jmpp.v6n1a2
7. Coccia, M.: Problem-driven innovation in drug discovery: co-evolution of the patterns of radical innovation with the evolution of problems. Health Policy Technol. **5**(2), 143–155 (2016)
8. Al-Imarah, A.A., Shields, R.: MOOCs, disruptive innovation and the future of higher education: a conceptual analysis. Innov. Educ. Teach. Int. **56**(3), 258–269 (2019). https://doi.org/10.1080/14703297.2018.1443828
9. Kolb, A., Kolb, D.: Learning to play, playing to learn: a case study of a ludic learning space. J. Organ. Chang. Manag. **23**(1), 26–50 (2010)
10. Hamari, J., Koivisto, J., Sarsa, H.: Does gamification work? – a literature review of empirical studies on gamification. In: Proceedings of the 47th Hawaii International Conference on System Sciences, Hawaii, USA, 6–9 January (2014)
11. Danelli, F.: Implementing game design in gamification. In: Reiners, T., Wood, Lincoln C. (eds.) Gamification in Education and Business, pp. 67–79. Springer, Cham (2015). https://doi.org/10.1007/978-3-319-10208-5_4
12. Neeli, B.K.: Gamification in the enterprise: differences from consumer market, implications, and a method to manage them. In: Reiners, T., Wood, Lincoln C. (eds.) Gamification in Education and Business, pp. 489–511. Springer, Cham (2015). https://doi.org/10.1007/978-3-319-10208-5_25

13. Nicholson, S.: A RECIPE for meaningful gamification. In: Reiners, T., Wood, Lincoln C. (eds.) Gamification in Education and Business, pp. 1–20. Springer, Cham (2015). https://doi.org/10.1007/978-3-319-10208-5_1
14. Taylor, C., et al.: Propagating the adoption of CS educational innovations. In: ITiCSE 2018, Larnaca, Cyprus (2018)
15. Fullan, M.: The New Meaning of Educational Change, 5th edn. Teachers College Press (2007)
16. Nicholls, A.: Managing Educational Innovations. Routledge (1983). https://doi.org/10.4324/9781351040860
17. Schlossberg, M., Larco, N., Slotterback, Carissa S., Connerly, C., Greco, M.: Educational partnerships for innovation in communities (EPIC): harnessing university resources to create change. In: Frank, Andrea I., Silver, C. (eds.) Urban Planning Education. TUBS, pp. 251–268. Springer, Cham (2018). https://doi.org/10.1007/978-3-319-55967-4_17
18. Havelock, R.: The Change Agent's Guide to Innovation in Education. Educational Technology Publications (1973)
19. Tidd, J., Bessant, J.: Innovation management challenges: from fads to fundamentals. Int. J. Innov. Manag. **22**(05), 1840007 (2018)
20. Uerz, D., Volman, M., Kral, M.: Teacher educators' competences in fostering student teachers' proficiency in teaching and learning with technology: an overview of relevant research literature. Teach. Teach. Educ. **70**, 12–23 (2018)
21. García-Alcaraz, P., Martínez-Loya, V., García-Alcaraz, J.L., Sánchez-Ramírez, C.: The role of ICT in educational innovation. In: Cortés-Robles, G., García-Alcaraz, J.L., Alor-Hernández, G. (eds.) Managing Innovation in Highly Restrictive Environments. MIE, pp. 143–165. Springer, Cham (2019). https://doi.org/10.1007/978-3-319-93716-8_7
22. Yordanova, Z.: User innovation as a basis of innovation network between universities and business. Int. J. Innov. **6**(2), 85–94 (2018). https://doi.org/10.5585/iji.v7i2.308
23. Drummond, DeYound: Understanding higher education admissions reforms in the eurasian context. J. Eur. Educ. **44**(1), 7–26 (2012). The New Educational Assessment Regimes in Eurasia: Impacts, Issues, and Implications
24. Paniagua, A., Istance, D.: Teachers as Designers of Learning Environments: The Importance of Innovative Pedagogies. Educational Research and Innovation. OECD Publishing (2018)
25. Young, S.: From disruption to innovation: thoughts on the future of MOOCs. Following The International Conference "ESTARS 2017" Innovation and Disruption in the Digital Age, Voprosy obrazovaniya/Educational Studies Moscow, no. 4 (2018)
26. Carlborg, P., et al.: The evolution of service innovation research: a critical review and synthesis. Serv. Ind. J. **34**(5), 373–398 (2014)
27. Djellal, F., et al.: Two decades of research on innovation in services: which place for public services? Struct. Chang. Econ. Dyn. **27**, 98–117 (2013)
28. Reinders, H., Nakamura, S., Ryan, S.: The scope of innovation in japanese language education. In: Reinders, H., Ryan, S., Nakamura, S. (eds.) Innovation in Language Teaching and Learning. NLLTE, pp. 1–8. Springer, Cham (2019). https://doi.org/10.1007/978-3-030-12567-7_1
29. Potting, K., Frie, L., (Frans) Jacobs, F.W.: Learning landscapes, a breeding ground for sustainable educational innovation: experiences of teachers working in a context that aims to support innovative behaviour. In: Jacobs, F., Sjoer, E. (eds.) Inspired to Change: A Kaleidoscoop of Transitions in Higher Education, Chap. 5, pp. 64–77 (2018). ISBN 978-90-73077-94-2
30. Huizinga, J.: Homo Ludens: A Study of the Play Element in Culture, 2nd edn. Routledge & Kegan Paul, London, Boston and Henley (1949). First edition published in German in Switzerland in I944

31. Pelling, N.: The (short) prehistory of gamification. Funding Startups (& other impossibilities). Haettu (2011)
32. Deterding, S., Dixon, D., Khaled, R., Nacke, L.: From game design elements to gamefulness: defining "gamification". In: Lugmayr, A., Franssila, H., Safran, C., Hammouda, I. (eds.) MindTrek 2011, pp. 9–15 (2011). https://doi.org/10.1145/2181037.2181040
33. Deterding, S., et al.: Gamification: toward a definition. In: CHI 2011, Vancouver, BC, Canada, 7–12 May 2011. ACM (2011). 978-1-4503-0268-5/11/05
34. Lee, J., Hammer, J.: Gamification in education: what, how, why bother? Acad. Exch. Q. **122**, 1–5 (2011)
35. Kapp, K.M.: The gamification of learning and instruction: game-based methods and strategies for training and education. Pfeiffer, San Francisco (2012)
36. Kiryakova, G., et al.: Gamification in Education. In: Conference: 9th International Balkan Education and Science Conference At: Edirne, Turkey (2014)
37. McGonigal, J.: Reality Is Broken: Why Games Make Us Better and How They Can Change the World. The Penguin Press, London (2011)
38. Shpakova, A., Dörfler, V., MacBryde, J.: Changing the game: a case for gamifying knowledge management. World J. Sci. Technol. Sustain. Dev. **14**, 143–154 (2017)
39. Deterding, S., et al.: Gamification: using game design elements in non-gaming contexts. In: CHI 2011, Vancouver, BC, Canada, 7–12 May 2011. ACM (2011). 978-1-4503-0268-5/11/05
40. Huotari, K., Hamari, J.: Defining gamification - a service marketing perspective. In: Proceedings of the 16th International Academic Mindtrek Conference, Tampere, Finland, 3–5 October 2012, pp. 17–22. ACM, New York (2012)
41. Zichermann, G., Cunningham, C.: Gamification by Design: Implementing Game Mechanics in Web and Mobile Apps. O'Reilly Media, Sebastopol (2011)
42. Burke, B.: Gamify: How Gamification Motivates People to Do Extraordinary Things, 1 edn. Routledge (2014)
43. Jakubowski, M.: Gamification in business and education, - project of gamified course for university students. Dev. Bus. Simul. Exp. Learn. **41**, 339–341 (2014)
44. Werbach, K., Hunter, D.: How Game Thinking Can Revolutionize Your Business. Wharton Digital Press (2012)
45. Werbach, K.: (Re)Defining gamification: a process approach. In: Spagnolli, A., Chittaro, L., Gamberini, L. (eds.) Persuasive Technology. PERSUASIVE 2014. LNCS, vol 8462. Springer, Cham (2014)
46. Staehr, L.: Understanding the role of managerial agency in achieving business benefits from ERP systems. Inf. Syst. J. **20**(3), 213–238 (2010)
47. Xue, Y., Liang, H., William, R.B., Snyde, C.A.: ERP implementation failures in China: case studies with implications for ERP vendor. Int. J. Prod. Econ. **97**, 279–295 (2005)
48. Salmela, H.: Analysing business losses caused by information systems risk: a business process analysis approach. J. Inf. Technol. **23**, 185 (2008). https://doi.org/10.1057/palgrave.jit.2000122
49. Soh, C., Sia, S.K., Tay-yap, J.: Cultural fits and misfits: is ERP a universal solution. Commun. ACM **43**(4), 47–51 (2000)
50. Gargeya, V.B., Brady, C.: Success and failure factors of adopting SAP in ERP system implementation. Bus. Process. Manag. J. **11**(5), 501–516 (2005)
51. Zach, O., Bjorn, E.M.: Identifying reasons for ERP system customization in SMEs: a multiple case study. J. Enterp. Inf. Manag. **25**(5), 462–478 (2012)
52. Zach, O., Bjørn, E.M., Olsen, D.H.: ERP system implementation in SMEs: exploring the influences of the SME context. Enterp. Inf. Syst. **8**(2), 309–335 (2014)

53. Metaxiotis, K., Zafeiropoulos, I., Nikolinakou, K., Psarras, J.: Goal directed management methodology for the support of ERP implementation and optimal adaptation procedure. Inf. Manag. Comput. Secur. **13**(1), 55–71 (2005)
54. Campbell, D.T., Stanley, J.C.: Experimental and Quasi-Experimental Designs for Research. Rand McNally, Chicago (1966)
55. Yordanova, Z.: Innovation project tool for outlining innovation projects. Int. J. Bus. Innov. Res. **16**(1), 63 (2018)
56. Bingi, P., Sharma, M.K., Godla, J.K.: Critical issues affecting an ERP implementation. Inf. Syst. Manag. **16**(3), 7–14 (1999). https://doi.org/10.1201/1078/43197.16.3.19990601/31310.2
57. Yordanova, Z.: Gamification for handing educational innovation challenges. In: Ashmarina, S., Mesquita, A., Vochozka, M. (eds.) Digital Transformation of the Economy: Challenges, Trends and New Opportunities. AISC, vol. 908, pp. 529–541. Springer, Cham (2020). https://doi.org/10.1007/978-3-030-11367-4_53
58. Stoimenov, N.: Innovative relative wear of lifters. In: XIV International Scientific Congress "Machines. Technologies. Materials, pp. 15–18

Improving a Startup Learning Framework Through an Expert Panel

Rafael Chanin(✉), Afonso Sales, Leandro Pompermaier, and Rafael Prikladnicki

School of Technology, PUCRS, Porto Alegre, Brazil
{rafael.chanin,afonso.sales,leandro.pompermaier,rafaelp}@pucrs.br

Abstract. It is not easy to provide real-world experience to students in an academic setting. When it comes to the development of a software startup, the connection with real users and customers is a must; otherwise, it becomes just a technical challenge. Furthermore, universities and the academic environment are paying more attention to this topic in the past years. One interesting work developed in this regard is the Challenge Based Startup Learning. In this sense, this paper aims at exploring, studying, and extending the Challenge Based Startup Learning Framework by running an expert panel. The idea behind this approach is to collect useful feedback in order to improve the framework to provide student with a better software startup development experience.

Keywords: Challenge Based Startup Learning · Challenge Based Learning · Startup education · Entrepreneurship education

1 Introduction

In the past few decades we have witnessed significant advances in terms of technology. Today, anyone with coding skills can develop an application that can be reached by millions (or even billions) of people [10]. Most of the services we use today, such as Netflix, Dropbox, Amazon, and Instagram, could only be developed after the popularization and the evolution of the Internet.

These innovative technological endeavors, which aim at providing a new product or service, or improve an existing one, are called *startups* [3]. Most startups follow the *lean startup* methodology, proposed by Eric Ries [20]. The idea behind this methodology is to maximize the learning process by constantly interacting with users through a minimum viable product (MVP).

Unfortunately, most startups fail in the first years of their existence [10]. There are definitely many factors that may lead to this destiny. However, bad use of software engineering practices is pointed out as one key reason [8,10,13].

This whole "startup movement" called the attention of the academic world. Researchers from all around the globe have already published relevant papers on how software development processes should be adapted to fit a startup context [10–12,16,18]. When it comes to software startup education, there are several studies in the literature reporting different approaches and best practices

S. Hyrynsalmi et al. (Eds.): ICSOB 2019, LNBIP 370, pp. 306–320, 2019.
https://doi.org/10.1007/978-3-030-33742-1_24

undertaken in the classroom, such as the one from Case *et al.* [4] and from Porter *et al.* [19]. One of these studies, which was developed by the authors, proposed a framework that combines Lean Startup and Challenge Based Learning (CBL) [17]. The authors called it the Challenge Based Startup Learning (CBSL) [6].

In this paper, we intend to continue the work started by the authors [6] by evaluating the CBSL framework through an expert panel [1]. The goal is to collect feedback from experienced practitioners and researchers in order to enhance the framework. In order to do so, we defined the following research question: "How instructors can improve the software startup learning process for their students using the CBSL framework?".

The remainder of this document is organized as follows. Section 2 presents the current version of the CBSL. In Sect. 3 we describe the methodology used to evaluate the framework. Section 4 depicts the results obtained from the expert panel. In Sect. 5 we present the evolution of the CBSL, which was based on the information gathered from the panel. Finally, we draw our conclusions in Sect. 6.

2 The Challenge Based Startup Learning Framework

The Challenge Based Startup Learning framework is a combination of the Challenge Based Learning [17], an active methodology based on solving real-world challenges, the Lean Startup methodology [20], and the Customer Development process [3]. The idea behind this approach is to bring students as close as possible to a real software startup development context. One key aspect mentioned by Chanin *et al.* [6] is that the framework allows students to develop both technical and soft skills. Since connecting to potential users is a must, students have the opportunity to interact and learn what it take to build a real startup.

The idea for this framework was born after the authors participated in several other studies, such as a systematic mapping review [7], a study on students' perception on learning startup methodologies [15], and a research on software startup education around the world [5].

Figure 1 presents the Challenge Based Startup Learning framework overview. By looking at the framework, we can identify the three CBL phases (*Engage*, *Investigate*, and *Act*), as well as Lean Startup and Customer Development components, such as the *pivots*, and the development cycles.

The *Engage* phase is supposed to be the same as in a "regular" CBL process. The goal here is for students to find a topic and a challenge that it is interesting enough for them. It is important to point out that instructors should never induce student to choose a given idea to work on. Startups are born because founders found something they care about and that they are excited to work on. According to Giardino *et al.* [11], founders tend to abandon their startups if they are not fully connected to the context.

After going through the *Engage* phase and having defined their challenge, students move to a phase in which investigation and action happens simultaneously. Students increase their action and decrease their investigation when

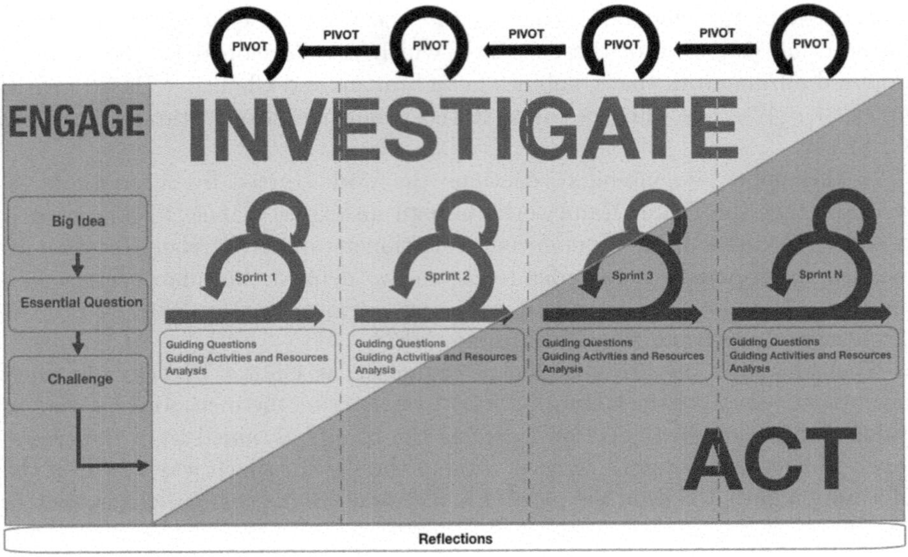

Fig. 1. Challenge Based Startup Learning framework [6].

moving forward into the process (see Fig. 1). The idea behind it is that as students learn more through their investigation, they can start acting more (for instance, developing features). On the other hand, if students fail in validating their hypothesis, they can pivot and change their assumptions.

In the case presented in Chanin *et al.* [6], the following activities were performed during the sprints (in this order):

1. Interview;
2. Value proposition testing;
3. Content creation;
4. Low-fidelity prototype;
5. High-fidelity prototype.

It is worth mentioning that each instructor needs to take their constraints into consideration when applying the framework. For instance, it may not be possible to pivot too many times due to time constraint in a course. In this scenario, instructors might have to ask students to assume the assumption was validated and move on into the process.

Throughout the whole process, students must reflect on their work. The reflection can be done in any format students feel comfortable with (video, audio, or text). This information can be very useful for instructors to understand how students are feeling regarding different aspects of the learning environment. More importantly, students learn more when they reflect over their own learning journey [17].

3 Methodology

In order to evaluate and analyze the framework proposed by Chanin *et al.* [6], we decided to run an expert panel. According to Beecham *et al.* [1], an expert panel is as exploratory study that focuses on analyzing a model, process, method, practice or technique in order to look for strengths, weaknesses, and improvement points. Experts' knowledge and experience bring a lot of value since they can come up with new ideas and thoughts, and they can help researchers avoiding taking the wrong directions [1].

The selected experts should have previous knowledge of some of the topics related to the research under evaluation. The information gathered from these panels are useful to evolve and to validate models [21]. Shepperd and Cartwright [21] also mention that an expert panel is a recognized way of performing an initial evaluation of a model. In addition, expert panels are appropriate when evaluating complex or technical contexts that may require a very specific knowledge [9].

The expert panel process was undertaking following the recommendations given by Slocum [9]. We have set three main goals for this research:

- Gather the view of experts about the current Challenge Based Startup Learning framework [6];
- Collect suggestions and improvement points for the framework; and
- Propose an evolution of the framework, based on the experts recommendations.

We have selected 14 experts to evaluate the current Challenge Based Startup Learning framework. According to Beecham *et al.* [1], there is no problem working with a small sample of experts. The goal is not to find statistical explanations, but rather to gain expert feedback on a given context. These experts were chosen due to their previous experience working with Challenge Based Learning.

3.1 Interview Protocol

The interview was performed face-to-face with each of the experts. At the beginning of each conversation the current model (as presented in Fig. 1) was presented and described in details. The paper describing the model [6] was also used in order to present an example of a case study.

After the presentation, the following questions were asked for each of the experts:

1. Your location (city/country/institution);
2. Academic experience (in years);
3. Industry experience (in years);
4. Challenge Based Learning experience (in years);
5. Challenge Based Learning knowledge (0–5);
6. Lean Startup experience (in years);
7. Lean Startup knowledge (0–5);

8. Positive aspects of the proposed framework;
9. Negative aspects of the proposed framework;
10. Improvement opportunities;
11. Suggestions/comments.

The idea behind asking for the expert's knowledge on Challenge Based Learning and Lean Startup on a scale from 0 to 5 was to clearly differentiate experience from knowledge. One may have studied Lean Startup for years, for instance, but may have never applied the methodology in a real startup.

In addition, it is important to point out that all experts involved in this process had at least one year of Challenge Based Learning experience. One might wonder how someone who had never seen Challenge Based Learning before would react to this framework. However, we decided that, for this study, we would only take into consideration experts that have worked with Challenge based Learning.

3.2 Experts Demographics

The details regarding the experts background and experience is presented in Table 1. The label presented in the table are depicted as follows:

- AE: Academic experience (in years);
- IE: Industry experience (in years);
- CBLE: Challenge Based Learning experience (in years);
- CBLK: Challenge Based Learning knowledge (scale from 0 to 5);
- LSE: Lean Startup experience (in years);
- LSK: Lean Startup knowledge (scale from 0 to 5).

Table 1. Experts' background.

Country	AE	IE	CBLE	CBLK	LSE	LSK
Brazil	10	8	1	3	5	3
Brazil	2	3	2	4	3	4
Brazil	11	2	5	5	3	4
Brazil	12	10	2	4	3	4
Brazil	4	6	4	5	2	2
Brazil	5	4	5	4	2	3
Brazil	17	9	4	5	1	2
Brazil	1	8	1	4	3	4
Brazil	4	25	4	4	0	4
Brazil	16	15	5	5	0	1
Brazil	5	4	3	5	2	3
Indonesia	3	17	1	3	0	0
Italy	3	25	3	5	3	3
Italy	3	5	3	5	1	1

There is a lot of diversity across all data presented in Table 1. The average academic experience of the group is 7 years, although it varies from 1 to 17 years. When it comes to industry experience, the average is 10 years. Regarding CBL experience, no expert knew CBL for more than 5 years, indicating that it is fairly new concept to them. The same happened to Lean Startup experience, although in this case three experts reported having no experience working with this methodology.

4 Expert Panel Results

Following the interview protocol described in Sect. 3.1 we gathered positive and negative aspects related to the proposed framework, as well as improvement opportunities and other suggestions by using an open coding strategy. The following sections depict the most relevant and important points related to each of these information.

4.1 Positive Aspects

To begin with, seven experts mentioned that it is interesting to see how all these processes and methodologies can fit well together. When it comes to the development of innovative projects using CBL, they could see how Lean Startup can really support the process. Since most of the time students do not have experience working with startups, the framework can give them a real feeling of what it takes to develop a startup. In sum, it is a good attempt to build bridges across learning methods that have a lot in common.

Four experts focused their positive feedback on the interview process suggested by the framework. They argued that this was a great idea, since software engineering students, in general, do not have any experience interviewing other people. One of the experts says "*students go to the streets with no background about how to talk to people in order to pull, and not to push information*". Another expert mentioned that "*the framework reflects the natural way to make validation. I liked the interviews*".

Regarding the *build-measure-learn* process, all experts emphasized that the framework gives a lot of room for experimentation, failure and learning. Interestingly, this is exactly what a startup is all about. In this sense, it seems the framework can help students understand in practice the process a startup go through. One expert mentioned that the framework "*provides structure during the investigation/act phase, which is often blurry because CBL is not explicitly tuned to designing a specific product or service*".

Finally, one expert pointed out that this framework can help instructors into motivating students to develop their own startups. Since it is easy to comprehend and to replicate, the framework can also be used as a way to bring more students into the entrepreneurship world.

4.2 Negative Aspects

One of the main issue that almost all experts pointed out as a negative aspect is that, depending on the type of project students are working on, it may take time to run experiments. In these situations, the framework should propose or suggest a way to avoid this problem. In addition, if the course is too short (for instance, two months or less), the framework might not work for the same reason: time constraints.

Six experts mentioned that the framework focuses more on agile development (scrum) rather than on Lean Startup. By looking at Fig. 1, aside from the *pivots*, in fact there is not any other reference to the Lean Startup methodology.

Regarding the reflections, a few experts did not quite understand its role throughout process. Moreover, it was also not clear to them how much guidance is embedded in the framework in terms of basic questions anyone should make. For instance, should students come up with guiding questions and activities or this structure would be provided by the instructor?

Half of the experts believed that there could be a risk working with this framework when students do not have prior CBL, Scrum and Lean Startup knowledge. They argued that either students should know them, or these concepts need to be presented and explored in advance.

An interesting point that one expert mentioned is that the framework is limited to four sprints. Even though this is actually not true (instructors can run as many sprints as needed), the framework - as presented today - might lead to this conclusion.

4.3 Improvement Opportunities

Several experts mentioned that the framework should guide students into the process. They agree that the proposed framework is a good start, but students might feel lost when they actually need to work on the activities. Suggestions on this issue were related to proposing at least a few guiding questions and activities for each sprint, but students can and should come up with more questions and activities. However, the main ones (such as "who is my customer?") have to be explicitly presented.

In regards to the *Engage* phase, some experts asked how students get to a challenge. Even though this process is suppose to be similar to the "regular" CBL methodology, experts suggested that tools and methods could be offered to help students into this process. For instance, they could learn how to run a brainstorming session in order to come up with as many ideas as possible, combine them and later agree upon a single one.

When it comes to Lean Startup processes and tools, experts suggested to explicitly present which tools or methods could be used in each part of the process. For instance, if students are validating a value proposition, the framework could suggest the use of a landing page.

One interesting point that was raised by most experts was related to content creation. In the current framework, content creation is performed in one of the sprints. Experts believed that this activity should begin as soon as possible and it should never stop. The sooner students begin to create a relationship with an audience, the sooner they have a chance to test out a hypothesis with real people.

Regarding pivoting, one expert observed that the framework does not allow pivoting during the *Engage* phase. Students need to know that they can change a *challenge*, an *essential question*, or even a *big idea*.

Even though the framework clearly shows that reflections happens throughout the whole process, some experts pointed out that it would be better if there was an explicit reflection moment after the end of each sprint. In this case, students would know that before moving to the next sprint, they have to reflect on the work performed in the previous sprint.

Finally, there was an interesting discussion on defining key achievements or learning goals for each sprint. In other words, how students know they can move to the next sprint? Is it a matter of hypothesis validation, achieving a set of milestones, or both?

4.4 Key Findings

After gathering all information from the expert panel, the authors analyzed the data in order to agree upon the main take aways. The goal was to further propose changes and improvements to the current Challenge Based Startup Learning framework.

We came across seven improvement points we believed that could be incorporated or adapted to the current framework in order to better deliver value to students:

1. Make it clear that the framework is not limit to a given number of sprints. Even though the framework depicted in Fig. 1 present the last sprint as "N", indicating that there can be more sprints, we understood this information can be more visible.
2. Guiding questions, activities and resources for each sprint (including the *Engage* phase) should be provided by instructors. Students can and should come up with other guiding questions and activities. However, it is important for them to have at least a few essential questions already defined, specially because in most cases students do not have any background on software startup development.
3. Lean Startup processes and tools could be explicit throughout the process. As pointed out by the experts, the framework does not refer to any Lean Startup tool or process aside from the *pivoting*.
4. Content creation can begin as soon as the challenge is defined. The idea is that students will have more chances to interact with real users if they start connecting with them as early as possible. In addition, this process should persevere until the end of the project/course.
5. Allow pivoting during the *Engage* phase. In fact, it is possible to revisit the *Engage* phase in the regular CBL methodology. The idea is to make it clear that students can change their main assumptions.

6. Reflections should happen at the end of each sprint. After running any experiment, it is a good idea to make students reflect on their work. By providing this opportunity at the end of each sprint, students can reflect more often on their learning process.
7. Defined key achievements and/or goals for each sprint. It is important that students know what is expected from them at the end of each sprint. By having clear goals students can create a vision on the path they have to take.

It is worth mentioning that the order of these items is random; we did not intend to prioritize them in any manner. The goal is to make changes in the framework in such a way we can accommodate all seven aforementioned improvements.

5 Proposed Framework

The updated overview version of the Challenge Based Startup Learning framework is presented in Fig. 2. We tried to translate most of the suggestions from the experts directly into one image. However, we could find a way to include the details regarding guiding questions, activities and resources, and sprint goals.

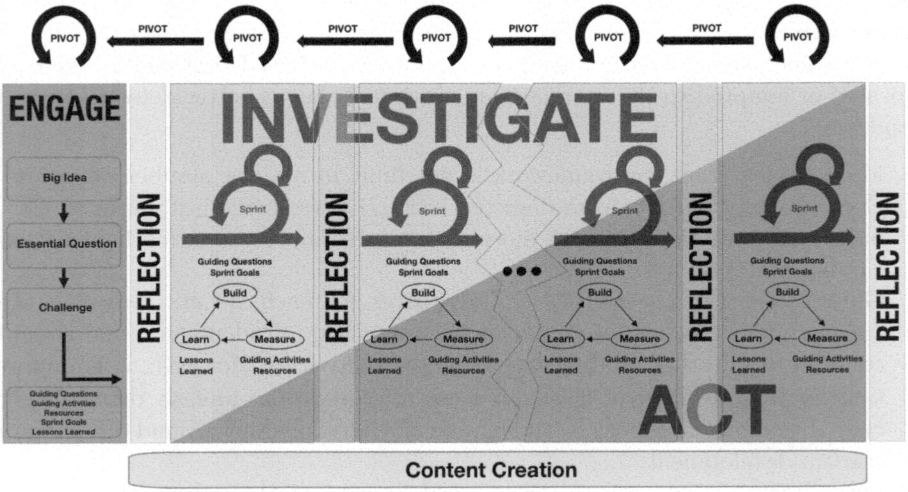

Fig. 2. Proposed Challenge Based Startup Learning framework.

Therefore, we decided to add extra layers to the framework in order to better guide students into the process. It is important to mention that all the suggested guiding questions, guiding activities, resources, and sprint goals are just a starting point; they were defined by the authors based on their own experience and the guidelines proposed by Blank [2]. However, students and instructors should add their own ideas according to the context of the class and of the project being developed.

The first layer, presented in Fig. 3, entailed the *Engage* phase. The goal is to define a big idea, an essential question and a challenge. In order to do so, it is crucial for students to discuss their passions and the problems they want to solve.

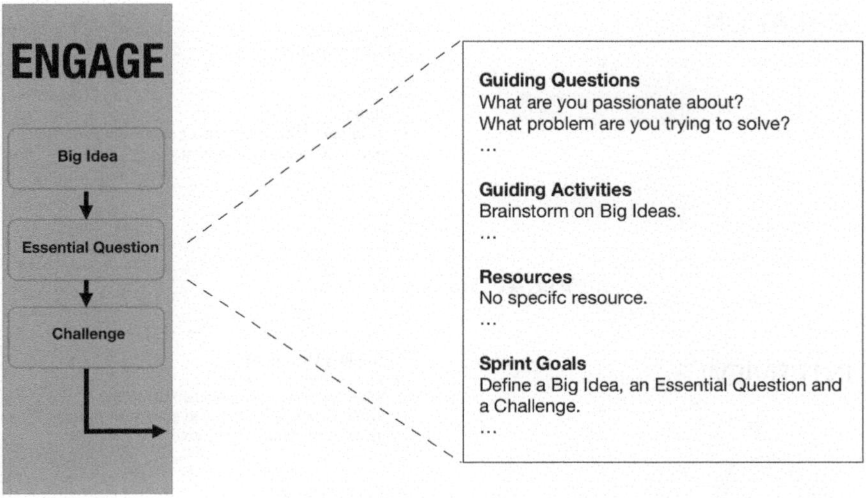

Fig. 3. Engage phase.

Once students have the topic they will be working on as well as the challenge, they can begin working on content creation (see Fig. 4). This is an ongoing process (see Fig. 2), and students should be aware that the sooner they are able to generate content and engage potential users/customers, the better the chances of having real people interacting with them.

Figure 5 entails examples of guiding questions, activities, and resources for the interview sprint. Students should reflect at least on who their customer is, what problems do they have, how they are dealing with these problems today, and where they can find these customers. This is an important step when developing a startup since one of the main reasons they fail, according to Steve Blank, is because founders focus on product development rather than on customer development [2].

When it comes to value proposition testing (see Fig. 6), students must focus on the benefits they would like to deliver to their customers. Developing a landing page can be an effective way to test it. In addition, students must be aware that it is important to measure customers' interest somehow. This measurement can be performed by asking them to fill out a form or just by providing their emails. In fact, any kind of currency a customer provides is a way to measure their interest.

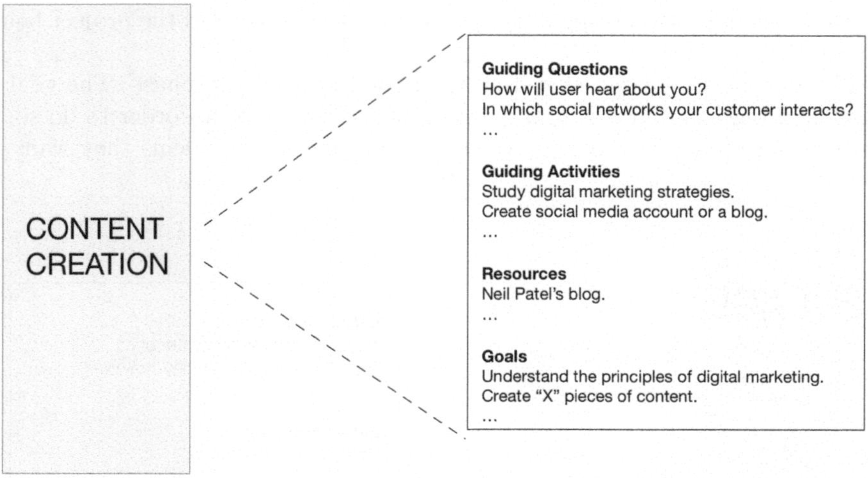

Fig. 4. Content creation.

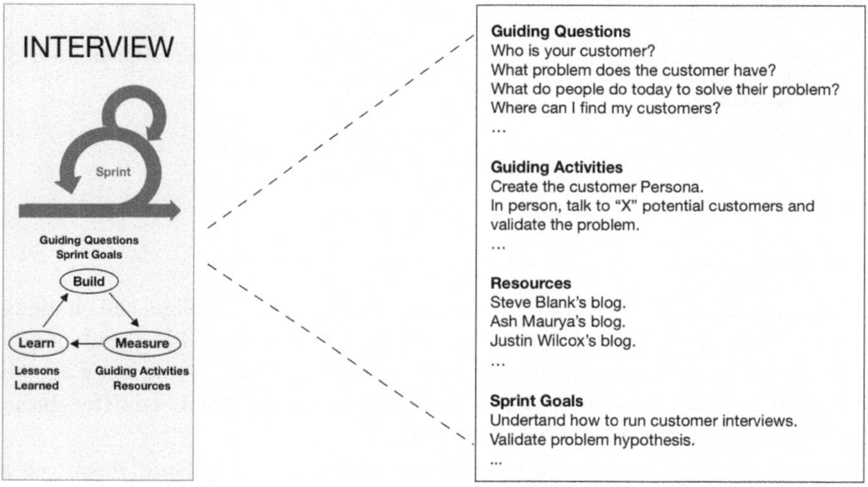

Fig. 5. Customer interview.

The prototyping sprint(s), depicted in Fig. 7, is the moment where students start thinking about their solution. Since they already gathered a lot of information from running interviews, testing their value proposition, and interacting with potential customers (through content creation), it is now time to develop prototypes in order to get more feedback from customers. If there is enough time, it is interesting that students develop both a low fidelity prototype as well as a high fidelity one. By doing so, students will have the opportunity to experience the evolution of the prototype development process.

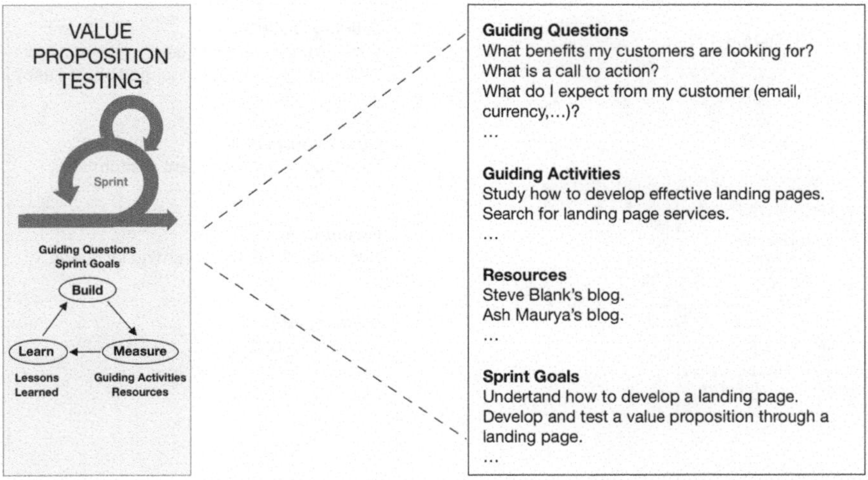

Fig. 6. Value proposition testing.

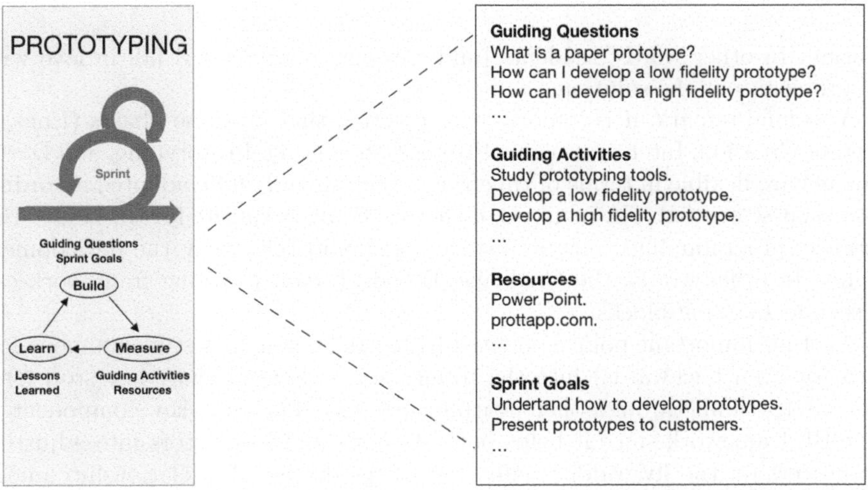

Fig. 7. Prototyping.

Finally, when there is an opportunity to actually develop a piece of software based on all knowledge acquired during the process, students can move to the development sprints (see Fig. 8). This is the moment where students can not only practice their software development skills, but also their knowledge on software startup processes.

It is important that instructors guide students into developing software based on the learnings acquired during the previous sprints. As Ash Maurya mentioned in one of his works [14], it is important to avoid the innovator's bias for the

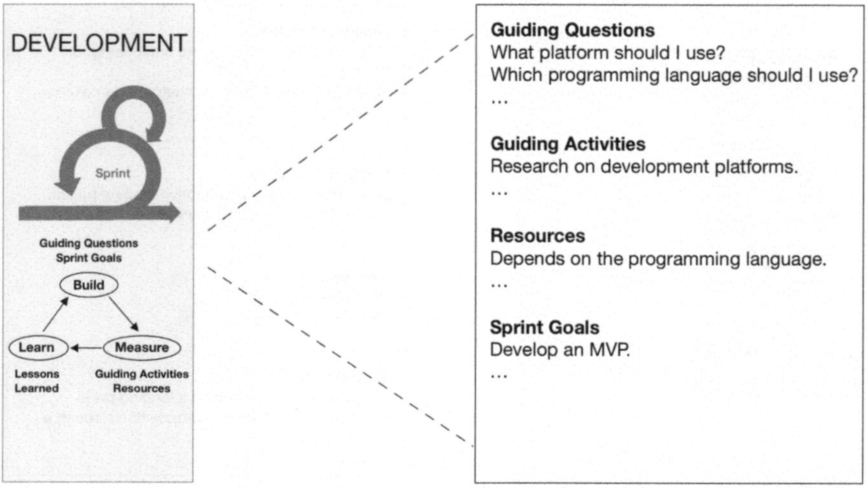

Fig. 8. Development.

solution. In other words, students (and entrepreneurs) should fall in love with the problem, not the solution.

As a final remark, it is important to mention that all these phases (Engage, Content Creation, Interview, Value Proposition Testing, Prototyping, and Development) are flexible in terms of timeframe; they should all be adapted according to the course context. For instance, if there is no pre-requisite for the course (for instance, programming), maybe instructors should take away the development sprints. In other words, the Challenge Based Startup Learning framework can be seen as building blocks.

Another important point is related to the reflections. As students move forward (or even backwards) into the framework, it is vital that they stop for a moment to think through their learning process. This is a key component of the CBL framework since it helps both students and instructors into adjusting the process on the fly. Additionally, reflections deepen the relationship among students as well as between students and instructors [17].

6 Conclusions

In this paper we presented an evaluation of the Challenge Based Startup Learning framework performed through an expert panel. The panel was formed by 14 people from different backgrounds and locations, and they all have previously worked with the Challenge Based Learning methodology. The process was very interesting since it resulted in great contribution for the future development of the Challenge Based Startup Learning framework.

Once the information gathered from the experts were fully analyzed, it was possible to identify improvement points on the framework. For instance, experts suggested that the framework should present a few pre-defined guiding questions, guiding resources, activities and goals for each sprint (or phase). By doing so, students can have a starting point on what is expected to be done, and it can also inspire them into coming up with additional questions they might have. Even though several teaching frameworks follow the same principles (specifying key questions, activities and goals), this was not the case for the Challenge Based Learning methodology.

It is worth mentioning that the framework should be adapted to the context of the educational setting; instructors must be sensitive to the course objectives and goals and use the framework accordingly. For instance, if the instructor would like to use the framework in a software development course, it is important to give students the opportunity to code their solution. On the other hand, if the course has no pre-requisite, it might be a good idea to stop at the prototyping phase (since students may not be coders).

Additionally, when it comes to startup development it is important to embrace the culture of failure and the "love for the problem" mindset. We believe that this framework can help students into understanding that a software startup journey differs from other software development contexts. There are several unknown variables that needed to be addressed along the way in order to increase the chances of success.

Acknowledgments. This work is partially funded by FAPERGS (17/2551-0001/205-4).

References

1. Beecham, S., Hall, T., Britton, C., Cottee, M., Rainer, A.: Using an expert panel to validate a requirements process improvement model. J. Syst. Softw. **76**(3), 251–275 (2005)
2. Blank, S.: The Four Steps to the Epiphany: Successful Strategies for Products That Win. K&S Ranch Incorporated, Pescadero (2013)
3. Blank, S., Dorf, B.: The Startup Owner's Manual: The Step-by-step Guide for Building a Great Company. K&S Ranch Incorporated, Pescadero (2012)
4. Case, S., Coleman, M., Deshpande, G.: The innovative and entrepreneurial university: Higher education, innovation and entrepreneurship in focus. US Department of Commerce, Economic Development Administration, Washington, DC (2013)
5. Chanin, R., et al.: Software startup education around the world: a preliminary analysis. In: Proceedings of the International Workshop on Software-intensive Business: Start-ups, Ecosystems and Platforms (SiBW 2018), Espoo, Finland, 3 December 2018, pp. 219–229 (2018)
6. Chanin, R., Sales, A., Pompermaier, L., Prikladnicki, R.: Challenge based startup learning: a framework to teach software startup. In: Proceedings of the 23rd Annual ACM Conference on Innovation and Technology in Computer Science Education, ITiCSE 2018, pp. 266–271. ACM, New York (2018)
7. Chanin, R., Sales, A., Pompermaier, L.B., Prikladnicki, R.: A systematic mapping study on software startups education. In: EASE, pp. 163–168 (2018)

8. Coleman, G.: An empirical study of software process in practice. In: Proceedings of the 38th Annual Hawaii International Conference on System Sciences (HICSS), pp. 315c 1–6. IEEE Computer Society, Big Island, January 2005
9. Elliott, J., Heesterbeek, S., Lukensmeyer, C.J., Slocum, N.: Participatory methods toolkit: A practitioner's manual. King Baudouin Foundation and the Flemish Institute for Science and Technology Assessment (viWTA) (2005)
10. Giardino, C., Paternoster, N., Unterkalmsteiner, M., Gorschek, T., Abrahamsson, P.: Software development in startup companies: the greenfield startup model. IEEE Trans. Softw. Eng. **42**(6), 585–604 (2016)
11. Giardino, C., Unterkalmsteiner, M., Paternoster, N., Gorschek, T., Abrahamsson, P.: What do we know about software development in startups? IEEE Softw. **31**(5), 28–32 (2014)
12. Giardino, C., Wang, X., Abrahamsson, P.: Why early-stage software startups fail: a behavioral framework. In: Lassenius, C., Smolander, K. (eds.) ICSOB 2014. LNBIP, vol. 182, pp. 27–41. Springer, Cham (2014). https://doi.org/10.1007/978-3-319-08738-2_3
13. Kajko-Mattsson, M., Nikitina, N.: From knowing nothing to knowing a little: experiences gained from process improvement in a start-up company. In: International Conference on Computer Science and Software Engineering, CSSE 2008, pp. 617–621, Wuhan, China, December 2008
14. Maurya, A.: Running Lean: Iterate from Plan A to a Plan That Works. O'Reilly Media Inc., Sebastopol (2012)
15. Melegati, J., Chanin, R., Wang, X., Sales, A., Prikladnicki, R.: Perceived benefits and challenges of learning startup methodologies for software engineering students. In: Proceedings of the 50th ACM Technical Symposium on Computer Science Education, SIGCSE 2019, Minneapolis, MN, USA, February 27–March 02 2019, pp. 204–210 (2019)
16. Nguyen-Duc, A., Seppänen, P., Abrahamsson, P.: Hunter-gatherer cycle: a conceptual model of the evolution of software startups. In: Proceedings of the 2015 International Conference on Software and System Process, Tallinn, Estonia, ICSSP 2015, pp. 199–203, August 2015
17. Nichols, M., Cator, K., Torres, M.: Challenge Based Learning Guide, Redwood City, CA, USA (2016)
18. Paternoster, N., Giardino, C., Unterkalmsteiner, M., Gorschek, T., Abrahamsson, P.: Software development in startup companies: a systematic mapping study. Inf. Softw. Technol. **56**(10), 1200–1218 (2014)
19. Porter, J., Morgan, J., Lester, R., Steele, A., Vanegas, J., Hill, R.: A course in innovative product design: a collaboration between architecture, business, and engineering. In: Proceedings of 2015 IEEE Frontiers in Education Conference (FIE), pp. 1–5. IEEE Computer Society, El Paso, October 2015
20. Ries, E.: The Lean Startup: How Today's Entrepreneurs Use Continuous Innovation to Create Radically Successful Businesses. Crown Business (2011)
21. Shepperd, M., Cartwright, M.: Predicting with sparse data. IEEE Trans. Softw. Eng. **27**(11), 987–998 (2001)

A Board Game to Teach Team Composition in Software Startups

Jorge Melegati[1](✉), Eduardo Guerra[2], Igor Knop[3], and Xiaofeng Wang[1]

[1] Free University of Bozen-Bolzano, Piazza Domenicani 3, 39100 Bolzano, Italy
{jmelegatigoncalves,xiaofeng.wang}@unibz.it

[2] National Institute for Space Research (INPE), Sao Jose dos Campos, Brazil
eduardo.guerra@inpe.br

[3] Universidade Federal de Juiz de Fora (UFJF), Juiz de Fora, Brazil
igorknop@ice.ufjf.br

Abstract. Startup education presence in Computer Science and Software Engineering curriculum has risen in the recent years. Currently, most reported courses focus on teaching innovation and business techniques and try to emulate real-world projects to convey the content. They have not focused on team composition which is a critical element for the success of startups since missing human capital increases the uncertainty involved in the process. In this paper, based on a literature review, we present a set of concepts about software startups team composition to be explored in a course. We also present a board game as a supplementary tool to convey these concepts. To evaluate the tool, we placed students in an artificial learning environment where they watched a video lesson about the topics and played the game. Then, participants answered a questionnaire about motivation, user experience, and perception of learning. The results indicate a first evidence of the value of the tool inducing a positive effect on learning as perceived by students.

Keywords: Startup education · Software engineering education · Software startups · Educational game

1 Introduction

In recent years, the interest in software startup education to technical students has risen [6]. Most entrepreneurship courses to technical students focus on teaching innovative and business thinking, and how a technical team can cope with this context by teaching methods like customer development process and agile [6].

These concepts, however, are not the only knowledge which is useful to create a successful startup. Another essential topic is team formation. One of the characteristics of startups is uncertain conditions [19], and missing human capital is a key reason for uncertainty [27]. Additionally, the ACM/IEEE curriculum guidelines [13] indicates that computer science education should be more holistic than

S. Hyrynsalmi et al. (Eds.): ICSOB 2019, LNBIP 370, pp. 321–335, 2019.
https://doi.org/10.1007/978-3-030-33742-1_25

"simply conveying technical facts" and mentions, as core elements, topics like team participation, team processes, roles and responsibilities. Nevertheless, to the best of our knowledge, no study has focused specifically on teaching software startups team composition to technical students.

Regarding teaching techniques in software startups education, flipped classrooms are ideal and front lectures are used only for presenting basic concepts [6]. Generally, courses on the topic consist of simulations where students create a team to emulate a startup with the objective of launching a product. Team formation is often challenging in these courses due to the fact that they may be targeted at a specific program where students will have the same type of expertise, or even if in multi-disciplinary contexts, students may prefer to create groups with friends from the same program instead of people from other programs or disciplines. Therefore, knowledge on how to compose a promising startup team is crucial for the learning experience of students.

An interesting approach to deliver active learning experience to students is the use of educational games. Some results show that these games can lead to effective learning, specially reinforcing previously presented content [20,33]. To the best of our knowledge, up to now, educational games have not been reported so far in software startup education.

In this paper, we aim at tackling both above mentioned under-explored topics. To this end, we firstly discuss topics related to team composition on software startups that a software startup course should cover, drawing upon a set of reviewed literature. Then we present an educational game - a board game - we designed as a teaching supporting tool to reinforce the concepts about software startup team composition. We evaluated the game regarding motivation, user experience, and perception of learning using MEEGA+ [21], a model to analyze educational games for computer science education.

The remaining of this paper is organized as follows: Sect. 2 displays previous work on entrepreneurship education and the use of games in software engineering and computer science education, Sect. 3 presents the learning goals about software startups team composition, Sect. 4 describes the developed board game and Sect. 5, its evaluation. Finally, Sect. 6 concludes the paper.

2 Background and Related Work

2.1 Software Startup Education

Software startups are companies that develop innovative, software-intensive products or services [31]. The impact that these companies have on our society and economy is enormous. For instance, companies like Google and Facebook changed the way people behave in modern society and employ a huge number of people. Such importance made even more important entrepreneurship education that already started in the last few decades [9].

Chanin et al. [6] performed a systematic mapping study to identify what were the topics taught and which teaching techniques were used in software startup education. The authors identified 31 papers, mainly experience reports on courses teaching startup topics, and few opinion or philosophical papers about the topics that should be covered in this discipline. The authors concluded that there were different topics discussed ranging from encouraging creativity to methods and attention to detail. The main methods taught were business model canvas, customer development process, design thinking, and agile, and, regarding techniques, most of the papers proposed project-based courses with student evaluation based on reports instead of exams. One challenge for this type of courses is to provide a realistic setting for students.

A common practice used by the courses is to mix students from technical programs such as computer science or software engineering with those from business disciplines in teams with the goal to develop a new product. Ford et al. [12] described a course where students from business and engineering programs had to develop new small products. Similarly, Buffardi et al. [4] described how parallel courses on software engineering and entrepreneurship had students collaborate to create products for real customers. Vitolo et al. [32] told their experience on developing a similar course and the difficulties found such as time constraints.

Fagerholm et al. [11] followed a design-based research approach and came up with patterns and anti-patterns on software startup education. These guidelines provide advice on how to run such courses regarding the learning environment, course design and its role in the curriculum, learning materials, teacher guidance, and educational interventions. None of the papers, though, discussed if they had covered for students the importance of mixed teams to startup success.

2.2 Games in Software Engineering Education

The use of games in education is connected to the concept of serious games. The first use of this oxymoron appeared in a book written by Clark Abt in 1970 [10]. Djaouti et al. [10] defined a *game* as "any contest (play) among adversaries (players) operating under constraints (rules) for an objective (winning, victory, or pay-off)." Then, *serious games* would have "an explicit and carefully thought-out educational purpose and are not intended to be played primarily for amusement", which however does not mean that they are not entertaining. Games can be digital or non-digital but, currently in research, the term *serious games* is generally used for digital games.

On a systematic literature review on games use in software engineering education, Kosa et al. [16] identified 53 studies and classified them in five categories: games that learners/students play; games that learners/students develop as projects; curriculum proposals; developing/coming up with new approaches, tools, frameworks or suggestions; and others. Regarding game types, only seven studies used non-digital games and one used both digital and non-digital games.

Problems and Programmers [1,2] is an educational card game to teach software engineering processes. Chang et al. [5] developed a card game with Rapid Application Development as the learning object. Taran [30] described a board game created at Carnegie Mellon University to teach risk management concepts. Von Wangenheim et al. [34] presented SCRUMIA, a paper and pencil game to teach SCRUM use in undergraduate programs. The authors evaluated the motivation, user and the game contribution to learning based on students perception. The results indicate that the game contributed positively to SCRUM learning with a pleasant activity. As far as the authors are aware of, no game has been developed for the purpose of software startup education on team related topics.

3 Learning Goals on Software Startup Team Composition

In the literature, the founding team importance has been studied for a long time. For instance, Kisfalvi [14] claimed that "an entrepreneurial firm will consistently pursue the strategic directions that most reflect the entrepreneur's set of life issues." Kollmann [15] described building blocks to set up a company in the net economy: one of them is the founders. According to the author, founders must have know-how on computer science, information management and business administration. It is also acknowledged that generally an e-venture is established by a team of founders since it is difficult for someone to have all the required capacities.

Correspondingly, in a software startup course or training, it is essential to address team composition. Based on a review of entrepreneurship and software startup literature, we identified three main topics related to team composition that are important to teach to future software startup founders: importance of a heterogeneous team, importance of growing the team according to the startup expansion, and importance of specialized roles.

Importance of a Heterogeneous Team. Several authors focused on the importance of team heterogeneity to ventures success. Muñoz-Bullon et al. [18] studied 1214 American nascent entrepreneurs in a longitudinal study on a six-year time frame. They concluded that the heterogeneity in founding team improved the likelihood of company establishment success. Besides that, industry experience also improved new company results. Ratzinger et al. [23] evaluated the impact of startup founding teams' education on the probability of securing equity investments and subsequent exits for investors using a sample of almost 5000 startups. The authors concluded that "increased formal business and technical education within founding teams increases the probability of reaching investment milestones for digital startups". Colombo and Grilli [7] concluded from a study with 506 Italian young firms that "there are synergistic gains from the combination of the complementary capabilities of founders economic-managerial and scientific-technical education and technical and commercial industry-specific work experiences".

Nevertheless, Ruef et al. [24] investigated the organizational founding teams formation and concluded that "homophily and network constraints based on strong ties have the most pronounced effect on group composition."

For software startups, the initial team composition has also been studied. Seppänen et al. [28] described what were the characteristics of a software startup team and how these characteristics were reflected in the composition. They broke down the competencies needed when building a software startup into two categories: innovation-related and implementation-related. The first set of competencies are more pertinent to the business value of the idea meanwhile the latter are to building the product. They found that, in the studied startups, the founder was the "sole owner of the innovation", hiring development teams to bring the idea to life, but some experts were needed in other areas such as process development or specific technological areas besides software development. The authors also acknowledged that in the studied companies, founders were "multi-talented individuals". The sample analyzed consisted of companies aged from one to six years.

Importance of Growing the Team. Crowne [8] investigated reasons for startup failure related to product development issues. He divided the maturity of a startup into three stages: startup, stabilization and growth, and for each of them, listed possible reasons for failure. In the growth stage, one of the factors is "skills shortage delays development". According to him, a lack of skilled individuals becomes a bottleneck in all activities. Therefore, it is important to be able to grow a team when needed by recruiting skilled individuals.

Importance of Specialized Roles. Crowne [8] also mentioned that, in the startup phase, a reason to failure was developers' inexperience. He acknowledged that the lack of resources made companies to rely on "clever, but inexperienced people" that may not be familiar with all issues on software engineering. According to the author, another reason is "the product has no owner" because nobody has the authority to decide the product features or the decision is made by a dysfunctional committee. Product managers could tackle these issues since their roles are authority, influence on collaboration and on the product, and access to resources [17]. Besides that, in a multiple-case study on 11 European software startups, Seppänen et al. [26] identified two domains where special knowledge was required: technical issues and abilities "to implement systematic routines and process."

In summary, various competencies are needed to transform an idea into a successful product/company. To bring together these competencies, a multidisciplinary team of founders must be formed but these teams are generally put together more based on personal affinities than on project needs. It is possible that an exceptional person can be the owner of an idea and be able to perform all activities demanded. But this is specially difficult for a software engineer who is generally not used to understanding the value creation objectives of a company [3]. Anyhow, the existence of a special type of persons capable of being solo entrepreneurs was already criticized by Sarasvathy and Venkataraman [25]. The authors drew a parallel between science and entrepreneurship. Once the first was considered something restricted to special people until the scientific method made it possible for any trained person to pursue science. They argued that the same should happen to entrepreneurship which nowadays was considered something to few: create an entrepreneurship method that could be taught.

4 The Board Game

Based on the learning goals described above, we developed a board game where each player controls a software startup, and should compose its team through the match. In order to make the game more fun and rich, two other concepts common in the software startup context were considered in the game creation: awareness of unexpected events and increased difficulty when a company grows. In the following section, we describe these two concepts. Then, Sect. 4.2 describes the game dynamics and Sect. 4.3 presents the process used to design the game.

4.1 Additional Concepts

Awareness of Unexpected Events. Shepherd et al. [29] argued that "the mortality risk of a new venture could increase, rather than decrease, as it ages." The authors explained that this could occur because of reversals or shocks, that is, "a low-probability, high-consequence event with an adverse economic impact." As examples, they mentioned: "the loss of a particular manager or other employee," "the actions of a manager may be so inept, bizarre, or unethical that the market loses confidence in the firm's managerial competence or even in its general abilities." Finally, the authors stated that if incidences and the effects of these disruptions are managed, managers could mitigate their company mortality risk.

Increased Difficulty When a Company Grows. Wang et al. [35] investigated the challenges software startups face in different life-cycle stages. They concluded that building the product is the biggest challenge faced by these companies at all stages and "market related challenges such as customer acquisition and scaling become increasingly perceivable" as learning and product development progress.

4.2 Game Dynamics

Startups Assemble! is a competitive board game for two to four players where each player represents a founder who needs to hire team members for her startup. The goal is after 12 months, each represented by a round, to have the startup with the best combination of team composition and profitability. A match usually lasts from 40 min to 1 h.

Professionals are from three categories: developers, designers, and business experts (Fig. 1b). Each player's startup is represented by a pawn in a board with coordinated axis system, where the horizontal axis represents the startup monthly income and the vertical axis the equilibrium observed in the team, that is, based on the number of developer-designer-business person trios as presented in Fig. 1a. Each startup team is represented by a set of cards in front of the respective player that represents its professionals.

Each player also starts with a double-sided card that represents herself as a founder and her abilities. There are also specialist cards (e.g. Fig. 1c) that represent professionals with specific expertise like cloud developer, product management, and head hunter. Each specialist is also categorized by the same professional card colors, as a developer, designer or business expert. The winner is the player who makes her company have the biggest score calculated based on the income at the end of the game and the team expertise equilibrium represented by the number of the expertise least represented in that team.

On each month, each player in her turn plays the number of dice equals to the number of developers the team has. The dice results are converted to drawbacks or success according to the developer cards. The player can re-roll or manipulate the dice based on the designers that the team has. Finally, business experts can be used to convert success into profit, increasing the monthly income by moving the pawn on the board. This flow mimics a startup since development work will not necessarily be translated to income. Frequently, users do not appreciate the result and do not buy the product. In this sense, a designer can help understanding the user and making the product more user-friendly. Then, not necessarily a popular product generates revenue for a company, for that reason, a business expert can think of ways of generating revenue to the company.

After rolling the dice and activating their effects, the player has the option to use part of the startup income to hire a new professional by getting another card. To represent the cost of having this new employee, the pawn should come back one position in the monthly income track. To promote a balanced team, the board has another scale on the vertical axis representing the number of the professional class less represented in that player's team. The more balanced the team is, the easier it is to go up in the monthly income scale.

On the beginning of each round, an event card is shown that contains a rule that affects all players on that month. This represents events that could happen in a startup life like a new technology that reaches market or a tech company hiring in the area that removes professionals from their teams. The effects can bring benefits or drawbacks to the players.

Specialist cards are special kinds of developers, designers or business experts that have unique effects on the game. Their availability is limited since their deck is shuffled and only three different specialists are available for hiring at each moment. Balancing between basic professionals and specialists is important for a good strategy on the game.

4.3 Game Design Process

The game was developed through a year following an iterative design process. This process was based on the following steps: (a) define a set of rules and components; (b) create a playable prototype; (c) perform playtests of the game; (d) get feedback from the playtests and reason about the rules. So, before the game's last version used to perform the evaluation presented in Sect. 5, several other playtests were performed to evaluate the rules.

The initial version had only basic professionals and the track had only the monthly income direction. The following iterations added respectively specialists and monthly events. The last addition was the two-dimension track considering the team composition. Additionally, in each iteration, some cards and rules changed focusing on balancing the fun with a close representation of the domain.

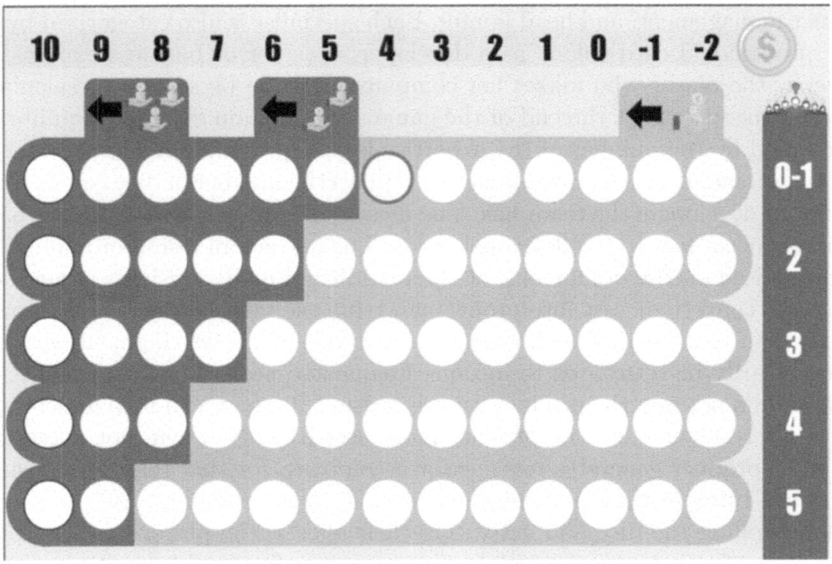

(a) The board of the game.

(b) Cards representing professionals, respectively, a business expert, a designer and a developer.

(c) An example of designer specialist.

(d) An example of a side of a card representing a founder: the founder can hire someone and have another die to roll.

(e) An example of card representing an event: on that month, on their turn, each player can get hire another professional without cost.

Fig. 1. Some components of the Startups Assemble! game: the board with axis representing income and team equilibrium, professionals cards from the three categories and an example of a specialist card.

5 Evaluation

5.1 Study Design

Assessing educational games is a complex task [20]. A common weakness in the evaluations of educational games for computer science education is the lack of scientific rigor [20]. In a recent systematic literature review (SLR) on this topic, Petri et al. [20] identified that 11 studies employed systematically two defined evaluation models (MEEGA and EGameFlow) and the first one seems to be the most used in practice. An improved version of MEEGA, MEEGA+, was proposed by Petri et al. [21] based on this SLR. MEEGA+ is a model to analyze educational games for computer science education in terms of motivation, user experience, and learning based on the students' perceptions [21]. It consists of a questionnaire to be answered by students after playing the game in the context of a discipline. The response format of the questionnaire is a 5-point Likert scale ranging from "strongly disagree" to "strong agree". The instrument concludes with three open questions asking to list three strong aspects of the game, three suggestions to improve the game, and if the respondent had any further comment. During data analysis process, these values were converted to numerical in a range from -2 to 2. The model has been evaluated in 40 case studies assessing 18 different games with a total of 718 students surveyed [21,22].

We performed the evaluation based on MEEGA+ with some adaptations. Since we are also proposing topics to be added to software startup courses, and there was no previous lesson on these topics, we prepared, presented, and recorded a lesson on the topics discussed. The video was 20 min long and allowed us to evaluate the game in an educational context without harming internal validity since all students were subjected to the same treatment. Some questions in the original questionnaire were changed to reflect this specific educational setting. Besides that, the last questions are based on the learning goals and were adapted properly. In the open questions, we removed the request of three elements leaving to the respondent to answer if and how he or she wanted.

5.2 Execution

We performed game sessions in three Brazilian cities (São José dos Campos, Juiz de Fora e Porto Alegre). Our sample consisted of vocational, undergraduate and graduate students. They were invited to watch the video lesson, to play the game and, later, to answer anonymously the questionnaire online. Figure 2 shows some students playing the game. The total number of responses is 24 where 2 were vocational students, 13 were undergraduate, and 9 were graduate students.

MEEGA+ proposes the use of descriptive statistics like frequency distribution and central tendency (median) for each quality factor as data analysis procedure [21]. Through a descriptive analysis, it is possible to identify the most positive and negative aspects of the game [34]. To perform data analysis, we used a spreadsheet that MEEGA+ authors made available.

Fig. 2. Students playing the board game.

5.3 Results and Analysis

The model divides the questions into player experience and usability. Figure 3 shows the results for the former and Fig. 4 for the latter.

For the player experience results, the first three sections (confidence, challenge, and satisfaction) are concerned with the player's perception on her own personal experience with the game. The results were good (one item with median "totally agree" and others with "agree"). The next two sections deal with social interaction and fun, and the results were extremely good with all medians being the most positive answer. The good results from the following section, focused attention, indicated that the game caught the students' attention. The results from the section relevance indicate that it was clear to the students that the game was related to the lesson content, but they may still prefer another teaching method in a first contact with a concept like a front class and perceives the game as a reinforcement tool. An explanation could be that concepts are not clear to someone not exposed previously to them before playing the game.

Regarding perceived learning, the results were extremely positive. For each question related to each of the five learning goals, more than half of the respondents answered "totally agree." The other question in this component, if the game contributed to the student learning in the lesson, the median answer was "agree," also a good result. These results provide an initial evidence that the game helped the students to reinforce the knowledge they obtained from the video lesson. The not-so-good result from the first question stresses the fact that the game acts as a support to, rather than a substitute of, traditional learning.

The results for usability indicate that the respondents found the game of good quality, specially regarding design qualities. The answers' median was also "agree" for the elements related to the ease to learn and to play the game.

In the answers for open questions, most comments concerned on game aspects like giving suggestions to change the dynamics or appraising the experience.

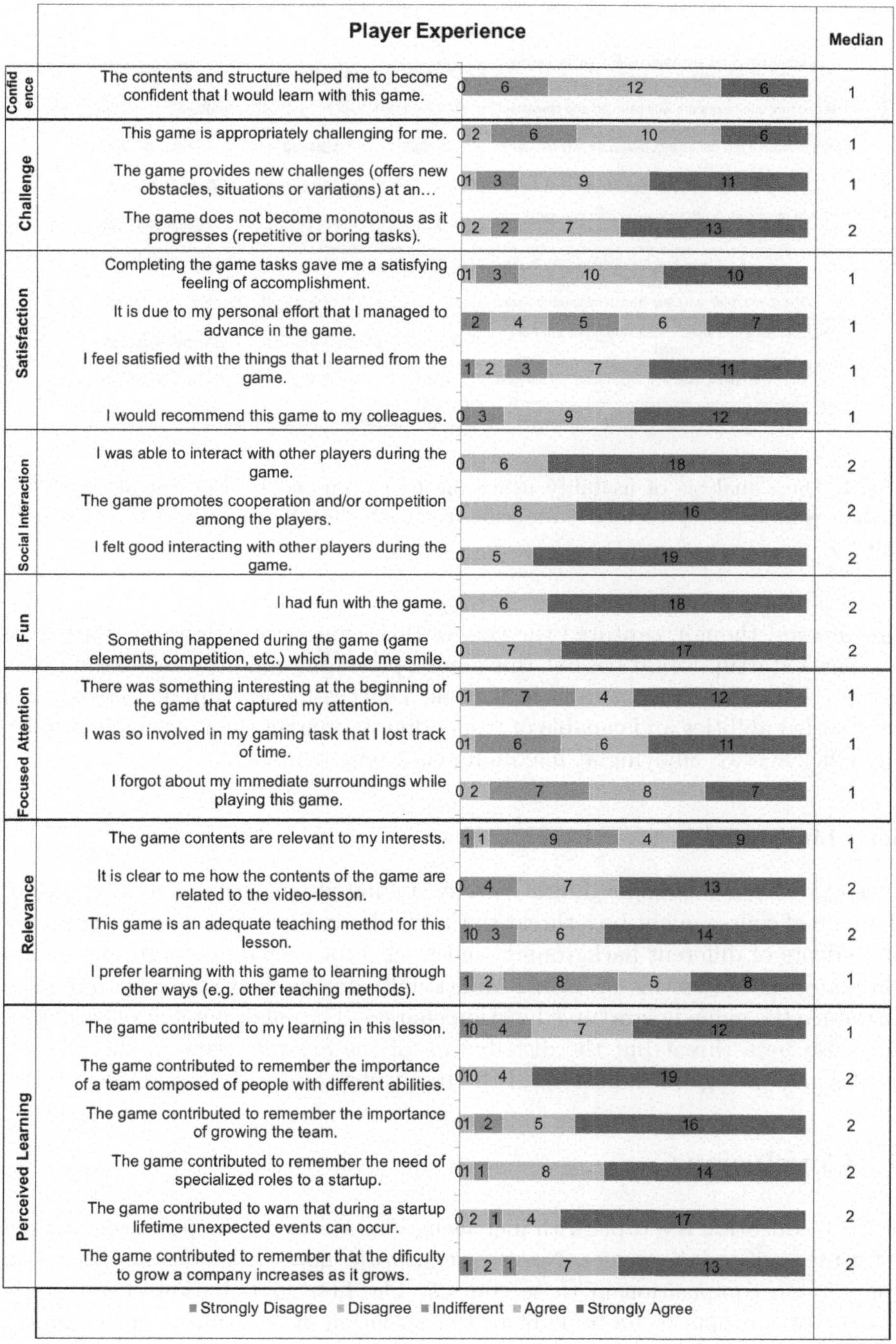

Fig. 3. Data analysis of player experience using the tool proposed by Petri et al. [21]. The median column is represented on a scale from −2 ("totally disagree") to 2 ("totally agree").

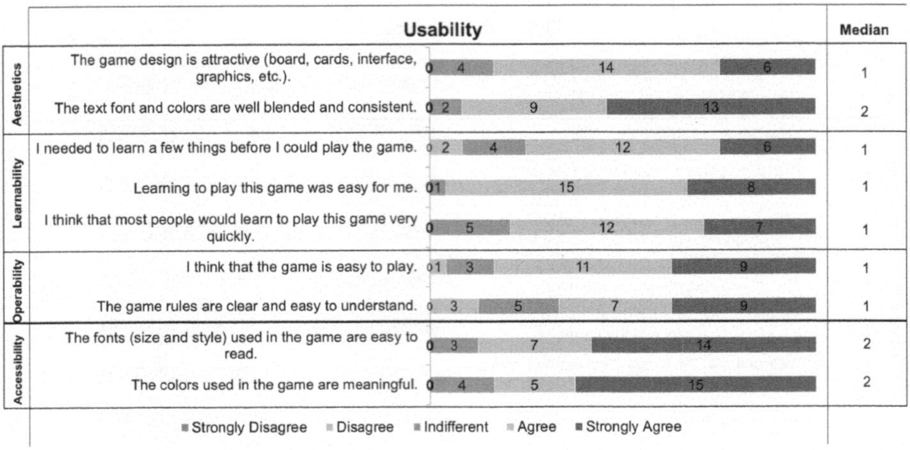

Fig. 4. Data analysis of usability using the tool proposed by Petri et al. [21]. The median column is represented on a scale from −2 ("totally disagree") to 2 ("totally agree").

One answer, though, captured the goal of this experience: "I only had a notion of what a startup would be, but this game opened my mind to understand that it is not enough to have a great idea to be a successful startup, it needs a team with varied abilities and capable of responding to market fluctuations in a quick and efficient way, enjoying at maximum each opportunity."

5.4 Limitations

This evaluation had some limitations. A simulated educational context rather than a real course might be a threat to the results validity. But, the participation of students of different backgrounds and levels (vocational, undergraduate, and graduate) mitigates this problem. Additionally, in the next steps, we intend to introduce the game in startup education courses. The small number of responses may also be a threat but the distribution of the answers skew to the positive results give us a good indication of the tool value.

6 Conclusions

Startup education is a topic with increasing importance in computer science and software engineering courses. Nevertheless, up to now, there was no discussion about team composition in these courses. The first contribution of our study is a list of concepts to be brought to the attention of students in such courses. The second contribution is a board game to reinforce the learning of these concepts. With the evaluation presented in this paper, we also extend the application of the MEEGA+ evaluation model to an environment beyond a classroom.

Based on our study, the model can be used in training and corporate environments to test, for instance, games used by a company to train their employees.

The version used in the evaluation is close to the final one. We intend to improve the graphic quality and evaluate the best way to publish it: either making it available online using a print-and-play format or producing it through a commercial publisher. Future work will focus on evaluating and, if needed, adapting the game to non-educational setups like accelerators or other initiatives to improve entrepreneurship that would like to train people to create new software startups. Another interesting follow-up would be to create a digital version of the game. Besides that, future work could focus on other games to be used in software startup education to reinforce topics on which hands-on experience is hard to achieve, such as funding or customer acquisition.

Acknowledgments. The authors would like to thank all the students that participated in the study and to Eduardo Pompermayer for running some game sessions.

References

1. Baker, A., Navarro, E., van der Hoek, A.: Problems and Programmers: an educational software engineering card game, pp. 614–619 (2004). https://doi.org/10.1109/icse.2003.1201245
2. Baker, A., Navarro, E.O., Van Der Hoek, A.: An experimental card game for teaching software engineering processes. J. Syst. Softw. **75**(1–2), 3–16 (2005). https://doi.org/10.1016/j.jss.2004.02.033
3. Boehm, B.W., Sullivan, K.J.: Software economics. In: Proceedings of the Conference on The Future of Software Engineering - ICSE 2000, pp. 319–343. ACM Press, New York (2000). https://doi.org/10.1145/336512.336584
4. Buffardi, K., Robb, C., Rahn, D.: Tech Startups: Realistic Software Engineering Projects with Interdisciplinary Collaboration. Journal of Computing Sciences in Colleges **32**(4), 93–98 (2017)
5. Chang, W.-C., Chen, Y.-L., Lee, T.-P.: Computer assisted learning with card game in system design concept. In: Leung, E.W.C., Wang, F.L., Miao, L., Zhao, J., He, J. (eds.) WBL 2008. LNCS, vol. 5328, pp. 93–101. Springer, Heidelberg (2008). https://doi.org/10.1007/978-3-540-89962-4_10
6. Chanin, R., Sales, A., Pompermaier, L., Prikladnicki, R.: A systematic mapping study on software startups education. In: 2018 Evaluation and Assessment in Software Engineering, EASE 2018, pp. 163–168 (2018). https://doi.org/10.1145/3210459.3210478
7. Colombo, M.G., Grilli, L.: Founders' human capital and the growth of new technology-based firms: a competence-based view. Res. Policy **34**(6), 795–816 (2005). https://doi.org/10.1016/j.respol.2005.03.010
8. Crowne, M.: Why software product startups fail and what to do about it. Evolution of software product development in startup companies. In: IEEE International Engineering Management Conference, vol. 1, pp. 338–343 (2002). https://doi.org/10.1109/IEMC.2002.1038454
9. Daimi, K., Rayess, N.: The role of software entrepreneurship in computer science curriculum. In: Proceedings of the 2008 International Conference on Frontiers in Education: Computer Science and Computer Engineering, FECS 2008, August 2008, pp. 332–338 (2008)

10. Djaouti, D., Alvarez, J., Jessel, J.P., Rampnoux, O.: Origins of serious games. In: Ma, M., Oikonomou, A., Jain, L. (eds.) Serious Games and Edutainment Applications, pp. 25–43. Springer, London (2011). https://doi.org/10.1007/978-1-4471-2161-9_3
11. Fagerholm, F., Hellas, A., Luukkainen, M., Kyllönen, K., Yaman, S., Mäenpää, H.: Designing and implementing an environment for software start-up education: patterns and anti-patterns. J. Syst. Softw. **146**, 1–13 (2018). https://doi.org/10.1016/j.jss.2018.08.060
12. Ford, R.M., Goodrich, J.G., Weissbach, R.S.: A multidisciplinary business and engineering course in product development and entrepreneurship. In: Proceedings of Frontiers in Education Conference, FIE 1, T2E/5-T2E10, vol. 1 (2004). https://doi.org/10.1109/FIE.2004.1408498
13. Joint Task Force on Computing Curricula, Association for Computing Machinery (ACM) and IEEE Computer Society: Computer Science Curricula: Curriculum Guidelines for Undergraduate Degree Programs in Computer Science, 999133. ACM, New York (2013)
14. Kisfalvi, V.: The entrepreneur's character, life issues, and strategy making. J. Bus. Ventur. **17**(5), 489–518 (2002). https://doi.org/10.1016/S0883-9026(01)00075-1
15. Kollmann, T.: What is e-entrepreneurship? Fundamentals of company founding in the net economy. Int. J. Technol. Manag. **33**(4), 322 (2006). https://doi.org/10.1504/IJTM.2006.009247
16. Kosa, M., Yilmaz, M., O'Connor, R.V., Clarke, P.M.: Software engineering education and games: a systematic literature review. J. Univers. Comput. Sci. **22**(12), 1558–1574 (2016)
17. Maglyas, A., Nikula, U., Smolander, K.: What are the roles of software product managers? An empirical investigation. J. Syst. Softw. **86**(12), 3071–3090 (2013). https://doi.org/10.1016/j.jss.2013.07.045
18. Muñoz-Bullon, F., Sanchez-Bueno, M.J., Vos-Saz, A.: Startup team contributions and new firm creation: the role of founding team experience. Entrep. Reg. Dev. **27**(1–2), 80–105 (2015). https://doi.org/10.1080/08985626.2014.999719
19. Paternoster, N., Giardino, C., Unterkalmsteiner, M., Gorschek, T., Abrahamsson, P.: Software development in startup companies: A systematic mapping study. Inf. Softw. Technol. **56**(10), 1200–1218 (2014). https://doi.org/10.1016/j.infsof.2014.04.014
20. Petri, G., Gresse von Wangenheim, C.: How games for computing education are evaluated? A systematic literature review. Comput. Educ. **107**, 68–90 (2017). https://doi.org/10.1016/j.compedu.2017.01.004
21. Petri, G., Gresse von Wangenheim, C., Borgatto, A.F.: MEEGA+, systematic model to evaluate educational games. In: Lee, N. (ed.) Encyclopedia of Computer Graphics and Games, pp. 1–7. Springer, Cham (2018). https://doi.org/10.1007/978-3-319-08234-9_214-1
22. Petri, G., Von Wangenheim, C.G., Borgatto, A.F.: A large-scale evaluation of a model for the evaluation of games for teaching software engineering. In: Proceedings of 2017 IEEE/ACM 39th International Conference on Software Engineering: Software Engineering and Education Track, ICSE-SEET 2017, pp. 180–189 (2017). https://doi.org/10.1109/ICSE-SEET.2017.11
23. Ratzinger, D., Amess, K., Greenman, A., Mosey, S.: The impact of digital start-up founders' higher education on reaching equity investment milestones. J. Technol. Transf. **43**(3), 1–19 (2017). https://doi.org/10.1007/s10961-017-9627-3

24. Ruef, M., Aldrich, H.E., Carter, N.M.: The structure of founding teams: homophily, strong ties, and isolation among U.S. entrepreneurs. Am. Sociol. Rev. **68**(2), 195 (2003). https://doi.org/10.2307/1519766
25. Sarasvathy, S.D., Venkataraman, S.: Entrepreneurship as method: open questions for an entrepreneurial future. Entrep. Theory Pract. **35**(1), 113–135 (2011). https://doi.org/10.1111/j.1540-6520.2010.00425.x
26. Seppänen, P., Liukkunen, K., Oivo, M.: Little big team: acquiring human capital in software startups. In: Turhan, B., et al. (eds.) PROFES 2017. LNCS, vol. 10611, pp. 280–296. Springer, Cham (2017). https://doi.org/10.1007/978-3-319-69926-4_20
27. Seppänen, P., Liukkunen, K., Oivo, M.: Opportunity exploitation in software startups. A human capital view. In: Wnuk, K., Brinkkemper, S. (eds.) ICSOB 2018. LNBIP, vol. 336, pp. 142–156. Springer, Cham (2018). https://doi.org/10.1007/978-3-030-04840-2_10
28. Seppänen, P., Oivo, M., Liukkunen, K.: The initial team of a software startup. In: 2016 International Conference on Engineering, Technology and Innovation (ICE) and IEEE International Technology Management Conference, pp. 57–65 (2016)
29. Shepherd, D.A., Douglas, E.J., Shanley, M.: New venture survival. J. Bus. Ventur. **15**(5–6), 393–410 (2000). https://doi.org/10.1016/S0883-9026(98)00032-9
30. Taran, G.: Using games in software engineering education to teach risk management. In: Proceedings of Software Engineering Education Conference, pp. 211–218 (2007). https://doi.org/10.1109/CSEET.2007.54
31. Unterkalmsteiner, M., et al.: Software startups - a research agenda. e-Informatica Softw. Eng. J. **10**(1), 1–28 (2016). https://doi.org/10.5277/e-Inf160105
32. Vitolo, T.M., Hersch, K.E., Brinkman, B.J.: Making the connection: successful cross campus collaboration among students. In: 2016 IEEE Frontiers in Education Conference (FIE), October–November 2016, vol. 2016, pp. 1–7. IEEE (2016). https://doi.org/10.1109/FIE.2016.7757614
33. Von Wangenheim, C., Shull, F.: To game or not to game? IEEE Softw. **26**(2), 92–94 (2009). https://doi.org/10.1109/MS.2009.54
34. Von Wangenheim, C.G., Savi, R., Borgatto, A.F.: SCRUMIA - an educational game for teaching SCRUM in computing courses. J. Syst. Softw. **86**(10), 2675–2687 (2013). https://doi.org/10.1016/j.jss.2013.05.030
35. Wang, X., Edison, H., Bajwa, S.S., Giardino, C., Abrahamsson, P.: Key challenges in software startups across life cycle stages. In: Sharp, H., Hall, T. (eds.) XP 2016. LNBIP, vol. 251, pp. 169–182. Springer, Cham (2016). https://doi.org/10.1007/978-3-319-33515-5_14

Does Self-efficacy Matter? On the Correlation of Self-efficacy and Creativity in IT Education

Juhani Risku[1(✉)], Kai-Kristian Kemell[1], Joni Kultanen[1], Polina Feschenko[1], Jeroen Carelse[2], and Krista Korpikoski[3]

[1] University of Jyväskylä, Jyväskylä, Finland
juhani.risku@jyu.fi
[2] Carelse Ltd., Hattula, Finland
[3] University of Lapland, Rovaniemi, Finland

Abstract. Self-efficacy belief affects humans in life, action and work. Higher self-efficacy enables stronger contribution in fulfilling tasks, helping others in a team, and survive when facing obstacles and failures. Also creativity correlates to higher self-efficacy. At the same time, design is a powerful skill in note-making, improving the student's understanding of the undergoing topic in a class. Note-making, when consisting of recorded writings, self-drawn images and other supportive subjects like structural analyses, charts, ad-hoc notes, detailed features and verbal links to related themes, forms a fundamental skill and ability in learning and applying new motifs and patterns. We executed during a design class an experiment with 22 students from various faculties at two universities by designing and creating visual notebooks. The students acted as designers and visualizers communicating to themselves and their teams with own creations. These notebooks were analyzed and reflected against the questionnaire results to evaluate the impact of the course in the progress in design skills and creativity.

Keywords: Self-efficacy · Creativity · Note-making · Education · Design

1 Introduction

Creativity, and more generally innovation potential, are skills that are almost universally useful. Creativity is not a skill only required by those working professions that are conventionally considered creative ones, such as architecture. For example, creativity and innovativeness have been extensively studied in relation to entrepreneurship, e.g. [1, 2], where innovative ideas can shape and create markets. In the context of Information Technology (IT), Graziotin et al. (2014) underlined the importance of creativity in relation to problem solving among programmers [3], and Carberry et al. (2018) stress the importance of innovativeness among engineering students [4].

In this study, we utilized the ISE Measure instrument by Carberry 2018 to measure the innovation self-efficacy of students. This was done before and after a university course intended to teach design and to support innovation self-efficacy. Additionally, we evaluated, using a panel of judges, the creativity of the students based on materials

S. Hyrynsalmi et al. (Eds.): ICSOB 2019, LNBIP 370, pp. 336–344, 2019.
https://doi.org/10.1007/978-3-030-33742-1_26

they produced during the course. Taking on an explorative approach, we then sought correlations between creative output and innovation self-efficacy.

RQ: Do the notebook qualities correlate to the students' creativity according to self-efficacy questionnaire results and notebook evaluations by creativity?

The rest of this paper is structured as follows. Section 2 presents the theoretical background of this study was we discuss self-efficacy, creativity, and creativity in the context of self-efficacy. In Sect. 3 we declare our research methodology from course design to data collection and analysis. We then explain the analysis of our data in Sect. 4, and discuss the implications of the results in Sect. 5. In Sect. 6 we present discussion and implications. Finally, Sect. 7 concludes the paper.

2 Theoretical Background

In this section, we discuss the theoretical background of the study. The first subsection discusses self-efficacy in general, while the second one discusses creativity in general. The third subsection then connects these two as we discuss creativity and its relationship with (different types of) self-efficacy.

2.1 Self-efficacy

Self-efficacy refers to the perception one has of their own abilities in the context of some task (Carberry 2018). E.g., one's own perception of whether their C ++ programming skills are sufficient to carry out an assignment. Self-efficacy is considered important in successfully performing various tasks. If one believes in their own abilities, they are more likely to persevere in the face of challenges, more likely to pursue the related tasks in the first place and more intrinsically motivated [5].

Bandura (1994) argues that self-efficacy is influenced by four factors: (1) mastery experiences, (2) vicarious experiences, (3) social persuasion, and (4) physiological states. Mastery experiences are past task completions (or failures) and hold a notable impact on one's self-efficacy. In the absence of, and in addition to, mastery experiences, vicarious experiences can weigh on one's self-efficacy. Vicarious experiences are gained by observing others with similar ability perform tasks. Social persuasion, then, refers to support from prestigious individuals or individuals we respect, and can positively affect self-efficacy. Finally, our current physiological states, such as stress or simply being tired, can influence our self-efficacy.

Self-efficacy is related to specific tasks (Carberry et al. 2018). Though we have our perception of e.g. our own ability to program, it is typically considered in relation to a specific task at hand. We may consider ourselves to be good at programming, and yet know that developing an autonomous vehicle from scratch is well beyond our means.

2.2 Creativity and Measuring Creativity

Creativity has been studied in a plethora of contexts and across varying fields of science. It can be seen as the production of novel and useful ideas in any domain [6].

While such a general definition for creativity can largely be agreed-upon, creativity often has to be further defined when seeking to measure it for the purpose of a study.

Creativity is typically measured by examining outcomes of the process that leads to the creation of creative results [7, 8]. In practice, this often means having participants generate creative solutions for uncommon problems [9, 10]. The problems should be uncommon to ensure that the participants are not familiar with the problem at hand, which would enable them to use solutions they know are well suited for solving it in a creative manner. These solutions are then scored by judges, e.g. (some of) the authors of the study, in order to assess the creativity of the solutions and simultaneously the individuals (Graziotin et al. 2014).

2.3 Self-efficacy in the Context of Creativity

Antecedents studied in relation to creativity also include *self-efficacy*, and specifically, *creative self-efficacy*, which Tierney and Farmer (2002) [11] define as being "the belief one has the ability to produce creative outcomes". Past studies have established a link between creative self-efficacy and creativity (Mathisen and Bronnick 2009) [12]. I.e. one's confidence in one's own creativity makes one more creative. Furthermore, Mathisen and Bronnick (2009) argued based on their data that creative self-efficacy can be improved by training, while going on to note that further studies on whether doing so also improved creative performance were required. This is something we seek to further address in this study, although extant studies on the matter also exist.

2.4 Note-Making and Notebooks

Note making is considered as an active and versatile method of ideation, creation, getting intentions, and note-taking a passive action capturing information more by dictation. As Neville 2014 expresses, that note-taking is the start of note recording, which leads to more fundamental note-making [13]. At the design course, we asked the students to focus on note-making, which meant planning, organizing, thinking creatively, making relationships as Buzan and Buzan (2010) explain [14]. During the course, note-making was seen as a designer's tool for collecting own ideas and designs in a visual and structured order for later use.

3 Research Methodology

3.1 Course Design and Participant Characteristics

The data for this study were collect from a design course (TJTS1000 Design Practices in Contemporary World) at the University of Jyväskylä (Faculty of Information Technology). The iteration of the course in question was an intensive four-day summer course held in June 2019.

Out of the 22 participants included in this study, 12 were female and 10 were male. Eight of the participants were between 18–24 years of age, 11 were between 25–34 years, two between 35–44 years, and one between 55–64 years. 19 of the participants were from the University of Jyväskylä and three from the Shanghai University. The degree of the participants' current studies divided as 10 bachelor's, 11 master's and one doctoral student. The major subjects of the participants were Information Systems Science (8), Information Technology (3), Business (2), Cognitive Sciences (2), Accounting (1), Art Education (1), Art History (1), Communication Ethnology (1), Digital Marketing (1), International Business (1), and Marketing (1).

3.2 Data Collection Methodology

Data were collected from the twenty-two participants who completed the previously described course. Three sets of data were collected for the study during the activities of the experimental procedure: (1) Innovation Self-Efficacy questionnaire, (2) notebook/course assignment, and (3) Innovation Self-Efficacy questionnaire.

The data measuring the level of participants' innovation self-efficacy were collected using the Innovation Self-Efficacy (ISE) Measure instrument developed by Carberry et al. (2018). The ISE Measure was developed to measure the innovation self-efficacy of engineering students. It can be used to evaluate the positive or negative impacts of an intervention, such as training, on the participants' judgment of their own innovation ability (Carberry et al. 2018), as we do in this paper.

The ISE measure is utilized by having an individual give a numeric rating to their confidence in an activity. There are 29 activities related to innovation and creativity in the survey (e.g. "Identify opportunities for new products and/or processes"). The activities are categorized into eight categories: creativity, exploration, iteration, implementation, communication, resourcefulness, synthesis, and vision (Carberry et al. 2018).

Participants completed the Innovation Self-Efficacy (ISE) Measure instrument based questionnaire (Carberry et al. 2018) twice during the course, first during the first lecture of the course and the second time during the final lecture.

For the creativity evaluation, students created a notebook during the course with the assignment to make five (5) pages of notes during each lecture. The students could choose ways of their own liking, e.g. writing, drawing, sketching or cutting and pasting pictures from a source of their own choice.

4 Data Analysis

The data set included answers on 29 questions of 22 participants. The questions were aimed at finding the respondents view (each graded 0–100) on his/her own self-efficacy. Thus, in order to calculate the self-efficacy variable for each participant, the average of all 29 responses has been calculated and used for checking the assumption of its correlation with the evaluated creativity variable.

To evaluate creativity, we followed the model Graziotin et al. (2014) used to measure creativity in their study. We utilized a panel of judges to evaluate the creative outputs of the student participants in the form of a notebook, based on the judges' own definitions of creativity. Each judge individually rated the notebooks on a 7 point Likert scale.

The panel of judges consisted of three experienced designers, who were industrial and service designers, architect, artist, art and design teacher and carpenter.

In this study measurements of quality were utilized for the assessment of creativity, which is where we diverted from Graziotin et al. (2014), who in addition used measurements of quantity. This diversion was due to our study only having one object to evaluate the creativity on, whereas Graziotin et al. (2014) had several outputs from each participant to measure. Graziotin et al. (2014) measured quality by two scores: the average score based on all the outputs of a participant evaluated for creativity (ACR) and the best score among the outputs of a participant (BCR). In our study only one score for creativity was assigned (scale 1–7) due to the quantity of the outputs for each participant being only one larger item that was evaluated.

5 Results

Both self-efficacy and evaluated creativity variables data has been found to be quite normally distributed. Nevertheless, since there are outliers in the data, that can be clearly noticed from the relationship between the two variables (Fig. 1), Pearson's correlation cannot be applied and the Spearman's correlation coefficient was computed instead to check the dependence between them. To do that, IBM SPSS software was used. As shown in the Table 1, the correlation coefficient turned out to be −0.53, what indicates the negative correlation between the variables (Freedman et al. 1978) [15]. However, since the significance is equal to 0.800, it is possible to conclude that there is not enough evidence to say that the correlation exists, even though in the sample a small negative correlation has been observed (Weinberg and Knapp 2002) [16].

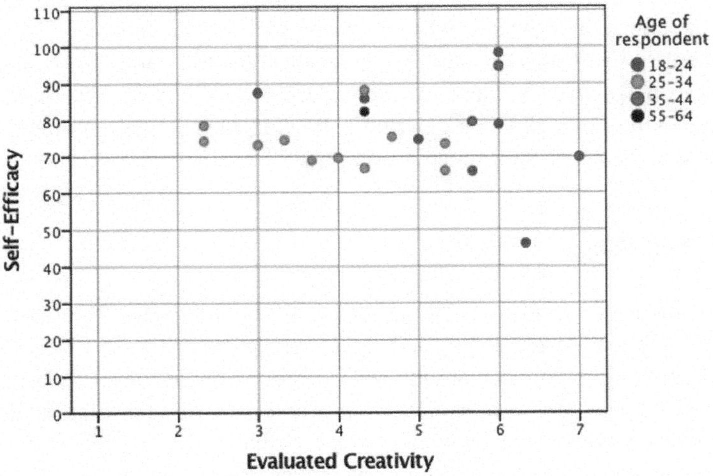

Fig. 1. The scatter plot of self-efficacy and evaluated creativity variables, with marked age of the respondents.

The was also no correlation of the age of the respondents with either self-efficacy or evaluated creativity noticed, what can be observed from Fig. 1.

Table 1 Spearman's correlation coefficient of self-efficacy and evaluated creativity variables.

			Evaluated creativity	Self-efficacy
Spearman's rho	Evaluated creativity	Correlation coefficient Sig. (2-tailed) N	1.000 . 22	−.036 .874 22
	Self-efficacy	Correlation coefficient Sig. (2-tailed) N	−0.36 .874 22	1.000 . 22

Another important finding was the existence of positive relationships between the categories of self-efficacy (as defined by Carberry 2018) within respondents' answers. In his article, Carberry defined 29 questions to measure self-efficacy that have been used in this study. The questions were based on 9 innovation-related clusters (8 were used for forming the questionnaire): creativity (questions 6, 12, 26), exploration (1, 8, 18, 29), iteration (9, 22, 27), implementation (7, 13, 21, 24), communication (16, 17, 23), resourcefulness (3, 14, 15, 19, 20, 28), synthesis (2, 10, 25) and vision (4, 5, 11) (Carberry 2018). The average score for each category of questions has been computed and used for correlation measurement. The Spearman's correlation coefficient was computed between the categories, as well as each category has been correlated with the evaluated creativity variable, to check if any specific dimension of self-efficacy correlates with the researched creativity. The results showed the strong linear relationship between all the categories (Fig. 2) and no any significant relationship between any category and evaluated creativity.

From the table above it is possible to conclude that, for example, exploration cluster has the most strong positive correlation with resourcefulness and communication clusters [with Spearman's correlation coefficient (rho) being 0.736 and 0.746 correspondingly]. Synthesis is also strongly correlated with resourcefulness, as well as with vision and implementation. The very high correlations can be also seen between resourcefulness and vision, resourcefulness and communication, iteration and implementation, communication and vision. Overall, all the categories are strongly correlated between each other. However, none of the categories have a significant correlation (either positive or negative) with evaluated creativity variable.

			Evaluated Creativity	Exploration	Synthesis	Resourcefulness	Vision	Creativity	Implementation	Iteration	Communication
Spearman's rho	Evaluated Creativity	Correlation Coefficient	1.000	.246	-.246	-.084	.015	-.06	-.226	-.046	.072
		Sig. (2-tailed)	.	.271	.270	.711	.948	.793	.311	.838	.752
		N	22	22	22	22	22	22	22	22	22
	Exploration	Correlation Coefficient	.246	1.000	.465*	.736**	.6**	.51*	.609**	.643**	.746**
		Sig. (2-tailed)	.271	.	.029	.000	.002	.016	.003	.001	.000
		N	22	22	22	22	22	22	22	22	22
	Synthesis	Correlation Coefficient	-.246	.465*	1.000	.797**	.7**	.50*	.732**	.596**	.608**
		Sig. (2-tailed)	.270	.029	.	.000	.000	.019	.000	.003	.003
		N	22	22	22	22	22	22	22	22	22
	Resourcefulness	Correlation Coefficient	-.084	.736**	.797**	1.000	.8**	.62**	.770**	.753**	.837**
		Sig. (2-tailed)	.711	.000	.000	.	.000	.002	.000	.000	.000
		N	22	22	22	22	22	22	22	22	22
	Vision	Correlation Coefficient	.015	.633**	.687**	.840**	1.0	.53*	.668**	.685**	.827**
		Sig. (2-tailed)	.948	.002	.000	.000	.	.011	.001	.000	.000
		N	22	22	22	22	22	22	22	22	22
	Creativity	Correlation Coefficient	-.059	.508*	.496*	.623**	.53*	1.00	.755**	.728**	.625**
		Sig. (2-tailed)	.793	.016	.019	.002	.011	.	.000	.000	.002
		N	22	22	22	22	22	22	22	22	22
	Implementation	Correlation Coefficient	-.226	.609**	.732**	.770**	.7**	.76**	1.000	.847**	.679**
		Sig. (2-tailed)	.311	.003	.000	.000	.001	.000	.	.000	.001
		N	22	22	22	22	22	22	22	22	22
	Iteration	Correlation Coefficient	-.046	.643**	.596**	.753**	.7**	.73**	.847**	1.000	.773**
		Sig. (2-tailed)	.838	.001	.003	.000	.000	.000	.000	.	.000
		N	22	22	22	22	22	22	22	22	22
	Communication	Correlation Coefficient	.072	.746**	.608**	.837**	.8**	.62**	.679**	.773**	1.000
		Sig. (2-tailed)	.752	.000	.003	.000	.000	.002	.001	.000	.
		N	22	22	22	22	22	22	22	22	22

*. Correlation is significant at the 0.05 level (2-tailed).
**. Correlation is significant at the 0.01 level (2-tailed).

Fig. 2. Correlations between the categories of self-efficacy (Carberry 2018) and between each category and evaluated creativity.

6 Discussion and Implications

Universities have a significant role in finding and developing methods and curricula to improve students' self-efficacy. A thorough program of research and development of design principles is needed, as well as design education according to traditional design methods and newfound design methods from CS and SWD research. Also design principles from CS and SWD can be transferred to traditional art and design to refresh the cooperation between SW startups and design professionals. Researchers and teaching staff with their upgraded and new design skills can create a new design culture to the academia (Risku et al. 2015) [17].

Startups are in the center of high creativity and self-efficacy on account of note-making and design, because practical skills in note-making is part of creation and design, and success in executing own ideas to the markets relates to self-efficacy source of mastery experiences. It means that the startupper performs the tasks in her own control. A positive vicarious experience can be in startuppers' context interpret to be as working in and for the team (Bandura 1994).

7 Conclusions

This study indicates, that self-efficacy beliefs do not describe the creativity grades of design class students. This leads to two conclusions: either run the research in a designer student class and in a non-designer student class, and compare the results.

Then the wider experience of design students may show differences with the other group. On the other hand, a comparative research made between specially design-trained non-designers versus ordinary non-designers may lead to differences, after which it is possible to know, if the training made the difference.

Future research on self-efficacy and its relation to creativity and innovation is important for present day companies and universities. By the same time with a theoretical, practical and educational procedure, new ways of working motivates students to meaningful studies and exploration.

Limitations were also found in this study. Self-efficacy and creativity was evaluated within one week and a definite group, but still on a sharp testbed. Now when started, a wider research and evaluation program at relevant academic course could be organized.

References

1. Ahlin, B., Drnovsek, M., Hisrich, R.D.: Entrepreneurs' creativity and firm innovation: the moderating role of entrepreneurial self-efficacy. Small Bus. Econ. **43**, 101–117 (2014)
2. Khedhaouria, A., Gurâu, C., Torrès, O.: Creativity, self-efficacy, and small-firm performance: the mediating role of entrepreneurial orientation. Small Bus. Econ. **44**(3), 485–504 (2015)
3. Graziotin, D., Wang, X., Abrahamsson, P.: Happy software developers solve problems better: psychological measurements in empirical software engineering. PeerJ **2**, e289 (2014)
4. Carberry, A.R., Gerber, E.M., Martin, C.K.: Measuring the innovation self-efficacy of engineers. Int. J. Eng. Educ. **34**(2B), 590–598 (2018)
5. Bandura, A.: Self-efficacy. In: Ramachaudran, V.S. (ed.) Encyclopedia of Human Behavior, pp. 71–81. Academic Press, New York (1994)
6. Amabile, T.M., Conti, R., Coon, H., Lazenby, J., Herron, M.: Assessing the work environment for creativity. Acad. Manag. J. **39**(5), 1154–1184 (1996)
7. Amabile, T.M.: Social psychology and creativity: a consensual assessment technique. J. Pers. Soc. Psychol. **43**, 997–1013 (1982)
8. Davis, M.: Understanding the relationship between mood and creativity: a meta-analysis. Organ. Behav. Hum. Decis. Process. **108**, 25–38 (2009)
9. Forgeard, M.J.: Happy people thrive on adversity: pre-existing mood moderates the effect of emotion inductions on creative thinking. Pers. Individ. Differ. **51**, 904–909 (2011)
10. Kaufman, J.C., Lee, J., Baer, J., Lee, S.: Captions, consistency, creativity, and the consensual assessment technique: new evidence of reliability. Think. Skills Creat. **2**, 96–106 (2007)
11. Tierney, P., Farmer, S.M.: Creative self-efficacy: its potential antecedents and relationship to creative performance. Acad. Manag. J. **45**, 1137–1148 (2002)
12. Mathisen, G.E., Bronnick, K.S.: Creative self-efficacy: an intervention study. Int. J. Educ. Res. **48**(1), 21–29 (2009)
13. Neville, C.: Effective Note-making. University of Bradford, School of Management, Digital Publication (2006, 2014). https://www.slideshare.net/itamardorneles/effectivenotemaking
14. Buzan, T., Buzan, B.: The Mind Map Book. BBC Worldwide Limited, London. Pearson Education Limited, Harlow (2010). ISBN 10 1406647160
15. Freedman, D., Pisani, R., Purves, R., Adhikari, A.: Statistics, 2nd edn, pp. 133–139. Norton & Company, Inc., New York (1978)

16. Weinberg, S.L., Knapp, S.A.: Data Analysis for the Behavioral Sciences Using SPSS, p. 425. Cambridge University Press, Cambridge (2002)
17. Risku, J., Abrahamsson, P.: What can software startuppers learn from the artistic design flow? Experiences, reflections and future avenues. In: Abrahamsson, P., Corral, L., Oivo, M., Russo, B. (eds.) PROFES 2015. LNCS, vol. 9459, pp. 584–599. Springer, Cham (2015). https://doi.org/10.1007/978-3-319-26844-6_44

Hard Competencies Satisfaction Levels for Software Engineers: A Unified Framework

Nana Assyne(✉)

Faculty of Information Technology, University of Jyväskylä, Jyväskylä, Finland
nana.m.a.assyne@student.jyu.fi

Abstract. Software engineer's/developer's competency has long been established as a key pillar for the development of software. Nevertheless, the satisfaction levels derived from using a competency needs more investigation. The aim of this paper is to propose a framework for identifying hard competencies and their satisfaction levels. The paper contributes to the software engineering competency research by highlighting the satisfaction levels of hard competence for the benefit of the educators (academia), software engineers and users of software competence (practitioner).

Keywords: Hard competency · Technical competency · Software engineers' competencies · Competence satisfaction levels

1 Introduction

Software are the principal driving force for hardware that currently run our daily lives. As such software development is propelled by the competency of the software developers. Competency is said to be the combination of abilities, knowledge, and skills for performing an assigned task. Competency then includes both soft and hard competencies [1]: a hard skill is or are the skill(s) one needs to be able to perform a job or assignment. Hard skills are teachable and acquired mostly through formal training and studies, and are sometimes referred to as technical skill. Often for example a trainee is required to be smart or must possess a good IQ to acquire the required skill. Thus, hard/technical skills are pre-requisite skills required by software engineers/developer in software development process.

Where as both practical and empirical knowledge on technical competencies of software developers is not lacking, competency study has become an important and fundamental strategic area for academic research. Colomo-palacios et al. identify the competency levels relevant to software engineering of professional profiles [2]. Turley and Bieman in an attempt to identify non-exceptional and exceptional competencies of software engineers, also provided the technical competencies of software engineers [3]. Yet – there is paucity of studies that examines the satisfaction levels derived for possessing or using a competence.

Though the works of [2, 4] and [5] establish the essence of hard or technical competence to software development, if we do not know the satisfaction level derived as assurance for the possessor or the user, beneficiary cannot know which competency

S. Hyrynsalmi et al. (Eds.): ICSOB 2019, LNBIP 370, pp. 345–350, 2019.
https://doi.org/10.1007/978-3-030-33742-1_27

will be demanded or be needed. Our initial study looked at [2] work, which examined relevant levels of profile of software engineers and professional. Also the work of [6] assesses base competencies necessary for software engineering students. We do agree with the said work and argue further that it gives credence to the software engineering competency. However, we are of the view that additional satisfaction levels of the competency will provide assurance for both possessor and users in the software engineering community. Thus, there is a need to provide strategic frameworks for the various satisfaction levels of hard or technical competencies of software developers. This paper forms part of broader research on software developer's competency study.

The goal of this paper is to use existing models to create classification levels for the benefit of the users and possessors of software engineering competency. We therefore set our research question as: how do we determine the benefit or satisfaction of a competency of technical or hard competencies for software developers, thus, the research question for this paper is:

What are the different satisfaction levels derived from using a software technical or hard competency?

Research on software competency is not necessarily lacking in software engineering studies [7], however, in this study the Kano model, which is the main framework for this study is being used for the first time on competencies as against it original use on products. To structure this study to fit into previous studies for practical use, we also made use of Competency Framework for Software Engineers (CFSE) [8]. The framework has two main areas, that is soft and hard competency. Since this paper focuses on hard competency, we make use of that as part of the framework. This paper, is structured as follow: Sect. 2 discusses the theoretical foundations, Sect. 3, methodology and the proposed framework, Sect. 4, conclusions and future work.

2 Theoretical Foundations

2.1 Kano Model

The Kano model provides a quality function-deployment framework that aids products or service developers to take into consideration the customer's voice and preferences in the development phase instead of a passive approach of only developers [9–15] employed the Kano model for ICT system development and established that the model highlights user involvement. The model assists in determining basic, performance and delighters of a product or service.

In this paper, we conceptualize the customer as the software community (organization using the competencies) and the product or service as the needed competency. According to Kano et al. [16], customer's decision-making options on product or service acquisition, are founded on conscious and subconscious deliberations. For effective product and or service development there is the need to understand these deliberative conscious and subconscious processes of decision-making. Kano et al.'s categorization of these processes into three-requirement levels (basic, performance and delighters) is relevant. For instance, basic requirements emanate from customer's expectations about a product or service, since their presence are immutable to influence customer options and opinion about the product. However, their absence may result in complaints from the customer. By extension, performance requirements, are expected pre-requisites knowledge factor vital in influencing customer decision-making options. These are critical pre-requisite requirements when appropriately adopted yields high levels of satisfaction. Meanwhile, at the delighter level, product and service developers are required to include surprise elements often referred to as 'wow' factors to entice, attract and influence customer choice options and preferences [16].

2.2 Competence Framework for Software Engineers

Competency Framework for Software Engineers (CFSE) is a framework proposed by [17]. It identifies the training needs of software community and also serves as a guide for competency identification. The framework is divided into two main categories with sub-categories under main categories. The main categories are hard and soft competency. The soft competency category has socials and personals. The hard competency category has subcategories similar to roles for software development identified in SWEBOK. These includes project management, requirement analysis, software design, programming, validation and verification tests, configuration management, quality, tests, documentation and maintenance.

Our study, forms part of a broader software engineering competency study, which aims at creating classification maps for the satisfaction levels of software engineers' competencies. Specifically, in this paper, we focus on hard competency. Since CFSE serve the purpose of identifying hard soft competencies, we make use of the hard category side. This framework provides a granularity which align closes with the roles of software engineering. Thus, we make use of hard category aspect and the kano model to create our desired framework for the study. The result will be a unified framework to identify and classify the satisfaction levels of hard competencies for the use of the software engineering community.

3 Methodology and Proposed Framework

According to [18] framework as design science artifact requires some iteration in the validation of the process in developing. Justification for the need of the artifact has been presented through using literature, but it also requires stakeholder input, Thus, we present the proposed model for validation in this conference.

3.1 Propose Model: A Unified Framework of Hardcompetency Satisfaction Levels for Software Engineers (UFHCSL)

This framework originates in the Kano model and CFSE. The Kano model as quality function-deployment model has been used for research work in software engineering. Our study is the first to apply the Kano model on human resources as a means to determine the competency satisfaction levels of software engineers. CFSE is a framework for identifying competencies of software engineers, and there are more compatible frameworks available, such as [19–22] which provide a means to identify competencies of software developers. However, in line with our objectives, the CFSE frame work provides required granularity and align with the roles of software engineering, we think the work of Rivera-ibarra et al. (2010) is suitable for our objectives.

To use the presented framework (UFHCSL), hard competencies are identified and classified using the hard category in [17] framework, followed by competency identification or classification subjected to the metrics of Kano model (we provide the metrics as Fig. 1) to determines its satisfaction levels. The Categorization metrics is divided into three main parts (satisfaction levels): (1) basic, (2) performance and (3) delighter competencies. In each part a number of parameters are considered e.g. socials (interpersonal relations, cooperation and work in a team, and handling and conflicts resolution) and personals (development in the job, personal development, rights and limits).

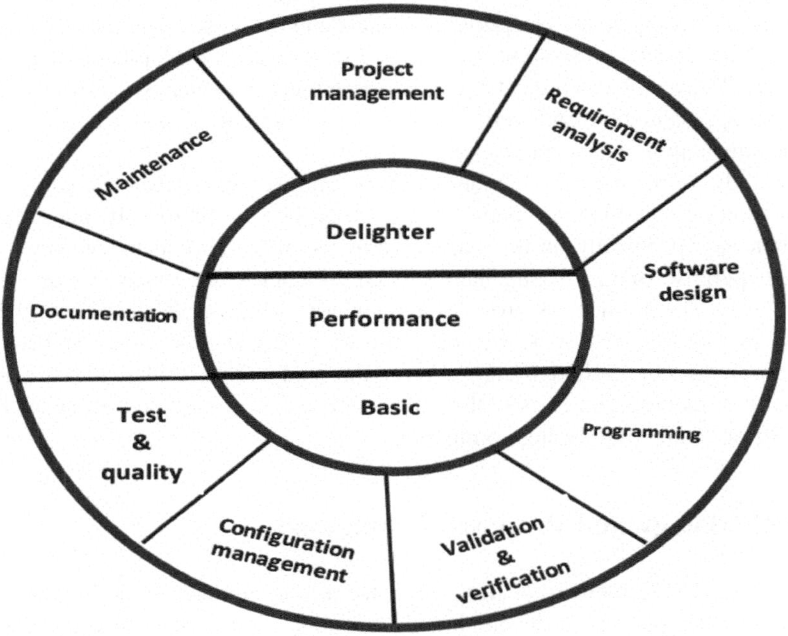

Fig. 1. Unified framework of hard competency satisfaction levels for software engineers

4 Conclusion and Future Work

The proposed framework UFHCSL uses the kano model and the CFSE framework to create framework that can be use to identify hard competencies of software developers, their satisfaction levels and the most valued competencies of the developers. This framework add to the work of [23]. Thus, we have provided a framework that can be beneficial to educators, competency users, and possessors of hard competencies. The future work will be to use empirical data to evaluated the framework.

References

1. Sedelmaier, Y., Landes, D.: Software engineering body of skills (SWEBOS). In: 2014 IEEE Global Engineering Education Conference (EDUCON), pp. 395–401 (2014)
2. Colomo-palacios, R., Carlos, U., De Madrid, I.I.I.: The case of software engineers identifying technical competences of IT professionals. Int. J. Hum. Capital Inf. Technol. Professionals **1**(March), 31–43 (2010)
3. Turley, T., Bieman, M.: Competencies nonexceptional of exceptional and software engineers. J. Syst. Software **28**(28), 19–38 (1995)
4. Patel, A., Benslimane, Y., Bahli, B., Yang, Z.: Addressing IT security in practice: key responsibilities, competencies and implications on related bodies of knowledge. In: 2012 IEEE International Conference on Industrial Engineering and Engineering Management, pp. 899–903 (2012)
5. Manawadu, C.D., Johar, M.G.M., Perera, S.S.N.: Essential technical competencies for software engineers: perspectives from Sri Lankan undergraduates. Int. J. Comput. Appl. **113** (17), 27–34 (2015)
6. Thurner, V., Axel, B., Andreas, K.: Identifying Base Competencies as Prerequisites for Software Engineering Education. In: IEEE Global Engineering Education Conference (EDUCON), pp. 1069–1076 (2014)
7. Lenberg, P., Feldt, R., Wallgren, L.G.: Behavioral software engineering: a definition and systematic literature review. J. Syst. Softw. **107**, 15–37 (2015)
8. Holtkamp, P., Jokinen, J.P.P., Pawlowski, J.M.: Soft competency requirements in requirements engineering, software design, implementation, and testing. J. Syst. Softw. **101**, 136–146 (2015)
9. Lee, Y.C., Sheu, L.C., Tsou, Y.G.: Quality function deployment implementation based on Fuzzy Kano model: an application in PLM system. Comput. Ind. Eng. **55**(1), 48–63 (2008)
10. Gangurde, S., Patil, S.: Benchmark product features using the Kano-QFD approach: a case study. Benchmarking Int. J. **25**(2), 450–470 (2018)
11. Huang, J.: Application of Kano model and IPA on improvement of service quality of mobile healthcare. Int. J. Mob. Commun. **16**(2), 227–246 (2018)
12. Lehtola, L., Kauppinen, M.: Suitability of requirements prioritization methods for market-driven software product development. Software Process Improv. Pract. **11**(1), 7–19 (2006)
13. Liu, X.F.: Software quality function deployment. IEEE Potentials **19**(5), 14–16 (2000)
14. Piaszczyk, C.: Model based systems engineering with department of defense architectural framework. Syst. Eng. **14**(3), 305–326 (2011)
15. Richardson, I.: Software process matrix: a small company SPI model. Software Process: Improv. Pract. **6**(Daft 1992), 157–165 (2001)
16. Kano, N., Seraku, N., Takahashi, F., Tsuji, S.: Kano. Attractive quality and must-be quality. J. Jpn. Soc. Qual. Control **14**, 39–48 (1984)
17. Rivera-ibarra, J.G., Rodríguez-jacobo, J., Fernández-zepeda, J.A., Serrano-vargas, M.A.: Competency framework for software engineers and. In: 2010 23rd IEEE Conference on Software Engineering Education and Training, pp. 33–40 (2010)
18. Peffers, K., Tuunanen, T., Rothenberger, M., Chatterjee, S.: A design science research methodology for information systems research. J. Manage. Inf. Syst. **24**(3), 45–77 (2008)
19. Linck, B., Ohrndorf, L., Kiel, T.D.L., Magenheim, J., Neugebauer, J.: Competence model for informatics modelling and system comprehension. In: 2013 IEEE Global Engineering Education Conference (EDUCON), pp. 85–93 (2013)
20. Tuffley, D.: Optimising virtual team leadership in Global Software Development. IET Software **6**(March 2011), 176–184 (2012)

21. André, M., Baldoquín, M.G., Acuña, S.T.: Formal model for assigning human resources to teams in software projects. Inf. Softw. Technol. **53**, 259–275 (2011)
22. Schulte, C., Magenheim, J., Kathrin, M., Budde, L.: The design and exploration cycle as research and development framework in computing education. In: 2017 IEEE Global Engineering Education Conference (EDUCON), pp. 867–876 (2017)
23. Rivera-Ibarra, J.G., Rodríguez-Jacobo, J., Serrano-Vargas, M.A.: Competency framework for software engineers. In: 2010 23rd IEEE Conference on Software Engineering Education and Training, pp. 33–40, 1 (2010)

Software Startups and Digital Business

How Software Startup Teams Reflect: Approaches, Triggers and Challenges

Dron Khanna(✉) and Xiaofeng Wang

Free University of Bozen-Bolzano, 39100 Bolzano, Italy
{dron.khanna,xiaofeng.wang}@unibz.it

Abstract. Learning from experience is essential for software startup teams. To obtain experiential learning, reflection should be conducted on experience. The existing research on reflection in software startups is much limited. In this study, we focused on reflection in software startup teams and identified formats, triggers and challenges used in such a context. To achieve this, we defined a conceptual framework of reflection. We conducted a multiple case study and analyzed the data obtained from two software startups. The initial finding shows that software startups do perform reflection of different types based on the factors like team size and collocation. We also found two new formats, three triggers and three challenges of reflection in software startups. Reflection sessions conducted by startups could mean tough moments, confrontations and sometimes involve the ego of team members. To conduct the session, it is important to be open, honest, raise key affair and straight to the point.

Keywords: Software startups · Reflection · Experience · Learning · Experiential learning

1 Introduction

Software startups are new ventures that build an innovative software-intensive product and aim at exponential growth. They operate under the conditions of extreme uncertainty [1] and are confronted by various challenges related to business, product, finance and team building [2]. To survive in such demanding environments, the capability of a software startup team to collectively reflect on their entrepreneurial journey and draw validated learning can be a decisive factor for the startup to succeed or fail.

Reflection inside software startups is important as it leads to various positive outcomes. First and foremost, it enhances learning from experience in startup teams. It also creates better understanding and coordination in a team. Finally, it influences directly on the behaviour of a startup team, since performing reflection on experience assists a startup team to refine their skills concerning finance and marketing [3]. However, not many software startup teams have the habit to reflect on their entrepreneurial experience, or they are not aware of the importance and value of performing reflection as a team.

S. Hyrynsalmi et al. (Eds.): ICSOB 2019, LNBIP 370, pp. 353–368, 2019.
https://doi.org/10.1007/978-3-030-33742-1_28

Compared to the general entrepreneurship literature in which entrepreneurial experiential learning and reflection have received some attention, there is a paucity of studies in the literature that investigate the reflection approaches adopted by software startup teams, the challenges of performing reflection in this specific context, and what could be done to improve the capabilities of a software startup team to reflect for the purpose of obtaining validated learning from team's entrepreneurial experience. Currently, the trend of research on software engineering aims at companies which are evolving software development product and services. Nevertheless, research has increased on software startups due to their emphasis on the development of new software-intensive product and services [4].

The objective of our study is to provide a better understanding of the current reflection practices in software startups and issues faced by them. This is a necessary step before any interventions to improve the state of the practice could be meaningfully conducted. To this end, we formulated the following research question to guide our study:

RQ: How do software startup teams perform reflection?

The research question can be further divided into three sub-questions:

- *RQ1: What are the approaches used by software startup teams to perform reflection?*
- *RQ2: What triggers software startup teams to perform reflection?*
- *RQ3: What are the challenges faced by software startup teams to perform reflection?*

To answer the research questions, we have built a conceptual framework of reflection approach using relevant literature and conducted a multiple case study of two software startups. The findings include a set of formats, triggers and challenges related to reflection in software startups.

The remaining part of the paper is organised as follows. In the Sect. 2 background literature, first we describe the concept of reflection and its importance in the team. Later in the section is stated the related reflection frameworks. Section 3 outlines the conceptual framework of reflection approach for a software startup with the reflective element and its gravid sub-elements in details. Next, we state the research approach in Sect. 4. The two software startup case details and interviews conducted is indicated in this section too. Section 5 reveals the two novel formats, three triggers and three challenges of reflection in software startup teams. Finally with discussion and conclusion in Sects. 6 and 7 we conclude the study.

2 Background Literature

As far as the authors are aware of, there is no study examining the reflective practice in the context of software startups. As the theoretical basis of the study, we needed to draw upon the general literature on reflection.

2.1 The Concept of Reflection

Reflection is one of the two crucial elements when conducted with experience results in experiential learning. Figure 1 represents the experiential learning model where reflection and experience are the two elements that lead to learning. The third element presented in the model is a team who perform reflection on an experience.

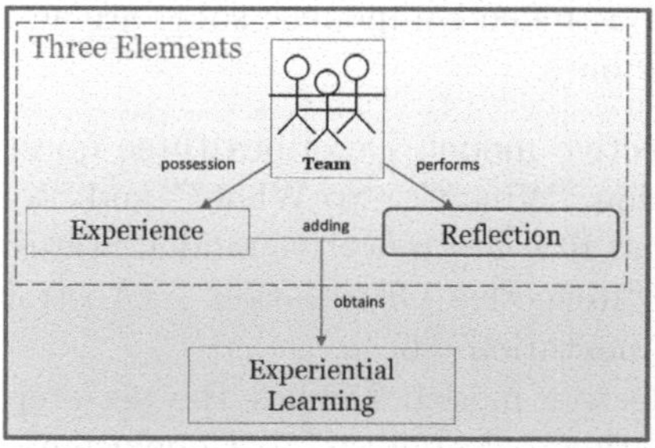

Fig. 1. Three Elements of Experiential learning model

Reflection is the mechanism to process experience to outcome experiential learning [5–10]. According to Dewy, reflection is an inactive "quietness" process [5], whereas for Kolb reflection is an active "transformation" process [6]. For instance, in a startup team, the mechanism of deliberating why or how a task is going on or already finished is a reflection, as the brain gets the time to judge willfully the event. Irrespective whether the task yields positive or negative results, the analysis on decisions, actions, emotions, and beliefs allows the experience to be transferred into learning [3]. To harness the experience to its potential, reflection is needed [5,7]. Although not all experiences lead to learning [11], the process of reflection enhances experiential learning [3,10,12,13].

When reflection is considered as a means to extract experiential learning at the team level, it is termed as collaborative reflection [14–16], by which a group of people or team reflect together, share the experience with each other and discuss in a team to collaboratively obtain insights for change in future work. In other words, reflection is taking place among several individuals, for example, in meetings when a team discuss on several problematic situations [17].

2.2 Reflection Frameworks/Models

Several reflection frameworks exist in the literature. Fowler describes a generic framework for experiential learning in the field of nursing, analysing the elements required that facilitate learning. Experience, reflection and learning are the three elements specified by Fowler [7]. The framework is of considerable interest but lacks in-depth analysis of each element. The framework explains learning as dependent outcome based on the two elements that are experience and reflection.

If any of the two elements are available in limited quality then learning will be limited. Experiential learning, as a result, is dependent on the significant synergy from both the elements [7]. Degeling and Prilla define a framework for the modes of collaborative reflection and the means of support.

The framework presents three modes of reflection: scheduled, concurrent and spontaneous reflection. To support these three elements, the framework further provides three means to support: articulation, scaffolding and guidance, and synergising [14,15].

There are also various reflective models; some are actively used in practice. Below is a list of major ones:

- Terry Borton's reflective model: Describes three questions which should be asked during reflection "What?", "So What?" and "Now What?" [18,19]
- David Allen Kolb and Ron Fry reflective model: States the four stages "Concrete Experience", "Reflective Observation", "Abstract Conceptualisation" and "Active Experimentation" [6]
- Graham Gibbs reflective model: Defines the six step cycle "Description", "Feelings", "Evaluation", "Analysis", "Conclusion" and "Action Plan" [20,21]
- Roger Greenaway: Outlines the four stage sequence"Experience", "Express", "Examine" and "Explore" [22]
- Daudelin Marilyn Wood: Specifies the four stages "Articulation of a problem", "Analysis of that problem", "Formulation and Testing" and "Action" [10]

2.3 Triggers for Reflection

Some triggers which provoke reflection are:

- Calm surroundings encouraging reflection without being distracted [5,7,9,23].
- Being attentive to and mindful of the present moment [9,23].
- Interpreting old experience [9] and making the relation with new experience [23].
- Thinking from another persons perspective [23].

2.4 Challenges of Reflection

Following in the list are the three challenges involved during the reflective session.

- Unwillingness to reflect: One of the challenges to reflect on experience is an unwillingness to reflect [7,24]. If an entrepreneur in a team is fanatic about certain assumptions on a particular point or subject, then he/she would be resistant to reflect upon an experience. Strong opinion for a particular subject makes an individual unwilling to reflect [7]. To overcome this challenge, according to Mezirow, when our belief or assumptions becomes problematic for a particular point or a subject, reflection is often triggered [25]. When the assumption about a particular task becomes blurry or not correct, causes the reflection to occur. Commonly, our mind is willing to obtain a satisfying feeling about a certain task, to remain in the comfort zone, until the problem occurs. The encounter of a problem triggers to step out the comfort zone and reflect on task [24].

- Vulnerable in a team: Another challenge to reflect on the team depends upon the involved members' ethnicity. In some situations, team members belonging to different cultural norms tend to preserve the reflection viewpoints if the situation within the team is uncomfortable for them. They may not reflect because by being open to reflect in a team, they are worried to make the mistakes, which can make them being vulnerable in a team. To overcome the feelings of embarrassment in a team as the reflected and shared viewpoint are not so crucial, the individuals tend to keep with themselves. Sometimes reflection can be too personal and interrogating on experience. Therefore, team members could be reluctant to reflect [26].
- Time: The time constraints is another challenge which makes the team not to reflect. The team members are so occupied by various tasks that reflection cannot take place, as the energy of the group members already get void due to the involvement with the daily working tasks. Sometimes this internal energy could also become null due to personal or social problems [7].

3 The Conceptual Framework of Reflection Approach

In this section, we examine the concept of reflection in greater depth and build a conceptual framework of reflection approach that serves as the theoretical basis for the empirical investigation. Figure 2 shows the elements of reflection. Format, type and technique are the elements which help the reflective session. Further, these elements comprise sub-elements which are being taken from the literature available on reflection and then grouped under each element.

3.1 Formats of Reflection

Following in the list are the four formats of reflection [23].

- **Writing**: Written reflection is a format which helps to develop and structure our thoughts in a meaningful experience. It could be a challenging technique but could lead to a written record or diary of experience as notes. The notes jotted down could include script, drawings, maps, etc.
- **Telling**: Telling is a type of format where an individual orally describes an experience. Also, while telling an individual could deepen his or her understanding of an experience. Storytelling is a powerful technique to practice this format of reflection. Presentation and discussions are other telling formats.
- **Multimedia**: Multimedia is a format of reflection where individuals could bind together various media of expression, maybe in an artistic manner too. Films or videos, snapshots or photos, a collage of visual representations are some formats to perform reflection on experience. Also drawing a painting is another way to capture the essence of an experience.

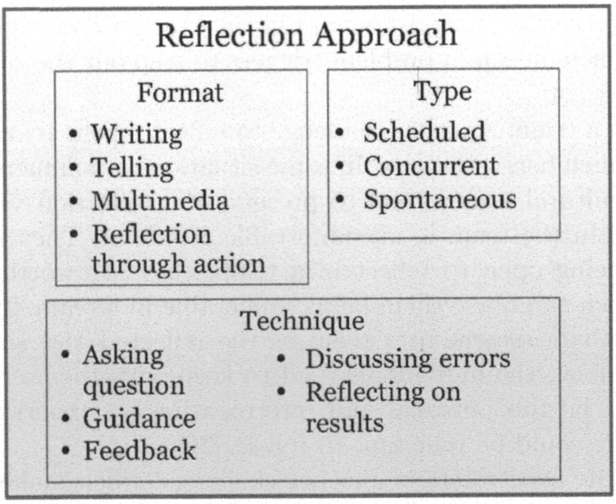

Fig. 2. The conceptual framework of reflection approach

- **Reflection through action**: An experience that can be obtained through action and then reflecting on it. Activity or exercise done is the way to encounter the experience. An individual can experience this format of reflection only by spending time in the environment or the same settings as of another individual. It is equivalent to encounter someone's experience.

3.2 Types of Reflection

Following in the list are the three types of reflection [14].

- **Scheduled reflection**: It is a type of reflection that happens in particularly dedicated sessions. This type of reflection could occur regularly (monthly) where critical feedback triggers reflection or irregularly (randomly scheduled) where problems or difficult situation could initiate reflection. Both regular or irregular schedule reflections could be accompanied by a group of facilitators where participants could explain the problems.
- **Concurrent reflection**: This type of reflection occurs without a scheduled or dedicated session. During work shifts or workflows when individuals meet, they reflect on the situation. Here a particular subject is not examined so thoroughly. The time invested is less as compared to a scheduled reflection. Feedback triggers this reflection.
- **Spontaneous reflection**: This reflection occurs when individuals carry out spontaneous reflection for shorter intervals than concurrent reflection but several times during their work shifts. A particular subject is discussed several times after various feedback's. The feedback's inv olved are corresponding to the same or different task.

3.3 Techniques for Reflection

Some of the techniques of reflection mentioned by Daudelin are asking questions, feedback discussions, mentoring guidance [10]. Along the same line, Harms illustrates techniques such as asking questions, seeking feedback, reflecting on results, and discussing errors or unexpected outcomes of actions [27]. Both authors emphasize primarily on asking questions, which is one powerful technique to reflect that can be dated back to the time of Socrates and Plato. The power of deliberate questions in a business environment is a healthy technique to advance commitment [10]. Depending on a reflective model and its stages, there are various type of reflective questions [10,19]. In an intense and demanding business environment, reflective questions can open up risks and make situations more expressive [10].

4 Research Approach

The objective of this study is to explore how software startup teams perform reflection. Since the study is exploratory in nature, a case study is considered by the researchers to be a suitable research approach. For our study, we employed a multiple qualitative case study approach [28]. The selected two cases are software startups. Both are founded in Italy. Case 1 which initiated five years ago with the idea of an online platform of selling and re-selling various things, did four pivots till date. Currently, the startup is the software developer kit provider. Case 2 within the first year did one pivot till date. The startup is the manufacturers for security and commercial devices. Table 1 provides the startup outline. The number of team members for Case 1 varies from three to five, as they outsource some work to other countries. For Case 2 startup, there are seven members including the CEO and a marketing manager.

Table 1. Software startups outline

Case	Startup age (in years)	No. of team members	Business domain	Interviewees
1	5	3 to 5	Software development Kit provider	CEO1 CEO2
2	1	7	Security & commercial Device producer	CEO Marketing manager

We used personal face-to-face interviews as the main data collection method. Semi-structured interviews were conducted with open-ended questions. The interview lasted from 23 min to 60 min. As the interviewees, we mainly involved the founders and co-founders because they are in the whole journeys of their startups. The questions used during the interviews are: what happened recently in your startup, that you remember and made you learn something? How did it happen? Why did it happen? How did you come to know? What made it reflect? How do you reflect? What did you do? Did you share it with other team members? What trigger this reflection? What are the challenges you encounter?

As suggested by Yin [28], we followed the multiple-case analysis. First, each case was analysed, and later cross-comparison was made. To code, the interview data followed the guidelines of Saldaña [29]. The formats, triggers and challenges involved were identified within each case and were compared and contrasted across cases. The data analysis process was aided by Nvivo 12, a qualitative data analysis software package.

5 Findings

We found out that scheduled reflection is common for both the startups. Case 2 performs scheduled reflection every week. Whereas Case 1 struggles to schedule a dedicated time for a reflective session. But the CEO2 of Case 1 said that in future they are planning to schedule reflection sessions as they realized the importance of it. Currently, they perform scheduled reflection when a tremendous problem exists in the startup and dedicating time to discuss it.

Commonly concurrent and spontaneous reflection is conducted by Case 1 because the team size is small, and they work in the same working space. Irrespective of the type of reflection, discussion as a format is found to be regularly practised by both the startups. From interviews, we found out two new formats, three triggers and three challenges. The two new formats are "speaking loudly" and "mental archive notes". Table 2 provides the outline of the reflection.

Table 2. Reflection outline (software startups)

Type	Format	Case
Scheduled	Telling - Discussion	Both
	Writing - Notes	Case 1
Concurrent	Telling - Discussion	Case 1
Spontaneous	Telling - Discussion	Case 1
	Other format	
	Telling - Speak Loudly	Case 1
	Mental - Archived notes	Case 2

5.1 Scheduled Reflection

Telling - Discussion. For Case 1 discussion as a format and telling as a type of reflection was performed. Both the CEO of Case 1 scheduled the reflection during the initial startup journey. Both of them examined thoroughly and discussed with each other about their competencies and skills to know where they can together lead the startup. For example, the CEO2 of Case 1 recalled: *"We divided our services, we sat down at the table and we decided, what is actually your field of interest? Where are your skills placed? And my skill placed."*.

Whereas, Case 2 team perform scheduled reflection every week with the team. The marketing manager mentioned: *"We do every week a call in order to, how did it happen? With our team, good? Bad? What happened? Yeah, we reflect."*. The feedback helps them trigger the scheduled reflection: *"We reflect about the feedback and also we try as the CEO said before, psychology, so we try to understand why our partner says one thing?"*. The CEO of Case 2 added: *"It is part I will say part to adapt and part to correct."*. Then both, the marketing manager and the CEO added the importance of discussion as a format of reflection. Also, during the reflection session be direct to the point: *"I think also importantly to discuss with them, we have discussions also between us and also with our partners essential parts, straight to the point, I think it is important."*.

Writing - Notes. Writing notes as a scheduled reflection is another method to reflect which comes in handy while a team reflects on the problems encountered. The CEO2 of Case 1 mentioned: *"Lets write down what is the problem? We wrote it down. We saw the problems actually."*. Also, he added writing notes as reflection acted as a reset button to the issues encountered in the startup: *"This problem we will solve it too and this was really good enough, for bringing your problems to paper, you have to bring your problems into paper in order to solve them. Because otherwise you have them in your mind, but really blurry and you are not really precise and to your problems. But if you write them down you will see that actually there is a solution for everything and yeah it was kind of reset button and then we started again"*.

5.2 Concurrent Reflection

Telling - Discussion. The CEO1 of Case 1 recalled when other entrepreneurs gave feedback to him on particular activities: *"We had a chance to meet really important people and you have the possibility to meet people that you will never meet again. For example, the CEO of... And you are talking, you are sharing, they can tell you may be trying this way or this way' because we just had this problem and we solve it in this way."*. Also, in Case 1, the CEO1 mentioned that they had a nice network outside their team too. They often meet for conversation where the entrepreneurs discuss information and provide guidance. The CEO1 also mentioned that being connected to a channel made them reflect: *"People sharing the product and asking for feedback, people also sharing the business model. For example, business pitches and then you have to give the feedback first, then explanation was good enough. Do you understand it, what are the questions?"*. Sharing feedback helps to reflect and nourishes the startup.

5.3 Spontaneous Reflection

Telling - Discussion. In Case 1, to collaborate the proper workflow, so for example if one person in a team is responsible for product and another is dealing with market analysis and business models, it is important to perform spontaneous reflection as the CEO2 mentioned: *"But this is a decision which actually has a necessary to be taken by both of us. Because I can't, I mean like there are decisions to, which will be the market? Which will be your entrance market? The other hand he would tell me for the market side, it would be the best thing to do this. But then I am telling. But in this case we can not do this, because of the product is not able to generate this kind of information. So probably we should switch this one."*. So without a dedicated session for reflection, to exchange feedback's during the working shifts is a good way to reflect.

5.4 Novel Formats of Reflection

Telling - Speak Loud. While telling is one of the ways to reflect where discussions and presentations could be a few techniques that could be used to reflect on a team. We found out that speaking loud could be another technique too. The team using the same working space could reflect on there working shift while applying this method. From Case 1 we found evidence to support this method, for example as the CEO2 said: *"Speak out loudly to your partners, what or you are thinking? Don't be kind, just speak out loudly what you are thinking? But it is a general, live thing, in my opinion. Everybody should do it everybody. But always be straight. Do what you think it is kind of right and explain that to your partners. Why do you think it is right? Yeah to be honest or be open and straight forward and honest like to the others"*. Later in the interview the CEO 2 again emphasized: *"If you then speak out loudly to each other"*. Speaking loudly helps to narrow down the issues encounter by the startup as Case 1, CEO2 mentioned: *"You have to change something. You have to make a step, a cut and then speak out together and think about it. What could we do different? What was the cause? Because we don't have this or. Was it because a client troubled you up? Then actually only by telling out loudly you will hear it. Be open to each other. Really the willing to speak out loudly"*.

Mental Archived Notes. From Case 2, we found that team members after reflecting stored their learning inside their mind. They use the brains as their hard drive to keep the information. The CEO of Case 2 said: *"I mean notes are stored in the mental archive"*. Also, the CEO commented that he shared the learning with other team member but not so much in detail: *"Perhaps not enough"* and as the other team was matured enough to get the information, where the marketing manager added: *"I think there is also a big difference with this team and the her team"*.

5.5 Triggers for Reflection

From the two cases, we also identified the three major triggers that provoked the two startups to reflect. The three categorized triggers are: "Work", "Team" and "Inner voice". For "Work" we found out six causes, "Team" three causes and one cause for "Inner Voice" that evoke reflection.

1. **WORK**
   - **Continuously decrease in revenue for three months** - Another insight what the CEO2 described: *"First thing, which you are looking at the revenues and this would like decreasing in the last 3 months. What? Why? I mean, of course, one month, it could be. Two months could be. Then third months you are, somehow, thinking about what is going wrong? Revenue is first thing."*.
   - **Workflow getting blurry** - The CEO2 from Case 1 highlighted that when the usual workflow is getting fuzzy in the usual tasks it is time to reflect: *"When your workflow is kind of getting blurry. Not strong. Which actually makes you working not that good as before."*.
   - **Dropping down the passion/energy/level of commitment/not enjoying work** - Also the CEO2 stated that when an entrepreneur passion or energy to work in startup environment is decreasing, the team should think about performing reflection: *"I will say you can see it from the passion for the job. The passion is the main thing I would say and if you see this passion likes smaller, smaller, smaller."*. Where he added: *"I would say in 4 years, it was one time said, also loud. Listen, we can't work anymore like this. I mean we get back our energy. As I know notice by myself and also the other CEO was noticing it that we both lost our energy."*. Similarly Case 2 CEO mentioned that the team has different level of commitment to work: *"The team does not, also different level of commitment to work, you are not loving anymore what you are doing."*.
   - **Change in approach to work** - In the Case 1, the CEO mentioned that the entire teams got aware, when the usual working approach changes: *"The other team members noticed it, that there was a big change in the approach. I mean if you don't say it, people will notice it. Whats going on with you? Then also, they noticed that we were kind of having a another rhythm of work."*.
   - **Deadlines trouble at work** - The CEO1 of Case 1 mentioned: *"Even deadlines and then your getting in troubles with deadlines. In my opinion, you don't want to do it anymore. Because if you want to do it, you will do it in time and you will do it good. If you don't want to do it, it is kind of something troubling you off."*. Where the Case 2 mentioned *"The team doesn't, respect the deadline"*.
   - **Stop working for extra office hours** - The CEO1 of Case1 mentioned: *"Because at the beginning you will, you have tasks. At the beginning always open a new task even if it is 5 pm in the evening. You will, initialise another task and you will sit down in the office till 7–8 clock. You finish*

the another task, after some period you notice. Myself and the other CEO also noticed yeah we have liked. The task is finished at 5 pm, quarter past 5, no. I am not getting another into a task. We do it tomorrow.".

2. **TEAM**
   - **Not discussing small personal issues with team members** - Often individuals tend to keep small personal issues within themselves. They do not bring up or discuss with the team members they encounter the issues with and which can breakdown the workflow momentum with other team members: *"There is kind of just mini things, which then they are accumulated. Then, in the end, you are getting like really angry and you will cry.".*
   - **Unpleasant exchange of messages/miscommunication in team** - Also CEO2 mentioned that team was exchanging unpleasant messages: *"I think where we got really, really two or three not so good messages. But if it is three or four messages which are not so good coming to you after continuously fighting for existence" for the startup "Then you should ask yourself.".* In Case 2 both the CEO and marketing manager acknowledged that miscommunication can create a sour environment in team: *"Miscommunication with the team.".*
   - **Not good previous experience with team** - The Case 2 marketing manager mentioned the need to reflect in there startup was because of the work failure in the team. The team didn't perform well, he mentioned: *"Why because our previous experience. Because of our team. Did not go good."* and the CEO agreed to it: *"Yes".*
3. **INNER VOICE**
   - **Inner voice or feeling, going on wrong track** - The Case 2: *"Now that the reason is certain, an inner feeling. Every entrepreneur has this inner feeling that is the same. I will say, interior compass, which other times while confronting with bad news or I mean obstacles or problems. So, the same inner voice. It was powerful warning, that we were on the wrong track. Therefore, I mean definitely we needed to change something."* where marketing manager added: *"Stop please. Stop please."* and then CEO said: *"The other times. Go forward."* to which the marketing manager agreed: *"Yes".*

5.6 Challenges of Reflection

We found three challenges of reflection:

1. **Trust between partners and postponing reflective sessions** - Sometimes when the co-founders of the startups are friends, they trust each other blindly so, for example, CEO2 mentioned: *"Working on separated things where he doesn't even know what I am exactly doing like right now. But he trusts me that I will do the best. The same with me I am not looking at him and asking him. I trust him blindly, I think he trusts me too."* and they often forget to reflect due to the busy in work schedule: *"Because you will always*

find other work to do. You can say, I can speak to you tomorrow. You could, but you can also speak with me after 2 years. So for this reason you have to sit down this time. To also do this thing too. To prevent the situation".

2. **Small team with collocated space** - When the team is small and collocated in the same working space they find it difficult to devote time for a reflective session: *"Since you are just two persons, sitting in room. It depends, on and we don't have fixed meetings for it. Because we are in two. We just actually not that good at all. We already spoke about it, and we will do it in future. Then of course every month. Every two months. Every three months. Like we will fix meetings. So every two months will be two hours of meeting. So we are kind of planning, it is necessary."*.
3. **Team member with old age and ego, intend to dominate** - From Case 2 we found out that when the team is comprised of the different age group the reflection is little biased and team members are not completely open and clear during the discussion session. Team members who are with elder age tend to emphasise their stories on the younger ones. The Marketing manager added, important is the experience, not the age: *"I think that because there are different egos and I think I am not having high ego. Here people you know, are the 50 years old. They say yes, I am 50 years old. So, I know that this is the story. Now the age is not important. Important is experience. You cannot impose. You have to explain why it is correct? Why it is not correct? May be the other two can accept. But if you say no, then this you need accept. After all, there are no emperor, there are no king."*.

6 Discussion

Software startups do perform particular types of reflection depending on the team size and working space. Commonly, if the team is comprised of three members and share the same working space, concurrent and spontaneous reflection occurs. The team reflect through speaking or thinking aloud during their working shifts. Mutual decisions, quick feedback, answers and discussions trigger this type of reflection. The dedicated scheduled reflection in a startup team comprised of around three people does take place either to analyse the team members skills or when they encounter big problems related to a workflow. Although the startup team do believe and agree on the importance of scheduled reflection, due to team size, same working space and trust, it is a challenge which postpones the dedicated reflection period.

Mostly, if the team is comprised of more than three members and does not share the same working space, scheduled reflection occurs. The team reflect every week and discuss what happened, how did it happen, why did it happen, and if it went good or bad? To trigger this type of refection, feedback and inner voice play a key role. Some entrepreneurs do reflect individually, then store experiential learning in mind as a mental archive and later discussed with the team. To reflect often, a team should encourage to keep track of the mentioned triggers that motivate the team to reflect.

We found from both the cases that it is important to be open, honest, to raise key affair and straight to the point in a reflection session. Sensitivity in a team can have problems during reflection as there are tough moments, confrontations during a reflective session and the ego should not be involved.

One cause from the "Team" trigger validates the trigger mentioned by literature that is "interpreting the old experience" [9]. Previous unsatisfactory experience with a team member leads to reflection. We found out from the literature time as a challenge of reflection [7]. The findings from the case study authenticate but time and trust together as a challenge. As the team members trust each other; and are involved in the daily work routines which postpone the reflection session. To overcome the challenge of unwillingness to reflect [7,24] according to Mezirow [25] one should monitor a task if it becomes blurry, problematic or not correct to trigger reflection. One of the CEOs mentioned the similar takeaway that is, the team should reflect if the workflow or task is getting blurry or not as good as before.

Regarding the threats to validity, we conducted just two software startup cases, one with a team size of around three and another with a team size of seven. The external validity of our findings is limited to similar case sizes and startup teams with a comparable level of entrepreneurial experiences. To increase it, we need to conduct more case studies with various levels of sizes and at different stages of maturity. Finally, the insights cannot be generalised at this point due to a few cases.

7 Conclusion

There has been less research done on the importance of reflection on experience inside software startup teams. The reflection is the mechanism which transfers the experience into experiential learning [5–10]. Various frameworks exist in the literature for performing reflection, but they lack an in-depth analysis of the reflection elements. We provided a framework with the elements inside the reflection concept. The framework describes the format, type and technique for reflection. We conducted a multiple case study and analyzed the data obtained from two software startups. We found out two new reflection formats, three triggers and three challenges of reflection. Apart from conducting more case studies with diversified profiles to consolidate the findings, we will also extend our research and investigate the other elements involved in entrepreneurial experiential learning: a better understanding of types and sources of experiences, and documentation and sharing of learning outcomes within team members.

References

1. Ries, E.: The Lean Startup: How Today's Entrepreneurs Use Continuous Innovation to Create Radically Successful Businesses. Crown Books (2011)

2. Giardino, C., Bajwa, S.S., Wang, X., Abrahamsson, P.: Key challenges in early-stage software startups. In: Lassenius, C., Dingsøyr, T., Paasivaara, M. (eds.) XP 2015. LNBIP, vol. 212, pp. 52–63. Springer, Cham (2015). https://doi.org/10.1007/978-3-319-18612-2_5
3. Le Roux, I., Steyn, B.: Experiential learning and critical reflection as a tool for transfer of business knowledge: an empirical case study of a start-up simulation intervention for nascent entrepreneurs. S. Afr. J. Econ. Manag. Sci. **10**(3), 330–347 (2007)
4. Seppänen, P., Liukkunen, K., Oivo, M.: On the feasibility of startup models as a framework for research on competence needs in software startups. In: Abrahamsson, P., Corral, L., Oivo, M., Russo, B. (eds.) PROFES 2015. LNCS, vol. 9459, pp. 569–576. Springer, Cham (2015). https://doi.org/10.1007/978-3-319-26844-6_42
5. Dewey, J.: Experience and education. In: The Educational Forum, vol. 50, no. 3, pp. 241–252. Taylor & Francis Group (1986)
6. Kolb, D.A.: Experiential Learning: Experience As the Source of Learning and Development. FT press, Upper Saddle River (2014)
7. Fowler, J.: Experiential learning and its facilitation. Nurse Educ. Today **28**(4), 427–433 (2008)
8. Andresen, L., Boud, D., Cohen, R.: Experience-based learning. Underst. Adult Educ. Train. **2**, 225–239 (2000)
9. Boud, D., Keogh, R., Walker, D.: Reflection: Turning Experience Into Learning. Routledge, Abingdon (2013)
10. Daudelin, M.W.: Learning from experience through reflection. Organ. Dyn. **24**(3), 36–48 (1996)
11. Beard, C., Wilson, J.P.: The Power of Experiential Learning: A Handbook for Trainers and Educators. Stylus Publishing, Sterling (2002)
12. Politis, D.: The process of entrepreneurial learning: a conceptual framework. Entrep. Theory Pract. **29**(4), 399–424 (2005)
13. Cope, J.: Entrepreneurial learning and critical reflection: discontinuous events as triggers for 'higherlevel' learning. Manag. Learn. **34**(4), 429–450 (2003)
14. Degeling, M., Prilla, M.: Modes of collaborative reflection (2011)
15. Prilla, M., Degeling, M., Herrmann, T.: Collaborative reflection at work: supporting informal learning at a healthcare workplace. In: Proceedings of the 17th ACM International Conference on Supporting Group Work, pp. 55–64 (2012)
16. Knipfer, K., Prilla, M., Cress, U., Herrmann, T.: Computer support for collaborative reflection on captured teamwork data. In: Proceedings of the 9th International Conference on Computer Supported Collaborative Learning, pp. 938–939 (2011)
17. Prilla, M.: Supporting collaborative reflection at work: a socio-technical analysis. AIS Trans. Hum. Comput. Interact. **7**(1), 1–17 (2015)
18. Borton, T.: Reach, Touch, and Teach. Saturday Rev. (1969)
19. Rolfe, G.: Reach touch and teach. Nurse Educ. Today **4**(34), 488–489 (2014)
20. Gibbs, G.: Learning by Doing: A Guide to Teaching and Learning Methods. Further Education Unit (1988)
21. Finlay, L.: Reflecting on reflective practice. PBPL Pap. **52**, 1–27 (2008)
22. Greenaway, R.: Reviewing by doing. J. Adventure Educ. Outdoor Lead. **9**(1), 21–25 (1992)
23. Collier, P.J., Williams, D.R.: Reflection in action. In: Cress, C.R., Collier, P.J. (eds.) no. 50, pp. 83–97 (2005)
24. Mälkki, K.: Building on Mezirow's theory of transformative learning: Theorizing the challenges to reflection. J. Transform. Educ. **8**(1), 42–62 (2010)

25. Mezirow, J.: Transformative Dimensions of Adult Learning (1991)
26. Fook, J., Askeland, G.A.: Challenges of critical reflection: 'Nothing ventured, nothing gained'. Soc. Work. Educ. **26**(5), 520–533 (2007)
27. Harms, R.: Self-regulated learning, team learning and project performance in entrepreneurship education: learning in a lean startup environment. Technol. Forecast. Soc. Chang. **100**, 21–28 (2015)
28. Yin, R.K.: Case Study Research and Applications: Design and Methods. Sage Publications, Thousand Oaks (2017)
29. Saldaña, J.: The Coding Manual for Qualitative Researchers. Sage, Thousand Oaks (2015)

Amidst Uncertainty – or Not? Decision-Making in Early-Stage Software Startups

Kai-Kristian Kemell[1(✉)], Eveliina Ventilä[1], Petri Kettunen[2], and Tommi Mikkonen[2]

[1] University of Jyväskylä, Jyväskylä, Finland
kai-kristian.o.kemell@jyu.fi
[2] University of Helsinki, Helsinki, Finland
{petri.kettunen,tommi.mikkonen}@helsinki.fi

Abstract. It is commonly claimed that the initial stages of any startup business are dominated by continuous, extended uncertainty, in an environment that has even been described as chaotic. Consequently, decisions are made in uncertain circumstances, so making the right decision is crucial to successful business. However, little currently exists in the way of empirical studies into this supposed uncertainty. In this paper, we study decision-making in early-stage software startups by means of a single, in-depth case study. Based on our data, we argue that software startups do not work in a chaotic environment, nor are they characterized by unique uncertainty unlike that experienced by other firms.

Keywords: Software startups · Entrepreneurship · Decision-making · Cynefin framework · In-depth case study

1 Introduction

Despite being extensively studied [10], startups still lack an accurate definition. Various characteristics have been attributed to startups to differentiate them from other firms. Characteristics typically associated with startups include (1) highly reactive, (2) innovation, (3) uncertainty, (4) rapidly evolving, (5) time-pressure, (6) third party dependency, (7) small team, (9) one product), (10) low-experienced team, (11) new company, (12) flat organization, (13) highly risky, (14) not self-sustained, (15) lack of resources, and (16) little working history [8]. In software startups, the role of software in the final offering may vary from being the core product to merely serving as an enabler or support of the main business idea (e.g. Uber) [11].

Klotins [3] highlighted the (lack of) empirical evidence behind many of these characteristics, questioning the uniqueness of software startups in relation to failure rates, lack of software engineering (SE) experience, innovativeness, market-related time pressure, and lack of resources. To this end, decision-making is another area where little is known empirically about software startups [10]. Software startups are considered to work amidst uncertainty that has even been described as a chaotic [2, 7, 8].

To provide empirical evidence into this on-going debate on software startup characteristics, we study software startup decision-making in relation to the uncertainty attributed to software startup in this paper. Wedo so by means of an in-depth case study

S. Hyrynsalmi et al. (Eds.): ICSOB 2019, LNBIP 370, pp. 369–377, 2019.
https://doi.org/10.1007/978-3-030-33742-1_29

executed in an ethnography-inspired fashion, utilizing the Cynefin framework [6] for data analysis. Specifically, wetackle the following research question in this paper:

RQ: Using the Cynefin framework, how can we characterize the context software startups operate in relation to decision-making?

2 Background

Few studies focusing on decision-making in the context of software startups currently exist [10]. On the other hand, organizational decision-making is a well-established area of research spanning various disciplines from economic ones to psychology and SE. Areas of research related to it are similarly diverse (e.g., business intelligence).

Some of the research on decision-making in the area of New Product Development (NPD) can be considered related to this context. Software startups search for new business models [10], whereas conventional business organizations *execute* business models. Software startups also make various decisions regarding SE [8].

In a literature review spanning multiple disciplines, Krisnan and Ulrich [5] presented a list of decisions related to setting up a product development project. They list various higher-level decisions related to product development that an organization needs to make when starting a product development project. Many of these decisions (e.g., "which technologies will be employed in the product(s)?") are relevant for software startups, while some are far more relevant to more established companies, (e.g., "will a functional, project, or development matrix organization be used?").

Extant literature has focused on conventional firms. The argument used to justify studies into software startups is that they differ from conventional firms, making the findings of such studies not (fully) applicable to them. Thus, studies seeking to understand how and whether startups differ from conventional firms are useful in this area.

3 Research Framework: Cynefin

To analyze our data, we utilize an existing theory: the Cynefin framework. Cynefin (Fig. 1) is a decision-making tool from the field of knowledge management and complexity science [6]. It a sense-making tool intended to help its users understand the current context they are in. It presents a typology for decision-making situations.

The Cynefin framework splits decisions into five domains. The domains are based on the assumption of order, i.e., perceived causality of cause and effect. Each domain contains characteristics describing decisions in that domain, recommended actions for decision-making in that domain, and what type of practices should be used in it.

For example, the *chaotic* domain is characterized by a lack of perceivable cause and effect relations, as well as time pressure. The recommended actions are act, sense, and respond. I.e., one has to act quickly in order to establish some facts (sense) after which one has to respond to the situation again. This continues iteratively until it is possible to exit the chaotic domain. Crisis management situations are typical examples of chaos.

In addition to the four main domains, *disorder* refers to a situation where the domain is unclear, necessitating further analysis of the situation.

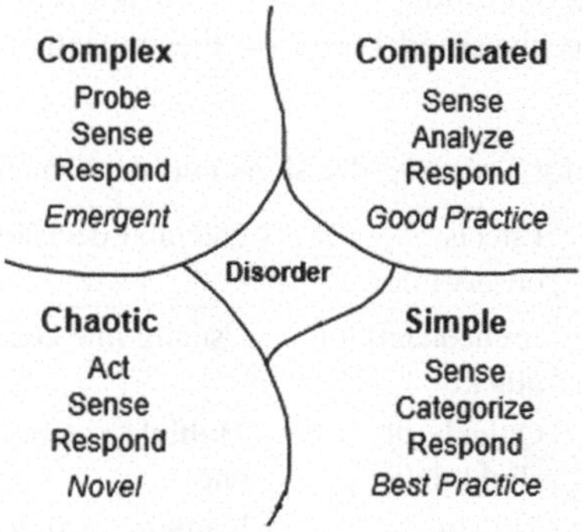

Fig. 1. The cynefin framework [6]

4 Research Methodology and Case Description

This study was carried out as a single in-depth case study, in an ethnography-inspired fashion. One of the authors worked as the founder of a software startup while collecting data. The case startup (from here on out Startup A) was founded in early 2018 by an inexperienced founder. Startup A produces a software service via a dedicated hardware solution: a wristband that would act as a replacement for business cards. Initially, it was unclear whether the company would develop only the software, or the hardware as well. The case startup is a real-life startup not founded to carry out this study.

The data collection started when the founder was the sole member of the team and the startup only had an idea to its name. Data from the case was collected from 30 April to 30 October 2018, in the form of video diary entries. Each evening, the founder produced a video recording detailing each decision they had made that day, or since the previous entry, along with detailing the current situation of Startup A. Occasionally, entries were produced less regularly, either because no decisions were made, or because the founder was not working on the startup e.g. during a weekend.

The recordings were later transcribed for analysis. These transcripts included a full transcript of each entry and a list of every decision discussed in each entry. From the transcripts, all decisions (136 total) were extracted into a list, which was then analyzed using the Cynefin framework (Sect. 3). Each decision was evaluated and placed into the corresponding domain according to the criteria described in Table 1.

In order to increase the rigor of the analysis, we followed the protocol below:

1. Author A (founder) categorizes the data and provides reasoning for each choice.
2. Author B categorizes the data independently, without seeing A's analysis.
3. Author B compares the results of their analysis with those of Author A.
4. Decisions classified into the same category by Authors A and B are included for analysis (89 decisions, 65,4% of the total 136).

5. Author B studies the reasoning provided by Author A in the case of conflicting classifications (47 decisions, 34,6% of the total 136), and either changes their classifications by agreeing with Author A or continues to disagree.
6. Author C discusses the remaining conflicts with B (22. 16,2% of 136 total).
7. Remaining conflicts are classified based on the consensus of Authors B and C.

Table 1. Criteria for assigning decisions into the Cynefin main domains.

	Decision speed	Effects observable	Potential decisions	Key action
Simple	Fast	Immediately or quickly	Usually one correct one	Categorize
Complicated	Slow	Quickly or slight delay	Multiple potentially correct ones	Analyze
Complex	(Very) slow	Slowly	Numerous, difficult to choose good ones	Experiment
Chaotic	Fast	Immediately or quickly	No correct option, minimize risks	Act

5 Results

This section is split into five subsections according to the Cynefin domains. In our analysis, we highlight key observations in the form of Primary Empirical Conclusions (PEC), which we then discuss in the discussion section. Each subsection contains some examples of decisions and the full list of decisions is on FigShare[1].

5.1 Simple Domain

Out of 136 decisions, 36 were simple. Indeed, an early-stage startup faces many tasks that can be considered universal for small firms, such as setting up a company website and social media profiles, as well as creating a logo. A new firm, startup or not, has to carry out a large number of menial tasks.

Aside from such decisions relevant for virtually any startup, Startup A also made various context-specific simple decisions. These included setting up meetings with organizations belonging to the local startup ecosystem, dressing up for said meetings, and creating a calendar for the team in order to keep track of events.

However, many simple decisions led to further decisions that were complicated or even complex in nature. The decision to set up a website is simple because it is a best practice but deciding on what content to put on the website requires analysis.

[1] https://doi.org/10.6084/m9.figshare.8298008.v1.

5.2 Complicated Domain

Out of 136 decisions, 46 were complicated. These complicated decisions required capabilities from different areas of business and IT. For an early-stage startup with a small team, finding the required capabilities can be challenging, as was the case here. The inexperience of Startup A's team made many of the complicated decisions more resource intensive. E.g., the team did not know how to find a limited company and thus had to devote resources towards studying how to.

PEC1: Inexperience increases the workload of a software startup team, contributing to the lack of resources typically associated with software startups.

Indeed, many of the complicated decisions were related to resource allocation. The team constantly weighed between different funding options, trying to analyze which ones were the most likely to yield funding if applied for. As funding applications required time to prepare, this further aggravated the lack of resources.

PEC2: A lack of financial resources contributes towards a lack of resources in terms of person-hours.

Startup A was able to tackle some of the complicated issues with the capabilities they had. However, they occasionally had to learn new skills (designing), enlist outside help (video making), or hire new team members (programming). Issues related to team capabilities were prominent in Startup A in the complex and complicated domains.

5.3 Complex Domain

Out of 136 decisions, only 21 were complex (15,4%). Complex decisions require experimentation and cannot be consistently solved with existing good or best practices.

PEC3: Only a small portion of the decisions (very) early stage software startups make requires experimentation over analytical decision-making based on existing good or best practices

Many complex decisions made by Startup A were related to funding. Startup A was constantly balancing between different funding options with no clear way to determine the most likely successful one. The team was eventually forced to pursue funding options that would have yielded funding the fastest. Some of the sources of funding also had conflicting requirements (e.g. requiring a limited company (to not exist yet)).

PEC4: A lack of financial resources notably increases the level of uncertainty experienced by a software startup.

Aside from funding, Startup A operated in a complex environment in relation to their service. Lacking hardware capabilities, they struggled to devise a technical MVP. With no technical MVP, they were forced to experiment with other ways of validation (e.g. surveys), and with no funding, they found it hard to experiment with existing hardware.

PEC5: A lack of technical know-how in the team is a critical issue for software startups and increases the uncertainty experienced by a software startup.

5.4 Chaotic Domain

No decisions were categorized as chaotic. Startup A never experienced time pressure that necessitated acting without experimentation or analysis. Though they struggled with funding, they had never paid themselves salaries and thus it was simply their normal situation. It is, nonetheless, arguably possible for a software startup to find itself in a chaotic situation in relation to funding e.g. upon failing to pay salaries.

PEC6: Software startups do not operate in a predominantly chaotic environment.

5.5 Disorder

Disorder is highly context-specific and difficult to identify retrospectively. Only some personal time management decisions of the founder were classified under disorder (e.g. whether to work weekends). Unforeseen events, fatigue, and one's own mood can affect such decisions, making it difficult to decide in advance what to do on such a high level.

6 Discussion

We have underlined our Primary Empirical Conclusions (PEC) in Table 2. In this section, we discuss each of them in relation to extant literature.

Table 2. Primary empirical conclusions based on analysis of the data

#	PEC description (from analysis section)
1	Inexperience increases the workload of a software startup team, contributing to the lack of resources typically associated with software startups
2	A lack of financial resources contributes towards a lack of resources in terms of person-hours
3	Only a small portion of the decisions (very) earlystage software startups make requires experimentation over analytical decision-making based on existing good or best practices
4	A lack of financial resources notably increases the level of uncertainty experienced by a software startup
5	A lack of technical know-how in the team is a critical issue for software startups and increases the uncertainty experienced by a software startup
6	Software startups do not operate in a predominantly chaotic environment

We identified no chaos in the case startup (PEC6). This contradicts extant literature that has suggested that software startups operate in a chaotic environment in the context of Cynefin. One of the papers that originally suggested that startups operate in a chaotic environment dates back to 1998 [2]. While this may have been the case in 1998, we now understand startups better based on both practice and research. E.g., startups now have good practices to utilize and startup entrepreneurship is taught in universities.

Indeed, software startups also do not seem to operate under as much uncertainty as is typically attributed to them. Only 15,4% of the decisions of Startup A were considered complex, and to thus involve notable levels of uncertainty, while the rest could be solved with good or best practices (PEC3). However, not all decisions are equal. Some decisions may have much larger impacts on the future of the firm than others. Moreover, the case startup was a very early stage one still working on the first version of its service. This may not be the case in more mature startups that have progressed further. Finally, chaotic situations are arguably possible in software startups (e.g. if a startup that has already been paying salaries runs out of funding), even if none were present in the case startup. However, software startups hardly seem characterized by chaos.

In this study, most of the uncertainty experienced by Startup A stemmed from (1) lack capabilities in the team, and (2) lack of funding. Extant research has studied team present from the start if they are required [9]. Our findings support this notion. However, problems related to securing technical know-how are not unique to startups[2].

The missing hardware capabilities quickly began to cause issues for Startup A as they struggled to validate their service idea, unable to develop an MVP. With no funding, they also found it difficult to experiment with hardware solutions. All in all, this resulted in an unreasonably long development cycle for an initial version of the product, which has been considered a key anti-pattern in software startups [4].

As for the lack of resources also experienced by Startup A, Klotins [3] recently argued that existing literature does not provide convincing arguments to support the uniqueness of startups in this regard. Our data does point towards software startups being unique in how they experience lack of resources (financial, person-hours). Lacking funding, startup A had to devote notable amounts of resources towards securing some (PEC4), which, due to their small team size, resulted in less resources being available for productive activities, e.g. programming (PEC2). A mature business would not task its developers with writing funding applications while lacking financial resources.

Finally, the inexperience of Startup A's team contributed to their lack of resources (PEC1). With no entrepreneurship experience, they were forced to devote resources towards e.g. studying different legal company forms. An experienced founder and team will arguably devote less time towards such menial activities, letting the team devote more resources towards productive activities. This supports extant literature which has linked business and technical experience with success in software startups [12]. Our findings help us better understand *why* this is the case.

6.1 Limitations of the Study

The single case approach is a limitation to the generalizability of the results. However, even a single case study can be enough to form a theory and is especially appropriate for new topic areas [1]. We do not consider our results conclusive and encourage further studies in the area. Moreover, data for this study were collected from the business-oriented founder, likely limiting the amount of SE-related decisions in the data.

[2] E.g., https://yle.fi/uutiset/3-10669492 ("More than 10 000 open programmer positions, but no one to fill them").

We also underline three limitations in the Cynefin framework: (1) it is a decision-making framework for making sense of a situation rather than a categorizing tool for retrospective use as we have done here; (2) the subjective perception of an expert can make a complicated decision seem simple; and (3) the level of detail is important in categorization (e.g. deciding on applying funding vs. actually doing so). We have tackled the second limitation by conducting the analysis with three authors.

7 Conclusions

In this paper, we have conducted a single, in-depth case study of a software startup in an ethnography-inspired fashion. Based on our results, we argue that software startups are not characterized by a *unique* uncertainty, or chaos. The sources of uncertainty faced by the case startup (lack of financial resources and team capabilities, as well as idea validation) are issues any new or even mature business can face. However, a mature business might tackle these issues differently.

To summarize our findings into practical implications, we underline the importance of: (i) understanding what capabilities are needed in the team, and aiming to secure them early on; and (ii) inexperienced software startup founders understanding the need to study various practical entrepreneurship skills (e.g. how to find a limited company).

Finally, we encourage further research into what makes startups unique. Aside from uncertainty, various other characteristics have been attributed to software startups (see Introduction). Out of these characteristics, the uniqueness of startups in relation to failure rates, lack of (SE) experience, innovativeness, and (external/market) time pressure lack empirical support [3]. E.g. most startups fail, but so do most new firms [3].

References

1. Eisenhardt, K.M.: Building theories from case study research. Acad. Manag. Rev. **14**(4), 532–550 (1989)
2. Eisenhardt, K.M., Brown, S.L.: Time pacing: competing in markets that won't stand still. Harv. Bus. Rev. **76**, 59–70 (1998)
3. Klotins, E.: Software start-ups through an empirical lens: are start-ups snowflakes? In Proceedings of the International Workshop on Software-intensive Business: Start-Ups, Ecosystems and Platforms (SiBW) (2018)
4. Klotins, E., Unterkalmsteiner, M., Gorschek, T.: Software engineering antipatterns in start-ups. IEEE Softw. **36**, 118–126 (2019)
5. Krisnan, V., Ulrich, K.T.: Product development decisions: a review of the literature. Manag. Sci. **47**(1), 1–21 (2001)
6. Kurtz, C.F., Snowden, D.J.: The new dynamics of strategy: Sensemaking in a complex and complicated world. IBM Syst. J. **42**(3), 462–483 (2003)
7. Nguyen-Duc, A., Seppänen, P., Abrahamsson, P.: Hunter-Gatherer cycle: a conceptual model of the evolution of software startups. In: Proceedings of the 2015 International Conference on Software and System Process, pp. 199–203 (2015)

8. Paternoster, N., Giardino, C., Unterkalmsteiner, M., Gorschek, T., Abrahamsson, P.: Software development in startup companies: a systematic mapping study. Inf. Softw. Technol. **56**, 1200–1218 (2014)
9. Seppänen, Pertti, Liukkunen, Kari, Oivo, Markku: Little big team: acquiring human capital in software startups. In: Felderer, Michael, Méndez Fernández, Daniel, Turhan, Burak, Kalinowski, Marcos, Sarro, Federica, Winkler, Dietmar (eds.) PROFES 2017. LNCS, vol. 10611, pp. 280–296. Springer, Cham (2017). https://doi.org/10.1007/978-3-319-69926-4_20
10. Unterkalmsteiner, M., et al.: Software startups – a research agenda. e-Informatica Softw. Eng. J. **10**(1), 89–123 (2016)
11. Wang, X., Edison, H., Bajwa, S.S., Giardino, C., Abrahamsson, P.: Key challenges in software startups across life cycle stages. In: Proceedings of the 2016 International Conference on Agile Software Development, pp. 169–182, May 2016
12. Zhang, J.: The advantage of experienced start-up founders in venture capital acquisition: evidence from serial entrepreneurs. Small Bus. Econ. **36**(2), 187–208 (2011)

Customer Churn Prediction in B2B Contexts

Iris Figalist[1](✉), Christoph Elsner[1], Jan Bosch[2], and Helena Holmström Olsson[3]

[1] Corporate Technology, Siemens AG, 81739 Munich, Germany
{iris.figalist,christoph.elsner}@siemens.com
[2] Department of Computer Science and Engineering, Chalmers University of Technology, Hörselgången 11, 412 96 Göteborg, Sweden
jan.bosch@chalmers.se
[3] Department of Computer Science and Media Technology, Malmö University, Nordenskiöldsgatan, 211 19 Malmö, Sweden
helena.holmstrom.olsson@mau.se

Abstract. While business-to-customer (B2C) companies, in the telecom sector for instance, have been making use of customer churn prediction for many years, churn prediction in the business-to-business (B2B) domain receives much less attention in existing literature. Nevertheless, B2B-specific characteristics, such as a lower number of customers with much higher transactional values, indicate the importance of identifying potentially churning customers. To achieve this, we implemented a prediction model for customer churn within a B2B software product and derived a model based on the results. For one, we present an approach that enables the mapping of customer- and end-user-data based on "customer phases" which allows the prediction model to take all critical influencing factors into consideration. In addition to that, we introduce a B2B customer churn prediction process based on the proposed data mapping.

Keywords: Customer churn prediction · B2B · Data analysis

1 Introduction

Data on customer behavior can provide valuable insights on future decisions made by a customer. Churn prediction models, for instance, identify customers "who stop using a product or service" [11]. This is of high interest to product providers since a large number of churning customers not only leads to a loss of revenue but can also have a negative impact on a company's reputation [14].

While the field of customer churn prediction is well-researched in the business-to-customer (B2C) domain, it receives much less attention in business-to-business (B2B) contexts [7]. The number of customers in B2B businesses is usually significantly lower but their transactional values are often a lot higher. Therefore, single customers are of high value to a company and the impact of

S. Hyrynsalmi et al. (Eds.): ICSOB 2019, LNBIP 370, pp. 378–386, 2019.
https://doi.org/10.1007/978-3-030-33742-1_30

losing one is much bigger [12]. This backs up the relevance of customer churn prediction in B2B contexts. However, approaches developed for B2C systems can often not be applied in B2B environments due to their complex setups. For instance, the customer buying a product is not necessarily the actual user of the product. While the customer makes the final decision of a purchase, the decision is to some extent influenced by the end-users.

For this reason, we conducted an exploratory study to answer the following research questions: (1) How can customer churn be predicted in B2B contexts while taking B2B-specific characteristics into consideration?; and (2) How can customer data as well as end-user data be combined in order to take all influencing factors into consideration?

In order to address these questions, we implemented a customer churn prediction model in a real-world product and derived the approach presented in this paper from the instantiation of the respective solutions. Specifically, we developed an approach that enables the mapping of end-user and usage data to customer data based on so called *customer phases* resulting in a shared data set that forms the basis of the prediction process. The shared data set is then used as the input for the prediction model itself.

The contribution of this paper is two-fold: First, we provide an approach for overcoming the challenge of combining and mapping data of different stakeholders who, either directly or indirectly, influence a certain decision, such as the purchasing behavior of a product's customers. Second, we present a step-wise process that enables the prediction of customer churn in a B2B context based on customer- as well as end-user-data by using the previously mapped data as input for the prediction model.

The remainder of this paper is structured as follows: Sect. 2 gives an overview of related work in this area, before we elaborate the research method as well as the research context in Sect. 3. In Sect. 4, we describe the implementational details of our approach. The results of our study are presented in Sect. 5, followed by a conclusion in Sect. 6 including a discussion on the generalizability of our approach.

2 Related Work

Oftentimes, subscriber data required for churn prediction models changes dynamically over time. This results in the need to retrain prediction models on a regular basis in order to "overcome data staleness and inconsistency" [16]. Moreover, most data sets in this area of applications are highly imbalanced in relation to class distribution. Precisely, the rate of accepting an offer is often much lower than the rate of a declined offer [16]. Since we discovered the same characteristics in our data set, we resampled it to overcome the imbalance as proposed by [16] or [15]. Additionally to retrain the model iteratively, we propose an approach based on different customer phases that depict the commonly changing behavior for each customer over time in the purchasing process.

Ullah et al. [13] propose an approach for customer churn prediction in the telecom sector (B2C) that additionally provides the reason or factors behind the churning of customers in order to derive retention strategies. Lastly, the k-means algorithm groups the customers into one of three categories (low, medium, or high) resembling their respective risk of churn. Recommendation systems can then propose strategies that worked on similarly behaving customers, using a collaborative approach [13]. In order to being able to act upon certain predictions, it is critical to know and understand the underlying factors of a churning customer. However, the perceived value of a product differs between B2C and B2B customers [9]. We, therefore, decided to tag the identified factors as either *customer factors* or *end-user factors*.

While the majority of studies in this area investigate business-to-customer (B2C) relationships, Kandeil et al. [8] use the outcome of the LRFM (Length, Recency, Frequency, Monetary) analysis [1,6] to cluster customers in a business-to-business (B2B) setting into different categories. These results can be used as a basis for customized marketing strategies [8]. Related to this, Jahromi et al. [7] use data mining techniques to predict churn of customers in a B2B non-contractual environment. Based on their predictions, they developed a retention campaign to maximize a company's profit. The case product in our study is in the contractual domain and the type of features used for classification go beyond the core customer behavior resembled by LRFM but also include the end-users' interaction with the product.

3 Research Method and Case Context

We chose to inductively derive the approach presented in this paper from instantiating it in a real-world product [5]. Specifically, we interviewed three stakeholders of a B2B software product provider in order to identify their challenges related to B2B customer churn prediction. Additionally, we examined their database and data structures to get an understanding of B2B-specific data characteristics. We strengthen the generalizability of these characteristics by comparing them to other B2B cases that we have studied in earlier publications (in [4] and [3]). In a next step, we developed and implemented an approach to predict customer churn in B2B contexts while addressing the previously identified challenges and characteristics. We extract the characteristics that our approach is based upon as well as the steps we have taken during the instantiation to build a generic model for B2B customer churn prediction taking B2B-specific factors into consideration. We validate the generalizability of our model by showing that each of the characteristics and single components has also been observed in other B2B products we have worked with or have been applied in a similar context in the literature.

The product itself is the platform of a software ecosystem that is established in the healthcare domain. Multiple platform-internal as well es external applications are developed based on the platform. The platform provider offers a variety of licensing options to its customers, including basic an premium licenses as well as trial phases. The decision about a purchase is made by the respective customer, while the users of the product are typically the customer's employees.

The decision is, therefore, directly influenced by the customer and indirectly influenced by the end-users of the product.

4 Implementation

In order to derive an approach for customer churn prediction in B2B contexts, we implemented a churn prediction model for a real-world B2B software product (see Sect. 3). We start by identifying questions and hypotheses related to churn, before exploring the available data and generating a shared feature set comprising both customer- and end-user data. Finally, we preprocess the data set, train the prediction model and evaluate and interpret the results. All (case-specific) implementation details of our approach will be provided in the following subsections.

4.1 Data Preparation

Before starting to implement the prediction approach, we conducted several unstructured interview sessions with a product owner, an operations engineer, and a data analyst of the platform's development teams. They provided us valuable insights on the available data, the platform provider's interactions and relationships with their customers as well as important events in the lifecycle of each customer. During the interviews the platform provider revealed a strong interest in the evolvement of customer and user behavior over time as well as the impact of features in different points in time. Therefore, we start by identifying the steps or phases that each customer goes through from registration to making a decision (churn vs. non-churn). Next, we process and extract the available platform data, before mapping it to the defined phases.

Customer Phases. In order to identify all relevant events that constitute the frame for the phases, we interviewed three stakeholders of the platform who provided us insights on the important events and phases each customer goes through from registration to the decision on whether to stick with a premium license or not. As a result, the first phase *"Onboarding"* covers the interval between the registration date of a customer and the effective date of that customer's basic license. At any later point in time, the customer can choose to enter a trial period during which its users can experience the premium features of a product. The second phase *"Basic"*, therefore, comprises the time between a customer's basic license effective date to the starting date of the trial period of that specific customer. At the end of that trial period, the customer needs to decide whether to keep the premium version of the product (non-churn) or whether to go back to the basic license (churn). Additionally, one of the interviewees hypothesis was that the last couple of days or week before the trial period expires have a greater impact on the decision than the weeks before that. For this reason, we decided to split up that time frame into two phases: *"Trial"* and *"Pre-Decision"*. The *pre-decision phase* starts ten days before the trial period expires. In order to validate the defined phases, we presented them to the interviewees once again who approved the described customer phases.

Data Extraction. The product's database stores four different types of data. For one, each table is either related to the *customer* or the *end-user* of the product. Second, the data can either be *static* (e.g. a customer's registration date) or *dynamic* (e.g. number of logins per day). Moreover, multiple measures (*direct* metrics) can be combined to generate *derived* metrics that also hold valuable information. Table 1 gives an overview of all extracted features organized by its type.

In order to generate a mapped data set that constitutes the foundation of our prediction approach, we define the time attribute as the main mapping criterion, specifically the customer phases. In a first step, all static features identified during the data selection and related to either the customer or the user of a customer are extracted and linked to the respective customer ID. Following this, the timeframes of each of the defined customer phases are extracted for each customer individually to generate a customer-specific timeline. Based on this, each of the dynamic features are extracted for each of the computed customer phases, and are, again, linked to their respective customer ID.

Table 1. Extracted features per type

	Customer data		User/Usage data	
	Static	Dynamic	Static	Dynamic
Direct	Purchase info	avg. uptime of receiver avg. downtime of receiver # of affiliated users		avg. time since registration
Derived	Time between registration & basic license	Availability of receiver (computed by uptime and errors)	avg. time between registration & affiliation	avg. # of logins per day avg. # of sessions per day avg. # of sessions per type, avg. # of uploads per day
Extraction Type	Once	Per phase	Once	Per phase

4.2 Prediction Model

In order to train our prediction model, we preprocessed the mapped data set into a labeled input data set by removing rows with missing values, standardizing the columns and adding a label for each customer on whether they downgraded to the basic license or not (binary classification).

We apply a feature selection technique [2] to the data set in order to identify the most relevant features for training the prediction model. As a result 25 out of 50 features are selected for further processing. The input data set is split up into a training data set (80%) and a test data set (20%). Next, we build a neural network using the 25 selected input features, one target variable and two hidden layers with twelve nodes each. We set the number of epochs to 300 and the batch size to ten before training the model. Finally, we evaluate our model by predicting the output variable of the test data set, achieving an accuracy of 88% with a precision of 0.89 and recall of 0.91.

5 Derived Data Mapping Model and Prediction Process

On an abstract level, the implementation of our study relies on two core mechanisms: (1) the generation of a mapped data set that combines customer as well as user/usage data by linking their respective behavior to shared customer phases; and (2) the construction of a process for predicting customer churn decisions based on the previously generated data set. Based on our implementation, we derive a generic model for both of these mechanisms which will be explained in a greater detail in the following subsections.

5.1 Data Mapping

One important characteristic of B2B businesses is the differentiation between customer and end-user. While the customer is behind the purchase of the product, the customer's customer or employee is the one using it [8]. The benefits and, therefore, perceived value of a product or feature is different for each of the stakeholders [9]. In previous studies [3,4] we worked with four different platform providers established in various B2B businesses, including the one studied in this paper. While investigating the communication structures, we found that even though the customers and end-users are two individual entities, they still share direct communication channels. As a result, an end-user's dissatisfaction might indirectly influence a customer's decision to renew, or not renew, a contract. We, therefore, argue that it is beneficial to also take end-user data into consideration when implementing churn prediction models for B2B businesses. This, however, results in the need for a shared data structure or data mapping. We propose a model that enables the mapping of customer- as well as end-user-data based on *customer phases.* For any type of product, customers usually trigger a series of product-specific events (e.g. registration, purchase, renewing a contract etc.). Customer phases are the timeframes between such events and serve as a basis for our mapping approach. The approach itself consists of three steps: the definition of customer phases, data selection, and data processing.

Step I: Definition of Customer Phases. Using customer phases as the main mapping criterion has two advantages. For one, it makes it easy to link customer as well as end-user behavior to each phase simply based on the timestamps. In addition to that, it can portray changes in behaviors over time and include these changes in the prediction model. In order to define the customer phases, we start by identifying the steps or phases that all customers go through before they make a decision to churn or not to churn. Oftentimes a series of events serves as the frame for the phases.

Step II: Data Selection. On an abstract level, each feature in the data set can be characterized by three different attributes. For one, a data point can either be related to the **customer** or the **end-user**. Furthermore, each data point can either be characterized as **static** or **dynamic**. Static data holds information that does not change over time. Dynamic data points, however, are dependent on their either pre-defined or event-driven recorded point of time. Lastly, some data points can be extracted as **direct metrics**, while other data points can be combined and further processed into **derived metrics**.

Step III: Data Processing. Based on the preceding steps, the data is now processed into a shared data model (see Fig. 1). We define the time attribute as the main mapping criterion, specifically the customer phases. First, all static features related to either the customer or the user of a customer are extracted and linked to the respective customer ID (see yellow boxes at top & bottom in Fig. 1). Derived metrics are computed by further processing one or more direct metrics. Following this, the timeframes of each of the defined customer phases are extracted for each customer individually to generate a customer-specific timeline (see *Customer Phases* in Fig. 1). Based on this, each of the dynamic features are extracted for each of the computed customer phases (see green boxes above and below customer phases in Fig. 1). After a customer passes through all the phases, it needs to decide for or against churning.

5.2 Prediction Process

The previously generated mapped data set is crucial to the entire prediction process since it serves as the input data of the procedure. Initially, the input data set is turned into a labeled data set by (a) mapping previous decision outcomes (churn or non-churn) to the respective customer ID; (b) cleaning, standardizing, and resampling the data; and (c) applying appropriate feature selection techniques [2] to identify the relevant feature set. Based on the labeled data set, a classification technique can be applied in order to train a prediction model.

In order to enable customer churn prediction in B2B contexts, we combine our data mapping approach with the described prediction procedure. Figure 2 shows the generic model we derived during our study. It consists of the following steps (linked to numbers in model): **S1–3:** Relevant metrics are identified and extracted by following the data mapping approach presented in Sect. 5.1. All metrics based on static data are extracted once for each customer while all metrics based on dynamic data are extracted for each phase and customer. All extracted metrics are combined to a shared data set. **S4–5:** The previously generated data set is then labeled (churn vs. non-churn) based on the previous decision of the customers. After preprocessing (standardizing, resampling,

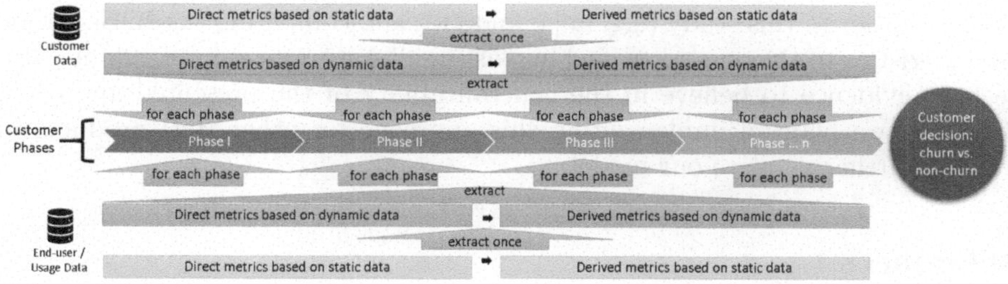

Fig. 1. Overview of the mapping approach based on customer phases (Color figure online)

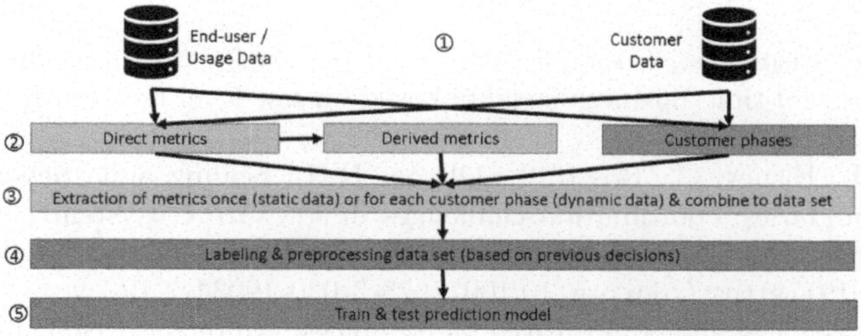

Fig. 2. Prediction process

feature selection etc.) the data set, it can be used as the input to train a prediction model. Ultimately, our model enables practitioners to predict customer churn based on customer- as well as end-user-data, thereby taking all influencing factors into consideration.

6 Conclusion

Single customers of B2B businesses are often of greater importance compared to B2C businesses since their number is typically much lower [12] but their transactional value is much higher [10]. Losing even one might have a significant impact on the provider of B2B products [12]. While this reinforces the importance of customer churn prediction in B2B contexts, there is a lack of research on how to achieve this [7].

The goal of this exploratory study was to investigate how to perform customer churn prediction in B2B contexts while taking B2B-specific characteristics into consideration. We implemented this in a real-world product and derived a two-stage process that consists of building a shared data model as well as the prediction process itself. During the data mapping, a shared data set of customer- as well as end-user-data is generated based on customer phases. This data set is then used as input for the prediction model.

One of the limitations and threat to validity of this study is the number of investigated cases. However, after working with multiple other B2B product providers prior to this study (e.g. in [4] and [3]), and comparing the B2B-specific characteristics to the ones identified in existing literature (e.g. in [8,12], or [10]), we have evidence to believe in the generalizability of the presented approach. Moreover, we plan on implementing this approach for other B2B products in order to further validate our model.

References

1. Chang, H., Tsay, S.: Integrating of SOM and K-mean in data mining clustering: an empirical study of CRM and profitability evaluation (2004)
2. Dash, M., Liu, H.: Feature selection for classification. Intell. Data Anal. **1**(3), 131–156 (1997)
3. Figalist, I., Elsner, C., Bosch, J., Olsson, H.H.: Business as unusual: a model for continuous real-time business insights based on low level metrics. In: Proceedings of SEAA. IEEE (2019)
4. Figalist, I., Elsner, C., Bosch, J., Olsson, H.H.: Scaling agile beyond organizational boundaries: coordination challenges in software ecosystems. In: Kruchten, P., Fraser, S., Coallier, F. (eds.) XP 2019. LNBIP, vol. 355, pp. 189–206. Springer, Cham (2019). https://doi.org/10.1007/978-3-030-19034-7_12
5. Goddard, W., Melville, S.: Research Methodology: An Introduction. Juta and Company Ltd., Cape Town (2004)
6. Hughes, A.M.: Strategic Database Marketing. McGraw-Hill Pub, Co., New York (2005)
7. Jahromi, A.T., Stakhovych, S., Ewing, M.: Managing B2B customer churn, retention and profitability. Ind. Mark. Manag. **43**(7), 1258–1268 (2014)
8. Kandeil, D.A., Saad, A.A., Youssef, S.M.: A two-phase clustering analysis for B2B customer segmentation. In: Proceedings of INCoS, pp. 221–228. IEEE (2014)
9. Mencarelli, R., Riviere, A.: Perceived value in B2B and B2C: a comparative approach and cross-fertilization. Mark. Theory **15**(2), 201–220 (2015)
10. Rauyruen, P., Miller, K.E.: Relationship quality as a predictor of B2B customer loyalty. J. Bus. Res. **60**(1), 21–31 (2007)
11. Sajjadi, S.: Introduction to churn prediction in Python (2018). https://www.datascience.com/blog/churn-prediction-python. Accessed 11 Sept 2019
12. Stevens, R.P.: B-to-B customer retention: seven strategies for keeping your customers. White Paper (2005). http://www.ruthstevens.com/
13. Ullah, I., Raza, B., Malik, A.K., Imran, M., Islam, S.U., Kim, S.W.: A churn prediction model using random forest: analysis of machine learning techniques for churn prediction and factor identification in telecom sector. IEEE Access **7**, 60134–60149 (2019)
14. Verbeke, W., Martens, D., Mues, C., Baesens, B.: Building comprehensible customer churn prediction models with advanced rule induction techniques. Expert. Syst. Appl. **38**(3), 2354–2364 (2011)
15. Wang, S., Liu, W., Wu, J., Cao, L., Meng, Q., Kennedy, P.J.: Training deep neural networks on imbalanced data sets. In: Proceedings of IJCNN, pp. 4368–4374. IEEE (2016)
16. Yan, L., Wolniewicz, R.H., Dodier, R.: Predicting customer behavior in telecommunications. IEEE Intell. Syst. **19**(2), 50–58 (2004)

Online Multiplayer Games for Crowdsourcing the Development of Digital Assets

The Case of Ingress

Samuli Laato[1,2], Sonja M. Hyrynsalmi[1(✉)], and Mauri Paloheimo[3]

[1] Department of Future Technologies, University of Turku, Turku, Finland
{sadala,smnyla}@utu.fi
[2] Department of Teacher Education, University of Turku, Turku, Finland
[3] Faculty of Humanities, University of Turku, Turku, Finland
mailpa@utu.fi

Abstract. Crowdsourcing has emerged as a cost-efficient solution for companies to resolve certain tasks requiring vast amounts of human input. In order to motivate participants to harness their best efforts for the crowdsourcing task, companies are gamifying or creating complete games around crowdsourcing problems. The location-based game Ingress integrated the development of a geographically distributed database of points of interest in its game design. Players submitted and later peer-reviewed PoI candidates for Niantic for free, who then used the crowd-sourced database as backbone for such popular games as Pokémon GO and Harry Potter: Wizards Unite. This study analyzes the solution in Ingress from two main perspectives: (1) how the game motivates players to participate in the crowdsourcing tasks and (2) how crowdsourcing fits into the game creator Niantic's revenue model. The results show that Ingress players are provided multi-layered motivation to participate in crowdsourcing. The crowdsourcing tasks influence the game world, but are not limited inside it, and can be used elsewhere. Adopting crowd-sourcing as a business strategy has served Niantic well, making Niantic an international multi-billion dollar company. Therefore it is predicted that more online multiplayer games implementing crowdsourcing as a revenue stream are likely to emerge in the near future.

Keywords: Crowdsourcing · Revenue stream · Location-based games · Ingress

1 Introduction

From the viewpoint of business, crowdsroucing is a sourcing model where part-products or services are produced by outsourced companies and/or individuals [1]. Typically crowdsourcing refers to externalizing the development of tasks requiring human input to a large disconnected crowd of people [2].

S. Hyrynsalmi et al. (Eds.): ICSOB 2019, LNBIP 370, pp. 387–401, 2019.
https://doi.org/10.1007/978-3-030-33742-1_31

Recently, crowdsourcing the development of digital assets has gained popularity as a more prominent part of companies' business model [3]. Successful crowdsourcing project rely on maintaining the participants' motivation, either intrinsic, extrinsic or both [4–8]. One of the most common extrinsic motivators for participating in crowdsourcing is money, and, platforms such as the Amazon Mechanical Turk provide crowdsourcing services in exchange for a monetary compensation [9,10]. This has lead to some scholars making predictions that participating in crowdsourced projects might be considered an employment in the future [11,12], and therefore, unsurprisingly, participants in for-profit crowdsourced projects have been found to be more extrinsically motivated [12]. However, recent studies highlight the importance of intrinsic motivation, especially in more complex crowdsourced projects, for good outcomes [13]. Intrinsic motivation is also cheaper to maintain, assuming that the main way to provide extrinsic motivation is money [14], and therefore, several crowdsourced projects have consorted to gamification, that is, the usage of game design elements in non-game contexts [15], in their crowdsourcing projects [16–18].

Moving beyond simple gamification such as awarding points for participating in crowdsourcing [13], recently, several popular multiplayer online games have emerged where players are tasked to create playable content for each other such as Super Mario Maker [19], Minecraft [20] and Ingress [21]. In the first two cases, the created content remains, at least mostly, context-specific to the game where it is created, and therefore has little value outside the game. The current study makes a difference between crowdsourced digital assets that can be utilized purely in the game-context they were created, and digital assets which extend beyond the game-context into other games and possibly other applications as well. Even though creating versatile multi-purpose digital assets via online multiplayer games might be the preferable option from a business standpoint, if the crowdsourcing task is completely unrelated to the game inside which participants are recruited, they might not have the intrinsic motivation to participate [22,23]. Thus, the ideal case for utilizing crowdsourcing as a way to generate digital assets by using online multiplayer gamers as the workforce, is to tie the crowdsourcing project into the gameplay. In addition to consciously created data, other kinds of data such as players movement and behavior can also be regarded as a digital assets, even though digital assets created this way do not fall under popular definitions of crowdsourcing [2]. Nontheless, not all games are suitable crowdsourcing platforms and not all projects are suitable to be crowdsourced via online multiplayer games [24].

Niantics' Ingress, shown in Fig. 1, is an example of an online multiplayer game where the creation of certain digital assets, mainly Niantics global database of geographic points of interest (PoIs), has been succesfully crowdsourced. This database is arguably one of Niantics currently most valuable assets, being part of the backbone for such megahits as the location-based games Pokémon GO and Harry Potter: Wizards Unite [25,26]. Most PoIs in the database are submitted by Ingress players, and since 2017 have also been peer-reviewed by players [27]. A big chunk of maintenance of the Niantic PoI database is also currently crowdsourced.

The case of Ingress is interesting from a scholarly perspective as at least up until the release of Ingress Prime in 2019, the game was free, contained no ads and provided only minimal incentive to players for in-app purchases. Even though there were other revenue streams for Ingress such as selling merchandise, the game can be seen as one of the pioneering examples of online multiplayer games utilizing crowdsourcing to generate assets.

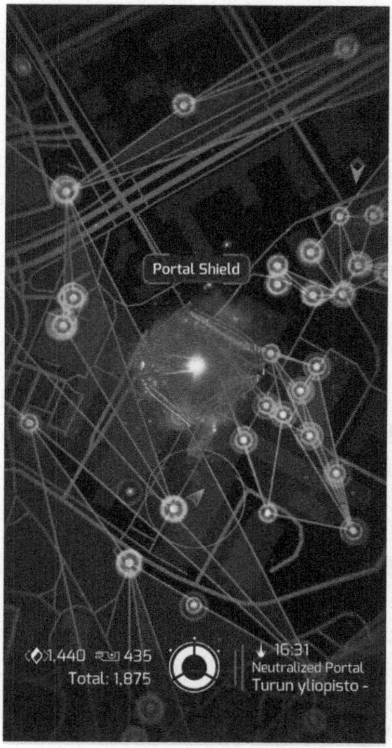

Fig. 1. A screenshot showing the main user interface of Ingress Prime.

This conceptual case study investigates crowdsourcing as a new emerging revenue stream for online multiplayer games and summarizes findings from previous studies for formulating an understand of crowdsourcing in the context of online games. Ingress is used as an example, as it is a prominent example of successfully harnessing crowdsourcing to create digital assets. Via Ingress and previous studies, the following research questions are investigated:

RQ1 How online multiplayer games, which utilize crowdsourcing, motivate players to participate in crowdsourcing?

RQ2 How Niantic has integrated crowdsourcing as a part of their revenue model?

As mainly Ingress is observed, critical evaluation is needed whether the findings translate to other games [28]. Due to the fact that both multiplayer games and crowdsourcing problems can be extremely complex, it is likely that repeating the success story of Ingress will not be a trivial challenge. However, recent studies have advanced the understanding of what makes crowdsourcing succeed to the degree where it seems now more feasible than ever to adopt in game design [18].

2 Background

2.1 Crowdsourcing as a Sourcing Model

In 2012, a study of revenue models of apps in the Android Market found free apps to generally have complex revenue models, with a single application often utilizing multiple revenue streams [29]. A closer look revealed there was no indications that any of these apps were utilizing the crowdsourced development of digital assets, however, one app relied on the donation model, which can be interpreted as a close relative of crowdsourcing [30]. It can thus be argued, that crowdsourcing in online games has only lately gained popularity. The difficulty of implementation as well as the challenge to find tasks suitable for crowdsourcing in online games are likely causes for this [31]. Furthermore, crowdsourcing is best utilized in cases where the collective wisdom of crowds outclasses that of a limited set of professionals [32].

Crowdsourcing can be divided into four categories: (1) crowdprocessing, (2) crowdsolving, (3) crowdcrating and (4) crowdcreating [33–35]. In the first two types of tasks, the value is derived from individual contributions whereas in the second two, value is derived from combining multiple solutions. Depending on the problem at hand, one or more of these can be utilized in online multiplayer games. For example, Ingress uses crowsolving for submitting new portal candidates and crowdrating for evaluating them. If a crowdsourcing task is simple, and over in short time frame, it might not be cost-effective to create an entire online multiplayer game for solving that problem, and monetary compensation for participants or simple gamification might work better. On the other hand, if the task requires a lot of focus from participants, gamification must be used with care [36]. For example, in the case of Wikipedia where participants are tasked to write, review and edit articles, the task itself is attention-demanding enough so that any additional gamification elements to the work process itself might only disrupt the flow of contributors [37].

2.2 Crowdsourcing and Gamification

Video games are a rapidly growing industry with the market size of US$ 96 billion in 2018, bypassing Hollywood as a biggest entertainment sector [38]. Gamification by definition means using game design element in non-game contexts. The origins of the term 'Gamification' dates back to the end of the first decade of

2000, the usage of the term increased explosively after mid-2010 [39]. The border between gamified application and a game is obscure, as even when the two are linked, the terms cannot co-exist because of the definition of gamification [40]. For example, it can be argued that the popular physical activity increasing location-based game Pokémon GO [41] is in fact not a game, but rather a gamified sport application.

Nowadays gamification has been successfully utilized in several crowdsourcing endeavors, and in many cases, has managed to increase engagement and participation rates [13,16,35]. Simple and straightforward tasks have generally used simple gamification tools such as points, however, more complex problems have been gamified in a more nuanced and creative fashion [13]. When discussing real games with built-in crowdsourcing, the motivating elements can be multi-layered. This can mean simple rewards such as points, but also things such as social pressure, new gameplay opportunities and gratifications from permanently influencing the game world among others [13,16]. Furthermore, people have been found to contribute more to gamified crowdsourcing systems when organized in teams, and cooperative elements increase users' willingness to recommend the crowdsource-system more, when compared to a competitive design [18]. When participating in crowdsourcing where participants create things together, motivators can include career advancement, peer recognition, contribution to a collaborative effort, self-expression, having fun, and learning new skills and knowledge [6]. Peer recognition, for example, can be highlighted in game design by showing other players what their peers have contributed.

Crowdsourcing the development of digital assets via online multiplayer games has been applied to such games as, for example, hand-crafted action and dialog generation models for a social robot [22,42] and analyzing images of infected thick blood smears [43]. From the business perspective, revenue models often consider revenue streams as money streams, however with crowdsourcing, the added value comes in the form of digital assets.

2.3 Ethical Considerations of Using Crowdsourcing in Games

As gamified crowdsourcing harnesses human resources for work, often without any need for signing legal documents, questions about the ethical aspect of such revenue model arise [44]. Can crowdsourcing potentially be utilized as means to circumvent existing legal protection for the working class? What about child labour? Transparency and quality control [45]? According to Brabham [6] motivators for participating in crowdcreating especially include contribution to a common effort among others. Thus, in addition to these pressing issues, participants in crowdsourcing projects can regard the end result as a shared property, even though it may legally be owned by a private company [6,35]. If participants consider the crowdsourced outcome as a common property, does the company with the legal rights to the created assets have a moral responsibility to keep providing participants the outcome of their work? To address the ethical concerns, four dimensions: privacy, accuracy, property and accessibility of information (PAPA) have been looked at in crowdsourcing business [46]. Participation in crowdsourcing runs the risk of exposing sensitive information to the crowdsourcing platform [47], however, with online multiplayer games this risk already exists, arguably even in greater magnitude [48]. Companies utilizing crowdsourcing should pay attention to include PAPA in their design to avoid legal and ethical misconduct [46].

The ethics of using gamification have also troubled researchers. The worries concerning gamification can be divided in two categories: *Limiting*, situations where player is optimizing the work required to complete task, or *harmful* distracting users from the main purpose of actions, issues. The dark side of gamifications can be discussed when the elements of gamification are used for example in casino environment or with game addicted people [40].

Finally, there are some risks of bias in crowdsourcing. First, there can also be large differences in who contributes to the crowdsourcing projects, with some participants perhaps working hundreds of times more than others, which can scew the outcome to the direction of those working more. In addition, there can be differences and biases in participants age, gender, situation in life and geographical location. For example, when Wikipedia's crowdsourcing was studied, a bias between men and women content creators was revealed [49]. Whenever a bias is significant, it can be questioned whether the content is biased.

3 Research Process

This study presents a conceptual analysis of crowdsourcing in the game Ingress. Ingress is a free-to-play game from the market leading company in terms of revenue in location-based games (LBGs), Niantic. Several studies have focused on the gamification of crowdsourcing [18], but analysis of success cases of crowdsourcing in online multiplayer games are missing. Ingress is ideal for this kind of a study, as the creation and partially also the maintenance of a geographically distributed global database of PoIs corresponding to real world locations was successfully outsourced to the players of the game [27]. What makes Niantic and Ingress further interesting is that there are two cases where the crowdsourced PoI database has been applied outside the context of Ingress: the LBGs Pokémon GO and Harry Potter: Wizards Unite. Thus, in the following sections the crowdsourcing solutions of Ingress are observed and analyzed and the motivating factors for participating in the crowdsourcing are derived by looking at the game design. Afterwards, crowdsourcing is looked at more broadly from the perspective of Niantics revenue model, in order to gain insight of how crowdsourcing can fit into the current video game ecosystem.

4 Case: Ingress

Ingress, initially released in November 2012 [50], is a pervasive LBG by Niantic. The gameplay revolves around travelling to PoIs called portals and linking them together to create triangles. Links between portals cannot cross existing links, and the bigger the created triangle, the more points (mind units) the player receives. The game world is shared with other players and there are two teams called factions competing against each other: Resistance and Enlightened. As Ingress is gameplay revolves around the PoIs called portals, their quality and location are important. Contrary to many other LBGs such as The Walking Dead: Our World and Jurassic World: Alive, Ingress PoIs corresponds to real world objects [51]. Many of the successful crowdsourcing projects in online multiplayer games have the game designed specifically for the crowdsourcing endeavour [23,42,43], and, as portal submissions became available right at the launch of Ingress, it is evident that crowdsourcing was embedded in the creation process of Ingress and possibly also influenced the design of the gameplay [52].

Besides crowdsourcing the development of their PoI database, Ingress allegedly monetizes itself via user data collection and their location surveillance [50]. Collecting user data and selling it onwards is becoming an increasingly popular revenue stream for online games [53–55], however, as a pervasive LBG, Ingress is able to generate data on users' movements and daily activities, something many other games are unable to do [26,50].

4.1 Crafting the Portal Network in Ingress

When Ingress launched, it contained a few pre-created PoIs as portals from the previous Niantic pilot game Field Trip and the social picture sharing platform Panoramio. Alternatively, these pre-existing candidates could have been obtained from other services such as Open Street Maps [27]. Some of the initial candidates were perhaps not entirely accurate, however, right from the beginning the evolution of the Portal Network can have been regarded as a continuous process where new candidates are being accepted and old obsolete ones are being removed. Immediately upon launch, players had the ability to submit new portal candidates for Niantic to review, but otherwise had no means to participate in the development of the PoI database. The submission screen the player sees inside their Ingress app is depicted in Fig. 2.

4.2 How Ingress Motivates Players to Participate in Crowdsourcing

Being a free to play game, Ingress provided several reasons for players to contribute portal submissions for their PoI database. These included (1) the ability to permanently influence the game world (2) the ability to create more playing opportunities in the local area (3) Obtaining score to "Seer" and (4) the willingness to support Niantic in their attempt to create a global database of cultural hotspots, among others. Soon however, Niantic became overburdened in their attempt to manually review all portal submissions and sometime around 2015–2016 the portal submission option was removed from players in several countries [27]. As a resolution, in addition to crowdsourcing the portal submission system, in 2017 Niantic released Operation Portal Recon (OPR), a browser-based system for players to peer-review the portal submissions. To motivate players to start working in OPR, Niantic gave the peer-review system a cool name

Fig. 2. A screen capture taken from the beginning of an Ingress Portal Submission using the Ingress Prime app.

and created a badge to Ingress which could be leveled up by doing OPR. The OPR system is currently handling new submissions, portal name edits, location changes and description changes which are all affected throughout all Niantic games utilizing their PoI database. However, some aspects Niantic employees are still responsible for themselves, such as portal appeals, portal removals and the acceptance of new picture submissions to existing portals. Sometime around 2018–2019 Niantic also gave Pokémon GO players the ability to submit new portal candidates [56], however only Ingress players above level 12 are allowed to review them. By limiting who can participate in crowdsourcing Niantic protects itself against possible abuse from, for example, scripted low level accounts trying to influence the crowdsourcing.

4.3 Crowdsourcing as Part of the Niantic's Revenue Model

In this section the observed revenue streams of Niantic related to the game Ingress will be looked at (Fig. 3) in the context of Karl Popp's Revenue Model model [57]. As mentioned before, Niantic currently maintains servers for three games they have developed or co-developed. Out of the three games Ingress has the largest amount of different revenue streams, even though in the light of revenue statistics, it seems to be making the least money. On the other hand, Niantic retains full ownnership of its Ingress brand, which gives them the ability to gain revenue from selling merchandise. This is contrasted by the Pokémon [58] and the Wizarding World [59] brands of which Niantic has no ownership. The estimated generated revenue of the most popular location-based mobile games during July 2019 (1 month) according to the mobile app store marketing intelligence company Sensor Tower are shown below.

- Pokémon GO 22 million USD
- Harry Potter: Wizards Unite 2 million USD
- Jurassic World: Alive 800 000 USD
- The Walking Dead: Our World 400 000 USD
- Landlord Tycoon: Real Estate Investor 50 000 USD
- Ingress Prime 20 000 USD
- Draconius GO <5000 USD

First, this data highlights the dominance of Niantic in the current LBG market. Second, it shows how Ingress created very little monetary revenue (20 000USD) compared to the other two Niantic games. However, this statistic does not take into account value received from crowdsourcing. Third, a thing to observe from the data is that the four most popular games are all based on pre-existing brands, which vaguely seem to correspond to the overall estimated value of the brand.

Looking at the observed revenue streams, partnerships are used in all thee Niantic games to attract big brands such as McDonalds and Starbucks, and they are also visible in the real life events organized by Niantic. For example, Pokemon Go Fest -events have been held in shopping centers, which have partnered with Niantic. Income from in-app purchases is the most visible revenue stream of Pokémon GO and Harry Potter: Wizards Unite. Especially with Pokemon Go, Niantic approach the potential business partnerships by telling them how often players are attracted by PoIs or how they are changing their regular walking route on a weekly basis to play Pokémon GO [60].

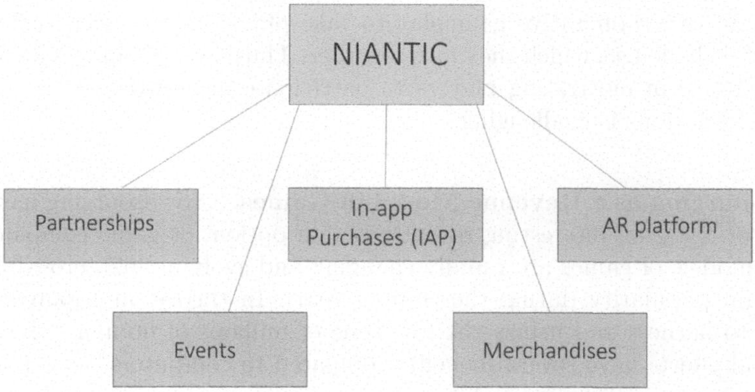

Fig. 3. Five observed revenue streams for Niantic

Currently, most of the development of the Niantic PoI database is crowdsourced and automated. This database is currently in use in three games: Ingress, Pokémon GO and Harry Potter: Wizards Unite. Out of these three games, Ingress is generating the least direct revenue whereas the other two currently make well over 20 million USD monthly. Recently Niantic launched its AR - platform, including the PoI database, for developers to rent and use as the backbone for their games [61]. One part of their business offer in AR platform is the content, which players have provided for them via Ingress. With the platform, Niantic has harnessed the content which players have created while playing, for a business outside the original game-context. It is plausible that this kind of a revenue model which utilizes crowdsourcing could also work with other gaming companies and industries. Managing, harnessing and correctly leveraging player motivation to get them contributing in crowdsourcing is the key challenge in this business approach. Designing the multiplayer online game with a specific crowdsourcing goal in mind in most cases helps the issue [42,43], as does the inclusion of collaborative multiplayer elements [18].

5 Discussion

5.1 Key Findings

Motivating Players to Participate in Crowdsourcing in Online Video Games. Online video games seem a promising platform for implementing crowdsourcing as long as a suitable crowdsourcing problem exists. The problem needs to be such that a game can be created around it so that players can be motivated to contribute. Video games can provide multi-layered motivation to contribute into crowdsourcing beyond simple gamification [13,16]. Ingress currently provided both simple direct rewards such as points for contributing both OPR reviews and portal submissions, but also higher abstraction level rewards such as recognition from peers and gratification from permanently influencing the augmented virtual world. Cooperative multiplayer elements have been recently linked to increased contributing in crowdsourcing tasks in online games [18], but for effective cooperative gameplay to take place, players need to be given meaningful challenges which they face together. Thus, even if online video games can be effetive in motivating players to participate in crowdsourcing, creating successful solutions is challenging.

Crowdsourcing as a Revenue Model in Games. Crowdsourcing has shown promise of being an interesting revenue stream option for game companies. As revenue models of games are rapidly changing and evolving [62], crowdsourcing might gain popularity during the coming years. In theory, multiplayer games are able to harness and utilize the free time of millions of humans whose computational efforts have several benefits compared to computers, especially with regards to solving complex problems or creating new assets. In order to optimize the crowdsourcing, companies might want to look at designing their games with the crowdsourcing task already in mind, to have an accordingly planned revenue model and to ensure that the gameplay seamlessly integrates with the task [42,43].

Ingress is not the only successful commercial game to leverage crowdsourcing as a means to generate income. For example, Super Mario Maker, based on the popular Super Mario platform games [63], has players create levels and upload them to a server for other players to enjoy. Studies have demonstrated that the Super Mario Games can be also used to crowdsource the development of game aesthetics [64]. These kinds of tasks share similarities with the PC modding scene [65,66] where game developers give tools for players to create all sorts of content around their core game. These kinds of co-created media [67] have been around for over 15 years, however only recently as crowdsourcing has moved beyond the context of individual games, has it become a feasible option for a revenue stream in online multiplayer games as demonstrated by Ingress.

5.2 Limitations and Issues with the Niantic Solution

The Niantic PoI database has received several criticisms, for example, for favoring major cities so that rural areas, and those inhabited by minorities, tend to have a significantly lower PoI-density [25]. There are two main reasons for this: (1) Lack of players and thus lack of support for the crowdsourced creation of portals in certain areas and (2) Causal effects of Niantics chosen PoI criteria for Ingress portals. The first reason is straightforward and has been combated by, for example, Niantic allowing Pokémon GO players to submit portals in addition to Ingress players. The second reason is more problematic, as compromising the portal criteria might result in low quality portals in well populated areas as well. Tregel et al. [27] proposed their own set of criteria with 21 priority levels to combat this issue, however, no such solution has yet been applied into practice.

There are also biases in the way OPR operates. Firstly, the system is supposed to be a blind peer-review, but at least in Finland, Ingress players have their own chats discussing how to vote for certain candidates, with instructions sometimes being against official Niantic guidelines. In addition, players might want to influence the portal network to favor themselves or to cause harm to players in the opposing faction. As portals located in places which are not easily accessible like islands can cause harm to Ingress players, OPR could show bias in accepting portal submissions in these places. However, because portals can be submitted repeatedly and players rank is punished if they vote against the general consensus, only systematic abuse of the system by several players can really influence the outcome of the peer review.

5.3 The Future of Crowdsourcing the Digital Assets in Games

Revenue models of games change fast. Every now and then a new type of revenue model emerges which disrupts the video game industry. Examples of these have been the shift from a bulk purchase price towards free-to-play games and more recently, loot boxes. Where loot boxes are quite specific to video games, with only minor applications elsewhere like gambling, crowdsourcing has mainly gained popularity outside video games and has only recently started to be gamified

[16,17] or embedded in games. Based on the success case of Ingress, it is likely that crowdsourcing will make its way into the design of many more future games as a part of their designed revenue stream.

6 Conclusion

In this study the crowdsourcing of digital assets in online multiplayer games was discussed. Results from previous studies suggest that as with many other revenue streams, crowdsourcing the creation of digital assets should be taken into account already in the design process of the online game to maximize potential. Crowdsourcing struggles constantly with how to motivate participants to contribute, and creating elaborate games around crowdsourcing problems might be a solution. Previous studies have shown that a multiplayer design, especially such which focuses on teamplay can have a positive impact on participants motivation to contribute to the crowdsourcing task [18]. Ingress provided players multilayered motivation to contribute in the crowdsourcing tasks from simple gamification elements such as rewarding points to higher abstraction level rewards such as recognition from peers or gratification derived from permanently influencing the virtual game world across several games. The success case of Ingress will likely motivate several future explorations on how to leverage crowdsourcing as a revenue stream in online multiplayer games.

References

1. Marjanovic, S., Fry, C., Chataway, J.: Crowdsourcing based business models: in search of evidence for innovation 2.0. Sci. Public policy **39**(3), 318–332 (2012)
2. Estellés-Arolas, E., González-Ladrón-De-Guevara, F.: Towards an integrated crowdsourcing definition. J. Inf. Sci. **38**(2), 189–200 (2012)
3. Zakariah, Z., Janom, N., Arshad, N.H.: Business model of crowdsourcing. In: 2015 IEEE 6th Control and System Graduate Research Colloquium (ICSGRC), pp. 66–69. IEEE (2015)
4. Hossain, M.: Users' motivation to participate in online crowdsourcing platforms. In: 2012 International Conference on Innovation Management and Technology Research, pp. 310–315. IEEE (2012)
5. Brabham, D.C.: Moving the crowd at threadless: motivations for participation in a crowdsourcing application. Inf. Commun. Soc. **13**(8), 1122–1145 (2010)
6. Brabham, D.C.: Motivations for participation in a crowdsourcing application to improve public engagement in transit planning. J. Appl. Commun. Res. **40**(3), 307–328 (2012)
7. Gerber, E.M., Hui, J.S., Kuo, P.Y.: Crowdfunding: why people are motivated to post and fund projects on crowdfunding platforms. In: Proceedings of the International Workshop on Design, Influence, and Social Technologies: Techniques, Impacts and Ethics, vol. 2, p. 10. Northwestern University Evanston, IL (2012)
8. Deng, X.N., Joshi, K.D.: Why individuals participate in micro-task crowdsourcing work environment: revealing crowdworkers' perceptions. J. Assoc. Inf. Syst. **17**(10), 648 (2016)

9. Ipeirotis, P.G.: Analyzing the amazon mechanical turk marketplace. XRDS: Crossroads, The ACM Magazine for Students, Forthcoming (2010)
10. Hara, K., et al.: Worker demographics and earnings on Amazon mechanical Turk: an exploratory analysis. In: Extended Abstracts of the 2019 CHI Conference on Human Factors in Computing Systems, LBW1217. ACM (2019)
11. Deng, X.N., Joshi, K.: Is crowdsourcing a source of worker empowerment or exploitation? understanding crowd workers' perceptions of crowdsourcing career (2013)
12. Pilz, D., Gewald, H.: Does money matter? motivational factors for participation in paid-and non-profit-crowdsourcing communities. Wirtschaftsinformatik **37**, 73–82 (2013)
13. Morschheuser, B., Hamari, J., Koivisto, J.: Gamification in crowdsourcing: a review. In: 2016 49th Hawaii International Conference on System Sciences (HICSS), pp. 4375–4384. IEEE (2016)
14. Kumaran, A., Densmore, M., Kumar, S.: Online gaming for crowd-sourcing phrase-equivalents. In: Proceedings of COLING 2014, the 25th International Conference on Computational Linguistics: Technical Papers, pp. 1238–1247 (2014)
15. Seaborn, K., Fels, D.I.: Gamification in theory and action: a survey. Int. J. Hum Comput Stud. **74**, 14–31 (2015)
16. Hamari, J., Koivisto, J., Sarsa, H., et al.: Does gamification work?-A literature review of empirical studies on gamification. HICSS **14**, 3025–3034 (2014)
17. Morschheuser, B., Hamari, J.: The gamification of work: lessons from crowdsourcing. J. Manag. Inq. **28**(2), 145–148 (2019)
18. Morschheuser, B., Hamari, J., Maedche, A.: Cooperation or competition-when do people contribute more? A field experiment on gamification of crowdsourcing. Int. J. Hum Comput Stud. **127**, 7–24 (2019)
19. Newman, J.: Kaizo mario maker: rom hacking, abusive game design and nintendo's super mario maker. Convergence **24**(4), 339–356 (2018)
20. Duncan, S.C.: Minecraft, beyond construction and survival. Well Played J. Video Games, Value Meaning **1**(1), 1–22 (2011)
21. Davis, M.: Ingress in geography: portals to academic success? J. Geogr. **116**(2), 89–97 (2017)
22. Chernova, S., Orkin, J., Breazeal, C.: Crowdsourcing HRI through online multiplayer games. In: 2010 AAAI Fall Symposium Series (2010)
23. Hantke, S., Eyben, F., Appel, T., Schuller, B.: ihearu-play: introducing a game for crowdsourced data collection for affective computing. In: 2015 International Conference on Affective Computing and Intelligent Interaction (ACII), pp. 891–897. IEEE (2015)
24. Brito, J., Vieira, V., Duran, A.: Towards a framework for gamification design on crowdsourcing systems: the game approach. In: 2015 12th International Conference on Information Technology-New Generations, pp. 445–450. IEEE (2015)
25. Juhász, L., Hochmair, H.H.: Where to catch 'em all?-a geographic analysis of pokémon go locations. Geo-spat. Inf. Sci. **20**(3), 241–251 (2017)
26. Colley, A., et al.: The geography of pokémon go: beneficial and problematic effects on places and movement. In: Proceedings of the 2017 CHI Conference on Human Factors in Computing Systems, pp. 1179–1192. ACM (2017)
27. Tregel, T., Raymann, L., Göbel, S., Steinmetz, R.: Geodata classification for automatic content creation in location-based games. In: Alcañiz, M., Göbel, S., Ma, M., Fradinho Oliveira, M., Baalsrud Hauge, J., Marsh, T. (eds.) JCSG 2017. LNCS, vol. 10622, pp. 212–223. Springer, Cham (2017). https://doi.org/10.1007/978-3-319-70111-0_20

28. Temple, B., Young, A.: Qualitative research and translation dilemmas. Qual. Res. **4**(2), 161–178 (2004)
29. Hyrynsalmi, S., Suominen, A., Mäkilä, T., Järvi, A., Knuutila, T.: Revenue models of application developers in android market ecosystem. In: Cusumano, M.A., Iyer, B., Venkatraman, N. (eds.) ICSOB 2012. LNBIP, vol. 114, pp. 209–222. Springer, Heidelberg (2012). https://doi.org/10.1007/978-3-642-30746-1_17
30. Hyrynsalmi, S.: Letters from the War of Ecosystems – An Analysis of Independent Software Vendors in Mobile Application Marketplaces. Doctoral dissertation, University of Turku, Turku, Finland (December 2014) TUCS Dissertations No. 188
31. Kohler, T., Nickel, M.: Crowdsourcing business models that last. J. Bus. Strategy **38**(2), 25–32 (2017)
32. Saxton, G.D., Oh, O., Kishore, R.: Rules of crowdsourcing: models, issues, and systems of control. Inf. Syst. Manag. **30**(1), 2–20 (2013)
33. Geiger, D., Schader, M.: Personalized task recommendation in crowdsourcing information systems–current state of the art. Decis. Support Syst. **65**, 3–16 (2014)
34. Prpić, J., Shukla, P.P., Kietzmann, J.H., McCarthy, I.P.: How to work a crowd: developing crowd capital through crowdsourcing. Bus. Horiz. **58**(1), 77–85 (2015)
35. Morschheuser, B., Hamari, J., Koivisto, J., Maedche, A.: Gamified crowdsourcing: conceptualization, literature review, and future agenda. Int. J. Hum Comput Stud. **106**, 26–43 (2017)
36. Bonfanti, A., Brunetti, F.: Crowdcrafting as a new manufacturing model: the experience of berto salotti. Sinergie **98**(Sep-Dec) (2015)
37. Talukdar, P.P., Cohen, W.W.: Crowdsourced comprehension: predicting prerequisite structure in wikipedia. In: Proceedings of the Seventh Workshop on Building Educational Applications Using NLP, pp. 307–315. Association for Computational Linguistics (2012)
38. Research Ltd, M.: Global video games industry: Strategies, trends and opportunities (2019)
39. Deterding, S., Dixon, D., Khaled, R., Nacke, L.: From game design elements to gamefulness: defining “gamification”. In: MindTrek 2011, pp. 9–15. ACM, New York (2011)
40. Hyrynsalmi, S., Smed, J., Kimppa, K.: The dark side of gamification: How we should stop worrying and study also the negative impacts of bringing game design elements to everywhere. In: GamiFIN (2017)
41. Althoff, T., White, R.W., Horvitz, E.: Influence of pokémon go on physical activity: study and implications. J. Med. Internet Res. **18**(12), e315 (2016)
42. Chernova, S., DePalma, N., Morant, E., Breazeal, C.: Crowdsourcing human-robot interaction: application from virtual to physical worlds. In: 2011 RO-MAN, pp. 21–26. IEEE (2011)
43. Luengo-Oroz, M.A., Arranz, A., Frean, J.: Crowdsourcing malaria parasite quantification: an online game for analyzing images of infected thick blood smears. J. Med. Internet Res. **14**(6), e167 (2012)
44. Standing, S., Standing, C.: The ethical use of crowdsourcing. Bus. Ethics Eur. Rev. **27**(1), 72–80 (2018)
45. Dolmaya, J.M.: The ethics of crowdsourcing. Linguistica Antverpiensia, New Ser. Themes Transl. Stud. (10) (2011)
46. Durward, D., Blohm, I., Leimeister, J.M.: Is there papa in crowd work?: a literature review on ethical dimensions in crowdsourcing. In: 2016 IEEE IoP, pp. 823-832. IEEE (2016)
47. Harris, C.G.: Dirty deeds done dirt cheap: a darker side to crowdsourcing. In: SocialCom 2011, pp. 1314–1317. IEEE (2011)

48. Martin, K., Shilton, K.: Putting mobile application privacy in context: an empirical study of user privacy expectations for mobile devices. Inf. Soc. **32**(3), 200–216 (2016)
49. Nov, O.: What motivates wikipedians? Commun. ACM **50**(11), 60–64 (2007)
50. Hulsey, N., Reeves, J.: The gift that keeps on giving: Google, ingress, and the gift of surveillance. Surveill. Soc. **12**(3), 389–400 (2014)
51. Laato, S., Pietarinen, T., Rauti, S., Paloheimo, M., Inaba, N., Sutinen, E.: A review of location-based games: do they all support exercise, social interaction and cartographical training? In: CSEDU 2019, INSTICC, pp. 616–627. SciTePress (2019)
52. Chess, S.: Augmented regionalism: ingress as geomediated gaming narrative. Inf. Commun. Soc. **17**(9), 1105–1117 (2014)
53. Venger, O.: Internet research in online environments for children: readability of privacy and terms of use policies; the uses of (non) personal data by online environments and third-party advertisers. J. Virt. Worlds Res. **10**(1) (2017)
54. Seok, S., DaCosta, B.: The cyber awareness of online video game players: an examination of their online safety practices and exposure to threats. Int. J. Cyber Res. Educ. (IJCRE) **1**(1), 69–77 (2019)
55. Cloos, J., et al.: Is your privacy for sale? An experiment on the willingness to reveal sensitive information. Games **10**(3), 28 (2019)
56. Pokéstop nomination beta comes to brazil and south korea! https://pokemongolive.com/en/post/poi-submission-beta/
57. Popp, K.M.: Software industry business models. IEEE Software 26–30 (2011)
58. Allison, A.: The cool brand, affective activism and Japanese youth. Theory Cult. Soc. **26**(2–3), 89–111 (2009)
59. Waysdorf, A., Reijnders, S.: Immersion, authenticity and the theme park as social space: experiencing the wizarding world of harry potter. Int. J. Cult. Stud. **21**(2), 173–188 (2018)
60. Make an impact with location-based AR marketing. https://nianticlabs.com/business/
61. Designing a planet-scale real-world AR platform. https://nianticlabs.com/blog/nrwp-update/
62. Alomari, K.M., Soomro, T.R., Shaalan, K.: Mobile gaming trends and revenue models. In: Fujita, H., Ali, M., Selamat, A., Sasaki, J., Kurematsu, M. (eds.) IEA/AIE 2016. LNCS (LNAI), vol. 9799, pp. 671–683. Springer, Cham (2016). https://doi.org/10.1007/978-3-319-42007-3_58
63. Kühn, S., Gleich, T., Lorenz, R.C., Lindenberger, U., Gallinat, J.: Playing super mario induces structural brain plasticity: gray matter changes resulting from training with a commercial video game. Mol. Psychiatry **19**(2), 265 (2014)
64. Shaker, N., Yannakakis, G.N., Togelius, J.: Crowdsourcing the aesthetics of platform games. IEEE Trans. Comput. Intell. AI Games **5**(3), 276–290 (2012)
65. Scacchi, W.: Computer game mods, modders, modding, and the mod scene. First Monday **15**(5), (2010)
66. Sotamaa, O.: When the game is not enough: motivations and practices among computer game modding culture. Games Cult. **5**(3), 239–255 (2010)
67. Morris, S.: Wads, bots and mods: Multiplayer fps games as co-creative media. In: DiGRA Conference. Citeseer (2003)

Emerging Research Topics

Organizational Innovativeness Relies on Business and IT Alignment

Zornitsa Yordanova(✉)

University of National and World Economy, 8mi dekemvri, Sofia, Bulgaria
zornitsayordanova@unwe.bg

Abstract. The purpose of the paper is to empirically research what is the interconnection between the efforts of business organizations to manage their organizational innovativeness and using management information systems in their management and operations. The organizational innovativeness in the study is narrowed by the prism of innovative potential and innovative capabilities that are defined by the Company Innovative Leadership model. The scope of IT when it comes to business and IT alignment is seen from the usage of ERP, CRM and BI systems for information and process management of operations. These three management information systems act as tools for Business and IT Alignment in the study. The methodology employed in the study relied on 51 middle and high level management respondents who explained what are the possible linkages between innovation goals of organizations and application of information and process information systems. The key findings of the results are concrete identified aspects of organizational innovativeness that may rely on information and process information systems. The practical implication of the study is its possible use as a high-level tool for organizations on how to approach and to address their organizational innovativeness by the already used systems.

Keywords: Innovation management · Organizational innovativeness · MIS · ERP · CRM · BI

1 Introduction

Innovation is considered to be the growth engine of business and economy from many researchers, companies and governments [1]. For many organizations, no matter of type, size or industry, improving and increasing innovativeness and ability to develop innovations is the most substantial factor for growth [2]. A knowledge gap has been identified about the interconnection, liaison and reciprocity between managing organizational innovativeness consistency and application of management and business information systems. In this research this interconnection has been researched as a narrowed Business to IT alignment study only on these matters, since innovation is a main factor for achieving competitiveness.

This paper presents some key findings from an empirical research amongst 51 organizations (the respondents were managers at middle and high management level) for these organizations' experience when it comes to organizational innovativeness and

S. Hyrynsalmi et al. (Eds.): ICSOB 2019, LNBIP 370, pp. 405–408, 2019.
https://doi.org/10.1007/978-3-030-33742-1_32

using management information systems. The practical implication of the results may be used for deepening the dependency and impact on organizational innovativeness by using different business information system processes and to strengthen Business to IT alignment his way.

2 Theoretical Background

Organizational innovativeness in the study is observed through the perspective of the ability of an organization to develop and commercialize innovations. By emphasizing on organizational innovativeness, the study does not focus on organizational innovation at any point. Organizational innovation is seen as (1) organizational structure and design theories, (2) organizational cognitive and learning theories, and (3) organizational change and adaptation theories [3]. The term innovativeness and organizational innovativeness in particular have been researched by Subramanian and Nilakanta [4] as the relationships between innovativeness of firms, their organizational characteristics, and organizational performance. The research of Kamaruddeen, Yusof and Said [5] went through all confusing and mixed up terms as innovation vs innovativeness and organizational innovation so as to define the organizational innovativeness as the inclination or the propensity to adopt innovative materials, methods/process, and business systems that are new to the organization not just for profit making but towards meeting the needs of the customers or end users, sustainability and environment consciousness. Wang and Ahmed [6] have identified innovativeness as "an organization's overall innovative capability of introducing new products to the market, or opening up new markets, through a combination of strategic orientation with innovative behavior and process". Foxall [7] describes innovativeness as a personality or organizational trait. Rogers defined innovativeness as "the degree to which an individual or other unit of adoption is relatively earlier in adopting new ideas than any other member of the system" [8]. Lumpkin and Dess (1996) perception of innovativeness includes both behavior related and product-related concepts [9].

3 Methodology of the Research

The methodology used in the study is based on the Company Innovation Leadership Model [10, 11]. It encompasses and measures innovative business organization management using three main groups of components and metrics. The groups are: Innovative competencies, Innovative potential and capabilities and Innovation activity. This study is based on the second set of indicators that are directly related to organizational innovation: Innovation potential and opportunities. The aim at measuring the organizational innovation potential as well as organizational current innovation outcomes. The five categories of indicators are: flexibility, social skills and competences, platform and data, leadership, strategy, business process. The survey was distributed amongst middle and senior executives from Bulgarian and international organizations operating in Bulgaria. The survey was conducted in 2018. The survey form was widespread through LinkedIn's professional network, allowing respondents with random access to the research and diversification of their organizations characteristics (size, industry, and management practices).

4 Results and Discussion

The results of the empirical research are shown in Fig. 1 and demonstrate a high dependence between the use of MIS and the organizational innovation as per these 51 organizations that participated in the study. For all of the surveyed criteria for organizational innovation under the Company Innovative Leadership Model, respondents responded that MIS were helping to manage and to perform innovation-related functions to a large extent. The blue and orange areas in Fig. 1 represent those answers which support the thesis for abundant help of MIS in this respect.

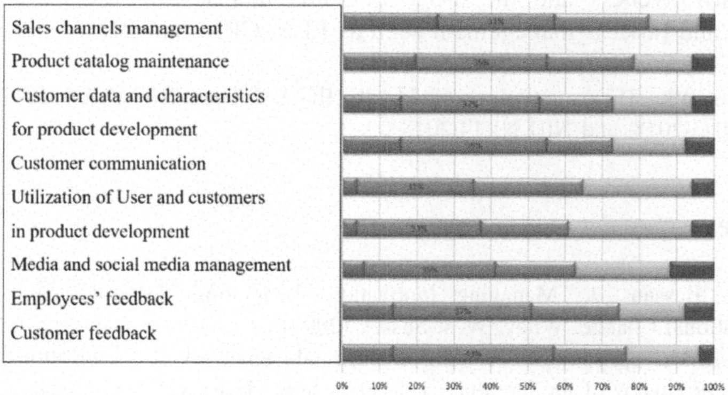

Fig. 1. Respondents answers of how MIS help the organizational innovativeness

Overall, the impact of MISon sales growth was assesses as positive by 59% of respondents. Customer feedback is an important indicator of the organization's innovativeness in terms of its innovative potential and innovative capabilities, especially for 75% of the respondents who consider it would not be achievable without using MIS. Employee feedback management is for 65% of the respondents is of primary interconnection of using of a business management program (for assigning tasks, orders, etc.) or mobile applications for sales representatives.

Managing customer communication for 55% of respondents is highly appreciate the use of MIS in managing customer communication. Given the specificity of the customer communication management activity and the existence of MIS that specifically manages this CRM system, a further section of the data is made to assess whether users of this type of system value their deployment. 82% of the responses evaluating the high use of MIS on this criterion come from managers working in organizations that develop product or process innovation. The use of client data implies the management of these data and this is usually only possible through MIS. Usually CRM systems perform this function. 68% of the organizations that indicated that they used CRM systems actually had greatly appreciated the use of MIS in the use of customer data and product development features. 64% of these respondents' organizations use ERP systems, which are also a tool for subtraction and subsequent analysis of client data and features. 66% of respondents who highly appreciate the use of MIS for this task respond to the fact that the organizations they work for are innovative. 72% of the respondents who have highly appreciated the use of MIS have indicated their organizations as innovative. 60% of respondents who rated MIS as indispensable to maintaining the product catalog developed mainly process innovation, and 72% of those who indicated that MIS are largely product-driven. 68% of organizations using CRM systems are highly rated for MIS for sales channel management and 72% of ERP systems are the same.

In conclusion, we may confirm with large level of confidence, that the stated hypothesis at the beginning of the paper has received arguments for confirmation. The empirical research supports that there is a strong relation between managing organizational innovativeness and the usage of some mainstream systems for business information and process management such as ERP, CRM and BI.

Acknowledgments. The paper is supported by the BG NSF Grant No M 15/4 -2017 (DM 15/1), KP-06 OPR01/3-2018, and NID NI 14/2018

References

1. Tidd, J., Bessant, J.: Managing Innovation: Integrating Technological, Market and Organizational Change. Wiley, West Sussex (2009)
2. Crossan, M.M., Apaydin, M.: A multi-dimensional framework of organizational innovation: a systematic review of the literature. J. Manag. Stud. **47**(6), 1154–1191 (2010)
3. Bruce, T.C., Packard, J.: Organizational innovation. In: Yamane, D. (ed.) Handbook of Religion and Society. HSSR, pp. 155–175. Springer, Cham (2016). https://doi.org/10.1007/978-3-319-31395-5_9
4. Subramanian, A., Nilakanta, S.: Organizational innovativeness: Exploring the relationship between organizational determinants of innovation, types of innovations, and measures of organizational performance. Omega **24**(6), 631–647 (1996)
5. Kamaruddeen, A., Yusof, N., Said, I.: Innovation and innovativeness: difference and antecedent relationship. IUP J. Architect. **II**(1), 12 (2004)
6. Wang, C.L., Ahmed, P.: The development and validation of the organizational innovativeness construct using confirmatory factor analysis. Eur. J. Innov. Manag. **4**(7), 303–313 (2004)
7. Foxall, G.: Corporate Innovation: Marketing and Strategy. St. Martin's Press, New York (1984)
8. Rogers, E.: Diffusion of Innovations, 5th edn. The Free Press, New York (2003)
9. Lumpkin, G.T., Dess, G.G.: Clarifying the entrepreneurial orientation construct and linking it to performance. Acad. Manag. Rev. **21**(1), 135–172 (1996)
10. Blagoev, D., Yordanova, Z.: Company innovative leadership model. Econ. Altern. **2**, 5–13 (2015)
11. Yordanova, Z., Blagoev, D.: Measuring the Bulgarian IT sector innovations capabilities through company innovative leadership model. Econ. Altern. **3**, 379–393 (2016)

MVP Development Process for Software Startups

Leandro Pompermaier(✉), Rafael Chanin(✉), Afonso Sales(✉), and Rafael Prikladnicki(✉)

School of Technology, PUCRS, Porto Alegre, Brazil
{leandro.pompermaier,rafael.chanin,afonso.sales,rafaelp}@pucrs.br

Abstract. This paper presents a proposal of a Minimal Viable Development Process for Software Startups that can be used during the MVP development process. Defining a methodology is a major challenge for startups because they are creative, flexible, and reluctant to include bureaucratic measures in their day-to-day procedures that may disrupt their natural attributes. Thus, to make the process simple, we defined it in 3 main phases: requirements gathering, software development, and market validation.

Keywords: Software startup · Process development · MVP · Software engineering

1 Introduction

There is a growing number of new companies, called startups, that develop innovative solutions. Ries [1] defined startup as a human institution designed to deliver a new product or service on conditions of extreme uncertainty. In this sense, Ries [1] defines the lean startup methodology as being a methodology for managing companies in environments of great uncertainty. A subset of startups that have their software-based solutions could be defined as software startups or digital startups [2].

These software startups are increasingly obsessed with delivering software products in an extremely short time so that the products can be validated directly by the end users. The use of lean software development methodology and the experimentation of business models has become popular in software startups, especially in the design of the minimal viable product (MVP) [3]. There are different types of MVP and this study is related just to MVPs that build some software products. In this context we know that some software engineering practices are used by the startups, however there is not a software development process that would focus on the creation of MVPs. We have observed in our studies that the use of some software development process is not a concern for entrepreneurs since they prioritize the validation of their market hypotheses without even minimal bureaucratization. For this reason this study aims to answer the following research question: What is the minimum development process for developing MVPs in software startups?

S. Hyrynsalmi et al. (Eds.): ICSOB 2019, LNBIP 370, pp. 409–412, 2019.
https://doi.org/10.1007/978-3-030-33742-1_33

2 Minimum Viable Software Development Methodology for Startups

Implementing a development methodology is a major challenge [4] for startups because they are creative, flexible, and reluctant to include bureaucratic measures in their day-to-day procedures that may disrupt their natural attributes. Several models were introduced to drive software development activities in startups, though without offering significant benefits [5].

In this context this work proposes a minimal viable methodology for software development for startups. As shown in Fig. 1, this methodology is defined in 3 main phases: requirements gathering, software development, and market validation. These phases are described as follow.

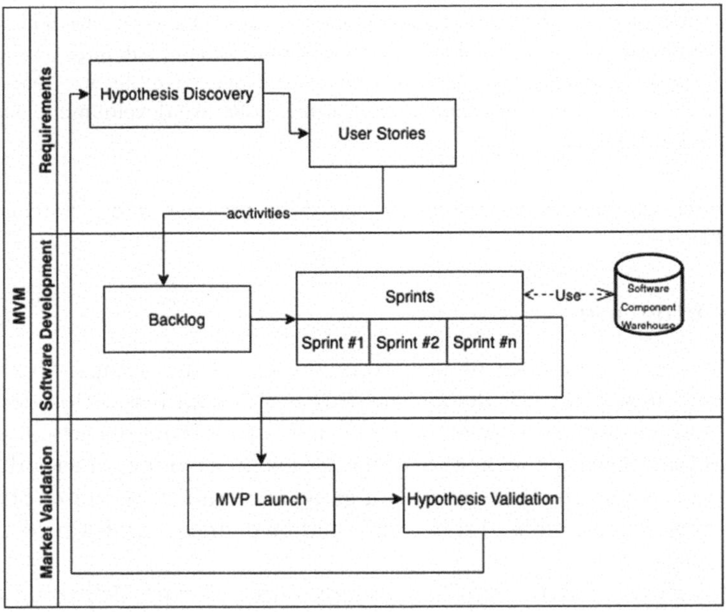

Fig. 1. Proposal of minimum viable process

2.1 Requirements Gathering

In a scenario where software startups work on defining the requirements of their solutions, problems with defining requirements grow exponentially due to the fact that: the customer is not fully defined and the problem was not specified and/or defined.

According to Melegati [6], software startups do not follow a specific activity when it comes to requirements engineering and are usually influenced by their founders, software development managers, developers, business models, market, and the ecosystem. In addition, the business model is a deciding factor in the choice of practices of requirements engineering [6].

Therefore, requirements engineering that contemplates elicitation, analysis, documentation, and revision must be adapted according to the maturity of the startup and its team and also aligned with the practices used in the process of Customer Development. And with that a set of User Stories must be mapped to forward them to the next step.

2.2 Software Development

All aspects of software production from the earliest stages to system maintenance involve specifying, developing, managing, and evolving software systems. This procedure is a function of Software Engineering (ES) which came about to solve problems of software systems with the purpose of supporting the development using processes, methods, techniques, and tools [8]. The reality is no different in startups.

In the world of startups, agile methodologies are common because they present characteristics that can easily be customized according to the team profile [9]. Agile methodologies are a group of software development methods based on an iterative and incremental process [10]. The four key characteristics of all agile methodologies are planning, iterative and evolutionary development, speed and flexible response to change, and promoting communication [11].

2.3 Market Validation

With each cycle all construction carried out by software startups should look at the market response to the assumptions made in the initial phase and coded later. Startups should thus be able to design and carry out previous activities quickly and effectively, releasing MVP as soon as possible.

After the release an analysis of what is happening and how the market is realizing the MVP should be controlled by the startup in order to generate the required learning at this stage.

According to Moogk [12] the key principles of the lean startup include omnipresence of entrepreneurs, uniqueness of the management style of startups, and learning from product testing against relevant metrics. Some measures that entrepreneur can use are: customer interviews, usability testing, split testing, usage monitoring and funnel analysis.

Analyzing these data and customer and market-related learning will help entrepreneurs make important decisions that will lead to a new cycle: either increment of the MVP with new features or flows, creating a new MVP by changing the customer or market focus, or making changes to the implemented functionalities.

3 Conclusion

The paper has presented a process proposal for the development of MVP's by software startups. Having a separate view of the requirements discovery part and an organization in the software development part is necessary, according to the dynamics commonly used by startups. Also, the grid part of the validation of the developed software product is performed through the use of this product by the market, thus justifying the validation phase with the market, presented in the process proposal. As future work, we intend to apply the process in startups and analyze its adequacy in the first steps of these companies.

Acknowledgments. This work is partially funded by FAPERGS (17/2551-0001/205-4).

References

1. Ries, E.: The Lean Startup: How Today's Entrepreneurs Use Continuous Innovation to Create Radically Successful Businesses. Crown Books (2011)
2. Paternoster, N., et al.: Software development in startup companies: a systematic mapping study. Inf. Softw. Technol. **56**(10), 1200–1218 (2014)
3. Nilsson, H., Petersson, L.: How to manage technical debt in a lean startup (2013)
4. Coleman, G., O'Connor, R.V.: An investigation into software development process formation in software start-ups. J. Enterp. Inf. Manag. **21**(6), 633–648 (2008)
5. Giardino, C., et al.: Software development in startup companies: the greenfield startup model. IEEE Trans. Softw. Eng. **42**(6), 585–604 (2016)
6. Melegati, J., et al.: A model of requirements engineering in software startups. Inf. Softw. Technol. **109**, 92–107 (2019)
7. Blank, S., Dorf, B.: The Startup Owner's Manual: The Step-by-step Guide for Building A Great Company. BookBaby (2012)
8. Sommerville, I.: Software Engineering, 9th edn. (2011). ISBN-10 137035152
9. Pantiuchina, J., Mondini, M., Khanna, D., Wang, X., Abrahamsson, P.: Are software startups applying agile practices? The state of the practice from a large survey. In: Baumeister, H., Lichter, H., Riebisch, M. (eds.) XP 2017. LNBIP, vol. 283, pp. 167–183. Springer, Cham (2017). https://doi.org/10.1007/978-3-319-57633-6_11
10. Sharma, S., Sarkar, D., Gupta, D.: Agile processes and methodologies: a conceptual study. Int. J. Comput. Sci. Eng. **4**(5), 892 (2012)
11. Maher, P.: Weaving agile software development techniques into a traditional computer science curriculum. In: 2009 Sixth International Conference on Information Technology: New Generations. IEEE (2009)
12. Moogk, D.R.: Minimum viable product and the importance of experimentation in technology startups. Technol. Innov. Manag. Rev. **2**(3) (2012)

Technical Debt Trade-Off - Experiences from Software Startups Becoming Grownups

Orges Cico(✉)

Norwegian University of Science and Technology, Trondheim, Norway
orges.cico@ntnu.no

Abstract. Software startups are software-intensive early-stage companies that have high growth rates. Their time to market is often regarded as short and decisive in establishing their product/service success, thus leading to short-cuts in software engineering decisions. High accumulation of the technical debt at early stages has been documented from previous investigations. How startups rapidly becoming grownups perceive technical debt, make the primary goal of our study. We conducted semi-structured interviews with six technical and executive officers from five software startups, selected using purposive sampling. We identified four critical perceptions (managing, accepting, avoiding, ignoring technical debt) which permit them to make technical debt trade-offs. We also found that no one size fits all. Startups need to make deliberate educated decisions on how to use technical debt in their advantage.

Keywords: Software startups · Technical debt · Software intensive

1 Introduction

Facing Technical Debt (TD)[1] is becoming even more of an urgent need for many software startups [2,5,8]. Empirical evidence on how TD is perceived from software startups is still meager, and the need for empirical evidence is reported from [1]. Software startups are known to accumulate TDs via their early-stage prototyping and product development, which eventually requires the companies to pay the debt, causing initial growth hinders productivity [6]. At the point in time when startups shift to an established stage in term of finance and resources, the management of such TDs becomes significance from managerial perspective. Compared to previous efforts studying TDs at different startup phases, the understanding of TD management at such transitions is very limited. We aimed at understanding effective approaches for managing TDs for startups in the scaling transitions. As the first step, we formulated the following research question: **RQ:** *How is Technical Debt perceived in Software Startups becoming Grownups?*

[1] Metaphoric concept of TD has been first introduced by Ward Cunningham [4] in 1992.

S. Hyrynsalmi et al. (Eds.): ICSOB 2019, LNBIP 370, pp. 413–418, 2019.
https://doi.org/10.1007/978-3-030-33742-1_34

To answer the RQ, we designed a survey-based semi-structured interview, conducted with six Chief Executive Officer (CEOs) and Chief Technical Officers (CTOs) from five software startups, selected using purposive sampling. We focused on those startups that are almost or have already made a successful transition towards becoming Grownups[2]. Aligned to previous studies findings, we also noticed that TD is deliberately embraced as long as product/service delivery deadlines and good enough quality are met. Furthermore, we found that a TD trade-off is required in the transition from early stages to grownup stages. Eventually, we identified (1) Managing TD, (2) Accepting TD, (3) Ignoring TD, (4) Avoiding TD are the main approaches perceived from TS to achieve the TD trade-offs. Providing empirical evidence on how transitioning startups have been able to conduct a smooth transition from Minimum Viable Products (MVPs) towards qualitative product/services can help future practitioners and entrepreneurs make educated decisions.

2 Research Methodology

We aim to understand the perception of technical debt in Software Startups becoming Grownups. Therefore, the research question guided our investigation. Based on recommendations from Runeson [7] we devised a qualitative approach with semi-structured face-to-face interviews with six CEOs/CTOs from the five Software Startups.

2.1 Case Selection and Demographics

We were able to collect the sample data from a significant event where participation involved 100+ startups. The sample population has been selected using a non-probability sampling technique. We collected data from the startups' online resources after initial contact (email or face-to-face acquaintance) and then later on from CEOs and CTOs. Demographics of the five software startups are reported in Table 1.

2.2 Interview Design, Data Collection and Analysis

We performed a pilot study in constructing our interview template, which was used for later data collection from all the cases. This allowed us to focus our interview questions in connection to the RQ. The interview process took place in three parts: (1) demographic information about the startup (2) broad context on software and technological aspects of the startup (3) perception of technical debt. We interviewed six CTOs/CEOs from five different startups located in the same country and conducting geographically proximate business activities with a high tech product focus. The interviews aimed to understand the perception of

[2] Grownups are well established companies with market revenue being primary source of income.

Table 1. Software startup sample demographics.

Startup Case Number	Role	Country	Product / Service	Establishment Year	Product Commercial. Year	Team Size	Gender Balance	Employee Average Age / Range
Startup 1	CTO CEO	USA	High tech software products	2008	2017	8	50% M 50% F	20s – 30s and 40+
Startup 2	CEO	USA	High tech software intensive and hardware system product	2016	2017	4	100% M	30s
Startup 3	CEO	USA	Software Development	2001	2012	65	60% M 40% F	30s
Startup 4	CEO	USA	High tech software intensive	2015	2016	7	90% M 10% F	30s
Startup 5	CTO	USA	High tech software intensive and hardware system product	2012	2017	34	80 % M 20 % F	30s

TD from startup founders, represented by both CEOs and CTOs, Table 1. After data collection, in order to obtain significant evidence, we used thematic analysis approach [3], consisting of identifying recurring patterns and themes within the interview data. The systematic analysis steps consisted in (1) **Reading the transcripts**, (2) **Coding**, (3) **Creating themes**, (4) **Labeling and connecting themes**, (5) **Drawing the results summary**, (6) **Writing results**. We also used thematic coding tools such as NVivo.

3 Results

During our analysis we created five major categories, namely TD trade-off, Managing TD, Avoiding TD, Accepting TD, and Ignoring TD, each helping to answer our RQ in the following subsections.

- **TD Trade-off.** In most cases, we noticed a repetition of the TD trade-off term. The term itself was mentioned from the interviewer, reporting positive connotation from the interviewees. This demonstrates that the perception of the TD is not totally negative or positive, but it is commonly agreed that a TD trade-off is required in the transition from early to grownup stages. For example, the CTO of Case 5 explicitly states: *"We accept TD can happen, take responsibility for it and this is all about trade-offs. Our team is highly deadline driven."*. Thus, here is where we identified different approaches (Managing TD, Accepting TD, Ignoring TD, Avoiding TD) part of TD trade-off while analyzing the perception of the CEOs/CTOs.
- **ManagingTD.** In many cases, TD management is reported as the most common option. The CEOs from two startups (Case 3, 5) emphasize the relevance the increased awareness helped them have better control over the TD. This was common even in large contingents of development teams adopting pair programming approach to software development. In Case 5, TD trade-off was

accepted, whenever deadlines had to be met. However, team members were fully aware of the situation and accepted that TD issues had to be dealt with later on. Likewise, managing and isolating code issues modules with low coupling helped in controlling TD, as reported in Case 3 (Fig. 1).

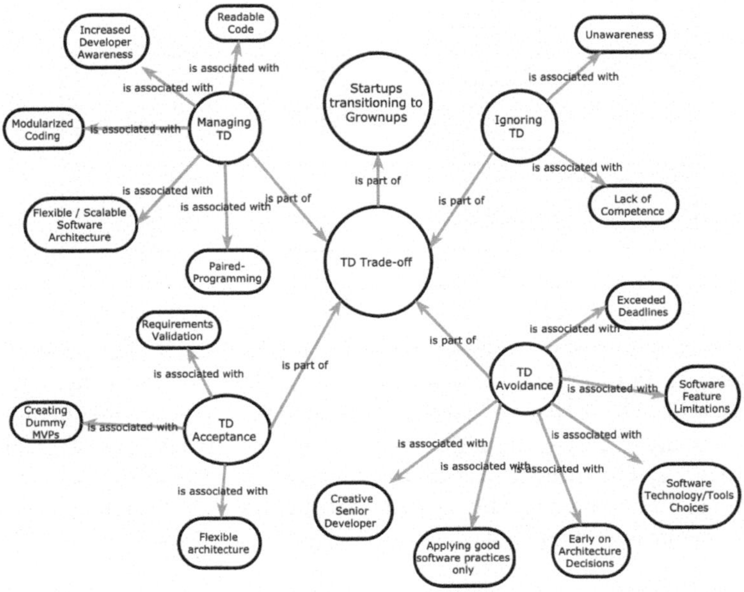

Fig. 1. Themes summary.

- **AvoidTD.** We found that avoiding TD is primarily perceived as positive when sacrificing software features seemed to be a good option. Case 3 reported that: *"We can develop anything but not everything within the given time limitations"*. However, in Case 1, avoiding TD was strongly connected with exceeded deadlines, or good software practices producing products that don't match the end-user needs. We found that early on architecture, programming language, and technology choices helped the software startups in taking precautions to avoid TD, Case 2.
- **AcceptingTD.** Although the acceptance of the TD term was a mere surprise for us, we discovered that the acting along with the TD was considered to be beneficial. Case 2, reported that requirement validation could be best achieved when introducing dummy MVPs that can be thrown away due to the large amount of TD introduced. Furthermore, the same case reports that TSs can widely accept TD if relying on easy to manipulate backend architectures. Accepting TD is perceived to be inappropriate, Case 3 reports: *"We always use best approaches, although we accept that we cannot achieve perfect software."*.

- **IgnoringTD.** We found that this category was strongly associated with a lack of TD awareness from the team, Case 3. Planning ahead to throw away prototypes can also lead to ignoring TD for those modules totally. Example made earlier with dummy MVPs from Case 2. However, to differentiate with the previous example, when a startup decides to ignore TDs they have made a deliberate long-lasting decision, which might or might not affect the product during its operational lifetime, but the reason for doing so is lack of team competence which is not possible for them to compensate.

We report **key findings:**

1. Managing TD is perceived to be an essential aspect of the TD trade-offs to be made in order to meet deadlines. Accountability for improving the software system is to be dealt with afterward. Readable code and flexible software architectures help along the process.
2. Avoiding TD can have positive as well as a negative connotation. If startups are able to cut-off features of their products, then it is recommended for them to try to avoid TDs, while applying good software development practices.
3. Accepting TD is found in two main beneficial scenarios: (1) acting along with TD to validate requirements (2) flexible backend software architectures that allow for rapid change.
4. Ignoring TD is primarily affected by lack of awareness and lack of competence.

4 Discussions

Many of the previous studies have focused on covering and addressing several startup life cycle phases by unfolding the TD challenges and benefits [2]. In our case, we focus more on a specific moment in time borderline to the transitioning from software startups to grownups. This is of significant interest because not knowing how to cope with TD at this later stage to make the big decisive jump has higher financial and technological risks. The perception of TD of succeeding startups having made the jump to grownups can be a winning and compelling choice for future ones. Another important reason for studying borderlines is also because it is there when disruptions are observed and successfully overcoming TD thresholds is required [2]. We believe that TD while transitioning to grown up company has a different perception compared to TD while at very early stage. We also provide **key recommendations:**

1. TD is going to be your best friend or best enemy, so making the right Trade-offs is crucial. No one size fits all.
2. Cut-off software features if you require less TD. This workaround can still allow software startups to meet deadlines without compromising future updates.
3. Accept TD and make it work in your advantage. Build as many dummy MVPs as possible until you are sure about requirements.

4. Hire if possible at least one highly creative senior developer. If they understand why you want to build the system, they can also tell you what you need to build.
5. Play it smart. Don't just ignore TD, because you are unaware or because you think you lack the competence. As per definition, the debt is later to be paid, unless you decide it is useful in staging your product.

5 Conclusions and Future Work

We focused on understanding how software startups transitioning in grownup, perceive TD. After interviewing five different software startups and six of the co-founders, holding either CEO or CTO roles, we identified four important perceptions (Managing TD, Avoiding TD, Ignoring TD, Accepting TD) which permit them to make TD trade-offs. We also found that no one size fits all. Startups need to make deliberate educated decisions on how to use TD in their advantage. This can only be obtained if they have a clear view of the options to cope with TD. This study provides a set of initial recommendations. We plan in the future to collect further data by surveying and interviewing larger sets of participants. The triangulation will allow us to generalize our findings and provide guidelines to be exploited by future startups.

Acknowledgement. This work was funded by the Norwegian Research Council under the project IPIT Project Number: 274816. Many thanks to Prof. Letizia Jaccheri, for the support as project leader.

References

1. Abrahamsson, P., et al.: Software startups - a research agenda. e-Informatica Softw. Eng. J **10**(1), 1–28 (2016)
2. Besker, T., et al.: Embracing technical debt, from a startup company perspective. In: 2018 IEEE International Conference on Software Maintenance and Evolution (ICSME), pp. 415–425. IEEE (2018)
3. Braun, V., Clarke, V.: Using thematic analysis in psychology. Qual. Res. Psychol. **3**(2), 77–101 (2006)
4. Cunningham, W.: The WyCash portfolio management system, Experience Report. In: Proceedings on Object-Oriented Programming Systems, Languages, and Applications (OOPSLA 1992) (1992)
5. Devos, N., Durieux, D., Ponsard, C.: Managing technical debt in IT start-ups-an industrial survey. In: International Conference on Software and System Engineering and Their Applications (ICSSEA) (2013)
6. Giardino, C., et al.: Software development in startup companies: the greenfield startup model. IEEE Trans. Softw. Eng. **42**(6), 585–604 (2016)
7. Runeson, P., Höost, M.: Guidelines for conducting and reporting case study research in software engineering. Empir. Softw. Eng. **14**(2), 131 (2009)
8. Tom, E., Aurum, A.K., Vidgen, R.: An exploration of technical debt. J. Syst. Softw. **86**(6), 1498–1516 (2013)

A Dynamic Software Startup Competency Model

Nana Assyne[1(✉)] and Isaac Wiafe[2]

[1] Faculty of Information Technology,
University of Jyväskylä, Jyväskylä, Finland
nana.m.a.assyne@student.jyu.fi
[2] Department of Computer Science, University of Ghana, Accra, Ghana
iwiafe@ug.edu.gh

Abstract. Current literature suggests that engineering activities of software engineering and software startup engineering differ. Thus, there is the need to elicit competencies specific for software startup engineering. This paper proposes a model that provides the various types of competencies and their respective relevance at the various stages of software startup evolution.

Keywords: Startups · Innovation · Startup engineering · Startup evolution

1 Introduction

The competency of startuppers and developers are ingredients for software startup success. Especially, how their competency needs addresses specific challenges of software startups [1]. Software startups are new companies with no operating history that produces cutting-edge technologies at extremely fast pace. Hence, there is the need for such startups to possess unique competencies that will propagate them to survive a competitive business environment. These competencies are the knowledge, skills and attitudes that a developer require to accomplish a software project. Due to lack of methods and frameworks for guiding the establishment and operations of startups, developers adopt ad hoc methods for starting ups and these mostly leads to failures [2].

Some attempts have been made to provide frameworks and methods to guide startups, but they have mainly focused on challenges, characteristics and growth [4]. Yet, competency needs have been identified a key issue in all successful startups. Consequently, it has become imperative to identify the key competencies required for successful startups. This study therefore reports initial findings of a research activity that seeks to expand existing work by [3].

2 Problems of Software Startup Competency Model

Although software startups appear promising by creating jobs, innovation and digital disruptions, its failure rate is discouraging. Over 60% of startups fail within the first 5 years [4]. This may be attributed to issues including, technology uncertainty, lack of problem or solution fit, neglected learning process, lack of resources, etc. Currently,

S. Hyrynsalmi et al. (Eds.): ICSOB 2019, LNBIP 370, pp. 419–422, 2019.
https://doi.org/10.1007/978-3-030-33742-1_35

existing startup competency models are static and address issues such as personnel experience, limited resources, and dependency on external parties. They fail to adequately address the dynamic nature of startups [5].

There are six (6) human capital areas that must be considered in startups [3]. These areas are application domain, software development, hardware development, mechanic development, systematic development, and difficult technology domain. The six areas can be acquired using nine (9) means (i.e. founder' experience, other products, prototyping and testing, customer cooperation, research, experience team growth, and unconventional team growth). This argument was derived from fundamental principles in human capital theory [6] and resource-based-view [7] in existing literature. Seppänen et al. [3] explained that human capital (competency needs) evolves as startups grow and thus calls for the need for competency needs models to be dynamic. Yet, studies that seek to understand the variables of human capital, particularly regarding software competencies fail to address questions on issues such as (i) what types of competencies (human capital) are required for successful startups, and (ii) what required levels of competencies are needed to ensure a successful startup as it goes through the different evolutionary stages.

3 A Software Competence Framework

In this study, it is argued that existing software competencies can be classified into three (3) main types. These are architecture competency, innovation competency and business competency. Innovation competency is perhaps the most important of all. It is a set of skills, attitude and knowledge possessed by startup professionals that enable them to translate ideas into product or service for money. It includes creative thinking, problem solving ability, visionary thinking and empathy. It can be observed that without any form of innovation, a startup does not exist. Architecture competency is the set of fundamental software and hardware related skills and knowledge that a startup professional need during a startup creation. They include competencies in programing language, database developing skills, networking skills, application framework skills, electronic and machine skills. These set of competencies are relevant because they provide the foundation upon which a startup can be initiated. There is a need for strong understanding of knowledge in the tools needed for converting the innovative idea into a reality. Although competencies in innovation (i.e. having a groundbreaking idea or concept), and architecture (having the prerequisite knowledge and skillset of hardware and software tools for converting an idea into a product or a service) is necessary, it is not sufficient for establishing a startup to maturity. Competency in business is required to ensure a successful transition from one stage to the other within a startup lifecycle. Business competency is the set of interpersonal knowledge and skills required by a startup professional to ensure that groundbreaking ideas are converted into matured businesses. These skills may include organizational skills, teamwork, leadership skills, communication skills, social skills, etc.

The relevance of these competencies (i.e. architecture, innovation, and business) differ as startup's evolve. Hence a particular competency may be classified as desired or required at a stage. Desire competencies are not urgent as compared to required competencies. They add value, however without their presence, a startup can survive. They are therefore not mandatory. A required competency is mandatory and without their presence a particular task cannot be performed. As compared to desired competency, it is the backbone need and the lifeline at a particular stage within the lifecycle.

	STARTUP	STABILIZATION	GROWTH	MATURITY
BUSINESS	Desired	Desired	Required	Required
ARCHITECTURE	Required	Desired	Desired	Required
INNOVATION	Required	Required	Require	Required

Fig. 1. Startup evolutionary competency Model

The Crowne [8] startup lifecycle model consist of four (4) main stages namely; startup, stabilization, growth and maturity. At the startup stage the product or service is still at the conceptualization state thus, innovation and architecture competencies are required whereas business competency is desired. Without a groundbreaking idea (innovation) a startup does not exist and for this idea to be realize as a product or service there is the need to have knowledge and skills in software and hardware tools.

Architecture competency is also a requirement. However, business competency is desirable at the first stage since the concepts and ideas can be improved at this stage without expert knowledge in business. As the startup progresses to stabilization, the relevance of architecture reduces whereas innovation remains "required". At the growth stage the ability to make the product or service a leading-edge is crucial. Thus, innovation and business competencies become required whilst architecture is a desire. Figure 1 represent the various stages in the lifecycle and their respective levels of need.

4 Discussions and Conclusion

The lifecycle of successful startups such as Facebook, Google, SpaceX, etc. can all be identified with these stages. They started as groundbreaking ideas and have been developed into full businesses. At the various levels, they focused and also exhibited different competencies. For instance, the founder of Facebook had programming competence (architecture) and aground breaking idea (innovation). The development of Facemash demonstrates that business competency was not a requirement at the startup stage. At stabilization, Facemash was used by student hence innovation was required to make it user friendly. At growth stage, additional users who were non-students joined. Thus, the need for business competency. Facebook started an initial public offering (IPO) and also found itself mingled in some legal issues. In addition, experienced market giants such as PayPal, Peter Thiel, joined Facebook. This confirms the assertion that there is a need for competencies in business and innovation at the growth stage. The maturity stage saw Facebook scaling into a large business industry and at this stage they demonstrated strong competencies in business, innovation and architecture. They hired more developers to enhance their architecture competence, they continued to innovate and added more features. They also put in place proper business structures.

From the above scenario, it can be observed that the classification of the various levels and relevance of competencies provide a thinking framework for both researchers and practitioners on how software startups can be managed through the lifecycle to achieve success. As argued earlier, successful software startups need competency models that are dynamic and capable of withstanding the extreme nature of startup lifecycle. This model therefore serves as a guide for practitioners and researchers to structure their thinking on the immature and volatile evolving environments of startups. Further studies need to be conducted to validate the efficacy of the proposed framework.

References

1. Abrahamsson, P., et al.: Software Startups - A Research Agenda **3**(1), 1–28 ((2016))
2. Wang, X., Edison, H., Bajwa, S., Giardino, C., Abrahamsson, P.: Key challenges in software startups across life. In: Sharp, H., Hall, T. (eds.) Agile Processes in Software Engineering and Extreme Programming, vol. 256, pp. 169–182 (2016)
3. Seppänen, P., Liukkunen, K., Oivo, M.: Little big team: acquiring human capital in software startups. In: Felderer, M., Méndez Fernández, D., Turhan, B., Kalinowski, M., Sarro, F., Winkler, D. (eds.) PROFES 2017. LNCS, vol. 10611, pp. 280–296. Springer, Cham (2017). https://doi.org/10.1007/978-3-319-69926-4_20
4. Nobel, C.: Teaching a 'Lean Startup' Strategy. Harvard Business School, pp. 1–2 (2011). http://hbswk.hbs.edu/pdf/item/6659.pdf
5. Seppänen, P., Liukkunen, K., Oivo, M.: On the feasibility of startup models as a framework for research on competence needs in software startups. In: Abrahamsson, P., Corral, L., Oivo, M., Russo, B. (eds.) PROFES 2015. LNCS, vol. 9459, pp. 569–576. Springer, Cham (2015). https://doi.org/10.1007/978-3-319-26844-6_42
6. Becker, G.: Human Capital: A Theoretical and Empirical Analysis, With Special Reference To Education (1993)
7. Barney, J.B.: Firm resources and sustained competitive advantage. J. Manag. **17**, 99–120 (1991)
8. Crowne, M.: Why software product startups fail and what to do about it. Evolution of software product development in startup companies. In: IEEE International Engineering Management Conference, vol. 1, pp. 338–343 (2002)

Objectives and Challenges in Finnish Software Companies 2018 - Interview of 99 Finnish Software Development Firms

Toni Luhti(✉)

IT Faculty, University of Jyväskylä, PL 35, 40014 Jyväskylä, Finland
toni.luhti@gmail.com

Abstract. The business domain of software development growth increasingly during 2018 and while software companies in Finland are taking benefit of this momentum, they are facing multiple internal and external challenges. We constructed annual software business survey for 99 enterprise to micro-size software companies in Finland. Based on our survey, software development firms aim at growing rather than improving efficiency or changing focus. The focus remains on strengthening the current business instead of aligning it with the market transition, although the lack of competence and resources is remarkable. This poster paper gives a prompt overview of the Finnish software business domain and how software companies are encountering it.

Keywords: Software business · Objectives · Challenges

1 Introduction

A vast growth in software development industry is needed the seize the opportunity for companies operating on that domain. The challenge comes along with the opportunity. A business transformation beginning from technological changes is one of the biggest reasons [1] why companies do change or transform their business. Also new potential market opportunities [2] and change on customer needs [3] can act as trigger to change business. Globally the development of new technologies, changing demand on markets and customers can transform entire business domain rapidly. Especially in software business new technologies and changes in competition are forcing companies to change their business strategies [4, 5]. Based on such overall understanding we expected that the same continuous change is also a part of the software business industry in Finland. We formed a research question "What are the objectives and challenges in Finnish software development companies" and conducted an understanding how the software business domain in Finland in transforming and how companies in it are experiencing it.

In order to do the right decisions, understand market situation and build proper competitive advantage, software companies must have overall neutral view for this business domain. Also, many companies, especially startups but also some incumbents, tend to prefer blue ocean strategy [6] which means that companies supposed to address a product or solution category instead of focusing on a market with fierce competition. This is part of an inherent principle embedded as a part of the lean startup approach [7]

S. Hyrynsalmi et al. (Eds.): ICSOB 2019, LNBIP 370, pp. 423–429, 2019.
https://doi.org/10.1007/978-3-030-33742-1_36

which is popular among software companies. Without proper understanding of the market and competitors it is difficult to focus on blue ocean strategy and execute lean startup strategy although the lean startups are typically created for acting under extreme high uncertainty.

2 Research

2.1 Research Process

Research conducted during late summer (July – August) 2018 as the annual Finnish Software Company Survey (OSKARI). Survey is a joint action of the Finnish Software and E-business Association, Technology Industries of Finland and University of Jyväskylä. All invited companies to the survey were members of the Finnish Software and E-business association, 99 of them participated. 8 of them all are large or midsize companies (more than 50 employees), 29 are small (10–49 employees) and the rest (62) are micro-firms, meaning less than 10 employees. The survey was executed in a phone interview of 5 questions (four of them open-ended). One interview lasted around 45 min. All interviews were recorded and stored to a cloud storage. All companies and individual persons were anonymized from the results.

2.2 Set of Questions

The following set of questions were asked from the participants without any guidance how to answer in order to get the eventual thoughts and respondents'personal opinion.

1. Name max. 10 technological or IT-business trends that you would like to learn or know more?
2. What are the most important trends or your own business domain that you are following?
3. Choose your main target in business development (only one)?
   a. Increase performance
   b. Grow current business
   c. Change existing business essentially
4. What things do you believe to be changed in your own business during next 3–5 years?
5. Point out matters that are hindering down the change or preventing success of your company?

2.3 Data Analysis

Collected data was coded and classified to multiple subcategories and instead of analyzing individual answers, we gathered a classified overview as a result. In order to validate classifications and interpret all answers correctly, we involved four persons to data analysis part. Analysis tasks were divided in four parts: (1) data transcription (executed by one person). (2) data classification (handled by two persons). (3) correlation findings (handled by three persons). (4) conclusions and discussions of the results (handled by three persons). After conclusions and discussions all results were presented for to the Finnish Software and E-business Association and they confirmed that our survey fulfills their needs and targets have been achieved.

3 Findings

3.1 Industry Details and Transformation

For the first questions ("Name max. 10 technological or IT-business trends that you would like to learn or know more?") interviewees mentioned 217 individual answers what we classified to 8 different categories (presented in Table 1). The TOP 3 most often mentioned categories are artificial intelligence (61 references), general other (56 references) and trends in software development (30 references).

For the second question ("What are the most important trends or your own business domain that you are following?") we identified 222 indications (presented in Table 1). TOP 3 trends what these software companies are following are general other (54 references), trends in software development (47 references) and trends in software business (42 references). Generally, it seems that the trends in software business are somehow scattered as we classified all answers that got 1–2 references to a category "general other" and that is in TOP 3 in both questions.

Almost half of the companies (42%) are following the trends in software development but at the same time more than one quarter (26%) suffers the lack of information of the trends in software development. The same pattern applies for the artificial intelligence, 31% of companies are following this trend actively and still 61% are lacking such information. It is also notable that for an example IoT and blockchain got relatively low amount of references in both categories. Both of these trends are actively followed by only 8% of companies and also less than one fifth needs more information (blockchain 15% and IoT 17%).

Table 1. Trends what companies would like to learn or know more (question 1), totally 217 references in 8 categories and trends that companies are actively following (question 2), totally 222 references.

Technological or IT-business trend	References	
	Learn and know more	Following
Artificial intelligence	61	31
General other	56	54
Trends in software development	30	47
Trends in software business	26	42
Internet-of-Things (IoT)	17	8
Blockchain	14	8
Change in demand	10	29
No trends	3	3

3.2 The Focus on Business Development and Change During Next 3–5 Years

Probably because of the form of the question, the only consensus in this survey comes from the question 3 ("Choose your main target in business development (only one)?"). 69% of companies are currently focusing on growing their existing business and 11% are looking the performance improvements when only 20% are transforming essentials parts of their present business (presented in Table 2). This is somehow remarkable when taking questions 4 ("What things do you believe to be changed in your own business during next 3–5 years?") into account (presented in Table 3).

Table 2. The main targets in business development (question 3).

The main target in business development	%
Grow current business	69,3
Change existing business essentially	19,8
Increase performance	10,9

Table 3. Things that companies do believe to be changed during next 3–5 years (question 4), totally 202 references in 9 categories.

Things that will change during next 3–5 years	References
International and new markets	44
Technology	35
Business	35
Competence	31
Customer needs	19
Financing and holding	13
Resources	10
Nothing	8
Speed of operations	7

Respondents referenced 202 times matters that will be changed in near future. Our classification covers 9 different categories. The most referenced category is changes in international and new markets (44 hits) and the least referenced is category "nothing" (8 hits) where companies cannot see any upcoming changes in ahead. Reading this result to another direction, 194/202 answers are pointing out a notable change in near future and still only 20% of the companies are looking to transforming their business.

3.3 Blockers and Obstacles

On the last part of the survey we asked all kinds of blockers and obstacles that are roadblocks for the change or preventing companies on their way to the success. As a result, we got scatter big picture where only two categories are considerably bigger than the rest of 10 categories. 21% of all answers referenced to a recruitment or the current number of employees (presented in Table 4). This understanding is fulfilled with 31 references to the competence which is the second biggest category. Combining only these two challenges together we have a situation where IT software companies in Finland do not have enough competent employees and that is potentially preventing development in the entire industry.

Table 4. Factors that are hindering down the change or preventing companies to success (question 5), totally 176 references in 12 categories.

Obstacle factors for success	References
Amount of employees/recruitment	37
Competence	31
Funding	20
Something else	16
Stakeholders	14
Desire to growth	13
Technology	12
Regulation	11
Internationalization	9
Nothing	6
Marketing	5
Productization	2

4 Discussion

Based on the information delivered from this survey, industry is in under a change and as answers shows that this will happen in vast scale in near future. Only some of all topics shares consensus among respondents and only few of all companies do not see a business transformation or roadblocks ahead. More than one out of three companies believe that their business will change during next 3–5 years. Parallel to that almost the same amount of companies does see that technologies what they are currently using will change in a same time frame. A surprising finding is that no actual consensus can be found in any – except in focus of business – perspective what we examined. Firms do see that some technological changes (like artificial intelligence, IoT and blockchain) are changing the market but there is not a single one megatrend that everyone are following.

As in any research, there are same limitations as well. As the participants for this survey are from any size of software development companies and answers cannot be divided by company size, the results might be too universal and superficial. For an example 63% of answers coming from micro-size companies which contains start-ups and entrepreneurs. This could directly mean why the focus of business development is on growing instead of transformation. Only 20% of companies are focusing on transformation and only 8% of participated companies are employing over 50 persons, meaning larger companies (also incumbents) who already have some serious business what they would like transform. For the validity and reliability of this research, the scope and context of this study must be considered. Relatively short number of participants and large portions of "general" answers in results might indicate that wider research, more interviews and possibility to map answers on company profiles could provide more deep and particular insights.

5 Conclusion

Companies do see that the entire industry is constantly changing, and new technologies are transforming their own business and also customer and market demands. Thus, when companies are already in trouble with recruitments and know-how, that will probably come as a bigger problem in near future. This issue was highlighted already in OSKARI survey 2017 [8]. The timeframe for viewing upcoming changes was 3–5 years which is relatively short period of time to educate enough new competent resources to the market. This conclusion indicates a major challenge to the software development industry and is probably transforming Finnish IT business to the competitors abroad.

Practical implication of this study is to highlight the importance of hiring highly competent resources almost at any cost. Software development companies who have enough capable resources will success in the future. Our implication for academic will hopefully direct more studies on what the consequences of such lack of competence and resources for the competitiveness of Finland are. To answer our research question "what are the objectives and challenges in Finnish software development companies", we can simply answer that the market in general is changing but the main focus on software companies is to strengthen their existing business instead transforming it. The most crucial challenges on the way to success are related to recruitment and competence.

References

1. Bucherer, E., Eisert, U., Gassmann, O.: Towards systematic business model innovation: lessons from product innovation management. Creativity Innov. Manage. **21**(2), 183–198 (2012)
2. Chesbrough, H.: Business model innovation: opportunities and barriers. Long Range Plann. **43**(2–3), 354–363 (2010)
3. Zott, C., Amit, R.: Business model design: an activity system perspective. Long Range Plan. **43**(2), 216–226 (2010)
4. Bharadwaj, A., El Sawy, O., Pavlou, P., Venkatraman, N.: Digital business strategy: toward a next generation of insights. MIS Q. **37**(2), 471–482 (2013)
5. Cusumano, M.: The changing software business: moving from products to services. IEEE Comput. **41**(1), 20–27 (2008)

6. Kim, W.C., Mauborgne, R.A.: Blue Ocean Strategy, Expanded Edition: How to Create Uncontested Market Space and Make the Competition Irrelevant. Harvard Business Review Press, Brighton (2014)
7. Ries, E.: The Lean Startup: How Today's Entrepreneurs Use Continuous Innovation to Create Radically Successful Businesses. Crown Books, New York (2011)
8. Ohjelmistoyrityskartoitus. https://teknologiateollisuus.fi/sites/default/files/file_attachments/oskari2017_final.pdf. Last accessed 18 Aug 2019

The Impact of IT Bootcamp on Student Learning - Experience from ICT Enabled Experiential-Based Course

Orges Cico(✉)

Norwegian University of Science and Technology, Trondheim, Norway
orges.cico@ntnu.no

Abstract. We have been teaching an experiential-based course for fist year master students. In the last two years, we have added to the course external activities such as Hackathon and Bootcamp. These external activities helped students internalize how important are soft skills and involvement of external stakeholders to succeed in developing relevant startup projects. This year, we wanted to evaluate if students were getting what we declared. We conducted a survey on students' perception of different dimensions: soft skills challenges (teamwork, communication with stakeholders, presentation, negotiation, and innovation), technical challenges and project management (PM) challenges, before and at the end of the Bootcamp days. We found out that the mean values regarding soft skill challenges and project management vary, while values regarding technical challenge have not changed before and after Bootcamp. The overall outcomes of the study contribute to conceptualizing an early model integrating student startup formation with course learning outcomes.

Keywords: Bootcamp · Experiential course · Soft skills · Technical challenges · External stakeholders

1 Introduction

The concern of the skill gap between students and industry expectations has repeatedly been raised during the years [10]. Universities have tried to increase student readiness and fulfill industry requirements [6]. To this end, different approaches have been adopted to tackle technical and soft skills, mainly relying on capstone courses [5]. In these cases, student projects adopt the idea of prototyping through industry customer-driven [1], startup-driven [2,3], innovation and creativity-driven [4]. All these team-based project courses have provided an adequate challenge for students to get acquainted with industry-related technical and soft skills, primarily because of the involvement of external stakeholders.

A strong emphasis is also put on inter- and multi-disciplinary teams in innovative courses [7,9], through experiential learning [8].

S. Hyrynsalmi et al. (Eds.): ICSOB 2019, LNBIP 370, pp. 430–435, 2019.
https://doi.org/10.1007/978-3-030-33742-1_37

We incorporated external activities to our course to provide students a concrete learning outcome: to emphasize how important are technical skills, soft skills, and exposure to external stakeholders to succeed in developing relevant projects. To this end, we formulated the following research question (RQ):

RQ: *What skills can students gain from external stakeholders within an experiential-based course?*

To address the RQ, we designed a survey that consisted on asking each team to grade the initial and final value of dimensions related to soft skills (teamwork, communication, presentation, negotiation, and innovation), project management, technical challenges concerning the Bootcamp activity and involvement of external stakeholders. Teams provided the initial values after the stakeholders presented them with their challenges in Bootcamp Day 1. Final values were provided at the end of the project final draft delivery ready to be pitched, Bootcamp Day 2. Within the course scope, these two Bootcamp Days occurred with a distance of 40 calendar days. The goal was to evaluate the variance of these two measurements and assess which dimensions have changed.

We found that the perceived value of soft skills and project management dimensions being a challenge towards delivering the final project varied after the Bootcamp. However, we did not notice any variance in technical skills. This is also justified from the fact that there was little input either from the course instructors or the stakeholders in this regard, due to the experiential learning nature of the course. We propose a conceptual model to be adopted and further evaluated in the future. Furthermore, students have gained practical experience in forming startups with multi-disciplinary teams.

2 The Course and Bootcamp Settings

2.1 The Course and Student Teams

Our course is based on the experiential learning approach [8]. A total of 21 students have participated in the course. Demographics show that the ration among female and male students is 52%/48%. Whereas, the age distribution primarily varies between 18–30 composing 95% of the students and only 5% being above 30 years old. Teams are commonly composed of students having different study background. The main character is the inter and multidisciplinary composition of each team. Every team makes an effort to come up with an innovative idea. Team composition is decided from the course leader before the start of the course, taking into account discipline and gender balance. The team size varies from 5 to 7 students at most. Self-structuring is common, and each team is required to apply group process theory, when coping with challenges and improving team dynamics.

2.2 The Bootcamp and External Stakeholders

The Bootcamp represents a three one-day event organized during the semester. It motivates students to develop relevant solutions and business concepts through

Minimum Viable Product (MVP) prototypes, which can be field-tested during and after the course, in realistic scenarios. Support is provided by the instructors and external stakeholders to help students develop developing their future startups. Students undergo several phases: (Phase 1) Practical exercises related to analogy thinking, brainstorming, idea selection, and solution proposal. (Phase 2) Focus on the idea development through lean methodology, prototyping, and business models. (Phase 3) Students learn how to pitch ideas, think international, and create future startups.

The external stakeholders participating in the Bootcamp are part of different sectors. Their role is to present a framework of practical social challenges, which can be tackled through information and communication technology (ICT) tools. Their participation in the Bootcamp days is key to the fostering of innovative ideas. We have tried to cover three crucial sectors (academia, government, and industry) when choosing stakeholders background.

3 Survey

Based on the **RQ:** *What skills can students gain from external stakeholders within an experiential-based course?* we guided our investigation. The survey involves questions regarding the Bootcamp external activity but with direct influence on the students learning outcome and performance. The investigation is performed based on a quantitative questionnaire where the same group receives the same treatment in different points in time. Dimensions considered for the investigation are grouped into soft skills (teamwork, communication, presentation, negotiation, and innovation) and technical skills (technical challenges, project management) acquired during the Bootcamp days.

3.1 Survey Design

Students are asked to answer the online questionnaires once after the initial Bootcamp presentation (Day 1) and after the first prototyping is developed (Day 2) based on MVP concept. Key dimensions related to technical, soft, and PM skills challenge perception are to be rated with a scale from 1 to 5. The calendar time difference between the two surveys is approximately 40 days. To minimize bias, the respondents do not have the answers from the first survey available during the second one.

3.2 Data Collection

We conducted the study during the spring semester 2019, where each of the four teams involving 21 students, chose to develop a project within the course theme. We noticed that all the projects are different in nature but with similar complexity. Project Halloo-Capeesh allows people to connect through a mobile application adopted from the original Capeesh language learning, mobile app. The project Sanku-Lions consists of a mobile application that can enhance the remote access of Sanku-Fortification. The Food-Waste projects tackle issues on how to give use of food wasted by supermarkets and redistribute foodstuffs to the final consumer that are in this case, students. The B-Social tackles the challenges that internationals face when moving to Trondheim in terms of social integration. The solution proposed is an app prototype and survey. The initial and final perceived values of correctly addressing soft, technical skills and project management challenges can be found from the online surveys[1].

3.3 Data Analysis

Since we didn't know what to expect from the investigation and the same group is taken into consideration, we analyzed the mean and variance of the obtained answers before and after Bootcamp and represented them in box plots, Fig. 1

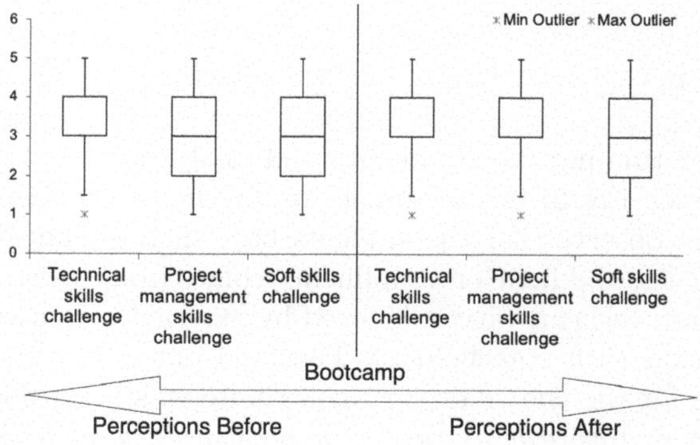

Fig. 1. Box plot distribution before and after Bootcamp activity.

Preliminary key findings are as follows:

1. **Technical Challenge.** The scope of the experiential learning approach is not to address the technical knowledge of the students. On the contrary, it relies on their previous technical knowledge. We would not expect a significant difference in this value neither after the Bootcamp or along the course, which eventually was true.
2. **Soft Skills Challenge.** This is the key knowledge acquired during the course setting; thus, we would hope that the Bootcamp contributes to this dimension significantly. We notice a slight dropping of this value.
3. **PM Challenge.** Some of the students within the teams might have previous knowledge regarding project management acquired from other courses. However, the setting changes in the Bootcamp since they have to cope with inter-disciplinary teams. We notice a slight dropping of this value, especially for the minimal outlier.

[1] Survey results can be made available on request.

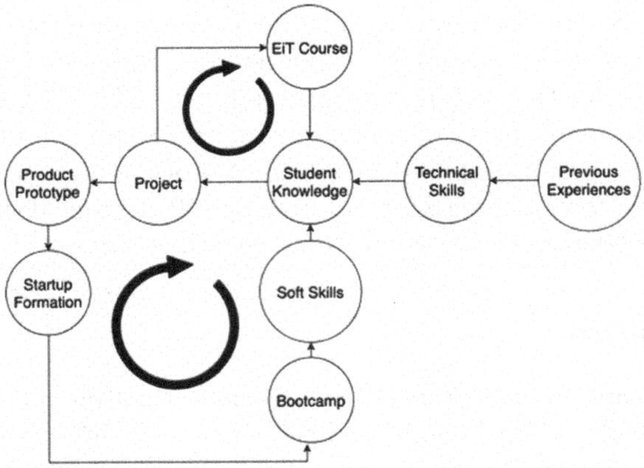

Fig. 2. Startup-driven experiential-based learning model for future courses.

4 Discussion

We are able after running the Bootcamp and analyzing the data to construct a conceptual model, Fig. 2. In the model, we internalize the benefit of external activities. We can observe that the students base their technical skills on their previous experiences, and little or no influence comes from the stakeholders. Soft and PM skills, however, can vary influenced by external activities which require active collaboration with stakeholders. The final outcome could be to deliver relevant projects for the course or even contribute to startup formation, which can become part of future activities, thus creating a loop within the courses in future academic years. To, validate the model we still need to analyze the remaining data qualitative gathered from interviews and observations during the Bootcamp Days.

5 Conclusion and Future Work

We designed our course to allow students to interact with external stakeholders by conducting Bootcamp activities. We found that challenge perception of soft and PM skills varied before and after the collaboration with the external stakeholders during the Bootcamp Days. The technical challenge, however, remained the same since there was a little contribution in this dimension either from the course or from the Bootcamp activities. Based on the gathered data, we were able to propose a model to be validated from qualitative data already gathered and adopted in the future to the other similar courses. Our study leaves open questions that can be answered in future research. What is the potential of developing realistic products based on startup formation within the course? How can we involve further the stakeholders, and what are their motivations and challenges to actively collaborate with students?

Acknowledgement. This work was funded by the Norwegian Research Council under the NOKUT center (2016–2018). Many thanks to Letizia Jaccheri.

References

1. Bruegge, B., Krusche, S., Alperowitz, L.: Software engineering project courses with industrial clients. Trans. Comput. Educ. **15**(4), 17:1–17:31 (2015)
2. Buffardi, K.: Tech Startup Learning Activities: A Formative Evaluation (2018)
3. Buffardi, K., Robb, C., Rahn, D.: Tech startups: realistic software engineering projects with interdisciplinary collaboration. J. Comput. Sci. Coll. **32**(4), 93–98 (2017). ISSN: 1937–4771
4. Dafnis, B.: The innovation diffusion paradox in undergraduate information technology student outcomes. In: Proceedings of the 16th Annual Conference on Information Technology Education, SIGITE 2015, Chicago, Illinois, USA, pp. 15–20. ACM (2015)
5. Dunlap, J.C.: Problem-based learning and self-efficacy: how a capstone course prepares students for a profession. Educ. Technol. Res. Dev. **53**(1), 65–83 (2005)
6. Jaakkola, H., Henno, J., Rudas, I.J.: IT curriculum as a complex emerging process. In: 2006 IEEE International Conference on Computational Cybernetics, pp. 1–5. August (2006)
7. Jaccheri, L., Sindre, G.: Software engineering students meet interdisciplinary project work and art. In: 11th International Conference Information Visualization (IV 2007), vol. 2007, pp. 925–934. IEEE (2007)
8. Kolb, D.A.: Experiential Learning: Experience as the Source of Learning and Development. FT Press, New Jersey (2014)
9. Pappas, I.O., et al.: Empowering social innovators through collaborative and experiential learning. In: 2018 IEEE Global Engineering Education Conference (EDUCON), pp. 1080–1088. April (2018)
10. Radermacher, A., Walia, G., Knudson, D.: Investigating the skill gap between graduating students and industry expectations. In: Companion Proceedings of the 36th International Conference on Software Engineering, pp. 291–300. ACM (2014)

Tutorial

Implementing Artificial Intelligence Ethics: A Tutorial

Ville Vakkuri(✉) and Kai-Kristian Kemell

Faculty of Information Technology, University of Jyväskylä, Jyväskylä, Finland
{ville.vakkuri,kai-kristian.kemell}@jyu.fi

Abstract. Artificial Intelligence (AI) Ethics have steadily gained attention following various real-world incidents surrounding both purely digital and cyber-physical AI systems. Concerns have been raised over the ethical aspects of these systems for example in relation to data privacy, or material harm in the case of cyber-physical systems. Though academic activity in the area has grown recently, much of the current corpus consists of theoretical and conceptual studies. Attempts to bring this ongoing discussion into practice have been primarily made in the form of various guidelines for ethical development of AI systems. However, these guidelines have not been adopted out on the field. The current situation in the area calls for more actionable methods for AI ethics, focusing on the point of view of developers. In this paper, we discuss current methods for implementing ethics in different contexts and then provide an introduction to a tutorial on a developer-focused method for implementing AI ethics, the Ethics Card Deck.

Keywords: Ethics · Artificial Intelligence · Design methods

1 Introduction

Artificial Intelligence (AI) Ethics have gained mainstream attention following real-life incidents surrounding AI systems. Especially Cyber-Physical Systems (CPSs) such as autonomous vehicles have sparked discussion, e.g. following accidents that have caused material damage and even loss of life. Data privacy and privacy in general have also been highlighted in the context of AI systems, with e.g. San Francisco pre-emptively banning facial recognition technologies from being used in surveillance systems. Purely digital systems have also been involved in ethics-related incidents, with the high-profile Cambridge Analytica incident also being enabled by an AI system.

This has also seen the scientific field of AI ethics grow steadily. Though discussion in the area has been active, most studies have been highly conceptual in nature, focusing on defining central AI ethics constructs. Despite the academic and public activity in the area, a clear gap exists between research and practice as developers have indicated that they do not currently systematically implement AI ethics. Currently, little exists in the way of tools or methods that would help

S. Hyrynsalmi et al. (Eds.): ICSOB 2019, LNBIP 370, pp. 439–442, 2019.
https://doi.org/10.1007/978-3-030-33742-1_38

developers implement AI ethics in practice. Attempts have mostly been made in the form of guidelines that have not had a notable impact out on the field.

We thus turn towards the areas of behavioral Software Engineering (SE) and Software Process Improvement (SPI). In bridging the gap between research and practice in AI Ethics, studies in the area should focus their point of view on the developers, utilizing extant literature dealing with SE methodologies and changing (improving) software processes. Actionable tools, methods, and practices are arguably needed to bring the current discussion and guidelines into practice. In this tutorial, we present our work on one such method, the Ethics Card Deck.

2 Background

Research on AI ethics has been largely conceptual in nature, with the goal of defining principles for AI ethics. This on-going discussion has thus far converged on a set of four central constructs: *Transparency* (T) [1,2], *Accountability* (A) [1,2], *Responsibility* (R) [2], and *Fairness* (F) (e.g. Greene et al. [5]). However, this set of constructs is not universally agreed-upon, with competing conceptual models present in the area (e.g. the ART and FAT model). Transparency and accountability, however, have come to form the core of AI ethics.

Yet, outside these four constructs, and in addition to them, the discussion on AI Ethics principles is still active. In early 2019, a set of EU guidelines for ethical AI was published, which focused on *Trustworthiness* as the goal for AI systems [3]. Moreover, in a recent study, Morley et al. [10] presented an entirely new set of more abstract constructs intended to summarize the existing discussion and the plethora of principles discussed so far in addition to the ones mentioned here.

Indeed, while ethics in AI as a field of research has been steadily growing, most research on the topic thus far has been theoretical or conceptual in nature. Perhaps because this discussion on the principles of AI ethics is still so active, few attempts to bring it into practice have been made. For the time being, few empirical studies exist, and even fewer studies proposing practical methods or tools based on that empirical data exist.

3 Implementing AI Ethics

Currently, ethical tools and methods for implementing AI ethics are scarce. Studies on AI ethics have largely been conceptual, focusing on defining principles for AI ethics as we discussed above. Attempts to bring this discussion into practice have thus far been made primarily via guidelines.

Guidelines for implementing AI ethics have been produced by organizations such as ISO [7] and IEEE [2], national or governmental actors such as the EU [3], as well as large practitioner organizations such as Google [11]. However, in a recent version of the IEEE EAD guidelines [2], a gap between research and practice in the area is acknowledged to likely exist, along with the notion that much work is still needed to bridge it. This is consistent with existing studies on ethical guidelines. McNamara et al. [9] studied the impact of the ACM ethical guidelines [6], concluding that they had not changed the way developers worked.

Tools and methods in the area have not seen much success either. Morley et al. [10] presented the preliminary results of a systematic review of current AI ethics methods and tools. Though they found as many as 253 different methods and tools that could be used to develop an ethical algorithmic system, these tools were largely focused on machine learning as opposed to design. These methods also paid little attention to evaluating the effects of the systems on various stakeholders, which is something considered to be highly important in AI ethics.

To address this issue, ethical tools from fields such as business ethics can potentially be utilized in AI ethics as well. The RESOLVEDD strategy is one example of such a tool. In a past study [12], we studied the use of RESOLVEDD in the context of AI ethics projects. Our results pointed towards it having some weaknesses in the context of AI ethics, namely that it did not feel like a natural part of project work to the participants. As it was not specific to the field of AI ethics, it also did not provide any support in resolving ethical issues specific to AI systems (how to handle user data etc.).

Moreover, in a preliminary study on the current state of practice in AI ethics [13], we found that none of the case companies used any formal methods or tools to implement ethics. We thus believe that there is a need for ethical methods specifically created for the context of AI ethics, a need we have begun to address by means of an ethical method we showcase in this tutorial.

4 A Tutorial on Developer-Focused Method for Implementing AI Ethics

Based on past studies in SE (e.g. [4]), we argue that a methods for AI ethics should be both lightweight and easy-to-use for developers to adopt them. As ethics is not considered a top priority by developers, resource-intensive tools are unlikely to see widespread utilization, unless necessitated by laws or regulations in the area. Following this line of reasoning, we have begun to develop a method for implementing AI ethics while focusing on the point of view of developers.

Software Engineering (SE) methods have occasionally utilized cards and card decks to aid in the implementation of methods. For example, the use of the Essence Theory of Software Engineering [8] in practice consists of utilizing various cards and playing card games[1] with them among the team. Another prominent example of card use in SE is the Planning Poker or Scrum Poker[2].

We choose to use this approach in developing our Ethics Card Deck as well. As developers are not well-versed on ethics in SE [9], and this seems to be the case in AI ethics as well [13], we consider this card-based approach to be a more tangible way to introduce developers to AI ethics.

Together, the cards form a process. The process supports iterative development that has become the norm in SE. Additionally, the process can be tailored

[1] https://queue.acm.org/detail.cfm?id=2389616.

[2] https://wingman-sw.com/articles/planning-poker.

to suit any situational context (project). The cards pose questions to the developers and answering these questions necessitates ethical consideration from the developers. Using the cards produces transparency by producing documentation, especially related to the development process. It produces justification for any ethical choices made, supporting accountability. The cards are also intended to encourage developers to be more responsible. The method is currently being evaluated in a real SE project out on the field, and the Ethics Card Deck will be showcased at a tutorial at ICSOB 2019.

References

1. Dignum, V.: Responsible autonomy. arXiv preprint arXiv:1706.02513 (2017). https://arxiv.org/abs/1706.02513
2. Ethically aligned design: A vision for prioritizing human well-being with autonomous and intelligent systems, first edition (2019). https://standards.ieee.org/content/ieee-standards/en/industry-connections/ec/autonomous-systems.html
3. Ethics guidelines for trustworthy AI (2019). https://ec.europa.eu/digital-single-market/en/news/ethics-guidelines-trustworthy-ai
4. Fitzgerald, B., Hartnett, G., Conboy, K.: Customising agile methods to software practices at Intel Shannon. EJIS **15**(2), 200–213 (2006). https://doi.org/10.1057/palgrave.ejis.3000605
5. Flores, A.W., Bechtel, K., Lowenkamp, C.T.: False positives, false negatives, and false analyses: a rejoinder to "machine bias: there's software used across the country to predict future criminals, and it's biased against blacks". Fed. Probat. **80**(2), 38 (2016)
6. Gotterbarn, D.W., et al.: ACM code of ethics and professional conduct (2018). https://www.acm.org/code-of-ethics
7. ISO/IEC JTC 1/SC 42 artificial intelligence. https://www.iso.org/committee/6794475.html
8. Jacobson, I., Lawson, H.B., Ng, P.W., McMahon, P.E., Goedicke, M.: The Essentials of Modern Software Engineering: Free the Practices from the Method Prisons! Morgan and Claypool Publishers, NY, USA, New York (2019)
9. McNamara, A., Smith, J., Murphy-Hill, E.: Does ACM's code of ethics change ethical decision making in software development? In: Proceedings of the 2018 26th ACM Joint Meeting on European Software Engineering Conference and Symposium on the Foundations of Software Engineering, ESEC/FSE 2018, pp. 729–733. ACM, New York (2018). https://doi.org/10.1145/3236024.3264833
10. Morley, J., Floridi, L., Kinsey, L., Elhalal, A.: From what to how. An overview of AI ethics tools, methods and research to translate principles into practices. arXiv preprint arXiv:1905.06876 (2019). https://arxiv.org/abs/1905.06876
11. Pichai, S.: AI at Google: our principles (2018). https://www.blog.google/technology/ai/ai-principles/
12. Vakkuri, V., Kemell, K., Abrahamsson, P.: Ethically aligned design: an empirical evaluation of the resolvedd-strategy in software and systems development context. arXiv preprint arXiv:1905.06417 (2019). http://arxiv.org/abs/1905.06417
13. Vakkuri, V., Kemell, K., Kultanen, J., Siponen, M.T., Abrahamsson, P.: Ethically aligned design of autonomous systems: Industry viewpoint and an empirical study. arXiv preprint arXiv:1906.07946 (2019). http://arxiv.org/abs/1906.07946

Author Index

The manufacturer's authorised representative in the EU is Springer
Nature Customer Service Centre GmbH, Europaplatz 3, 69115 Heidelberg,
Germany. If you have any concerns regarding our products, please
contact ProductSafety@springernature.com

Printed and bound by CPI Group (UK) Ltd, Croydon, CR0 4YY
02/10/2026
02227135-0005